THE MUNSEE INDIANS

The Civilization of the American Indian Series

Detail of *Manatus gelegen op de Noot Rivier*, 1639. Projection (attributed to Johannes Vingboons) showing Manhattan and its nearby hinterlands. Manuscript map on vellum in pen and ink and watercolor wash. Courtesy of the Library of Congress.

THE MUNSEE INDIANS

A History

ROBERT S. GRUMET

FOREWORD BY DANIEL K. RICHTER

University of Oklahoma Press : Norman

Also by Robert S. Grumet

Native Americans of the Northwest Coast (Bloomington, Ind., 1979)
Native American Place Names in New York City (New York, 1981)
The Lenapes (New York, 1989)
Historic Contact (Norman, 1995)
(ed.) *Northeastern Indian Lives* (Amherst, Mass., 1996)
(ed.) *Journey on the Forbidden Path* (Philadelphia, 1999)
Bay, Plain, and Piedmont (Annapolis, Md., 2000)
(ed.) *Voices from the Delaware Big House Ceremony* (Norman,
2001)(ed.) *Revitalizations and Mazeways* (Lincoln, Nebr., 2003)
(ed.) *Modernity and Mind* (Lincoln, Nebr., 2004)

*This book is published with the generous assistance of
Furthermore: a program of the J. M. Kaplan Fund.*

Library of Congress Cataloging-in-Publication Data Grumet,
Robert Steven.
   The Munsee Indians : a history / Robert S. Grumet ; foreword by Daniel K.
Richter.

      p.   cm.
   Includes bibliographical references and index.
   ISBN   978-0-8061-4062-9   (hardcover)
   ISBN   978-0-8061-8652-8   (paper)   1. Munsee Indians—History.
2. Community life—Northeastern States—History.   3. Northeastern States—History.
4. Northeastern States—Ethnic relations.   I. Title.
   E99.M93G78 2009
   974'.00497345—dc22

                                                          2009011630

The Munsee Indians: A History is Volume 262 in The Civilization of the American
Indian Series.

   The paper in this book meets the guidelines for permanence and durability of the
Committee on Production Guidelines for Book Longevity of the Council on Library
Resources, Inc. ∞

For Eleanor Burke Leacock (1922–1987)

CONTENTS

ILLUSTRATIONS

FOREWORD

Look up "Munsee" in the *Oxford English Dictionary.* You will read that the term, "now chiefly historical," refers to "a member of a North American Indian people formerly inhabiting the headwaters of the Delaware River in eastern North America." The vague geographical placement (a bit too far to the northwest), the implication that the people are now long dead (as Mark Twain would say, greatly exaggerated), the semi-active verb "inhabiting"— all sum up the place (or lack of place) of the people known as Munsees in our usual stories of American history. Indeed, as Robert S. Grumet reminds us, "although their place and personal names fill maps and books, they seem to flit unnoticed through American history as unseen as ghosts." *The Munsee Indians* painstakingly reconstructs what we can know—and frankly admits what we cannot know—about the people who lived in the lower Hudson and upper Delaware river valleys and around New York Bay, who traded and fought with the early Dutch colonists at Manhattan, and who created a human landscape that endures in far more than just place names on books and maps.

Those maps tell many stories; the most familiar, perhaps, is the chain of places called Muncy or Muncie, a chain that traces the people's eighteenth- and nineteenth-century migrations across Pennsylvania, Ohio, Indiana, and Illinois to the locations in Wisconsin, Ontario, Kansas, and Oklahoma where their descendants live today. But Grumet's emphasis is on a much earlier period, when an astonishing variety of local Munsee communities in their traditional eastern homeland surmounted horrific epidemics, wars with both Native and European foes, and relentless pressure from an expanding colonial population to remain very much in charge of their own fate and—to a degree their would-be Dutch and English overlords could never admit—of the fate of the Europeans who settled among them.

No one but Robert Grumet could have written this book. He has devoted the better part of a scholarly career spanning nearly forty years to tracking down every possible scrap of paper relating to Munsee people in the seventeenth and eighteenth centuries and to compiling a remarkable database of land deeds, treaty records, and other materials that enables him to identify communities, leaders, and relationships with a level of detail one would not have thought possible. This volume's copious notes are an impressive piece of scholarship in their own right, with their careful identification of nearly thirty major subgroups and their locations and the notes' capsule biographies of important figures. The chronological narrative that provides the core of this book is equally encyclopedic in scope, deploying an unparalleled mastery of archaeological, ethnological, and historical literature to build a story that always remains firmly rooted in Munsee country. Those who seek information on where Munsee people lived, how they interacted with each other and with Europeans, and how they adapted to the wrenching changes they faced will find no surer guide.

And yet the Munsees of the colonial period remain elusive. Their language has not been in everyday use in their homeland for more than two centuries. The deeds and other scraps of paper that Grumet so carefully mined preserve few of the Munsees' own words, even in translation, and give few direct insights into what they thought, how they felt, and what it meant for them to be in the world. The environmental setting in which they lived—the world of islands and waterways that Grumet's opening chapters evoke—can be reconstructed. The death toll from epidemics and warfare can be estimated, their horrors inferred from the sudden disappearance of chiefly and community names from surviving documents. The ever-shifting political arrangements that provided the flexibility crucial to cultural survival can be mapped. The threads that, from an outsider's perspective, give continuity to historical experience can be traced. But to get from these to deeper realms of human experience is more than anyone, Native or non-Native, can do at this historical distance. That Grumet has been able to do so much, with such scrupulous care, is a remarkable achievement.

Daniel K. Richter

A FEW THANKS

Who to thank before glazed eyes roll and the music starts to play me off? Thanks first to National Park Service Northeast Region anthropologist Chuck Smythe for administering Cooperative Agreement CA4560B0028, under which the writing of this book was first undertaken as a Cultural Affiliation Study. Thanks also to Daniel K. Richter, professor of history at the University of Pennsylvania and director of the university's McNeil Center for Early American Studies, who oversaw the study's development, provided much good advice, and was kind enough to provide a research associateship that among other things gave me access to university libraries and the many scholarly websites that play an ever-increasing research role. Both Chuck and Dan gave careful line readings of successive manuscript drafts over a period of three years. They raised key questions and concerns, showed how important points could be presented more clearly, encouraged revision where needful, and corrected many errors. The final manuscript is a much better product than it would have been without their help. Adrienne Gruver drafted the maps for this study, and Leah Webb-Halpern located illustrations, most of which can be found readily on the Web. The initial version of the report submitted to the NPS Northeast Region Ethnography Program is entitled "From Manhattan to Minisink" and is on file in the National Park Service Ethnography Program regional office in Boston. It contains appendices surveying past research, theoretical and methodological issues, and a bibliographic essay not included in this volume.

I owe much to Eleanor Burke Leacock, known to friends and colleagues as Happy, to whom this study is dedicated. Along the way, Lambert P.

Lockett, Sr., Frederick J. Dockstader, Leigh Marlowe, Robert E. L. Schuyler, Mark D. Dornstreich, Scott Chapin, Mary Lou Ganim, Robert Karlin, Robin Fox, Warren Susman, William K. Powers, Anna Kline, Francis Jennings, and Raymond D. Fogelson also helped in their own ways when their support was really needed.

John Bierhorst, Laurence Hauptman, John A. Strong, Anthony F. C. Wallace, and Kees Waterman critiqued an early draft of the entire manuscript. Lion Miles and Ray Whritenour helped set things straight on more than a few etymologies while correcting other mistakes. Others who made material available or reviewed early draft text include Paul D. Boyd, Ray Daugherty, Joseph E. Diamond, Dena Dincauze, Maria K. Fell, Henry T. Gitner, Charles T. Gehring, Elspeth Hart, Seth Kupferburg, Paul Huey, Nathaniel Johnson, Alice B. Kehoe, Elspeth Leacock, Nancy O. Lurie, Julia Thompson Margulies, Sheila Miller, Bruce Pearson, Lynn M. Pietak, William Reese, Jim Rementer, Paul Robinson, John Michael Smith, Darryl Stonefish, and Richard S. Walling. At the University of Oklahoma Press, thanks go to Senior Associate Director and Publisher John Drayton, Acquisitions Editor Alessandra Jacobi Tamulevich, Managing Editor Steven B. Baker, and Marketing Assistant Lauren Ballard. Thanks also to copyeditor Melanie Mallon. To these and others who helped see this book into print, I am truly grateful.

TECHNICAL NOTES

Dates documented in primary manuscript records used in this study were recorded during the years Europeans shifted from the Julian, or Old Style, calendar to the Gregorian, or New Style, calendar during historic contact period times. Proclaimed by Pope Gregory XIII in 1582, the New Style calendar moved the beginning of the year from March to January and advanced the Old Style calendar ahead eleven days, reckoning the day following its first adoption on October 4, 1582, as October 15. Protestant countries only gradually adopted the New Style calendar: Holland by 1699, and Great Britain in 1752. All dates are presented as they appear in the primary literature, with the exception of clearly identifiable Old Style dates using numbers instead of names to identify months. Such dates are advanced eleven days to conform to New Style usage. Thus, notation of "the 18th day of the 11th month in the year 1679," is rendered here as January 29, 1680. Uncited dates and names of significant world events are drawn from Stearns (2002). Also uncited are inclusive dates for Europeans, largely drawn from genealogical websites currently proliferating on the Internet. Unless otherwise noted, monetary sums represent values in provincial currency.

Spellings of Indian names are presented in their original forms within quotations and in notes. Those not presented within quotation marks in the narrative are systematized. Group names follow standardized orthographies published in the Northeast volume of the *Handbook of North American Indians* (Trigger 1978). Frequently used place names and personal names of prominent people like Oratam, Tackapousha, and Teedyuscung follow conventional forms used in existing literature. Most, but not all, spellings for names of lesser-known people and places are adapted from those first presented in Grumet (1979 and NAPN).

Wilt, wilden, or *naturvolker,* which are translated into "savage" in earlier sources, appear as Indian here. Spellings of proper nouns and words like "savage" and "barbarian" in original manuscripts appear unchanged.[1] Scholarly jargon is avoided wherever possible and explained when no substitute will do. Spellings of Dutch names follow those in J. Jacobs (2005). Spellings of all but proper nouns in quoted materials are modernized within reason. Those of well-known figures like Pieter Schuyler are presented in their best-known forms. Modernized spellings and punctuation make writers and events seem less quaint, add a degree of contemporary feel that I find particularly valuable, and provide the real benefit of reducing, to one extent or another, the alienating effects of time and cultural distance. This choice, I believe, gives readers a better chance to more closely appreciate the sense of immediacy that writers must have felt when chronicling the events they documented.

TIMELINE

11,500 years ago	The earliest scientifically verifiable physical evidence of the first people arriving in northeastern North America, called Paleo-Indians by archaeologists, coincides with the end of the last glacial epoch.
10,000 years ago	People belonging to what archaeologists call archaic cultural traditions begin hunting small game like deer and start gathering plants more intensively as moderating conditions cause forests to replace park tundra in the Northeast.
3,000–4,000 years ago	People in the Northeast increasingly adopt technological innovations, like pottery developed farther south and west, as modern climatic conditions emerge.
1,000 years ago	Bows and arrows; ceramic pots and pipes; longhouses; signs of corn, bean, and squash cultivation; and other tools and technologies resembling those used by historically chronicled Munsee people appear in archaeological sites about the time the medieval warm period moderates climate throughout the Northern Hemisphere.
500 years ago	Europeans begin sailing to northeastern North American shores.
1524	Giovanni da Verrazano, an Italian sailing in French service, writes the earliest known visitor's account mentioning Indians in New York Harbor.

1607	Total Indian population in Munsee country may have been as large as fifteen thousand people.
	The English establish their first permanent North American colony at Jamestown, Virginia.
1609	Holland and Spain agree to what becomes known as the Twelve Year Truce.
	Dutch merchants commission an Englishman named Henry Hudson to sail east to find a northern passage to the Orient. He sails across the Atlantic to find a northwest passage instead and becomes the first European known to sail up the river that today bears his name.
	Accompanying a Canadian Algonquin raiding party, Samuel de Champlain gets into a fight with Iroquois on the lake that bears his name.
	The First Anglo-Powhatan War breaks out in Virginia. Fighting ends in 1613.
1614	Dutch trading vessels sailing for the newly established New Netherland Company are given the right to cruise, chart, and trade along Northeast Coast shores for a three-year period.
	The Dutch build Fort Nassau on the banks of the Hudson River in present-day Albany, New York.
1616	An epidemic that may have been pneumonic plague breaks out among Indians in New England. Sickness does not end until 1619.
1618	The Thirty Years' War begins in Europe.
1620	English settlers establish their first colony on Massachusetts Bay at Plymouth.
1621	The Twelve Year Truce between Holland and Spain ends.
	The Dutch States General charters the Dutch West India Company to establish and maintain outposts in New Netherland, West Africa, Brazil, and the Caribbean to attack Spanish shipping, trade with local people, and, if feasible, establish mines and plantations.
1622	The Second Anglo-Powhatan War breaks out in Virginia. Fighting ends in 1624.
1624	The Dutch build Fort Orange near the site of the abandoned Fort Nassau.

The First Mohawk–Mahican War breaks out. Fighting ends in 1628.

Johannes de Laet publishes the first edition of *Nieuwe Wereldt,* presenting the first detailed descriptions of Indians in New Netherland.

1626   The Dutch report purchase of Manhattan from the Indians for sixty guilders' worth of goods. They build Fort Amsterdam at the island's southern tip. The village of New Amsterdam soon grows up next to the fort.

1630   The Dutch West India Company authorizes the patroon system, giving wealthy corporate investors the right to administer self-governing manors directly purchased from Indians.

Agents of patroon Michiel Pauw obtain the first deeds from Munsee sachems for land in their homeland. His patroonship, named Pavonia after himself, takes in Staten Island, the Bayonne Peninsula, and Jersey City.

English Puritans, operating under a charter granted to the Massachusetts Bay Company, establish their first colony at Boston.

1633   Smallpox ravages New England and spreads to Iroquoia by 1634.

1634   Indian population in Munsee country declines to somewhere around six thousand people.

English Catholics led by Lord Baltimore establish the capital of the new Maryland colony at St. Mary's City on the Potomac River.

1637   The Pequot War breaks out in Connecticut. English massacre of noncombatants in the Pequot Fort at Mystic becomes a byword for terror in the region.

1638   Pequots surrender to the English. The English break the Pequot nation apart and scatter most among colonial Indian allies.

A consortium of Swedish and Dutch investors establish the colony of New Sweden along the lower Delaware River.

1640	The first phase of Kieft's War begins when the Dutch attack Raritan Indians on Staten Island. Confined to the New York Harbor area, fighting sputters out by 1641.
1642	Civil war begins in England. Parliamentary forces defeat King Charles I and execute him in 1649. Fighting ends in 1651.
1643	The second and most violent phase of Kieft's War begins when the Dutch massacre Lower River Indians taking refuge among them.
	Massapequa sachem Tackapousha and Hackensack leader Oratam first appear in Dutch records.
1644	Dutch settlers led by immigrant English veterans of the Pequot War attack Lower River Indian towns and massacre their inhabitants on the mainland and on Long Island.
	The Third (and final) Anglo-Powhatan War breaks out in Virginia. Fighting ends in 1646.
1645	The Treaty of August 30 ends the worst of the fighting during Kieft's War. Hostilities drag on in Raritan country till 1649.
	Indian population in Munsee country drops to four thousand.
1647	Influenza is reported in New England.
1648	The Peace of Westphalia ends the Thirty Years' War.
1649	South Bay sachem Mattano is first mentioned in Dutch records.
1650	The Treaty of Fort Hope (present-day Hartford, Connecticut) establishes a boundary between New Netherland and New England.
1652	The First Anglo-Dutch Naval War begins. The Treaty of Westminster reestablishes peace in 1654.
	Esopus sachem Harman Hekan, better known among settlers as Ankerop, starts appearing in Dutch records.
1653	Matinecock sachem Suscaneman makes his documentary debut.
1655	The Peach War begins in New Netherland. Hostilities last until 1657.

A Dutch expedition launched from New Amsterdam seizes the colony of New Sweden on the Delaware River. Adriaen Van der Donck publishes the first edition of his *Description of New Netherland*.

1657   Having driven off settlers in 1640 and 1655, Indians sell Staten Island for a second time.

1658   Malaria is reported on the Delaware River.

1659   Fighting breaks out between Indians and settlers at Esopus.

1661   Smallpox breaks out in New York.

1662   The Second Mohawk-Mahican War begins. Fighting drags on until 1675.

1663   Esopus warriors destroy Nieuwdorp (Hurley, New York) and devastate Dutch settlements at and around Wiltwijck (Kingston, New York).

Dutch soldiers aided by Long Island Indians burn two Esopus forts and scatter their occupants.

One hundred Indians from the Delaware River help the Susquehannocks defend their fort against a besieging Iroquois force.

Hackensack leader Pierwim, also known as Hans, is first mentioned in colonial records.

1664   Numbers of Indian people living in Munsee country are reduced to less than three thousand as the colonial population in New Netherland reaches nine thousand.

The Dutch sign a treaty ending their war with the Esopus.

New Netherland falls to an English fleet and is renamed New York.

New Jersey is established by the English Crown while the British invasion fleet is en route to Manhattan.

New York governor Richard Nicolls grants patents encompassing 750,000 acres west of the Hudson River at Elizabethtown and Navesink before news of New Jersey's establishment arrives. These remain trouble spots for the remainder of the colonial era.

Smallpox continues to ravage the region.

1665	Nicolls and his agents sign treaties establishing enduring alliances with the Esopus and Mohawk nations.
	The Second Anglo-Dutch Naval War begins.
1666	French troops destroy the Mohawk towns.
	Mamanuchqua, an Esopus woman who later rises to the rank of sachem, and a key Lower River Indian culture broker called Claes the Indian make their first appearances in colonial records.
1667	The Treaty of Breda ends the Second Anglo-Dutch Naval War. The English keep New York.
	Pequannock, Connecticut, sachem Taphow, later referred to in several deeds as "the commander in chief of all Indians living in Northern New Jersey," is first mentioned.
1669	Mohawks defeat and destroy a large invading force of Mahican and Northern Indians led by Josia Chickataubut.
1670	Indians sell Staten Island for the third and last time.
1672	The Third Anglo-Dutch Naval War begins. New York is recaptured by a Dutch fleet.
	The Rebellion of 1672 breaks out in New Jersey.
1674	The Second Treaty of Westminister ends the Third Anglo-Dutch Naval War. New York is returned to English rule for the second and final time.
1675	King Philip's War begins in New England.
	Bacon's Rebellion breaks out in Virginia and Maryland. Susquehannocks are forced to abandon their homeland. Fighting drags on in these locales for several years.
	Weequehela, later known as the King of New Jersey, is first mentioned in English records.
1676	The Quintipartite deed establishes the separate colonies of East and West Jersey.
	The New York government erects a sanctuary north of Albany at Schaghticoke, New York, for Indian refugees from New England and establishes another above the Falls of the Delaware River for Susquehannocks.
	Influenza ravages Seneca country.
1677	Treaties at Albany establish the Covenant Chain alliance linking the Five Nations and the Upper and Lower River

	Indians with English provincial governments from New England to Maryland and Virginia.
1679	Smallpox ravages the region until 1680.
1681	Pennsylvania is established.
	René-Robert Cavalier, Sieur de la Salle, encounters a large party of Eastern Algonquians from Massachusetts, New York, and Virginia, including a number of Munsees, near the mouth of the St. Joseph River in Michigan. He refers to these people collectively as Loups.
1684	Malaria devastates communities throughout the Northeast until 1685. Mamanuchqua, Pierwim, and many other Lower River Indian leaders disappear from European records within two years.
	Total Indian population along the lower Hudson and upper Delaware rivers drops to approximately 2,800.
1685	Louis XIV revokes the Edict of Nantes, which protected rights of Huguenots in France. Many of the thousands who flee to England and the Netherlands soon move to New York and the Jerseys to join coreligionists from Belgium who had migrated earlier.
1686	Separate New England colonies are joined into one dominion administered by a single royal governor. New York and the Jerseys are annexed to the Dominion of New England in 1688.
1687	Loups in Ottawa country ask permission to return to New York.
1688	Revolutionaries oust King James II and crown Dutch stadtholder Prince Willem of Orange as King William III of England.
1689	Colonists arrest or drive out dominion officials and reestablish their separate provinces.
	Jacob Leisler seizes control of government in New York and the Jerseys in the name of King William without royal authority.
	King William's War against France begins.
	Iroquois warriors destroy Lachine just outside Montreal.

1690	Soldiers and warriors returning from an abortive expedition against Canada inadvertently spread smallpox through Munsee country.
	Susquehannocks regather in the Susquehanna Valley at Conestoga town under joint Pennsylvania and Five Nations supervision.
	French raiders burn Schenectady.
1691	Smallpox continues to ravage the region.
	Refusing to surrender authority promptly to the representative of the newly appointed royal governor, Leisler is arrested and executed for treason.
1693	French troops destroy the Mohawk towns.
1694	Shawnees abandon their alliance with the French farther west and move to the Delaware Water Gap.
1696	French troops destroy the Onondaga and Oneida towns.
1697	The Treaty of Ryswick ends King William's War.
1699	Tackapousha makes his final documentary appearance.
1701	Indian population in Munsee country reaches a low point of a little more than one thousand; nearly fifty thousand Europeans and almost four thousand enslaved Africans live between the Delaware and Hudson river valleys.
	The Great Peace of Montreal ends wars between the Five Nations and the French and their Indian allies.
	The Five Nations place lands claimed farther west under English protection.
	The Society for the Propagation of the Gospel in Foreign Parts (later called the New England Company) is founded in London to promote Anglicanism and convert Indians and enslaved Africans in the Americas.
1702	Queen Anne's War begins.
	Yellow fever kills 570 colonists in New York.
	Smallpox sweeps across the region until 1703.
1709	Delaware Valley sachem Nutimus is first mentioned in the records.
	Plans for a land-sea invasion of Canada miscarry when a promised English fleet fails to arrive.

1710	The Four Indian Kings (three Mohawks and an Upper River Indian sachem) visit England to drum up support for another attack on Canada.
1711	The second invasion attempt on Canada is aborted when a substantial part of the English fleet sent to reduce Quebec is lost in the Gulf of St. Lawrence.
	The Tuscarora War breaks out in North Carolina. Yamasees, Cherokees, and Catawbas help the Carolinians defeat the Tuscaroras.
1712	Tuscarora refugees begin to seek asylum among Unami- and Munsee-Delaware people in Pennsylvania and New York.
	A slave revolt in New York City is savagely repressed.
	An unsuccessful Mesquakie and Mascouten siege of Detroit sparks the beginning of the Fox Wars. Fighting drags on until 1733, scattering and nearly destroying the Mesquakie nation.
1713	The Treaty of Utrecht ends Queen Anne's War.
1714	Munsee country Indians sell the last of their major landholdings east of the Delaware River.
	The Five Nations formally invite the Tuscaroras to settle under their protection in the Susquehanna Valley.
1715	River Indian warriors join Tuscarora and Iroquois war parties traveling south to attack Yamasees at war with North Carolina.
1716	Iroquois diplomats tell Covenant Chain allies in Albany that henceforth gifts to their confederacy should be divided into six parts so that they might be properly shared by the Tuscaroras. Shortly thereafter, colonists begin to refer to the confederacy as the Six Nations.
	Smallpox rages until 1717.
1720	The population of Indians from Munsee country, mostly spread out between the Housatonic and Susquehanna valleys, hovers around the 1,000 mark; 92,300 Europeans and nearly 11,000 enslaved Africans live in Pennsylvania, New Jersey, and New York.
1722	War between Abenakis and settlers begins in New England. Fighting ends by 1726.

Expatriate River Indians are living among other Indian refugees at Ochquaga, Tioga, and other towns along the upper parts of the West and North branches of the Susquehanna River.

1727   The name Munsee first appears in colonial records in a reference to Indians living along the upper branches of the Susquehanna River.

Weequehela is hanged for killing a settler in New Jersey. Shortly thereafter, most of his people move to the Lehigh Valley at the Forks of Delaware.

1728   The Shawnees move away from Minisink country. Weequehela's cousin Manawkyhickon tries to spark a general war against the English.

1731   Intermittent outbreaks of smallpox strike the region at five-year intervals throughout the remaining decades of the colonial era.

1734   The Society in Scotland for Propagating Christian Knowledge, known as the Scotch Society (founded in 1709), starts its first mission among Mahicans at Stockbridge, Massachusetts.

1735   Pennsylvania governor Thomas Penn approaches Indians at the Forks of Delaware with an unregistered deed dated 1686 to all land within a day and a half's walk of the village of Wrightstown.

1736   The Six Nations sell the lands between the Delaware and Susquehanna rivers below the Kittatiny Ridge belonging to Munsee- and Unami-speaking Delawares.

1737   Indians from Minisink and the mid-Delaware Valley sign the confirmatory Walking Purchase deed. Runners sprinting along a road made for the purpose stake the province's claim to the bulk of remaining Munsee lands west of the Delaware River.

1739   Moravians arrive at the Forks of Delaware. They begin building their central community on the banks of the Lehigh River at a place they christen Bethlehem one year later.

1740	Most Munsees and Unamis live farther north, east, or west of the 204,000 Europeans and 16,500 enslaved Africans residing in their former homeland.
	Moravians start their missions at Shekomeko and Pine Plains in present-day Columbia County, New York, and at Pachgatgoch in Kent, Connecticut.
1742	At a treaty meeting in Philadelphia, the Six Nations order the Munsees to leave lands within Walking Purchase bounds and move to the Susquehanna Valley.
1743	Scotch Society missionary David Brainerd starts working at the mixed Munsee-Mahican community of Kaunaumeek in the Berkshire foothills of New York.
1744	King George's War begins.
	Brainerd begins his mission among the Munsees at the Forks after urging his Kaunaumeek converts to relocate to Stockbridge.
1745	French and Indian raiders burn Saratoga.
	Minisink and Esopus Indians living among settlers on the Hudson River, fearing attacks from colonial neighbors, move to their winter hunting camps in the upper Delaware Valley.
	Brainerd's followers at the Forks begin moving back to New Jersey. They complete the move the following year.
1746	Dutchess County officials drive the Moravians from Shekomeko and Pine Plains.
1747	Malaria breaks out in New York.
1748	The Treaty of Aix-la-Chapelle ends King George's War.
1754	Six Nations sachems sign over nearly all Indian lands in Pennsylvania at private meetings with Pennsylvania and Connecticut colonists held during the Albany Congress.
	George Washington's attack on a French patrol outside present-day Pittsburgh, Pennsylvania, starts the French and Indian War, whose European phase is known as the Seven Years' War.
	Abenaki Indians convince the few Indians still living at Schaghticoke to move to Canada.
1755	Substantial numbers of Munsee warriors join other dispossessed former English allies attacking colonial

settlements along the Pennsylvania, New Jersey, and New York frontier after a French and Indian force destroys General Edward Braddock's army at the Battle of the Monongahela.

An Indian force destroys Gnadenhuetten, killing its missionaries and carrying off many of the community's Indian converts.

Another army led by William Johnson stops a French force at the Battle of Lake George.

A planned British campaign meant to take Fort Niagara miscarries.

1756   Pennsylvania formally declares war on the Delawares and Shawnees.

Pennsylvania militiamen burn the Delaware town of Kittanning on the Allegheny River.

Colonists kill Munsee families living in the settlements at Peapack, New Jersey, and Walden, New York.

1758   Most Munsees join other Delawares signing peace treaties with the English.

Munsees and Wappingers give up all but their hunting and fishing rights in northern New Jersey in the treaty signed at Easton, Pennsylvania.

Unamis and Munsees exchange remaining land claims in New Jersey south of the Raritan River and Delaware Water Gap for a reservation at Edgepillock (Indian Mills, New Jersey).

Most Munsees signing these treaties live in exile with the majority of their countryfolk; a couple of hundred Munsees continue to hang on to small reservations and isolated, otherwise untenanted tracts scattered at various places in their homeland in the midst of a colonial population in New York, New Jersey, and Pennsylvania totaling 428,000 people, a figure that includes 29,000 mostly enslaved Africans.

1759   Yellow fever devastates the region.

1762   The Treaty of Paris ends the Seven Years' War.

1765   Pontiac's War begins.

	A column led by Andrew Montour destroys the Chemung Valley Munsee towns. Major fighting ends in 1766.
1775	The War of Independence begins.
1783	The Treaty of Paris ends the War of Independence.
1801	Munsees and Unamis at Edgepillock agree to sell their Brotherton Reservation in the pinelands and move north among the Oneidas.

Part I

THE MUNSEES
AND THEIR COUNTRY

1

MUNSEES

Just four hundred years ago, forebears of Delaware-speaking people who would later be known as Munsees lived quietly in an ancestral homeland that was wholly their own. It was a land of dense forests, broad marsh lands, and clear waters that stretched across the Mid-Atlantic slope of North America between the lower Hudson and upper Delaware river valleys. Two islands, Manhattan on the lower Hudson and Minisink on the upper Delaware, lay at the margins of this homeland. Near its eastern end, Indians on Manhattan, looking out on the bay on a fall morning in 1609, saw Henry Hudson's ship *de Halve Maen,* "the Half Moon," sail into and up the river that would bear its captain's name. One hundred and fifty years later, descendants of these same Manhattan islanders living at Minisink would be forced to leave what had become for many a last refuge in a homeland seized by Europeans.

Although the homeland of these people is now the location of one of world's great metropolises, the Indians who called it their home are a forgotten people. So thoroughly have they receded from memory that no one is completely sure where their lands were or what they originally called themselves. Linguists, tracing origins of Indian place and personal names recorded on maps and other documents left behind by Europeans, think most of these people spoke Munsee, the northernmost dialect of the Eastern Algonquian language they call Delaware. Their descendants became known as Munsees only after 1727, while colonists were driving them from their last ancestral lands. The name Munsee, appropriately enough, means "People from Minisink." Most Munsees, in turn, became part of the Delaware Indian nation that formed in exile in Pennsylvania and Ohio shortly after Minisink was finally abandoned by its original inhabitants, just before the American Revolution. Today, descendants of these people, some of whom still call themselves Munsees and others who identify themselves as Delawares or Mohicans, live scattered in exile in places like Wisconsin, Oklahoma, Kansas, and Ontario.[1]

The homeland of the Munsees' ancestors lay across a twelve thousand-square-mile expanse of tidewater and timberland that stretched from the Atlantic Ocean across piedmont foothills and ridge valleys to the Appalachian Mountains one hundred miles farther inland (see map 1). Their country took in the westernmost reaches of Long Island Sound and present-day Connecticut, extended across New York Harbor and its adjoining hinterland, and reached over the Hudson Highlands and through the Great Valley of southeastern New York and northern New Jersey to northeastern Pennsylvania's Pocono Plateau and Lehigh Valley. The Catskill Mountains marked its northern borders; the Berkshires, the Taconic Mountains, and central Long Island's pine barrens framed the territory's eastern limits. New Jersey's pinelands stood watch over the southern frontiers. The upland divide separating the Delaware from the Susquehanna river drainages formed its western boundary.[2]

Towns were located at favorable locales throughout this region. Most were small communities scattered across oceanic expanses of woodland like islands in a chain. Many, like Manhattan and Minisink, were literally islands. Others were in clearings on well-drained terraces overlooking rivers, streams, farm fields, swamps, marshes, or stretches of sandy beach. Networks of families and friends linked these island communities to each other. Although surging tidewater and breaking waves washed against the shores of the coastal sections of this land, its inhabitants were not a maritime people. They instead followed a deeply rooted woodland way of life based on hunting, foraging, and farming in fields and forests that stretched inland from the region's beaches and riverbanks.[3]

This study gathers the many scattered pieces of physical evidence, mostly archival and archaeological, to reconstruct the history of the Munsee people in their homeland. It primarily focuses on the period of contact that began when Europeans started colonizing Munsee land and that ended when these colonists finally forced most of its remaining original inhabitants into exile just ten years before the start of the American Revolution.

No comprehensive up-to-date account of the history and culture of the Munsee people in their homeland exists. Most people interested in the subject depend on studies written more than seventy-five years ago by local historians and amateur archaeologists. Much is owed these early investigators.

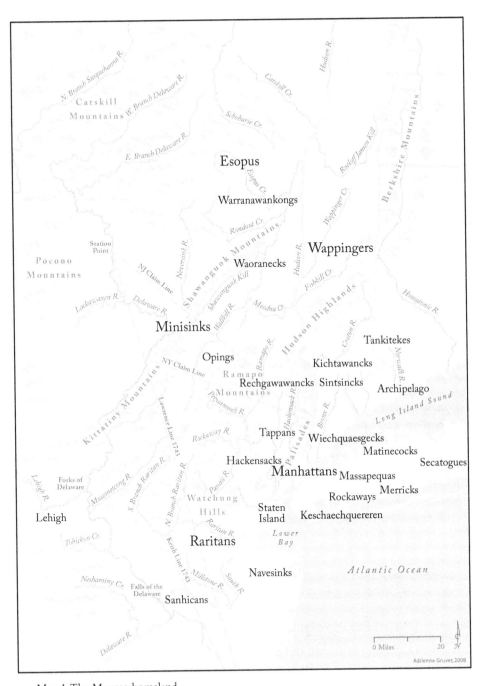

Map 1. The Munsee homeland

Many of them unearthed sites and copied documents that have long since vanished. The best of them crafted remarkably detailed histories from the sources then available. More recently, scholars trained in various disciplines have discovered new sites; located, transcribed, and translated masses of rediscovered or long-lost manuscripts; and developed methods that can extract new insights from old evidence.

Writers using fresh findings and new techniques to reconstruct histories and cultures of Indians in northeastern North America have largely overlooked Munsees. Information documenting events that occurred in Munsee country tends to be folded into histories of the Delaware nation and their closely related Mohican linguistic cousins. This has helped make the names of Delawares and Mohicans, who played major roles in America's founding, as recognizable today as they were during colonial times. The same practice has caused the Munsees to be forgotten. Although their place and personal names fill maps and books, they seem to flit unnoticed through American history as unseen as ghosts. In the more than two hundred years that have passed since Munsee was last spoken in everyday conversation in their homeland, most Munsee descendants have had little access to records documenting their history and heritage.[4]

The fact that Munsees are forgotten cannot be blamed on any lack of evidence. Munsee people left behind reminders of their existence everywhere they lived and traveled. Worked stone and bits of shell and pottery scattered around smudged soil stains mark their workshops, house sites, and fishing spots. Parks, plaques, and monuments mark their town sites, battlegrounds, and council places. Rivers, mountains, villages, towns, and cities bear their names, while many roads and travel corridors still follow their trail and trade routes. Thousands of deeds, court proceedings, journals, council minutes, treaty documents, and other writings, many with dates and locations, chronicle major and minor events in their colonial contact history. I have connected a little less than half of the more than 10,000 Munsee personal names thus far found in these documents to 210 individuals prominent enough to warrant repeated mention in colonial records. I call this compilation of named individuals and associated documentation, cross-indexed by date, location, and community, the Munsee File. Information on the 210 men and women in this database often includes aliases and nicknames, status, location, and family and political affiliations. Although dates of birth, marriage, or death are rarely revealed in colonial documents, correlations of first and last appearance rates of people in the Munsee File provide indirect indicators of relative impacts of wars, epidemics, and other factors affecting Indian communities in the lower Hudson and upper Delaware river valleys during the first two centuries of contact with colonists.[5]

The sheer mass of the surviving record shows that ancestors of Munsees have been hidden in very plain sight for quite some time. In many ways, the history of forgotten Munsees is as extensively documented as those of the better-remembered Delaware and Mohican nations. At a time when it is unthinkable to ignore in accounts of America's founding, the question can be asked, what is it about Munsees that makes forgetting them so thinkable?

In the broadest sense, values placed on particular people and places often determine who and what gets remembered. Glamorous associations can give a memorably strong sense of importance to otherwise overlooked lives or remote backwaters. Local histories of long-forgotten original inhabitants of world centers like Manhattan, for their part, do not seem to resonate either strongly or widely. Those interested in such things may connect Gauls with Paris. Far fewer readily associate ancient Jomon people with Tokyo or Baghdad with ancient Mesopotamians.

Consideration of the relative significance of one or another group in historical narratives also determines how writers chronicle particular people. In the past, lumping Munsees together with Delawares or Mohicans has been seen as a harmless way to more clearly present a complex cast of characters embedded in a complicated narrative. The result, however, is most like what would happen if colonial historians lumped Dutch, English, and Palatine German settlers together as a single Germanic people. The effect of such lumping has robbed Munsees of their identity and blotted out memory of the part they played in the early history of America. Most of their present-day descendants probably regard this with little more than a rueful shrug of weary recognition. It may also be that their ancestors had a hand in cultivating this attitude. Caught between powerful nations intent on taking their lands, lives, and livelihoods, these never-populous but determinedly self-reliant people have long recognized the value of maintaining a low profile.

Another clue may lie in the different ways people relate to the dead. Like most traditional people, Munsee ancestors believed that death occurred when the soul that animated and maintained a body left its host. Sickness, in this view, was regarded as a temporary death that could become permanent if soul and body were not reunited in time. Among Munsee ancestors, this task was the responsibility of healers they called *metewak,* capable of enlisting the help of *manitowak* (their word for spirits) in recovering lost souls.

Those mourning over bodies no longer habitable by souls also interred names of the deceased. They felt that mentioning a dead person's name could rekindle old longings and revive lingering animosities among the dead as well as the living. Souls of the dead hearing their names spoken by the living might respond by returning to old haunts. Once there, they might entice spirits of beloved relatives and old enemies to join them in death. By the same logic, mentioning names of lost places might do the same thing, kindling unappeasable longing for an irretrievably lost homeland. Such beliefs would have helped convince many people that they should at least put potentially magical names of past places and people behind them.[6]

This does not mean that traditional people like Munsees somehow lived in an unending present where the past did not exist. Their myths, songs, and stories distilled wisdom safely removed from pains and passions of personal recollection. Ritually consecrated ceremonial names also kept memories of long dead individuals alive at a safe distance. The Iroquois League of Nations, for example, still maintains a stock of fifty names linked to league founders. Turned into ceremonial titles used when transacting league business, each is given to a man selected by senior kinswomen. The man holds the name for the duration of his tenure as a league chief. Kinswomen who can remove unwanted leaders and replace dead ones also pass the name on to successors.[7]

More independent-minded people like Munsees, who were loath to legitimate even the most unintrusive higher authority, tended to use names differently. Rather than draw on specific stores of names symbolizing powers of particular families, clans, or nations, such people preferred to cast significant past events in a more egalitarian light. Egalitarian societies, as defined by anthropologist Morton H. Fried, are not communities where everyone is equal. Neither are they places where differences in power, wealth, and authority do not exist. They are instead societies where ability tends to count more than heredity. Egalitarian people try to achieve consensus when making decisions, maintain broadest possible access to resources, equitably redistribute wealth, and discourage growth of ingrained hierarchical inequalities. They do this by rewarding generosity, ridiculing excessive pride, and recognizing accomplishments of the living rather than the dead to limit prospects of passing power on to descendants lacking ability.[8]

It is easy to understand how descendants might want to forget the pain of losing much-loved places, friends, and relatives along with their names. It is also easy to see why egalitarian people carefully edit usable pasts to maintain freedom of action. It is just as easy to understand why people like Americans have a passion for keeping records. Americans would be swamped by the past, however, if passion for writing things down was the sole reason for chronicling history. On the other hand, Americans would have almost no history if shame and sorrow were enough to blot out unpleasant memories. So the question remains.

The homeland of Munsee ancestors, forgotten by Americans, was delimited by borders that were neither static nor sealed. Welcoming help of people from other places, they valued hospitality and mandated marriage with proper strangers from appropriate families and communities. This latter practice, known among anthropologists as exogamy, reflects the kind of choices required of people who must, as Edward B. Tylor pointed out, marry out or die out. Traditions of hospitality and out-marriage welcomed outsiders and assured safe harbors to travelers. Other traditions of consensus-based decision making gave those disagreeing with local decisions the option to vote with their feet and move elsewhere. This further ensured that present and former friends and relatives could be found in different Munsee-speaking communities as well as among other nearby Eastern Algonquian nations.[9]

In these ways, Munsee and other Eastern Algonquian homelands served as social and political arenas open, in varying degrees, to friends, relatives, and invited guests. In Munsee country, these mostly included neighbors on their northern, eastern, and southern frontiers. People speaking a closely related dialect of Delaware called Northern Unami lived just to the south in what is today central New Jersey and adjacent portions of southeastern Pennsylvania. Neighbors to the north and east spoke slightly more distantly related Eastern Algonquian Mahican and Quiripi languages. Members of the Minisink community also allowed a large number of Central Algonquian–speaking Shawnees to settle between Minisink Island and the Delaware Water Gap between 1694 and 1727.[10]

Mohawks and Susquehannocks living just beyond the mountain ramparts of the Munsee homeland spoke Iroquoian languages as different from Algonquian as Japanese is from English (see map 2). The Mohawk homeland centered on a long stretch of the Mohawk River in upstate New York. They were the easternmost member of the Iroquois Confederacy of Five (later Six) Nations whose heartland stretched across central New York from the Mohawk to the Genesee river valleys. The Susquehannocks were a closely related but independent Iroquoian-speaking nation who moved from the upper branches of the Susquehanna River to its lowermost reaches sometime during the mid-1550s. Relations between both nations and the people of Munsee country were often strained during the colonial era. Iroquoian populations were much larger than those of people living in the Munsee and other Eastern Algonquian homelands. Unlike the scattered settlement pattern favored by people living in Munsee country, most Iroquoians lived close to one another in densely packed clusters of longhouses. These were often surrounded by palisade fortifications during periods of protracted warfare. The first century of European colonization was one such period. Populous centrally organized Mohawks and Susquehannocks would increasingly look beyond their borders to the countries of their neighbors for needed resources as wars with colonists and devastating new diseases brought by strangers reduced Eastern Algonquian ability to resist Iroquoian demands.[11]

Power differences between people in Munsee and Mohawk countries during contact period times were expressed in various ways. Surviving records indicate that Mohawks and other Five Nations people rarely moved away to marry into Indian families in the Munsee homeland. Instead, they made it their practice to adopt and marry Munsees and other foreigners forced or invited to live among them. This allowed them to draw increasing numbers of foreign children and marriageable spouses into their towns to recoup losses and bolster strength. Successes and failures of such efforts were reflected in terms their diplomats used to address foreigners in councils. The initial Iroquois use of terms like brethren, cousin, and nephew when referring to those of smaller nations like Munsees in early councils gave way to the later practice of calling them women and children on formal occasions. These changes show that, in councils at least, Five Nations people increasingly saw themselves more as husbands and fathers than as siblings or age mates as their power grew and that of smaller nations declined.

Indians in the lower Hudson and upper Delaware river valleys found themselves increasingly pressed between Iroquois nations in the interior and Western Europeans from Great Britain and the Netherlands claiming their homeland as colonial possessions. The coming of Europeans presented unique challenges to Indian people along the rivers. Wars with newcomers and the far more lethal diseases they brought with them would devastate Indian communities. The vast numbers of settlers flooding into their homeland overwhelmed and ultimately drove these River Indians from their ancestral lands.

Relations between Natives and newcomers in Munsee country during the 250 years between the time Europeans first came to the region in the

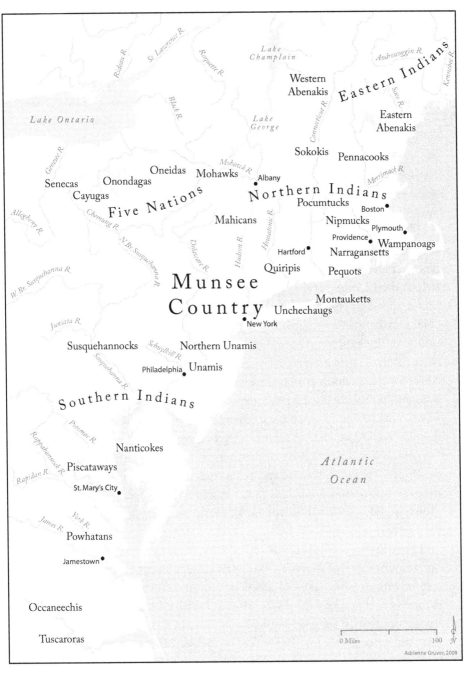

Map 2. Munsee country in the Northeast

Rideau R.
St. Lawrence R.
Raquette R.
Lake Champlain
Androscoggin R.
Kennebec R.

Western Abenakis
Eastern Indians
Black R.
Connecticut R.
Lake George
Eastern Abenakis

Lake Ontario

Sokokis Pennacooks

Genesee R.
Mohawk R.
Oneidas Mohawks Albany
Merrimack R.
Senecas Onondagas
Northern Indians
Cayugas
Five Nations
Pocumtucks Boston
Allegheny R.
Chemung R.
Mahicans
Housatonic R.
Nipmucks
Plymouth
N. Br. Susquehanna R.
Delaware R.
Hudson R.
Providence Wampanoags
Hartford Narragansetts
W. Br. Susquehanna R.
Quiripis Pequots

Munsee Country
Montauketts
Juniata R.
Unchechaugs
New York

Susquehannocks Schuylkill R. Northern Unamis
Susquehanna R.
Philadelphia Unamis

Southern Indians

Potomac R.
Rappahannock R.
Nanticokes
Rapidan R. Piscataways
St. Mary's City

Atlantic Ocean

James R.
York R.
Powhatans

Jamestown

Occaneechis

Tuscaroras

0 Miles 100
N
Adrienne Gruver, 2008

early 1500s to the final dispossession of the Munsees by the mid-1700s were not simple and their result not inevitable. The story of contact in the region is neither a triumphant march of civilization nor an edifying morality play featuring oppressed victims or heroic resisters. Outnumbered and technologically outclassed as they were, the people of Munsee country were not hopelessly outmatched by all-powerful Dutch and English hegemonists who could take their lands whenever they wanted. Although Munsee people in their homeland were never able to achieve a united front, unity also eluded the Dutch and the English as well. Dutch and English and New Yorkers and New Englanders fought among themselves and each other. All, at one time or another, also joined with or fought their Indian neighbors.

This tangle of kaleidoscopically shifting alliances and relationships created a political climate that alert Indian leaders in Munsee country could exploit. Their ability to take advantage of ambiguities by playing off adversaries helped their nation survive to join the ranks of what anthropologist Edward Spicer called an enduring people. According to Spicer, enduring people are able to sustain persistent identity systems that allow them "to maintain continuity in the experience and conception of themselves in a wide variety of sociocultural environments." This emphasis on different ways people like Munsees see themselves at various times in their history helps explain how a people going under different names and compelled to live in different places with different people can maintain a coherent sense of their own identity during challenging times that overwhelm other nations. Munsee "experience and conception of themselves" as a unique people and culture developed, persisted, waned, and recovered as the specifics of their lives—their tools, clothing, languages (both Indian and European), locations, religious beliefs, national allegiances, memories, even their names for themselves—changed.[12]

The idea that cultures are, as anthropologist Anthony F. C. Wallace points out, organizations of diversity is important here. People identified as Munsees in one context and Mahicans in another did not suddenly become members of different cultures. Neither did references to people by different names necessarily suggest confusion or disorganization. Names used like this can reflect what may be called situational identity. Different names identifying the same people in different situations serve as markers of social flexibility that can allow a person to function as a Munsee in one context and a Mahican in another. Flexibility has its limits, of course. As Wallace also points out, too much or too little can destabilize things to the point where

revitalization, a resorting of identities and their underlying customs and beliefs, is necessary if cultural values are to endure.[13]

Few indicators convey cultural continuity in the midst of changing contexts more graphically than the many and various names used by Munsees
to identify themselves as distinct people at different times in their history. Although sources are far from clear on the subject, Munsee use of their dialect's variant of the Delaware word Lenape probably most closely reflected
their shared sense of ethnicity in their home country. Lenape means "man."
Munsees and other Delaware speakers used varieties of their word *xkwe,*
similar to the widely adopted and originally inoffensive Massachusett word
"squaw" when talking about a woman. They used the word Lenape when
referring to family, friends, or fellows much as people today use words like
mensch (German and Yiddish for "man") and expressions like "she is a real
human being" when talking about someone they really like.[14]

Today, many writers regard Lenape as the most appropriate term to use
when talking about Delaware-speaking people. The word itself, however,
only rarely appears in colonial-era documents. Both Indians and colonists
evidently found it too blunt an instrument for everyday use. Indians in particular tended to identify themselves as people from a particular place or a
certain river. This practice is reflected in the way they used "Delaware," a
loan word adopted from English. "Delaware" comes from the name of
Thomas West, Baron de la Warr, second governor of the Virginia colony.
Early Virginian explorers gave his name to the river that Unami-speaking
Delawares called Lenapewihittuck and that Munsees called Kithanne, "Large
River." Colonists and Indians both began calling the river Delaware by the
early 1700s. At about the same time, most Unami- and some Munsee-
speaking people living along the river's shores began using the word when
referring to themselves. Most of their descendants continue to identify
themselves as Delawares, as do municipalities, towns, counties, corporations,
clubs, and the small state at the river's mouth.[15]

As might be imagined, absence of a single universally accepted term for
Munsees, Unamis, Lenapes, and Delawares is a source of confusion. This is
particularly the case for those who believe that names are unequivocal re-
flections of stable social systems. Seeking order in seemingly contradictory
documentation marked by the use of different and sometimes seemingly
confused names, most early writers tended to regard what they considered
the earliest or most suitable name for a town, region, or nation as the
appropriate term of identification for all subsequent inhabitants associated

with the locale, feature, or polity in question. Those favoring this approach would continue to identify otherwise unidentified inhabitants as members of earlier mentioned nations or towns long after the name and composition of the community may have changed. This practice also led to invention of communities and confederacies where none existed. The persistent belief that all Indians living between the Hudson and Connecticut rivers belonged to a Mahican- (sometimes confusingly spelled Mohegan) speaking Wappinger Confederacy represents the best-known and most enduring example of the impact of this practice on Munsee studies.

Web surfers may be forgiven for believing that few facts of regional history seem more self-evident than the existence of a Wappinger Confederacy. Many would doubtless be surprised to learn that the confederacy is actually the creation of a nineteenth-century Newburgh, New York, newspaperman named Edward Manning Ruttenber. Ruttenber first proposed the existence of the confederacy in his *History of the Indian Tribes of Hudson's River,* published in 1872 and the first modern study of its type.[16]

Just as no clearly unambiguous name collectively identifies the original inhabitants of the Munsee homeland, no reliable figure tallies their aboriginal population. This, however, also is not unusual. Few societies of any sort kept track of population numbers before modern times. Some numbers do exist. Writing in 1628, a Dutch colonial official named Isaack de Rasiere penned the only known enumeration of Indian communities in the Munsee homeland counting both sexes. He estimated that eighty to ninety people lived on Staten Island, while another two hundred to three hundred people he called Manhattans, "women and men, under different chiefs," lived farther north. Other colonists, evidently preoccupied with matters of safety and security, only took note of what they called fighting men. In one example of this type of counting, Charles Wolley, an English clergyman who visited the region between 1678 and 1680, noted that Indians living between the Hudson and Delaware rivers could call on a total of more than 500 men of military age. By multiplying such numbers by factors of three, four, or five to account for women, children, and elders (an impressionistic if often used yardstick), Wolley's estimates can suggest population totals varying from 1,500 to 2,500 in those communities at this time.[17]

The dynamic nature of Indian settlement patterns in the Munsee homeland placed further obstacles in the paths of would-be census takers. Hometowns of particular extended families that usually sheltered a few dozen households occasionally became sites of substantial gatherings of hundreds or even thousands. The very same places could be totally abandoned at other times. Demographic impacts of wars, epidemics, and other disasters are even harder to determine in the absence of hard numbers. Although nearly every colonial commentator recognized declines in Indian populations, almost all observations were impressionistic. Writing in his journal of his visit to New York in 1680, Labadist missionary Jasper Danckaerts, for example, noted that he had "heard tell by the oldest New Netherlanders that there is now not one-tenth part of the Indians there once were, indeed, not one-twentieth or one-thirtieth." Reflecting on the fact that two small villages remained in 1645 where six towns once stood on Long Island, another commentator named Daniel Denton mused "how strangely they have decreased by the hand of God since the English settling of those parts." He went on to ascribe their destruction to a "divine hand . . . removing or cutting off the Indians, either by wars one with the other, or by some raging mortal disease."[18]

By their own accounts, settlers claimed to have killed between one thousand and two thousand Indian men, women, and children in attacks on communities in Munsee country made during the costliest war with the Dutch, fought between 1640 and 1645. Hundreds more died in other colonial conflicts and in wars with other Indians. Drink also caused its share of damage. As a story recalling first contact at Manhattan as the "place where we all got drunk" indicates, the particularly dramatic effects of alcohol on Indians were clear from the start. Fights broke out over it, exposure killed those befuddled by it, leaders complained about it in public (and quietly asked for it in private), and colonial authorities tried to stop settlers from selling it. Towards the end of the seventeenth century, a Minisink leader named Tomachkapay put a number on the problem. Speaking to English officials in 1681, he said "that about 60 of his people have been killed by knives in their drink in three years."[19]

Whatever the effects of booze and bullets, microbes were the biggest killers in Munsee country. Elders with weakened immune systems and very young people who had yet to develop resistance were particularly susceptible to epidemics of influenza, measles, and smallpox not known to have infected Indians before contact. These struck communities throughout the region with increasing frequency and dreadful regularity as the pace of colonization quickened.[20]

Epidemiological research findings show that diseases like smallpox and influenza can kill as much as 90 percent of an unexposed population. It is also clear that the people of Munsee country and their neighbors were afflicted by successive waves of the same diseases throughout the first centuries of contact. It is far from clear, however, that repeated infections by the same disease caused the same rates of mortality.

Attempts to assess the effects of war and disease usually start from baseline population figures. Most estimates of the aboriginal population in the Hudson and Delaware river valleys when Europeans first sailed to the region range between 10,000 and 30,000. Most earlier scholarly estimates varied from 20,000 to 22,600 based on crude population densities of 0.75 per square mile thought typical for hunters, gatherers, and farmers. More recently, investigators raised these figures by a factor of 50 percent, suggesting an extrapolated total Delaware population of 30,000. The more conservative figures most widely accepted today divide early estimates in half to produce a total aboriginal Delaware population estimate of from 10,000 to 12,000 people. In the absence of anything more substantial, a median number of 15,000 halfway between high and low counters will have to serve here as a population baseline figure at the time of contact. Whatever the number used, all estimates yield a total population that was tiny compared to the millions living in societies that started sending colonists to Munsee country shores during the early 1600s.[21]

Some scholars use small population size to support arguments asserting that aboriginal inhabitants in the Munsee homeland were hunters and gatherers living in small nomadic bands similar to those of Arctic Innuits, Australian Aborigines, and Kalahari Bushmen. Estimates of the crude population densities of these peoples range from 1 to 25 people per one hundred square miles of all territory, habitable and otherwise. Even the lowest estimate of Indian numbers in Munsee country yields a crude population density more closely resembling the 0.66 people per square mile figure more typical of sedentary hunting and gathering farmers like the Iroquois. This density is twenty-five to one hundred times larger than that usually found among nomadic hunting and gathering bands.[22]

Notions of population size directly influence what is thought about the structure of past societies. Nowhere is this fact more evident than in arguments over whether people in Munsee country lived in settled farming communities or belonged to less populous nomadic band communities. Many writers refer to their communities as bands only because they find alternatives like tribe and chiefdom even more of a problem. This issue is more than an academic quibble; words like "band," "nomad," and "tribe" reflect very specific social science concepts. Even their casual use evokes vivid images of the way of life followed by people addressed by particular terms.[23]

If one must categorize Munsees at all, Fried's term egalitarian seems to most closely fit the situation here. Egalitarianism in the Munsee homeland was governed by particular sets of principles regulating ancestry, descent, affiliation, and sociability. Munsees favored customs fostering traditions of flexibility, maximizing chances of dealing successfully with change and uncertainty. Such traditions often provided a degree of adaptive creativity needed to take advantage of opportunities and rise to challenges. They were tailor-made for dealing with the ambiguities of contact, often providing margins of flexibility, helping Munsees counter colonial intrusions that overwhelmed other, more rigidly regimented societies.[24]

Like other speakers of the Delaware language, those using the Munsee dialect were matrilineal people, who traced descent through successive generations of women related by blood to one another. Lineages were responsible for lands handed down by female blood-kin. Most but not all women stayed on family lands all their lives. Family rituals and ceremonies cemented temporal and spiritual ties between lineage members and their ancestors. Leaders and councils disposed of lineage land use rights held in trust for ancestral spirits.

Colonists preserved only the scantiest records of lineage names in Munsee- and other Delaware-speaking communities. Moravian chroniclers were probably referring to lineages when they talked about Delaware *hauptstammen,* "head stems or lines," and *freundschaften* (literally "friendships"). Some lineages took on the names of honored ancestors. The Amogarickakan, Mahow, Kettyspowy, and Kakatawis families first mentioned at a meeting with local authorities in Kingston, New York, in 1677 and the Mogewehogh, Mahaw, Kighshepaw, and Kaghkatewees families mentioned nearly seventy years later at another meeting in 1743 bore the names of four leaders who played significant roles during the wars of the 1650s and 1660s. Other family lineages in Munsee country evidently adopted the European practice of using names of notable ancestors like Nimham and Hekan as surnames.[25]

Marriage between lineage members, no matter how distantly related, was considered incest. This ensured that boys and men moved out and through households, towns, and territories of other families of women at different times during their lives. Most resided with their mothers at home when they were children and elsewhere with maternal uncles (who were addressed as and acted in the capacity of fathers) as they grew into adolescence. They lived in various places with different wives when they became adults (several simultaneously for influential polygamous men and one at a time for most monogamous others), and, very often, moved back where they started with sisters and maternal aunts as elders.[26]

Matriliny, however, was not the only kinship principle at work in Delaware society. The prominent leader Nutimus brought this point home to Quaker founder of Pennsylvania William Penn's agent James Logan at a meeting on May 8, 1735. When asked how he came to have rights to lands at the Forks of Delaware in Pennsylvania when he had been born on the other side of the river in New Jersey, Nutimus replied that "his mother came from this side of the river and by her he had a right here as likewise had to some land in the Jerseys which his father left him." Later writers used statements like this to support the idea that Munsees and other Delawares also had patrilineally descended family hunting territories.[27]

In their homeland, Munsees tended to organize their lives around matrilocal households. Husbands moved into their new wives' households after marriage as new spouses from other families moved into their mother's house. Thus, the sixteen to eighteen families living together in the one house chronicled by Van der Donck in 1655 probably represent a group of closely related extended families comprising a single matrilineage and their in-laws. A few years later, Danckaerts corroborated this observation when he noted that the twenty-eight people he saw living in a longhouse in Brooklyn in 1679 were "generally of one stock, as mother and father with their offspring."[28]

Whether they are called extended families, clans, or lineages, each of these matrilineally linked households probably belonged to larger groupings anthropologists call phratries. Members of lineages belonging to particular phratries all see themselves as people of one blood. Following the rule of phratry exogamy, they regard marriages between members of the same phratry, no matter how distantly related their lineages, as incestuous. This assures that members of at least two phratries can be found in every community no matter how small. For Munsees, people connected to this kind of kinship network had a high expectation of finding blood relatives from whom they could expect hospitality and protection wherever they traveled in the Delaware-speaking world. Particular lineages and phratries could dominate specific areas of the Munsee homeland only so long as they maintained the degree of cohesion sufficient to keep numbers up and affairs in order.[29]

The animal-named divisions usually translated as wolf, turtle, and turkey widely chronicled after Munsees and their kin were driven into exile are the most widely known features of Delaware Indian social organization. The social formations they represent have been a subject of much speculation since the Moravian missionary John Heckewelder first stated that Munsees of his acquaintance in Ohio linked Wolves with themselves, turtles with Unamis, and turkeys with people he called Unilachtegos. Subsequent investigators have pointed out that no other writers made the same connections. It is hard to imagine that Heckewelder, a fluent speaker of Munsee, completely misunderstood his friends. More probably, they were telling the missionary that members from particular animal divisions dominated particular Delaware nations. In their new lives out west, Munsees and other Delawares tried their best to use already existing family and national names as rallying points around which scattered people could organize themselves for specific purposes. Although use of the three animal divisions has receded into memory among present-day Delawares and Munsees, they would become particularly important in apportioning responsibilities for annual Big House religious get-togethers in Oklahoma and Ontario during the nineteenth and early twentieth centuries.[30]

Ties of blood with maternal kin and marriage links to paternal relatives helped Munsees preserve knowledge and secure and share tools needed to support a hunting, gathering, fishing, and farming society living in a region of widely scattered seasonally available resources. Networks formed by these ties allowed Munsees to travel to different places in their homeland that usually could support only small numbers of people for limited periods. Munsees did what they could to sustain ties when it made sense to do so and altered them when situations warranted. They came together, moved apart, and gathered again into different social, political, and ritual groups in different places at different times. Horizontally distributed and vertically organized, they ordered their society at different levels of what some anthropologists call sociopolitical integration.[31]

Like most other egalitarian people, the inhabitants of Munsee country did not maintain strictly static or hermetically sealed social boundaries beyond the blood ties of their matrilineages. Trying to reconcile personal autonomy with community needs, they had to make decisions about which task groups to join, what work to do, and how long to remain with the group. Unlike citizens of more rigid societies where bureaucrats give orders and where walls, visas, and border guards limit movement, Indians in and around the Munsee homeland could and did pursue wider ranges of available options. Opportunities were never unlimited, however. Choices were determined by a combination of social conventions, political realities, and environmental constraints that did not always neatly coincide. Feelings of desire, fear, piety, and pride mingled with practical considerations to further complicate matters.

Men called sachems, women addressed as squaw sachems, and spiritually blessed metewak whom settlers called doctors, magicians, and, much later, medicine men and women, stood ready to help guide people in Munsee country in making decisions. Depending on the situation, the roles of sachems and metewak could and often were combined in one person. Whatever their knowledge, skills, and abilities, sachems tended to be drawn from particular families and lineages giving evidence of being on good terms with the spirit world, with proven track records for leadership. As in most egalitarian societies, ability usually trumped heredity in matters of succession. At the same time, influential families employed their society's preferential marriage patterns and orchestrated kinship terms and connections to transfer authority and maintain politically advantageous linkages among themselves.[32]

Documented kinship connections of prominent seventeenth-century Massapequa sachem Tackapousha show how people belonging to influential lineages used kinship and marriage rules to maintain power and authority during colonial times. Tackapousha was one of the most widely known Indian culture brokers of his time. His evident ability to mediate between colonists and Indians helped him rise to the rank of paramount sachem of western Long Island, a position he held for more than fifty years, between the 1640s and 1690s.[33]

Tackapousha's immediate predecessors, Mechoswodt and his cousin Penhawitz, were the area's two most influential sachems during the first decades of Dutch colonization. Penhawitz was a leader of the Keschaechquereren community in the present-day Canarsie section of Brooklyn. Mechoswodt was leader of the Massapequa community farther west in present day Queens and Nassau counties. Both men referred to Tackapousha as a son. These claims make sense if western Long Island Indians employed what anthropologists call a Crow kinship term system. Among people using the Crow system, a child born into a matrilineal kin-group uses the word "father" to address both his mother's husband (who is a member of a different phratry and therefore unrelated by blood to his children) and his mother's

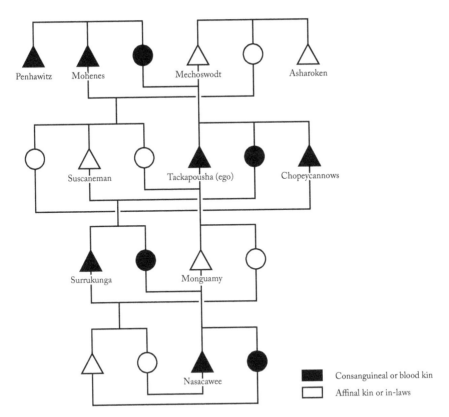

Figure 1. Cross-cousin marriage in western Long Island

brothers (who are related by blood). People using such terminologies often contract cross-cousin marriages between children of a mother and her brothers that would be considered incestuous unions of first cousins in American society (see figure 1). This, however, is not the case in Munsee and other unilineal societies. Children in such societies would belong to their mother's lineage and would inherit the rights and privileges of their mother's brothers. They would not necessarily succeed to the rights and obligations of their mother's husband; he would pass on his rights and obligations to his own sister's children.[34]

Multiple unions of cross-cousins, either through polygyny (marriage to more than one wife at one time) or by marrying brothers off to wives from different phratries, helped particular lineages in each phratry retain power and influence over several generations. The evidence indicates that Tackapousha was adept at extending and maintaining his lineage's influence by

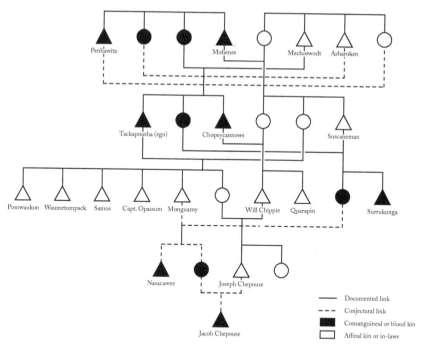

Figure 2. Tackapousha and his kin

contracting strategic marriages and arranging for sons born from these unions to be sachems of their communities. Marriage of his younger brother Chopeycannows to the sister of the influential sachem Suscaneman of the nearby Matinecock community, for example, assured close relations between the Massapequa and Matinecock communities. Six men identified in colonial records as Tackapousha's sons, noted on the kinship graph (see figure 2), each served as sachems of different western Long Island Indian communities.[35]

Thus Tackapousha, son of Penhawitz of Keschaechquereren, could inherit the sachemship of Massapequa from his maternal uncle, the Massapequa sachem Mechoswodt. As a person who addressed both men as father and whom both called son, Tackapousha would have been ideally situated to inherit the area's most influential sachemship if he could show that he was up to the job.[36]

Sachems like Tackapousha could maintain authority, however, only by demonstrating skill and ability. They were authoritative, not authoritarian. As Penn put it, they moved "by the breath of their people." Those capable of appealing to people's feelings won their support. Those that did not could swiftly lose followers. Relying more on the power of persuasion than on the persuasion of power, they worked together with councilors to hammer out a consensus. Consensus in Indian societies in the region did not mean unanimity. Rather, it meant consent, sometimes grudgingly given. Sachems engineering consensus helped direct labor, organize production, redistribute goods, and mediate disputes. They could also exact fines, order exile or execution, select experienced warriors to serve as captains during wartime, and order war captains to step down when it came time to make peace.[37]

Often represented by speakers with stronger oratorical and rhetorical skills, civil sachems conducted public business in councils. These were occasions for stately rituals ordering relations between people who were sometimes enemies, who often spoke different languages, and who frequently lived far away. The soothing rhetoric of the condolence ceremony and formal exchanges of pleasingly powerful gifts like wampum smoothed paths between strangers and friends everywhere in Munsee country and throughout the Indian Northeast. European strangers required rituals of their own, many involving formal speeches, solemn pledges, gift exchanges, and ceremonial placements of pen to paper. Treaty proceedings and deeds preserve records of their encounters mixing Indian and European beliefs, customs, and rituals.[38]

Whether expressed in the formal rhetoric of council meetings or in conversations between friends and family, information traveled quickly and widely in Munsee country. This helped people linked to one another by interconnecting networks hear about opportunities and threats. People free to travel along network lines could leave places where raiders were rumored to strike and move to places where deer were said to gather. This legacy of swift communication and direct observation maintained traditions of flexibility that would help Munsees effectively confront the challenges of European colonization.

2

MUNSEE COUNTRY

The ancestral homeland of the Munsee people was a land of old and new terrains jumbled together and resting atop some of the world's oldest and most ancient bedrock. Wind and fast-moving water melting from glacial ice sheets whose most recent retreat north began some 20,000 years ago did most of the mixing. The thick layers of clay, sand, and gravel left behind by the glaciers initially supported tundra, then dense cold-weather conifer forests similar to those found in Canada and Siberia today. These forests covered the land between the Hudson and Delaware rivers when most scholars think people first came to the region, around 11,500 years ago. They extended from the Appalachian Highlands across broad flat plains whose now-flooded easternmost reaches extended as much as sixty miles offshore beyond the present-day shoreline.

The mixed-hardwood forests that would be familiar to Munsees and present-day residents only emerged when regional climate warmed to modern levels some six millennia later. Archaeological evidence of tools, implements, house types, and foods similar to those in use by historically chronicled Munsee people dates their first appearance in the lower Hudson and upper Delaware river valleys to at least one thousand years ago.[1]

Munsee traditions concerning their origins are clear and unequivocal—whether they fell from the sky or emerged from deep beneath the earth, their first ancestors made their first earthly homes on what they called the Turtle Island, today's North America. Archaeological remains currently provide the only physical evidence of firstcomers to the region. The remains are scant indeed. Most of what survives consists of worked stone artifacts, manufacturing debris, and tiny bits of fortuitously preserved antler, bone, shell, charcoal, and pollen. While these remains speak volumes about the ways their makers made their livings, they reveal little about who they were and nothing of their inner lives.[2]

Archaeologists call the people who created the earliest known remains Paleo-Indians. Most think that Paleo-Indians first came to the region at the end of the most recent ice age. Although some believe that people arrived as much as ten thousand years earlier, the most solid evidence indicates that Paleo-Indians first journeyed to the region between thirteen thousand and ten thousand years ago, during a long stretch of cold weather climatologists call the Younger Dryas event. By that time, the great Wisconsin ice sheets that had advanced as far south as Perth Amboy had retreated north to the St. Lawrence Valley. Most of the land south of the ice sheets was covered by an unbroken expanse of conifers most closely resembling modern-day Siberian taiga and Canadian boreal forests. With considerable amounts of water still locked in glacial ice, lower sea levels exposed since-inundated coastal plains far beyond present-day shorelines.

Paleo-Indians had to travel light and far to make a living in this cold, dry environment. Those parts of their tool kit that survive, a mix of scrapers, gravers, knives, and projectile points, appear well suited for hunting and skinning game animals. Much of this technology was based on stone tools chipped from narrow straight blades struck from cores of the finest available stone. Paleo-Indians' most distinctive implement, what archaeologists call a diagnostic artifact, was the finely crafted lance-shaped fluted projectile point. Paleo-Indian toolmakers carefully sharpened the business ends of fluted points, roughly grinding their bases to provide firm purchase for bindings securing them to handles and shafts. The most distinctive attribute of these diagnostic tools was created by striking a long, narrow flake from the center of each point. This required considerable skill. The resulting channel, the flute for which the projectiles are named, thinned and lightened the point. Fluting also allowed makers to deeply embed all but the point's sharp edges into its handle. This enhanced the lance's aerodynamic qualities while providing a stout casing, protecting thin but brittle points against chipping and breakage.

Sharp, light, and lethal lances tipped with fluted points joined other parts of an eminently portable toolkit that allowed small bands of Paleo-Indian hunters and gatherers to travel on foot the long distances required to track and kill caribou and other game animals in ice age forests. Collectors have picked up hundreds of these fluted points on the surfaces of freshly plowed fields everywhere in the region. Archaeologists frequently led to find spots by their amateur discoverers have found substantial numbers of Paleo-Indian artifacts in places like the Plenge site in New Jersey's Muscontecong Valley and at Port Mobil on Staten Island (see map 3). More rarely, fluted points have been found in and around hearths and pits containing charred seeds, nut shells, and fish bones at places like the Shawnee-Minisink site near the Delaware Water Gap.

Paleo-Indians occupying these sites primarily depended on locally available sources for stone and other raw materials. Most commonly used were chert, quartz, and chalcedony cobbles found in nearby rivers. Other rock came from farther stone outcrops just west of the Hudson River north of the Catskill Mountains. Rare finds, like discoveries at the Dutchess Quarry Cave in Orange County, New York, of two Cumberland points most commonly found in places like the Tennessee Valley suggest contact with distant people living farther south. Other finds of tools and flakes made from green- and tan-banded Flint Ridge cherts and lustrous brown-red Ramah chert indicate that some Paleo-Indians in the region also traveled to or traded with people living as far away as Ohio and Nova Scotia.

For reasons that still remain unclear, Paleo-Indian toolmakers stopped passing on knowledge and skills needed to craft fluted points and other tools from blades about the time the ice age climate began to moderate, around ten thousand years ago. Fluting specialists died off or adopted new techniques. For the next seven millennia, hunters and gatherers everywhere in the Northeast made a succession of stone tool types suited to life lived in increasingly warmer and wetter temperate forests. Woodworkers used axes, adzes, and gouges pecked or ground from basalt and sandstone to fell trees and fashion timber into tool handles, house posts, and dugout canoes. Tool makers chipped sharp edged points, knives, scrapers, choppers, drills, and other implements from flakes struck from cobbles of lower quality but perfectly serviceable cherts, quartzes, quartzites, and argillites. Most of these stones were either collected from local riverbeds or pried from nearby outcrops.

Untold thousands of stone tools produced in a wide variety of notched and stemmed styles dating to these years, called the Archaic period by archaeologists, have been found everywhere in eastern North America. Like all styles, each was popular for a time before newer varieties proved more attractive. Although local tool makers may have invented some of these innovations, most came from places farther north, west, or south. It is impossible

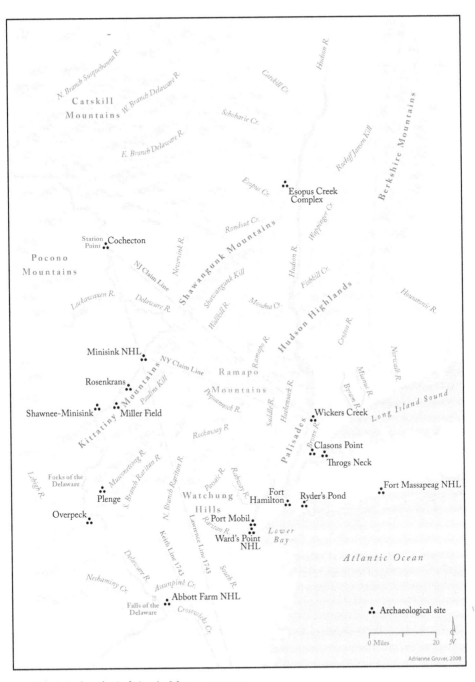

Map 3. Archaeological sites in Munsee country

to know at the present time whether changing stylistic patterns reflect spreading ideas or population movements.

Major changes again occurred between three thousand and four thousand years ago. Heaps of clams, oysters, and mussels found around New York Harbor and the lower Hudson reflect the rising importance of shellfish to inhabitants in the region. New forms of ground-stone implements joined those already in service. Slate bannerstones served as counterweights on handles of spear throwers. Also called atlatls or throwing sticks, implements weighted with bannerstones increased velocity, range, and killing power of formerly hand-thrown spears and lances. Hunters and fisherfolk using ground stone bolas, plummets, and netsinkers took greater numbers of fish and birds. Milling stones crushed seeds, roots, and anything else requiring grinding. Shallow bowls crafted from soapstone began to appear toward the end of this period. New stone point styles, known among archaeologists as Orient, Perkiomen, and Susquehanna broad spear points, also appeared at this time. Their makers increasingly favored stones not widely used earlier, like purplish argillites from the mid-Delaware Valley and creamy brown jaspers quarried from deposits in Pennsylvania's Lehigh Valley.

More dramatic changes began transforming people's lives farther west in the continent's interior at this time. Foragers in the Ohio and Mississippi valleys started intensively collecting seeds from amaranth, goosefoot, and other wild plants. They ground these seeds into flour, baked it into cakes and breads, or boiled it in stews and porridges cooked in stone bowls and, increasingly, in clay pots resembling those made by people living farther south. People also began planting seeds of squash plants originally domesticated in Mexico and Central America. They left broad-bladed points showing few or no signs of wear, shell beads from distant locales, red ochre powder, and tablets, gorgets, beads, and smoking pipes of copper, stone, and clay in what we think were storage caches.

These and other new products and ideas, and the people spreading them, soon began influencing neighbors in the Great Lakes region and Tennessee River valley. Innovations spread from these places to the coastal Northeast. Meadowood people from upstate New York, for example, left remains of small campsites, caches of distinctive unfinished stone blades (sometimes covered with a coating of powdered red ochre), equally distinctive ground slate birdstone counterweights, and a few burials in and around the Hudson River valley. They also introduced smoking pipes and pottery. The earliest of these ceramics were coarse soapstone-tempered pots known as Vinette 1 wares. Initially crafted as flat-bottomed vessels resembling soapstone bowls, potters later fashioned them into pointy-ended vase-shaped vessels.

People belonging to or influenced by the Ohio Valley Adena culture also left signs of their presence at various locales along northeastern shores and valleys from Chesapeake Bay to the Canadian Maritimes around this time. Archaeologists know them locally as Middlesex people. They deposited extremely well-made large stemmed and side-notched points, tubular sandstone and copper beads and smoking pipes, and slate gorgets and boatstones in caches and burials. One of these cemeteries, the Rosenkrans site, is located on a high bluff overlooking Wallpack Bend in the Delaware Water Gap National Recreation Area.

Evidence of several archaeological complexes postdating Meadowood and Middlesex is found throughout the region between 2,000 and 2,500 years ago. Distinctive point types, pottery styles, and mortuary customs continued to characterize cultures known to archaeologists as Bushkill, Fox Creek, and Kipp Island phase people. Clay pots and tobacco smoking pipes broadly similar to those produced by people in Munsee country at the time of colonial contact also first started appearing in the region around the same time. These were made by what archaeologists call members of the Point Peninsula tradition. The Point Peninsula archaeological tradition first appeared in the same part of the Great Lakes where many linguists believe the ancestral Proto-Algonquian language spread to the Northeast. Innovations like smaller stone points capable of being fixed to tips of arrow shafts and the first evidence of bean and squash cultivation began turning up with Point Peninsula artifacts in sites along the Hudson and Delaware rivers about 2,300 years ago, the same time Munsee and other Eastern Algonquian languages might have split from their Proto-Algonquian antecedents.

Archaeological materials more closely resembling those made and used by Eastern Algonquian–speaking people at the time of European contact first appeared in various places throughout the Northeast around one thousand years ago. Archaeologists have unearthed carbonized corncobs and tobacco seeds at several sites in the upper Delaware Valley and found triangular stone arrowheads throughout the region. These discoveries reflect adoptions of new crops and the advent of the bow and arrow as a widely used hunting tool and war weapon. The disappearance of ritual objects crafted from imported shells, stones, and metals, by contrast, signals an inward turn away from interaction spheres that had radiated outward from the continent's interior during preceding millennia. These developments occurred during an interval of moderating climate conditions called the medieval warm period. Weather during this time tended to be temperate, decidedly seasonal, and distinctly moist. Such conditions favored spread of corn and bows and arrows from warmer places to the region. Although no data exist to confirm or deny the possibility, better-fed, larger populations supported by new developments would have been better able to detach themselves from relationships with foreigners they may have regarded as dangerous, distasteful, or needlessly intrusive.

House types and pottery styles similar to those made by historically documented people living in Munsee country emerged in the archaeological record around eight hundred years ago. Postmold patterns of round-ended longhouses unearthed at Miller Field and other upper Delaware Valley sites suggest the beginnings of settled village life. These round-ended buildings had doors on the sides rather than at the ends like the square-sided longhouses found farther north around the same time in Iroquois country. Large cone-shaped Owasco-style wares and, somewhat later, squatter round-bodied Minisink series pots are also found in these sites. Pots of the latter style were often surmounted with elaborately incised castlelike rims. Human and animal effigies pressed or incised into pot rims and pipe bowls also make their first appearances in sites throughout the lower Hudson and upper Delaware river valleys sometime between six hundred and seven hundred years ago.

These house types and ceramic styles generally resemble those preferred by Iroquoian-speaking people living farther north and west and by Mahicans and Northern Indians in New England to the northeast. They differ from the roundhouse wigwams and bag-shaped Riggins and Bowmans Brook pots found in contemporary Lower Delaware Valley sites. These latter house and pottery forms more closely resemble similar types used by Nanticokes, Piscataways, Powhatans, and other more southerly historically documented Eastern Algonquian–speaking people. Findings of this sort suggest that differences between Munsee- and Unami Delaware-speaking people documented by Europeans probably began emerging at this time.

People almost certainly ancestral to the Munsees began gathering in snug longhouses to cook warming soups and stews in Owasco-style pots at about the same time colder little ice age weather patterns began making themselves felt, sometime around the 1300s and 1400s. Although temperatures dropped only an average of 3 or 4 degrees Fahrenheit (F) in most places during the four centuries of this climatic event, it was enough to ice over New York Harbor and the lower Hudson River estuary during particularly cold winters.

Little ice age climate conditions continued to dominate life in Munsee country throughout the first centuries of contact with Europeans. Average winter temperatures tended to hover between 15 and 20 degrees F in interior sections and from 32 to 36 degrees F closer to shore. Summers averaged between 72 and 76 degrees F along the coast and 62 to 66 degrees F farther inland. Temperature extremes in the region ranged from highs around the 100-degree-Fahrenheit mark to lows of more than -25 degrees F. Although yearly rainfall averaged around forty-five inches inland and fifty-five inches at the shore, drought, torrential downpours, and five-foot-deep snowfalls could significantly affect precipitation totals.

Then as now, winds constantly blew moisture-laden storm clouds across Munsee country. Delawares living in Oklahoma affirm that their ancestors regarded the powerful winds brought by northeasters, hurricanes, and tornadoes with a mixture of awe, fear, and respect. They also continue to consider the four cardinal directions from which the winds blow as grandparents. Three of these they think of as grandfathers; the fourth, the one that blows winds from the south, they call "Our Grandmother Where It Is Warm." Seasonal change is thought to reflect their changing fortunes on the gambling mat. Spring comes when South Grandmother is defeating North Grandfather; autumn signals a change in his luck. Their constant play assures seasonal change. Chance sees to it that the winds never blow the same way twice.

The breath of these grandparents blew over ramparts of stone, sand, and sea that guarded the borders of Munsee country. The open waters of the Atlantic Ocean, Long Island Sound, New York Harbor, and the Hudson Estuary formed water barriers securing the eastern frontiers of the Munsee heartland. Appalachian foothills known today as the Kittatiny (from the Munsee word for "Big Mountain"), Catskill, Taconic, and Berkshire mountains rose along the region's northeastern, northern, and western margins. Ice age glaciers scouring these and other uplands farther north pushed vast masses of stony rubble into broad terminal moraines stretching along the spine of Long Island across central New Jersey to the Delaware Water Gap. The pervasive presence of rock rubble and outcrops everywhere in the region is reflected in place names like Ossining, from *ashunusung*, "place of little stones."

Another Munsee place name, Rockaway (from *leekuwii ahkiing,* "at the sandy land"), marks locales where wind and water deposited thick blankets of sand and gravel. Wide swathes of sand lying across Long Island's midsection and the southern approaches to Munsee territory support dense pinelands. Often called barrens, they form thick thorny barriers that still extend across the southern and eastern reaches of the region. On Long Island, pinelands separated Munsee communities from those of Montauketts, Shinnecocks, and other more easterly nations.

The Munsee heartland protected by these bulwarks of rock, sand, and salt water was and is a world of water. Stretching inland from the open waters of the North Atlantic and its bays, sounds, and harbors, the heart of Munsee territory lay astride two of the region's greatest rivers. The larger of the two, the Hudson, called the North River and the River of the Mountains by the Dutch, is a broad arm of the ocean. Its tidal character is reflected in its Mahican name, Muhheahkkunnuck, "River that Flows Both Ways." The Delaware River, by contrast, is a mountain stream in Munsee country running between the Catskill and Pocono plateaus, where stretches of boulder-strewn rapids separate broad sluggish reaches of placid flat water called eddies.

Gaps cut by these two great rivers through inland mountain walls opened the Munsee heartland to waterborne travelers journeying between the coast and the interior. Along the Delaware, its gap lay more than fifty miles north of the falls marking the head of navigation at present-day Trenton, New Jersey. The Hudson, by contrast, extended unobstructed by falls or rapids much farther inland beyond mountain walls than any other river in eastern North America.

Political and place names indicate how the watery web traced by these rivers and their tributary creeks and streams loomed large in the minds of the region's inhabitants. Colonists used the term River Indians to identify Indians living beside regional waterways. As mentioned earlier, Indians living along the Delaware ultimately accepted the English name of their river as their own. Colonists collectively referred to people living along the Walkill, Rondout, and Esopus drainage wending its way across the Great Valley between the Catskills and Hudson Highlands as Esopus Indians, from the Munsee word *siipuw,* "creek." Massapequa (as indicated by parsing out its earliest known written forms as Maros-sepi-inck) and Paramus, an apparent contraction of the place name Paramp Seapus (possibly a composite mixing the way the English word "plum" sounded to Munsees with their word for creek), are also built around the word. Fishkill provides a less immediately recognizable example. Colonists applied this name, the Dutch equivalent of the Munsee name *nameesii siipuw*, "fish creek," to the West Branch of the Delaware River above Hancock, New York. It is preserved today as the name of a village and creek in Dutchess County, New York.[3]

The Munsee word *pequa*, "stream," also appears with some frequency on regional maps. One translation of the name Pequannock, a word that may have been brought to northern New Jersey by immigrants from Connecticut where it is also found, suggests an original meaning approximating "a stream between two hills." Although some specialists believe Massapequa was a word meaning "big stream," Munsees used *kicht* rather than *massa* to express large size.[4]

Other place names indicate that the people of Munsee country and their neighbors evidently paid particular attention to shapes, forms, features, and conditions of waterways that ran through their homelands. Connecticut means "at the Long River" in the Quiripi-Unquachog dialect. Susquehannock is probably a Nanticoke or Powhatan word for "Muddy River." Musconetcong is a Munsee word meaning "rapid running stream." One of the first etymologies suggested for Hackensack translates as "the stream which discharges into itself on low level ground." Tankiteke, "Little River," probably refers to a small tributary of the Housatonic River that coursed through the heart of the homeland of people identified by that name in western Connecticut. The shallow branching character of many upland waterways is reflected in names like Wawayanda, "ditch," and Lehigh, Lackawaxen, Lackawack, and Lackawanna, all of which contain variants of the Munsee word for river fork or branch. Woaraneck, "a very fine stream, one without rapids," may refer to the quiet upper course of the Walkill River as it winds its way through Great Valley–drowned lands in Orange County, New York.[5]

Names also indicate where particular places along the courses of regional rivers figured prominently in the minds of Munsee country's first people. The area's inhabitants regarded islands as singularly secure places of habitation. As already seen, place names like Manhattan reflect the importance of islands safely surrounded by streams, swamps, and steep-sided bluffs to the people of the region. Other names, like Wallpack, "a turn hole or a deep and still place in a stream," the name of a bend in the upper Delaware River, and Ashokan, "there is walking in water," the present-day reservoir that flooded a ford along the upper Esopus Creek, focus on stream characteristics. Necks, hooks, and other promontories were particularly desirable fishing places, crossings, and observation points. Neversink, for example, probably comes from the words meaning "place you can see from far off." Nyack, a word that appears on past and present regional maps in many forms, may mean "neck or point of land" or may come from *aanayiik*, "there are trails."[6]

Regional waterways flowed across a domain of forests, grasslands, and wetlands resting on and, in some places, overlooked by towering rock walls. The most indestructible of these are the solid magma diabases and trap rock basalts of the Palisades and the Reading Prong that stretches across north-central New Jersey into eastern Pennsylvania and the quartz- and mica-flecked metamorphic marbles, gneisses, and schists of New York's Hudson Highlands and New Jersey's Ramapo ("underneath the rock," i.e., a rock shelter) and Watchung (from the Munsee *wachtsu*, "mountain," and *ahkiing*, "place") mountains. Multilayered sandstone and shale ridges interlaid at intervals with flaky chert nodules and argillite outcrops ideal for chipping into stone tools extend across both sides of the upper Delaware River. These become the Shawangunk Mountains (from a Munsee expression meaning "in the smoky air") as they trend northeastward to their terminus in the mid-Hudson Valley.[7]

Other place names reflect the importance of flat land to the region's people. Wetlands valued for their fish, waterfowl, reeds, and roots lined the shores of Long Island's Mosquito Cove (an English pun merging their word for the bug with the Eastern Algonquian word for "swamp") and the present-day Harlem River, originally called Kil Muscota by the Dutch. All are derived from Munsee variants of *muskeg*, still widely used in Canada. Wiechquaesgeck, "at the end of the swamp" (anglicized as Wickers Creek), was the Munsee name for the area around present-day Dobbs Ferry in Westchester County. Another place name, Pascack in present-day Rockland County, appears to come from *seekapaskahk*, "wet grass."

Indians living in the Munsee homeland also valued fertile bottomlands blanketed by forests and grasslands growing from on deep soils ground and grated by glacial ice from softer sedimentary sandstones and limestones. Names of places like Tacony in the Lower Delaware Valley and the East River island of Tenkenas (present-day Wards Island) may trace their origins to the Munsee word *tekene*, "forest." Passaic in the upper Hackensack Valley comes from the Munsee word for valley. Wyoming, from the Unami *m'ch-wewamunk*, "at the extensive river flats," is preserved most prominently on modern maps as the name of the broad valley along the North Branch of the Susquehanna River around Wilkes Barre, Pennsylvania, and as the name of the state whose wide vistas reminded nostalgic settlers of their homes back east.[8]

Particularly salubrious ecologies of weather, water, and land came together only at certain times and places in Munsee country. Climatic, technological, political, social, and other limiting factors further narrowed the number and availability of niche settings. Shifting locations, sizes, and functions of settlements in tidewater locales, for example, reflected changes in season, salinity, and sea level. Factors like time of year, terrain and forest conditions, skill levels and availability of people, traveling distance, and tool efficiency governed choices of hunting and foraging grounds. Access to good trails and navigable waterways, ample supplies of wood and water, prospects for adequate sanitation, and sufficient distance from pests and potentially quarrelsome neighbors helped determine locations of large or lengthy gatherings. Rock art, stone cairns, and pictographs incised into tree trunks marked caves, whirlpools, and other places believed to connect their country to the world of spirit powers.

Settlers tended to build their first settlements on lands already cleared by Indian people. Later, cities, towns, and villages grew around many early colonial settlements. Plowing, development, road building, and vandalism have destroyed much physical evidence of Indian life in these places. The extent of site destruction is particularly severe in heavily urbanized areas like Manhattan, the lower Passaic River, and the Lehigh Valley. Landfill, urban sprawl, and looting, moreover, have damaged or destroyed most tidewater sites. Not all has been lost, however. Museum collections and pages of local histories, for example, preserve records of discoveries made at long-obliterated sites like Ryder's Pond and Fort Hamilton in Brooklyn and the Throgs Neck and Clasons Point locales in the Bronx. The National Park Service has designated two of the small number of tidewater sites escaping total destruction as National Historic Landmarks. The Ward's Point National Historic Landmark at the southern tip of Staten Island still preserves evidence of more than six millennia of occupation despite years of looting. Thirty miles farther east, much-disturbed archaeological deposits in the Fort Massapeag National Historic Landmark in Nassau County contain the only surviving remains of a palisaded fortification used by Indians in the Greater New York area.

Farmers, potters, and foundry men long ago carted off most shells heaped in more readily accessible middens at Croton Point and other locales along the lower Hudson. Some deposits, however, still survive. Recent excavations at the

Wickers Creek site in Dobbs Ferry, New York, for example, uncovered large numbers of stone tools and much manufacturing debris. Other substantial deposits are also preserved farther upriver. A number of rock shelters have been excavated in and above the Hudson Highlands. Small scatterings of flaked and shattered stone debris and other materials also still mark locations of campsites on flat lands in many places throughout the region. Few of these campsites, however, contain diagnostic artifacts clearly linking them to Munsee ancestors.

Cities like Newark, Newton, Clinton, and Phillipsburg in New Jersey; Kingston, Newburgh, and Port Jervis in New York; and Allentown, Bethlehem, and Easton in Pennsylvania now lie atop centers of former Munsee occupations. Despite this fact, development has not obliterated such evidence at every locale favored by the region's Indian people. Archaeologists have found evidence of particularly dense concentrations of settlement, for example, in the historically chronicled Esopus heartland. Most of this material lies on terraces rising above broad flats lining both banks of the Esopus Creek in and around present-day Hurley, New York. Other sites have been found on shorter stretches of flat land in the Huguenot Street National Historic Landmark, overlooking the Walkill River at New Paltz, as well as along the Ramapo, Musconetcong, Millstone, and other inland streams.[9]

Investigators have unearthed particularly substantial amounts of archaeological material at several historically documented locales along the upper reaches of the Delaware River. Dense concentrations of evidence still lie buried beneath fields and forests at the Minisink National Historic Landmark, Miller Field, and other sites protected by the National Park Service within the Delaware Water Gap National Recreation Area. Farther downriver, the Abbott Farm National Historic Landmark preserves remains of fishing camps and other settlements at the head of navigation around Trenton, New Jersey. Sites of smaller, but still substantial settlements like Cochecton, "finished, completed," and Overpeck (in Kintnersville, Pennsylvania) lie on stretches of flat land north of the falls at Trenton.[10]

Existence of sites dating to the period of colonial contact north and south of the Lehigh Valley suggests that sites of similar vintage in modern-day Allentown, Bethlehem, and Easton were buried or destroyed before they could be recorded. New construction and innovative technological developments like ground-penetrating radar may reveal deeply buried or other intact deposits in these and other places that possessed resources and conditions favored by the aboriginal inhabitants of Munsee country.

Pollen grains and other evidence preserved in soil siphoned up in cores drilled at various places in the region show that in the warm months, forests were still vast oceans of shade dominated by gigantic ancient maples and oaks during Late Woodland times. Leafy canopies rising high above forest floors covered the region's mountains and ridges to their crests. Charcoal smudges on growth rings of still-standing ancient trees in places like Rutgers University's Hutcheson Memorial Forest in central New Jersey affirm that fires set by Indians in the fall or spring to burn off brush and drive game cleared floors of forests to such an extent that the first European visitors thought they looked like Old World game parks. Burned-over forest floors lit by light streaming through tree branches that shed their leaves in fall also eased travel by snowshoe and toboggan during cold months. Fires were set in areas where accumulations of brush were not large enough to sustain blazes hot enough to reach tree tops. During warm months, the sun shone directly only on wetlands, prairies, beaches, open waters, and rivers, which must have looked like brightly lit highways running through otherwise dark forest expanses.[11]

Indian people linked to one another by rituals and relationships traveled along the region's forest paths and waterways to forage, farm, hunt, and fish. Rhythms of tide and season set the tone and tempo of these peoples' passages through networks as dark and as light as they were both symbolic and substantial that joined them to their land and each other. They hunted summer-fattened deer and bear during the cold months, taking spawning striped bass, shad, sturgeon, eels, and herring, and planting corn, beans, and squash when warm weather came. Those living closest to salt water followed the ebb and flow of tidal waters to net, spear, and hook flounder, fluke, striped bass, and bluefish. At low tide they dug clams and mussels from sand flats and gathered fish, crabs, and other creatures stranded in tidal pools.

Munsee families and invited guests often gathered during shad runs or after harvest time. Amounts of available food and firewood joined with sanitary considerations to limit the size and duration of such gatherings. Thousands could assemble at places like the rock wall of the Falls of the Passaic at Paterson, New Jersey, or the Falls of the Delaware at Trenton, where fish waited their turns to cross rapids that slowed progress to upriver spawning grounds.

Tidal forces of war and belief also pushed and pulled on Munsee communities. Evidence preserved in the ground at Fort Massapeag and on paper in colonial documents and drawings indicate that some communities barricaded themselves behind fortifications during times of trouble. Others scattered, sometimes moving far from ancestral territories until danger passed. Large gatherings answered calls of dreamers and religious leaders to pray and give thanks together. These same leaders could convince people to move away from places rendered uninhabitable by forces beyond their control.

Although some very brief descriptions survive, no single account fully describes what an Indian community looked like around the time Europeans began colonizing the Munsee homeland. An idea of one community's appearance can be had by putting Late Woodland and early contact period house patterns together with drawings and descriptions written by Adriaen van der Donck and others. This imaginary composite may be placed in a small clearing in today's Bronx County, hacked and burned out of the dense forest canopy whose remnants can still be seen along the Bronx River in Bronx Park. It lies on a well-drained, level piece of land above and a bit behind the floodplain of a fast-running section of the river, just above the falls marking the uppermost reach of tidewater at present-day West Farms. Small streams like the Bronx River, known as Ranachquahung in the Munsee language, are preferable to big rivers like the Hudson, which can swell with floodwaters and where uninvited strangers can happen by without warning at any time.

Ranachquahung's swift current provides drinking water as it washes away eggs and larvae of mosquitoes and other pests. Fish are speared and netted from rocks overlooking pools and holes below ledges and between boulders. Some rocks leaving sharp edges when cracked in just the right way are ideal raw material for stone tools. Other water-worn fine-grained rocks found on the river bottom do not burst when heated. These are just right for hot-rock cooking and sweat lodges. Stone gouges chip away wood charred from tulip tree trunks hollowed to make long, slender dugout canoes. Stone adzes shape and smooth the outer hulls of these boats. Finished craft are launched from the shore of a quiet, wide, slow-moving eddy above the rift where the creek starts to tumble past the town.

Surrounding shady woods are filled with clearings lit by shafts of light. In these clearings, leafless trees girdled and scorched by fires set to burn brush stand dead in garden plots cleared by the cooperative labor of men and women. Women and children swinging horn, bone, and wooden hoes till and weed low mounds of soil where clumps of corn, beans, squashes, and melons are grown. Although they do not have to, loving husbands and accommodating grandfathers help out. They take turns guarding fields, drive away pests, and assist in the harvest. Some men also care for small plots of tobacco. Most of the clearings, however, lay fallow and uncultivated. Townsfolk practice a long fallow form of shifting slash-and-burn agriculture. Fields planted one season need several more to recover fertility. During warmer months, berries, greens, roots, and milkweed pods bursting with soft down that can be twisted into sewing thread and yarn cord grow in the resting fields. Saplings, young trees, and deadfalls in and around field clearings provide firewood and furnish poles and bark for building materials as well as for dugout canoe hulls. Willow, dogwood, maple, and other hardwood branches gathered nearby are fashioned into bows, bent into frames for drying skins, and whittled down into handles and tool shafts. Craftsfolk wrap raw hide and sinew around bases of pecked-stone axes, adzes, and gouges and chipped-stone knife blades, scrapers, drills, and arrow points inserted into shaft notches or fitted into handle grooves. Glues made from tree sap or boiled fish and other animal bones and fat secure tools to handles. Men find the arrows and spears that craftsfolk produce particularly useful when hunting deer, bear, and other animals attracted to cleared fields.

Women use chipped stone knives and scrapers to prepare meat and fish for cooking and storage and to scrape, tan, and tailor animal skins into skirts, loincloths, shoes, and other apparel. Hats and other headgear are not needed to ward off sun rays in this shady forest world and are rarely seen. Shoes and mantles, on the other hand, are important. Shoes protect the feet of people whose canoes are their only other way of getting around. Mantles worn over the shoulder protect against branches and brambles, ward off rain and snow, warm wearers in winter, and absorb cooling sweat when the weather gets hot.

The ground is increasingly beaten hard by footprints as the town center is neared. Standing trees become fewer and larger. Woodworkers, stone knappers, and lounging townsfolk shelter under small bark-roofed tents and lean-tos built to deflect wind, rain, and sunlight. Smoky fires drive away insects and broil cuts of meat and fish set on sticks and wooden racks placed around the fires. Leaf-wrapped corn cakes bake in hot ashes. Women use sapling tongs to place rocks heated in the fires into clay pots filled with fixings for stews and soups.

The town center boils with dogs and children. They run and play around fireplaces in clearings containing one or two low-slung longhouses. Each is around sixty to eighty feet long, around ten feet wide, and from eight to ten feet high. They are bent pole–framed affairs covered with bark slabs and mats woven from fresh and saltwater sedge grasses and reeds. Sapling-framed doors or skins hung at the far sides of each house open into a dark windowless interior lit only by fires in rock-lined fireplaces and holes in the ceiling where bark sheets have been moved aside to let out smoke and let light and air in. Several of these fireplaces are located at intervals along a central corridor. Each lies at the center of a small apartment divided from others by bark and mat walls. Woven baskets and other containers store possessions stashed beneath sleeping platforms built along apartment walls and in the eaves above the apartments. Plaited corncobs and dried strips of squash and meat hanging from apartment ceilings help keep hunger away during good years. Dried herbs for teas hang in their place during lean times. Combined with tightened belts, they curb appetites.

The apartments are mostly empty during the day and whenever weather is dry and warm. Couples make love in the fields, and almost everyone sleeps under tents or lean-tos. There is no plumbing. Water is drawn from the creek or from nearby springs. There are no toilets and no town dump. People bathe in the creek and take sweat baths in hot-rock heated lodges. They relieve themselves in the woods. Refuse is thrown into the fire or thrown to the dogs. There is also no cemetery. Those who die when the ground outside is frozen are often buried indoors beneath fireplaces until the ground thaws and they can be decently interred in the forest. Bodies of infants and young children are frequently buried beneath trails so that their spirits, it is believed, can reenter passing mothers and have another chance at life. Small pots or bows and arrows are often hung in nearby trees and bushes to mark the graves of girls or boys.

Townsfolk still move to new home sites five, ten, or twenty miles away when they exhaust local soils and strip forests of readily accessible firewood and workable timber. Although much remains the same as it was for hundreds of years before contact, a person visiting this community during the early decades of European contact will notice many changes. Many children have blue eyes and curly blonde or red hair. There are also more graves around than formerly. Epidemics have carried off many of the town's inhabitants. Pockmarks scarring the faces of survivors testify as much to the protection of spirit guardians as to their immunological good fortune. More people seem to live in the town despite the epidemics. Some speak the Quiripi dialect used by friends and relatives farther east. Others speak the languages of more distant Mahican and Susquehannock nations. A few practice what sound to them like odd-sounding Dutch words and expressions on one another.

The place also seems to be busy. Many deer carcasses hang from hooks, and more pelts than formerly dry on frames. Larger and more numerous gardens flourish near the houses. Townsfolk exchange furs, deer meat, and garden produce for Dutch goods. In the past, they could get only a few beads, some iron nails, and a few scraps of copper and brass from occasionally visiting sailors. Now traders at Fort Amsterdam, the post built at the tip of lower Manhattan in 1626, just fifteen miles away, offer finished goods like woven blankets; iron knives, axes, and awls; and copper pots. The latter are increasingly used for cooking rather than as raw material cut up into triangular arrowheads or tube-shaped beads.

Not everything brought by the Dutch winds up at Ranachquahung. Dutch laws, for example, prohibit trade of guns, lead, and powder to Munsees. They do, however, give them beer, brandy, and wine, also banned by law. Drink makes them part with goods as easily as it separates them from their senses. Bad feelings rise as colonial lust for Indian furs and Indian desire for drink fuels arguments and encourages abuses. Fights break out, and people are hurt and killed. Although condolence presents and soothing words quiet passions for a time, fear and resentments begin to build along Ranachquahung as they do elsewhere throughout the region.

Part II

EUROPEANS
COME TO MUNSEE COUNTRY,
1524–1664

3

CONTACT, 1524–1640

Munsees knew nothing of Europe or its people when Giovanni da Verrazano wrote the earliest known eyewitness description of his visit to New York Harbor in 1524. A Florentine navigator sailing in the service of King Francis I of France, Verrazano hove into the bay one blustery day in early March 1524. Christening the place Santa Margarita, after the patron saint of the king's eldest sister, he conferred the name Angoleme, Francis's family name, on the surrounding countryside.[1]

Verrazano piloted his ship through the Narrows separating Brooklyn from Staten Island. Beyond in the upper harbor, he saw people "clothed with feathers of birds of various colors." He wrote that the harbor was "a beautiful lake with a circuit of about three leagues; over which [Indians] went to and fro in 30 of their little boats, with innumerable people who passed from one shore to the other in order to meet us." A rising breeze blew his ship back out to sea before he had a chance to speak with anyone.

Tantalizing bits of evidence suggest other visits in the decades following this voyage. Reports of French strangers sailing up the St. Lawrence River in 1535 and 1542 almost certainly made their way south to Munsee country. Other messages probably brought word of the Spanish James River mission built in 1570 in what later became Virginia and destroyed a year later by local Indians. Indians in Munsee country may have seen or met Englishmen who also began sailing along regional shores following the disappearance of their Roanoke Colony in North Carolina in 1585. And they almost assuredly knew that some Englishmen built a small fort they christened Jamestown on the Virginia coast in 1607. Sustained direct contact, however, did not begin in Munsee country until a few years after Hudson sailed into what he called the River of the Mountains in 1609.[2]

Dutch merchant companies specially chartered to raid Spanish shipping and to trade for furs with Indians soon began granting licenses to independent free traders, allowing them to make voyages to what shortly became known as New Netherland. Few records document these initial voyages. What was written was terse and almost wholly devoted to matters of trade and navigation. Most used only the broadest of terms when describing local inhabitants.[3]

This incurious attitude did not matter much so long as contacts were infrequent, brief, and conducted over ships' rails or on beach tent blankets. Most of the writers of these logs and diaries were neither ready penmen nor much interested in guiding potential rivals to favored trading spots. Because of this, little can be gleaned from their writings. This does not mean that nothing happened or that what did happen was entirely peaceful. Log entries record that on occasion, Indians attacked voyagers. Others note that sailors stole from, kidnapped, and killed Indians. Even Hudson's voyage was marred by shootings that claimed the lives of several Indians and one of his crew.

Despite this, both Hudson and one of his ship's officers, Robert Juet, managed to record the first Munsee word documented in European chronicles. The word was Manhattan, penned in the forms Manahata and Manahatin. The name was soon inscribed on a map evidently furtively copied from their papers and secretly sent by Don Alonso de Velasco, the Spanish ambassador to England, to his sovereign Phillip III in 1610.[4]

Other Munsee words soon appeared on maps drawn by free traders Adriaen Block and Cornelis Hendrickszen van Monnickendam, two of the five skippers who first sailed to Hudson's river under trade charter licenses in 1614. Block ventured along the coast from Delaware Bay to the island that today bears his name. He overwintered on Manhattan, building a small yacht that he christened the *Onrust,* "Restless," after his ship, the *Tijger,* "Tiger," burned just off the island's southern tip. Block placed names and locations of people and places he visited, heard about, or saw on John Smith's map (drawn in 1612 and entitled "Map of Virginia") onto his own projection.[5]

Block's map brought several Munsee place names to international notice. These included Sangicans, placed on the map across the Hudson River from the island Block called Manhates. His map also contained some of the earliest references to nations farther inland, like the Mahicans, Mohawks (written Maquaas), Senecas, and Susquehannocks (written Minqua). Block was also the first Dutchman to give the name Archipelago to the rocky island-strewn fifty-mile-long stretch of coastline extending eastward along the north shore of Long Island Sound from Manhattan, which encompassed the territory of people he called Quiripeys (Quinnipiacs, who lived along the river of the same name that empties into the sound at New Haven, Connecticut) and ran west to the Hellgate of the East River.

Cornelis Hendrickszen van Monnickendam sailed Block's Onrust back to New Netherland and made two voyages of his own during the next two years. The map he made of his voyages added Indian names of places and polities not on Block's projection. Among them were references to the Woranecks, Esopus, and Pachami on the east bank of the Hudson above the Highlands and to the Waranawanka on the west bank. The first references to the east bank Wiechquaesgecks (noted in the form Wikagyl in their historically chronicled location on the southeastern shore of the Hudson) and Tappans and Mechkentiwoom across the river from what he styled Manhattes, also appear, as do two variants of Block's Sanhican. Hendrickszen placed his Sangicans near Newark Bay and located what he called Stankekans farther southwest, alongside symbols indicating the location of longhouses on both shores of the Delaware River at the important fisheries at its falls at Trenton. The place's value was enhanced by its location at the river's head of navigation, midway along the best level land route linking New York Harbor with the Lower Delaware Valley. This value only increased as trade with Europeans grew in importance during the next few decades.[6]

Block's and Hendrickszen's maps join other surviving records confirming that the early Dutch visitors limited themselves to a maritime commerce carried on in open bay and river waters, at safe anchorages, and within their first tiny outpost at Fort Nassau in present-day Albany. Indians doing business with these Dutchmen wanted iron and their copper pots, pans, knives, awls, and axes. Those intending to fashion or repair their own tools and implements also found sheets of metal scrap acceptable. Woven wool, flax, and cotton textiles traded in bolt rolls, cut into sections called blankets, or tailored into shirts, coats, and other apparel were also desirable, as were glass beads, mirrors, and vermillion. In return, the Indians offered beaver and other pelts and gave visitors food, fresh water, information, and other things.

The era of free-trading ventures commanded by captains whose words were law quickly passed. Their place was taken by men employed by a group of influential merchant-investors who formed themselves into the Dutch West India Company in 1621. The company started up just as the Twelve Year Truce with Spain ended. Like the already established Dutch East India Company and the English Virginia Company chartered by King James I in 1606, the Dutch West India Company was expected to challenge Spanish dominance on the Atlantic and funnel booty and trade goods back to the mother country. The Dutch West India Company's outposts in West Africa, Brazil, the Caribbean, and New Netherland were intended to be self-governing profit centers. They were also depots used to supply and shelter Dutch privateers and warships sailing against Spain and other hostile powers.[7]

Unlike other Dutch colonies, the strategic and economic virtues of the tiny New Netherland colony were not readily apparent to investors. The densely forested, rocky strip of land between what the Dutch now called the Fresh, North, and South rivers (today's Connecticut, Hudson, and Delaware rivers) nestled uncomfortably on territory claimed by both Spain and England, midway between Jamestown and the New Plymouth colony established by the Virginia Company in 1620. Some directors thought that efforts in New Netherland should focus on fur trade with the Indians. Others felt it should be an agricultural colony. Debate shifted between those arguing for company control of all activities in the colony and those trying to increase revenue by throwing commerce open to all comers. Whatever point of view they argued from, all thought the place should be a money-maker.[8]

The company began its search for profits by appointing as its first resident director a veteran of several trading voyages named Cornelis Jacobszen May. Cape May, at the southern tip of New Jersey, preserves the memory of his name. A new director, Willem Verhulst, was in command by the time the company was able to send the first ships carrying a few dozen families, soldiers, and traders in 1625. Intended to consolidate Dutch control over the area, the vessels debarked their passengers at several newly built outposts. One of these, a small piece of land surrounded by the waters of New York Harbor that Indians called Pagganck, "nut island," lay in the heart of Munsee country. Selected as the location of Verhulst's headquarters, the place was soon known as Governor's Island. Pieter Minuit, who replaced Verhulst a year later, felt that the island was not a suitable site for a trade center. Instead, he bought Manhattan from the Indians and began to build the colony's capital of New Amsterdam at its southern tip.

BUYING MANHATTAN

Manhattan was the first place formally purchased by the Dutch West India Company in Munsee country. In the years following its purchase, Minuit and his successors, most notably Wouter van Twiller, who became director in 1633, and Willem Kieft, who replaced him in 1638, worked to settle colonists on land in and around the island. From the start, Manhattan was more than just a place name. The maker of the 1610 Velasco map acknowledged this fact when he took care to distinguish what he called Manahatin the place from Manahata the people.

In his *Nieuwe Wereldt* (New World), a promotional pamphlet first published in 1624, Dutch West India Company director Johannes de Laet published the first account referring to Manhattans as a people. De Laet himself never visited New Netherland. Staying at home in Holland, he based his account of goings-on at Manhattan on voyagers' accounts. Writing about the Hudson River, "called by some the Manhattes River," he observed that "on the east side, upon the main land, dwell the Manatthans, a bad race of Indians, who have always been very obstinate and unfriendly toward our countrymen." This reflected the general Dutch attitude toward the people of the bay, a bad reputation that had clung to them after warriors there retaliated for the killing of several of their own people by attacking the *Halve Maen's* crew.[9]

Few documents chronicle the purchase of Manhattan. Significantly, none of these are deeds. In the 1633 edition of his pamphlet, De Laet noted that "our people have bought from [the Manatthans] the island separated from the rest of the land by the Hellgate." A letter from a company agent notifying the States General of the safe arrival of the ship *Arms of Amsterdam* from New Netherland on November 5, 1626, dryly observes that colonists "purchased the island Manhattes from the Indians for the value of 60 guilders; it is 11,000 morgens [22,000 acres] in size." Only afterward did another early pamphleteer who never set foot on New Netherland, a man named Nicolaes Janszoon van Wassenaer, write that the purchasers established their new settlement among "a nation called Manates."[10]

No bill of sale documenting the Indian sale of Manhattan has ever been found (a fake deed most likely produced in 1677 is on file in the New York Archives in Albany). The identity of the Indians who sold the island, moreover, is not known. Rarely mentioned after the sale, evidently Manhattan Indians did not immediately leave their island or its surrounding hinterland.

Two years after the purchase, for example, then-resident company secretary Isaack de Rasiere may have been writing about Manhattan Indians when he noted that "up the river the east side is high, full of trees, and in some places there is a little good land, where formerly many people have dwelt, but who for the most part have died or been driven away by the Wappenos" in a passage describing development opportunities on Manhattan Island at the time of its purchase.[11]

De Rasiere went on to note that the Manhattan nation consisted of several communities: "the old Manhatans [Manhatesen] are about 200 to 300 strong, women and men, under different chiefs, whom they call Sackimas." Adriaen van der Donck, who resided in New Netherland for many years, later distinguished these people as members of a distinct speech community. In his book, first published in 1655, Van der Donck listed Manhattan among the four languages spoken by Indians in New Netherland. He also furnished some indication of the extent and composition of this community, writing, "with the Manhattans, we include those who live in the neighboring places along the North River, on Long Island, and at the Neversink."[12]

No document clearly identifies a specific individual as a Manhattan Indian. This does not mean that no person can be linked to a Manhattan Indian community. An affidavit written on February 14, 1652, twenty-six years after the sale of the island, talks about "Manhattans Indians of New Netherland, living at Nayack, a place on Long Island directly opposite Staten Island." Other contemporary documents note that a man named Mattano was then sachem of Nayack and Staten Island.[13]

Mattano belonged to a particularly influential lineage, several of whose more prominent members were sachems of Northern Unami- and Munsee-speaking communities located between the Falls of the Delaware and Raritan Bay. Connections revealed through a genealogical reconstruction of prominent members of this lineage show how Mattano could have rights to lands extending from the western end of Long Island across the Narrows through Staten Island to the Raritan and Navesink country and beyond (see figure 3). This reconstruction linking the Manhattans with Nayack, Mattano, and his relatives and descendants also represents the first documentary link in a genealogical chain that joins members of present-day descendant Munsee communities with ancestral Manhattan Indians.[14]

Whoever was a Manhattan, it seems clear that Manhattan country embraced more than the island at its center. People speaking languages belonging to Van der Donck's Manhattan speech community also lived along

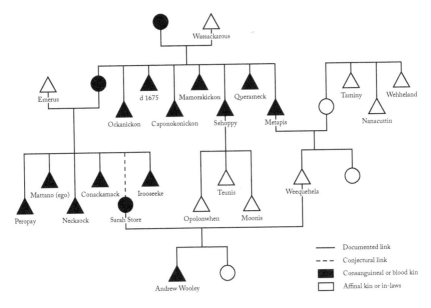

Figure 3. Mattano and his kin

both banks of the lower Hudson River estuary and western Long Island. Although early records preserve Indian names for Long Island, like Suanhacky, Metoac, and Pamanack, no surviving general term collectively identifies Munsee-speaking people living on the island's western end. Records instead document names of communities and places like Keschaechquereren, Rockaway, Massapequa, and Matinecock. All were situated on well-drained pieces of land close to good planting lands and seasonally available resources. Sketches of individual longhouses drawn on the Manatus map, a projection showing Manhattan and its nearby hinterlands first drafted in 1639, shows the locations of four Indian towns in present-day Brooklyn (see Figure 4). Two of these places, Techkonis, in the present-day Gravesend section, and Wichquawanck, near where Nayack later stood, appear on the Manatus map and nowhere else. The locations of the other two, Keskachauwe (in Flatbush) and Mareckewich (in downtown Brooklyn), are verified in other references and marked by archaeological remains.[15]

Territories of other nations belonging to Van der Donck's Manhattan language community centered on places like Wiechquaesgeck in present-day Dobbs Ferry, New York, and Hackensack, along the river of the same name across the Hudson River in nearby New Jersey. It is not known if people living in these and nearby towns also considered themselves Manhattans. The Dutch would only begin noting more than just names and locations after they began buying Indian land in earnest in 1630. Afterwards, increasing amounts of information would stream into New Amsterdam as contacts with local Indians and with colonists in New England and Chesapeake Bay became more frequent.[16]

News tended to travel faster and farther whenever violence flared. Dutch writers ground out an unprecedentedly substantial body of paperwork after Mohawks killed the local commander of Fort Orange (which had been built in present-day Albany, New York, in 1624 to replace Fort Nassau) and several of his men, who had joined a Mahican expedition on its way to attack Mohawk towns in 1628. Another Dutch commander, at Fort Hope in today's Hartford, Connecticut, brought on another considerable round of wordsmithing when he murdered a visiting Pequot sachem a few years later. Surviving documents show how company officials refused to pile one mistake onto another by swallowing their pride and quickly restoring peace in both places. In so doing, they managed to avoid the interminable fighting that devastated Indian and colonial communities in Virginia between 1610 and 1646 and sidestep the brief but vicious war that ended in the defeat, dispersal, and near destruction of the Pequot nation in New England in 1637.[17]

FIRST DEEDS

In 1630, Dutch settlers began offering Indians in and around Munsee country goods in exchange for handwritten marks made on sheets of paper—deeds that the Dutch intended to be conclusive transfers of title and ownership. Earlier agreements like the 1626 Manhattan purchase, made by the director for the company, were probably informal accommodations sealed with gift exchanges and hand shakes or their equivalent. Although it cannot be known with any certainty, Indians probably regarded these deals as temporary arrangements with Dutchmen that could be renewed or cancelled by either party at any time. This changed in 1629 after the Dutch West India Company passed an act allowing directors to set up largely self-governing estates of their own. The new rule gave investors willing to use their own capital to buy Indian land and settle fifty colonists on it the right to establish a patroonship. Similar in concept to English manors, patroonships conferred rights of limited self-government to private landowners called patroons, "patrons or masters." At this time the company also began issuing permits to private persons wishing to purchase lands directly from their Indian owners. This established three interest groups competing for Indian territory in New Netherland: the company, the patroons, and private purchasers acting alone or banding together in syndicates.[18]

On July 12, 1630, agents for the prospective patroon Michiel Pauw made the first land purchase formalized with a deed from Indians in Munsee country. It was the first of several deeds, signed by the first sachems from the area identified by personal names in Dutch records, that gave Pauw title to Staten Island, the Bayonne Peninsula, and present-day Jersey City. Pauw, who never visited his estate in New Netherland, named the new patroonship after himself. Pavonia did not prosper. Unable to attract a sufficient number of settlers to the place, he sold his rights to the land to the company in 1635.[19]

Patroons went through the trouble of obtaining deeds from Indians to secure their estates against the possibility that the company might later make competing claims. Sachems identified by name subsequently signed six deeds to lands in and around present-day Brooklyn for other private purchasers between 1636 and 1637. New Netherland director Van Twiller obtained three of these deeds (including one for Governor's Island) as a private citizen before being recalled to Holland in 1637 to answer charges that he was improperly profiting from his position. His replacement, Willem Kieft, obtained the first company deed to land near Manhattan, this one in the Bushwick section of Brooklyn, on August 1, 1638. During the following year, he would obtain a tract of land for the company in the southwestern corner of the Bronx and another taking in the whole of western Long Island. This latter deed, whose language clearly indicates that it was negotiated as a peremptory purchase evidently made to protect the company's right to land being eyed by New Englanders, would become a major bone of contention between Indians and colonists for generations to come.[20]

4

CONFLICT, 1640–1645

Although hindsight shows that the first seeds of discord had been sown early, relations between Indians and colonists were generally amicable on the surface during the first decade and a half of intensive colonial settlement on and around Manhattan. The first signs of serious tension appeared only after English settlers from New England began approaching Indians to sell lands on the still-unsurveyed border with New Netherland. New Englanders began looking to acquire land west of Massachusetts Bay, Plymouth, and Connecticut even before they defeated the Pequots in 1637, dividing up Pequot territory as well as the Pequot people among themselves and their Indian allies. The latter included Uncas, the founder of the Mohegan nation in eastern Connecticut, and Montauketts on eastern Long Island. Following their victory, the English turned their attention to the lands of other Indians they thought supported the Pequots in the late war. Only one nation west of the Connecticut River, the Sasquas, was known to have openly sided with the Pequots. This did not stop Connecticut settlers in newly built Hartford from treating like defeated enemies all other nations known to have submitted to some degree to Pequot authority before the war.

Even before the fighting stopped, Connecticut government emissaries met near Norwalk with a gathering of "old men and captains from about Milford to Hudson River" during the last week of March 1638. They told the assembled sachems that they had been sent to establish their colony's authority over "the Indians along the coast from Quilipioke [Quinnipiac] to the Manhatoes." After consulting among themselves, the sachems reached consensus and agreed to place themselves, their people, and their lands under English control.[1]

Within two years, Connecticut colonists were purchasing their first tracts of land from Indians around Norwalk. News of these purchases alarmed Kieft and his council in New Amsterdam. On April 19, 1640, Kieft dispatched his second-in-command Van Tienhoven to the Archipelago with an order "to purchase the adjacent lands there; to set up the arms of the Lords States General; to take the Indians under our protection, and to prevent any other nation committing any usurpation on our limits and encroaching further on our territory."[2]

Van Tienhoven failed to purchase any Indian land at Norwalk. He evidently spent much of his time trying to confirm rumors that other men from Connecticut and New Haven (separate colonies at the time) were setting up settlements on Long Island land placed under Dutch authority the previous year. Sailing across the sound from Norwalk to Hempstead Harbor, Van Tienhoven met with Penhawitz, who had moved near Hempstead after selling "all the lands left as an inheritance to him by his ancestors" to the Dutch West India Company. Penhawitz confirmed reports that Englishmen from the mainland had "begun to build houses, cut trees, and . . . pulled down their High Mightiness's arms." This latter act was an open challenge to Dutch hegemony. Shortly afterward, another Dutch emissary reported that the English had added insult to defiance, writing that he "found the [metal plate bearing the embossed company arms] torn off and that on a tree to which they had been nailed a fool's head was carved."[3]

Annoyed by the taunt, Kieft dispatched troops, who succeeded in evicting the English homesteaders. Needing settlers to screen his colony's exposed eastern frontier, Kieft soon invited the English to return. Those accepting the invitation were neither numerous nor entirely strangers to the Dutch. Many Dutch families knew and liked their Protestant English coreligionists. English soldiers fought alongside the Dutch in their long war against Catholic Spain, and dissident families took refuge in Dutch cities when things were difficult for them in England. Although England and Holland would go to war with one another at least three times during the following decades, the Dutch stadtholder Willem Hendrijck would marry an English queen and become King William III of England in 1689.

Kieft allowed colonists forced from Puritan New England to settle in the Dutch colony so long as they lived quietly and obeyed company laws. Among these émigrés was Puritan nonconformist Anne Hutchinson, who settled in Westchester. Another was John Underhill, who as a commander of the force that took the Pequot fort at Mystic had indiscriminately massacred its occupants.

Kieft permitted Underhill to settle in Hempstead, where he and other townsfolk obtained company permits to begin land-purchase negotiations with the Indians. Kieft allowed those successfully getting deeds to establish their own communities, issuing patents for the lands and assuming jurisdiction over the towns. The arrangement benefited both parties. New England exiles found a haven in New Netherland. They would provide fighting men, produce, and business in a colony ill-supported by its mother country.

Kieft's determination to get Indians to give up produce without compensation brought on the colony's first crisis. It started on September 15, 1639, when Kieft and his council ordered collection of "peltries, maize or wampum from the Indians residing hereabout, whom we have hitherto protected." The fact that the Indians had not asked to be protected and that the Dutch had not provided protection evidently did not enter into the decision. To make matters worse, ominous wording in the act authorized levy collectors to use "the most suitable means" to get Indians along the lower Hudson to pay. It was an open invitation to violence.[4]

A year and a half later, De Vries observed Tappans sullenly paying the resented impost. He noted that the tax was laid upon "Indian Christians," a fact evidently forgotten when the Tappans and Wiechquaesgecks on the opposite bank of the Tappan Zee were made to pay. It is not known who these Indian Christians might have been. Few colonists and even fewer Indians are known to have shown much interest in conversion at the time.[5]

In 1642, Wiechquaesgecks joined Tappans and other Indians from the Manhattan area meeting Kieft to protest the tax. It soon became apparent that Dutch authorities were not the only ones extorting protection money from the local Indians. Other Indian nations living far upriver wanted some as well. Armed with Dutch muskets, they regarded Indian towns around the bay, mostly defended by warriors denied similar weapons by the company, as easy pickings. Mohawks and Mahicans demanded a cut of the heap of wampum, pelts, and trade goods they imagined piled up in bayside longhouse rafters and storage pits.[6]

FIGHTING BREAKS OUT ON STATEN ISLAND

The corn levy was just the most visible problem threatening the peace between Indians and Dutch colonists at this time. It can only be guessed what traders' abuses and Indian retaliations led up to the violent confrontation on waters off Staten Island in the late spring of 1640. A company trader reporting the incident told Kieft that trouble began soon after he and his party sailed to meet Raritans at what they called "the usual trading place" on the Arthur Kill, the narrow tidal stream separating Staten Island from the New Jersey mainland. The trader went on to state that the clearly angry Indians meeting him there proceeded to insult them and derisively wave marten skins at them. Things began to get out of hand after they slapped one of the traders in the face with a squirrel skin. They then stole canoes tethered to the Dutch sloop, showering the traders with arrows as they sailed away.[7]

Provocative as the incident was, it took the theft of a hog on Staten Island a few weeks later to spark open war. It later turned out that the pig had been stolen by one of De Vries' servants. The report reaching Fort Amsterdam, however, identified the culprits as Raritans. On July 16, 1640, Kieft dispatched Van Tienhoven with some troops to sort things out. To hear Van Tienhoven tell it, the troops refused to obey his orders to deal peaceably with the Indians. He went on to report that he had to turn his back and walk away after his men broke into Indian houses and storage pits. They subsequently burned the Indians' fields, tortured a sachem's son, and killed several of the townspeople before returning to Manhattan. Outraged Raritans left the island, returning a year later to kill or carry off De Vries' tenants and burn his farms to the ground. The war started by Van Tienhoven's reportedly mutinous troops has since come to bear the name of the governor who dispatched them to the island.[8]

Kieft responded by calling for help from the same Indians he was taxing for protection. Realizing that people forced to pay for protection might not be anxious to die for the privilege, Kieft offered a bounty of ten fathoms (sixty feet) of wampum to anyone bringing him the head of any Raritan and twice that for the head of someone who killed a settler. One report noted that Indians from Long Island taking up Kieft's offer "voluntarily killed some of the Raritans, our enemies." Another document, dated November 2, 1641, noting a Tankiteke sachem named Pacham bringing the hand of a dead Raritan to Fort Amsterdam shows that the Long Islanders were not the only Indians accepting Kieft's bounty.[9]

TROUBLED TRUCE

Tankiteke and Long Island Indian attacks on behalf of the colonists evidently compelled Raritan people to make peace sometime in late 1641. This did not, however, put an end to the troubles. Settlers moving onto lands sold by Indians put both peoples in closer contact than ever before. Settler's horses and cattle trampled nearby Indian gardens while pigs broke into homes and fields of Indian neighbors. Colonists demanded compensation for livestock shot by Indians or killed by their dogs. Authorities ordered Indians to fence their fields and kill their dogs. Relations worsened as rumors of Indian conspiracies, fueled by the realities of Indian wars in Canada, Virginia, Connecticut, and elsewhere, spread insidiously throughout New Netherland. Arguments, petty thefts, and drunken brawls further poisoned the atmosphere. Finally, a string of killings brought things to a boiling point. A Wiechquaesgeck man killed a Dutch settler on northern Manhattan. Other Indians reportedly "made crazy" by drink killed two Dutch settlers in Pavonia.[10]

De Vries wrote that a Hackensack sachem, probably the leader colonists would soon know as Oratam, quickly moved to defuse the situation. Meeting with Kieft at Fort Amsterdam, the sachem publicly promised that his people would turn over the suspect, who had fled inland to the Tankitekes, as soon as possible. Privately, he told De Vries that the killer was a chief's son and would not be given up.[11]

The conciliatory note sounded by the Hackensack leader was not repeated by the Wiechquaesgeck sachem when he next met with Kieft at the fort. He told the governor that the killing was vengeance for a settler's murder of one of his people many years earlier. Refusing to turn the man over, the obviously angry sachem added "that he was sorry that 20 Christians had not been murdered."[12] The response infuriated Kieft. He dispatched two expeditions to punish the Wiechquaesgecks for their defiance during the spring of 1642. Both got lost and returned after killing and capturing some Indians they came across in the woods. Frustrated by these failures, Kieft waited for an opportunity to, as he put it, "put a bit into the mouth of the heathen."[13]

The opportunity came during the winter of 1642–1643, two weeks after a party of eighty or ninety musket-bearing Indians from the upper Hudson River attacked Tappan and Wiechquaesgeck towns. Sources differ on who the attackers were. Some claim they were Mahicans. Others think they were Mohawks.[14] Whoever they were, the raiders took several captives and reportedly killed between seventeen and seventy people. Indians from every community around the Tappan Zee fled through deep snow to New Amsterdam and Pavonia. Nearby settlers let them put up shelters;

brought food, fuel, and blankets; and helped tend children, elders, and the wounded.[15]

Tappans and Wiechquaesgecks were not the only people taking refuge at these camps. Many were Marechkawicks and other western Long Islanders whose warriors had helped hunt down Raritans two years earlier. Most of these people joined those Tappans and Wiechquaesgecks taking shelter at the small cluster of huts maintained by the enterprising Keschaechquereren sachem Numerus. The little settlement, called Nechtanck, was located at Corlaers Hook, a neck of land jutting into the East River just beyond the northeast end of the Dutch town.[16]

Past services provided by Marechkawicks and their kinsfolk did not prevent Kieft from ordering surprise attacks on both camps. Company soldiers and armed settlers carried out the order on the night of February 24, 1643. By the time the shooting stopped, eighty Indian people lay dead at Pavonia. Another forty were killed at Nechtanck. A graphic description of the Pavonia attack, best known in the version later published in De Vries' memoirs of his time in New Netherland, still shocks and appalls readers.[17]

Outraged by the brutality of the attack and anxious to know why their people had been massacred in their sleep, Indians living around New Amsterdam quickly pressed for talks. Two coalitions appear in records documenting the meetings that followed. A delegation from a group of Long Island nations arrived at the fort a few days after the massacre. They asked De Vries to come with them to Rockaway to start negotiations. Arriving there together on March 5, 1643, they were greeted by a man identified as the one-eyed sachem (probably Penhawitz). De Vries wrote that two hundred to three hundred people from Long Island were taking refuge at the place. After hearing grievances presented by a speaker representing the sixteen Long Island chiefs attending the meeting, he agreed to accompany them to Fort Amsterdam to reestablish peace with Kieft. On March 25, 1643, Penhawitz signed a peace treaty on behalf of the Indians of Long Island at the fort. Two weeks later, on April 23, 1643, Oratam signed a treaty agreement on behalf of another coalition consisting of Hackensacks, Tappans, Rechgawawancks, Kichtawancks, and Sintsincks.[18]

RETALIATION AND DEVASTATION

The killing of a settler along the Hudson by a Wappinger on August 7, 1643, was an indication that the treaties signed earlier that spring had not taken.

The Dutch offense had been great, and presents they gave too meager to condole bereaved survivors or erase the memory of lost kinsfolk. Wappingers, Wiechquaesgecks, and their allies were soon waylaying other settlers and burning outlying farms throughout the lower Hudson Valley. De Vries attributed the renewal of open conflict to dissatisfaction with Dutch condolence payments and their outrage at Kieft's offer of two hundred fathoms (four hundred yards) of wampum as a reward to sachems who killed what he called "madcaps" agitating for war. This time he found few takers. Pacham's change in attitude reflected the feelings of many River Indians. Just two years earlier he had called "the Swannekens . . . his best friends." Now he called for relentless war against them.[19]

Warriors from nearly every community along the lower Hudson attacked with a ferocity and resolve that astonished colonists. One party destroyed Vriesendael. Another attacked Anne Hutchinson's newly built farm on the banks of the river that today bears her name in present-day Pelham, New York. Contemporary accounts report that Indians killed Hutchinson and five of her fifteen children on the homestead sometime in September 1643.[20]

Reeling from these and other attacks, colonists throughout the outlying settlements abandoned their farms. Some took refuge in and around Fort Amsterdam. Others, including the now ruined De Vries, finally gave up and left the colony altogether. Anxious to stem the flow of fleeing settlers, Kieft quickly moved to augment the meager forces available to him. He enlisted Underhill and fifty English colonists from Hempstead and the Archipelago towns. He also authorized slave owners to arm servants and ordered the commander at Fort Orange to send some of its garrison downriver.[21]

Kieft soon sent his men against Indians in Westchester and Staten Island. Both expeditions failed to bring Indians to battle. Easily detecting the oncoming columns, the Indians withdrew farther into the interior. Frustrated commanders contented themselves with killing or capturing the few stragglers they caught, burning crops, pillaging Indian houses, and rifling storage pits.[22]

The ability of colonial troops to move freely if clumsily through their territories did have a sobering effect on many Munsees. Sachems representing Kichtawancks, Massapequas, Wiechquaesgecks, Nochpeems, and Wappingers met with Underhill at Stamford, Connecticut, on April 6, 1644. Alarmed by the prospect of more lethal incursions, they asked Underhill to "appeal to the governor of New Netherland for peace." One week later, the Matinecock sachem Gauwaroe made peace for his people and neighboring Massapequa and Secatogue townsfolk. He promised that his people would not help still defiant "Indians of Reckonhacky, the bays, and Marechkawieck."[23]

Peace with the Matinecocks and their confederates further isolated Rockaways and others refusing to end the fighting. Kieft waited until the fall harvest was gathered in before ordering assaults on the remaining belligerent communities. The force, led by Underhill, was stiffened with English veterans of the Pequot War. The first attack, made with 120 men, swept across western Long Island, reportedly killing a total of 120 Indian people at Massapequa and an unnamed larger town. The little army then sailed to the recently established English village at Greenwich, Connecticut, and headed inland. Slogging along snow-choked trails, the force, now numbering 130 men, managed to surprise a large town in the interior uplands of Westchester at the end of their first day's march. Using the same strategy employed at Mystic, Underhill ordered his men to burn the town. It was later reported that all but eight of the five hundred trapped people died in the hail of bullets fired into the flaming houses. In contrast, Underhill lost one man killed and fifteen wounded in the attack.[24]

Desolated Indians everywhere around Manhattan soon sent emissaries to make a lasting peace. On May 24, 1645, Massapequa sachem Tackapousha, accompanied by forty-seven warriors, came to Fort Amsterdam after Hempstead settlers murdered five of seven Indians they had captured with the intent of bringing them to the fort. Evidently swept up in the murderous mood prevailing at the time, Dutch soldiers at the post wantonly killed the other two captives. Tackapousha, however, was more intent on ending the war than in bringing the latest murderers to justice. Telling Kieft that he had been sent to represent every Indian community on Long Island, he made peace for all and offered warriors for service against Indians continuing to fight against the Dutch.[25]

News of the arrival of 130 Dutch soldiers brought in from Brazil in July compelled most of the remaining combatants to come to the conference table at Fort Amsterdam a month later, on August 30, 1645. Exhausted after four years of war, all parties accepted a restoration of the status quo ante bellum. The list of participants included most of the prominent Indian leaders from Long Island and the Hudson Valley. Tackapousha made peace for the last Marechkawick and Nayack diehards. Oratam and his colleagues represented Hackensacks, Tappans, Rechgawawancks, and a community from the Archipelago identified as Onany (the Uncowa or Unckaway community in Fairfield, Connecticut). Mahican sachem Aepjen (Ape in Dutch) represented Wappingers, Wiechquaesgecks, Sintsincks, and Kichtawancks. The record also shows that a group of Mohawk ambassadors, accompanied by Fort Orange trader and translator Cornelis Antonisen van Slijck, helped serve as mediators.[26]

These leaders probably represented three Munsee coalitions gathered at high levels of sociopolitical integration. Each would have contained several communities, all consisting of one, two, or more longhouses sheltering groups of related extended families, in-laws, and friends. Deeds to lands in present-day Brooklyn signed between 1636 and 1639, for example, listed both sachems of particular towns and more influential "chiefs of the district" like Penhawitz, who served as witnesses and gave their blessings to the bargains. Such examples show how local Indian communities fitted into larger polities led by influential sachems. Considerably larger gatherings at places like Rockaway in 1643 and at the upland town above Stamford destroyed by Underhill's men a year later suggest that many nations gathering at particular places could form more populous coalitions.

Taken together, corporate identities of delegations chronicled at meetings with Dutch authorities during the war suggest that Lower River Indians formed at least four large-scale coalitions between 1643 and 1645. These included the coalition of towns between Raritan Bay and the Falls of the Delaware, the united western Long Island Indian communities, the coalition of Lower River Indian communities on both banks of the Tappan Zee, and their closely related kinsfolk from the Archipelago and the interior all but annihilated by Underhill's force. Not identified as such in the August 30, 1645, treaty, the Long Island and Tappan Zee coalitions almost certainly constituted the major part of what Van der Donck later identified as the Manhattan speech community.

The presence of these coalitions and the absence of emissaries representing Raritan Valley people, mid-Hudson Esopus communities, and upper Delaware Valley Minisinks at the August 30 treaty shows that terrible as it was, the crucible of Kieft's War failed to forge the closely connected, independent-minded people of Munsee country into a single unified polity. Lingering Sanhican hostility toward Manhattans, western Long Island and Tankiteke attacks on Raritan communities in 1641, and Tackapousha's promise to send warriors against Lower River Indians still fighting the Dutch in 1645 represent only three examples of divisive enmities standing in the way of unity. Stronger pressures would be required before shared language and culture translated into social solidarity.[27]

In terms of understanding Munsee history, the fighting brought many sachems and communities around the bay and the lower river to Dutch notice for the first time. War records, especially those chronicling peace negotiations, documented acts and affiliations of Indian nations and leaders previously known only by name to European chroniclers. The war also revealed something of their composition. Disappearances of the names of towns, sachems, and entire nations provide indirect indices of the impacts of depopulation and dispossession. Extant records also indicate that war and land loss did not affect all Lower River Indian communities in the same ways. No records directly document involvement of Minisink, Esopus, and other inland Indians in either fighting or land sales at this time. Although negatives prove nothing, the absence of records documenting involvement of these communities suggests that their sachems managed to at least avoid noticeable participation in the conflict.

The immediate effects of the war were further indicated by the subsequent disappearance of many people and places near the center of Dutch colonization from written records after 1645. The Indian towns of Keschaechquereren, Marechkawick, Wichquawanck, and Techkonis in Brooklyn on lands purchased before the war or burned during the fighting never again appear. Neither Tankitekes, Nochpeems, nor Sintsincks are ever mentioned again. Shippan, Toquams, and other locales on lands bought by Englishmen along the Archipelago disappeared from colonial records after Underhill's men slaughtered their inhabitants in the winter of 1644–1645. Sachems like Penhawitz and Pacham were also never again heard from.

MAKING A DESOLATION

In the way of nations already ancient when Roman historian Tacitus wrote the phrase, the men who signed the August 30, 1645, treaty at Fort Amsterdam ending Kieft's War made a desolation and called it peace. Company soldiers and militiamen had destroyed every Indian town within fifty miles of the fort's walls. Sparing neither women nor children, they cut down standing crops, pillaged stored supplies, and burned what they could not carry away. By their own estimates, they killed between 800 and 1,200 Indian people. Unknown numbers of other Indians died of hunger, disease, or exposure or were killed or carried off in internecine fighting or by Upper River raiders.[28]

New Netherland suffered as well. Nearly every outlying settlement around Manhattan had been attacked. Many colonists were killed, and more than a few were taken captive. More disheartened colonists entirely abandoned the colony. Farm families not killed or captured outright huddled in New Amsterdam and the few towns stout enough to discourage attack. Their farms, bread baskets of the colony, were nearly all destroyed. Fields lay fallow, livestock was killed, and the fur trade, the mainstay of the colony's economy and one of the main reasons it was established in the first place, ground to a halt.

The war also stopped colonial expansion into Indian territory. Indians signed only one deed during the three years following the end of the fighting. Settlers going back to their land had enough to do rebuilding what had been destroyed. Lower River Indians did not show much interest in parting with additional tracts of land. The one deed signed at this time was a purchase of lands along the far western shore of Long Island from Gowanus to Coney Island, acquired earlier by other colonists. Kieft made the purchase on behalf of the company from Seyseychkimus and several other chiefs on September 10, 1645. The deal evidently ruffled feathers on both sides of the Atlantic. Perhaps because it included some lands already sold by the Indians, company officials in Amsterdam subsequently invalidated the deed.[29]

Although the war curbed colonial expansion for a time, the desolated colony began recovering soon after peace talks were concluded. Settlers fanned out across the charred landscape, gathering firewood and salvaging what they could of the year's harvest. Working late into autumn evenings, they managed to lay up sufficient food, fuel, and fodder to make it through the winter. Their links with neighboring colonies, and with the broader North Atlantic world, speeded recovery. Ships from Virginia and from old and New England soon joined vessels from Holland landing seed, supplies, and livestock. New infusions of goods needed to buy pelts from Indians and to provision Dutch settlers and ships revived commerce. Most important for New Netherland, new immigrants replenished populations thinned by death and desertion.[30]

There is every reason to think that Indians living around the bay and the lower river estuary also set to work to recover from the recent fighting. They were accustomed to building new homes, clearing new fields, planting new crops, and restocking depleted larders when moving from one place to another. Although the scale of devastation inflicted during Kieft's War has no recorded parallel in their history either before or since, the war was not their first experience with terrible loss. Newly introduced epidemic diseases had already devastated their communities. In the past, before they had to cope with European wars and diseases, Indians replenished their numbers by natural increase, by adopting war captives and immigrants, and perhaps with wholesale replacements of the kind also made that summer by Mohawks, who reportedly presented their Oneida neighbors with more than fifty of their own men to replace sons and spouses killed fighting Hurons and Algonquins in Canada.[31]

Indian hopes for recovery on their coastal lands had to have withered in the face of harsh new realities. They did not have home populations in the millions like colonists, who were soon able to more than make up for lost numbers. Colonists now held most of the best tidewater territories (see map 4). Indian losses along the coast in the late war, moreover, were immense. Diseases brought by European mariners and the first colonists probably reduced Indian population in Munsee country from fifteen thousand to six thousand by 1634. If twice the approximately one thousand people killed according to colonist's own accounts died or abandoned the region during Kieft's War, only four thousand Indians may have still lived in their homeland in 1645. Division of this number by the twelve prominent sachems in the Munsee File still mentioned in colonial documents in 1645 indicates that each of these leaders hypothetically represented somewhere in the neighborhood of three hundred people.

Whatever the actual numbers and representation ratios, losses were nothing short of catastrophic. Entire clans, along with their ability to maintain title to landed estates, almost certainly were wiped out. Having neither families nor land to return to, many captives and most refugees driven from their shoreline homes probably chose to stay with new friends and relatives in the interior farther from colonists. Forced to give up adopted colonists captured during the fighting who might have replaced lost loved ones, surviving Indian families along the coast had neither sufficient numbers, resources, nor time to reconstitute themselves on remaining bits of ancestral territory directly in the path of colonial expansion.

Hopes that another Indian nation might come to their aid or push back colonists on the coast also dimmed at this time. Nations farther north and east had not yet recovered from smallpox epidemics that had ravaged their towns between 1631 and 1634. The impact of epidemic mortality differs significantly between populations numbering in the thousands and those whose numbers run in the tens of millions. Although high birthrates allow

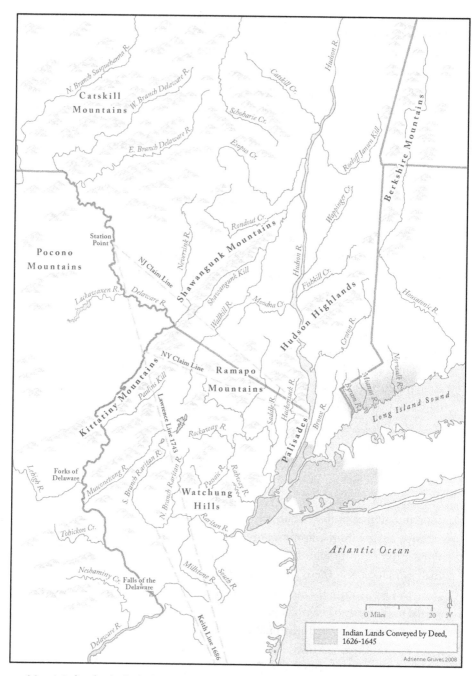

Map 4. Indian land sales in Munsee country, 1626–1645

even small populations to rebound quickly, devastating epidemic and war losses all but overwhelmed the Munsees. Higher survival rates among adults possessing acquired immunity to epidemic diseases like smallpox in colonial communities further tipped demographic scales in favor of settlers.

People surviving smallpox tend to develop immunities that help them endure subsequent epidemics. Such survivors do not, however, transmit acquired immunities to their children. In the grim arithmetic of mass death, although the percentages may not change, larger populations ensure higher numbers of survivors. These, in turn, can produce ever larger populations of survivors. Thus, while there is no clear evidence suggesting that Indians were inherently more vulnerable to epidemics like smallpox, their smaller numbers and lack of earlier exposure significantly increased overall demographic susceptibility to new epidemics brought by Europeans.

No amount of immunity protected people from wars like those that had just desolated much of Munsee country and threatened Oneida survival. Fighting swept up Indians throughout the region. New England Indians still reeled from the Pequot bloodbath of 1637. To the north, Mohawks, Oneidas, and their Iroquois brethren intent on avenging lost relatives and dominating fur trade seemed trapped in an endless round of bloody conflicts with all nations on their borders. Farther south, warriors led by Opechcancanough were making their last futile attempt to drive out Virginian colonists. Struggling for survival in their own homelands, few Indian nations anywhere in the Northeast, even if so inclined, could help Indians in Munsee country rebuild, much less migrate to or otherwise occupy their lands.

Only colonists possessed the resources and power to hold and occupy coastal lands in Munsee country during the desolate summer of 1645. Continued fighting and a series of epidemics striking local Indian communities in quick succession over the next twenty years would sweep over the region in a drumfire of devastation that would leave few survivors or memories untouched or unchanged when a career soldier named Petrus Stuyvesant, who replaced Kieft in 1647, finally had to surrender the still insufficiently supported New Netherland colony to the English in 1664.

5

DRUMFIRE, 1645–1664

A seemingly endless succession of wars and rumors of wars rolled over the Hudson and Delaware valleys like a smothering artillery barrage during the final two decades of Dutch rule. More than a century later, in 1762, a New Jersey Indian living in exile in Ohio named John Doubty put his people's memory of this era of ceaseless conflict into words while talking with a visiting Quaker trader: "After the white people came the Dutch about New York shot an Indian for pulling peaches off his trees, which caused wars, and after peace, the Indians being settled thick in a Town near the Dutch, in very deep snow, the Dutch taking the advantage killed the Indians[;] only one made his escape, who alarmed others so that two other wars and peaces ensued."[1]

Dutch chronicles substantiate Doubty's story of the three wars in Munsee country. His conflation of the signature incident of the midmost of these conflicts, the Peach War fought between 1655 and 1657, with the preceding Kieft's and the following Esopus wars, shows that at least one descendant from the area remembered the final three decades of the Dutch colonization as a period of seemingly continuous conflict.

Fighting beyond the borders of New Netherland intensified the impact of seemingly interminable warfare in the colony. Some, like the Dutch seizure of New Sweden on the Delaware in 1655, were isolated incidents that did not lead to wider war. A truce agreed to by Dutch and New England colonists prevented the First Anglo-Dutch Naval War of 1652–1654, waged mostly in Europe, from spreading to the region. And both Dutch and English colonists avoided formal involvement in the Five Nations' wars against the Mahicans and their Northern Indian allies, with the French in Canada, and with the Susquehannocks and other Indian nations during these years.[2]

Fear that these and other conflicts might spread fueled rumors, alarms, and conspiracy theories. Killings, assaults, robberies, and insults joined disputes both foreign and domestic to create a tense atmosphere thick with retaliatory threats and talk of fighting. Local disputes that broke out into open warfare seemed continuous because they were brush-fire conflicts of the kind typically waged by more or less evenly matched opponents not strong enough to prevail over one another. Flaring and sputtering over time, such wars often merge into one another to form memories of continuous conflict.

Fighting during Kieft's War conformed to this pattern, flaring into periods of intense violence followed by shaky truces, renewed raids, and inconclusive diplomacy. Even the Treaty of 1645 did not end the violence. As we have seen, the continuing hostility of Raritan people and unreconciled refugees from the lower Hudson River living with them made life hazardous for colonists traversing the lowlands between the Hudson and Delaware valleys.

Remaining belligerents were finally brought to the conference table at the insistence of the Susquehannocks, who probably did not appreciate the way hostilities blocked their most direct trade route with Fort Amsterdam. At a July 19, 1649, meeting meant to resolve all outstanding differences, sachems representing the Raritan, Wiechquaesgeck, Rechgawawanck, and Nayack communities put their marks onto a peace treaty alongside the signature of a new Dutch governor, Petrus Stuyvesant. Kieft, who went down with most of the crew and passengers of *de Prinses Amelia* (the Princess Amelia) when she sank off the coast of Ireland in a storm in the late summer of 1647, did not live to answer charges that he was the cause of the troubles finally put to rest by Stuyvesant's treaty in 1649. Stuyvesant turned out to be a capable administrator. Dutch West India Company directors in Holland gave him the new title of director-general, reflecting his past accomplishments as both a diplomat and a soldier in the Caribbean, where he lost a leg in battle. He was vigorous, willing to travel to trouble spots to protect company interests and settle disputes. Stuyvesant's often (but not always) patient diplomacy with Indians contrasts sharply with the more popular image of him as an irascible hothead.[3]

Five Nations diplomats, traders, and warriors seemed to turn up everywhere throughout the Northeast at this time. Their warriors subjugated, destroyed, or drove away nearly every Indian nation along their borders by

the third quarter of the seventeenth century. Lower River Indians and Mahican warriors were reportedly sometimes seen accompanying Five Nations
war parties ambushing trappers and carrying off unwary settlers from New
France to the New England frontier. Colonists in these places knew that the
Dutch would openly support neither the Mohawks nor any Indians allied
with them during those brief intervals when their home governments were
fighting one another in Europe. Even Minisink and Esopus Indians allied
with Susquehannock enemies of the Five Nations knew that colonists might
attack them if war broke out between settlers and Mohawks.[4]

Reports that New Englanders planned to attack the Wappingers during
the spring of 1650 reached New Amsterdam at a time when the Esopus, the
Mahicans, and five other Indian nations from New England allied with the
Wappingers reportedly promised the French that they would attack their
Iroquois enemies. The Dutch feared that English conquest of the Wappingers, whose territories lay astride the disputed border with New England, would allow the English to extend their boundary claims to Hudson
shores. The prospect of such an unwelcome possibility helped convince
Stuyvesant to agree to a meeting with New Englanders to hammer out mutually acceptable borders in the late summer of 1650.[5]

The resulting Fort Hope treaty did more than settle this boundary dispute for a time. Alarmed by growing Iroquois military ascendancy,
Stuyvesant asked the New Englanders if they would consider joining in an
alliance against them. The New Englanders took the proposal under advise-
ment. River Indians eager to get out from under Mohawk thumbs tried to
help things along by spreading rumors that Iroquois warriors planned to attack Dutch settlements. None of this came to anything, however. Although
the colonists managed to stay out of it, the outbreak of the First Anglo-
Dutch Naval War prevented any union of Dutch and English settlers against
anyone. River Indian hopes that Europeans would enter into an alliance
against the Iroquois were finally dashed when the governor of New France
concluded peace treaties with each of the Five Nations in 1653.[6]

Peach War

Memories of the horrors of Indian war had hardly faded around the Hudson
Valley when a party of Indian warriors said to number close to one thousand men in sixty-four canoes descended on New Amsterdam on September 15, 1655. They arrived while the city's garrison, then numbering some

three hundred soldiers and militiamen, was away subjugating the Swedish settlements. Neither the identities nor the intentions of the Indians constituting the force were clear to the colonists. Some said that Indians "living back of Onckeway and Stamford" were in the flotilla. Others thought they recognized Indians from Westchester among them. Stuyvesant cast the net widely, including among them "Maquasas, Mahicanders, Indians from the Upper and Lower North River, from Paham's Land, Northern Indians and others." Later, Wappingers and Esopus sachems affirmed that some of their warriors had been with the Indian army.[7]

Some thought Susquehannocks friendly with the Swedes put the River Indians up to it. The Indians themselves said they were on their way to fight people they called Northern Indians, a claim supported shortly thereafter when Tackapousha asked for Dutch help against an expected Narragansett attack from Rhode Island, just across Long Island Sound. Still others alleged that the Indians were only out to avenge themselves on Dutch colonists and would leave alone English, Finnish, and other settlers belonging to the eighteen other nationalities said to be residing in New Netherland. Whatever the facts of the matter, shots were soon fired, and people died. It began when warriors saying they were searching for Northern Indians allegedly hiding in town shot and wounded Hendrick van Dijck. Van Dijck had been one of Kieft's chief lieutenants during the last war. Recently fired by Stuyvesant from his position as state attorney, he was the man the Indians believed had wantonly killed a woman picking peaches in his garden some time earlier.[8]

The warriors subsequently embarked on a three-day rampage. Settlements at Pavonia and Staten Island were once again burned. Other attacks destroyed or forced evacuation of nearly every other outlying farmstead. Warriors reportedly killed between fifty and one hundred colonists and captured one hundred more. Unable or unwilling to do further damage, representatives were dispatched to hold peace talks. These reached an impasse when Dutch authorities refused to pay ransoms demanded for captives. Both sides finally settled for a working disagreement in which Dutch authorities refusing to give in to ransom demands presented Indian families with even larger gifts than those demanded. In return, Indian families pleased with their presents encouraged newly adopted captives to return to their homes.[9]

Represented by his speaker Pennekeck, Hackensack sachem Oratam was a primary intermediary in these exchanges. Tackapousha also again stepped forward. Meeting with Stuyvesant on March 12, 1656, Tackapousha promised that neither the Massapequas nor the Matinecocks, Secatogues, Merricks, Rockaways, or Canarsees, all of whom had recently acknowledged him as their sachem, would break the peace so long as they could be sure of Dutch protection. A dense cloud of stolid belligerence nevertheless settled over the region for another year until the last exchanges of presents and prisoners finally restored some quiet along the lower river estuary.[10]

TROUBLE AT ESOPUS

Settlers from Fort Orange began buying land for farms in Esopus country soon after news of the peace treaties signed by the Five Nations and the French in 1653 removed fears of attack by marauding war parties in what to colonists was a remote borderland. Their sense of security was shaken just two years later when word of the Indian attacks at and around Manhattan reached them. Most abandoned their farms and fled back upriver. Proof that they were well advised to do so soon emerged when it was found that the rampaging flotilla included many Esopus warriors.[11]

Esopus families did not welcome the sixty or so settlers returning to plant their fields in 1657 after danger of attack faded. Resentment was fueled by Fort Orange fur traders who continued sailing to their shores during the fighting. Most if not all of these men engaged in sharp trading practices that left many of their clients little more than drunk at the close of business. Relations quickly went from bad to worse during the spring of 1658 when Indians shot down a trader on his yacht near Esopus, burned two nearby farm houses, killed or carried off livestock, and threatened further harm.[12]

Responding to news of the troubles at Esopus, Stuyvesant sailed upriver with sixty-one soldiers to find out what was going on during the last week of May. After hearing out both sides, he ordered them to settle their differences. Sensing a thinly veiled threat in a sachem's statement that he could not control drink-befuddled young warriors, who were spoiling for a fight, Stuyvesant replied that he "would match man with man, or 20 against 30, yes even 40" of the Indians. Finding no one to take up the challenge, Stuyvesant told the sachems that he wanted to buy land for a fort near the mouth of the Rondout Creek (in present-day Kingston, New York). He then advised settlers to move their houses into the fort once it was completed. A stockade was erected by the end of June. Settlers moving behind its walls named the place Wiltwijck, "Indian town."[13]

Things moved closer to an open break when reports of further provocations and rumors of a secret meeting of perhaps as many as five hundred Indians caused Stuyvesant to travel back to Esopus on October 15. Placing the blame for the unrest on the Indians, Stuyvesant demanded that the sachems pay a punitively high indemnity of nearly one hundred strings of wampum and, in an unprecedented move, ordered them to give up their lands around Wiltwijck to cover costs of settler losses, relocation, and fort construction. Promising to give them presents, he also urged them to entirely leave the region if they wanted to avoid further difficulties. The stunned sachems tried to moderate Stuyvesant's demands. Failing that, they told the director-general that they would come back in the spring to give up the demanded territory.[14]

Spring passed into summer, and the Esopus still did not come to surrender their land. On August 17, 1659, some Esopus sachems reminded settlers that Stuyvesant had not yet given them presents promised the preceding spring. That September 4, a large delegation of Esopus sachems accompanied by women and children appeared at the fort. They began by telling the settlers that they had recently met with "two Minquaes [Susquehannock] sachems, Sinnekins [in this case probably used as a general term for the four westernmost Five Nations who were themselves then at war with the Susquehannocks], and Southern Indians [probably Hackensacks and their neighbors]" who strongly urged them to keep the peace. Reminding their listeners that both sides were at fault in this dispute, they delivered seventy-five of the one hundred wampum strings demanded by Stuyvesant to show they were serious about wanting to live in peace with the settlers. No one, however, made any mention of land.[15]

Open fighting broke out before Stuyvesant could return upriver to compose matters. On the night of September 20, 1659, settlers fired into an Indian drinking party, killing one man, wounding two, and seizing another. The next day a large body of warriors, estimated by terrified settlers at between four hundred and six hundred men, appeared before the walls of Wiltwijck. Threatening to abandon the unruly settlers to Indian vengeance, the disgusted fort commandant swallowed his anger and dispatched a messenger to inform Stuyvesant of developments. The Indians captured the courier and the detachment of twelve men sent to protect him just outside the fort's walls. They then lay siege to the place.[16]

Word of the troubles reached New Amsterdam hard on the heels of reports that other Indians killed some settlers at Maspeth, just across the East River from Manhattan. Settlers from outlying farms once again soon began fleeing to the protection of Fort Amsterdam. Gathering what men he could, Stuyvesant led a scratch force of 150 soldiers, militiamen, conscripts, servants, and some Long Island Indians upriver. They landed two days after news of their impending arrival caused the Indians to raise their siege on October 8. Unwilling to send his small band out against an enemy of unknown strength, Stuyvesant order about half of his troops to join settlers defending the fort and returned with the remainder to New Amsterdam.[17]

As in earlier conflicts, leaders quickly tried to stop hostilities before fighting spread. Mohawk and Mahican sachems set aside their own differences to work out a cease fire agreement and secure the release of two prisoners during the last weeks of October. The resulting truce held through the winter despite Esopus refusal to meet with Stuyvesant when he again sailed upriver in late November.[18]

Evidently angered by the snub and incensed by reports of continued Esopus defiance, Stuyvesant used the winter months to prepare quietly for war in the spring. He began by calling for reinforcements from the company since efforts to raise troops among settlers reluctant to abandon families during dangerous times did not prosper. Stuyvesant tried to remove some of the settlers' fears at a March 6, 1660, meeting with Tackapousha and other sachems from Long Island and the lower river estuary. Stuyvesant accepted Tackapousha's explanation that the Maspeth killers had fled to Navesink. More interested in securing the heartland of his province than in apprehending fugitives, Stuyvesant renewed friendship with the sachems. Three days later he received company permission to begin hostilities against the Esopus and a promise of men and material. Attending to the spirits of his colonists, Stuyvesant appointed March 24 as a day of fasting, prayer, and meditation. Refusing a last-minute Esopus peace offer made through Wappinger intermediaries, Stuyvesant formally declared war and sent troops north.[19]

The commander of the one hundred men in the Wiltwijck garrison, recently reinforced by the twenty-five soldiers sent from Manhattan, soon ordered raiding parties to fan out across Esopus country. They struck during April and May, the hungry time when Indians living on the last of their winter stores concentrated on planting and the spring hunt. Dutch raiders killed and captured a number of Esopus people, destroyed settlements and supplies, and reportedly killed eleven visiting Minisink Indians. Stuyvesant ordered eleven of the more defiant Esopus captives sent to Curacao as slaves. Two or three others suspected of killing settlers were held for later punishment.[20]

Intent on humbling the Esopus, Stuyvesant rebuffed repeated peace over-tures. Keeping up the attacks, he further isolated them by securing neutral-ity pledges from their Wappinger and Lower River Indian friends. Stuyvesant finally agreed to a truce on June 3, after receiving word that his troops had captured and killed Preuwamakan, the oldest and most influen-tial of the Esopus sachems. He subsequently met with the Esopus chiefs at Wiltwijck to conclude a general peace on July 15, 1660. The chiefs prom-ised to give up their lands around the fort, return prisoners, indemnify Dutch losses with substantial payments of corn, and keep the peace. Stuyvesant gave them gifts and three prisoners, holding the eleven sent to Curacao as hostages for the good behavior of their nation. The sachems put their marks on the treaty instrument in the presence of chiefs from nearly every other Hudson Valley Indian nation, whose promise to attack the Eso-pus in the event they renewed the war served as a further surety for the treaty terms.[21]

Developments in Raritan-Navesink Country

The absence of Indians from the Lower Bay at the July 15, 1660, treaty evi-dently was not a casual omission. Stuyvesant had constantly received reports of killings and other hostile acts allegedly committed by Indians from that quar-ter since coming to the colony. An "Indian from Raretany," for example, was the prime suspect in the murder of the Dutch settler at Pavonia that brought Raritan sachems to the treaty table in 1649. A few years later, reports reached Stuyvesant's desk alleging that Cornelis Melijn, a banished political enemy of Kieft who returned to New Netherland in 1649, had hired more than one hundred musket-armed Raritan and Southern Indian bodyguards to defend his farm on Staten Island. It was also bruited about that Melijn encouraged the Indians to assassinate the director-general. Other reports identified a man from Navesink as the man who shot the trader on the deck of his yacht near Esopus in 1658. Both this man and Wassackarous, who would later openly boast about killing a Dutch settler at Maspeth, evidently were the murderers who reportedly sought sanctuary in Navesink country.[22]

Indians along the lowland corridor between the Falls of the Delaware and Raritan Bay continued to find themselves pressed from both sides during these years. Dutch sources indicate that Susquehannock attacks from the west and threats of other assaults from Indian enemies on Long Island drove most Indians away from the Raritan Valley by 1650. Further pressure from the east came from Dutch buyers from Brooklyn determined to purchase Indian territory around the Lower Bay from the mouth of the Raritan to Sandy Hook.[23]

Preoccupied with troubles at Esopus, Stuyvesant was unable to settle accounts with "the Neuwesink and Raritan tribes, among whom most of the perpetrators of all the single murders keep themselves." Susquehannock protectors may have helped the alleged murderers slip farther from his grasp. On April 18, 1660, Stuyvesant received word from company employees on the Delaware that Mohawk ambassadors urged Susquehannocks to offer asylum to Raritan or Navesink people "living near the Manhattans," fearing Dutch attack. There is every reason to believe Susquehannocks, desperate to replenish their own dwindling numbers, took the Mohawks up on their suggestion. They were mired in a seemingly interminable conflict with the westernmost Iroquois nations and faced the prospect of renewed war with Piscataway Indians in Maryland, whom they had been fighting since the late 1640s. Contemporary reports affirm that Indians from the Delaware River, moving one hundred or so miles from their territories to the Susquehanna River, helped Susquehannocks fight these enemies. Navesink and Raritan people, whose numbers may have included some or all alleged murderers of Dutch settlers, were probably among the one hundred Indians from the Delaware River helping Susquehannocks withstand a Seneca siege of their town in the spring of 1663.[24]

After receiving word of the July 15, 1660, Esopus peace treaty, company directors ordered Stuyvesant to either attack the Raritans and Navesinks or make peace with them. Their sachems rebuffed Stuyvesant's subsequent demands for surrender of alleged murderers, sending instead gifts to see "that the matter should be adjusted and forgotten." Stuyvesant rejected the presents. Unwilling to compromise and unable to attack, he had to settle for a stalemate in Raritan-Navesink country as he turned his attention northward when fighting again broke out at Esopus.[25]

MORE FIGHTING AT ESOPUS

Like so many others, the July 15, 1660, peace agreement proved to be more truce than treaty. Unwilling to admit defeat, many warriors at Esopus remained defiant. Stuyvesant's refusal to repatriate the eleven Esopus prisoners sent to Curacao became a troublesome sticking point. Both Esopus and Five Nations diplomats meeting with Stuyvesant during the following summer urged him to order the return of the men. Later that year, a concerned Stuyvesant wrote that the Esopus Indians were losing patience and looking for an excuse to renew fighting. The winter of 1661–1662 passed, however, without an Esopus attack. A relieved Stuyvesant wrote to his counterpart at Curcao, ordering the return of two of the captives and directing that the remaining nine be told "that if they behaved well [they] too shall be released and sent back in due time."[26]

Relations with the still-resentful Esopus took a turn for the worse during the spring of 1662. Ignoring Stuyvesant's warnings and Esopus threats, Wiltwijck settlers began to build what they named Nieuwdorp, "New Village." Now called Hurley, it was located a few miles west of Kingston on a piece of upland overlooking the broad fertile flats lining the lower courses of the Esopus Creek. A year passed without incident before alarmed residents threatened by angry Esopus neighbors wrote to Stuyvesant on May 10, 1663, asking that he send troops and preserve the peace by sending gifts to the Indians "at the first opportunity." Stuyvesant refused to send soldiers or subsidize local expansion efforts. Settlers girded for an Esopus attack.[27]

They did not have to wait long. Esopus warriors struck both Nieuwdorp and Wiltwijck on the morning of June 7, 1663. Firing on farmers in the fields and burning houses within the villages, they quickly destroyed Nieuwdorp and nearly burned Wiltwijck to the ground. They killed at least twenty settlers and captured another forty-five. Once again, Stuyvesant declared war, called for volunteers, and asked Mohawk and Mahican sachems to begin negotiating for the release of captives. He also met again with Oratam and other Lower River Indian chiefs to satisfy himself that they would not help the Esopus and to obtain information about the hostile Indians. Tackapousha once again pledged his support, this time more tangibly in the form of twenty warriors, under the command of his brother Chopeycannows, sent to fight alongside seventeen Indians already helping protect colonists at Wiltwijck.[28]

Stuyvesant sent a force of sixty men upriver under the command of his reliable captain-lieutenant Marten Kregier. On July 26, 1663, Kregier led these men, reinforced with another one hundred he found at Wiltwijck and thirty-seven Long Island warriors, out against a fort reported to be the center of Esopus resistance. Guided by a Wappinger captive and a former prisoner who had escaped from the fort, the force reached the place only to find it empty. Kregier's troops spent the next few days burning crops and spoiling stores before putting the stockade to the torch and returning to Wiltwijck.[29]

Distressed by the ease with which Kregier's force moved through their country, Esopus people scattered to friends and relatives among the Minisinks, Catskills, and Wappingers. Most busied themselves with planting new cornfields while their young people worked to erect a new fort farther from Wiltwijck. While this went on, Stuyvesant worked to convince nations known to be sympathetic to the Esopus to abandon their friends.[30]

In the meantime, Kregier kept up pressure by sending patrols out into the heart of Esopus country. On September 3, 1663, one of these patrols brought word of the new fort's location. Kregier immediately gathered fifty of his men and headed up the Walkill River. Traveling with great care, they managed to surprise and take the fort two days later. Deep in Esopus territory and fearing counterattack, Kregier's men did not have enough time to burn the place. Instead, they plundered the houses and destroyed what they could not carry away. Withdrawing with nineteen prisoners and twenty-three liberated captives, they left the corpses of at least thirty Esopus people behind.[31]

The attack broke the back of Esopus resistance. Oratam and Mattano helped work out a truce with Esopus sachems, one of whom, Sewackenamo, had emerged as their most visible pro-peace advocate. The truce they hammered out was a shaky one. Unknown Indians killed settlers at Communipaw and in Wappinger country during the winter and spring of 1663–1664. Determined to uphold the cease fire, both sides chose to regard the killings as isolated incidents. A renewed outbreak of fighting in the old feud between the Mohawks and Mahicans and their Northern Indian allies in the fall of 1663 presented a more serious threat to peace. The Dutch dealt with the threat by brokering a truce between the adversaries at Fort Orange in December, persuading both to keep pressure on the Esopus to maintain their own cease fire.[32]

Representatives from nearly every Indian nation along the Hudson finally gathered at Fort Amsterdam to conclude a general peace on May 15, 1664. One day later, the assembled dignitaries signed the treaty document. Like the Treaty of 1645, the terms largely restored things as they were before the fighting began. Speaking for all Esopus sachems, Sewackenamo agreed to give up the lands demanded by the Dutch, this time specified as territory extending as far as the old and new forts. The Dutch allowed them to harvest crops in both places before leaving. Both sides further pledged to meet yearly to air grievances and preserve peace. Treaty minutes do not mention exchanges of wampum, pelts, or gifts sealing the agreements. Both sides evidently believed they had already paid the price of peace in full.[33]

Epidemics, War, and Dispossession

More than anything else, disease exacted the stiffest price from those it struck. Smallpox reported at New Amsterdam during the winter of 1660–1661 swiftly spread to every Indian and colonial community in and around Munsee country. Several Indians "of the Highland and Northern tribes" bringing news of the epidemic from Manhattan to Fort Orange on January 29, 1661, inadvertently helped spread contagion wherever they stopped in the Hudson Valley. By summer, Dutch chroniclers reported that the disease was causing what they said was "a great mortality" among the Susquehannocks.[33]

Reports of a renewed outbreak of smallpox devastating lower Delaware River communities reached New Amsterdam on February 1, 1663. By May, the disease had again spread to the Susquehannocks, and from them to the Senecas and other westernmost Iroquois warriors then besieging their town. Sickened men returning home following the failure of their siege, and Indian messengers bringing the news traveling across the Raritan corridor to New Amsterdam, again spread smallpox throughout the region.[34]

The impacts of these epidemics on Munsee communities can be assessed only indirectly. Effects of the 1663–1664 epidemic may have played a greater role than the burning of crops and forts in reducing Esopus ability to continue the war. Illness also may have kept senior Esopus sachems Caelcop I, Pemmyrawech, and Neskahewan (all of whom had been conspicuously absent) away from the May 15, 1664, treaty meeting.[35]

Twelve of the forty-three people in the Munsee File chronicled in Dutch records written between 1645 and 1664 were no longer mentioned after 1664. If Indian population in Munsee country was four thousand in 1645, each of the forty-three sachems mentioned during those years could hypothetically be seen as representing somewhere around one hundred people. Disappearance of twelve of these leaders after 1664 suggests a loss of more than one thousand persons to disease and war. This renders a hypothetical total Indian population of around three thousand in the Munsee homeland in 1664.

Whatever their immediate impact or proximate causes, the constant barrages of war, disease, and other calamities killed or drove away a substantial part of the total Indian population in the lower Hudson and upper Delaware valleys between the 1640s and 1660s. Death, destruction, and dispossession reached into every River Indian community. Epidemic contagion, wars, and rumors of war also desolated and demoralized colonists with unfeeling impartiality. Hundreds died in the nearly interminable fighting. More were carried off by epidemics. Immigrants from Europe would more than replenish colonial losses. Indian population numbers, by contrast, plummeted into decline. Many who survived war and epidemic contagion accepted adoption into more powerful Indian nations like the Susquehannocks and Iroquois, intent on making up their own dwindling numbers. Others began leaving their lands for new homes farther from colonists and their diseases.

Although again not documented, it is hard to imagine that feelings of unappeasable anger and inconsolable grief did not threaten to overwhelm those surviving these calamities. Possibilities of River Indians or colonists achieving the level of empathy needed to recognize each other's common humanity were increasingly reduced by growing hatred and unregenerate indifference. Whatever their descendants may think, both peoples could fall prey to these very human feelings. Although present-day writers rarely fail to condemn colonists for their overweeningly self-righteous ethnocentric pride in their cultural superiority, there is no reason to assume that River Indians loved their own traditions with passions any less intense or self-regarding.[36]

Most people are motivated to one extent or another by the contradictory but always intermingled impulses that fuel greed and generosity. These impulses blend in particular ways in different places at different times. Initially similar mixtures of greed and generosity among both Indians and colonists gradually diverged as the region was drawn into the world market system. Progressively impoverished River Indians increasingly relied on customs of hospitality, sharing, and generosity. Colonists prospering on former Indian lands, by contrast, increasingly used their laws to ensure that their beliefs in those parts of the Protestant ethic encouraging efficient wealth accumulation continued to represent a sign of divine favor as much as evidence of political power.[37]

Upheavals caused by war and disease widened economic differences between Indians and colonists and rearranged world views at critical intervals. It was during such times that colonial authorities felt strong enough to force River Indians to sign away rights to particular pieces of territory, give up long valued rights and privileges, and submit to their authority.

Indian warriors and military leaders tried to reverse the tidal surge of change that threatened to overwhelm their people by killing and driving away settlers, and by fighting mourning wars to avenge lost loved ones. Their efforts only caused more mourning. Increasingly outnumbered and technologically outclassed, Indians in Munsee country began to recognize that war was no longer a productive way to resolve differences. They had to find new ways to cope with ever-growing numbers of colonists flooding their lands. Accommodation, however, presented its own set of challenges. How, for example, could they secure protection without becoming slaves of their protectors? How could they obtain now-essential trade goods with fewer producers, less land, and dwindling resources? And, most perplexingly, how could they slow or stop colonists from taking their land altogether and driving them away?

6

COPING, 1630-1664

Even if settlers miraculously disappeared, Indians of Munsee country could never return to the life they had lived before their coming. Whatever happened, they would have to put the past behind them and move forward. That meant trying to remember what might be most helpful and forgetting everything else.

Everyone in Munsee country, settlers as well as Indians, had much to forget. Their relationships with one another thus far had been neither harmonious nor uplifting. Epidemics suffered by both peoples had left behind ugly trails of death, disfigurement, and sorrow. Their wars were inglorious, unredemptive, inconclusive, and brutally squalid affairs marked by massacre, pillage, and destruction in discouraging dimensions.

Although the scourges of war, disease, death, and dispossession had not fallen equally on both peoples, each sacrificed much and lost more. Everyone could point to offenses offered, outrages suffered, and sicknesses endured. Most almost certainly believed that these were punishments brought down or allowed by divine protectors somehow angered by sinful living and willful or accidental ritual and ceremonial mistakes or omissions. It is equally certain that both Indians and colonists willingly paid the costs of spiritual and moral rearmament as they poured energy and treasure into defense efforts.

For all that, it is doubtful anyone could claim that they had gained a sense of security and satisfaction anywhere near worth the costs. Colonists paid high material and moral prices in wars against the Indians. Even though they might still claim ethical high ground, most River Indians had been forced from the coast, and their power was clearly in decline. Despite these facts, the Indians still possessed vast reserves of strength to counter expansion by colonists divided by provincial discord at home and pressed by international tensions abroad.

Neither people had gained complete ascendancy. Forced to deal with each other, both had to give far more than they wanted and get less than they thought they needed. Most settled for cobbled-together creative working disagreements that both parties could blithely deny and easily forget when no longer necessary. River Indians buried the names of lost coastal towns like Marechkawick with those of their lost loved ones. Settlers adopted Munsee names like Manhattan as their own and briefly kept others like Marechkawick alive as a kind of toponymical cat's paw before finally retiring it in favor of a name of their own, Wallabout Bay. Indians and colonists could forget names and mutually deny distasteful compromises. No matter what they did or how they felt, however, their lives and histories had been joined. Stuck with each other, they would have to remember enough to get on with life and forget enough to be able to grudgingly, reluctantly, but unavoidably live together in the homeland they now shared.

DEEDS AND LAND

Nowhere were the impacts of choices made by Indians and colonists compelled to live together on territory each wanted for their own more evident than in their land dealings with one another. Then as now, land was everything; its stewardship, care, and management were vital concerns essential for survival.

The Indians of Munsee country signed more than six hundred deeds to land in their ancestral homeland between 1630 and 1779 (see, for example, map 5). Through these deeds, signed over a period of nearly 150 years, at least 210 prominent Munsee individuals and several hundred other signatories ultimately conveyed the whole of their lands to colonists. The pattern formed by this vast body of documents signed over such a long period suggests that land sales were more than simple wholesale surrenders of territory. Much more was at work. Otherwise, why did Europeans not simply take all the land they wanted at one time from the Indians? Despite obvious differences, Indian and European power and ideas must have been equivalent enough to sustain a relationship corresponding to the size, complexity, and duration of this documentary record.

One significant area of equivalence lay in the respect both peoples had for spiritual power. Everyone living in the Hudson and Delaware valleys not only believed in spirits, they believed that they held their land in trust from them. Munsees believed that Kiisheelumukweenk, "he who creates us with his thoughts," gave the land to their ancestors. Sachems representing families descended from these ancestors upheld customs protecting their ancient rights to these lands. Settlers believed that their rulers and governments had God-given rights to lawfully claimed land. However they held the land, whether through statutory law or customary tradition, Indians and colonists clearly defined and resolutely guarded rights to ground holding graves of ancestors whose numbers they would join when their own time came.[1]

This is not to say there were not significant differences. Indian custom supported communal ownership. Sachems and councils charged with administering family lands used a custom anthropologists call usufruct to allocate use rights for town sites, planting fields, fishing spots, hunting and foraging territories, and other places so long as they were utilized. Usafruct did not mean that Indians thought land was free like air and water open to anyone wishing to share it. This is a crucially important point often missed by writers who think that land held in common under usufruct was available to anyone in the way open oceans are free to ships sailing upon them. Usufruct rights were available only to people with rights to land who were willing to properly respect local customs and concerns. Land was not free to strangers from foreign places who did not have these rights. Such people could only accept land as a granted gift or seize it outright.[2]

European law, by contrast, defined land consecrated to Crown or corporate control as private property and regarded land sales as final. Officials dispensed and protected fee simple ownership to purchasers meeting ownership requirements and paying deed prices, survey costs, and title fees. Concepts like private and communal ownership are neither cross-culturally incomprehensible nor necessarily absolute, however. Words used in land transactions like "give," "promise," and "forever" mean much the same thing in most languages. Ideas behind land tenure concepts, moreover, are neither simple nor unequivocal abstractions. However they differ, all such ideas vary in meaning as well as substance, making them susceptible to interpretation and thus to manipulation.

Fee simple ownership, for example, does not completely privatize property. Covenants of one sort or another limit extent or length of ownership. Needs of the state expressed through regal fiat, eminent domain, zoning

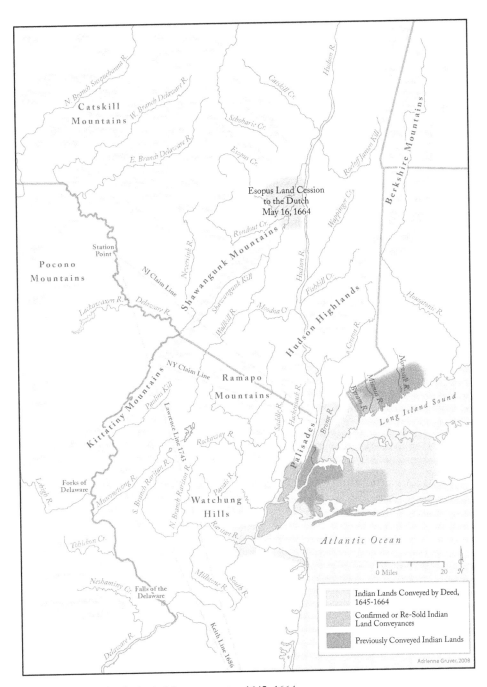

Map 5. Indian land sales in Munsee country, 1645–1664

regulations, and other forms of legal control and confiscation ensure that public necessity can trump private privilege. Although data documenting similar customs among the Indian people of Munsee country do not exist, it is difficult to imagine that people intensely tied to particular places always honored customs encouraging communal sharing. Failure of colonists to pay rents and taxes mandated by colonial law and omissions of Indians forgetting to give presents required by custom also probably met with similar responses in both societies.[3]

Other similarities suggest further common ground for cross-cultural comprehension. Much data exists, for example, showing that Indians and colonists cared deeply about territorial integrity and paid close attention to property rights and boundaries. Both peoples also evidently took great care to grant resource rights to particular places to particular people for specified lengths of time. Both also accepted the fact that land could be militarily conquered as well as peaceably transferred. And both further felt that no transfer, whether forced or voluntary, was complete without performance of appropriate rites and ceremonies. Indians and colonists marked all stages of property transfer with rituals validated by presentations of acceptable agreed-upon gifts and payments. Both peoples, moreover, keep records of their transactions. Indians used wampum shell bead strings and belts supplemented with notched or painted sticks to jog memories. Europeans favored pen and ink writings on paper or parchment.[4]

Some twenty years passed between the time Hudson sailed to the region in 1609 and 1630, the year the first deeds were signed, before Indians and colonists settled on deeds as the instrument of choice in land dealings with one another in Munsee country. The fact that both accepted the European deed form shows that land affairs were not conducted on a completely level playing field. Unlike deeds signed among themselves, those used by colonists to obtain title to Indian land also secured sovereignty over purchased property. Land sold by Indians thus passed from Native to colonial jurisdiction subject to the rules and laws of the colonizing nation. This would not happen when a Finn bought land from a Dutch landowner in New Netherland. Although title would pass to the Finn, the land would not become sovereign Finnish territory. Under international law, transfers of sovereignty in and among nations could only be accomplished through treaty agreement. In this way, Indian deeds served as a kind of treaty between Native people and colonists.

Not all colonies used deeds to acquire Indian lands. Maryland, Virginia, and New France, for example, did not recognize private purchases from Indians. Officials in these provinces claimed all territory granted under charters issued by their sovereigns as Crown lands. Like the modern-day United States, where the Supreme Court has consistently upheld the federal government's constitutional right to be the sole arbiter in dealings with tribes defined as domestic dependent nations, administrators in provinces not using Indian deeds acquired their land through treaty cessions. Barring private Indian purchases, they kept a tight leash on land affairs and made sure that conditions conducive to what Francis Jennings called deed game shenanigans, in which rival colonists used privately obtained deeds to support contending land claims, did not arise in their provinces.[5]

This was not the case in the provinces between Boston Harbor and Delaware Bay. In these places, private individuals, corporations, and government officials concluded land deals with Indians at every level of governance from the municipality, town, and county, to the province, and, for the brief period of its existence, to the dominion. Many thousands of documents recording these transactions lie in state and county archives scattered across a vast swath of territory. The sheer quantity of these documents bears witness to the complexity of an inter-cultural relationship through which deeds divided owners from nonowners as gifts, presents, cash payments, loans, taxes, rents, fees, and a vast body of customary and statutory law linked buyers and sellers alike to clan, Crown, corporate, or private interests.

Like the ideas behind them, deeds were susceptible to varying degrees of interpretation, manipulation, and worse. As an instrument, however, their wording was usually clear and their structure simple. It is not for nothing that deeds were among the first forms printed on colonial presses. Their standardized structure, straightforward format, and requirements stipulating that they be read aloud before signing helped both lettered and unlettered people understand and endorse their contents. All specified time and place of sale, identified interested parties, listed considerations to be paid, and described tract boundaries. Each also contained wording that described the nature of the title that passed to the grantee and set out covenants obliging one or the other party to fulfill certain conditions. All were then signed with signatures or marks and sealed by officials in the presence of witnesses.[6]

Even if both parties involved in transactions did not exactly understand everything written or said, the endlessly repeated structure of deed contents and the ceremonial readings and signings of deed documents composed what can be thought of as a ritual formula. Literate or illiterate, Indian or colonist, all people in colonial America were attuned to the nuances of social etiquette, political procedure, and religious ceremony. Respect for proper performance of reading and signing rituals during land deals went far in assuring all parties that appropriate ceremonies and forms were being observed. It is unlikely that many would casually overlook or unquestioningly countenance omissions of particular parts of these rituals or alterations in their order of presentation.[7]

The uniform format followed in deed-signing rituals was replicated in the strict order of administrative processes provincial authorities required to convert communal Indian land into private property under colonial sovereignty. While specifics varied somewhat from colony to colony, jurisdiction to jurisdiction, and time to time, all essentially required prospective buyers to obtain permits or licenses to purchase Indian lands. Each also required that purchasers obtaining signed Indian deeds register the document; obtain a survey warrant; hire a surveyor with it; get the surveyor to lay out, describe, and map tract boundaries; and secure a patent formalizing ownership of the surveyed property. All steps were papered over with records mostly filed in separate record groups. Although their forms were as standardized as those used in deeds, they nevertheless also remained susceptible to differing interpretations by those wishing to contest their contents or validity.[8]

Land purchase was an expensive proposition in provinces where cash money was in short supply. So scarce was hard money that settlers in Munsee country and elsewhere used Indian wampum beads as currency among themselves into the 1700s. Whether paid in coin, wampum, or goods, prices paid to Indians were only a part, and often only a small part, of the assets laid out by buyers. Purchasers had to pay a multitude of publicly posted and scheduled filing fees for every required license, warrant, and finished form. Although the records say little of substance on the subject, endless complaints, accusations, and legal actions alleging bribery and corruption indicate that buyers just as surely had to discreetly pay off strategically placed officials at every step of the process. Payments, moreover, did not end when purchasers proved titles and received patents. Landowners in proprietary colonies like Pennsylvania and East and West Jersey were expected to pay annual quit rents to proprietors who purchased the original Indian titles, although the actual payments were often never made. Those buying land directly from Indians in New Netherland and New York more regularly paid taxes on their property. The high cost of doing business and maintaining property ensured that would-be landowners had to be both well heeled and well connected.[9]

Did Colonists Use Deeds to Dupe Indians out of Their Lands?

The comparatively low prices Indians usually accepted for their lands sustain the nearly universal belief that colonists duped them out of their territory. Most versions of the story fall into one of two camps. The first and formerly the more prevalent of these story lines traces descent to the barbarous savage stereotype. In it, greedy Indian-givers are outdone by quick-witted settlers. The other and currently most widely accepted view repeats variations on the equally venerable noble savage theme. Holders of this view tend to see Indians as guileless innocents whose sense of spirituality and wholesome communal cultural values did not allow them to fully grasp or willingly accept the selfish values of private property and exclusive land ownership.[10]

Of course, few narratives in either tradition ever lay things out so simply. On one level or another, most writers know that all people weigh costs and benefits. Those recognizing that similar choices can be based on different cultural calculi more clearly appreciate how those negotiating across divides of language and custom nevertheless try to extract maximum benefits for minimal costs, however they are defined. This viewpoint helps investigators more clearly see how people involved in negotiations adjust wishful thinking to hard realities.

Just as beliefs of Indians and Europeans involved in land negotiations did not differ to the point where neither could comprehend the other's concepts, buyers and sellers differed among themselves regarding what they wanted deeds to do. Whatever they thought they were doing, tangible commodities obviously changed hands. Commodity prices always reflect notions of value. Although these fluctuate from one culture and situation to another, all people invest land with cultural value. Such values may be expressed symbolically in terms of supernatural power and pollution by spiritually inclined people and by market prices in societies relying on capital. People holding the former point of view often exchange essential but ritually polluted perishables for highly prized spiritually pure ritual objects. Skagit Indians in the Pacific Northwest, for example, exchanged essential ritually polluted perishable food that ultimately turned to dung, sweat, and urine for incorruptibly inedible spiritually pure masks and dentalium shells.

Pure things were needed to please keepers of game or delight spirits of plants and animals who might then give themselves to people for food.[11]

Exchanges of land for trade goods may have been guided by similar logic among Indians in Munsee country. It is entirely possible that Indians may have regarded places vulnerable to military and microbial assaults, denuded of game, and ruinously close to Europeans as ritually defiled land that had become, in the words of one of their sachems, mere dirt. On the other hand, many sources clearly affirm that Indians considered glass beads, tobacco pipes, vermillion, and other European trade goods as spiritually powerful as wampum. Like copper, shells, and other objects that had long been brought to Munsee country from distant places, strange Europeans brought mysteriously produced foreign goods. Those believing such goods were charged with alien spirit powers often also believed that such powers were not necessarily effective in foreign territory. Unlike local products, newly traded objects still in their original boxes, so to speak, and untouched by local magic could easily be considered spiritually pure objects unpolluted by everyday contact.[12]

Other less tangible desires were satisfied through material exchanges documented in deeds. One of the more compelling of these was the desire for protection both parties expected deeds to provide. Settlers wanted the protection of lawful title in an often inscrutably intimidating legal system controlled and manipulated by officials backed up by sheriffs, militiamen, and armies. They also used deeds as a shield to protect them from Indian retribution that would surely follow outright seizure of their lands. Indians wanted legal protection of colonial administrators in peacetime and military protection in times of war. One deed contained wording explicitly expressing this expectation. In it, the Indian signatories stated that "to promote the good and general welfare of both nations, we think it fit and convenient on settle some of our lands [with] Englishmen who have from time to time and in times of greatest necessity been our benefactors."[13]

And what of the low prices Indians accepted for their lands? A number of sources show that Indians in Munsee country soon learned that prices paid them rarely matched those charged settlers. A closely related kinsman of Nutimus named Teedyuscung, from the Munsee–Northern Unami borderlands of central New Jersey, put this awareness into words at a treaty meeting at Easton, Pennsylvania, in 1756. Underscoring Indian resentment of land frauds perpetrated by Englishmen, he reminded his listeners that "I have sold great tracts of land at unreasonably low rates, to the English, far below what any person would allow to be their value." And in the dense inter-locking networks of a society where, as Penn wrote in the Quaker style, "wealth circulateth like the blood," information of such critical importance to so many people almost surely traveled fast and far.[14]

Did awareness of this information make the Indians feel cheated? It prob-ably did at the most elemental level. Who would not want to get as much as they could for something most did not necessarily want to part with in the first place? People forced to deal with vastly more powerful colonizers in-sisting that they sell their lands had to put aside such thoughts. Efforts to drive up prices had very little effect on buyers facing the immediate prospect of vastly larger payouts before any benefit or profit could be ex-pected. How then could Indians use desire for their lands to get protections they needed?

Teedyuscung expressed Indian expectations succinctly in his Easton speech, saying the "proprietor has purchased the lands so cheap, yet he sells them again too dear to the poor people, that they do not use the Indians well and think they owe us nothing." Teedyuscung expected colonists to feel obligated to give something more for the low prices they paid for land. Scholars have a word for this sense of obligation. They call it reciprocity.[15]

DEED EXCHANGES AS RECIPROCAL RELATIONSHIPS

Reciprocity as defined by economists is clearly expressed in the form of give and take recorded in deeds to Indian land in Munsee country. Just as they use the term egalitarian to identify societies that do not institutionalize so-cial or political inequality, anthropologists use the word reciprocity to de-scribe a wide range of often unequal economic exchanges. Anthropologist Annette Weiner neatly defined reciprocity as a cultural process that "creates social relations, establishes friendships, validates alliances, sustains order in so-cieties, and establishes political authority."

Reciprocity according to this definition exists in various forms. The best known of these is balanced reciprocity, which occurs when more or less po-litically equal parties give and receive commodities both regard as equivalent in value. Negative reciprocity occurs when one party accepts less for what both parties consider a more valuable commodity. This kind of reciprocity, which most often occurs in relationships between unequal parties signifi-cantly differing in population size, productive potential, and political power, characterized transactions between Indians and colonists in Munsee country throughout the colonial era. Less powerful Indians accepted negatively reciprocal asymmetrical value and exchange rates when parting with much more than they almost certainly usually wanted to give.

There was no question that Indians in Munsee country had to part with land they did not want to sell after epidemics and military defeats ended their ability to resist colonial demands. Knowing that continued resistance would result in the loss of their lives as well as their lands, Indians with few other choices decided to sell lands they would much rather have kept at prices they knew were much lower than their resale value among colonists. Following the strategy often chosen by people compelled to accept unequal exchanges, they worked hard to make colonists promise to protect them militarily, give them just treatment in colonial courts, and take on other obligations settlers might not otherwise have accepted if Indians had been powerful enough to demand and receive much higher colonial market values for their land.[16]

In this way, the treatylike nature of Indian deeds tacitly sanctioned by Native custom and sealed according to colonial law allowed Indians to exchange land for a degree of protection and justice. Like all treaties, deeds established as well as renewed relationships. As long as these relationships existed, Indians in Munsee country constantly worked to oblige colonists to protect them. Sometimes they succeeded; sometimes they did not. And sometimes the price of protection was more than they were willing or wanted to pay. Evidence of their efforts to obtain protection is preserved in the records of assembly meetings, court proceedings, and governor's councils. These forums provided opportunities for Indians and colonists to air grievances, resolve disputes, and come to one another's assistance.

The January 15, 1639, Massapequa deed was the first conveyance promising protection and justice. All deeds signed previously simply transferred Indian ownership rights to purchasers. Although the Massapequa deed included language far more explicit than that found in alienation clauses in earlier deeds, it went further in specifying residual rights and obligations. Mechoswodt, the deed's primary Indian signatory, made it a condition that he "be allowed, with his people and friends, to remain upon the aforesaid land, plant corn, fish, hunt and make a living there as well as they can, while he himself and his people place themselves under the protection of the [Dutch West India Company]."[17] This wording provided openings for many interpretations. What did alienation mean when Indians could continue to live on sold lands? What would happen when Indians and colonists wanted to use the same tracts? What did protection mean? Would failure to provide protection invalidate the agreement?

In 1639, protection offered the prospect of survival in a country that soon would be rent by decades of brushfire warfare. By the time the fighting stopped in 1664, few if any Indians in Munsee country had any lingering illusions about the quality of colonial protection. As we have seen, the Dutch tried to force Lower River Indians to pay taxes for protection even before the ink of the 1639 deed had dried. All saw that authorities protected them only when Indians' interests coincided with colonial policy or squared with European notions of equity and justice. Justice, even in its inconsistent and unequal applications in courts, only allowing Indian testimony when it suited provincial interests, nevertheless helped keep the peace. And peace would forestall seizure of the type forced on the Esopus, whose most productive territories were taken, in the words of the May 16, 1664, treaty ending the Esopus War, by the sword.

Indian demands that settlers again repurchase Staten Island show that colonists were not the only people in Munsee country who believed swords could be used to regain lost lands. The unnamed Staten Island Indians telling Melijn that "there must be a new bargain made" for Staten Island in 1649 belonged to the same nations whose warriors had driven De Vries' settlers away in 1641. Mattano, his brother Neckaock, Oratam, and the other chiefs who negotiated the 1657 deed specifically represented Hackensacks, Raritans, and other nations whose warriors had again taken the island back in 1655.[18]

A speech made by Wiechquaesgeck sachem Romackqua shows that while swords could be used to take lives and force people to give up moveable property, they could not by themselves pry land away from those unwilling to sell it. Meeting on October 30, 1671, with Francis Lovelace, New York's governor from 1668 to 1673, who was then trying to tie up his colony's territorial loose ends, Romackqua and other Wiechquaesgeck sachems offered the western half of territory they had promised to sell only to the now-ousted Dutch West Indies Company in the deed signed on July 14, 1649. Aware of the latest bout of fighting pitting Mahicans and their Lower River Indian allies against the Mohawks, Lovelace asked if Romackqua's people still had the right to sell lands from which they had been "beaten off by the Maques." Romackqua replied, "the Maques will not say they have any pretense to their land, though being at war, they would destroy their persons and take away their beavers and goods."[19]

However they were used, no one questioned who had the biggest swords in Munsee country. Sachems could neither ignore nor hide the eroding effects of disease, defeat, and depopulation on their bargaining positions. This does not mean that they gave up hope that their political fortunes would improve or that the epidemics that threatened everyone in the region might at some point strike only colonists. But by mid-century, Indians throughout the region had to face the fact that, barring a raft of miracles, they could no longer effectively protect their lands and lives on battlefields.

A Better Battlefield

Losses suffered during the drumfire midcentury wars also convinced settlers that the sword was a poor tool for prying land from Indians in Munsee country.[20] After 1664 both peoples would use council chambers and court rooms to wage their land battles. Then as now, Indians preferred to go straight to the top when dealing with officials. Governors, directors-general, and other high authorities served as agents of distant corporate, proprietary, or imperial interests. Men like Stuyvesant and his successors were usually at odds with more self-seeking colonists like Melijn. Indians knew from long experience that high officials determined to keep the peace would make time to hear their complaints. They also learned that upper-level administrators often supported them when their interests did not conflict with official policy. Stuyvesant's successors soon found out that they could use Indian concerns as handy wedge issues in disputes with refractory provincials.

Although differing in form and content, custom and public opinion in Indian and colonial societies worked to restrain destructive self-interest and discourage acts threatening peace or outraging prevailing morality. Colonists added a further coercive layer of law to this regulatory mix. Colonial law did not then meddle in purely internal Indian matters. Authorities, however, made sure that Indians accepted colonial jurisdiction in all legal actions involving settlers. Colonial courts were normally places where Indians could only be defendants tried under provincial laws. Indians could neither serve on juries nor, in many cases, provide evidence or present testimony in any but the most serious capital cases.

This was not the case in actions involving long-standing sources of intercultural trouble like land disputes, liquor smuggling, and illicit firearms trade. In such cases, Indians could be called by plaintiffs as well as defendants, serve as witnesses, make depositions, testify in open court, and sometimes, as a significant symbolic gesture in signal instances, join juries. Sachems soon saw how conflicting interpretations of words and meanings could embroil contending landowners in lengthy disputes that dragged on inconclusively for decades at a time. The vast body of land dispute documentation preserved in libraries and archives attests to lengths Indians and colonists went to exploit differing word readings and less-than-exact boundary descriptions to cultivate the modest measures of reasonable doubt needed to support particular points of view in colonial courts.

Although the endlessly repeated formal structure of deeds helped make them comprehensible, sections detailing property boundary descriptions contained place-names and other information subject to differing interpretations. Land transactions throughout the seventeenth century were conducted at a time before formally trained licensed surveyors became a fixture of provincial life. Deed boundary descriptions and surveys made during these years were mostly amateur affairs. Many were notoriously inexact, often hazy, and sometimes just plain wrong. The impermanent character of boundary markers like winding streams, rock piles, and blazed trees caused further problems. This latter practice provided particularly fertile soil for litigators exploiting boundary disagreements. Trees marked with numbers or letters carved into or painted onto trunks often could not be found when officials and Indians walked boundaries together at later dates. Other markers were no more dependable. Streams could change course and piles of stones disappear. And, most important to the Indians, locations and meanings of place names recorded in their language were subject to their own interpretations.

Indian efforts to impress their views of things on colonial authorities are clearly discernible in records documenting debates over the meanings of several deeds to particularly large portions of Indians' ancestral heartland. Two of the earliest of these lengthily contested deals were the January 15, 1639, and November 13, 1643, deeds that took in nearly all land on western Long Island. Not every aspect of these deeds was subject to debate. No one, for example, ever denied that the deals had been made. And no question ever arose challenging the rights of the chiefs to the lands involved. Both of Tackapousha's fathers fixed their marks on the 1639 deed, and Tackapousha himself signed the 1643 conveyance.

Neither the signatories nor their successors, however, wound up regarding these cessions as unconditional surrenders. All instead evidently came to treat them more as species of promissory notes guaranteeing exclusive future purchase rights to the nation of the colonists signing the deeds. Mechoswodt made this view clear to Dutch authorities in the 1639 deed, whose terms explicitly allowing his people to remain upon their lands had to have been the result of considerable negotiation.[21]

No colonist formally accepted Indian interpretations as matters of law. Colonial administrators could not, however, afford to alienate Indians by simply ignoring their demands or rejecting their claims out of hand. Instead, both parties compromised. By hedging things just a little, Stuyvesant and his successors could deny they were repurchasing any part of already sold land. Sachems doing the same thing could graciously allow colonists to settle on a little more land, accept generous gifts as signs of enduring friendship, and still retain rights to remaining territory.

Just as contact between Indians and colonists in Munsee country was not a simple morality play of oppressed victims or heroic resisters, the story of intercultural relations in the ancestral Munsee homeland is also not a mere cautionary tale of lamentable and easily dismissed folly, blunders, and missteps caused by failures of will, communication, and understanding. Cultural, linguistic, and temperamental differences certainly got in the way of perfect understanding. It is nevertheless difficult to imagine either Indians or colonists mistaking one another's intentions for long after they made the first deals or broke the first promises.

It seems instead that both peoples arrived at working disagreements based on a form of creative misunderstanding. Providing a kind of plausible deniability, creative misunderstandings allowed people to conduct business otherwise discouraged by moral scruples or cultural prohibitions. Creative misunderstandings helped people establish relationships and make decisions that would otherwise be unacceptable. Bending truth short of breaking trust, people used the polite fictions of their creative misunderstandings and working disagreements to lessen the disruptive effects of all-too-human impulses like intolerance and greed. By blending subtle tints of half-truths and white lies into weightier mixes capable of sustaining deed agreements and treaty pledges, people willing to reach across cultural divides could still find common ground. The level playing field provided by discreet and courteous acceptance of readily denounceable untruths helped people work together in the face of otherwise overwhelming differences in belief, numbers, and political power. The system worked, however, only so long as it forwarded everyone's interests.[22]

The many deeds and other land records signed by Munsee people conveying both title and sovereignty over to settlers provide a particularly lengthy record of working disagreements in action. It is not clear if Indians professed an unshakable belief that people could not sell their Mother Earth during colonial times. The custom of usufruct followed by Indians depended on relationships among kinsfolk, friends, and strangers that required frequent adjustment and periodic renewal. Usufruct beliefs did not prevent Indians from signing deeds that colonial purchasers considered full and final sales (although Indians reserved residual rights). Colonists repeatedly paid off sachems continuing to claim rights to sold lands with what both sides called gifts or presents. These presentations allowed colonists to make a show of generosity while satisfying Indian needs for traditional renewal payments long after initial bargains were sealed.[23]

Playing Off Rivals

The balance of power in Munsee country affecting working disagreements had shifted in favor of the colonists by the time the English took over New Netherland in 1664. Things still had not reached the point that settlers could use swords, deeds, or any other instruments to take what they wanted or force unwilling Indians to accept their claims or interpretations. Although colonists now vastly outnumbered Indians, the fractious character of their local politics and nearly constant international tensions prevented settlers from fully exploiting their numerical and technological advantages. Company men vied with free traders, yeoman farmers with large landholders, townspeople with countryfolk, English settlers with Hollanders, New Netherlanders with New Englanders, French colonists to the north in New France, and Marylanders and Virginians farther south. Competing with and against one another in a bewildering and ever-changing variety of combinations, contending parties, factions, and communities at every level of society created a swirlingly bewildering political environment.[24]

Differences between contending colonists created manipulable divisions. Preoccupied Europeans inadvertently helped Indians exploit rivalries by conferring a unique sort of legal immunity upon those cooperating in investigations into smuggling, liquor trade, gunrunning, fencing of stolen goods, and other illicit activities. Sachems were constantly encouraged to provide evidence against settlers peddling guns and liquor to their people. Like all contraband, proscribed firearms and strong drink were always in great demand. The sachems were thus often able to hold the whip hand over smugglers all too aware that Indians could turn in those who cheated them without fear of being prosecuted for buying or trying to buy highly desirable forbidden commodities.[25]

It is difficult to imagine that sachems were displeased when colonial authorities punished settlers and partisan rivals guilty of harassing, assaulting, or robbing them. They also welcomed gifts and promises of protection given at meetings encouraging their cooperation in suppressing contraband trade. They were more ambivalent about supporting prohibitions against alcohol and positively opposed bans on munitions.[26]

Conflicts like the Pequot and Kieft's wars provided unmistakable evidence of the decisive advantages firearms could confer in warfare. Lower River Indians appreciating the need for the range and striking power offered by firearms looked with much misgiving on Dutch policies banning open sale of guns to their warriors and hunters while allowing Mahicans, Mohawks, and Susquehannocks to acquire muskets, lead, and powder. It is not surprising that they did not help company officials prosecute settlers like Melijn who gave them guns and ammunition without authorization.[27]

The thicket of laws, ordinances, and regulatory procedures mandated by authorities at home and enacted in the provinces presented a particularly productive environment encouraging emergence of exploitable disputes. Lacking firearms needed to forcibly stop settlers from taking their lands, Indians in Munsee country could and did play contending parties in land controversies off against one another to slow, deflect, and even halt sales. Different figures and factions alternately worked with and against Indian interests with baffling unpredictability. Embattled Indians, however, could usually expect support from one side or another in most land disputes.

Some rifts, like corporate struggles between patroons and company officials, were private affairs discreetly worked out in the privacy of boardrooms and council chambers. Others, like Melijn's very public feuds with Kieft and Stuyvesant and the often poor relations between Dutch and English settlers in the colony, were common knowledge and easily seen by anyone taking the trouble to look. Such public disagreements were tailor-made for Indian exploitation. When looked at from this perspective, most of the records mentioning Indians in the Munsee homeland chronicle attempts to exploit colonial differences. Three well-documented examples, at Matinecock, Brooklyn, and Navesink-Raritan country, will have to stand for the many incidents of this type documented during the Dutch regime.

Power Plays and Manipulations

One of the most long-lasting land disputes in Munsee country occurred at Matinecock in the present-day Long Island towns of Hempstead and Oyster Bay. Much of this dispute centered on contested meanings of deed provisions and locations of deeded boundaries. Dutch officials, who had an entire colony to worry about, tended to take more nuanced views of things than local townsfolk. They could afford to see these deeds as preemptive agreements requiring future confirmations. Poorer, preoccupied, and the ones who paid to turn Indian land into colonial property in the first place, townsfolk usually favored strictly literal, conclusive interpretations. Hempstead settlers in particular chose to regard their 1643 deed as a final sale. They did not feel that it was their job to keep paying off Indians to maintain peace in New Netherland. They only wanted them gone as soon as possible.

The Indians, however, refused to go. Frustrated townsfolk dispatched a delegation to meet with Stuyvesant at Fort Amsterdam on August 23, 1647, to get the Dutch to drive them out. Hoping to appeal to Stuyvesant's reportedly suspicious nature, they told him that the Massapequas were plotting their destruction. Stuyvesant did not jump to the bait. He regarded the Hempstead settlers with even more suspicion as subversives loyal to New England. Unlike the English at Gravesend and other towns nearer New Amsterdam, the Hempstead settlers openly maintained contact with New Englanders just across Long Island Sound. Neither Stuyvesant nor, as it turned out, the company directors were inclined to indulge them at the expense of one of the colony's more dependable Indian allies.[28]

Massapequa and Matinecock sachems managed to sow further dissension among their English neighbors by subsequently selling unclearly bounded adjoining tracts to rival townsfolk. In 1653, for example, Suscaneman's predecessor Asharoken sold tracts of land in what later became the centers of Oyster Bay and Huntington to the town's founders. Five years later, Suscaneman's brother-in-law Tackapousha signed deeds conveying land farther west along the contested border between Hempstead and Oyster Bay to rival purchasers. Arguments over both pairs of sales would embroil settlers for decades.[29]

Settlers were not the only Long Islanders tangled up in these land wrangles. Having already inserted himself into arguments over Indian title to lands west of Secatogue, Montaukett sachem Wyandanch used border disputes between Oyster Bay, Hempstead, and Huntington to further his efforts to exert influence over Indian affairs in western Long Island. In a codicil to the March 17, 1658, deed, he promised Oyster Bay settlers that he would support them against Huntington claims to land sold earlier by Tackapousha. Later that month, Wyandanch dispatched his adviser Cockenoe to mark out the boundary subsequently described in the May 11, 1658, deed.[30]

For a time it looked like Wyandanch's efforts to sidestep Tackapousha would succeed. A year later, death, perhaps with a little help from what one settler said was poison, put an end to Wyandanch's machinations. His attempts to involve himself in land matters in western Long Island had represented a major threat to Massapequa and Matinecock autonomy. His involvement in their affairs would have ended any chances they had to deal independently with colonists. What was worse, this involvement would have made it possible for Wyandanch to sell their lands from under them, leaving them with the choice of moving where others wished or abandoning Long Island entirely.

Mattano tried to manipulate suspicions that divided rival Dutch and English claimants to Indian lands in Brooklyn. His first efforts to exploit this rivalry in Brooklyn met with limited success. The Dutch claimed what amounted to nearly all his people's lands on Long Island under the terms of both Tackapousha's broad conveyance of November 13, 1643, and Seyseychkimus's later cancelled September 10, 1645, deed to the most westerly portion of lands within the bounds covered by the 1643 deed. A small patch in this latter area was also claimed by yet another group of New England exiles led by Lady Deborah Moody, who settled at Gravesend with Dutch permission during Kieft's War. After the war, English settlers there secured their claim in a sale, again arranged with Dutch approval, concluded with Seyseychkimus and Mattano's father, Emerus, on November 1, 1650.[31]

Mattano made his first move as unsettling news of the killings of three colonists by unknown Indians in nearby Hellgate reached New Amsterdam in the spring of 1652. On June 17, a group of unnamed Nayack sachems, almost certainly including Mattano, offered to sell land at Flatbush, which they said the company had not yet paid for, to an agent of Utrecht merchant and would-be patroon Cornelius van Werckhoven. Stuyvesant did not welcome the offer. He was first concerned by what he regarded as the unusually high price offered to the Indians for the land by the agent of a man he did not want to see rise to the eminence of patroon. He also worried that the Indians would see any deal as a concession to the recent killings. Stuyvesant put his concerns into a letter to the directors, asking if it was wise "to encourage and embolden the Indians" by repurchasing "the same lands which they previously have, of their own good will, sold, given, ceded and received payment for, and which since have been partly occupied." He went on to write that it might "lead to serious consequences, if it can be proved, that there is in the midst of the purchased land some which has not been bought (although we are not quite convinced of it), or what would be the consequence of the situation if we gave a small gift to the Indians?"[32]

Stuyvesant was convinced that paying twice for even the least productive vacant plots within tracts sold earlier by the most prominent sachems in the region would be "an inducement to murder more Christians, imagining them to be fainthearted, and threaten a massacre so that later on they may again obtain money and goods for another piece of wild and waste land." He called things correctly. Alarmed by the rumor spread by Melijn that the Dutch plotted to join with the English at Gravesend to kill his people, Mattano threatened war if colonists took the land without paying for it. Although Stuyvesant doubted that Indians had a greater "claim to the wild and waste bush, upon which God and nature had grown trees, than any other Christian people," he nevertheless recommended that the Indians be given a gift to prevent "blame and new troubles."[33]

Mattano and the Nayacks immediately took advantage of Stuyvesant's offer to make new gifts to the Indians by concluding two deals for land at Flatbush with contending colonists. The first was made on July 29, 1652. It conveyed to an English colonist from Gravesend an island in southern Brooklyn originally presented by Kieft to John Underhill as a gift for his services during Kieft's War. In the second deal made on the following November 22, Van Werckhoven bought land at Nayack and New Utrecht "for which payment was yet to be made" from Mattano and Seyseychkimus.[34]

Mattano's manipulations helped him secure de facto recognition of his rights to lands included in earlier purchases. They did not, however, prevent Van Werckhoven from inserting what amounted to an order of eviction into the Nayack deed. While deed conditions required that Mattano and his people move to nearby Staten Island, it did not put an end to Indian occupation at Nayack. More than twenty-five years later, Jasper Danckaerts visited Indians living at Nayack with the permission of Jacques Corteljou, who had started out by managing Van Werckhoven's business interests in New Utrecht.[35]

Mattano and his kinsmen had more success manipulating land rivalries across the Narrows in Staten Island and in the nearby Raritan-Navesink country. Mattano sold two tracts of land along the southern shores of Raritan Bay on March 28, 1651, and December 26, 1652, to another of Van Werckhoven's silent partners, a prominent trader named Augustine Heermann. Mattano's father, Emerus, had sold land along the Navesink Highlands one year earlier to Lubbertus van Dincklagen, vice director of the colony and the agent of another prospective patroon named Hendrick Van der Capellen toe Ryssel. Van der Capellen was a well-connected nobleman whose agents had been buying up Indian land around the Lower Bay in partnership with Melijn since the 1640s.[36]

All three purchases were made along the same political fault lines that Mattano and Emerus had tried to exploit in Brooklyn. Stuyvesant openly hated Melijn and made no pretense of hiding his dislike for aspiring absentee patroons like Van Werckhoven and Van der Capellen, whose possession of feudal manorial privileges would openly infringe on his authority. Determined to protect his prerogatives, he demanded and received company authorization to invalidate private purchases of Indian land made without his authorization.[37]

This had the effect of stymieing the would-be patroons. Unable to find settlers willing to move to a dangerous place like Navesink, Van Werckhoven gave in as gracefully as he could to Stuyvesant. The director-general allowed him to exchange the claim for his erstwhile patroonship into a title for land purchased as a private citizen at New Utrecht. Van Werckhoven's manager there, Corteljou, abandoned further efforts to turn the lands into a patroonship of his own after his employer died in 1655. The outbreak of the Peach War that same year put an end to all efforts to acquire Indian lands until the fighting ended.

Van der Capellen was less easily deterred. He was one of the first colonists to resume Indian land acquisitions after peace returned to New Netherland in 1657. On July 10 of that year, Van Dincklagen negotiated a new deed to Staten Island for his associate. The deed was signed by Mattano and a consortium of other Hackensack and Lower Bay sachems. Oratam added his prestige to the deal by signing on as a witness. Stuyvesant was alarmed by Van der Capellen's continuing efforts to establish a patroonship by sidestepping his authority. He particularly resented his private unsanctioned acquisition of land first purchased from Indians nearly thirty years earlier. It did not help that Van der Capellen had Melijn as a partner. Refusing to give in to either man, Stuyvesant again asked for and received company permission to annul their Indian purchases. The company directed Stuyvesant to negotiate a new deal with the Indians. They tried to sweeten the pill for the influential Van der Capellen by advising Stuyvesant to resell the land to him under the same terms offered all free settlers.[38]

Having received the company's blessing to protect their land interests, Stuyvesant then moved to forestall further acquisitions by Melijn and

Van der Capellen by negotiating a new deed with Indians for land at Pavonia on January 30, 1658. He need not have bothered. Van der Capellen died
a year later. His heirs subsequently sold his land rights to the company for
three thousand guilders.[39]

Van der Capellen's death did not stop efforts to acquire Indian lands at
Raritan and Navesink. Stuyvesant received word that Gravesend men were
negotiating for Navesink land just as rumors that an English fleet was sailing
to seize the colony made both Indians and English settlers more willing to
defy company authority. Determined to stop the Gravesend settlers from
getting the land at Navesink, Stuyvesant hurriedly dispatched the energetic
Marten Kregier to look into the matter. Kregier had just returned to New
Amsterdam after the arrival of winter closed campaigning season in Esopus
country. Hiring several Indian guides, he arrived at the mouth of the Raritan at the head of a small party on December 6, 1663.

A concerned Stuyvesant authorized Kregier to promise the openly unfriendly Raritan and Navesink people "that all former acts and claims shall
be forgotten and forgiven, if [they would] sell the land to nobody but the director-general and council." The sachems could not miss the note of desperation evident in this offer to overturn earlier purchases. They were
already negotiating a sale to Corteljou at the Indian town of Ramenesing
(Munsee for "place of a small paint-stone"), south of the Navesink Highlands. Unable to sail up the Raritan, Kregier had to cool his heels while one
of his guides went inland to meet with the chiefs. The guide returned with
several Raritan and Navesink Indians promising to sell some lands to the
Dutch. On December 12, 1663, Stuyvesant extracted a promissory note
framed in the form of a deed for land at the Navesink Highlands from
Mattano and several other men representing his brother, the Navesink
sachem Peropay. The goods listed in the deed evidently represented a pledge
of earnest money rather than a final payment for the land. Even more intriguingly, Corteljou signed the deed as a witness and an interpreter.[40]

Two weeks later, the Navesink sachems sent a message to Stuyvesant
setting their price for the territory in question. They demanded additional payment of goods worth four thousand guilders. A stunned
Stuyvesant responded by ordering troops to Navesink to stop Gravesend
men from entering the country. The men needed to garrison such a post
were then on duty at Wiltwijck, however, and could not be spared. It did
not matter. On February 16, 1664, Stuyvesant heard that Peropay had

been in Brooklyn. While there, he told the Gravesend men that he preferred to sell the Navesink land to them.

Things quieted down until March 25, 1664, when a Navesink messenger suddenly burst into a meeting at New Amsterdam with Lower River chiefs negotiating the release of prisoners held by the Esopus. He told Stuyvesant that the Navesink chief had sent him to report that "the English pressed him very hard, to sell the land of the Newesinghs, but the chief had answered, he could not sell it to them, they had received already from us wampum and goods for it." He went on to say that the sachem said "that we had to make haste, if we wanted to buy the land, they could not keep off the English any longer and we must come immediately after having bought it and erect a house there." Stuyvesant was preoccupied with more pressing concerns, however. He told the messenger that he could not "make a contract for the land and put up a house there . . . as long as we were engaged in a war and had no stable peace." He asked the sachem to put off the Gravesend men and promised to travel to Navesink to seal the deal "when the corn planting began."[41]

Stuyvesant could do nothing else. He had to give the months running up to corn planting time over to restoring peace along the war-torn Hudson. The Navesink people did not wait. Peropay signed over the land at Navesink to the Gravesend settlers the same day his messenger spoke with Stuyvesant. Stuyvesant may have vented his rage by preventing Raritan and Navesink representatives from attending the May 15, 1664, treaty meeting ending the Esopus War. This may not, however, be the only reason why they were not included in the treaty. The extensive preparations made for the force then organizing in England for the conquest of New Netherland could not be concealed. Raritan and Navesink people surely heard the rumors circulating through Gravesend and other English communities. Their nonappearance at the treaty meeting may therefore also reflect a certain reluctance to show any attachment to a regime whose days were evidently numbered.[42]

By playing off rivals, Mattano, Peropay, Tackapousha, Suscaneman, and the others managed to maintain strong bargaining positions. This allowed them to continue accepting gifts and receiving payments to testify for or against one or another rival in subsequent provincial town meetings, courts, and council chambers. They could also still pick and choose land buyers. Once large tracts were sold, they could still slow occupation by selling small and often unclearly bounded tracts in, between, or near already purchased lands to unsure, unscrupulous, or uninformed settlers. Pursuing such strategies, Indian sachems throughout Munsee country ultimately signed a very large number of deeds over a very long period of time. In Oyster Bay alone, a township containing 160 square miles, Asharoken, Suscaneman, Tackapousha, and their relations managed to conclude the aforementioned 138 real estate deals with townsfolk before descendants of the Indians who first sold a neck of land on Long Island Sound there in 1658 put their marks on the last Indian land sale—a confirmation deed signed in the town in 1711.[43]

This delaying strategy was a makeshift stopgap built on desperate hopes. It could neither stop land loss nor win back lost territories. It could, however, accomplish another goal. Those sachems grudgingly giving up portions of ancestral land to different and often mutually hostile purchasers bought time during which the balance of power might shift in their favor. If they were patient and lucky, they might stop settlement, take back lost lands, and maybe even oversee a revival that could convert their nation into a populous people powerful enough to turn the tables on colonists.

Despite their best efforts, sachems surrendered very nearly all of their remaining coastal and tidewater lands in the Munsee homeland to colonists by 1664. The amount of lost land came to a bit more than 10 percent of the total ancestral Munsee estate. At first glance, the number does not seem high. Formal conveyances to settlers, moreover, did not necessarily mean settlement. Speculators like the would-be patroons Van Werckhoven and Van der Capellen often could not attract settlers. Most smaller purchasers were cash poor and could only afford to take up, clear, fence, and occupy a fraction of acquired lands. Both colonists and Indians regarded unfenced lands as commons open to hunt, forage, run livestock, and fish upon. Indians did not shy from exercising reserved rights to camp, plant, cut timber for fuel and canoes, gather berries and herbs, and take bark, grass, and reeds for housemats and baskets on lands already deeded to colonists. The fact that they often had to ask permission to gain access to sold land reduced, but did not end, their ability to extract resources from these territories.

The 10 percent deeded over to settlers by 1664 still included a good part of the most productive Munsee lands, however. Reduced access to these territories significantly affected their ability to maintain themselves on the large but generally less productive interior lands to which they still held title. Compelled to turn inland, they increasingly relied on bark slabs and cattail reeds for house walls and bedding; deer, bear, and other woodland game for meat, bone, and fur; and forest clearings for corn, bean, and squash planting. Although they continued to camp on vacant beaches and unfenced marshlands, they would never again enjoy unchallenged access to wetlands, mud flats, and stretches of shoreline where sedge grasses for sleeping mats and shelter walls or flesh from sea birds, bass, bluefish, and oysters could be gotten. Although all but toll roads were free to all travelers, most paths going to the shore led to fences, docks, wharfs, or landings. The need to ask permission to cross onto private land reduced the degree of access needed to gather numbers of clams and whelks of adequate quality required to produce wampum. Land owners interested in making a profit in wampum may have demanded a cut of Indian production. Some may have barred Indians altogether from particularly productive stretches of beach. Loss of untrammeled access to their best saltwater territories played its role in transforming Indian life everywhere in Munsee country during the final decades of Dutch colonization.

Thrown farther back into the less productive and more remote lands in the interior, many Indians in Munsee country found themselves increasingly distant from commercial centers at New Amsterdam and Wiltwijck that they increasingly depended on for goods and services. On the positive side of the ledger, they still held sole title and unchallenged ownership to 90 percent of their ancestral homeland. The remaining readily habitable portions of this territory, however, consisted mostly of small stretches of level land tucked into narrow valleys surrounded by rocky uplands, swampy meadows, or sandy pinelands. Colonists would soon press them to sell the best pieces of these inland tracts. If they were to endure as a people, they would have to find ways to slow colonial takeover of their remaining productive lands as they struggled to learn how to live on ever-shrinking and increasingly separated pieces of good terrain.

Part III

MUNSEES AND COLONISTS DURING

THE EARLY ENGLISH YEARS,

1664–1685

7

CONTENTIONS, 1664-1674

In the spring of 1664, King Charles II presented a proprietary grant for a vast new territory to his younger brother, James, the Duke of York and Albany and the future James II of England. The new proprietary took in all of Munsee country and included the Dutch colony of New Netherland as well as Nantucket, Martha's Vineyard, and a piece of Maine. The king made the grant while his nation was at peace with the Netherlands. Just as Stuyvesant's seizure of New Sweden had not otherwise disturbed world peace in 1655, Charles II's decision to press the Crown's claim to land held by a Dutch trading company in faraway New Netherland did not necessarily mean wider war between the two mother countries.

Determined to swiftly reduce the Dutch outpost, the Duke of York put together a small but formidable force of three hundred men and placed it under the command of Colonel Richard Nicolls. Nicolls was an experienced soldier, loyal to the king, and a retainer of the duke's household. York promised him governorship of lands he was able to take from the Dutch West India Company. Nicolls and the three frigates carrying his men and supplies sailed from Portsmouth, England, in the early summer of 1664. News of their arrival off the Lower Bay reached New Amsterdam by the end of August. The arrival of another one hundred New Englanders under the command of Connecticut governor John Winthrop, Jr., stiffened Nicolls' little force.

Small as it was, Stuyvesant was unable to marshal forces sufficient to resist them. On September 6, 1664, the Dutch director-general surrendered New Amsterdam. Fort Orange capitulated two weeks later, and the Delaware

River settlements a month after that. During this time, both the Indians of Munsee country and the more than nine thousand settlers living in the New Netherlands came to grips with the fact that the English now controlled the whole of the Atlantic coastline from Virginia to New England.

The English invasion probably caused little surprise among Indians already aware of contentions that preoccupied colonists. Sachems and settlers watching Nicolls' ships darkly lolling in the quiet waters off Gravesend Bay could only take their coming as reminder, if one was needed, that they now had to contend with ever-broadening forces and events. Indians in the region, survivors of wars and epidemics, could still believe that storms brewed in other men's worlds might yet be dealt with locally. Once the commotion died down, more astute sachems found that the nearly bloodless English takeover simply added new levels of complexity to the already contentious maelstrom of interests, pitting colonists against one another. Many quietly began looking for ways to take advantage of opportunities presented by the new competitions that almost immediately arose between colonists and conquerors.[1]

Nicolls and his men did their best to bring order to the contending colonial factions as they moved to reconcile fractious colonists and suspicious Indians to proprietary rule. They enacted new laws, appointed new officials, and fixed new names onto old places. In his role as the new province's governor, Nicolls met with representatives from the predominantly English towns in Long Island and Westchester in assembly during the summer of 1665 to announce a fresh set of regulatory ordinances. These came to be known as the Duke's Laws. The code tread lightly on existing rights, respecting established religions, guaranteeing jury trials, and permitting elections of sheriffs, justices, and other minor officials. The code did not, however, provide for elected representation or a regularly convened legislative assembly. Although the laws recognized existing land titles granted by Dutch authorities, the code ordered owners to acquire new patents from the proprietor by April 1, 1667. Larger landowners were required to pay registration fees of two shillings, six pence, for every one hundred acres of property.[2]

Names as well as laws changed as New Netherland became New York, and New Amsterdam was transformed into the city of New York. The areas of predominantly English settlement on Long Island, Staten Island, and much of what later became Westchester (pointedly known among the Dutch as their Oostdorp, "East Village") became the east, west, and north ridings of the newly erected county of Yorkshire. Fort Amsterdam was renamed Fort James, Fort Orange became Fort Albany, and Wiltwijck was christened Kingston. Nicolls gave the name Albania to the land between the Hudson and Delaware today known as New Jersey.

Everyone in the region knew that Nicolls would need more than his three hundred-man army if he was to secure his conquest for the duke. Support of English settlers already living in New York could not be counted on. Nearly all were Puritan expatriates who still passionately hated the restored royal regime. Proprietary demands for new payments on already purchased lands increased reluctance to come to the aid of the new government. Many settlers living east of Manhattan, moreover, preferred to consider themselves citizens of Connecticut. Few would willingly support Nicolls if any challenge to his administration arose.

Luckily for Nicolls, New York was enjoying a rare season of peace during the first months of proprietary rule. As far as any of the locals knew, England and the Netherlands were still at peace. The bold English move to take a Dutch possession during peacetime was, however, a clear indication of strained relations. England's mercantile squabbles with Holland and France had flared into open warfare in the past. Every indication suggested that the then-quiet economic cold war would soon turn hot again.

No one could know how complicated the region's already volatile political situation was about to become. The prospect of new invasions loomed when news of the outbreak of the Second Anglo-Dutch Naval War reached New York during the spring of 1665. A year later, France unexpectedly joined the fighting against England. Suddenly, Nicolls and his meager forces faced the twin possibilities of Dutch counterattack from the sea and a landward invasion from the north by newly reinforced French forces already at war with the Five Nations.[3]

The king himself made Nicolls' position even more difficult. More in need of money and political support than policy coherence or undivided family loyalty, Charles split his brother York's yet-to-be-conquered proprietary in half while Nicolls' fleet was still en route to its destination. On June 23 and 24, 1664, Charles presented deeds to land Nicolls had already named Albania to two of his more loyal stalwarts. The first of these, Lord John Berkeley, was a royalist general with close ties to the Duke of York's household. The other, Sir George Carteret, was a native of the Island of Jersey. The new proprietors named their colony New Jersey in honor of Carteret's celebrated defense of his native island during the civil war. Both men soon dispatched Captain Philip Carteret, a distant cousin of Sir George's, to govern the new proprietary. Cousin Carteret arrived in New York, commission in hand, on July 29, 1665.[4]

NICOLLS' TREATIES

Sachems of mainland Indian communities across from Manhattan quickly realized that Carteret's arrival signaled emergence of new exploitable divisions at the very epicenter of colonization in their country. They also shared the opinions held by many settlers that wars against them had weakened the divided and often poorly provisioned Dutch colony, making New Netherland easier prey to the English takeover. Still embroiled in their own war with the Five Nations, Lower River Indians knew that ongoing Iroquois wars against the Susquehannocks, Mahicans, Northern Indians in New England, and others threatened catastrophically wider and potentially more divisive involvements. Most could plainly see that the disunited English would, at the very least, need to establish peace with and among Indians, especially with those living in the heart of their settlements, if they were to hold onto their newly won territories.

Lower River Indian and Five Nations leaders moved quickly to make their peace with Nicolls' new government. Their price remained the same: justice in legal disputes, fair dealing in trade, and military protection in war. Nicolls pledged to meet these demands in a series of treaties signed during the first two years of his administration. Colonel George Cartwright, one of a group of royal commissioners dispatched to assist Nicolls, negotiated the first of these treaties as his agent shortly after taking Fort Orange. Meeting at freshly rechristened Fort Albany with Mohawk and other Five Nations leaders on September 25, 1664, Cartwright promised the sachems equal protection under English law and assured them that trade would continue as before. Aware of the fact that the River Indians and their allies were then at war with the Mohawks, Cartwright affirmed that the English would remain neutral. They would not support moves against the Iroquois made by Wappingers, Esopus, or any Indians "as have submitted themselves under the protection of his majesty . . . in these articles of agreement and peace."[5]

A year later, Nicolls himself traveled upriver to convince the Esopus sachems to submit to the same articles of peace and agreement accepted by the Five Nations. He met with their civil sachems and a group of war captains representing the humbled but still defiant younger Esopus warriors at Kingston on October 7, 1665. After settling several unresolved land disputes and adjusting boundaries of lands ceded in the peace treaty with the Dutch, concluded just before the English takeover, Nicolls got the sachems to accept a general treaty of friendship. The sachems and the governor agreed to work together to keep the peace. The Indians also agreed to accept jurisdiction of English courts in actions involving settlers. Thanking the governor for the particularly generous gifts given to seal their new accord, the sachems pledged to "come once every year and bring some of their young people to acknowledge every part of this agreement in the Sopus to the end that it may be kept in perpetual memory."[6]

The October 7, 1665, agreement became known as the Nicolls Treaty. Meetings initially held annually a few years after the signing and more irregularly thereafter helped maintain peace between the Esopus nation and the English for the next hundred years. Neither it nor Cartwright's earlier treaty, however, put an end to the threat of widening hostilities posed by the wars carried on by the Five Nations. An opportunity for a comprehensive peace unexpectedly presented itself in the form of a French army a few months later. Governor of New France Daniel Remy, Sieur de Courcelles, led a force large enough to destroy the Mohawk towns south to the New York frontier during the winter of 1665–1666. The force got lost in the snow. Reaching the Mohawk Valley, the troops found that they had missed their mark by some fifty miles. They came out of the forest near the newly established village of Schenectady. Some settlers there gave food and blankets to the hungry freezing soldiers while others sent word of their coming to the Mohawks. Having lost the element of surprise, the French column returned to Canada, harried all the way by Mohawk warriors.[7]

Courcelles' superior, the French viceroy to North America, Alexandre de Prouville, Sieur de Tracy, led a second expedition the following summer. This time the French did not lose their way. Unwilling to fight such a strong enemy force in the bowels of their country, the Mohawks evacuated every one of their towns. Tracy had to content himself with plundering the villages before marching away.[8]

Sobered by the successful summer attack, the Five Nations quickly made peace with the French. Chastened Mohawks also began negotiations aimed at ending their chronic warfare with the Mahicans and their Indian allies in Munsee country and New England. They convinced their Oneida and Onondaga confederates to accept an offer made by Connecticut governor Winthrop to broker a peace conference. Sachems representing the belligerent nations subsequently signed a peace treaty at Albany on September 10,

1666, in the presence of representatives from New York, Connecticut, and Massachusetts Bay.[9]

The treaty was signed just as France joined the Dutch in their war against England. The hard-won peace agreements hammered out during the late summer of 1666, however, discouraged further military adventures in the region for the present. Unwilling to involve themselves in a war largely being fought elsewhere unless ordered to do so by their home governments, settlers in New France and New York quietly pursued their long-standing and profitable clandestine smuggling trade. As they had done during the First Anglo-Dutch Naval War, and as they would continue to do in other conflicts whose primary theaters of operations lay elsewhere, everyone along the frontier observed an informal truce until diplomats in Europe signed the Treaty of Breda, formally ending the war on July 21, 1667. Exhausted by the struggle, the treaty signatories largely accepted the way things stood at Breda. The English gave a little by recognizing the recent Dutch conquest of Surinam. The States General reciprocated by letting the English keep New York.[10]

Affairs to the North and Consolidation Problems

Unlike the Breda treaty, which was more like a truce than anything else, Nicolls' treaty with the Esopus effected a more lasting settlement. At their yearly meetings in Kingston and, as the years passed, at Albany and New York, sachems and settlers ritually reaffirmed friendship. The cordial atmosphere created by ceremonial exchanges of pelts, presents, and pleasantries helped participants iron out most problems on meeting agendas. So peaceable did relations become that the Kingston magistrates finally ordered the watch at the town fort to permanently stand down on January 25, 1672.[11]

The hard-hammered agreement restoring peace between the Iroquois Confederacy and the Lower River Indians and their Mahican and Northern Indian allies made at Albany on September 10, 1666, did not hold. Old enmities died hard, and many Indians in Munsee country continued to help Susquehannock allies still at war with the Five Nations. The fighting sputtered on largely unnoticed by colonists until word reached New York during the winter of 1668–1669 that Esopus and Navesink sachems were among Susquehannock emissaries offering to make peace with the Mohawks.

The Mohawks evidently favorably received the proposal. They felt a particular closeness toward Susquehannocks. Both nations acknowledged a common ancestry. Mohawks were not, however, interested in ending their war against Mahicans, Wappingers, and Wiechquaesgecks closely allied with Northern Indians who were also again fighting against them. The diplomats settled for what could be achieved. On August 11, 1669, Hackensack sachem Pierwim showed New York governor Francis Lovelace, who had succeeded Nicolls in 1668, a belt from the Mohawks affirming that they had made a separate peace with the Lower River Indians.[12]

Fighting continued farther up the Hudson. Mahicans, whose numbers may have included a few Lower River Indians, were among the three hundred Northern Indian warriors that invaded Mohawk country in late August 1669. Led by the Massachusett war chief Chickataubit, the force laid siege to the easternmost Mohawk castle at Caughnawaga for several days. The brief siege ended when a large force gathered from the Western Iroquois nations relieved the town. Five Nations warriors soon trapped and defeated retreating Northern Indians at Kinaquariones near Schenectady. Most of the invading force was killed on the field. The few warriors taken prisoner were later mostly put to death.[13]

Mahicans and many Lower River Indians fled from their homes when news of the defeat reached their towns. Some moved far to the west, to the lower Great Lakes. The majority, including many Wiechquaesgecks, took shelter closer by among friends and relatives in the Housatonic Valley and other nearby parts of New England. Disheartened Wiechquaesgecks represented by their sachem Romackqua, along with twenty of his people (many of whom were probably local community leaders and councilors), finally sent word to New York offering to sell the remaining half of their homeland to the English and move away permanently on February 24, 1671. Romackqua subsequently met with Lovelace in New York City to discuss the sale. This was the meeting alluded to when Romackqua told the governor that the Mohawks might take their lives, beavers, and property, but they could not claim their land. Lovelace agreed to the sale, and the Wiechquaesgeck sachem signed a deed turning over title to all but a small planting plot to the New York government.[14]

Shortly afterwards, New York, Massachusetts Bay, and Connecticut merchants, determined to end fighting that suppressed the Indian trade, managed to cobble together another peace agreement. Meeting in Albany on November 8, 1671, sachems representing the interested parties once again put their marks to yet another treaty meant to end the long-festering blood feud.[15]

Meanwhile, the English still struggled to consolidate a measure of control over their ramshackle domain in New York. Lovelace would need more and better cooperation from both settlers and Indians if he was to secure the English conquest. Colonists living in the new New York did not seem to be in a particularly cooperative frame of mind. It was not so much that they minded being ruled by a foreign government whose seat of power lay three thousand miles away, across a vast ocean. They were more interested in things closer to home. Far from settling existing squabbles, the transition to English control sparked new and increasingly rancorous boundary disputes and power struggles. As they had in the past, contending colonists continued to use promises and presents to get Indians from Munsee country to support their sides in the many disputes. Needing the Five Nations to be at peace to safeguard the border, the English were even more in need of good relations with River Indians in the heart of their colony.

Only Manhattan, home to a largely Dutch majority at least outwardly willing enough to accept English rule, seemed secure. Farther east on the mainland, Connecticut colonists used charter bounds awarding their province all land from the Atlantic to the Pacific oceans lying between their north and south borderlines to press claims to territories farther west. On Long Island, Hempstead and Oyster Bay settlers seemed more interested in their ongoing boundary dispute than in provincial security.

Philip Carteret, who had assumed control of Albania and renamed the place New Jersey shortly after his arrival, was soon at odds with newly arrived local settlers and New York officials. Puritan colonists from western Long Island, whose recent purchases of Indian lands in Albania were secured by patents issued by the New York government, had begun building houses in and around the soon-to-be-named town of Elizabeth before anyone in the region knew about Charles's division of the duke's province. They preferred to remain within the New York government and flatly refused to acknowledge Carteret's authority over them.[16]

In New York, town governments in the county of Yorkshire scrambled to secure new patent applications by the April 1, 1667, deadline specified in the Duke's Laws. Representatives from Long Island towns like Amersfoort and Newtown and other towns on the mainland renegotiated new deeds with Indians, confirming earlier purchases to strengthen their titles. Anxious to get new deeds patented and old patents grandfathered in under the code, settlers rushed to make deals with Indians everywhere around Manhattan.[17]

As Stuyvesant had done after the Peach War, the first English governors worked hard to settle land disputes amid the flurry of new purchases. Disputes were numerous and many were lingering sore points. All prevented or slowed collection of expected rent money, fee payments, and tax revenue. Uncooperative town governments and defiant townsfolk worked just as hard to protect their interests and stop rental agents and tax collectors from taking a cut of their wampum, trade goods, and scanty stocks of hard currency. River Indian sachems worked even harder to find ways to get the most out of these disputes.

Matinecock was the site of one of the most intractable disputes over land in Munsee country. Tackapousha, who had signed the first deeds to land in the area, distrusted all Englishmen, especially those who allied themselves with his Northern Indian enemies from across Long Island Sound. He also took seriously the many treaties of peace and friendship he signed with the Dutch. Honoring his Dutch alliance and unconvinced that they would not return, Tackapousha remained aloof. Staying quietly at home, he was among the few sachems who did not formally welcome Nicolls to Munsee country at the time of the English takeover.

Tackapousha would soon have to change his position. Emboldened English settlers at Hempstead made increasingly strident demands, ordering his people to leave lands he denied selling. Their efforts forced the sachem to swallow his pride and ask the new governor for help. Nicolls responded by ordering both parties to present their cases for his consideration in New York on February 29, 1665. The meeting solved nothing. Hempstead settlers presented a deposition seven months later complaining that twenty armed Massapequa Indians had forcibly stopped a survey of land at Matinecock. Some months later, Nicolls wrote to the Hempstead magistrates, advising them to settle the matter by giving Tackapousha a small gift and, if this did not work, to allow him to treat with the Massapequa sachem on their behalf. The magistrates rejected both proposals.[18]

A now frustrated Nicolls ordered the antagonists to come to Fort James on October 18, 1666. Frustration turned into anger after both parties refused to accept Nicolls' compromise that would have allowed colonists already living in the disputed territory to remain so long as they paid the Indians and allowed them to have a small planting ground. Tackapousha subsequently produced a map showing where lands now claimed by Hempstead exceeded original purchase boundaries to explain why he rejected the compromise offer. Nicolls later learned that settlers there claimed they had already paid the Hempstead magistrates for the land at Matinecock and had suggested that the magistrates should be ordered to give their purchase money to the Indians.[19]

In the middle of this, Asharoken and several of his associates (including the young Suscaneman) stepped in to support Tackapousha and sell some land to firm up their ties with the Oyster Bay settlers. In a series of ten deeds, including four signed in a single day on June 22, 1667, they conveyed several small tracts and an island to prominent townsmen between February 2, 1667, and May 29, 1669. This marked the beginning of the Matinecock practice of selling large numbers of small plots to influential neighbors during brief spaces of time. Asharoken's successor, Suscaneman, would soon pursue this strategy with even greater vigor.[20]

There the matter lay until June 8, 1669, when Lovelace ordered the Hempstead magistrates to produce proof that they had paid the Indians for the Matinecock lands. A little more than a year later, the governor gave Oyster Bay settlers permission to buy the land after Hempstead authorities evidently failed to provide the requested evidence. Tackapousha, however, refused to either sell the land to anyone or meet with Lovelace to discuss a sale after receiving an order to appear at Fort James on June 26, 1671. Patience exhausted, Lovelace ordered up a session of the province's Court of Assizes and put the issue before them. The court directed Tackapousha to sell the disputed land to whoever would pay for it. Bowing to the court order, Tackapousha demanded that the governor make the purchase. Lovelace agreed and promised to sell the property to Hempstead. The court gave Tackapousha a month to set a price agreeable to all concerned and allowed him to reserve a small place within its bounds for his people to plant on. It was a compromise, but one that had slowed settlement, provided a measure of compensation for already occupied land, and, most important for the Indians, assured that the governor would set aside and defend their right to a small but tillable plot of cultivable land in the ceded territory.[21]

RESISTING EXPANSION INTO NEW JERSEY

Unlike Long Island, where broad stretches of sandy shoreline lay places like Matinecock open to intruders, a less tractable geography discouraged outsiders interested in those parts of the Munsee homeland west of Manhattan. Ice floes in winter and high winds and strong tidal cross-currents the year-round made the watery high road of the Hudson River especially treacherous for anyone crossing in small boats and canoes. The steep cliffs of the Palisades rising above its western banks presented an unbroken rock rampart that stretched from the Hudson Highlands south to Pavonia. In and around

Newark Bay, Mattano, Oratam, and other sachems guarded the marshland approaches to their home territories around Hackensack using the same play-off strategies employed by their Long Island brethren. Farther south, Raritan and Navesink warriors cultivated a reputation for implacable hostility that kept all but the boldest colonists away from the otherwise attractive lowlands.

The lowlands across from Staten Island presented the widest avenue of approach into the interior. Stuyvesant had tried to get Oratam to surrender the key to this area in 1663, a year before the English conquest, by asking him to convey land on the west bank of Newark Bay. Oratam refused to sell. Like the Navesink sachem Peropay, Oratam felt that all signs indicated that Stuyvesant's days as director-general of a Dutch colony were numbered. He put Stuyvesant off, saying that his old men, fearing that they would be robbed by Indians in the interior if they moved away, did not wish to part with the land. Oratam went on to tell Stuyvesant that he could not move discussions forward until the young men returned from their hunting. Transparently flimsy as the excuses were, the much-harried Stuyvesant had to accept them with as good a grace as possible. The colony fell before talks went further.[22]

Oratam's 1663 politic demurral was one last act of defiance toward the end of a long career. Worn down by war and disease, neither Oratam nor his people could put off colonists any longer. Settlers finally got their chance to breach the meadowland barrier guarding the heart of Hackensack country less than one month after Stuyvesant surrendered New Amsterdam. On October 1, 1664, Nicolls issued a license to purchase land on the west bank of Newark Bay to some English settlers from the town of Jamaica (then known to the Dutch as Rustdorp, "Restful or Peaceful Village").[23]

Three of the settlers, including the promotional pamphleteer Daniel Denton, quickly traveled to Newark Bay (then called Achter Col) to discuss a purchase. On October 28, 1664, they secured a deed from three Indians representing owners who lived nearby on Staten Island. It was later stated that Oratam gave his blessing to the deal. Nicolls acted quickly, issuing a patent for the tract on December 1, 1664, without waiting for a survey. The patent affirmed that the Indians had signed over an unprecedentedly large expanse of 500,000 acres, extending seventeen miles north to south between the mouths of the Raritan and Passaic, and reaching twice that distance into the interior, almost to the east bank of the Delaware River.[24]

The October 28, 1664, deed patented by Nicolls later became known as the Elizabethtown Purchase (see map 6). Other Long Islanders obtaining another license from Nicolls made another substantial purchase at Navesink, called the Monmouth Patent. Both places were intended to be keystones in Nicolls' plan to consolidate control over Albania by settling colonists willing to accept his authority on untenanted lands close to Fort James. The plan did not work. What was meant to unite settlers under a strong central government instead became a source of dissension in what became bitterly divided colonies.

Elizabethtown in particular became disputed territory immediately after Carteret announced that he was taking over the lands covered by Nicolls' patents in Albania for his proprietary masters in England. Among Carteret's first acts as governor of New Jersey was an order requiring that settlers holding patents from New York obtain new patents from his government. New York charter holders, who soon came to be known as the Elizabethtown Associates, refused to obey the order. For much of the next century, Elizabethtown Associates faced off against proprietors in a seemingly interminable legal battle that occasionally flared into open violence. Proprietary authorities determined to collect quit rents from associates living in this very sizable chunk of their charter territory ultimately challenged the validity of every aspect of the original Elizabethtown deed. They focused their most penetrating questions on the deed's boundaries and disputed both the rights and identities of the Indians who signed the document.[25]

Modern-day scholars often seem to play proxy for one side or another in old disputes. In the case of Elizabethtown, both proprietary lawyers and later researchers have pointed to several apparent irregularities in the original deed to show that the associates' purchase was fraudulent. Several have noted that Oratam did not sign the 1664 conveyance. Others have branded Mattano and the two other Staten Island Indians who signed the deed as foreign Indians lacking the right to sell the tract. Mattano's participation in the 1651 sale of land within the patent boundaries and later payment demands made by other Indians for the same territory, moreover, has been used to brand Mattano as a duplicitous double-dealer. It has also been pointed out that the names of two of the three Indians listed in the body of the deed clearly differed from those used to identify two of the document's three Indian signatories.[26]

As the centerpiece of their defiant refusal to accept Carteret's demand for new patents requiring quit rents, the associates took special care to chronicle all aspects of the 1664 deed transaction. Extant copies of many of these documents survive. These include the settlers' original petition, Nicolls'

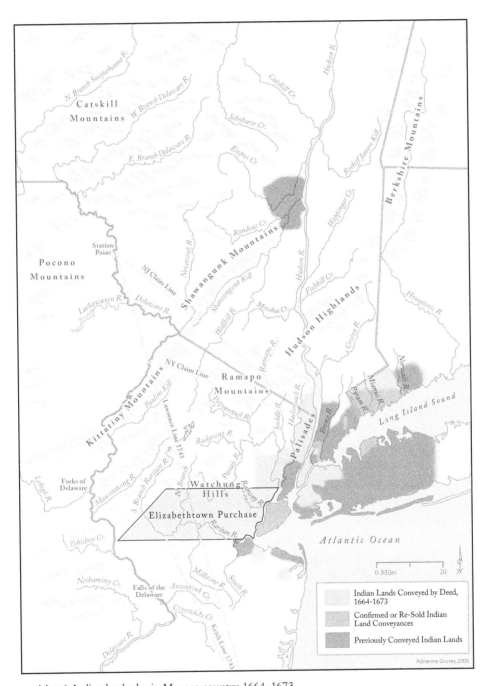

Map 6. Indian land sales in Munsee country, 1664–1673

license, several states of the deed and patent, a receipt in which the Indians acknowledge payment for the land, and several later depositions made by both Indians and settlers. Even though the size and scope of this mass of documentation has no parallel in the contemporary literature, modern-day analysts do not have to depend solely on either of the contending parties to this dispute for information. A number of other records penned by colonists uninvolved in the controversy help to identify the Indians who signed the deed and provide insights into how they used the sale to hold onto their remaining lands in Hackensack country.[27]

Hackensack Interregnum and Staten Island Redux

Although old and ailing, Oratam's decision not to sign the Elizabethtown deed does not mean he was inactive. Less than one month after the English takeover, Oratam sold Hackensack Neck in present-day Kearny, New Jersey, to one of Nicolls' ship captains. A few years later, Sarah Kierstede, a former captive of the Indians who often served as an interpreter, claimed that Oratam made her a present of 2,300 acres of land at Overpeck Creek at about the same time.[28]

No record reports that Oratam came down with the smallpox then running rampant throughout the region. His public announcement designating Pierwim as his successor at a February 23, 1664, meeting with Stuyvesant, however, clearly shows that he had mortality on his mind. Oratam furnished further evidence indicating the possible impact of illness or infirmity on meeting attendance six months later. Speaking for Sewackenamo at other discussions with Stuyvesant on July 8, 1664, he apologized for the continued absence of several Esopus sachems, saying they were sick, and promised they would come by the time they recovered, about the time the corn was ripe.[29]

Relations between Oratam, Mattano, Pierwim, and Sewackenamo became increasingly close when the Esopus sachem took refuge at Hackensack during the late war. The three Hackensack leaders served as sureties guaranteeing that Sewackenamo's people would honor the peace treaty signed on May 16, 1664. Pierwim evidently became particularly close to Sewackenamo. He took the Esopus sachem's name, identifying himself as Sewackenamo in the Elizabethtown deed and several later documents. In order to minimize possible confusion, he carefully noted his alias Hans. when using Sewackenamo's name.[30]

Pierwim first appeared in colonial records during the winter of 1663–1664 as Hans, the Indian guide who sailed from Manhattan to Raritan Bay with Captain Kregier. Both Pierwim and Oratam maintained their connections with the seat of power on Manhattan after Nicolls took over New Amsterdam during the following summer. Pierwim's participation in the sale of Elizabethtown to settlers bearing Nicolls' license signaled his acceptance of New York's authority over land affairs in Albania. Oratam also limited his final land sales to purchasers bearing New York licenses.

Neither Oratam nor Pierwim formally welcomed Carteret when he came ashore at the muddy landing he later christened Elizabethport in honor of his patron's wife, Lady Carteret. The new governor was made to feel even less welcome after publishing his commission in the new settlement he soon named Elizabethtown. In spite of this, Carteret did what he could to secure the colony for his proprietary backers. On May 26, 1666, he reached out to Oratam with an offer to officially establish friendly relations. The offer, made shortly after the sachem reportedly had been poorly treated while visiting New York, was accompanied by a request to buy land at present-day Newark. Oratam did not respond on the record to the governor's clumsily self-serving proffer of friendship and respect. Off the record, Pierwim later stated that the elder Hackensack sachem quietly gave him permission to sell the tract to Carteret. The younger sachem subsequently witnessed the July 11, 1667, deed to Newark lands as "Pierwim, the sachem of Pau."[31]

The Newark Tract deed marked a turning point in Pierwim's brief career as Oratam's successor-designate. Pierwin was not the primary Hackensack sachem signing the Newark deed. That role was played by a newcomer named Taptawappamund, a son of Metapis who was closely connected with his Navesink kinsmen Emerus and Peropay. Like them, he participated in many subsequent land sales in and around Navesink country as a sachem of Ramenesing.[32]

Elizabethtown signatories Machopoikan and Waerhinnis Couwee also signed the Newark deed. Another sachem putting his mark on the Newark deed was Memshe, a soon-to-be prominent leader who first appeared in colonial records as Wemessamy, one of three Minisink sachems who asked Stuyvesant for cannon for their fort on August 15, 1663. His participation in Newark deed negotiations provided the first direct evidence of inclusion of someone from the Upper Delaware Valley Minisink community northwest of New York in the network linking Indian towns across the Lower Hudson River Valley.[33]

The rest of the names on the Newark deed list read like a genealogy of the Mattano family network. The signatory Mamustome was Mamarikickon, one of Mattano's father's many influential brothers. The others, Peropay (listed as

Perawe), Conackamack (listed as Cakanackque), Neckaock (listed as Napeam), and Irooseeke (one of Weequehela's fathers and listed as Harish) were all Mattano's brothers.[34]

Each of these men subsequently closely aligned themselves with the New Jersey proprietors. Pierwim, by contrast, evidently remained loyal to New York. On August 11, 1669, he was mentioned as "Perewyn, sachem of the Hackensack, Toppan, and Staten Island Indians . . . lately chosen their sachem" at the head of an Indian delegation welcoming Lovelace to Fort James. Lovelace evidently had been told to expect Oratam to greet him. Asking whether they accepted Pierwim as their sachem, "the Indians then present (in owning him so to be) held up their hands."[35]

This was the first and last time anyone would raise their hands in public to acknowledge Pierwim as the Hackensack sachem. His refusal to switch loyalties from New York to New Jersey revealed an inflexibility at this point in his life that probably made him a liability in the eyes of his followers. His people needed a wilier leader willing to quietly play off contending colonists. Pierwim evidently did not then possess such qualities, and his followers apparently quickly deserted him. For a time, Hackensacks failed to even mention his name when dealing with New Jersey authorities. He does not appear, for example, in lists of Hackensacks signing deeds to the next two tracts of land above Newark purchased on July 20, 1668, and February 28, 1672, by buyers holding licenses from Carteret. He would not, however, disappear from public life. Casting his lot with the New Yorkers, he moved north, closer to the duke's proprietary lands.[36]

Staten Island turned out to be another persistent trouble spot. The place remained an intractably stubborn sore point even after Stuyvesant repurchased it from the local Indians on behalf of the company in 1657. Both New York and New Jersey proprietors contended that Staten Island lay within the boundaries of their provinces. Lovelace saw his chance to kill two birds with one stone when reports of new troubles on the island reached Fort James in February 1670. Settlers there complained that Indians refusing to move away threatened to kill livestock trampling and eating their crops. Determined to evict the Indians and affirm New York's title to the island once and for all, he ordered a local sachem named Agapou and several other sachems to bring in or secure representations from every Indian who still claimed land on Staten Island.[37]

The list of Indians demanding payment included several sachems and four children. The latter had not yet been born when the second deed had been signed thirteen years earlier. On April 13, 1670, Agapou, Taptawappamund, and Pierwim finally signed the third and final deed to Staten Island. The arrangement helped Lovelace address his most pressing concerns in the area. It satisfied the last Indian claimants to the island, removed a lingering source of discontent, and helped establish New York's authority over the place. It did not, however, completely put an end to Indian occupation. Locals needing help on their farms and in their fields and homes continued to hire Indians as farmhands, laborers, and servants. Most allowed families and friends of Indian workers to set up campsites in vacant out-of-the-way parts of their properties. Indians continued to come to the island to work, fish, collect shells and shellfish, and gather wood and grasses for baskets and brooms for the next hundred years.[38]

BREACHING THE PALISADES

Seven years after the English conquest, the lush valley drained by the Hackensack and Passaic rivers still lay tantalizingly out of settlers' reach. It must have seemed like a fertile crescent, as alluring and as unattainable then as another half a world away would be centuries later. Then as now, internal dissension, diplomatic disarray, poor planning, and problems of supply and geography stymied outlanders even after they secured the watery approaches to the beckoning twin valleys.[39]

Trying to build new communities in a political atmosphere riven by local disputes and cross-provincial rivalries, still-struggling settlers now controlling the approaches to the meadowlands had little time to pressure Hackensacks for more territory. Hackensack country was further protected by the Palisades. The line of formidable cliffs was not a perfect barrier, however. Inroads into the valley beyond could be made along a dried-up section of former Hudson riverbed that cut through the cliff walls at the Sparkill Gap at Old Tappan Landing (present-day Piermont, New Jersey). Just north of Old Tappan, around Nyack, the cliffs drew back from the river. There they threw out a concave cordon ringing the broad low-lying basin. Colonists like De Vries had attempted settlements at Tappan during the early decades of Dutch colonization. Huddled between towering cliffs and the fast-moving river, it and similarly isolated outposts were easily swept away during troubled times.

Like Nicolls before him, Lovelace was determined to jump-start the lagging rate of expansion in his province. And like his predecessor, Lovelace believed that Munsee lands to the west of Manhattan in Carteret's rival province were just the place for expansive development. Lovelace accordingly issued an order allowing private citizens in New York to purchase territory, especially on the mainland, directly from Indians. A pair of Walloon Huguenot immigrants from the Spanish Netherlands named Balthazar de Harte and Isaac Bedloe were among the first New Yorkers to take advantage of this new dispensation. Fortified by licenses from Lovelace, they and a retinue of translators, scribes, and witnesses met with Hackensack, Tappan, Rechgawawanck, and Minisink sachems during the spring of 1671 to discuss sale of the strategic Palisades cliff line.[40]

Two deeds came out of these get-togethers. The first, bearing a date of April 13, 1671, gave Bedloe and De Harte title to all land between the Hudson River and Overpeck Creek "on the north side of the Sir Governor Philip Carteret's" from Hespatingh in present-day Jersey City to Tappan. The second, finalized on May 19, 1671, gave De Harte a still larger tract taking in all lands north of the April purchase line from Tappan to Haverstraw between the Hudson and Hackensack Rivers. Together, these deeds turned the whole of the Palisades into the property of buyers from New York, who promptly registered their new purchases, written in Dutch, in Manhattan.[41]

As they had in Staten Island a year earlier, New Yorkers had purchased land coyly referred to in both deeds as "under the jurisdiction of the province of New Jersey," but not necessarily within its charter borders. With patience and perhaps some well-placed payoffs, De Harte and Bedloe might use these deeds to help Lovelace extend New York's sovereignty over the desired land. They certainly seemed to have the support of the Indians. The list of sachems who signed the deeds for the New Yorkers included leaders from every major Indian community between the lower Hudson and upper Delaware rivers below the Highlands. The primary signatory was Aroorhikan, who identified himself in both documents as a Tappan sachem. Like Seyseychkimus, whose interest in land at Haverstraw was represented in the May 19, 1671, deed, Aroorhikan was another expatriate from Brooklyn. New York's faithful ally Pierwim also signed both deeds. Tomachkapay put his mark on the April 13 conveyance as sachem of Minisink. Among other signatories were Memshe, Waerhinnis Couwee, and a man new to colonial records, who had a talent for languages named Towakhachi (Munsee for "Mudpuppy").[42]

Towakhachi was probably originally from Wiechquaesgeck country, where he first appeared in a September 21, 1666, deed as Claes the Indian. He was listed by various spellings of his Indian name in the bodies of both Palisades deeds. He also appeared in both as a translator, identified as Jan Clausen in the April 13 document and Claes de Wilt in the May 19, 1671, deed. Towakhachi and the rest were accompanied by a conclave of local sachems, witnesses, and other translators. The latter were especially needed. Negotiations were probably carried out in a patois of trade jargon Munsee, Dutch, and English, originally written down in Dutch. Only the May 19, 1671, deed was translated into English before insertion into New York records. Intriguingly, neither deed is preserved in New York; the only known examples are proprietary copies filed in the New Jersey State Archives.[43]

Both transactions brought together uncommonly large gatherings of local leaders from the region, unusual in peacetime and all but unprecedented for land deals up to that point. Inclusion of every major sachem and many local leaders in the proceedings indicates that they had formed themselves into an unusually large and complex coalition for the purpose. The gravity of the issue at hand almost certainly convinced the sachems to gather at a level of organization of sufficient size, order, and complexity needed to deal with sales of land of such strategic importance. The buyers probably encouraged Indians to include all possible claimants in order to maximally secure their title as they girded for an almost inevitable land battle with New Jersey proprietary authorities.

New Jersey Revolt and Dutch Reconquest

The expected battle did not take place. Although the deals openly challenged Carteret's authority, he could do little about it. A revolt led by rebellious deputies in the New Jersey assembly demanded all of his attention. New Jersey's laws, unlike those of New York at the time, gave settlers the right to elect a general assembly of twelve deputies to serve in the legislature with the governor and his council. In 1668, settlers elected an antiproprietary slate. The new deputies declined to take the oath of allegiance to the proprietors. Openly defiant, they refused to acknowledge the proprietor's right to require new patents, did not pay quit rents or fees demanded, and promptly set about arresting provincial officials trying to collect imposts.

A movement that began as a rent strike soon grew into an insurrection known as the Rebellion of 1672. Carteret fled the province and sailed for England on July 1. Alarmed by the rebellion, the Crown quickly confirmed the proprietary rights granted six years earlier. Fortified by this confirmation, the proprietors published a declaration on the following December 6, ordering settlers to either submit to their authority or be declared rebels. In the event, resolution of the issue had to be put on hold. On the morning of July 30, 1673, proprietary partisans and rebellious associates both woke to an incredible sight. Just off Sandy Hook, a fleet of twenty-three Dutch warships (including eight captured prize vessels) prepared to sail into New York Harbor.[44]

The previous invasion had occurred during peacetime nearly a year before the belligerents issued formal declarations of war. This fleet, however, arrived sixteen months into the conflict today known as the Third Anglo-Dutch Naval War. The war started pretty much where the last one had left off five years earlier. As in the earlier Anglo-Dutch wars, most of the fighting was done elsewhere. And like the previous conquest, surrender at Manhattan seemed just as inevitable and was just as complete.

The formidable fleet arrayed before Fort James on August 8, 1673, projected much the same impression of irresistible force that Nicolls' far smaller flotilla made in 1664. The man in command at the time (Lovelace was away visiting his colleague Winthrop in Connecticut), a captain named John Manning, nevertheless refused to surrender his tiny garrison of fifty men without a fight. The Dutch commanders, Cornelis Evertsen, the younger, and Jacob Benckes, obliged, bombarding Fort James for four hours before landing six hundred marines under the command of Captain Anthonij Colve. Running out of powder, Manning lowered the fort's flag and surrendered, an action he would later have to defend in front of a court martial in England. Evertsen and Benckes accepted the capitulation, and New York became New Orange.

Aside from replacing some officials, administering loyalty oaths, and changing a few other names (Kingston, for example, became Swaenenburgh, and Fort James was renamed Fort Willem Hendrijck), the new Dutch conquerors interfered very little in the province's affairs. Their interest in the region throughout the war instead focused on commerce raiding and the capture of small, isolated, and hopefully booty-laden outposts like the French fort at Pentagoet in present-day Castine, Maine.

Evertsen, Benckes, and Colve held numerous meetings with locals at Fort Willem Hendrijck during the weeks immediately following the English surrender. They were careful to politely welcome, discreetly impress, and generously give gifts to Indian delegations coming to greet them. One group of unnamed Hackensack chiefs, accompanied by twenty of their people and arriving at the fort on September 13, 1673, presented a speech and exchanged presents, formally affirming their nation's friendship. Other nations were more diffident. A Mohawk delegation appeared five days later, counted troops, and took a good look at the fleet before decorously welcoming the Dutch. They then returned upriver to "make a report thereon." Like most River Indian communities, who did not send delegates to New Orange, the Mohawks and their confederates decided to bide their time before formally acknowledging the Dutch reconquest.[45]

In the meantime, Evertsen and Benckes sailed off with the fleet and most of their men in search of fresh conquests after a brief stay in Manhattan. They left Colve in charge to complete the reduction of the English colony and manage affairs till the outcome of the war was decided. Colve did not wish to add troubles with the Indians to his list of problems. Reminding settlers that this was wartime, he told them that he would deal harshly with those cheating Indians and declared a virtual moratorium on new purchases of Indian lands. The effectiveness of these actions is imperfectly known. Few records document Indian relations during Colve's tenure in New Orange.[46]

Surviving papers documenting two examples of Colve's conduct of Indian diplomacy show that in these instances at least he continued the moderate policies of Lovelace and Nicolls. Colve faced his first severe test when a Dutch sentry evidently accidentally shot and killed an allegedly drunken Indian who had failed to answer his challenge just outside the gates of Fort Willem Hendrijck one night in early 1674. The man turned out to be one of Mamarikickon, Metapis, and Ockanickon's brothers. Colve acted quickly. Inviting the dead man's relatives to the fort, he formally condoled their loss at a council meeting on January 22. Evidently well coached by his advisers, he backed up his words with generous presents of cloth coats and wampum. The sachems accepted both Colve's words and gifts and, in the words of the scribe taking down the notes of the meeting, "thanked the governor and departed well pleased."[47]

Three months later, Colve faced a less trying test. A group of Indians came to the fort on April 23 to complain that they had not sold Secaucus but "only Espatingh and its dependencies" in the 1658 deed to Stuyvesant. They further told Colve that "other Indians blamed them for selling land that was not theirs." A copy of the 1658 deed was taken out of the files and examined in the presence of the sachems. Both agreed that Secaucus had indeed been included in the deal. Colve, however, was determined not to send the Indians away without something to show for their trouble. Reminding the sachems that he always stood ready to hear their grievances, "to obviate further difficulty" he presented them with an anker of rum to share with those still claiming the land.[48]

Neither Colve nor anyone else in New Orange knew that the colony had already been returned to England by diplomats signing the Treaty of Westminster, ending the war on February 4, 1674. The journey across the ocean still took many weeks. And the wheels of bureaucracy ground as slowly then as they do today. Several months passed before Charles II appointed a new man to govern the province. More passed before the new governor set foot on New York shores on October 22, carrying instructions authorizing sweeping changes in the ways things were done with Indians and everyone else in the region.

STILL POINT IN THE STORM

Cannier sachems had been able to use the confusion and uncertainty created by invasions and fears of invasion that preoccupied colonists during the decade between 1664 and 1674 to parry some of the more worrying colonial thrusts into their territories. Many could, if they chose to, reflect on the preceding ten years with some relief and more than a small sense of achievement. They had passed on much of their people's remaining birthright more or less intact. Some important lands had been lost in the process. The sachems had done their best, however, to sow confusion, cloud title, and slow settlement at more vulnerable points like Elizabethtown, Navesink, and the Palisades. Although Mohawks still warred on them, most River Indians enjoyed a season of peace far longer and less nerve wracking than the brief intervals afforded their embattled European neighbors. More important, they had been spared further outbreaks of the epidemic contagions that had ravaged their communities ten years earlier.

The great dying had stopped, at least for a time. Wampum, words, and more condoled those mourning lost loved ones at treaties and soothed the sadness of those having to sign deeds selling ancestral lands. To be sure, seasoned elders like Oratam, Mattano, and Sauwenaroque had passed from the scene. Aroorhikan, Seyseychkimus, and others, however, remained to pass on experience tempering traditional ideals with sobering experience. Material evidence of this is preserved in documentary records indicating no appreciable falloff in Indian diplomatic skills.

Not only that, findings made in archaeological sites dating to this period also show that traditional craftspeople still worked skins, manufactured wampum, fashioned clay pots, and chipped or ground stone tools from local rocks. Quality of some domestically produced wares had slipped somewhat.

Just as freely available, high-quality cheap imports always drive out more pricey and increasingly shoddier domestic products. Textiles, glass beads, and iron, steel, copper, lead, and brass tools and weapons made in Europe were drying up age-old Indian demand for domestically produced painstakingly hand-crafted goods. What they lost in autonomy, however, they gained in convenience and, in the case of high-tech items like firearms, in quality. For the last time in their history, Indians in the Munsee homeland looking for the best tool for the job could choose from the best of both worlds.

A healthy new generation was growing up on poorer but still productive interior parts of their homeland. Many of those who survived the epidemics now possessed antibodies that afforded the same degree of protection from further outbreaks enjoyed by similarly immunized settlers. The final decades of Dutch rule also were a time of plenty for Indian people in Munsee country. Game driven from lands cleared by colonists flocked to inland forests dotted by Indian farmsteads located on good soils near clean fresh water. Locally, the beaver were gone and Indians hoping to trap or trade for their pelts had to travel farther into the interior. Powerful nations still stood between them and the western fur country beyond the Appalachians. Susquehannocks helped. Many among them were grateful for River Indian assistance in their ongoing wars with the Five Nations. They reciprocated by allowing River Indians to pass through their territory to trap and trade in the Far country around the Great Lakes.

On the debit side, Indians had given up title to their best lands along the coast by 1674. Most, however, still lived within a few hours of still accessible ancestral shores. Friendly relations with agreeable colonists assured continued access to particularly prized fishing spots, landings, and clam beds. Many Indians still possessed small but well-placed plots of land reserved for their sole use on or near favored locales. Others quietly camped in remote marshes and beaches or set up shelters in vacant back lots of agreeable landowners.

The preceding decade had turned out to be a quiet recuperative interval. Although the serious problems challenging continuing survival in their ancestral homeland had not disappeared, ten years of health and peace had given the people of Munsee country an important respite. More reflective souls among them must have suspected that they were only passing through the quiet eye of the colonial storm. The leading edge of that storm had brought death and devastation on an almost mythical scale. They could only prepare as well as possible for the trailing edge that was sure to follow.

8

RESPITE, 1674–1679

The coming of Edmund Andros, stormy figure in his own right, to Munsee country did not in and of itself signal a return to tumultuous times. The duke wanted his turbulent province placed on a paying basis. The strong-willed new captain-governor of New York was expected to accomplish the task by reining in troublemakers who he judged placed private self-interest above public well-being. Powers that be in England gave him several tools to do the job.

Andros brought a new charter from the king that rejoined New Jersey to New York. Many thousands of Indians and more than twenty thousand colonists, slave and free, now lived within his charter bounds. Andros chose to rule over the whole of the duke's proprietary as well as former Dutch lands west of the Delaware also claimed by Maryland. Erstwhile New Jersey governor Philip Carteret, who had returned on the same ship as Andros, had to make do as his deputy in New Jersey until that troublesome colony could again be brought into some order.

Although he did not know it yet, Andros was also supported back home by a new bureaucracy specially designed to streamline administration, reduce waste, and maximize profit. On March 12, 1675, the king established a powerful and professionalized Board of Trade. He ordered the twenty-four privy councilors selected as his Lords of Trade on the board to make English commerce more profitable by integrating all foreign trade, colonial and otherwise, into the domestic economy. Their tools of choice were supplied by the Navigation Acts. These gave them the power to regularize customs duty collection; suppress illicit trade, smuggling, and piracy; and, in North America, regulate all trade with Indians. They expected colonial governors like Andros to treat their directives as royal orders and felt certain that he would impress this fact on Indians and everyone else placed under his authority.

A number of Indians were probably in the crowd watching Andros step off the long boat that landed him on Manhattan in October 22, 1674. They would have instantly recognized him by his regal demeanor, by his fashionably form-fitting armor, and by the ostentatious deference paid to him. Although sumptuary laws restricting such clothing to the upper classes were no longer on the books in England, they were still in force in some provinces (though not in New York). Indians as well as settlers would have been able to easily pick out of any crowd someone so well dressed and deferentially treated. Elders who had taken the measure of club man Kieft, stolidly efficient Stuyvesant, and their successors also would have immediately recognized a lifetime of obedience and command in Andros's stiff military bearing. Although only a gentleman at the time, Andros would be knighted and given the title Seigneur of Sausmarez during a short visit home in 1678. The title made him lord of Saltmarsh, Andros's ancestral family seat on the Island of Guernsey in the English Channel.

Those who came to know him would learn that Andros was cultured, well born, and fluent in both Dutch and French. He was also well connected, with extensive experience in European courts. He was on particularly good terms with Dutch stadtholder Willem Hendrijck of Orange, his enemy during the late war and the man whose marriage to York's eldest sister and Willem's first cousin, Mary Stuart, enabled Willem to succeed her brother and become King William III of England in 1689. More readily in evidence were the leadership qualities that made Andros a good choice to oversee a smooth, complete transition back to proprietary rule. An energetic, passionate man, Andros was careful to act with outward decorum. He civilly offered the king's protection to those pledging loyalty to the new government and gave those choosing to leave time to get things in order before formally accepting the Dutch surrender on November 10, 1674.[1]

Andros had come to a colony controlled and still largely populated by strangers, many of whom owned slaves from lands that were considered even stranger by the province's other inhabitants. After 150 years of contact and a half century of colonization, most newcomers in the region were still largely pinned to a narrow winding ribbon of tidewater wedged between the coastal uplands and the sea. They were held in place by still-strange geography and Indian nations. York had ordered his man to make this strange land accept new borders and work together in ways that may have seemed even stranger to the region's inhabitants.

Vast parts of Andros's New York were still sovereign territory of powerful Indian nations. Although still substantial, the total Indian population in the Northeast had dropped considerably by this time; little more than thirty thousand Native people probably continued to live in lands claimed by the English Crown between Chesapeake Bay and the Bay of Fundy in 1674. They still, however, vastly outnumbered settlers where it counted, along the frontier where scattered settlements were often far from towns and cities, where most colonists lived. The number of warriors Five Nations sachems could call on alone equaled the entire force of two thousand soldiers and militia then available to Andros. Most of these Indian men, moreover, were more experienced and skilled in forest warfare than their colonial counterparts.

Andros arrived at a time when colonial relations with many Indian nations were in disarray. The only thing that seemed to prevent Indians from uniting together against colonists was the endemic warfare that continued to pit them against each other. There had been peace between settlers and Indians everywhere along the mid-Atlantic coast since 1664. All signs, however, indicated that Indians and colonists tired of trying to live together in New England and Chesapeake Bay were again edging toward war. From the first, Andros would have to work with sullenly suspicious antagonists from different cultures, nations, and provinces eager to get at one another. His ability to see the big picture, broadened by years of foreign service, would be particularly valuable when open warfare finally broke out on every side of New York in 1675. Working with River Indian, Mohawk, and other Indian diplomats, he would play a pivotal role in forging new policies and forming new relationships that would dramatically transform social and political life in Munsee country and throughout the surrounding region.

All this was in the future when River Indian delegations started coming to the once-again renamed towns of New York, Kingston, and Albany to welcome the new governor as he made his grand tour of the province. Haltingly at first, they soon queued up in a constant procession once it was plain that a Dutch counterattack was not immediately in the offing. Tappan sachem Aroorhikan and his councilor Claes made the first Indian state visit to the fort on December 4, 1674. Tackapousha paid the next courtesy call on the following January 12, performing the now customary greeting ritual on behalf of all the Long Island Indians "so far as beyond Seatalcott." One month later, a party of Mahican sachems performed the same ceremony in Albany. Meeting with the town magistrates on February 14, they announced that they were now confederated with the Wappinger, Wiechquaesgeck, and Esopus Indians. They asked the magistrates to protect them in case their shaky truce with the Mohawks collapsed and promised to maintain their friendship with New York on behalf of the new confederacy. It was a short-lived coalition; no other record of it survives.

Two months later, on April 20, a delegation of thirty Navesink Indians, headed by Peropay and including Metapis and Taptawappamund, officially greeted Andros and Carteret in New York. The size of their retinue doubt-less reflected the sense of apprehension they must have felt at the time. Bad news from Raritan country had reached the city before them. The body of an Indian who drank himself to death near Raritan Bay, and those of two settlers found dead on the banks of the Millstone River, had only just been interred. Four wampum belts presented to the governor clearly conveyed the sachems' concern. Holding up three belts, their speaker reminded Andros that they were allies, lamented the recent deaths, and promised that they would not harbor Indians hostile to the English. Metapis then held up a fourth belt and asked if they might not give asylum to seventeen Susque-hannocks then being held captive by the Mohawks.[2]

Susquehannock Crisis

Metapis's unexpected request must have brought Andros and his council up short. Even at that late date, the Susquehannocks were still one of the most powerful Indian nations in the region. Although River Indians had long-standing ties with them (it was widely known that more than a few Min-isink and Esopus people had moved among them during and after the Esopus War), these were almost always marked by some degree of deference on the part of the River Indians. But this was something different. How was it that Navesink people could suddenly reverse roles and offer asylum to Susquehannocks, the terrors of the Five Nations and members of a power-ful, populous, and well-armed nation, whose traders controlled a vast west-ern fur empire and whose farmers tilled some of the most productive soils in the Northeast?

The answers to this question lay far from Susquehannock country. Com-petition for control of western trapping grounds and trade markets had long been one of many bones of contention feeding the maw of the endless war embroiling the Susquehannocks and the Five Nations. French arms and aid had helped keep the Susquehannocks in the fight. Now the French were friends of the Five Nations. Even more remarkable, Iroquois Confederacy diplomats were managing to convince the French that they should shift their support to them. Although still formidable, Susquehannock strength was sapped by war and disease. The French were realists. It might not take much to get them to look the other way if their longtime Susquehannock allies started looking like losers.

The Five Nations prepared their ground carefully. They let a decent interval pass before working to build trust with old enemies. After several years of undocumented but clearly careful negotiations, they concluded a peace and trade agreement with the people of Ottawa country in 1673. Five Nations sachems knew that the Susquehannocks would have to find a way to break up this new meeting of minds if they wanted to maintain access to vital western trade markets and trapping grounds. Susquehannocks knew that they ran the risk of making enemies out of the French if they openly attacked their allies in the Ottawa country. The Five Nations raised the stakes by promising to carry any furs obtained from the Ottawas east to Montreal instead of Albany. Intimating that the Susquehannocks might be an unnecessary impediment to this new flow of furs, they asked the French for help against a people they characterized as "the sole enemies remaining on their hands."[3]

Susquehannocks quickly found out about the Iroquois maneuvers. Refusing to openly rise to the bait, they evidently got River Indians to do the dirty work for them. In his annual report for 1674, Louis de Buade, Comte de Frontenac et de Pallau, who had replaced Courcelles as governor of New France two years earlier, informed his superiors in Paris that Esopus warriors had killed eight or nine Ottawas. Unable to get at the Susquehannocks directly, Iroquois Confederacy diplomats used the incident to try to detach the Esopus from their Susquehannock allies. On April 8, 1675, Mohawk emissaries carried a note to Albany from Frontenac demanding compensation and cessation of further Esopus attacks. Ruffled Albanians ordered Kingston authorities to straighten the mess out. Coming to Kingston on April 21, Sewackenamo, Mamanuchqua, and a young sachem named Assenerakan told the magistrates that their warriors had not yet returned. Although they claimed to know nothing about the incident, they acknowledged past trouble with French Indians. The sachems promised they would look into the matter, presented four strings of wampum to satisfy Mohawk honor and condole families and friends of the dead, and offered substantially larger payments if they found out that their men did the killings.[4]

Little more than a month later, on June 28, an embassy of Wappingers dropped in on Andros. They carried with them an extraordinarily large amount of wampum, some twenty-four belts and another band woven into a circle. They told Andros that these belts carried a major Mohawk offer to the Susquehannocks, proposing that they put the last sixteen years of war behind them, make their peace with the living and the dead, and move among them.[5]

Peace was something the Susquehannocks very much needed. They were stuck in the fight of their lives. The fight was not, as almost universally thought, with the Five Nations, however. Sometime in February 1675, the entire Susquehannock nation showed up in St. Mary's City looking for a new home in Maryland. On the face of it, they were simply accepting an invitation made by the Maryland government. More probably, Marylanders had issued them an order they dared not refuse. Unwilling to wage an almost surely suicidal war on two fronts, they agreed to move where the Marylanders put them. Their new home would be the non-vacant site of a fort of their old Piscataway enemies where Piscataway Creek flows into the Potomac River. Known today as the Accokeek Creek National Historic Landmark, the place was just a few miles south of present-day Washington, D.C., on what was then Maryland's western frontier.[6]

Isolated on a hostile frontier and surrounded by old adversaries, the Susquehannocks soon found themselves in serious trouble. Their problems began during the early summer of 1675 when several of their people were evidently inadvertently caught in the line of fire of Maryland settlers shooting it out with local Doeg Indians over a theft of hogs that had taken a deadly turn. No one condoled the deaths, and grieving Susquehannock relatives soon began avenging their dead kinsfolk in the age-old way.

Concerned authorities in Maryland and Virginia put together a combined force of nearly one thousand militiamen and a contingent of Piscataway warriors over the next few months. Placed under the overall command of John Washington, George's great-grandfather, they were sent to the Susquehannock Fort to look into the matter. As Dutch settlers had done over another hog theft in their own province thirty-five years earlier, unruly militiamen took matters into their own hands. Arriving at the Susquehannock town on September 26, they decided to murder the five chiefs sent out to parley with them. This began a siege that only ended six weeks later when the fort's occupants managed to slip away unnoticed.

The Susquehannocks scattered for a time. Many gathered near the Occaneechi towns along the Roanoke River just north of the present-day Virginia–North Carolina border. Their warriors there continued to launch raids until the spring of 1676, when word of a planned Virginian attack convinced them to leave the province. Virginia troops led by Nathaniel Bacon, whose subsequent rebellion against the province's royal governor would bear his name, arrived to find the Susquehannocks gone. Bacon's men took their frustrations out on the hapless Occaneechis. In the meantime, the Susquehannocks decamped again. Some took up the Mohawk offer and moved among the Five Nations. Most, however, would not live with their ancient antagonists just yet. Unable to return to their homeland, they did the next best thing and accepted a Unami invitation to live with them on lands around Delaware Bay.[7]

Although retreating Susquehannocks managed to escape the Virginians, those moving to Delaware Bay still had to contend with Maryland. That province's leaders had claimed the Delaware Valley as their territory since the colony's founding in 1634. Susquehannock opposition had long played a major role in frustrating Maryland's territorial ambitions there. Maryland finally removed that obstacle when they got the Susquehannocks to move to the Potomac. Suddenly, distant distracted New York stood as the only significant impediment to Maryland's long-hoped-for expansion into the Delaware Valley.

Although recent troubles strained relations with New Yorkers, neither Unami- and Northern Unami–speaking people living along the lower Delaware River nor Munsee-speaking townsfolk living farther upriver wanted to fall under Maryland's control. They much preferred dealing with more faraway New York. Brothers Ockanickon from the Falls of the Delaware and Mamarikickon, who was then living on the Millstone River, publicly strengthened their ties with the latter province at a meeting with Andros on September 22, 1675. Both parties used the meeting as an occasion to forget past differences (including the recent killing of a trader) and ostentatiously display solidarity.

Andros took advantage of the sachems' anxieties over the recent killing to press for further land cessions. He was able to purchase a considerable tract of land running eight or nine miles north and south of the falls on the west bank of the Delaware. The tract was on land claimed by New York but not officially included in the duke's patent. Andros's offer to the chiefs included 60 fathoms (120 yards) of wampum, many axes and knives, and most notably, six of the guns and a considerable amount of powder and lead still denied by law to Indians living around Manhattan. The governor's unusually generous offer was clearly meant to buy more than land. His meaning could not have been lost on the chiefs. Their acceptance of the presents therefore had the dual effect of stiffening New York's hold over the region and discouraging bolder interlopers from Maryland.[8]

The appearance of the Susquehannock main body in Unami country during the early summer of 1676 threatened to undo Andros's efforts to keep Maryland away from the Delaware Valley. The presence of their Susquehannock enemies there gave Maryland a clear excuse to occupy and annex land of strategic importance to the Crown that evidently could not be properly defended by ineffective caretakers in New York. Distressed by the prospect of such a seizure, Andros wanted the Susquehannocks gone as quickly as possible. He told them as much at a meeting with two of their sachems in Albany on June 2. Reminding them of the Mohawk invitation made the previous year, Andros urged them to make the move.[9]

The Susquehannocks politely demurred. Two months later, Andros learned that rather than become part of the Mohawk nation, they preferred to remain an independent people. Few would risk returning to the Susquehanna Valley, however. Most instead planned to take refuge in the Minisink country along the closer Unami-Munsee borderlands above the Falls of the Delaware, shielded from attack by the Pocono Plateau and the northern New Jersey Highlands.[10]

KING PHILIP'S WAR

In the meantime, Northern Indians became locked in a struggle for survival with New England colonists. The conflict became known as King Philip's War, after the English name of the prominent Wampanoag sachem Metacom, who came to embody the Indian cause in the minds of colonists and their descendants. Unlike the Susquehannock troubles, which have been largely forgotten, King Philip's War is one of the nation's best-remembered Indian conflicts.

The conflict reached into every corner of Indian New England, spreading into what is present-day Maine before the fighting finally sputtered out in 1677. The war took the lives of more than three thousand Indians and at least six hundred colonists. Hundreds of colonists were herded into harsh Indian captivities. Many Indians captured by colonists were sold into slavery in faraway places like Bermuda. Hundreds of Praying Indian Christian converts were miserably interned on barren windswept islands in Boston Harbor, where famine and disease ran rampant. A large number of Indian towns and more than half of all colonial settlements outside the larger villages suffered attack. Many were destroyed. Uprooted colonists flooded into Boston and its environs. Entire townships were depopulated, some lying abandoned years after the fighting ended.[11]

Indians in Munsee country greeted news of the war with varying degrees of dread and enthusiasm. Most living along the coast had little sympathy for Indians locked in the struggle. There had been bad blood with the Pequots and, after 1637, with Narragansetts and Niantics taking up where they left off. Western Long Island Indians as well as Montauketts suffered from their attacks, and all Indians on Long Island sullenly paid the wampum tribute they demanded to forestall further assaults.

Other Indians at Esopus, Minisink, and locales farther inland along the Hudson Valley must have felt a strong obligation to help Pocumtucks, Sokokis, Pennacooks, and kindred Northern Indian allies. They had fought alongside one another for decades against the Mohawks and had given each other food and shelter when fighting went against them. These experiences doubtless strengthened bonds of kinship and friendship forged in battles that took little notice of colonial province lines.

Whatever their feelings, hardheaded Lower River Indian sachems shared Andros's belief that there was little to be gained by plunging headlong into someone else's fight. Most therefore did what they could to work with the governor to prevent the spread of hostilities into New York. Andros had the easier task. He could order his soldiers to stand down and remain in their quarters. Sachems could thwart ambitious war captains through the simple expedient of not turning control over to them. They could not, however, order warriors to stay out of the fighting. Their task of persuasion was made all the harder by the way many warriors regarded the war. They saw battle as a chance to settle old scores, curry a bit of favor with the powers that be, and with some luck, perhaps win a name for themselves. Sachems denying warriors their chance to win glory while helping embattled friends and kinsfolk could easily lose followers.

Tackapousha and other sachems on Long Island managed to keep both their followers and their warriors at home by working out a face-saving arrangement with Andros. Warriors could not go into battle unarmed. Wanting to make sure that no belligerents could use their involvement as an excuse to widen the war, and willing to promise them protection, Andros wanted the Long Island Indians disarmed. Protesting loudly, but not too loudly, Tackapousha and like-minded elders made a show of reluctantly obeying Andros's order to surrender their people's guns as the governor progressed through their towns in a grand tour of the island during the spring of 1675.

Other sachems from Munsee country soon trooped to Manhattan in groups of twos and threes to assure Andros that their people also would remain neutral and only support the English if fighting was in prospect. Andros thanked them and gave presents to show his gratitude. He also demanded and impounded guns owned by Wiechquaesgecks and Wappingers with known ties to Northern Indians. To keep them out of harm's way, he invited both nations to move closer to Manhattan and gave their sachems passes authorizing safe conduct in nervous times. Andros also put a stop to all trade of guns, lead, and powder to Indians. To all Indians, that is, except the Five Nations. The governor, of course, knew about the long-standing war between the Mohawks and the Northern Indians. Although he did not want them crossing over into New England just yet, he let the Mohawks know that he expected them to use their guns to kill or capture any Northern Indians entering his province.[12]

Not all River Indian warriors stayed at home. A number of Wappingers and Wiechquaesgecks joined Mahicans helping Northern Indians against the New Englanders. Even some western Long Islanders got into the fighting. On February 29, 1676, an evidently concerned Tackapousha sent two of his warriors carrying the scalp of a Pequot man they had just killed in Connecticut to authorities at New York. He need not have worried. Even though the dead man was probably a friend to colonists, no complaint was forthcoming. The Connecticut colonists were preoccupied, and Andros was focusing on more momentous developments far up the Hudson. Nothing more was heard of the incident.[13]

Although no one knew it yet, the tide of the war was turning. Buoyed by their warm weather successes against the New Englanders, many Northern Indians withdrew inland to sit out the winter of 1675–1676. Safe from English attacks like the one that destroyed the main Narragansett fort in December, they were not far enough away to escape detection and assault from other quarters. On February 25, 1676, an exhausted Massachusetts settler named Thomas Warner stumbled into Albany. He told the magistrates he had just slipped away from captors camping on the Hoosic River some forty miles to the north. He said there were 2,100 mostly young Indian men, including five hundred or six hundred "French Indians with straws in their noses" planning spring operations at the encampment. Although his numbers sounded incredible to the Albanians, they were not all that far from the mark. Just then, two bodies of Northern Indian warriors totaling nine hundred men were camping with Mahican friends somewhere along the Hoosic. Metacom was there, helping to conduct negotiations with French Indians bringing guns and ammunition from Canada.[14]

This was an opportunity Andros would not resist. He quietly invited the Mohawks to camp around Albany, gave food and shelter to their families, and provisioned their warriors. An overwhelming force of Mohawk warriors soon fell on the Hoosic encampment, killing and capturing many and driving off survivors. Sending their captives back to New York, the Mohawks pressed eastward, attacking Northern Indians wherever they found them. Reeling from the assaults and unable to break through what in effect became a Mohawk cordon sanitaire, the Northern Indians could not bring in supplies or reinforcements from Canada. Cut off from their lines of retreat, Northern Indians losing operational mobility finally had to turn and face their English antagonists in New England. Praying Indians fighting on the side of the English killed Metacom himself at his Mount Hope home in Bristol, Rhode Island, in August 1676. Increasingly disorganized and pinned between Mohawk warriors and vengeful settlers, Northern Indian resistance in New England collapsed by the end of the year.[15]

NIBBLING AT THE EDGES OF MUNSEE COUNTRY

Catastrophes north and south of the duke's province dislocated lives everywhere in English America. Colonists ruined by war flocked to the unravaged Hudson Valley during and after the troubles of 1675–1676. Some moved north from Chesapeake Bay. Most, however, came from New England. Like other immigrants before them, the majority initially settled in and around Manhattan. More enterprising individuals, many joining together into partnerships and syndicates, began buying mostly small holdings directly from Indians or from town authorities. Land jobbers started purchasing larger tracts from sachems in anticipation of resales to newcomers at marked-up prices.

As in the past, Indians in Munsee country could not stop colonists from pressing them for lands. They could and did, however, continue to find ways to limit expansion into their territory. Most did so by contesting past deeds or restricting numbers of new sales. Uncertainty caused by civil unrest, English surrender and reconquest, and changes in proprietary governance encouraged Indians and settlers in East Jersey to pursue a singularly wide range of mutually accommodative strategies.

East Jersey came into being when Lord Berkeley sold his interest in New Jersey to a couple of Quaker purchasers for £1,000 in 1674. Two years later, William Penn and two other trustees for the now-bankrupt senior Quaker purchaser persuaded Sir Carteret to divide the proprietary into two provinces. The new Quaker proprietors signing what became known as the Quintipartite deed on July 1, 1676, erected West Jersey on the far side of a diagonal boundary line separating the new province from East Jersey at a point starting at Little Egg Harbor. The hazily defined line ran north-northwest through unsurveyed Indian territory to a place where the 41 degrees, 40 minutes north latitude line was supposed to cross the upper Delaware River. Later surveys, and there would be many, ultimately placed this northern station point just beyond the site of what colonists would come to know as the Cochecton Indian town.[16]

Arguments over the course of province line would furnish fertile ground for dispute for decades to come. In the meantime, Philip Carteret assumed the governorship of East Jersey. He planned to move the new province's capital to the mouth of the Raritan River, where he hoped to build a port capable of drawing trade away from New York. Ensuing arguments over revenue and jurisdiction caused a falling-out between Andros and Carteret that led to the latter's arrest, trial, and release in New York in 1680 and the former's recall to England a year later.

Confusion created a tangled state of affairs further complicated by uncertainty over the extent of patent lands. Unlike other sachems in East Jersey, who mostly moved farther upriver after selling land to settlers along the lower reaches of the Hackensack and Passaic valleys, most Indians whose sachems put their marks onto the 1665 Navesink deed continued to live in Ramenesing, Wickatunk, Toponemesing, and other towns within the purchase bounds. Rather than evict them, settlers instead moved past and around them. Navesink people saw little reason to give up their towns. Settlers dreaded the prospect of having to call on meddlesome provincial authorities for help in ousting recalcitrant Indians. Middletown and Shrewsbury township magistrates instead quietly worked out another working disagreement with the Indians. Like others elsewhere, both sides tacitly treated the 1665 deed less like a final sale and more like a preemptive option warranty legally required to obtain the necessary patent. Township elders authorized purchases of settled and unsettled tracts claimed by Indians within previously patented town bounds. Colonists ultimately obtained twenty-four deeds to much of this land from Peropay, Taptawappamund, Emerus, Metapis, Wassackarous, and the other local sachems between 1674 and 1680. Many of these deeds were later discreetly registered with proprietary authorities. Some were only registered in the county record hall. Others were never registered at all.[17]

One of these deals, a deed to a neck of land near Shrewsbury Inlet signed on August 16, 1675, contained the first reference to a young son of Metapis. The young man was given pride of place as the first-mentioned son in the deed. Identified as Quicacahuland, he would grow up to become Weequehela, the man known among colonists as the Indian King of New Jersey.[18]

Farther to the east across the South Bay on Long Island, Tackapousha used the years between 1675 and 1680 to continue looking for opportunities to slow colonial expansion into his people's remaining lands at Matinecock, Massapequa, and Merrick. On August 5, 1675, he entered yet another complaint that Hempstead settlers had failed to pay for their lands at Merrick. The settlers admitted never making the payment, saying they did not have to because the Dutch had bought the land for them. Besides, they insisted, Wyandanch, whom they believed was Tackapousha's overlord, had confirmed the colonist's rights to the lands in question by right of conquest during Kieft's War.[19]

As it had during earlier times, the dispute dragged on through Andros's administration. No matter how much he threatened, cajoled, or tried to reason with the aggrieved parties, no one gave ground. Like later disputes between similarly stubborn opponents, the outlines of a final settlement, in this case two government-guaranteed reservation tracts on the banks of Hempstead Harbor on the north side of the island and a small tract at Fort Neck along the south shore near the ocean, had emerged years earlier. More years would pass before everyone finally realized they could not get everything they wanted and settled for a compromise.[20]

Meanwhile, farther west in Hackensack country, Aroorhikan, Memshe, Mindawassa (a war captain who became a Tappan sachem), Tantaqua (also called Jasper), and Pierwim signed another seven deeds or deed confirmations during Andros's tenure as New York governor. Varying in size from small tracts to larger hunks of territory, the lands granted by these deeds only nibbled at the southern and eastern edges of the still sovereign Hackensack heartland. Farther north, Esopus Indians sold and, in two unusual deeds, bought land.[21]

Esopus sachems also began negotiations with a group of Huguenot exiles, while confirming existing deed boundaries at the annual Nicolls Treaty renewal meeting in Kingston on April 26, 1677. The parties agreed on the purchase price for a large tract of lower Walkill Valley land east of the Shawangunks exactly one month later on May 26. The stone houses that the children of the original purchasers later built in the heart of the tract are preserved as the Huguenot Street National Historic Landmark. The Huguenots named the new settlement die Pfalz, the German name for the Rhenish Palatinate refuge from religious persecution they left for New York. The village that grew up around this New World sanctuary is now known as New Paltz.[22]

SANCTUARY

Sanctuaries of a different sort were on offer for Indians from foreign parts willing to submit to the protection of others. On April 14, 1676, Andros asked Wiechquaesgeck sachems Wessecanoe and Amond to send messengers to New England offering protection and land to Northern Indians who would agree to move to New York. Hackensacks, Tappans, and Mahicans soon joined Wiechquaesgecks sweeping through New England looking for Northern Indians interested in starting new lives in the Hudson Valley.[23]

On April 27, Wessecanoe returned with fifty Indians from a place along the uppermost reaches of the Housatonic River he called Wayattano. Speaking for the party, he affirmed their desire to live in friendship and politely told Andros they would consider a move to New York. A few months later, on July 20, Connecticut authorities advised Andros to attack "some hundreds" of Northern Indians fleeing from what was almost certainly the Wayattano locale toward Esopus. One month later, the same authorities suggested in another letter to Andros dated August 19 that he take the same course of action against another group of one hundred or so Northern Indians making the same journey. Connecticut troops attacking the first group reportedly killed or captured about one-third of the 150 making up the party. The destination of both groups was identified as Paquiage, a Mahican town in the present-day Catskill Creek village of Leeds, New York.[24]

Andros neither delivered up Northern Indian refugees claiming his protection nor allowed Connecticut troops or Mohawk warriors to attack them once they crossed into New York. Instead, he offered asylum to any

Northern Indians who had stayed out of the fighting. Directed to avoid asking too many questions (the governor could not give sanctuary to admitted killers of colonists), Andros's agents relocated asylum seekers at a new village established for them on the Hoosic River along New York's northeastern frontier, near the site of the Northern Indian encampment recently attacked by the Mohawks. The place was called Schaghticoke (Mahican for "at the fork of the river"), not to be confused with the Connecticut town of the same name on the upper Housatonic River. Schaghticoke on the Hoosic soon became a major frontier settlement astride the main river and road route between New York and New France.

Only a few of the one hundred to three hundred people who moved to Schaghticoke during the first years of its existence were originally from the Hudson Valley. This, however, did not stop people from referring to everyone living in the place as Mahicans or lumping them together with people they collectively called the Upper River Indian Nation. At the same time, colonists began regularly referring to all Native people living below Albany as Lower River Indians.[25]

Growing numbers of Susquehannocks evidently also took up Andros's offer to move to the duke's province. Several sources report their movements into the Mohawk and Delaware river valleys at this time. Few records of their presence have been found in either place. This is due in part to the fact that no one in New York had much interest in admitting that Mohawks and Delaware River Indians were sheltering open enemies of Maryland, Virginia, and the Five Nations. Susquehannocks also had a strong interest in maintaining a low profile. They almost certainly avoided gathering in numbers anywhere that might attract unwelcome attention.

Changing consumption and production patterns also make it difficult to distinguish different Indian communities living together at particular places at this time. By the third quarter of the seventeenth century, European manufactures largely replaced stylistically distinct domestically produced clay pots and pipes that had tended to act as markers associated with particular communities or locales everywhere in the Northeast. Although archaeologists can discern differences between European goods produced in different places at different times, brass kettles, glass beads, gun barrels, and other goods traded to one Indian nation did not much differ from those traded by the same trader to its neighbors. Contemporary maps and descriptions, by contrast, clearly show that members of different Indian nations were then living together in many places. Disappearance of traditional domestically produced diagnostic artifacts currently hinders efforts to link different Indian nations with what now appear to be uniform assemblages of European imports found in these sites.[26]

An absence of Strickler ceramics and other diagnostic Susquehannock artifacts at Minisink Island and nearby late seventeenth-century sites in the Munsee homeland does not mean that all Susquehannocks abandoned their national identity or moved to Iroquoia. A scattering of brief documentary notices shows that some Susquehannocks continued to live in communities of their own in the Delaware Valley. One writer, for example, clearly referred to a Susquehanna Indian town on the north bank of the Schuylkill River above Philadelphia in 1689. This community was gone by 1696, when it was reported that Indians "that removed from Schoolkill" now resided with other Susquehannocks who left homes among the Five Nations to live at Conestoga near present-day Lancaster, Pennsylvania. Like Schaghticoke, Conestoga would also become a major polyglot frontier Indian outpost.[27]

River Indians in the Covenant Chain

River Indians and Mohawks had been negotiating diplomatic agreements with colonists for more than half a century when Andros arrived in New York. During this time, they and Europeans had adopted aspects of each other's diplomatic styles. Europeans came to use Indian expressions characterizing diplomatic linkages metaphorically, first as ropes and later as iron chains. They understood that blood, liquor, and tears rusted and weakened figurative iron chains. So they worked together with Indians to do what they could to make sure that frequent meetings and constant exchanges of presents and pleasantries burnished and brightened the links that bound them together.

Francis Jennings characterized the functional expression of this figurative Covenant Chain as "an organization of peers, unequal in power and status, but equal in the right of each to govern itself." Evolving over time, the alliance provided a framework for mobilizing allies in times of war and maintaining forums for airing grievances and discussing trade arrangements.[28]

Andros ushered in a series of what Jennings called constitutional changes to Covenant Chain relationships. In keeping with his mandate to centralize royal authority, the governor instituted a series of alterations in Covenant Chain ground rules that would profoundly, although not immediately, change how Indians in Munsee country and every other Indian community in the Northeast did business with the English. These came into being during talks carried on during the spring and summer of 1677 that established a more substantial Covenant Chain figuratively forged from gold or silver, less brittle and significantly farther reaching than the iron chain it replaced.

Andros worked to anneal his metaphorical precious metal chain into a broad bond binding every Indian nation and British province in the Northeast to the Crown's interest. He was not an altruist, however. Andros did everything he could to ensure that his patron, the Duke of York, and his patron's province would be dominant in this new arrangement. He started by making sure Mohawks and River Indians supported his insistence that Albany be the central meeting place for Covenant Chain conferences. They further secured New York's pride of place by giving Andros and subsequent New York governors the ceremonial title "Corlaer," the name of Arendt van Curler, a recently deceased Dutch trader remembered as a faithful friend and reliable culture broker.[29]

Jennings makes a good case for the idea that Andros established his new Covenant Chain during a series of talks held at Albany, Kingston, and New York City between April and July 1677. Andros began on or about April 24, when he gathered River Indians and emissaries from Connecticut and Massachusetts together in Albany to air grievances and put the sorrows of the recent fighting behind them. He then went south to Kingston, where he sat in on a meeting renewing the Nicolls Treaty with the Esopus Indians on April 27. After helping to mediate lingering payment and boundary disputes there, Andros returned to Fort James. He spent much of the following May haggling over talking points to be discussed at meetings scheduled for the summer with representatives from the New England and Chesapeake Bay colonies.[30]

Mohawk emissaries met with New Englanders at the first of these meetings in Albany on June 4. Making sure that everyone stayed on script, Andros oversaw the ritual renewals of friendship and sat quietly by as the participants pledged to settle future disagreements at the Albany fort. He also saw to it that everyone accepted a nonaggression pact that protected Northern Indians at Schaghticoke from Puritan vengeance. It was at this meeting that Mohawks, lamenting the loss of the "Old Corlaer," gave his name to Andros in hopes that the governor and his successors would embody similar qualities of reliability and devotion to duty.[31]

One month later, Andros returned to Albany, this time in the company of commissioners from Maryland and Virginia. There they met with embassies from each of the Five Nations (and as Maryland records note, from Indian communities throughout the Hudson and Delaware valleys) between July 20 and August 24. Explaining that they could not recall war parties that had already left for the south, the Indians asked that Marylanders and Virginians overlook losses of farm animals or produce that might disappear when hungry warriors hunting down their mutual Susquehannock enemies were nearby. Promising to make good any losses caused by their warriors, they pledged that they would thereafter act peaceably toward settlers and friendly Indians alike when traveling through both provinces. As the Mohawks had done with the New Englanders, all of the Five Nations and the Hudson and Delaware valley Indians agreed to make Albany the site for future meetings with Marylanders and Virginians as well.[32]

Subsequent records of Albany meetings show that these negotiations did much to establish the town as a central meeting place for colonists and Indians. The Albany magistrates appointed by Andros to oversee Indian affairs there ultimately became the influential Board of Indian Commissioners. The board's first secretary, Robert Livingston, a bilingual Scotsman who had grown up in the Netherlands, would become a major force in New York politics. This, however, was all in the future. For the present, the Albany magistrates and the newly arrived mayor's secretary Livingston did what they could to make frontier diplomats welcome in their city.

Their immediate work centered on finding means to safeguard the security of Northern Indian refugees at Schaghticoke and those Susquehannocks taking shelter in territory claimed by New York along the Delaware River. Five Nations warriors did not, however, stop killing and carrying off Indians who ran afoul of raiding parties that continued to range along the northern borders of New England and the western frontiers of the other English colonies. Authorities in other colonies also did not stop trying to end Iroquois Confederacy depredations by making separate deals of their own that bypassed Andros and Albany. And Lower River Indians living nearer settled towns most often preferred to travel to Kingston, Elizabethtown, and New York to affirm old treaties and transact new business.[33]

At one of these meetings in New York, River Indians informed Andros that they had decided to divide themselves into Upper and Lower nations. On July 10, 1679, Joris, a young Esopus sachem (sometimes also identified as a Mahican leader), told Andros that he had been chosen sachem of the Indians living on the river below Albany two years earlier. Speaking for all River Indians, he went on to inform the governor that the Mahicans and Northern Indians at Schaghticoke had consolidated into a single nation. He finished by asking that Wamsachko be appointed sachem of those "that live above the river at Albany, as Joris was below."[34]

Metaphorical Children

The July 10, meeting was also the place where Joris made what appears to have been an extraordinary declaration. He told Andros "that heretofore they were brethren to the English but now they are their children." Here, for the first time, a sachem from Munsee country ceremonially referred to his people in council as children. Up until that time, colonists trying to rhetorically subordinate Indians in the Munsee homeland by metaphorically referring to them by the term were firmly countered by circumspect sachems responding as brothers, cousins, or friends.

Colonists were familiar with Indian use of kinship and gender terms when formally addressing others at meetings. Metaphor meaning and usage, however, vary considerably over time and between cultures. Take, for example, Joris's use of the word "child." By the standards of American society, parents, fathers, mothers, and in appropriate circumstances any elder or authority figure may properly address a person as a child. The terms are reciprocal and imply some sort of relationship marked by dominance and submission.

Use and meaning of the term "child" can differ, however, in matrilineal societies that order relations along succeeding generations linked by women. As discussed earlier, a father's brother, the person Americans call an uncle, usually had more of a say over the life of a child than someone Americans would call father. Looked at this way, a person might be expected to pay a decorous degree of respect to the man or woman who addressed them as a child. The same person addressed as nephew, niece, or cousin, however, might be called on to respond in an altogether more obligatory way to a maternal uncle acting as his or her father.

Use of reciprocal uncle-nephew metaphors occurs frequently in rhetoric used by Five Nations and River Indian speakers at meetings throughout the later colonial era. Most, but not all, investigators regard such usage as rhetorical evidence of ties binding both societies together in specific ways. Since these vary with changing times and circumstances, people may use the same terms to address people standing in different relationships to them. Whatever metaphors they used, the realities governing their relations soon took dark and unexpected turns as war and disease returned to devastate Munsee country.[35]

9

DEVASTATION, 1679–1685

Although it cannot be known for sure, things must have looked bright for the people of Munsee country as the new year dawned in 1679. The luck of sachems and metewak blessed by spirit powers seemed to be holding. Their towns were still free from epidemics like the influenza outbreak that had struck the Senecas three years earlier and the smallpox that continued to periodically ravage Boston and other ports harboring ocean-going vessels. Their sachems kept them out of wars farther north and south and continued to limit land loss. The late misfortunes suffered by Indians from neighboring regions presented new possibilities for further recovery and regeneration. Many people living in the Munsee homeland looked inward for ways to best assimilate the hundreds of refugees now living among them. Others looked outward to suddenly open roads leading to distant trapping and trading grounds. To be sure, the Five Nations still stood in the way. River Indians, however, no longer had to depend on Susquehannock forbearance to travel farther south and west. Closer links with Northern Indians through friends and kinsfolk at Schaghticoke and the Upper River Mahican towns further opened clear roads to Canada and the Great Lakes. New prospects beckoned.[1]

KINDERMORD

A slaughter of innocents of biblical proportions, what Germans call a Kindermord, abruptly dashed such bright hopes. It arrived in the form of a smallpox epidemic that struck New York City sometime in August 1679. The disease progressed rapidly, striking the Five Nations in September and reaching Quebec one month later. The epidemic virus, apparently accompanied by an endemic fever that may have been malarial, sickened people everywhere. The fifteen-year respite from smallpox enjoyed by everyone in the Hudson and Delaware valleys made it particularly deadly to young people who had not had the chance to develop immunities to the disease.[2]

The virulence of the 1679 smallpox epidemic stunned everyone who witnessed its impact. One eyewitness was the Labadist diarist Jasper Danckaerts. In one settler's house in Brooklyn where a child had died a week earlier, Danckaerts saw three sick children lying next to two dead siblings. He wrote that the disease "was more fatal this year than usual," observing that a "great number" of Indians had succumbed to the contagion by the early winter. One year later, West Jersey settler Mahlon Stacy, one of the first Englishmen to move to the Falls of the Delaware after its purchase in 1675, and a future leading light in the West Jersey proprietary council, wrote that "it is hardly credible to believe how the Indians are wasted in two years time, and especially last summer." Although everyone suffered, River Indians seem to have suffered most. In one awful stroke, smallpox carried off much of their entire coming generation, casting whole communities into grief and scarring those who survived.[3]

Desolated survivors lived in the kind of society where spirits were thought to cause everything and where nothing happened by chance. Despite the fact that no records document the fact, the people of Munsee country surely turned to their spiritual leaders to identify the malevolent spirits that had attacked them and find out why they had done so. As spiritually inclined people still do everywhere, metewak probably blamed the devastation on lax observance of proper rituals, insufficient offerings, and spells cast by enemies. No evidence indicates that they hunted among themselves for guilty witches to destroy; that sad development would have to wait for more than a century for the Delaware witch hunts in Ohio and Indiana. Instead, Indians in Munsee country almost certainly focused their grief and anger on foreigners thought to have unleashed evil spirits against them. The most likely culprits in their eyes could not be their overwhelmingly powerful colonial neighbors, who did not need the help of spirits to crush them in a single blow. The evildoers must be unreconciled relatives of dead enemies whose restless spirits remained unappeased by treaty wampum, condolence gifts, and soothing words. In the time-honored ways of mourning war, grieving warriors set out to avenge their dead by attacking people belonging to suspect nations. They killed or captured strangers waylaid on their travels and took whatever possessions they could carry away, hunting, trapping, and trading wherever they went.[4]

Colonial records were soon full of reports of Indians venturing far from their homelands. Most duly noted that they were traveling to avenge past injuries and get furs. On March 23, 1680, Danckaerts heard that a large party of Indians from the Albany area "had gone south to make war against the Indians of Carolina, beyond Virginia." Reflecting again that they had lost many people to smallpox, he went on to note that their now-essential pelt inventories had run low and needed replenishment. On September 12, 1681, Tomachkapay at Minisink furnished evidence indicating that his people had joined the expedition. Speaking to Anthony Brockholls, acting governor of New York following Andros's recall earlier in the year, Tomachkapay said that his warriors had just killed six Indians and brought back another five as captives from another nation far to the south. He went on to explain that they had done this to avenge the deaths of two Minisinks killed by what he called "angry people" from that nation during a recent hunting trip "as far as the Spanish Indians" (see map 7).[5]

The identities of some of these southerners were revealed when Maryland and Virginian commissioners came to the Covenant Chain meeting place in Albany on June 13, 1682. They complained that a party of "Maquase and Mahikanders" had attacked their Piscataway friends somewhere in the more western parts of their provinces. They demanded compensation, called for the return of surviving prisoners, and insisted that the sachems promise to restrain their warriors and stop further attacks.[6]

On the following July 19, sachems representing the Mahicans, Catskills, and Esopus gathered at Albany to hear the complaints against them. The sachems, whose numbers included Joris (identified as a Mahikander), Esopus leader Mamanuchqua (identified as a *squae*), and her grandson the Esopus sachem Pemmyrawech (see figure 4), politely responded on the following day. Presenting two wampum belts, they renewed their Covenant Chain bonds and apologized for all offenses offered and damages done. They also presented a beaver pelt in token of a promise to travel farther westward beyond Maryland and Virginia when again "going out a hunting beaver."[7]

Wolves on the Miami River and Grief at Home

Tomachkapay's Minisinks were not the only Indians from Munsee country traveling far in search of beaver. The French explorer René-Robert Cavalier,

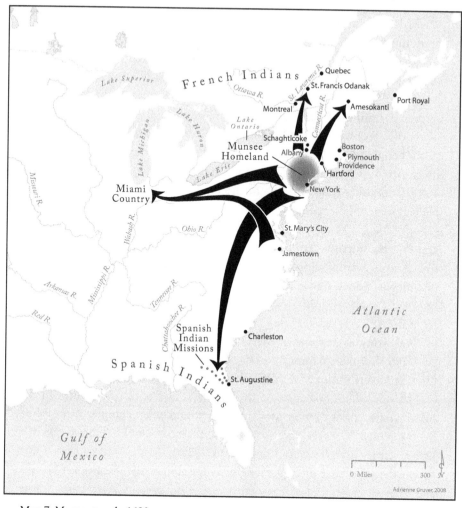

Map 7. Munsee travels, 1680s

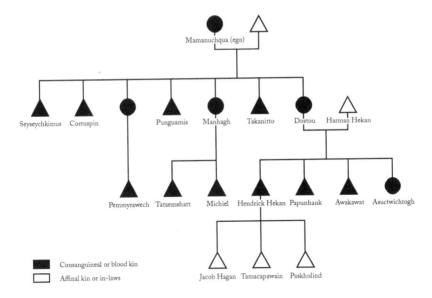

Figure 4. Mamanuchqua and her kin

Sieur de la Salle, came upon others in company with thirty or so hunters he called Loups ("Wolves," the general term the French used when talking about Eastern Algonquians) and their families near the mouth of the Miami River in February 1681. This group of hunting families probably numbered between 90 and 150 people. The Miami River they were living along is now known as the St. Joseph River, a 215-mile-long stream that runs across the base of Michigan's Lower Peninsula before emptying into Lake Michigan near the city bearing the river's name. It was then an important communication and trade route that, with a short portage, bypassed more northerly French posts like Michilimackinac to link lakes Erie and Michigan.[8]

La Salle wrote that members of this party had been living in the region for at least two years before his arrival. He identified them as Indians who had left homes from the east between New England and Virginia "partly because the beaver had become very scarce and partly because of the hate they bore the English." Speaking through an Indian interpreter from Boston that La Salle identified as Ouiouilamet, the Loups told the Frenchman that they were there to hunt up enough beaver to buy their way into the Iroquois Confederacy or any other nation willing to offer them lands and fields far from the English. Their numbers included Wampanoags and their neighbors, Narragansetts, Mohegans, Mahicans, Minisinks, Esopus, and, it appears, some Piscataways, Conoys, or Powhatans. The list appears comprehensive and reads like a directory of Eastern Algonquian nations between Boston and Virginia. It is tempting to speculate that the group represented a deliberately organized expedition formed to explore possibilities for a general emigration.[9]

The Indian from Boston La Salle called Ouiouilamet may have been Wawanolewat, the Anglophobic pro-French Northern Indian war leader better known among colonists as Grey Lock. Other prominent figures in the group included "Nanangoucy from Menissen," a man who subsequently served as La Salle's intermediary, and a "Mahigane Indian" named Klas. Nanangoucy was almost certainly the Delaware Valley sachem Nanacuttin, later noted as an uncle of one of Ockanickon's sons. Klas, for his part, may have been Claes de Wilt, the already mentioned Hudson Valley culture broker. Both Klas and Claes were known for having a talent for languages. Both were also evidently adventurous. Chroniclers along the Hudson and Delaware valleys do not include Claes's or Nanacuttin's names among Indians dealing with colonists in or around the Munsee homeland at the time La Salle wrote about them at Miami. If they were one and the same, both Klas/Claes and Nanangoucy/Nanacuttin were back east by 1682.[10]

Munsee Indians remaining in their homeland were still reeling from the epidemic that had carried off so many of their young people and inexplicably spared so many elders. Of the latter, only Seyseychkimus, Waerhinnis Couwee, Caelcop I, and a couple of minor sachems disappeared from colonial records just before or immediately after 1679. Immunities acquired during previous contagions probably protected older survivors of earlier epidemics. Elders mentioned by colonists thereafter, and there were many, would have credited spiritual help rather than antibodies for their survival. Nevertheless, they and their grieving families must have wondered why the spirits allowed so many of their children to die.

As Indian interments throughout the Northeast attest, European manufactures tended to comprise the largest share of offerings placed in children's graves. Such goods were intended to equip the dead in the afterlife. Grieving parents evidently placed European goods in graves of children who had not lived long enough to enjoy them in this world. Traders and trappers in places like Miami country could only bring home those furs they were able to fit in canoes to trade for colonial wares. War parties could bring back prisoners for adoption or sacrifice to avenge deaths and mollify restless spirits. Threats of retaliation might also discourage enemies from casting spells, although this could only be a forlorn hope. Neither warriors nor traders, however, could get the vast quantities of furs needed to acquire sufficient quantities of European goods to appropriately outfit the heartbreakingly large number of children for their journeys to the next world. Only land sales could provide the requisite amount of goods required.[11]

Colonists knew what the epidemic had done to the Indian communities. Mourning their own losses, their worries were multiplied by increasingly sure knowledge that disruptive and potentially expensive administrative and political changes were in the wind. Andros had been recalled in seeming disgrace, and his return appeared doubtful. No one knew who his successor would be or what he would do. Regime change meant at the very least that those officials fortunate to keep their jobs would have to pay steep fees for new commissions. Other fees for sale, survey, and registration of new deeds and confirmation of old patents would require further outlays. Some of these could be considerable. The entire province of East Jersey was up for sale. Quakers who had already bought West Jersey for £1,000 showed great interest in acquiring the rest of the duke's domains beyond the Hudson. They and nearly everyone else in and around the region were ready to trade goods Indians needed for titles to land they wanted.

In East Jersey, things were being run in the name of Lady Elizabeth Carteret after her husband died deep in debt on January 14, 1680. Working with trustees appointed under the terms of her husband's will, she immediately began looking for buyers interested in taking the unprofitable and troublesome colony off her hands. Determined to remove legal impediments that might put off prospective purchasers, she and her trustees ordered their governor to clear Indian title to as much land in the province as possible without delay. Indians living on what must have seemed like blighted lands along the Raritan and Hackensack rivers, near hostile neighbors, redolent with memories of lost loved ones and evidently cursed by angry or indifferent spirits knew something was up. Alert to all rumors floating through the region, they may have heard that New York might be giving up its claim to the Jerseys, ending opportunities to exploit uncertainties that had helped them slow settlement for nearly a generation. Whatever they knew, they could not have anticipated the relentless persistence of Governor Carteret's agents, who started swooping down on Indians in East Jersey in earnest in the late spring of 1681.

More Land Sales

Emerus, Metapis, Querameck, Conackamack, Taptawappamund, and their compatriots signed over the whole of the long-denied main stem of the

Raritan River in a series of nine deeds between May 4, 1681, and April 22, 1682. Memshe (signing as the Tappan sachem), Mindawassa, and their colleagues conveyed two tracts in Hackensack country on October 29, 1681, and March 17, 1682. Pressure ended only after the governor received a letter from Lady Carteret and her trustees written on February 16, 1682, and received many weeks later. The letter directed him "not to purchase any Indian lands, make patents, or suffer any settlements to be made until further orders."[12]

The order was sent because buyers for the province had been found. Between February 1 and 2, 1682, a syndicate of twelve merchant associates headed by the apparently omnipresent William Penn purchased East Jersey for the sum of £3,400. It was a bargain, considerably less than the original £5,000 to £10,000 price asked by the trustees. Farther east at Oyster Bay, Suscaneman was running a fire sale of his own. Concerned town fathers embroiled in generations-old land disputes with Tackapousha and neighboring towns worried about what the coming of a new governor would mean to their patents. Following lessons probably learned at the feet of his predecessor Asharoken, Suscaneman (often in company with his compatriots Syhar and Werah) signed twenty-seven deeds selling or securing title to house and wood lots to prominent residents in the heart of the town within the space of little more than a year's time. Negotiated between March 1, 1681, and June 1, 1682, most of these deeds ceded small tracts ranging in size from ten to fifty acres in extent. The nearly identical wording of these evidently mass-produced handwritten deeds anticipates the printed forms that would come into common use during the next century.

Suscaneman signed these deeds in batches, putting his mark on four deeds to ten-acre tracts on July 5, 1681, three more tracts of ten acres on October 18, 1681, six deeds to tracts mostly fifty acres in extent on March 1, 1682, three more for like amounts on April 26, 1682, and a hithertofore unheard of ten deeds to tracts ranging in size from fifteen to eighty acres on June 10, 1682.[13]

Farther north, other sachems signed several deeds for settlers wishing to shore up their own titles to lands within boundaries of what both Indians and settlers regarded as earlier preemptive deeds in soon-to-be-established Westchester County. Wessecanoe, Claes, and several local sachems signed four deeds giving over rights to lands along the east bank of the Hudson to the New York merchant Frederick Philipse I. Intent on establishing a grand manor in the style of the former patroons, Philipse added these tracts to territory he had purchased from the family of the late patroon Adriaen Van der Donck in 1672. Local sachems also sold small tracts to less imposing merchant princes. On June 3, 1682, for example, Amond, local sachems Sherikham and Askawanos, and seventeen of their friends and relatives sold Croton Point to a baker from New York.[14]

Farther east, Mamarranack and several other local sachems signed over two deeds (one with Wessecanoe's blessings) to Rye settlers for tracts on the still unclear border with Connecticut. Rye townsfolk added these to an arsenal of Indian titles defending rights to borderlands that increasingly insistent Connecticut authorities claimed lay within their own province's jurisdiction. Katonah, a young survivor of the recent epidemic from Connecticut's Pequannock Valley, was first mentioned in another transaction in the same area. On December 23, 1680, he participated in the sale of a tract known as the Hop Ground in the town of Bedford, New York. Like Taphow and other, lesser-known country folk from westernmost Connecticut, Katonah would become a prominent Lower River Indian sachem in the Highlands. Unlike the more highly placed Taphow, Katonah would limit his theater of operations to the contested borderlands separating the rival provinces of New York and Connecticut.[15]

Regime Change in Pennsylvania and the Jerseys

Farther south, a procession of new governors, both expected and unexpected, began arriving. On August 3, 1681, William Penn's first cousin William Markham presented his credentials to the magistrates of Upland, then the only English town in the newly established province of Pennsylvania. Markham's arrival marked the advent of his cousin's ownership of the newly established proprietary province of Pennsylvania, "Penn's Woods." The king had granted the province to Penn in recognition of his uncle's support during the civil war. Setting out the boundaries for the new capital at Philadelphia and erecting the first counties of Bucks, Philadelphia, and Chester, Markham began buying land from Indians as he waited for the new proprietor to arrive. Penn and Markham subsequently completed their initial series of purchases of Indian lands along the lower reaches of the Delaware and Susquehanna rivers by the end of 1683.[16]

Although Unami-speaking people signed most of these deeds, people from Munsee country also participated in some as well. The restless Wassackarous, the man from western Long Island who had moved to the lower part of the Delaware Valley after selling his last lands at Navesink in 1675, put his mark on the last of the initial purchases, a deed to land between Upland and Christina creeks on December 19, 1683. Taptawappamund, Peropay, and Metapis joined Ockanickon, Orecton (who signed for Nanacuttin in his absence), and several other sachems with close ties to Munsee country signing the first of these deeds. Negotiated between July 15 and August 1, 1682, this deed included a memorandum couched in treaty language guaranteeing Penn's title and calling for yearly renewal meetings. The sale largely took in land around the Falls of the Delaware purchased by Andros for the duke seven years earlier. Like the other Indian purchases negotiated by Penn and Markham at this time, the deed was signed by well-known local sachems and properly indorsed, registered, and patented in accordance with provincial law and regulations. Although it only took in land some five miles above the falls, the deed agreement marked the uppermost limit of Pennsylvania's initial expansion into the Delaware Valley.[17]

In East Jersey, another Quaker, Thomas Rudyard, replaced the now ailing Philip Carteret as governor. Carteret died a year later. On November 13, 1682, Rudyard assumed administrative responsibilities for a largely Quaker-owned province mostly peopled by Protestant Congregationalists and Puritans. Already hostile to the proprietors, most of these people loathed Quakers on general principle. Preferring to focus their efforts on friendlier ground in West Jersey and Pennsylvania, the twelve mostly Quaker East Jersey proprietors each took on a partner. This new board, now dominated by Scots and led by the newly appointed governor, Scottish Quaker Robert Barclay, began taking steps to end civil unrest and put the province on a paying basis.

Barclay replaced Rudyard with Gawren Lawrie during the summer of 1683. Lawrie soon completed the division of the province into the four administrative counties of Bergen, Essex, Middlesex, and Monmouth. This had the effect of centralizing proprietary authority and diluting opposition by legally separating contentious settlers and hostile towns. Lawrie also devoted himself to the task of finally building the new provincial port and capital at the mouth of the recently secured Raritan River. The provincial government moved to the new capital, christened Perth Amboy, in 1686. The first part of the place's name honored prominent board member James Drummond, Fourth Earl of Perth of Scotland. It was hoped that the name would help attract Scottish immigrants to a province whose still low population board members were anxious to increase. Quaker immigrants who would have earlier settled in East Jersey were instead moving on to Pennsylvania, where they could live by themselves far from hostile Puritans who energetically persecuted them in the old country throughout the Restoration era.[18]

Lawrie in East Jersey and Samuel Jennings, who served as resident deputy governor of West Jersey from 1681 until he was replaced by Thomas Olive in 1684, turned their attention to putting their provinces into fiscal and political order. Many residents in rebellious Elizabethtown and Middletown still refused to pay rents or acknowledge any other expression of proprietary authority. More defiant townsfolk continued to ignore proprietary orders prohibiting private land purchases from Indians. Even those willing to pay the proprietors often owed absurdly low quit rents. Energy had to be devoted to correcting abuses and bringing refractory townsfolk into line. This initially meant limiting outlays for still much-desired Indian purchases until already acquired lands were resold and recalcitrant townsfolk made to pay higher quit rents and accept proprietary rule.[19]

This does not mean that proprietary authorities stopped approaching Indians to sell lands. In East Jersey, the board authorized the newly installed Governor Lawrie to use every resource at his disposal to acquire Indian title to all land in the province. Lawrie subsequently authorized purchases of several tracts along the lower South River from Querameck and Irooseeke in 1684 and 1685. He also turned his attention north to strategic passes into the interior still in Indian hands. On October 12, 1684, his agents convinced Mindawassa, a son of Pierwim named Wewanapo, and several others to sell a strip of land where the Rahway River passes through a gap in the Watchung Mountain wall near the present-day village of Springfield. Four days later, Memshe and a cavalcade of sachems whose ranks included Claes, Mindawassa, and Sehoppy, the young brother of the recently deseased Ockanickon, signed a deed to a similarly strategically placed piece of territory, this one along the Pascack Creek linking lands in the Hackensack River drainage to the western interior.[20]

On July 16, 1684, defiant Middletown residents sidestepped the province's private purchase prohibition by acquiring a 315-year lease to a tract of land near their town center. This was secured from Irooseeke, who had his uncle Sehoppy and his brothers Neckaock and Peropay mark out its bounds. On May 14 of the following year, an aroused proprietary board authorized an expenditure of £250 to acquire thirty-six thousand acres at nearby Wickatunk. Less than a year later, Lawrie personally negotiated purchase of the Wickatunk tract from Irooseeke, Neckaock, and Metapis. This purchase required a considerable outlay of limited proprietary funds. The rest of the lands bought from Indians at this time were acquired on the cheap. East Jersey penury had nevertheless helped Indians in that portion of Munsee country again avoid more damaging cessions. Taken together, the lands they had to give up amounted to little more than a nip here and a tuck there along the edge of colonial settlement.[21]

DEED FRENZY IN NEW YORK

In New York, charges of mismanagement and worse in 1681 had again led to Andros's recall. Although Andros successfully defended himself against the charges, the duke decided to replace him. His deputy Brockholls acted as caretaker until New York's new governor, another experienced royalist officer, named Thomas Dongan, arrived in New York on August 3, 1683. An Irishman and the only Catholic to hold the post in colonial times, Dongan set foot on New York soil on August 3, 1683, with orders to consolidate Crown authority, more closely regulate commerce, and, by so doing, finally make the province a paying proposition.

Dongan started by instituting administrative reforms ordered by the king. He convened the provincial assembly for a final session and reorganized the courts. Like his colleagues in Pennsylvania and East Jersey, he formed the province's disparate ridings into counties soon after his arrival. Ten of these (two were in New England) became the nuclei of all New York counties in Munsee country. He also soon began looking into existing patents and started issuing new ones. Dongan's first reforms were neither as drastic nor as costly as some colonists feared. They did, however, do much to extend Crown authority over still independent-minded settlers in refractory towns.

Dongan's concentration of power in counties, and in new courts set up in them run by placemen in his pay, terrified many already anxious colonists. Farmers and merchants in increasingly well-to-do Long Island towns near Manhattan knew that the revenue-hungry governor would use his new county courts and fee collectors to extract money and land from them. They braced for orders to prove validity of existing titles and require them to take out expensive new patents for their towns. Perhaps most worrying of all, they dreaded the prospect of facing court officials appointed by an importunate governor ordering them to show cause why they should not surrender to the Crown unpurchased Indian lands within town boundaries.

Goaded by a sense of urgency bordering on desperation, they deluged their Indian neighbors with demands for new deeds and confirmation of earlier sales.

Deed frenzy reached its peak in Oyster Bay. Having been colonized by New Englanders hoping for union with Connecticut, the openly seditious town was an ideal target for Dongan's placemen. Dongan's new county courts could make short work of titles based on hazily worded and unclearly bounded Indian deeds that already mired the town in seemingly endless squabbles with Indians, neighbors, and provincial authorities. Few beyond town boundaries worried if decisions putting an end to these protracted and distracting disputes went against Oyster Bay settlers.

Concerned Oyster Bay townsfolk desperate to shore up shaky titles promptly hunted up their reliable deed signer Suscaneman. They had him put his mark on documents affirming that Tackapousha gave him permission to sell or confirm earlier deeds to land on behalf of himself and his relatives. They also secured three letters on as many occasions confirming Suscaneman's understanding that he would equitably share land sale proceeds with all Indians with interests in the properties. Relatives served as sureties for this promise. These included Suscaneman's sister's oldest son Quarapin, Suscaneman's elder son Surrukunga, a son of Tackapousha named Samos, their kinsfolk Werah and Syhar, and their sisters' heirs. All put their marks next to Suscaneman's on thirty-five deeds to lands in the town between 1683 and 1686. In one of the last and largest of these, a deed known as the New Purchase, signed on January 9, 1686, Suscaneman accepted £60 for all unsold lands at the west end of the north part of Oyster Bay from a syndicate of twenty townsfolk.[22]

Some of these deeds documented gifts of land given to old friends and, in one case, to a settler who had married a Narragansett woman living among them. Most, however, were cash transactions. Although some only noted the usual payment of "valuable considerations," the majority specified payouts in cheap local paper or equivalents in trade goods and hard silver currency. These mostly involved outlays worth between £10 to £20 for tracts ranging between fifty to one hundred acres.[23]

Similar goings-on were occurring elsewhere in the duke's province. On April 14, 1684, for example, Tackapousha, Suscaneman, and several of their sons, heirs, and retainers confirmed earlier sales in Flushing for anxious town fathers. Reserving only the right to cut bulrushes for themselves and their posterity, they pledged not to make further claims on the town. In Brooklyn, several sachems confirming sale of land in the town of Gravesend put their marks on the last Indian deed to land in newly founded Kings County on July 20, 1684. On the mainland, Katonah and several of his kinsfolk sold a tract called Quaroppas in and around White Plains to Rye town fathers intent on acquiring all remaining unsold Indian lands within their town's charter boundaries on November 22, 1683.[24]

Private citizens were also busy amassing enormous personal holdings of their own on the shores of the lower Hudson. Dongan's instructions empowered him to grant manors, English equivalents of the earlier Dutch patroonships, to colonists wealthy enough to purchase and patent large expanses of Indian territory. Robert Livingston was among the more ambitious of these prospective manor lords. In 1679, the Albany secretary married the recently widowed, well-placed, and very wealthy Alida van Rensselaer. She was the daughter of prominent Albanian Philip Pietersz Schuyler and sister of Pieter Schuyler, the influential frontier diplomat who became the first mayor of the City of Albany after it received its first municipal patent in 1686. This was a considerable step up for the humble Van Rensselaer family employee who had only just arrived in Albany four years earlier.

The Van Rensselaers were among the richest and most powerful families in New York. Unlike most other patroonships that had gone out of business by the time New Netherland fell, massive Rensselaerswijck, around Albany (founded in 1630), remained a going concern. In 1664, Governor Nicolls made the first formal presentation of manorial privileges in New York to Jeremias Van Rensselaer in return for his cession to the province of land comprising Albany. Led by Jeremias's widow, Maria, after his death in 1674, the family jealously worked to keep their 750,000-acre manor and its privileges intact. They increased their holdings to an unmatched total of 1,000,000 acres when they received a grant of 250,000 acres for what they called the Lower Manor in present-day Columbia County from Governor Dongan in 1685.

Although Livingston was close to them, the family would not give him a share in their manor lands. The determined secretary was not deterred. He looked elsewhere to acquire land to erect the manor needed to rise to the highest rungs of colonial society. His attention soon turned to the still-unpurchased Indian lands on the east bank of the Hudson just below the Lower Manor.[25]

Wealthy merchants based in New York City also began amassing lands in hopes of securing estates of their own at this time. On February 7, 1685, a very young and very ambitious Lewis Morris obtained an Indian deed confirming an earlier purchase made by his father, Robert Morris, of a tract that included land originally bought by Jonas Bronck. He would patent 1,900 acres of this land as the Manor of Morrisania in 1697. Witnessed by Claes, the confirmation document was signed by Wessecanoe, Askawanos, and several other signatories claiming to be descendants of the original sellers. Farther north, New York merchant Frederick Philipse I had just finished acquiring the last pieces of the vast personal estate he also started assembling many years before. Buying out his partners, Philipse put together a 92,000-acre domain that ultimately stretched between the Hudson and Bronx rivers from Spuyten Duyvil in the Bronx north to the Croton River. He would patent these lands as the Manor of Philipsburg in 1693. Operating on a less grandiose scale, Jacobus Theuniszen de Kay, a New York baker, and several partners purchased two small tracts of land in the Highlands from the local sachem Sherikham and his associates on April 21 and 25, 1685. Wessecanoe and the increasingly influential Taphow signed both deeds as witnesses.[26]

Wessecanoe and a number of senior sachems signed or witnessed other deeds to lands on both sides of the Hudson at and above the Highlands at this time. Pierwim, still listed in many deeds under various spellings of his honorific name Seweckenamo, signed three conveyances as a senior sachem from Haverstraw along with Sherikham, Askawanos, and a number of other local leaders. These deeds conveyed some eighty-six thousand acres above Peekskill on the east bank of the river to Stephanus van Cortlandt, Francis Rombouts, and Guleyn Verplanck between July 13 and August 24, 1683. All three were prominent New York businessmen who had formed a partnership to acquire lands above Philipse's domain. Ultimately buying out the other men, Van Cortlandt obtained a manorial patent for the estate in 1697.[27]

Dongan also acquired an even more massive estate for himself on the west side of the river above the Highlands in two deeds signed between the fall of 1684 and the following spring. Esopus leaders Pemmyrawech and Harman Hekan, three local sachems, and several others put their marks on the first of these deeds on September 10, 1684. Witnessed by Pierwim and Wessecanoe, this deed gave Dongan rights to lands making up much of the northern part of newly formed Orange County. The property extended from the New Paltz line south to the Moodna Creek. Several months later, on April, 15, 1685, Dongan acquired all the land east of Schunnemunk Mountain from the Moodna Creek south to Haverstraw from Wessecanoe, Pierwim, Maringoman, and several others. Together, these deeds put an unprecedentedly large amount of Lower River Indian land, totaling three hundred thousand acres, into the hands of a single purchaser.[28]

Pierwim, Wessecanoe, and their compatriots did not stop with these sales. Sensing an opportunity, they let Dongan know that they had not been paid for their May 19, 1671, deed to land at Haverstraw registered in East Jersey. Dongan was determined to secure the property for New York. He allowed a couple of New York traders named Nicholas Depui and Peter Jacob Marius to obtain another deed to the same land from the same Indians and their descendants. Claiming they were acting for the original and long-dead purchasers, Depui and Marius sealed what now appears to be a shady deal on July 9, 1686.[29]

Private deals and quiet toleration of corners cut by cronies like Livingston involved Dongan in relationships with buyers and Indians every bit as close, and as uncomfortable, as those binding them publicly in treaties. The governor needed the publicly posted fees and the under-the-table payoffs made by private purchasers as much as he needed to maintain peace and amity with the province's Indians. His personal participation in the rush on Indian lands was made in public and on the cheap without the usual cover of pricey agents or unreliable middlemen. This increased his dependence on the discretion and forbearance of both Indian clients and his fellow colonists. He would need their silence and assent if he was to wring profit from his purchases and avoid corruption charges that could bring him and his administration down.

LOSING ELDERS

Names and numbers of Indians mentioned in deeds and other documents began to change as age and infirmity began removing experienced sachems from public life between 1680 and 1686. Many of the men and women whose names disappeared during these years had been leaders since Dutch times. More than a few were probably well on in years. Although they never openly worked together in one body, their individual efforts as family, town, and coalition leaders had seen their people through wars, epidemics, and relentlessly intensifying pressure to sell land and move away. Their very survival indicated to followers that they were backed by powerful spirits as much as by skill and good connections. They maintained influence by making new ways of doing things work with old ways of thinking. This was the key to their effectiveness, and it helped them grapple with developments that could and did overwhelm larger and more powerful Indian nations.

The heart of this Indian leadership cadre and its reserve of hard-won wisdom suddenly began disappearing sometime during the fall of 1684. By 1686, 41 of the 80 people documented in 1680 in the Munsee File were no longer mentioned in colonial records. If we divide the 1664 guesstimate of 3,000 by 80, each of these sachems could be thought of as leading between 30 and 40 people. A drop in the representation ratio of sachems to people from 1 to 100 to 1 to 30 or 40 could reflect changing political, social, and demographic realities. The lower ratio of 1 to 30 or 40 would correspond with more limited spans of authority of larger numbers of younger and less influential leaders more involved in local land sales than in larger-scale intercultural diplomacy. Although the 24 people who first appeared between 1680 and 1686 somewhat offsets the disappearance of the 41 sachems, subtraction of 17 persons suggests that total Indian population in the Munsee homeland may have dropped to something like 2,400 by 1686. Given that surviving sachems generally led smaller communities by this time, the more probable hypothetical guesstimate should probably be even smaller.

The disappearance of 41 of the 80 people from European records written between 1664 and 1686 represents a loss of more than 20 percent of the total of 210 people in the Munsee File. This was the single highest disappearance of individuals in the file, both in terms of numbers and percentages, at any time between 1630 and 1802. Although the 24 people who appeared for the first time between 1680 and 1686 represented more than half the 41 that disappeared, they constituted a much higher percentage of the overall number of the surviving group. Taken together, these figures constitute an indirect but nevertheless striking index suggesting that Indians in Munsee country lost many of the people who had been their leaders and advisers during most of the preceding twenty to forty years. They were replaced by a much smaller group of successors each of whom almost certainly represented a much higher percentage of the total population after 1686.[30]

Word of a demographic disaster only slowly leaked out. The reasons for this, like so many other things left unsaid in contemporary records, can only be guessed. It is not likely that colonists were indifferent or eager to hide developments in Munsee country that might decisively affect their own lives. It is more likely that Indians, worried that settlers might take advantage of a disaster, tried to keep catastrophic news to themselves. Whatever its whys or wherefores, news that sickness had caused a delegation of Wiechquaesgeck sachems to miss their appointed meeting in New York first reached the city on January 28, 1684. Eight months later, Antoine-Lefebvre, Sieur de la Barre, the man who had replaced Frontenac as governor of New France in 1682, reported that an outbreak of "tertian and double tertian fever" raging through Iroquoia forced his army to return from an expedition sent up the St. Lawrence River to open trade routes through Seneca country. By September 27, 1684, Abenakis who had accompanied La Barre's expedition were spreading "a malignant fever" among their people at the mission towns of Sillery and nearby Three Rivers around Quebec City. On December 21, 1685, the Schaghticoke-speaker Soquans told Albany magistrates that "all the Indians upon the North River were dead" and that "the Indians that live upon [the Hoosic] River are few in number." Something of an overstatement, it nevertheless did not fall far short of the grim reality.[31]

The disease that struck these people was probably malaria. Although the name itself did not exist at the time, the fever of 1684 bore all the classic hallmarks of the disease. Contemporaries knew it by its most visible symptom, an uncontrollable intermittent feverish shaking they called ague. Particularly bad cases were described as tertian or double tertian agues. These "third degree shakes" were marked by three-day-long fevers that redoubled in strength in particularly severe cases. It is not known if the disease was native to North America. Mosquitoes carrying the disease-causing *plasmodium* protozoa, however, flourished wherever conditions were warm and wet enough to support agriculture in the Northeast during colonial times.

Acute diseases like smallpox killed most of their victims within a few days. Malarial protozoa had the opposite effect, causing a wasting disease that weakened those not overcome in its initial onslaught. Many sufferers, especially elders and very young children, often succumbed to pneumonia and other secondary infections. Reported elsewhere in the colonies, earlier outbreaks of malaria may not have caused devastatingly high mortality. Then as now, the disease existed in a number of forms, some more virulent than others. The fever that struck in 1684 may have been a deadlier, recently mutated or newly introduced variety or a familiar form that struck at a time when there were many vulnerable elders to attack.[32]

Whatever the cause, nearly two generations of the most experienced Indian leaders in Munsee country vanished from colonial records during the two years before and after the 1684 fever. Rates of disappearance were the same everywhere in nearly every part of the Munsee homeland. In Esopus country, Pemmyrawech, Mamanuchqua, and Assenerakan were never mentioned again. Farther south at Tappan and Minisink, Aroorhikan and Tomachkapay disappeared from the records. Colonists across the Hudson stopped recording references to Romackqua, Meghtsewakes, and Mamarranack at the same time Tackapousha's sons Pomwaukon, Waumetompack, and Monguamy vanished from colonial records on Long Island. To the west, Peropay, Querameck, and Conackamack in Raritan-Navesink country and Ockanickon, Mamarikickon, and Wassackarous in the Delaware Valley were no longer mentioned. Whether they died or retired from public life, disappearance of so many prominent people over so short a span of time was unprecedented. A similar rate of disappearance would never again occur during the remaining years of the colonial era. Much disappeared with them. They were parents, diplomats, religious leaders, breadwinners, storytellers, craftspeople, and soldiers. Their memories held stores of knowledge and tradition. The smallpox that killed so many young people in 1679 had carried off most of their most promising pupils. Those who survived were few in number and mostly untested. Their elders had had little time to pass on lessons they had learned before they too joined their ancestors.

Part IV

LOSING MUNSEE COUNTRY, 1686–1766

10

SOLDIERING ON, 1686-1701

Tried and tested sachems like Tackapousha, Suscaneman, Pierwim, Memshe, and Wessecanoe soldiered on in the face of demographic catastrophe and land loss. Younger sachems like Taphow and Weequehela joined new leaders like Katonah, Quarapin, and a sachem from northern New Jersey named Meshocorrang making up some of the losses. It is not known if these survivors tried to revitalize old religions that had failed to protect their most dedicated adherents. Awareness that colonists also suffered from the same diseases that afflicted them, combined with general colonial disinterest in missionary enterprises, probably explains why many Indians in the region did not feel the need to seek the help of Christian spirit power. All, however, needed material support available only from Christians. Loss of so many sachems, metewak, captains, hunters, and warriors made them vulnerable as never before. Loss of experienced artisans capable of crafting stone and bone tools and fashioning clay pots and pipes made them dependent on European metal implements, glasswares, and other manufactures. They had also lost all productive lands fronting on the Hudson River and tidal stretches of the Delaware. These losses forced further movements inland to less productive territories.

Deeds where many Indians made final appearances in colonial records did more than force the move inland. They were also a conduit pumping goods into Munsee country. Payments of at least £1,000 in goods and money were stipulated in those deeds that specified payout amounts. Even when subtracting for what was drunk away, used to pay debts, or simply unpaid, the total amount of wealth listed in these deeds was considerable. Quantities of goods and money suddenly available for sharing among much smaller numbers of people were much higher than what most Indians in the Munsee homeland were used to.[1]

It is not known what happened to this wealth. Although few undamaged sites from the era have been found in the Munsee homeland, a sizable proportion of the small amounts of European manufactures recovered indicates that a good portion of this material was probably placed in the graves of children. Much also probably wound up in places like the present-day Boughton Hill National Historic Landmark in Ganondagan State Park in Seneca country. Archaeologists working at this and contemporary town sites in Iroquoia have unearthed substantial amounts of European wares. The occupants of these towns are known to have extracted tribute in the forms of trade goods, wampum, and peltry from River Indians and other nations.[2]

These goods did more than accompany the dead or pay off tribute takers. New leaders got their chances to show respect, skill, and good sense at funerals and other get-togethers where gifts were offered and exchanged. As in the past, those placing goods in the right hands won friends and followers. The mere survival of sensibly generous men and women indicated that they had supernatural support in a region where as noted, everyone, settlers as well as Indians, believed in spirits. Munsee leaders in particular needed all the support they could muster as they made decisions that affected their people's future. Should they stay or leave? Move farther inland or relocate entirely in Canada or in the Far country? If they left, should they stay away or come back like the 156 men, women, and children who returned to Schaghticoke from Canada on July 1, 1685, or those from the Loups in Ottawa country who asked permission to return east to settle among the Wappingers two years later?[3]

Decisions of sachems in Munsee country now tended to affect fewer numbers of followers. It is not certain, however, that this made consensus any easier to achieve. Survivors facing difficult decisions almost certainly felt exposed, unsure, and unsafe. These kinds of feelings often but not always make people more willing to tolerate leaders concentrating power and authority in their hands. In earlier times, colonists often used the word "king" to describe any sachem. After 1686, settlers increasingly familiar with Indian customs largely limited use of the term to particularly influential leaders like Taphow and Weequehela. Although these Indian kings could not in any way be considered despots, they tended to act more forcefully than their predecessors. Their followers, in turn, tolerated more authoritative sachems. Whatever their status, all Munsees had to learn new ways of relating to each other and the outside world if they expected to keep their suddenly smaller, scattered, and increasingly isolated communities intact.

CONSOLIDATION AND ITS COSTS

The Indians of Munsee country were not the only people weighing costs and benefits of increased concentrations of authority during these years. Settlers were also looking for ways to deal with governors and other officials implementing policies meant to bring their provinces closer into the imperial fold and bind them more tightly to royal interests. Colonial administrators charged with these tasks were expected to enact laws and negotiate treaties aimed at maintaining peaceful relations with Indians, especially with Indians like those in Munsee country, who lived, as the expression went, within the bowels of the settlements. Past promises were repeated and new assurances given. Indians were to be equitably treated in courts, council chambers, and board rooms; protected from those who would enslave them or abuse them with alcohol; and be fairly dealt with in trade and land matters. They were also expected to limit their trading to specifically designated places like Albany and were prohibited from sheltering Indians from foreign parts and strangers of any sort without first notifying local authorities.

Local communities still played major roles in Indian relations. Towns continued to form committees to buy Indian land. Many also kept up the practice of appointing overseers to manage relations with Indian neighbors. The trend, however, was toward increasing centralization. Dealings with River Indians and others were quickly taken over by increasingly formal organizations vested with greater powers and wider areas of responsibility. One of the most important of these was Albany's Board of Commissioners of Indian Affairs.

Dongan increasingly relied on Albany magistrates to manage an ever-widening web of Covenant Chain responsibilities. He named Pieter Schuyler, his choice for mayor of the city, and Robert Livingston, who was given the key position of town clerk, to manage Indian affairs north and west of Albany after granting the place its first charter as New York's second city on July 22, 1686. They would be helped by a board made up of aldermen also appointed by the governor. As the informal board's secretary, Livingston was uniquely placed to get news of developments in Indian country long before anyone else knew about them in New York. Livingston was usually smart enough to distinguish rumor from fact and devious enough to use either when he thought it would help make him indispensable to his superiors. Working closely with his colleague and brother-in-law Pieter Schuyler, Livingston became powerful as well as rich.

Letters carrying news of fast-breaking developments in Europe made the two- to three-month Atlantic crossing in increasing numbers at this time. Among the bigger stories was the death of Charles II on February 2, 1685. His brother York, who openly embraced Catholicism, was crowned King James II of England on April 23, 1685. The new king James quickly moved to consolidate royal power in the Northeast by binding the fractious provinces into a single dominion. He started by upholding his late brother's 1684 revocation of Massachusetts Bay's charter. Determined to bring all of New England's provinces into line, he joined Massachussetts Bay with Plymouth, Rhode Island, Connecticut, and New Haven to form a single royal colony. On June 3, 1686, the king appointed Sir Edmund Andros to be royal governor of this new Dominion of New England.[4]

New York became a royal colony when its proprietor ascended to the English throne. Now-royal governor Dongan finally felt secure enough to implement policies crafted to maximally extract revenue from balky colonists and recalcitrant towns. Dongan began by issuing long-dreaded orders directing towns to prove old titles and take out expensive new patents. He chose for his first targets the towns on Long Island. Each had to pay fees of several hundred pounds for new New York patents. On the plus side, these Dongan Patents, as they are still known, affirmed titles of existing landholders. Provisions in new patents required towns to select boards of trustees made up of freeholders to administer commons and unpurchased town lands for the public good. Although new trustees had to pay the governor for their commissions, their appointments ended fears that Dongan or his minions might seize vacant or unpurchased town lands for their own purposes and profits. In order to make the new patents more palatable, trustees also were given first rights to purchase all common and public lands in town bounds on condition that they pay annual fees. Although fee structures and reporting obligations have changed over time, boards of trustees and freeholders and their authority to manage open lands and waters in Long Island remain as intact today as they were when first instituted more than three hundred years ago.

Dongan also used his revenue-raising efforts on Long Island to convince Indians and settlers alike that it was time to finally put an end to expensive and unproductive land wrangles. Hempstead and Oyster Bay settlers, determined to leave as little as possible for royal authorities to confiscate, had already acquired or confirmed purchase of almost all remaining Indian lands in their towns by 1687. No one in Hempstead raised a voice in opposition when Dongan granted a 150-acre reservation on the east side of Cow Neck to Tackapousha on June 24, 1687. Taking the power to sell reservation land out of the Indians' hands, the deed stipulated that Tackapousha and his heirs pay "yearly and every year forever unto his sacred treaty . . . one shilling current money." Three days later, Dongan granted Suscaneman a 200-acre reservation for his people in the town of Oyster Bay, just across Hempstead Harbor from Cow Neck, on the same terms (see map 8).[5]

These tiny reservations must have felt uncomfortably cramped to people used to having the run of the country. Tackapousha and his relatives subsequently spent increasing amounts of their time farther south in the still uncircumscribed bayside Indian towns at Fort Neck, Merrick, and Rockaway, discreetly screened from colonial view by thick stands of salt grass. Far from colonial settlements, these out-of-the-way places lay in small clearings deep within marshlands, bordering bays sheltered from Atlantic waters by narrow sand spits. Suscaneman himself moved westward for a time, settling and joining with friends and relatives in central New Jersey putting their marks onto five sales of tracts in East Jersey astride the contested border with West Jersey.[6]

Ten years had passed since Jersey proprietors had agreed to split their province in two. During that time, they had not managed to agree on a mutually satisfactory border. A 1686 meeting between the governors of New York and the Jersey provinces failed to resolve the problem. Taking matters into their own hands, East Jersey proprietors had their surveyor-general, Scottish Quaker apostate George Keith, run a partial line from Little Egg Harbor on the south to the south branch of Raritan River between April and May 1687. The Keith Line blatantly favored East Jersey and was promptly rejected by the other province. It was at this delicate point in proceedings that word reached the West Jersey capital at Burlington that the province had once again changed hands. Daniel Coxe, physician to Charles II and a naturalist intensely interested in the Americas, had purchased the right to govern West Jersey the previous February. The new governor, who was not a Quaker and who never managed to visit his province, chose to administer the proprietary through the Quaker-dominated government of deputy-governor John Skene, who had been appointed by Coxe's predecessor two years earlier.[7]

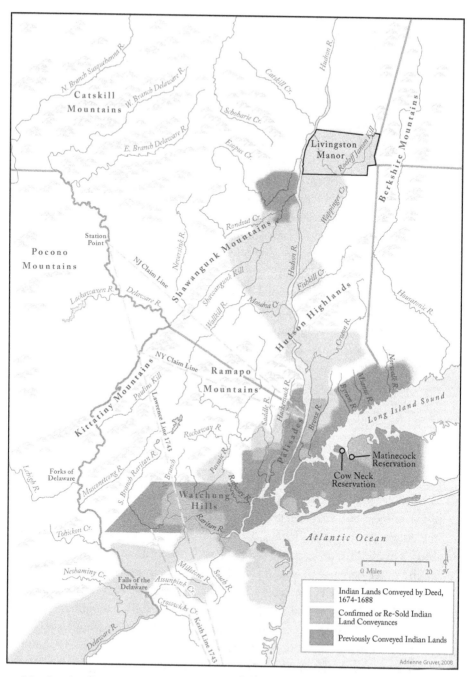

Map 8. Indian land sales in Munsee country, 1674–1688

Wealthy and powerful, Coxe was determined to become the largest landowner in West Jersey. He acquired more than 120,000 acres along with the proprietary shares he bought to gain the controlling interest he needed to get himself appointed governor of the province. Working through West Jersey land agent Adlorde Bowde and his successors, Coxe would ultimately amass an estate of over 1,000,000 acres. Bowde made the first two of these purchases from Metapis, Irooseeke, Taptawappamund, Suscaneman, Sehoppy, and a newcomer named Caponokonickon. As the name suggests, this latter sachem was either one of Ockanickon's close relatives or someone allowed to build on his reputation. These purchases took in large blocks of land above and around the Falls of the Delaware and did more than simply add land to Coxe's growing holdings. They finally opened the long-desired direct route between Raritan Bay and the Delaware River. For the first time, deepwater ports at the East Jersey provincial capital, Perth Amboy, and at West Jersey's capital at Burlington were joined by a secure overland passage.[8]

Like most other purchases, the prices paid to the Indians for these lands were small compared with the vastly larger outlay Coxe paid to royal authorities for the right to govern the province. Like Dongan in New York, Coxe and his opposite numbers in Pennsylvania and East Jersey soon looked west for trade profits as they worked within their provinces for ways to more reliably extract revenue from refractory settlers for themselves and their monarch (whose recent Indulgence Declaration protected the rights of Governor Penn and other Quakers living in Pennsylvania and West Jersey). Coxe and the other governors also made it their business to follow royal instructions ordering them to preserve good relations with Indians who could lead them to western wealth and whose grievances could quickly cloud title and clog cash flow. Indians bringing news of furs in the Ottawa country were quickly heard, as were complaints about surveys taking in too much land and settlers failing to pay land purchase prices. Grievances found to be valid, and there were many, were promptly adjudicated.[9]

Proprietary land reform in Pennsylvania and the Jerseys presented Indians and provincial authorities with abundant opportunities to rake in revenues and build closer relationships. Settlers unable to produce Indian deeds were directed to pay original signatories or their descendants for new copies and ordered to pony up fees for new surveys and patents. Proprietors reluctant to drive away potential rate payers gave those possessing unregistered titles issued by Nicolls or privately obtained from Indians opportunities to settle accounts and buy new patents. Many Quaker and Scotch settlers in Navesink finally decided to obtain proprietary titles to long-encumbered lands. More refractory Puritans in Elizabethtown were less forthcoming. They refused to ask proprietors belonging to sects they detested for dispensations to lands they considered their own. They had used their own money to buy their land from its Indian owners and had paid for patents and all other necessary paperwork required by a lawful English governor before the Jerseys even existed. No one offered to reimburse them for their past expenses. Instead, proprietors made it clear that they intended to milk them for quit rents, fees, and any other cash they could safely extract under color of law.[10]

Acts and intentions meant to concentrate power in fewer hands threatened more than colonial purses or Indian notions of communal autonomy. Consolidation could put an end to arrangements that allowed the weak to play off the powerful. Functionaries unfettered by all but absolute authority could enforce laws and regulations made by distant masters. Individuals, communities, even entire nations and nationalities might be disenfranchised, arbitrarily moved about, or driven away. Consolidation would at minimum rearrange things in favor of the privileged few who possessed the largest estates and the best connections. Less well-off people in colonial and Indian communities faced prospects that would only grow dimmer as power was increasingly concentrated in fewer hands.

Pressure Increases

More experienced Indian leaders in the Munsee homeland must have seen both threats and opportunities in the king's consolidation efforts. The few remaining elder sachems with close relations to merchants and officials could reasonably expect continued dispensations. The majority of Indian leaders after 1686 were much younger and less well-connected than their predecessors. These new men and women must have looked to the future with less assurance. Like their equally apprehensive colonial neighbors dealing with King James's appointees, they almost certainly wondered what would happen if the faraway English monarch succeeded in bringing all of their country under his complete control.

People in nearby New England were already getting a taste of what it would be like to live under imperial rule. Andros, who long cherished dreams of consolidating Crown authority, arrived in Boston with more than a mandate to dissolve existing freestanding chartered governments into a single dominion. Andros also carried orders directing him to combine separate provincial militias into a single military force under his command. Andros tried to assure suspicious colonists that the king had issued the order only to prepare for war with France. Whether he knew it or not, he made this assurance as James quietly negotiated a secret alliance with the French king.

Louis XIV's recent October 18, 1685, revocation of the Edict of Nantes guaranteeing freedom of conscience convinced many French Huguenot Protestants to move to England and the Netherlands. Although the revocation did not lead to massacres or mass expulsions, it intensified traditional Protestant English rancor against Catholics in general and French Catholics in particular. In New York, Huguenot refugees like Louis du Bois and his compatriots at New Paltz and the Depui, De Harte, and related families farther downriver joined with others in the province regarding James's growing closeness with Louis with unconcealed concern.[11]

This was not the least of it. The king gave Andros the power to put an end to town meetings; impose new duties, fees, and taxes; and treat sachems' signatures on Indian deeds as little more than what the governor characterized as "scratches of bear's paws." Unsurprisingly, Andros's efforts in exercising such powers fueled widespread unrest. Connecticut officials refused to surrender their charter, famously and perhaps figuratively hiding it instead in the hollow of a tree since known as the Charter Oak. Other acts of defiance followed. None of this stopped James from issuing still more edicts. Armed with a second royal commission sent from London on April 7, 1688, Andros personally led a force that compelled Dongan to give over governance of the province of New York to the Dominion of New England on September 11, 1688. Leaving a career officer, Francis Nicholson, in charge of New York as his lieutenant governor, Andros went on to receive equally sullen submissions of the proprietary governments of the Jerseys a week later.[12]

Not too far away, another newly arrived governor, Jacques-René de Brisay, Marquis de Denonville, was implementing his own sovereign's consolidation plans. Denonville started by trying to convince the Five Nations to submit to French authority. Iroquois diplomats politely but firmly refused. Determined to bring the Five Nations to heel, Denonville led a mixed force of three thousand French troops and Indian warriors through Seneca country during the summer of 1687. The Senecas withdrew before this overwhelming force. Marching through their country, Denonville burned Ganondagan and other hastily abandoned Seneca towns and began constructing a fort at the strategic pass at Niagara. Satisfied that the one hundred men he stationed at the post would be enough to cut the Five Nations off from the west, Denonville returned to Montreal.[13]

His army reached Montreal just as an epidemic of measles ravaged the St. Lawrence Valley. Most of the Indians living at Caughnawaga and other mission towns, including some expatriate River Indians and even more from New England, fell ill from the disease. Hundreds reportedly succumbed to the spotted fever before it disappeared with the return of warm weather. Spring also brought starvation and sickness to the post at Niagara that had been immediately besieged by vengeful Senecas. Farther east, River Indian warriors joined Mohawk war parties striking outlying French settlements along the St. Lawrence. A chastened Denonville received the seven survivors from abandoned Niagara, who had been carried back to Montreal by a passing party of Mesquakie Indians, and accepted a truce offered by the three central Iroquois Confederacy nations. The Senecas and Mohawks at the western and eastern doors of the league longhouse would have none of it. Only a Mohawk ambush of an Onondaga delegation on its way to treat with the governor at Montreal cut off negotiations that may have split the confederacy and detached the Five Nations from the Covenant Chain alliance.[14]

River Indian sachems must have followed these developments with growing concern as they gingerly grasped their ends of the Covenant Chain. Their young men, to be sure, probably welcomed the opportunity to win battle honors in Canada. The sachems, however, could not help knowing that the other end of their Covenant Chain bound them to an increasingly detested monarch, resented by visibly incensed colonial neighbors openly talking insurrection. The situation posed an uncomfortable but familiar dilemma. Munsee leaders had to find a middle way to ensure continued royal protection from land-hungry colonists without incurring their antagonism. This would have been a daunting task for experienced leaders at the head of stable sizable communities. It would be a hard classroom for new sachems trying to hold together demoralized survivors confronting seemingly continual epidemics and facing imminent war and dispossession.

Whatever their age or experience, sachems in the Munsee homeland were not without their own resources, however. They could still shelter Five Nations families taking refuge at Catskill and other Hudson Valley locales while their warriors helped Covenant Chain Indian allies against the French. They still held land that settlers could only peacefully acquire with deeds approved by royal officials. News of growing unrest throughout England and its empire could only have encouraged sachems relying upon continued existence of exploitable divisions for their people's survival.

REVOLUTION AND WAR

James's dream of a consolidated dominion under his complete control came to a sudden end when a force of fifty-three Dutch warships, four hundred transports, and twenty thousand men appeared off the south English coast in November 1688. Under the nominal command of an English admiral, the force was actually led by the same Cornelis Evertsen, the younger, who had taken New York in 1673. The force encountered no opposition and quickly gathered considerable support. Among the men Evertsen landed without incident was the Dutch stadtholder Willem Hendrijck of Orange, Andros's old friend, James's brother-in-law, and the figure rebellious English Protestants decided should replace their wildly unpopular current king. After a confusing but largely bloodless month of machinations, marches, and countermarches, Willem's supporters prevailed over James's divided forces. James fled to France, where Louis gave him asylum and promises of arms and men that ultimately went nowhere. Willem and his wife were subsequently crowned King William III and Queen Mary II of England on February 13, 1689. They accepted a new bill of rights acknowledging Parliament's right to limit royal authority and prepared England for the inevitable war with France that soon followed.

News of William and Mary's ascension reached the North America a few months later. Colonists in the English provinces rushed to proclaim themselves loyal subjects of the new sovereigns. James's detested dominion was promptly dismantled and Andros was arrested in Boston. In New York City, Nicholson got away before five hundred armed colonists led by a militia captain named Jacob Leisler seized Fort James. Acting on his own initiative, Leisler set up a caretaker government to hold the province for the Crown until duly constituted authorities arrived from London.

In the meantime, William and Mary declared war on France on May 7, 1689. Known in the colonies as King William's War, this wide-ranging conflict would embroil most European nations and their empires in a struggle that would drag on until 1697. Like the English takeover in 1664, and George Washington's fight with the French at Fort Necessity in Western Pennsylvania in 1754, it can be said that the first shots of this war were fired in America by Denonville's troops in Seneca country in 1687. Like

the arbitrary borders erected by royal decrees and disputed by colonists, formal commencement of hostilities was little noticed by River Indian and
other Covenant Chain allies who were already fighting against the French.
Regime change, however, was another thing. Sachems could not help
noticing that a mob carried Leisler to power. They also noticed that magistrates at Albany and other places rejected Leisler's initial efforts to make
them submit to his authority. As they had during uncertain power transi-
tions in the past, they did what they could to keep colonists guessing and
options open. Sachems delayed performing rituals formally recognizing
Leisler as their acting governor as long as possible. They may have also
helped spread rumors that they loyally planned to help Andros retake the
government if and when he returned to New York.[15]

In the meantime, men from the Upper and Lower River Indian towns
were among the 1,500 warriors under Five Nations command that fell on the
French village of Lachine just outside Montreal on the morning of July 26,
1689. They burned the village, killed more than 200 of its inhabitants, and carried 120 prisoners back to their towns. Denonville responded by ordering that
all remaining western garrisons burn their stores, demolish their forts, and
withdraw to Montreal. In one stroke, Denonville's policy of western expansion
ended as New France went on the defensive. Frontenac, who arrived with
fresh troops from Europe a month later to replace Denonville, could do little
more than guard against further Indian attacks as he reorganized his forces and
trained the troops to march and fight in North American forests.

Like their other Covenant Chain allies, River Indian war captains did not
see the need to send out large scouting parties to screen the frontier with
New France during the snowy winter of 1689–1690. No one was standing
guard when 210 soldiers and warriors dispatched by Frontenac poured out
of the snow-filled forest through the open gates of Schenectady during the
night of February 8, 1690. They killed over sixty townsfolk, took another
eighty prisoner, and burned the town down. The raid was not an isolated incident. Two other French columns destroyed English frontier settlements at
Salmon Falls, New Hampshire, and Casco Bay, Maine.

The raids shocked divided and uncertain colonists into realizing that
they needed to focus their energies on the French and not on each other.
Just seventeen miles east of Schenectady, Albany magistrates finally accepted
Leisler as their caretaker commander after his chief lieutenant arrived with
160 men to reinforce the city garrison on April 4, 1690. Wessecanoe and
Mindawassa allowed 18 of their warriors to join a second group of rein-

forcements after reluctantly recognizing Leisler as Corlear. They promised to send another 60 young men when the 900 militiamen pledged by Leisler and the governors of neighboring provinces assembled at Albany for a concerted assault on Montreal, planned for the coming summer.[16]

A motley assemblage of 150 New York militiamen and another 100 or so Mohawk and River Indian warriors gradually straggled into Albany during the next few months. They were joined by a few hundred Connecticut men. Massachusetts and Plymouth held back their promised contingents, preferring to send most of their men to join a seaborne attack on Quebec. The little army at Albany finally marched to the lower end of Lake Champlain in July 1690. There it stopped to wait for additional supplies and reinforcements from the other four Iroquois nations. These never came. Instead, a veteran Albany frontier merchant-diplomat and Leislerian partisan with strong ties to the Five Nations named Aernout Cornelissen Viele brought news that smallpox was ravaging their towns. Men and women in the camp were soon down with the disease. The army fell apart as stricken sufferers made for homes in New York and Connecticut. The sickness they carried spread wherever they went. Thousands fell ill, and hundreds reportedly died.[17]

The impact of this epidemic on Indian communities in the Munsee homeland is unknown. Munsee File documentation does not show appreciable rises or falls in documentary appearance-disappearance rates either in 1690 or during the years that immediately followed. This does not mean this smallpox epidemic passed without effect in Munsee country. The experienced sachems Metapis, Wessecanoe, Mindawassa, and Askawanos were last mentioned in 1690. Each had been in close contact with authorities in New York at the time they disappeared from colonial records. Unlike their colleagues in other River Indian communities, they had sent some of their warriors to Albany. All but Metapis lived directly along the Hudson River route taken by men returning to their homes after smallpox broke up their luckless little force on the shores of Lake Champlain. These factors increase the likelihood that the contagion either carried off or debilitated some if not all of these leaders.

News of the failure of New England's Quebec expedition in October put a sad end to a dismal year. Indians in the Munsee homeland contending with an epidemic that did not let up when cold weather came could only look back ruefully at the sorry performance of their Covenant Chain allies. Exhausted and exasperated, everyone stayed home during the plague winter of 1690–1691. Luckily for them, neither the French nor their Indian allies mounted attacks. In New York, people turned their attention to a slowly unfolding political drama being played out in Manhattan.

A company of royal troops led by Major Richard Ingoldsby arrived at the tip of lower Manhattan in front of the post Leisler had rechristened Fort William Henry on February 18, 1691. Ingoldsby's ship had been separated from the vessel carrying both his credentials and the newly appointed royal governor Colonel Henry Sloughter. Leisler decided to wait until the governor arrived before giving up the colony to someone not carrying the proper papers. Sloughter's ship sailed into the harbor a month later. In the meantime, several men were killed in fighting that broke out between Leisler's and Ingoldsby's troops. Sloughter and Ingoldsby finally forced Fort William Henry's surrender with the help of a local ship captain named William Kidd on March 20, 1691. Resenting Leisler's resistance and knowing that the king had not formally recognized the caretaker government, Sloughter gave his ear to the many enemies Leisler made during his brief stewardship. The new governor acted quickly, trying, convicting, and ordering the execution of Leisler and eight of his closest supporters for treason. Although Sloughter commuted the sentences of six of the condemned men, he had Leisler and his chief lieutenant Jacob Milbourne hanged, drawn, and quartered on May 26, 1691.

Whether they succumbed to disease or fell from favor, Munsee leaders last mentioned in documents by 1686 had not returned to colonial notice by 1691. Sachems like Wessecanoe and Mindawassa who supported Leisler never again appeared in colonial documents. Tackapousha, who never formally recognized Leisler's authority, quickly stepped forward to welcome Sloughter to his new province. Sachems from the Highlands and Schaghticoke soon followed suit.[18]

At these meetings, Sloughter gave Pieter Schuyler permission to attempt another assault on Montreal. Scraping together a force of 120 settlers, 80 Mohawks, and 66 Schaghticoke and River Indians, Schuyler set out on June 21, 1691. It took more than a month of hacking through deep forests to reach Montreal. On August 1, 1691, they fought a bloody but inconclusive battle with the city's defenders. Unable to advance farther, the army retreated to Albany. Nearly 20 percent of the force, including six River Indians, were killed during the campaign.[19]

Sloughter did not live long enough to hear about the latest failure. He died suddenly on July 23, 1691, and was replaced by Ingoldsby. The interim governor traveled up to Albany on September 2, 1691, to shore up the dispirited garrison and condole his Covenant Chain Indian allies for their losses. He had to sit quietly while Five Nations speakers scolded the English for squandering the lives of their men in piecemeal attacks. Ingoldsby distributed gifts and assured the assembled sachems that the English would soon bring their collective power to bear on the French. Renewing their Covenant Chain alliance, he asked that they put at least a temporary halt to their attacks on Waganis Indians.[20]

FAR COUNTRY INDIANS TRY TO MOVE EAST

Waganis was short for Dowaganhaes, an Iroquois name for people who today call themselves Anishinabeg. Also known as Chippewas or Ojibwas, in 1691 Dowaganhaes territories extended around the upper Great Lakes just west of Ottawa country. Like other inhabitants of what the French called the Pays d'en Haut, "Upper Country," people in the fur-rich Dowaganhaes lands had been trading with the French for generations and fighting successfully against the Five Nations since at least 1670. Working in part from the theory that the enemy of my enemy is my friend, Dowaganhaes allowed Northern Indians, River Indians, and other nations often at odds with the Five Nations to trap, trade, and, if they wanted, settle among them.

Daniel Coxe, the man who had opened the overland route across New Jersey and dreamed of funneling trade through a Delaware Water Gap still firmly in Indian hands, was not the only would-be fur-trade empire builder looking longingly to the west. Albanians like Aernout Viele, Robert Livingston, and Pieter Schuyler also dreamed of opening a way to the Dowaganhaes lands and other places in the Far country as the war with France and her Indian allies raged on. Dowaganhaes people tired of war found themselves attracted by the cheaper prices of higher-quality English wares. Hoping to pull out of the fighting and open a way to Albany, they asked River Indian friends to help them make a separate peace with their English and Iroquois enemies. A Dowaganhaes delegation traveled to Esopus to begin talks during the summer of 1690. They arrived just as men returning from the abortive Montreal expedition spread smallpox across the Hudson Valley. The entire delegation came down with the disease and died.[21]

This did not stop the New Yorkers from sending a delegation of their own. On October 2, 1691, Ingoldsby gave Albany and Esopus magistrates permission to each dispatch six men west in the company of no more than twenty-five Indians. Led by Pieter Schuyler's younger brother Arent, the party stayed away for nearly a year. They did not, however, return with any

Dowaganhaes people. On August 14, 1692, the younger Schuyler instead sent word to Ingoldsby announcing that he had arrived at Minisink with a party of Shawnees. The message included the minutes of a meeting with Shawnees and Minisinks he had attended in the Far country the previous May. At the meeting, a Minisink man named Mattaseet, who had been living among the Shawnees for the past nine years, offered them land above the Delaware Water Gap and promised that the governor would make peace with the Five Nations on their behalf.[22]

The Shawnees were a much-scattered people who were probably living somewhere along the upper Ohio Valley when Europeans first came to Munsee country. They had been living with River Indian and other Eastern Algonquian expatriates at various spots in the Far country at least since La Salle noted that one hundred Chaouanans joined with Loups and Miamis against the Iroquois on the St. Joseph River in 1681. Many moved west the following year among Indians from many nations settling together in the vast Grand Village of Kaskaskia. There they helped La Salle build Fort St. Louis atop the high bluff of Starved Rock, dominating the sprawling Indian metropolis on the banks of the Illinois River in present-day Utica, Illinois.[23]

People from many nations gathered at Kaskaskia to escape Iroquois war parties then ranging unchecked throughout the region. Five Nations warriors laying siege to the town for six days in 1684 evidently shattered whatever illusory sense of security its inhabitants may have felt. Most scattered after the Iroquois warriors burned their fields and withdrew. Although information is sketchy, Shawnees and their Loup companions evidently moved south and east. Some among the latter party were probably with Indians from Wawyachtenokse requesting asylum among the Wappingers in 1687. Five years later, Five Nations sachems, knowing that New York officials needed allies to press their war against New France, were in a less belligerent frame of mind. Meeting with the Shawnees at Manhattan in Fort William Henry on August 18, 1692, Ingoldsby assured them that they would be safe from Iroquois attack, and welcome if their people came to New York. Four days later, Ingoldsby ordered that Arent Schuyler escort the ambassadors on their return journey to bring their people back "to settle among our Indians with their peltry."[24]

A letter from Arent's older brother temporarily halted proceedings. The elder Schuyler reminded Ingoldsby that the Shawnees were still formally at war with the Five Nations. He went on to suggest that the governor ask "10 or 12 of the most important Schowaenos" to stay behind in Albany while his brother accompanied five or six prominent men from each of the Five Nations to conclude a formal peace treaty with their people. Ingoldsby had barely responded to Schuyler's letter when his replacement, Colonel Benjamin Fletcher, arrived to officially take up the governorship of New York on September 8, 1692. Fletcher wasted little time. Meeting with the Shawnees in the presence of their Minisink sponsors on September 17, he promised to help make peace with the Five Nations on their behalf and asked them to hurry back with their people. Fletcher made a slight change in personnel before sending them off. He replaced Arent Schuyler with the far more experienced Aernout Viele. Although Viele was only slightly less out of favor as a Leislerian, his firing by Leisler from his post as translator in 1690 put him in better odor with the anti-Leislerians. Together with Mattaseet, Viele and the Shawnees made their way west. Meanwhile, on October 25, 1692, Fletcher secured Five Nations approval for a Shawnee relocation and the promise that they would make peace with Far Indians at his first Covenant Chain meeting with them. For the next year or so, the English heard little but vague rumors concerning the progress made by their western embassy.[25]

Swift Arrow Shores Things Up

Fletcher arrived with explicit orders to reconcile divided colonists, strengthen the frayed Covenant Chain alliance, root out any lingering opposition, and form a united front against the French. He hardly had time to get the lay of the land before word of yet another unexpected mid-winter attack reached New York. On February 6, 1693, six hundred men sent by Frontenac suddenly appeared in the Mohawk Valley. The surprised Mohawks barely had enough time to escape before Frontenac's men marched into and burned all three of their towns. In less than a week they destroyed most of the Mohawk winter stores and captured more than three hundred of their people. Only Frontenac's determination to systematically lay waste to Mohawk country gave the Covenant Chain allies time to respond. A force of nearly six hundred Englishmen, Mohawks, Oneidas, and Schaghticokes led by Pieter Schuyler caught up with the heavily encumbered withdrawing French column, slowed by prisoners and a sudden thaw. In a running battle Schuyler's force killed between thirty and eighty of the raiders and liberated most of their prisoners.[26]

Fletcher reacted to news of the attack with a swiftness that surprised those used to more dilatory responses by governors. Although he arrived in Albany too late to help local forces chase the French back to Canada, he impressed returning soldiers, militiamen, and warriors by personally accompanying the several hundred soldiers sent to buck up the city's defenses. Mohawk sachems sat quietly while he chided them for allowing the French to surprise their towns. They listened politely as he praised their courage during the counterattack, and brightened considerably when he ordered Schuyler to find shelter for their families in the town and replenish their corn stores. Pleased to meet a governor whom they hoped would do more than fight the French to the last Mohawk, they pledged continued loyalty, announced plans to rebuild their towns closer to Albany, and conferred the title Cayenquiragoe, "Swift Arrow," on a man whose name meant arrow maker in his own tongue.[27]

When the roads cleared the following spring, Fletcher traveled throughout his new province replacing undependable officials with obedient placemen. He was determined, like Andros before him, to forge the provinces into a united front against the French. Fletcher was a hard-bitten campaigner rather than a cultured staff officer like Andros. He spared few feelings and personally looked at all reports, tolerating few fools. The governor lost little time quieting fears sparked by an improbable report that 350 Tappans and Hackensacks were preparing to avenge Leisler and swiftly squelched similarly false rumors of French and Indian attacks.[28]

Fletcher kept a careful ear open for news of real threats. He got an earful from a delegation of Indians from the upper part of the Delaware River on May 10, 1693. He was then in Philadelphia to take control of the province. Quakers had not sent men to fight against the French and were suspected as secret supporters of the ousted James. A wary William and Mary temporarily suspended Penn's charter to Pennsylvania and put the colony under Fletcher's supervision. He met with Delaware River Indians between meetings, interviews, and interrogations with various office holders and aspirants. Their speaker complained that Senecas angered by their failure to help them against the French had attacked their people while out hunting the previous summer. Fletcher promised that he would order the Senecas and other Covenant Chain Iroquois allies to halt further attacks and suggested that the Senecas and the Delaware River Indians send some men to Albany.[29]

Fletcher made his request as Indians in Munsee country were trying to keep as low a profile as possible in the foreign wars and colonial infighting that threatened the fortunate few who survived the late epidemics. On the Hudson, inexperienced sachems, unsure of what to make of recent political developments in New York, kept their warriors at home and put off welcoming Fletcher until things cleared up. A miffed Fletcher would have none of it. On July 6, 1693, he addressed the River Indian sachems as children when they finally met with him in Albany on the last day of Covenant Chain renewal meetings with the Five Nations and Schaghticokes. Taking his time to make his points, Fletcher reprimanded them for not coming sooner and rebuked them for leaving their families defenseless while they went off hunting and drinking. He ordered them to send warriors to scout the frontier, offering a substantial reward for the head of any enemy killed within three miles of Albany or Schenectady.[30]

Rumors that Indians on Long Island both planned an insurrection and feared an English attack kept their sachems away from Manhattan. Sachems representing a reportedly ailing Tackapousha finally officially paid their respects to Fletcher on May 4, 1694. Tales allegedly spread by a River Indian three months later evidently panicked the inexperienced young Long Island sachems. It took Fletcher another round of good words and gifts to finally assure Tackapousha's successors of his friendship on October 1, 1694.[31]

SHAWNEES ARRIVE AND KING WILLIAM'S WAR ENDS

A distressingly plausible rumor suddenly reached New York from New Jersey on February 3, 1694. Fletcher's deputy in East Jersey, Andrew Hamilton, sent word that 150 French and Indians were said to be on their way to detach the Minisinks from the Covenant Chain. Knowing that Frontenac liked to launch raids during snowy weather, Fletcher dispatched Arent Schuyler to Minisink country that same day to look into things. He arrived at the main Minisink town on February 7 to find that the alleged French and Indians were in fact three New Yorkers and two Shawnees who had stopped by the town six days earlier. They were sent by Viele to bring news of his progress with the Shawnees and to fetch gunpowder and supplies from Albany. These provisions, they said, would be needed by the seven hundred Shawnees who planned to come loaded down with beavers in the spring. The Minisink sachems also told Schuyler that they were afraid that Senecas may have waylaid an overdue hunting party in reprisal for not paying their tribute that year. Schuyler promised to inform the governor of these developments and immediately left. He arrived in New York three days later with the news.[32]

It is not known exactly when the Shawnees arrived, how many came east, or where they first settled. The group guided by Viele probably traveled along the ancient route leading to Ottawa country that troops led by Edward Braddock later cut into a wagon road. This route, still followed by U.S. Route 40, linked the Potomac River with the Monongahela River just below where it joins the Allegheny at Pittsburgh to form the Ohio River. European records mentioning later Shawnee communities along this route further suggest that this was the path Viele's party took to the Delaware Valley.

The first Shawnee contingent probably made its way to Minisink country by the summer of 1694. Others soon settled along the Susquehanna and Potomac rivers. Like the Susquehannocks who moved from the Delaware to the new town of Conestoga built under Anglo-Iroquois auspices in their old country in 1690, Shawnees settling on the west side of the river just above the Delaware Water Gap lived inconspicuously. They had good reason to do so. They evidently moved among the Minisinks before making peace with the Five Nations. In New York on June 11, 1696, Fletcher heard their complaints that Senecas had killed thirty of their people during the journey east. Fletcher sent Arent Schuyler to Albany to confirm the disturbing report and to ask the Five Nations if they would receive the Shawnees as friends. Several years would pass before an invitation was issued.[33]

Seneca attacks on Shawnees seeking English protection did nothing to further formation of a united front against the French. Infighting and defections threatened to tear the Covenant Chain alliance apart from within. Senecas ignored Fletcher's appeals to stop attacking the "few miserable Indians upon Delaware River . . . who hurt nobody and belong to Pennsylvania which is in the Covenant Chain and under my government." Farther east, River Indians were so frequently assaulted when traveling in New England that Fletcher ordered that they not cross into Massachusetts until the war was over. And in the crucial center, Iroquois who had suffered most from the fighting listened with increasing interest to Frontenac's invitations to join their relatives at Caughnawaga.[34]

Warriors armed and supplied by Europeans feeding and sheltering their displaced families were tired of the endlessly inconclusive war of raids and counterstrikes. Although many had died and entire villages like Schenectady and Lachine, and nearly every Seneca and Mohawk town, had been destroyed, no decisive blows were struck. And nothing could hide the fact that the Five Nations and their Indian allies were bearing the brunt of the war. Frontenac emphatically drove the point home during the summer of 1696. Leading two thousand men from the newly reconstructed Fort Frontenac at the head of the St. Lawrence, the governor of New France swept through Onondaga and Oneida towns thus far untouched by the fighting. As they had done with almost every other Iroquois town, they burned the hastily abandoned settlements and destroyed everything they could not carry away. Moving quickly during the height of the campaigning season, Frontenac's force was able to return to Montreal unmolested.

Fletcher knew that the gifts, promises, and supplies he distributed to Five Nations sachems when he met with them a month later could not condole them for their losses. In his report to the home government, Fletcher wrote, "we cannot expect the assistance from the Five Nations as formerly." Although some River Indian warriors continued to guard the frontier, the governor also knew that he could no longer depend on their support. Fletcher's request that the River Indians concentrate their settlements at a few designated locales was ignored. Many had already left for Canada or moved east among Abenaki friends still fighting against the New Englanders. Several of the latter were probably among the River Indians arrested by New Englanders for killing some settlers while out hunting during the spring of 1697. Two women from the party escaped from jail and made their way back to Schaghticoke after the settlers put two of their companions to death for the killings. On hearing the news, the Schaghticoke sachem Soquans quickly traveled to Albany, where he reported the arrests and demanded release of the surviving prisoners.[35]

In Europe, exhausted combatants signed the Treaty of Ryswick, ending the war on September 30, 1697. As most earlier treaties had done, the peace of Ryswick left things pretty much as they were at the start of the fighting. There were of course some changes. Louis XIV recognized William III as king of England. Prisoners were exchanged, and captured territory was mostly returned.

The years between 1689 and 1697 had been a disaster. Smallpox and war had ravaged the region. Less than half of 2,550 Iroquois warriors and 90 of 160 River Indian and Schaghticoke men counted by the English at the beginning of the war remained within what the English regarded as their sphere of influence when the Treaty of Ryswick was signed. Few of these men had died in battle. Many had perished with their loved ones in the

1690–1691 epidemic. Others either left or were carried off along with their families to New France.[36]

LAND SALES IN A TIME OF WAR AND PESTILENCE

River Indians and their Five Nations Covenant Chain allies were still formally at war with France when Fletcher received word that orders for his replacement had been prepared in London on March 17, 1696. Determined to do everything possible to secure Indian support for the war, Fletcher had held a tight rein over purchases of Indian lands up to that time. This did not mean that he halted all sales. Fletcher and his predecessor Leisler sanctioned at least fifty sales of lands in Munsee country and granted purchase licenses for others between 1689 and 1696. The frequency of these sales increased in direct proportion to their distance from the frontier. Few colonists wanted to buy, and even fewer Indians wanted to sell, land liberally watered by the blood of its defenders. More than half of lands sold at this time were on western Long Island, far from the fighting (see map 9). In deeds identifying them as Massapequa Indians, Tackapousha, his sons Samos and Chopeycannows, the latter's grandson Will Chippie, Suscaneman's son Surrukunga, and Suscaneman's old cronies Syhar and Werah conveyed fourteen tracts at the south end of the town of Oyster Bay. The same people mostly identified farther east as Secatogue Indians sold several necks and tracts of sandy pinelands in the town of Huntington in ten deeds. At this time, a man named Wamehas rose to prominence as one of the more influential Secatogue sachems as he signed twenty-six alienation and confirmation deeds to Indian lands mostly within Huntington town bounds.[37]

Suscaneman returned to Oyster Bay as well. In two deeds signed with Werah and Syhar on March 7, 1693, he gave three town residents gifts of land around and overlapping part of the unsurveyed two hundred–acre reservation Dongan had set aside for his people at the head of Hempstead Harbor. The reservation, which straddled the long-contested border between Oyster Bay and Hempstead, remained a sore point. A little more than one year later, Suscaneman complained to Fletcher that Hempstead men were cutting timber on reservation lands. Determined to prevent problems there from further adding to the worries of Indians and settlers already suspecting one another of dark plots and evil intentions, Fletcher ordered new surveys for both the town border and the reservation.[38]

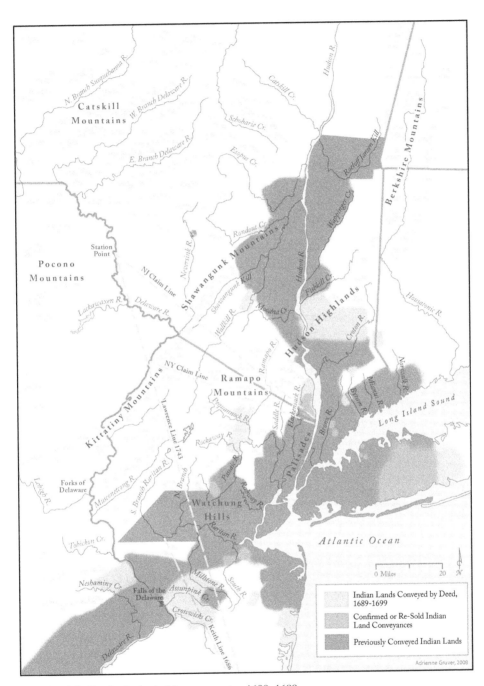

Map 9. Indian land sales in Munsee country, 1689–1699

Other sachems primarily sold gores (wedges of unsold land between purchased properties revealed during surveys) elsewhere in Munsee country. Katonah, Patthunck (an older man who rose to notice in deeds signed at this time), Patthunck's son Wapeto Patthunck, and several compatriots sold five small tracts on both sides of the lower Hudson. Farther southwest, Taphow, Memshe, Claes, and a young sachem named Nowenock sold three tracts. Nowenock conveyed the first, a parcel of land along the Dead River in and around the present-day Great Swamp National Wildlife Refuge at the headwaters of the Passaic, on March 10, 1690. Taphow sold a second tract where the Pequannock River joins the Wanaque River above Pompton Lakes on April 1, 1694. On June 6, 1695, Tatapagh (noted in the deed as Jaiapagh, sachem of Menissing), Memshe, and several associates that included young sachems named Renap and Nackpunck, sold a third tract, comprising 5,500 acres on the Pequannock River to Arent Schuyler. Schuyler had passed through the Pequannock Valley on his way to Minisink a year earlier. His purchase of land there shows why sachems often did their best to discourage visitors whose view of their country frequently excited more acquisitive inclinations.[39]

Fletcher gave his blessings to much larger grants, and collected much higher commissions, once it was clear that the war was ending and he was returning to England. In the space of less than a year, the lame-duck governor sanctioned twenty purchases of land from Indians in every corner of Munsee country. Fletcher is best remembered for giving vast estates to cronies like John Evans and permitting others to purchase enormous expanses of Indian land. The most extravagant of these vaguely bounded and even more vaguely worded grants took in hundreds of thousands of acres north and west of Albany. Only one was made on a comparable scale in Munsee country. On June 25, 1696, Taphow, Sherikham, Maringoman, Apiskaemo, and several others signed over the Kakiate Patent, a territory embracing over one hundred thousand acres west of Dongan's former three hundred thousand-acre estate sold to Evans by Fletcher and christened Fletcherdon by the appreciative purchaser.[40]

On Long Island, Tackapousha made his last appearance in colonial records as the primary signatory to a deed turning his people's share of land at Fort Neck over to Oyster Bay townsfolk. Signing the deed on October 6, 1696, the aged sachem stipulated that his people be allowed "to live upon, plant, or sow upon any of the land of said neck that has been already improved by the Indians both for ourselves, our sons, and our son's sons." His children sold their rights to other parts of Fort Neck as well as several small tracts in the interior of Huntington around the same time. Among other sales, Harman Hekan, Tatapagh, Renap, and a number of others signed over a tract between Maghkaghkemeck and Napanoch above Minisink on June 8, 1696, while Nimham I sold land at Fishkill, in Dutchess County, on June 24, 1696. In East Jersey, Weequehela and Quanolam sold land at Manalapan, Pennypack Creek, Manasquan, and Crosswicks Creek in four sales made between September 2, 1696, and March 12, 1698. On the other side of the still-disputed Keith Line, the West Jersey Society, a syndicate of forty-eight London merchants and gentlemen, purchased controlling interest in the province in 1692. Not limiting themselves to one province, they also bought up a goodly chunk of East Jersey proprietary shares. Indian land in Munsee country along the Delaware within West Jersey charter bounds remained largely unmolested while new proprietors fought old for control of proprietary interests in the province.[41]

POSTWAR LAND AFFAIRS

The arrival of Richard Coote, Earl of Bellomont, on April 12, 1698, brought a temporary halt to the reckless land spree. Like everyone else in British America, Bellomont knew that the new peace with France was little more than an uneasy truce that could be easily broken and in any event would not last very long. He was also aware that feelings over the Leisler affair still ran high. Making matters worse, Fletcher's extravagant land grants angered the overwhelming majority of settlers, who did not benefit from them, and alienated the Indians who lost their lands. Bellomont carefully felt things out before granting privileges and handing out positions. He knew his placemen would waste little time pressuring already sorely pressed Indians for ever-larger portions of their shrinking ancestral estate.

The question of how much was too much assumed new dimensions as the Indians of Munsee country, for the first time since the coming of Europeans, faced the real possibility of losing virtually all of their remaining ancestral territory. Bellomont was determined to prevent even the remnants of Indian communities clinging to remaining lands in Westchester and Long Island from leaving their homeland. Most, he knew, would surely go to Canada. Once there, their knowledge of the English and local geography would provide a help to the French out of proportion to their small numbers. Such help would put the English at a severe disadvantage when hostilities inevitably broke out again. Bellomont would have to move cautiously to prevent the defection of River Indians and friends and relatives who might follow their example.

The Indians of Munsee country were by no means the only constituency Bellomont had to worry about where land was concerned. The new governor arrived as opportunities to acquire cheap lands, long a major drawing point for immigrants, were shrinking to insignificance. In the Jerseys and in Pennsylvania, which regained its charter in 1696, proprietors monopolized access to all but the contested unsurveyed borderlands of their provinces. Along the Hudson River in New York, the Van Rensselaer, Evans, Livingston, Philipse, and Van Cortlandt families alone held more than 75 percent of all unfenced open land not still in Indian hands. Bellomont had to deal with an angry, apprehensive, and war-weary citizenry still polarized by Leislerian rifts, who felt they owed little to Indians and cared even less about Indian rights to land or life.[42]

Bellomont attempted to mollify settlers outraged by some of Fletcher's more flagrantly excessive grants by starting annulment proceedings that finally threw the three hundred thousand acres of Evans's Fletcherdon Manor open to new buyers in 1699. Determined to keep restive River Indians in the English fold, he had officials all but halt new acquisitions of Indian land for two years. Settlers were able to make only three purchases from Indians in Munsee country during the year following receipt of word that King William's War had ended. Suscaneman sold one small tract in Oyster Bay. In Huntington, Charles Pamequa sold another plot of land. A young sachem named Wackemane and his compatriots sold a third small plot to the town of Bedford in Westchester County. No longer able to easily play off rivals at these locales, sachems in each place increasingly concentrated on reducing sources of friction with their neighbors in order to maintain access to vacant sections of sold lands. In pursuit of this goal, several sachems confirmed earlier sales while others helped local townsfolk mark out more precise borders of earlier purchases.[43]

This temporary respite did not last long. Colonial officials started reissuing purchase licenses whose halt had all but stopped the transformation of stretches of Munsee homeland into colonial private property in 1699. Indians subsequently signed no fewer than fifty-one deeds to lands in every part of Munsee country by the time a new governor arrived from England in late 1702 to replace Bellomont, who had died suddenly on March 5, 1701. Most of these deeds conveyed small tracts around the edges of settlement. The names of Taphow, Nowenock, Meshocorrang, and Memerescum began to appear above and before those of older leaders like Memshe and Claes in signing orders of Indians placing marks on the twelve deeds to land in northern East Jersey negotiated at this time (see map 10). Taphow's particular rise to prominence was explicitly put into words in the July 29, 1702, deed to land along the Rockaway River that identified him as the "sagamore and commander in chief of all the Indians inhabiting what the English call the northern part of the Jerseys."[44]

Farther south, the primary position of Weequehela's mark on six deeds to lands near the provincial capital at Perth Amboy signaled his rise to prominence as the Indian King of New Jersey. Just to the west, Caponokonickon conveyed two small tracts at Assunpink and Doctors creeks. In Esopus country, Mamanuchqua's daughter Dostou sold some land at Coxsingh around present-day High Falls about the same time her son Hendrick Hekan and some colleagues conveyed two tracts closer to Port Jervis.[45]

On Long Island, Will Chippie, Charles Pamequa, and several others continuing to identify themselves as Secatogue Indians sold six more tracts to Huntington townsfolk between December 16, 1699, and May 22, 1702. Wishing perhaps to avoid being troubled by landless Indians and certainly interested in attracting Indian laborers, New York's then–chief justice William "Tangier" Smith set aside four small tracts in his vast Manor of St. George as Indian planting and fishing reserves on July 2, 1700. Terms of the deed allowed Indians to plant, sow, but not sell reservation lands. The tracts were guaranteed to them in perpetuity on condition that they annually pay Smith or his assigns two ears of yellow Indian corn.[46]

The reserves comprised a total of 175 acres of the 64,000-acre estate Smith had put together in the Suffolk County town of Brookhaven just east of Huntington. Smith was a prominent anti-Leislerian who had been a justice on the court that sentenced the luckless caretaker governor to death. He became a strong supporter of Governor Fletcher, who rewarded him, as he did many others, with a manor. Smith set aside the reservations for descendants of local sachems who had sold the lands composing his manor with what may have been Tackapousha's blessings (the 1700 deed includes a man identified as Tapshana). Many descendants of these people continue to live on this reservation to the present day. Reduced to fifty acres at Poosepatuck, the reservation is located just northeast of the William Floyd Estate unit of the National Park Service's Fire Island National Seashore.[47]

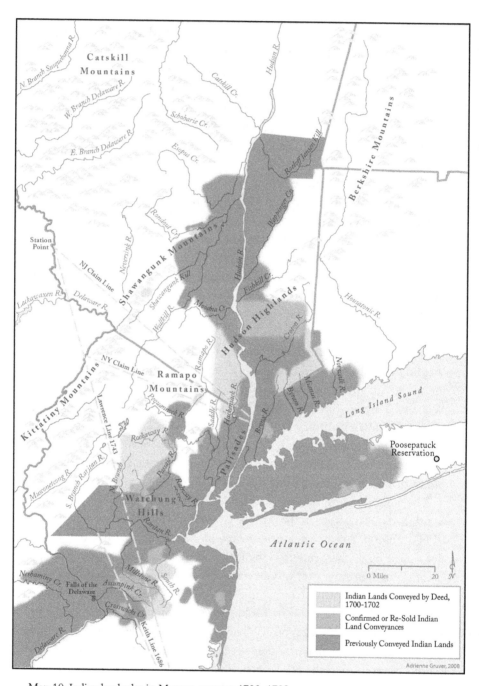

Map 10. Indian land sales in Munsee country, 1700–1702

Katonah and his colleagues still held title to much territory in the north-easternmost hills of Westchester County. Farther south, River Indian communities represented by Patthunck, Sherikham, and their associates retained lands closer to Long Island Sound. Surveys of hazily bounded earlier Indian deed boundaries, moreover, revealed other gores and gaps of unsold land that Indians could still claim. Katonah, Patthunck, Sherikham, Claes de Wilt, and a number of others accepted gifts and took payments in return for signing deeds to gore lands and confirming or clarifying the boundaries of several earlier conveyances.[48]

Caleb Heathcote, mayor of New York City and a member of the governor's council, acquired the lion's share of land taken up by these sales. He was a well-connected merchant close to Chief Justice Smith and married to his daughter. Inspired by his father-in-law's example, Heathcote determined to rise to the rank of a manor lord as soon as possible. Over the course of several years, he joined purchased lands bought earlier by other settlers with new purchases and confirmations from Patthunck and Sherikham. On March 21, 1702, he finally patented 11,500 of these acres into a manor he named Scarsdale, after the Derbyshire valley where he had been born and raised. Like most other large land owners, Heathcote allowed Indians who signed over their lands to camp, hunt, and fish on unfenced open lands within his manor. Unfortunately for his Indian associates, the manor lapsed after Heathcote died before his son reached his majority. The tract was broken up and resold. Like other colonists who bought their land from the Crown, town authorities, or private owners, new purchasers thought they owed nothing to the original River Indian proprietors or their descendants. Most resented visits of Indians they regarded as trespassers and beggars. More than a few started barring Indians from their property.[49]

Forging the Great Peace

New landowners were not the only people forgetting the Indians of Munsee country. Neither French nor English diplomats signing the Treaty of Ryswick made any provisions for them or any other Indians fighting at their sides. Although formally at peace, the former adversaries continued to try to use Indians as cat's-paws for imperial ambitions. Louis-Hector de Callières, the governor of Montreal who became governor-general of New France after Frontenac died in 1698, urged his Indian allies to continue fighting until the Five Nations repudiated their Covenant Chain alliance. Bellomont in New York continued to provide arms and supplies to Covenant Chain Indian allies resisting French blandishments and French Indian threats until his own death in 1701.

It made little difference. The Five Nations had had enough. They dispatched an embassy to Montreal, where they agreed to an armistice with the French and their Indian allies on July 18, 1700. Two delegations of Five Nations diplomats traveled from Iroquoia the following summer. At a meeting in Albany held between July 12 and 21, 1701, with Bellomont's temporary replacement, John Nanfan, the first delegation, largely consisting of Mohawks, Oneidas, and Onondagas, assured the New Yorkers that although they might stop fighting the French, they would not abandon the Covenant Chain alliance. Pledging enduring friendship, they deeded over what they claimed were their western hunting lands around the Great Lakes. Scholars continue to debate the meaning and validity of this deed. It appears, however, that Allen W. Trelease had it right when he wrote that Iroquois diplomats signing the deed only intended to give the English king what he called "the dubious privilege" of protecting Iroquois interests to lands they did not own.[50]

Farther north, the other and much larger Iroquois delegation, made up of sachems from the four western nations, assembled in Montreal by July 22, 1701. At a conclave attended by over one thousand Native people lasting until August 9, they made peace with representatives of thirty Indian nations allied with the French and proclaimed their neutrality in all future wars between England and France. A small Mohawk delegation belatedly signed on to the agreement a few days after the meeting ended. In two close-cut strokes, Five Nations diplomats simultaneously formally ended nearly a century of warfare and extricated themselves from involvements in political differences between France and England. These agreements helped set the pattern for separate peaces that Indians would make in pursuit of their own interests to the end of the colonial era and beyond.[51]

11

GREAT PEACE, 1702-1713

No one at the 1701 Montreal meeting mentioned anyone from Munsee country. This was not an oversight. It was instead a statement made by the Five Nations and tacitly accepted by the French and their Indian allies. Through this simple act of omission, this nonevent, the Five Nations signaled that they regarded Munsees and other lesser Covenant Chain affiliates as women whom they would represent at diplomatic conclaves.[1]

Only a very few and very late references, mostly dating to the second half of the 1700s, chronicle the Five Nations practice of addressing Munsees, Shawnees, and others they regarded as more or less subservient client nations as women in council. Scholars argue over when the Five Nations first started using the term, wonder if the term was flattering or derogatory, and speculate whether River Indians and others addressed as women were compelled, cajoled, or hoodwinked into assuming figurative petticoats.[2]

A little more than fifteen years passed between Joris's reference to his people as children of the English in 1679 and the earliest known Iroquois reference likening Lower Delaware Valley Indians to women. The reference was first made at a Pennsylvania Council meeting on July 6, 1694. Laying down a belt of wampum sent by the Onondagas and Senecas, the Indian speaker conveyed their message, complaining that Indians on the lower Delaware River "stay at home and boil . . . pots, and are like women" instead of sending warriors to fight alongside them like men against their common French enemy. Fifteen years later, a Minisink sachem took advantage of the Iroquois practice. Responding to a July 19, 1709, request that he send young men off to fight in faraway Canada for New York during Queen Anne's War, the sachem, almost certainly Tatapagh, politely refused by dryly affirming that "they were only squaws and not fighting men." The New Yorkers accepted this obvious evasion without protest. Both parties knew that the much-diminished River Indians could not provide many men. What was more important to the colonists was the power symbolically reaffirmed and wielded by the Iroquois, important clients of New York, over the restive River Indian community.[3]

Iroquois used the metaphor, and Indians living within their sphere of influence evidently accepted it, in the peculiarly Iroquoian sense of the term. Women played important roles in all decisions made in Northeastern Indian societies. Places where women's council might be given or taken differed from culture to culture and changed from time to time. Among Indians in Munsee country, some women, like Mamanuchqua, strode late seventeenth-century diplomatic floor boards as full-fledged sachems signing treaties and selling land. In Mamanuchqua's case, her sex was of so little relevance to her role as sachem that it was often not even mentioned in meeting minutes. Iroquois clan mothers worked more discreetly, quietly meeting among themselves to select and remove kinsmen as leaders.[4]

Iroquois use of the term "woman" to address River Indians and others they considered lesser links in the Covenant Chain did not do much to change existing relationships. Five Nations and other tribute takers had compelled less powerful nations to pay for protection for many decades. Metaphorical violence threatened against those failing to pay was made real in many chronicled assaults. Far from ending tribute taking or mitigating consequences of nonpayment, symbolic references to people like River Indians as women reflected the view that tribute payment was the proper province of women.[5]

Although much has been made of women's roles in Indian diplomacy to prove that the metaphor was not pejorative, contemporary records provide little evidence of Five Nations women taking the lead in negotiations. This was not the same among Iroquoians who were not part of the Five Nations. Ojuncho, the Indian queen at Conestoga, for example, was one of several documented nonconfederacy Iroquoian female leaders. Iroquois Confederacy sachems addressing tribute payers as women, however, did not expect them to bar their own mothers and sisters from leadership positions. Nor did they interfere in their meetings, land sales, legal wrangles, and other dealings. They expected tribute payers to act in international diplomacy with the

French and other nations outside the Covenant Chain as most Five Nations women acted at home, discreetly and behind the scenes.[6]

It is hard to imagine that Indians in Munsee country would have resented lack of formal inclusion in the faraway political affairs between the French and the Five Nations. They had always acted as their own agents in affairs that really mattered to them. Nothing French governors or Five Nations sachems could do or say would change that. Acting in concert with Schaghticokes and Mahicans as River Indians, more independently as Lower River Indians, or individually as residents of particular places or members of particular kin groups, Indians in Munsee country continued to represent themselves at meetings with English authorities at all political levels for a long time after 1701. English and Iroquois Confederacy Covenant Chain partners might use varying degrees of emphasis when suggesting particular courses of action to them. Indians living in the Munsee homeland with other places to move remained free to make their own choices.

This freedom to choose was reflected in their settlement patterns. Unlike most Iroquoians, River Indians and many other Eastern Algonquians traditionally tended to avoid living close to one another for any extended period of time. Neighborliness, of course, can be a virtue. Concentrations of people in one place at one time can help communities focus attention on problems and opportunities. Closeness also has its equally well-known drawbacks. Familiarity breeds contempt; contentions born of contempt can often quickly lead to conflict. Proximity can also lose its charms in tightly clustered towns filled with cramped houses lacking sanitation and running water. Large numbers of people stuck within stifling confines of smoky, insect-ridden, combustible, perishable mat, bark, and sapling walled houses can quickly burn through accessible timber fuel, exhaust fertility of nearby soils, and foul springs and other water sources.

Firsthand observations made by colonial surveyors and travelers confirm archaeological findings that people throughout the Northeast spread out across their territories following restoration of lasting peace. Even the Iroquois adopted a more expansive settlement pattern once the Great Peace removed the need to concentrate in fortified towns. River Indians already moving along networks long held together by ties of family and friendship continued to go to and from places whose limited resources could only briefly support larger populations. They could no longer gather in more salubrious places now densely settled by colonists like Keschaechquereren, Wiechquaesgeck, and Ramenesing. Just as they never again uttered dead ancestors' names, these and those of most other lost places gradually fell into disuse.

How, then, to account for survival of so many names never again uttered by Indians observing postmortem prohibitions? Europeans documented virtually all Munsee-language names that have come down to us. They were not, however, the only people who kept dead Munsee names alive. Some Indian families began getting around prohibitions banning utterance of names of ancestors like Chopeycannows (often spelled "Chippie," "Cheppie," or "Chepy"), Hekan, and Nimham by turning them into European-style surnames representing living families and lineages. And all Munsees continued to use names of socially functioning places like Manhattan, Raritan, and Hackensack no longer owned by them but adopted, and thus kept alive, like the symbolic name "Corlaer," by colonists.

Large numbers of River Indians continued to congregate on Manhattan and other colonial cities for treaty meetings. Focal points for their social networks, however, shifted farther inland to opposite ends of the Great Valley during the decades immediately following 1701. To the north, River Indian towns on both sides of the Hudson nestled within Catskill and Berkshire mountain hollows. Mahican was the dominant tongue at Catskill, Taghkanick, and other more northerly towns. Munsee, by contrast, was probably the language most often heard at Wappinger settlements along the Fishkill and other streams flowing into the Hudson from the Highlands. Off the beaten path of colonial expansion, these places ultimately served as gathering points of departure for destinations farther north and east.

At the other end of the Great Valley, mostly Munsee-speaking families found a refuge in the long narrow valley at and around Minisink behind the mountain wall of the Kittatiny Ridge. Located on and around an easily defensible island far but not too far from big colonial settlements, Minisink contained the largest expanse of level, well-watered land left under Indian ownership in the Munsee homeland. Steep ridges and a stone-choked river that only pierced the mountain wall at the Delaware Water Gap many miles downriver screened Minisink from three sides. Trails winding through high passes joined at Minisink to link the place with other locales beyond its mountain fastness. For many years after 1701, Minisink was the last best gathering place for Indians traveling to and from more westerly Indian towns in the Susquehanna, Allegheny, and Ohio river valleys.

Growing numbers of Munsee- and other Eastern Algonquian–speaking people congregated at places like Minisink, Catskill, Taghkanick, and Fishkill on their ways from coastal lowlands to more distant inland locales that the Great Peace had finally made it safe to travel to. These trips grew in distance, duration, and frequency as successive waves of European immigrants took up the last open lands around colonial centers and pressed outward into what remained of Munsee territory. Pressures brought to bear by land-hungry settlers were most keenly felt along tidal reaches of Munsee country. Shorelands were places where colonial population was thickest and Indian numbers fewest.

In western Long Island, descendants of Tackapousha's and Suscaneman's people still held title to the two small reservations on Hempstead Harbor established for their use by Dongan in 1687. Indian people also continued to hold on to the four tiny tracts Smith had granted them in and around Poosepatuck. Aside from these reserves, Indians also still held title to substantial expanses of sandy pinelands and a few necks in the towns of Brookhaven, Huntington, and Oyster Bay. Elsewhere on Long Island, Indians had given up title to nearly all of their remaining along-shore lands by 1701.

Then as earlier, conveyance of title still did not necessarily mean loss of access. Almost all rivers, wetlands, and bodies of open water were treated as freely accessible unregulated commons. On Indian lands, formal and informal arrangements continued to allow colonists to graze cattle, hunt, travel, and do other things agreeable to both parties when permission was asked and given. The same types of agreements let Indians camp in vacant lots designated for the purpose when visiting cities and set aside for them to plant, hunt, and fish.[7]

There is no evidence of grand annual mass migrations from the mountains to the shore. It is difficult to imagine, however, that friends and families of well-connected coast dwellers like Suscaneman living farther inland did not take advantage of their connections to travel to the shore at times of year when it made the most sense to fish, clam, and gather reeds and grasses for mats, brooms, and baskets. It is equally hard to imagine that shore people did not journey to interior locales like Minisink at one time or another to hunt; to spear and net their share of spawning shad, herrings, and eels congregating at falls and rapids; and to participate in Indian trade fairs and religious festivals.[8]

Journeys to and from tidewater locales decreased in frequency as colonial population growth along the coastlands increasingly limited shore access and colonial demand diminished for shore products provided by Indians. Fish and shellfish formerly provided by Indians were now caught or gathered and brought to markets by settlers. Colonists who used wampum as currency increasingly preferred to use growing stocks of hard cash and paper money flowing into the provinces. Inmates confined to poor houses in New York and Albany began making wampum still in demand among Indians.[9]

Although they would never entirely abandon the shore until finally forced from their homeland, most River Indians gradually turned inland. Those not leaving Munsee country altogether spread themselves out across the considerable expanses of their remaining interior territories. Among other benefits best appreciated by those who prefer wide-open spaces, spreading out allowed the Indians to maintain a presence on lands that colonists might otherwise claim for themselves as vacant wastes unwanted by their owners. Those spending time outside Munsee country built on existing relations with Northern Indians, Conestogas, Shawnees, Miamis, Dowaganhaes, and other Far Indians. Contacts in these communities allowed them to move across an increasingly far-flung network extending from New England and the Mid-Atlantic provinces beyond Iroquoia to Acadia, the St. Lawrence Valley, the Great Lakes, and Ohio country.

Dramatic Shifts in Population

The physical as well as cultural survival of Indians in Munsee country increasingly depended on network maintenance and extension as sachems surrendered their last remaining ancestral lands and their population plummeted. By 1701, the Indian population of the Munsee homeland was nearly 95 percent less than what it was when colonists purchased their first tracts of land from River Indians some seventy years before. During that time, the Indians had lost all but tiny bits of their saltwater lands and very nearly all of their productive territories closer inland. Although they still held millions of acres, all of it was in the interior, away from tidal waters. While some inland flats like those at Minisink contained fairly large expanses of level arable land, nearly all the rest consisted of rocky upland, boggy (and buggy) drowned lands, or sandy barrens.

Fifty-one prominent men and women listed in the Munsee File were involved in some form of transaction with colonists in 1701. Applying the 56 percent drop in River Indian population between 1689 to 1697 made by the Albany magistrates, the hypothetical Indian population in the Munsee homeland of around 2,400 in 1686 may have sunk to little more than 1,000 in the years immediately following the end of King William's War. Division of this latter figure by 51 produces a result suggesting that each sachem may have had an average of 20 followers—a figure that when matched with areas of occupation, finally yielded crude population densities most typically found in bands.[10]

These guesstimated population figures were neither uniformly nor evenly distributed within Munsee country. Documents recording activities of nine sachems in the central Long Island pinelands and lower Berkshire Mountain borderlands between New York and New England suggest that sachems in both places may each have led between 150 and 200 people. Using the same equation, five sachems represented around 100 people west of the Shawangunks in Esopus country. The eight sachems active in Indian communities astride the border between East and West Jersey would also have represented between 150 and 200 people. By the far the largest number, the twenty sachems at Minisink and the surrounding area, may have represented around 400 people in their refuge at the southern end of the Great Valley. In addition, between 100 and 300 Shawnees probably were then living above the Delaware Water Gap.

Small numbers of Munsee people also continued to live beyond the borders of their ancestral homeland in 1701. Most were probably associated with Mahican and Northern Indian people moving between Schaghticoke, the long-established Catholic missions at Sillery and Three Rivers near Quebec, the newly erected St. Francis Odanak mission near Montreal, and the Jesuit mission stations built between 1693 and 1695 at Amesoconti on the Sandy River (where Farmington, Maine, stands today) and Norridgewock (twenty miles downstream, where the Sandy River flows into the Penobscot River at present-day Madison). Other French sources indicate that at least some of the Loups encountered by La Salle in 1681 remained among Miamis, Potawatomis, Sauks, Mesquakies, and Wyandots living on the banks of the Miami River during the height of the fur-trapping season in the winter of 1700–1701. Although the population and composition of the Loup community at Miami at this time is unknown, the percentage of people from Munsee country among them probably continued to be small. Put together, a hypothetical total of 300 River Indian expatriates may have been living at various locales from Maine to Michigan. Adding this number to the 1,300 or so Indian people in the Munsee homeland (a number that includes 300 Shawnees), a total of around 1,600 Indians maintained connections of one sort or another in or with Munsee country in 1701.[11]

The composition as well as the numbers and percentages of total population of prominent individuals noted in colonial records in the Munsee File also changed at this time. Much of the Indian leadership in Munsee territory in 1701 was fairly new to European records. Although only thirteen out of the fifty-one first appeared after 1686, the majority of the remainder had been junior or local leaders who were only first mentioned in colonial documents just a few years before that year. Communities centering around Navesink, Raritan, and Crosswicks territory were mostly led by young or newly appointed descendants of Ockanickon and his brothers. Most of these people rose to prominence during the late 1680s and early 1690s.

The largest concentrations of experienced sachems lived in central Long Island and Minisink. Elders like Suscaneman, Werah, and Wamehas on Long Island and Memshe, Joris, Nimham I, and Taphow in the Great Valley and the North Jersey uplands would continue to be mentioned in colonial records for only a few years after 1701. During that time, they and other experienced sachems concerned for the future of their communities would have worked closely with younger people. Together, they would preserve the measure of continuity sorely needed by demographically devastated and increasingly dislocated Native people in the Munsee homeland.

Colonial population, at least in the English possessions, was set to explode in 1701. Immigrants primarily from the Celtic fringe of the British Isles and the German-speaking areas in Europe would join native-born colonists moving outward from large regional centers in Boston, New York, and Philadelphia. Many would stop at smaller staging areas along the edges of remaining Indian territory, such as Albany and Kingston in New York, Newark and Trenton in soon-to-be-reunified New Jersey, and Newtown and Wrightstown in Pennsylvania.

Population numbers and growth rates in the English settlements were considerable. Colonial population in New York, for example, had nearly doubled from 9,000 in 1664 to 17,000 by 1701. Growth was even more explosive in Pennsylvania and the Jerseys. The combined colonial population of East and West Jersey rose from nearly nothing in 1664 to more than 16,000 in 1701. As much as three-fifths of these people concentrated near the margins of remaining Indian lands in the northern counties of both provinces. Pennsylvania had grown fastest and largest, expanding from a few hundred settlers in 1664 to 21,000 colonists in 1701. Philadelphia's 4,400 people made it English America's third largest city. Only Boston, with 6,800 people, and New York City, with 5,000, were larger.[12]

Of a total colonial population of 53,500 in New York, the Jerseys, and Pennsylvania, the vast majority were Europeans of mostly English, Scottish, or Dutch descent. Growing numbers of Germans and Irish added to this total. Some 3,700 were enslaved Africans and their descendants, mostly confined to farms and households in New York and the Jerseys. Within twenty years, the number of African slaves nearly tripled as European population almost doubled in size. European population doubled again to more than 204,000 by 1740. Although the rate of increase in the enslaved population slowed somewhat during this time, more than 16,500 enslaved Africans were living in the Mid-Atlantic colonies in 1740. And both European and African populations all but doubled again after 1740 to a combined total of almost 428,000 in 1760.[13]

Nearby, even larger colonial populations burgeoned in New England and Chesapeake Bay. Only the French colonies remained small. Unlike the densely settled English provinces, whose ever-growing immigrant population farmed fields and built up new markets, France regarded its North American possessions in Canada and Acadia more as trading outposts and strategic assets. Of the 27,000 people who came to New France by 1760 to trade, trap, or work as farmers, fishermen, or soldiers, only one-third had stayed on after their contracts expired.

Numbers, however, are not everything. Divided as they were among themselves, the few thousand determined French and Indians were protected by a barrier of forbiddingly mountainous forests and desolate barren lands. French colonists, Indians, and mountain walls pinned the vastly more populous English to the Atlantic seaboard. Coastal colonists did not necessarily feel unduly confined. Most were content to tend their fields and manage their business affairs. The more enterprising among them engaged in maritime commerce, sending ships loaded with grain, furs, and timber to England. These would be loaded with British manufactures for the return trip. Vessels sailed directly back to the colonies or ventured to the Guinea Coast to purchase enslaved Africans. Those surviving the Middle Passage were sold for sugar or indigo in the West Indies; for rice, deerskins, or enslaved Indians in the Carolinas; for tobacco and wheat in Maryland and Virginia; or for corn, furs, and timber farther north in Philadelphia, New York, and Boston. More visionary entrepreneurs dreaming of western fur empires and vast open lands often bankrolled privateers, of whom the more luckless, like William Kidd, were hanged as pirates. Most commercially minded settlers concentrated on acquiring remaining Indian lands east of timber-picketed mountain barriers for resale or rent to ever-growing numbers of settlers.

Lies, Damned Lies, and Hard Realities

The little more than 1,300 Indians in the Munsee homeland found themselves in the way of more than 50,000 expansion-minded settlers in New York, the Jerseys, and Pennsylvania in 1701. Several times that number from New England, Maryland, and Virginia also hungrily eyed Indian lands. Royal officials in all colonies faced a common dilemma when weighing matters of equity and expedience. First and foremost, all were charged with implementing policies intended to manage colonial growth rather than help Indians. Even the most venal official knew, however, that growth and profits depended on peace with all Indian nations, not just the powerful ones. Unjust treatment of small nations could alienate more powerful Indian allies and displease royal authorities at home. Governors recognizing this fact extended a considerable measure of legal protection to Indians living under Crown rule. They investigated thefts, assaults, and killings of Indians and settlers alike. Malefactors from both communities often escaped justice by fleeing to other jurisdictions. Those caught were tried, and those found guilty punished.[14]

Although ordinances prohibiting sales of guns and alcohol to Indians were openly flouted, laws regulating purchases of Indian lands were strictly enforced. Land meant life; title to it ordered everything. Anything disrupting title threatened everyone's well-being. This is why officials who did little to stop Indians from pawning guns and furs tended to draw the line on land. Few examples document takings of Indian lands in Munsee country for debt. Only four examples of Indians mortgaging land in Munsee territory are known. Harman Hekan took out the first two of these, payable in wheat and corn, when he agreed to purchase his two tracts in Marbletown in accordance with provincial law on April 18, 1674, during the Dutch reoccupation of New York.[15]

To one extent or another, misrepresentation, corner cutting, and on occasion outright lies were part of intercultural relationships in Munsee country from the very beginning. Creative misunderstandings were not limited to relations between Indians and colonists. Colonists living in Munsee country also maintained working disagreements with covert competitors in other English colonies, open enemies in New France, and government officials and businessmen in their home countries. Like those arranged with Indians, these provided profits and other benefits that could not be had through official channels. Quiet accommodations helped colonists circumvent highly restrictive mercantile trade regulations in times of peace. Others maintained informal truces in places where royal forces failed to safeguard settlers or commerce in wartime.

The great distances of space and time separating colonies from imperial centers further fostered working disagreements and creative misunderstandings. Frontier improvisations necessary for survival at the edges of empire created opportunities for profit and freedom of action unavailable in Europe. These expressed themselves in what might best be described as waves of enthusiasms. Enthusiasm for land ownership sparked deed frenzies. Enthusiasms for greater degrees of self-government and personal freedom triggered everything from rent strikes to revolutions. Enthusiasm for extralegal profits made Albany a center of clandestine smuggling trade with New France and turned New York Harbor into an actual pirates' nest by 1700. And spiritual enthusiasms set off religious revivals and sustained great awakenings everywhere.

Lord Cornbury Comes to New York

A new governor, singularly enthused by the prospects for profit, landed on Manhattan on May 13, 1702. He was Edward Hyde, the Third Earl of Clarendon, Viscount Cornbury, most widely known as Lord Cornbury. Cornbury arrived just as another smallpox epidemic was raging through the region. Around the heads of the sick and scared, the North Atlantic world was again tumbling toward war.[16]

Lord Cornbury could not know that England had declared war on France just one day after his ship hove into New York Harbor. The new governor was not, however, totally surprised when the news finally arrived. He had left England expecting a fight. Cornbury started putting his province on a war footing shortly after informing East and West Jersey officials that the queen had united the governments of their fractious proprietaries into a single royal colony. Allowing the proprietors to maintain control over lands within their respective charter bounds, the queen grafted the new royal government of New Jersey onto New York and placed the consolidated provinces under her cousin's control. These decisions went far in easing political differences that were bringing East and West Jersey to the edge of anarchy. They did not, however, put an end to contentions between resident and nonresident proprietors, or proprietary and antiproprietary factions. Nor did they do anything to ease tensions between high church Anglicans and Calvinists, Quakers, Lutherans, and other nonconformists.[17]

In New York, old political hatreds continued to crystallize around Leislerian and anti-Leislerian factions. Power, however, was still in the hands of the anti-Leislerians. Lord Cornbury had no trouble finding properly placed politically powerful partisans from every faction willing to take positions and fill contracts to help themselves as they furthered the war effort. Preparations for the war, however, progressed slowly in smallpox-ravaged New York. Although privateers and war contracts promised spectacular short-term profits, few merchants in the province had much stomach for a struggle that would only throttle the fur trade. Indians trapping or trading furs from as far away as the Great Lakes and Hudson's Bay carried beaver and other pelts to merchants in Albany and Montreal for more than ninety years. Indian trade made up as much as 25 percent of the exports shipped out of New York City at the time. Fur commerce, however, was marked by sharp fluctuations in supply and volatile market demand. Prices paid and product quality and quantity constantly changed as supply and demand rose and fell.[18]

Merchants extended loans and offered other inducements to more closely bind Indian clients to their interests. Such efforts were only partially successful. Indians could and would take their furs where they pleased. They worked along what strategists would call interior lines. Their relative proximity to rival markets allowed them to carry pelts to merchants offering products they wanted at the best possible prices. News and rumors traveling as swiftly as people carrying produce along these interior lines could quickly stanch or shift the flow of furs to competitors. The fluid nature of this commerce, and the practical needs and desires of those serving it, made trade possible even between enemies formally at war with one another.

The supposedly covert trade between New York and New France was the worst-kept official secret in the colonies. Mohawks and River Indians had been quietly transporting furs, manufactured goods, and anything else that could be carried in a boat, bag, or brain in peace and war for a long time. Montreal merchants and Albany traders were notoriously reluctant to let either restrictive mercantile regulations or conflict between their mother countries cut into profits. Traders in both places had to maintain sufficient stocks of furs and trade goods needed to attract Indian clients, pay share-holders, and keep creditors and officials off their backs. Officials in both places found it difficult to drum up interest in any military enterprise that threatened the trade. Having just concluded their Great Peace with the Five Nations, Indians and colonists in New France had little stomach for any action that might bring them or their friends in New York into the fighting. Real animus was directed toward New England, where calls for holy war still fell on willing ears, and fresh memories of attacks and atrocities still rankled. During the first years of Queen Anne's War, Massachusetts sustained the brunt of the fighting while New York and colonies farther from the French frontier quietly kept their troops on watch.

Despite losses suffered during the last war and diseases that even then were ravaging their towns, Indians still held the balance of power on the frontier. A political realist, Cornbury really only cared about the most powerful of these nations. Although they carefully cultivated their image as the region's most powerful Indian nation, the Iroquois Confederacy no longer totally dominated military equations in Covenant Chain councils by this time. Having attracted hundreds of displaced Northern Indian expatriates to their town, Upper River Indians at Schaghticoke could call on over two hundred warriors when Queen Anne's War broke out. Shawnees living in Minisink country could field nearly as many men. Only the Senecas could raise a larger body of troops. The new governor would have to move carefully if he was to keep powerful allies on the frontier happy while giving in to pent-up enthusiasms for remaining Munsee lands near settlement centers.[19]

As Indian numbers declined to their nadir and Indian people in Munsee country ran out of lands to sell, many colonists, especially newcomers, increasingly came to feel that they no longer needed to fear or depend on Indians. Many were prepared to abandon discreet fictions in favor of naked lies and outright fraud. More thoughtful leaders like Cornbury, however, knew that the time was not right to give up pretenses and run roughshod over Indians who still had powerful friends and influential connections. This does not mean that he or any other officials maintained things as they were. Deals struck with Indians in Munsee country after the governor reopened the floodgates to Indian lands around New York City reflected new demographic and political realities.

Settlers began to petition Cornbury for permission to purchase tracts of Munsee territory almost as soon as he settled into his office at the newly renamed Fort Anne. A group of merchants, lawyers, and placemen quickly lined up at his door, clamoring for licenses granting exclusive access to sachems acting as agents for particular tracts of lands. Many but not all successful licensees were anti-Leislerians, derided as greedy opportunists by their equally ambitious but out-of-favor political enemies. Far too divided among themselves to ever form a fully unified bloc, those succeeding in gaining the governor's favor and favors came to be known collectively as the Cornbury Ring.

Unlike Livingston and his prestige-hungry brethren, few members of the Cornbury Ring were interested in taking on the burdens and responsibilities of manor lordship. At home in the city, and only on the lookout for a country seat or two for themselves, they were speculators who intended to resell newly acquired Indian lands at a profit as soon as possible. They and their mostly anti-Leislerian rivals quickly formed syndicates of investors. Each investor received title to particular portions of syndicate lands in particular places proportionate to his connections, size of investment, and other factors.

Like the go-ahead men they were, rival partners vied with one another to snap up licenses to purchase Indian lands. Most turned their attention north and west of Manhattan where the largest expanses of still unsold Munsee territory remained. These mostly mountainous territories had not been taken up previously because the more habitable small stretches of valley lowlands within them tended to be mosquito-ridden brush-clogged drowned lands underlain by clay, sand, and rocky rubble left behind by the last glaciers. Most colonists considered the farther reaches of these territories howling wastelands inhabited by wild animals and open to depredations of French raiders and passing Indian war parties. Promises of mineral riches in the stony uplands and fertile bottomlands at places like Minisink, however, beckoned investors. They soon started setting up meetings with sachems from those places to arrange purchases.[20]

MINISINK PATENT

Syndicate partners worked with the speed of driven men in wartime to purchase and patent as much Indian land as they could in Orange County. Within the space of two years, they managed to get sachems like Taphow and Dostou's son Maringoman to sign deeds conveying considerable tracts within what became known as the Wawayanda and Cheesecocks patents. Just west across the Kittatiny Ridge, rival anti-Leislerian syndicates from New York City contended with pro-Leislerian country gentry like Thomas Swartwout and Jacob Rutsen for the glittering prize of Minisink.[21]

More than a few colonists wanted the fertile upper Delaware bottom-lands on and around Minisink Island. Lucas Kierstede tried to claim the place with a story that older officials familiar with old land records might have recognized. In a statement made on January 8, 1707, he pressed his claim by insisting that grateful Minisink sachems had renamed their island Sarah's Island in honor of his mother (actually his grandmother). Evidently not feeling that was enough, Kierstede said they then gave the place to her as a gift for her services as a translator.[22]

Other claimants had more plausible stories. The most compelling was of-fered by a Schenectady raid survivor and blacksmith named William Tiet-soort. On September 10, 1707, Tietsoort petitioned the governor to patent a deed for land at Minisink obtained from local Indians. He obtained the deed, he explained, because other claimants were ordering him off land that he had been living on with Indian permission for the more than twenty years. Un-like Kierstede's improbable tale, Tietsoort's story made sense. Blacksmiths were thin on the ground in the colonies and even rarer in Munsee country. Minisink sachems would have been happy to provide a few acres to a friendly man possessing such skills. Cornbury agreed. He gave Tietsoort title to a modest tract just north of present-day Port Jervis, New York.[23]

Minisink was a desirable prize. Both New Jersey proprietors and New York merchants lusted after land there long before Arent Schuyler first showed on June 6, 1695, that colonists could obtain Indian deeds in the re-gion. Swartwout and Rutsen began jockeying to get possession of Minisink Island for themselves less than a year after Schuyler got his deed to lands nearby at Pequannock. Like Schuyler, they could not get sachems at Min-isink to sell territory at the heart of their country. The closest they were able to get was a probably preemptive deed to lands above Minisink west of the Shawangunk Mountains. The deal apparently did not go down well with everyone. In a petition to then-acting governor Nanfan made on October 18, 1699, before Cornbury arrived, Thomas Swartwout's younger brother Bernardus complained that Indians had beaten both him and his brother up, destroyed what they did not rob, and threatened to burn their houses and kill them if they did not leave. He identified Hendrick Hekan, Tindamunge, and Maringoman among the assailants, and claimed that their erstwhile partner Rutsen had put them up to it.[24]

The real struggle for Minisink began on September 12, 1702, when rival syndicates represented by the elder Swartwout and a New York businessman named Gerrit Aertsen petitioned Cornbury for permission to purchase Minisink Island from the Indians. This touched off a competition that resulted in one of the more controversial of the many suspect Indian land deals made by Cornbury Ring men. Neither Aertsen nor Swartwout seem to have made it to the final cut in the competition. The two syndicates that wound up vying for Minisink were instead wholly made up of Cornbury's men. The first was headed by Ebenezer Wilson (then sheriff of New York County); Cornbury's secretary, Daniel Honan; and Dirck Vandenbergh, a New York mason and avid speculator in Orange and Ulster county lands who had been forgiven his former Leislerian sympathies. They purchased the westernmost of the two tracts of land sold between Minisink Island and the drowned lands by their Indian owners for unspecified amounts of cash and goods in deeds negotiated over a two-day period between March 5 and 6, 1703. The second group was led by New York City mayor Philip French, a member of Cornbury's council named Matthew Ling, and Stephen De Lancey, lawyer, merchant, and patriarch of one of the most powerful trading families in the city. This second syndicate secured a deed to a large tract at Minisink from Indians for £400 on June 11, 1703.[25]

Spellings of Indian names on these and many other deeds written at the time were peculiarly garbled. There is no clear evidence, however, supporting French's assertion that his rivals purchased their tracts from "strange Indians not inhabiting on or claiming any right to the same." In addition to familiar figures like Taphow, Claes, and Sherikham, the names of what were then less-prominent local sachems like Nowenock, Nackpunck, Renap, and Jan Conelle, a man originally from Catskill who apparently moved to Schaghticoke after the sales, can be picked out of the orthographic haze of the March 5 and 6, 1703, conveyances. If anything, the particularly tortured renderings of Indian names on French's June 11, 1703, deed make it harder to verify the identities of the signatories mentioned in his purchase.[26]

This does not mean that Wilson and his backers were playing the game straight. On March 30, 1703, two men identified as Wawasowaw and Kisowaw, who had signed the Wilson syndicate's March 6, 1703, deed, told Pieter Schuyler that they had sold only two small tracts. They emphatically stated that they had not sold Minisink Island in this or any other deed. They further affirmed that Tatapagh, whom they described as the only person with the authority to sell the island, had not signed the deed. This did not stop Wilson and company from applying for a patent that included the place. The overreaching claims of the rival syndicates went beyond Minisink itself. Together, they claimed twice the amount of the sixty thousand acres thought to have been originally purchased. Unwilling to spend too much time haggling over land claims while a war was going on, Cornbury ordered the syndicates to come to some understanding. Both groups put aside their differences and came together long enough to allow the governor to grant their new partnership, now made up of twenty-three of his most loyal and generous supporters, a patent to 175 square miles of Minisink land in August 1704. Predictably, the grant included Minisink Island.[27]

HARDENBERGH'S PATENT AND OTHER LAND AFFAIRS

Even greater chicanery was afoot just to the north. On April 20, 1708, Cornbury granted what became known as the Hardenbergh Patent to another syndicate. The deal was the brainchild of Johannis Hardenbergh, an Albany-born soldier determined to make his fortune in real estate. He began on July 18, 1706, by petitioning Cornbury for a license giving him permission to purchase "a small tract [of] vacant . . . unappropriated land." He used his license to purchase a small tract of land just beyond Marbletown from Maringoman for £60 on March 22, 1707. Using this deed as his base, he threw in with his brother-in-law Jacob Rutsen and six other men who had also purchased interests in Indian lands west of the Shawangunks to form a partnership. This allowed the men to extend their claims beyond the recently enacted two thousand-acre legal limit placed on individual Indian land purchases. The partners petitioned the governor for a patent to secure title to their purchases on February 4, 1708. Despite their failure to provide a good survey, Cornbury granted letters patent to Hardenbergh's syndicate two months later. The amount of land granted under this patent ballooned individual takings of six thousand or so acres into syndicate property totaling 1.5 million acres comprising most of the present-day Catskill Mountains in Sullivan, Delaware, and Otsego counties (see map 11). In one stroke of a pen, the New York governor signed over the largest single taking of Munsee territory made during the colonial era.[28]

Like the Minisink Patent syndicate associates, Hardenbergh and his partners had difficulty finding settlers interested in purchasing property in their unsurveyed and unpromising-looking stony Catskill Mountain lands. The patent lay unsurveyed and fully in Indian hands when a much older and

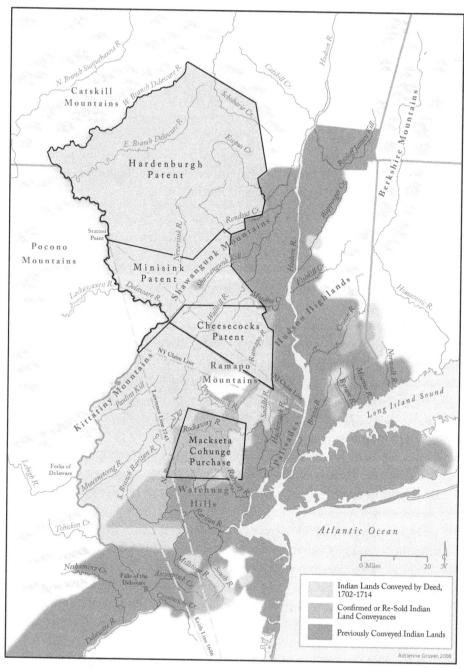

Map 11. Indian land sales in Munsee country, 1702–1714

long-frustrated Hardenbergh finally decided to sell one-third of his interest in it to the Livingston family around 1742. The late Robert Livingston's son, also named Robert, took the lead, sending surveyors to lay out parcels to sell to immigrants pouring into the province. The Indians, however, had other ideas. They turned back the surveyors after making it clear that they felt that neither Maringoman nor Sherikam represented their interests in the deeds signed in 1706 and 1707. As his father had done, Robert decided to negotiate new deals with the local Indians. He obtained his first deed there on June 6, 1746, and the second two months later on August 2. Both were signed by an assemblage of Indians representing every remaining Indian family and interest group in the area. A very elderly Hendrick Hekan signed both instruments as the principal sachem, selling remaining Indian rights to the lands for a total of £300 in trade goods.[29]

Although this arrangement confirmed the new partnership's title to the Hardenbergh Patent lands, it neither attracted many new buyers nor ended Indian occupation in the still mostly unfenced and untenanted territory. Like Minisink, most of the Hardenbergh lands would largely remain Indian territory colonized by a few squatters up through the Revolution. Although the Indians would leave by the end of the war in 1783, squatters who remained continued to frustrate efforts of large landowners to get them to pay for their properties well into the next century.[30]

It would be a great while before Hardenbergh, Wilson, or anyone else would be able to take up any land at Minisink Island or farther upriver. Whatever the motives of buyers or sellers, jealousy and acrimony among the purchasers made it impossible to clearly establish who owned what in the Catskills west of the Shawangunk Mountains. The Indian signatories to the first deeds and their descendants made a cottage industry out of boundary marking and place name identification for these and other purchases sunk in political controversy and endless litigation.[31]

East and West Jersey proprietors also did what they could to obtain title to as much land in Munsee country as possible in what they regarded as their parts of New Jersey while the exigencies of Queen Anne's War distracted the attention of royal administrators. Many Cornbury Ring cronies who became partners in the Minisink and other Orange County patent ventures also bought shares of proprietary interests in East Jersey. While rival syndicates in New York haggled over claims at Minisink, many of these same partners pressed Indians in northern New Jersey for land. Initially, Indians there acknowledging Taphow as their sachem and commander in chief were able to put off most demands. They were inadvertently helped by Cornbury cartel opponents like Lewis Morris, determined to prevent the governor, who had taken over New Jersey's government in 1702, from taking the province's land as well. Cornbury Ring men were able to confirm only an earlier sale at Saddle River and make a somewhat more substantial purchase of land between the Rockaway and Whippany rivers while Cornbury was in power.[32]

Farther south, Weequehela and retainers like Quanolam sold some, but again not all, of their remaining ancestral lands in Monmouth and Middlesex counties during the same period. West Jersey Society proprietors had greater success getting Sehoppy, Caponokonickon, Nimham I, and Weequehela to sell more lands around and above the Falls of the Delaware River. Although they gained considerable ground in what is today Hunterdon County, the longed-for goal of the Delaware Water Gap still remained tantalizingly out of reach.[33]

In Dutchess and northern Westchester counties. Katonah, Sherikham, and Wackemane headed lists of Highland Indians selling much of their remaining lands. Farther south, Patthunck, Raresquash, and Ann Hook sold their family's last parcels around Rye and Byram Pond. Across Long Island Sound, Wamehas and his people conveyed nearly all of their remaining title to lands in Huntington to town fathers between 1703 and 1707. Farther north in Esopus country, Harman and Hendrick Hekan placed their marks alongside those of Tatapagh, Renap, and several other sachems on deeds in Ulster County.[34]

Dwindling Trade and Queen Anne's War

No one, by contrast, seems to have made any demands on Shawnees for lands at the Delaware Water Gap during these years. Although they kept a low profile, they did occasionally put in appearances at New York and Philadelphia. A substantial number of Shawnees, for example, showed up at Philadelphia on April 23, 1702, in company with "Sasquehannah Minquays or Conestogo Indians" and Conoys from Maryland. Meeting with proprietary representatives and the governor, they signed a treaty guaranteeing trade and security so long as they conducted themselves peaceably.[35]

Another delegation of Shawnees met with Cornbury at New York between July 15 and 16, 1703. Nothing of the propositions discussed at the meeting can be made out from the badly scorched pages recording the get-together. Some idea of Shawnee concerns can be formed from contemporary records. Threats made by the Five Nations to carry off "those Shawanah Indians, both those settled near Conestogoe and those near Lechay" (at the Water Gap) were subjects of a message carried to Philadelphia on May 18, 1704, by one of the French traders who had accompanied the Shawnees on their eastward migration. Trade, it seems, was also on their minds. On March 6, 1705, "two Indians from the Shawannais upon Delaware" came to Philadelphia to inquire after trade opportunities. The Pennsylvanians told them that they then had little more than powder and lead in stock. They said that they were expecting another shipment in the fall and invited them to come down with their furs then.[36]

Trade was on a lot of minds as the war restricted free movement on land while privateers and warships swept merchantmen from the seas. The arrival in Albany on June 20, 1704, of Indians identified as Waganhaers (i.e., Dowaganhaes) from the recently established French trading center at Detroit shows how far Indians were willing to go to get goods they needed. Known allies of the French, the Waganhaers said they came in search of cheap prices. This did not stop them from suggestively intimating other possibilities. They made their priorities clear; speaking directly to the magistrates, they stated that "we esteem a good market above any other thing."[37]

There was little the Albanians could then do to take advantage of the opportunity. As short of inventory as the Pennsylvanians, the magistrates had to tell the Waganhaers that goods were also scarce and expensive in Albany. Like the Philadelphians, they invited them to return in the spring, when new shipments would allow them to "endeavor to be plentifully supplied with goods suitable to your minds." They further encouraged them with a present of twelve kegs of rum, a half vat of strong beer, a couple of guns, and some powder and lead.

Trade stocks everywhere in the colonies continued to dwindle as Queen Anne's War dragged on. Anger over a collapsing economy played as much of a role in Cornbury's recall in 1708 as attacks made by his political enemies. He was replaced when a ship carrying John Lord Lovelace, Fourth Baron of Hurley, and fifty-two Palatine German immigrant families landed in New York on December 28, 1708. As far as Indian affairs were concerned, Lovelace was able to do little more than suspend issuance of new land-purchase license permits before dying suddenly on May 15, 1709.

Richard Ingoldsby once again stepped in as interim governor until another replacement arrived from England. In the meantime, Ingoldsby, who had been a member of the Cornbury Ring, kept access open for those wanting land in Munsee country.

A career soldier by trade, Ingoldsby also showed a passion for combat with the French. He quickly committed New York to an ambitious scheme to seize both Acadia and Canada simultaneously in a coordinated two-prong assault. The northern wing of the attack, to consist of 1,000 Massachusetts militiamen, two battalions of regulars, and six British warships, would move on Port Royal before sailing to take Quebec. Ingoldsby would send 1,500 men to join a mixed force of 4,000 colonists and nearly 600 Iroquois and River Indians set to gather above Albany at Schuyler Flatts under the command of former New York lieutenant governor Nicholson for an overland strike aimed at Montreal.[38]

Ingoldsby had difficulty convincing Indians in Munsee country to join the expedition. In New Jersey, Weequehela politely told authorities in Perth Amboy that he would look into the matter and get back to them. Shawnees on the Delaware refused several invitations. And, as mentioned earlier, the Minisink sachem rebuffed recruiters, saying his people "were only squas." Orders requiring sheriffs in Queens and Suffolk counties to bring in Indians produced few warriors.

Not all Indians, however, were uninterested in joining the expedition. At least sixty River Indians, mostly from Schaghticoke, joined Mohawk and other Iroquois warriors from all but the Seneca nation assembling at Schuyler Flatts during the early summer. The small force, minus promised Pennsylvania troops held back to guard against a feared French seaborne assault up the Delaware that never happened, got as far as the south end of Lake Champlain. Arriving at Wood Creek, they erected a post they christened Fort Anne. Once again, an army poised to advance on Montreal wound up cooling its heels at its jumping-off point. And once again, the expected British support never arrived in Boston. Staying on until September frosts put an end to the fighting season, Nicholson finally disbanded the little army and sent his men home.[39]

Indians and Albany traders were probably secretly glad that the expedition had failed. Neither really wanted to break the informal truce with New France nor did either wish to give up their smuggling operations. Ingoldsby and other war hawks, however, were determined to strike a blow against the French. They packed three Mohawk men and a Schaghticoke sachem off to

England during the spring of 1710 to drum up support for another attempt. Chaperoned by Pieter Schuyler, his brother Abraham, and David Pigeon, a British officer who served as an interpreter, the Four Indian Kings of America, as they were called, created a sensation wherever they went. The trip was a public relations success. They got their portraits painted and made a favorable impression in a royal audience with the queen. The entourage left London with a firm promise that more than adequate support for a major effort against New France would be forthcoming by the time spring opened the next campaign season.[40]

This time the British were better than their word. It helped that the Board of Trade had already authorized a more limited strike against Acadia before the Four Kings arrived. The fleet of warships carrying five hundred marines left Portsmouth a short time after the Four Kings and their escorts took ship for New York. After stopping off at Boston in July to take on supplies and board several thousand militiamen and a small contingent of warriors that included some River Indians, the fleet sailed north under Nicholson's command. The force arrived in front of the Acadian capital of Port Royal on September, 24, 1710. After a enduring a short but honor-saving cannonade, the French governor surrendered the whole of Acadia to Nicholson on October 2, 1710. Nicholson promptly renamed the little outpost Annapolis Royal in honor of his queen. He also christened the newly recaptured province (it had been seized by a fleet from New England in 1690 and returned in 1697 to France in the last war) Nova Scotia. The new name honored the recent uniting of England and Scotland into Great Britain through the Act of Union passed by both nation's parliaments just three years earlier, in 1707.

Nicholson's success emboldened members of the Board of Trade intent on taking complete control over Atlantic commerce from France and Spain. They saw to it that the largest force yet sent to America left harbor on May 4, 1711. Under the command of Rear Admiral Sir Hovenden Walker, eleven warships manned by their crews and 600 marines guarded sixty transports carrying seven regiments of British regulars, a force of some 5,000 men under the command of Brigadier General John Hill. The force was further stiffened with the addition of 1,500 Massachusetts militiamen taken on in Boston before the fleet sailed north for Canada. Although the French could have done little more than surrender in the face of such an overwhelming force, they never got the chance. Walker neglected to enlist the help of a knowledgeable pilot to guide his ships safely through the shoal-ridden Gulf of St. Lawrence. Ten transports floundered on the rocks on August 20, 1711, drowning more than 700 soldiers and 200 sailors. Utterly disheartened, Walker ordered the expedition to return to England.

News of the disaster reached the 2,300 militiamen and 814 warriors gathered by a still-game Nicholson at Fort Anne. About 160 of these warriors were Shawnees, Upper River Indians, or Long Islanders. Once again, Schaghticokes made up the lion's share of Upper River Indian recruits. Press gangs had been able to round up only 50 of the hoped-for 150 Long Island Indians wanted to portage loads and handle canoes and shallow-draft long boats known as batteaus on the waterways between Fort Anne and Montreal. Some 40 Indians from Connecticut had to partially make up the shortfall. Once again, Munsee country Indians in New Jersey and the Lower Hudson declined requests to join the expedition.

In the short run, their presence or absence made little immediate difference on the outcome of the campaign or the war. Again left on the lurch after receiving news of Walker's debacle, Nicholson had to order his men to withdraw. This time, they burned Fort Anne behind them to deny it to the French. Two years later, diplomats in Europe signed the Treaty of Utrecht on April 11, 1713. Giving up Nova Scotia, Newfoundland, and the Hudson's Bay territories, France finally agreed to a peace with England that would last for the next thirty years. The treaty made at Utrecht finally allowed British colonists to share the benefits of peace with France that Indians in Munsee country and their Indian Covenant Chain allies enjoyed much to the consternation of provincial authorities since 1701.[41]

Tuscaroras Come North

Formal protestations of peace and amity to the north did little to end animosities that had long kept conflict on the broil farther south. The first intimations that old problems were causing new troubles filtered north when a delegation of Tuscarora sachems appeared at the Conestoga Town on June 8, 1710. Defrauded by North Carolina traders and abused by squatters trespassing on their lands, worried Tuscaroras carried wampum belts and messages to the Senecas asking permission to join Shawnees and others living under Five Nations' protection in the Susquehanna Valley. A delegation of Conoys from Maryland making a similar asylum request soon followed.[42]

Open war broke out between the Tuscaroras and North Carolinians a year later. The war was a calamity. Cherokee, Creek, Catawba, and Yamasee warriors helped provincial militiamen kill Tuscaroras and burn their towns. Hundreds of Tuscaroras died in the fighting. Captives taken by other Indians were put to death or adopted. Most taken by the colonists mostly were enslaved.

Tuscarora refugees started showing up seeking asylum at various spots in Pennsylvania and New York by the spring of 1712. They arrived at a bad time. Nearly bankrupted by the collapse of trade caused by the still-raging war with France and panicked by rumors of French, Shawnee, Seneca, and River Indian attacks, colonists in New York were in the process of savagely suppressing a slave revolt. On April 6, 1712, a small group of enslaved Africans and Indians killed nine colonists and wounded some others. Rounding up suspects quickly, city authorities tortured, tried, and executed at least twenty-one of the accused prisoners, transported others from the colony, and began enacting harsher slave codes.

In the middle of all this, Harman Hekan told magistrates at a Nicolls Treaty renewal meeting at Kingston on June 2, 1712, that about six hundred "Shawannos who cannot live at peace in their own native country" had asked to settle "among them to the west and northwest of the blew hills in Ulster County where said Esopus Indians now reside" as his subjects. Ordered to return to Kingston to clear up a rumor that three strange Indians had been circulating wampum calling on the Esopus to rise up and massacre their neighbors just three weeks later, a chastened Harman Hekan denied the report. He further denied that any of his people were heading south to help Indians "going against North Carolina." He then tried to ease the fears of the nervous officials by admitting that the six hundred Indians mentioned at the last meeting were actually "but one sachimo and about 30 or 40 souls." Remembering that New York authorities had dispatched a River Indian envoy to the Susquehanna River on May 20, 1708, to invite Shawnee Indians living there to come to New York, he tried to convince the magistrates that his Shawannos "had lived about menesinck above 12 years."[43]

The magistrates were not fooled. They soon found out that Harman Hekan's shawannos were actually Tuscaroras. On July 3, 1712, Governor Robert Hunter, who had arrived to take over the government of New York and New Jersey on June 13, 1710, formally gave the Tuscaroras permission to remain at a fort they had built "beyond the blue hills." This was not, however, on the Delaware headwaters, nor did the Tuscaroras become subjects of Esopus. More than five hundred families of Tuscaroras instead gradually settled along the Susquehanna River during the next few years. By September 24,

1714, Five Nations sachems were telling Hunter that the Tuscarora Indians "are come to shelter themselves among" them. They were more specific in a speech made at Albany two years later, on September 15, 1716. At the meeting, their speaker informed Albany magistrates that Tuscaroras were living under their sponsorship and protection "about the branches of the Susquahanna River." The speaker went on to say that presents to the Five Nations should thenceforth be divided into six portions. Colonists themselves began referring to Tuscaroras as the sixth Iroquois nation, and the confederacy as a whole as the Six Nations, by 1722.[44]

Iroquois warriors and their Covenant Chain affiliates joined Tuscaroras sending warriors out against the Yamasees, Cherokees, Catawbas, and other Indian nations in league with the North Carolinians. The narrow Appalachian ridge valleys traversed by the ever-shifting route of the Warrior's Path became desolated no-man's-lands as the Great Southern War intensified. Those at the southern end of the Great Valley, like the Yamasees, who had taken an active part in the war against the Tuscaroras, were soon destroyed in their own war with North Carolina in 1715. Indians from Munsee country joined Iroquois warriors helping Tuscaroras take their revenge on the Yamasees. Among "the sachims of Susquahanna" reporting receipt of several presumably Yamasee scalps and captives from Carolina on September 26, 1715, was the Minisink sachem Tatapagh and a young cousin of Weequehela named Manawkyhickon.[45]

Nations like the Shawnees and Conoys living along those parts of the Great Valley traversed by the Potomac River and its tributaries moved entirely to refugee communities along the main stem of the Susquehanna River around this time. Farther south, Siouan-speaking nations caught in the middle had to split up. Some, like the Tuteloes, mostly moved north to the Susquehanna. A few, like the Saponis and Occaneechis, tried to stay put in safe havens like Fort Christanna, on the south side of Virginia in the Roanoke River valley. Others moved farther south and west.[46]

Except for warriors joining parties heading south, most Indians in Munsee country limited their travels to destinations farther north or west. Although vengeance, glory, captives, and peltry worked their enduring charms on those willing to be seduced by them, few from the Munsee homeland were interested in journeying to places where Virginian and Carolinian slavers lurked, waiting to drag unwary Indians off to markets in Williamsburg and Charleston. Even fewer were willing to journey on paths where mourning warriors might kill or capture the first people they encountered. Indians in Munsee country still had friends and relatives farther west, where furs, game, and fertile soils could be found in abundance. Beyond the Appalachians and distant from Iroquoia, Far nations like the Miamis respectfully addressed River Indians and other easterners as grandfathers whose long experience with colonists had made them seem wiser than any may have wanted to be. Assistance provided by metaphorical grandchildren would help grandparents forced from Munsee country endure the strains and stresses of dispossession and dislocation during the decades that followed.

12

UNMOORED, 1708–1742

Trips farther north and west became more frequent as Indians in Munsee country finally began to give up title to nearly all of their remaining ancestral lands east of the Delaware River. Syndicate partners in New York and New Jersey had cut out vast hunks of their territory for themselves at Minisink and other places during Cornbury's administration. Buoyed by these successes, colonists finally felt the time was right to press Indians for their remaining lands in the combined provinces. Although the settlers were divided as ever, they would no longer allow themselves to be manipulated by the few Indians still living on those parts of Munsee ancestral lands they were determined to own. There was little Indians could do about the situation. They knew that colonists were fully aware of their weakness. They also knew that they now had few friends among them. The generations that had put up with working disagreements and creative misunderstandings were passing away. The reluctance of Indians in Minisink, central New Jersey, and western Long Island to step forward during Queen Anne's War, moreover, added substance to rumors that they were conspiring with slaves, Senecas, and Shawnees to drive settlers away and regain lost lands. Distrusted and alone, they had to face hard-nosed businessmen intent on extinguishing remaining Indian title to land in their provinces.

On September 30, 1708, Norwalk town fathers from Connecticut convinced Katonah to sign over title to his people's last twenty thousand acres along the border with New York. Four years later, on October 8, Nimham I headed the list of sachems selling a tract of land at Matapan behind Beacon in Dutchess County. A bit farther north, Robert Livingston purchased yet another piece of Indian land within his manor boundaries from its Munsee- and Mahican-speaking residents on May 13, 1713.[1]

One by one and in small groups, Taphow, Weequehela, Memerescum, Meshocorrang, and their compatriots had to give ground in northeastern and central New Jersey. Between 1708 and 1710, East Jersey proprietor Peter Sonmans and his agents used licenses granted during Cornbury's and In- goldsby's administrations to acquire vast tracts of land in the higher upland reaches of the Passaic and Raritan valleys. The largest of these East Jersey pur- chases, the Makseta Cohung deed, signed on August 13, 1708, conveyed a vast block of land (see map 11) west of the Watchung Mountains, that in- cluded most of present-day Morris County. This and the other deeds signed at this time transferred title to thousands of acres to well-placed former Cornbury Ring partners like Ebenezer Wilson and Peter Fauconnier, and to Lucas Kierstede, who finally got some land of his own in the November 18, 1709, deed to territory along the Ramapo and Pequannock rivers. Other proprietors acquired tracts in the same region from the same sachems around the same time.[2]

On the other side of the Province Line, agents working for Lewis Morris, Daniel Coxe, and other West Jersey Society shareholders finally acquired the long-desired lands at the Delaware Water Gap. They got Taphow, Nowenock, Memerescum, Manawkyhickon, a young sachem from the Forks named Lappawinza, and several other leaders to sign a series of deeds to land there between 1709 and 1714. All of the tracts were large. A group of four deeds to lands directly at and around the Delaware Water Gap signed over to Daniel Coxe and his partners in one day on August 18, 1713, and another fi- nalized on November 1, 1714, represented the single largest group of takings of Indian land in West Jersey.[3]

Together, these deeds conveyed title to more than 1.25 million acres of Munsee country to West Jersey Society buyers. The land lost through these deeds represented virtually all remaining ancestral Indian territory east of the Delaware River. From a vantage point three hundred years away from the event, it looks like nothing less than a collapse. Incessant demands seem to have finally worn away the resolve of sachems whose people's depleted numbers could no longer hold back the flood of settlers. The several hun- dred pounds' worth of cash and trade goods accepted for these lands did not come close to offsetting so much loss. Bright spots were few and far between. Although surveyors showed up far sooner than many deed granters expected, it would be some time before they were followed by settlers dead set on driving Indians off their lands.

Taphow and the other sachems, who had held settlers back from the Kittatinys for so long, could take small comfort in knowing that the Water Gap gateway that had so dazzled Daniel Coxe and his proprietary partners was actually a blind door. Munsee- and Northern Unami–speaking Indians still held title to all Great Valley lands west of the gap. With a little help from Pennsylvanians just as eager to draw trade to their own province, they could block West Jersey efforts to press farther west. Even if the Jersey men could somehow get through, it would be many years before settlers would obtain Indian title to the passes through the Kittatiny or Blue Mountains. By then, the focus of the fast-dwindling fur trade would shift much farther away. To the north, trade increasingly gravitated toward Fort Oswego, built by New Yorkers in 1722, where the Oswego River flows into Lake Ontario. Trade from the west and south flowed into key Susquehanna Valley Indian towns at Conestoga and farther upriver at the river-fork town of Shamokin, "place of eels."[4]

NOMADS IN THEIR OWN HOMELAND

It took less than five years to extinguish most remaining ancestral Indian title to lands east of the Delaware River. It had taken colonists more than a century, however, to turn the Indians of Munsee country into the nomads they originally thought they were. Not that they had been entirely sedentary, settled agrarian farmers when Europeans first sailed to their country. Unlike Europeans, who drew on winds, and wheels to carry their bodies and bundles from place to place, Indians relied on mind and muscle power. People with limited mobility, like elders, the infirm, and mothers with very young children tended to stay with family and friends on ancestral lands. Hunters, warriors, traders, and sachems, especially men with wives in different towns, traveled farther from home. Even with firearms, fruit trees, fine fabrics, and other labor-saving innovations introduced by colonists, most Indian people, and especially the young and fit among them, preferred to travel to places where desired goods awaited.

Most Indians living in Munsee country did not had to travel terribly far to such places when they had held sole and absolute title to their homeland.

Loss of their coastal lands by the third quarter of the seventeenth century largely meant that they had to travel longer distances from inland towns to along-shore locales still owned by relatives or accessible by permission from new owners. Sale of all but a few scattered spots east of the Delaware River changed all that. Some Indians from the region held on in Lehigh Valley towns at the Forks, in small towns in and around the Great Valley, in other small tracts of central New Jersey pinelands, and on small reservations and pieces of vacant land on western Long Island. Most, however, soon moved to Munsee Indian towns and Christian missions west along the Susquehanna River or to Mahican towns farther east in the Housatonic Valley. Those who still wanted to live for at least part of each year on now-sold lands in ancestral Munsee country, and their numbers were not small, became wanderers.

They spent the year as travelers, camping in out-of-the-way spots as they moved between towns, missions, and reservations. Small knots of friends and families began moving along increasingly far-flung networks that could carry them from trapping grounds in Ottawa country or the Wabash Valley in present-day Indiana in winter to spring trade fairs at Oswego, Montreal, Albany, or Shamokin. Joining up with new partners and saying goodbye to old companions, some might journey during warmer months to relatives living in Long Island reservations or to oceanside back lots at Rockaway, Merrick, and Massapequa. Others might visit families and friends still hanging onto tiny tracts in Monmouth, Somerset, or Westchester counties. Some could also settle for the summer by still-unfenced old planting fields and orchards in the Great Valley. Munsees, as most of these people were increasingly called, might gather again in places like Albany, Kingston, and New York City for treaty meetings. They could then journey to Minisink or to Susquehanna Valley towns for fall religious festivals. After mending political fences and giving thanks for their blessings, young families and lively elders would leave to hunt deer and tend winter trap lines in nearby Pocono and Catskill mountain valleys or journey to Far country forests beyond the Appalachians.

Just as no document records Indian views on the patterns of land sales chronicled in this study, no single set of sources chronicles movement of a person or group through a network of the kind reconstructed here. The existing record comprises scores of references noting the presence of people from Munsee country in the above-mentioned places and others at various times during the decades following the loss of most of their last ancestral lands. An idea of what this network might have looked like can be had by glancing at references documenting the changing residences of Manawky-hickon, the cousin of Weequehela who became a prominent Munsee sachem.

Manawkyhickon first appeared in colonial documents as one of the more important sachems selling land between the Musconetcong River and the Delaware Water Gap between 1711 and 1713. He was next mentioned as one of the sachems on the Susquehanna whose warriors were going to war against Indians to the south in 1715. In 1728, he was noted as a relative of Weequehela's living at a place called Chenastry, on the upper reaches of the West Branch of the Susquehanna River. That same year, he was also report-edly circulating war belts, calling Miamis, Shawnees, and the Six Nations to war against the British.[5] By 1737, Manawkyhickon had returned to the Delaware River, where he was repeatedly mentioned in colonial documents as a senior sachem at Minisink until his last archival appearance on October 23, 1758.[6]

HAVENS ON LOST LANDS AND IN FOREIGN TERRITORIES

Munsees maintained their preference for living in towns consisting of single longhouses that sheltered family lines when living in their former homeland well into the eighteenth century. Initially depicted symbolically on early maps, this settlement pattern was first directly documented in deeds to Rar-itan Valley lands signed during the last quarter of the 1600s. These towns were known by names like Metapas's Wigwam and Amirent's (Emerus's) Plantation, after the names of their most prominent residents. Such places tended to come to colonial attention following conclusion of some kind of land agreement, and most disappeared shortly thereafter. This does not mean that Indian settlements in the Munsee homeland appeared and disappeared when noted in documents. Instead, deeds and surveys revealed specifics of Indian settlement geography in Munsee country that had earlier been over-looked, ignored, or kept from colonial notice.[7]

The single most comprehensive surveying exercise revealing the cultural landscape of a major section of Munsee country was undertaken by a young man named John Reading, Jr. In 1715, he became the first surveyor to view Indian lands in northwestern New Jersey when he was sent to lay out tracts for proprietors in the vast territories acquired between 1708 and 1714.[8]

Like most surveyors, he was careful to chronicle notable resources and prominent features as well as property boundaries. His journals documented an Indian world in northern New Jersey that had been largely hidden from colonial view. Three of these notebooks, chronicling surveying trips made in 1715, 1716, and 1719, are preserved by the New Jersey Historical Society. Among observations assessing land quality, reporting weather conditions, and chronicling finds of potentially exploitable lead, iron, and copper deposits are records of Indian fields and houses he saw and, on occasion, slept in. The upper Delaware Valley town of Cochecton, Pomptown on the Ramapo River, Whippany and Peapack in present-day Morris County, and the Shawnee towns at the Water Gap that Reading was able to glimpse only from a distance were all by then familiar places well known to colonists. Others, like the formidable mouthful Essakauqueamenshehikkon; towns called Allamuch-Ahokkin, Chanongong, and Mensalockauke; a settlement in the upper Walkill Valley named Chechong (noted as "an Indian plantation in good fence and well improved [whose people] raise wheat and horses"); and several unnamed houses and campsites unoccupied when Reading rode by, appear only in his journals.

Except for the knot of settlers around Maghkaghkemeck and others living alone along the fringes of frontier settlement, he encountered no other colonists in the Minisink region. Ironically, Reading never got the chance to see the Minisink town itself. Indians living in a house where the Minisink Path crossed the Tohockonetcong River (today's Paulins Kill), refused to let his party pass farther west in 1715. Maringoman, who was Reading's Indian guide, refused to help with a second attempt at a different spot, saying "that Tohokkonetkong Indians would be angry with him for showing their land." When the party decided to press on, the guide went home. Without Maringoman, Reading finally thought better of the decision and quietly redirected the party east of the Paulins Kill.[9]

Reading also avoided Minisink when he returned to the region in 1719 to help survey the New York–New Jersey border. Passing by the Shawnee towns on the Pennsylvania side of the Delaware, he left the river three miles below Minisink and took a more inland route to Maghkaghkemeck before traveling on to Cochecton. Even with this detour, armed Munsees again stopped his party short of his goal. Like the Tohokkonetkong Indians four years earlier and Manawkyhickon some twenty years further on, Munsees at Minisink refused to acknowledge that they had sold their land to anyone. They let the surveyors pass only when assured that they were only establishing a station point marking the provincial border and not taking their lands. It would take a war and a final comprehensive settlement to finally shake their grip from their beloved upper valley island fastness. Even then, Munsees would take care to retain their rights to hunt and fish on the land.[10]

Many Munsees maintaining old ties with Mahicans intensified close connections with Pocumtucks Pennacooks, Sokokis, and other Northern Indians. Indians and colonists living farther north and west increasingly extended the name Abenaki, "easterner," when collectively referring to these people. Schaghticoke residents began making longer and more frequent visits to Abenaki towns at Norridgewock, Becancour, and St. Francis Odanak as their putative protectors, the Albany commissioners led by Pieter Schuyler, started buying up the lands of those they were supposed to protect. Although authorities in New York regarded the Upper River Indians as their first line of defense against Canada, Schuyler himself never trusted the Indians living at Schaghticoke. He knew that nearly all were at least nominal Catholics with strong ties to French missions. He was also aware of the fact that many Schaghticokes still cherished ancient hatreds for New Englanders, and that most, including the people from Munsee country living among them, were considered spies and smugglers.

These beliefs led Schuyler and his board to be less than careful in protecting Schaghticoke interests. The board men started small, using the highly irregular tactic of calling in a mortgage for sixty beaver pelts and other skins from one "Taspelalet alias Murhank" to claim land at Schaghticoke on January 19, 1702. Five years later, they obtained a deed to all but twelve acres of Schaghticoke land between the mouths of the Mohawk and Hoosic rivers from a group of sachems that included Jan Conelle on February 28, 1707.[11]

By 1714, the Indians at Schaghticoke were desperate. Meeting with the board at Albany on September 27, they listened while the same men who were taking their territory promised to "allot them so much land and more than you and your children can cultivate and plant." Insisting that they needed more than promises, their speaker demanded to be "confirmed in some particular place under certain metes and bounds, that they might live no more like dogs." Many did not wait for the Albany men to break their promises. Schaghticokes suddenly released from wartime duties following the restoration of peace that same year began to drift away from the Hoosic Valley. After a long string of violent incidents, most finally left for Canada to join their Abenaki brethren against the New Englanders when open war again broke out between the old adversaries in 1722.[12]

At about the same time, other people born in and around Munsee country, like Manawkyhickon, were spending increasing amounts of time in fast-growing settlements above the forks at Shamokin along the upper reaches of the West and North branches of the Susquehanna River. Although records from this time are sketchy, it appears that Munsees were already building houses and planting crops near Tuscarora and other expatriate communities at sites of later multicultural Indian towns like Wyalusing, Tioga, and Ochquaga on the North Branch. On the West Branch, Manawkyhickon and his people lived near Shawnee and Six Nations people in towns built on the flats between present-day Muncy, Williamsport, and Lock Haven, Pennsylvania. Farther south, Munsees visited other Delaware-speaking friends and relatives living among Shawnees, Conoys, and other Indian expatriates on the main stem of the river between Shamokin and Conestoga.[13]

One of the earliest recorded statements made by an Iroquois claiming suzerainty over expatriate Indian communities in the Susquehanna Valley appears in a speech made on September 12, 1722. Addressing Virginia governor Alexander Spotswood during a Covenant Chain meeting convened in Albany to end the Great Southern War, the speaker started by asserting parity with his British brothers by noting that they and his people each represented ten nations. He went on to list the "Tuskarores, Conestogoes, Chuanoes [Shawnees], Ocghtachquanawicroones [Ochquagas], and Ostanghaes [Ostonwackin on the Lycoming River at Williamsport], which live upon Susquehana" among those ten nations. Several years would pass, however, before an Oneida man who lived along the West Branch named Shikellamy moved to Shamokin and presented Pennsylvania authorities with his credentials as the official Iroquois viceroy over the Susquehanna River expatriates.[14]

It is not known what happened to the people from Munsee country living among the Loups along the St. Joseph River after 1687. Governor Dongan asked the Five Nations to invite "Mahikanders that are at Ottowawa and further nations" to return east that year. It is unclear whether the invitation was proffered nor, if it was, whether it was accepted. It may be that warfare brought on by King William's War forced Loups remaining in Miami country to finally come back east with Viele, Mattaseet, and the Shawnees in 1694. Although negative evidence cannot prove anything, Jacques-Charles Renaud Dubuisson's very detailed account of the Mesquakie and Mascouten siege of Fort Pontchartrain at Detroit during the spring of 1712 contains no references to anyone representing themselves as Loups or easterners during this pivotal event in that region's history.[15]

PATIENTLY TRYING TO LIVE QUIETLY

Wherever they moved, the original inhabitants of Munsee country trod softly. Whether traveling through or beyond the borders of their much-colonized homeland, they fell into routines that helped them lead unobtrusive lives on lands now dominated by strangers. This approach was a sensible if not particularly ennobling way of dealing with the loss of a homeland. Although defiant voices like Manawkyhickon's occasionally threatened more memorable retaliation, most Munsee people resigned themselves to lives lived obscurely, leaving the risks and worries of power politics that had brought them to a low point behind for the time being. Ceding center stage to others, Munsees focused on rebuilding their families as they struggled to come to grips with hard new realities.

Their decision to minimize involvement in wider developments had risks as well as benefits. Munsees were a small nation of independent-minded folk who now had to live mostly on other people's land. Safety depended largely on maintaining as low a profile as possible without being entirely disregarded. Sachems determined to remind others of past promises and pledges paid special attention to the diplomatic niceties. They took care to periodically sign new agreements and renew old ones like the Nicolls Treaty. Munsee delegations also continued to welcome arrivals and condole deaths of Crown officials. At major meetings, Munsees mostly conducted themselves unobtrusively. Although they would always have a day or two of their own to have their say, they tended to remain in the background as Six Nations diplomats and colonial officials made the big decisions.[16]

Authorities who forgot about Munsees most of the time always seemed to remember them when they had need of their services. Munsee sachems always made a show of answering summons and responding to requests. They were careful, however, to minimize expectations. Assured of their fidelity and constantly reminded of the constraints they operated under, officials tended to forgive and forget when Munsees failed to obey orders or fulfill promises. Sachems pledging enduring friendship did not forget to remind authorities of laws and treaties when their people were cheated, assaulted, or arrested. Although feelings might run high, Indians and colonists had to forget about murderers and lesser offenders when miscreants from either community escaped retribution by fleeing to other jurisdictions.[17]

The desire for land that had kept Munsees firmly in the minds of colonists did not pass with acquisition of most of their last territory in their homeland east of the Delaware in 1714. Now deeds mostly preserved fading memories of past deals and arrangements. This did not mean that Munsees stopped doing land deals or colonists stopped producing records to remind them of who owned what. Land records, however, increasingly took the forms of terser affidavits confirming earlier sales and depositions identifying buyers, sellers, place names, and boundary markers. A substantial body of this documentation chronicled proceedings dealing with unfulfilled promises, blocked boundary-marking parties, and survey plats and property patents that always managed to take in far more land than anyone intended to sell.

Weequehela and other sachems regarded as Indian spokesmen worked hard with Governor Hunter and William Burnet, the man who replaced him in 1720, to keep the peace that Indians and colonists dreamed about during long decades of struggle and uncertainty. They kept contacts open with one another and relied on customs and laws short of war to deal with problems severe enough to circulate wampum belts or set pens to paper.

This tranquil state of affairs was threatened only once during the era of the Great Peace. Like the incidents that led to so much trouble in 1675, problems began with a string of unpleasant but not overly uncommon incidents occurring in several places at about the same time. The first of these took place in New Jersey. One day in the spring of 1727, Weequehela shot and killed a local tavern keeper and sometime ship captain and pilot named John Leonard during what most seem to agree was a drunken argument.[18]

By any measure, Weequehela was the best-known and most influential sachem in New Jersey. Depending on who was talking about him, he was a respected or feared head of a powerful family with close connections in Munsee- and Northern Unami–speaking communities. He was also a highly cultivated man with refined and expensive tastes, unusual among Indians and settlers at the time. He is said to have lived in a well-furnished frame house, with barns housing cattle and horses, surrounded by fields of wheat tended by enslaved Africans. It is also thought that he operated at least one mill on the banks of the Manalapan River.[19]

The circumstances of the shooting and the subsequent trial were murky. The result was not. At Perth Amboy on June 30, 1727, New Jersey authorities hanged Weequehela for murder. Two months later, newspapers reported that three "Indian Kings" gathered with fifty of their principal men at the late sachem's plantation to "crown a new king." Nearly all of Weequehela's people packed up and moved to the Forks of Delaware shortly thereafter.[20]

Trouble broke out in Pennsylvania almost as soon as the New Jersey Indians arrived at the Forks. A message reaching Philadelphia on September 27, 1727, containing the earliest known written reference to Munsees by name, reported that "Munscoes Indians, who live on an eastern branch of the Sasquehannah" killed a trader at a place called Snake Town. Just two months later, Indians from the Forks of Delaware drove off surveyors trying to lay out lands at Durham where Penn proprietary secretary James Logan was setting up an iron furnace. Durham was located just below where South Mountain formed the natural border between the piedmont lands to the south and the part of the Great Valley drained by the Lehigh River immediately to the north. The Indians claimed that they had not been paid for the land. Logan responded by dramatically producing what he claimed was a ten-year-old deed bearing the marks of Delaware Valley sachems to Indians attending the June 5, 1728, meeting convened at Philadelphia to deal with tensions caused by this and other, more serious incidents.[21]

News of these incidents began reaching Philadelphia in a flurry of panicky reports received between April and May 1728. Several reports stated that Manawkyhickon was circulating war belts among the Six Nations and the Miamis, calling on them to help him avenge his cousin Weequehela's execution. Even more worried messengers brought word that a brawl had broken out at earlier constructed ironworks at Maxantawny (near present-day Kutztown) between some "Shawanese from about Pechoquealin" and local colonists. Bands of settlers were said to be gathering to defend their families from further attacks. Shortly thereafter, Philadelphia authorities learned that three colonists belonging to one of these bands had murdered two Delaware women and an elderly Delaware man passing through their village at Cacoosing in the nearby Tuplehocken Valley.[22]

Determined to stop these outrages from spiraling into war, Pennsylvania's resident lieutenant governor, Sir Patrick Gordon, who had taken over from William Keith only a year earlier, acted quickly. On May 16, 1728, he issued a proclamation that called for calm and ordered vigilante bands to disperse. He also saw to it that the murderers of the Indians at Cacoosing were swiftly captured and brought to trial. Gordon then met with Susquehanna Valley sachems at Conestoga on May 26, 1728, and the leaders of the Schuylkill and Delaware Valley nations ten days later at the June 5 meeting in Philadelphia.[23]

Gordon condoled the Indians for their losses at both meetings. Announcing that two of the three Cacoosing murderers had been executed, he assured the sachems that his feelings of friendship toward them remained unchanged and urged them to put the late unpleasantness out of their minds. He also promised to hold a more general convocation in the fall to formally reaffirm friendship with all Indians in Pennsylvania.

Several developments that would dramatically affect future intercultural relations in the region came out at these meetings. At Conestoga, everyone agreed to recognize Shikellamy as the Six Nations regent over Indians living on the Susquehanna. Shortly thereafter in Philadelphia, James Logan browbeat the Delaware sachem Sassoonan and his people, then living mostly in the upper Schuylkil Valley, into acknowledging the validity of the irregular unrecorded 1718 deed to their lands below "the mountains on this side Lechay" between the Delaware and Susquehanna that he had produced on June 5. And more ominously, neither Manawkyhickon nor Shawnees from the Delaware Water Gap attended these or other meetings convened at the time.[24]

It is not that invitations were not issued. Gordon had sent substantial gifts along with his invitation to Manawkyhickon, whom he addressed as a man of worth and note among his people. Neither these sentiments nor the proffered gifts evidently mollified the sachem. Subsequent Six Nations and Miami rejections of his war belts, however, forced Manawkyhickon to reconsider his options. Hoping to ease tensions with the Shawnees on the Delaware, as well, Gordon's secretary, Logan, dispatched a message to their sachem Kakowatchy at Pechoquealin on May 21, 1728, reaffirming his government's wish for peace and inviting him to meet at Durham in the fall. Logan then sat back and waited for the Shawnees to come to him.[25]

From Anger to Alienation

Logan would have to wait a long time if he thought the Shawnees would answer a call to a meeting where he would have a chance to spring another unexpected deed on them. As summer began, the Shawnees seemed to be avoiding any contact with settlers. Then news reached Philadelphia in late August that Shawnees had hanged a trader from one of the rafters of a cabin at Shamokin in what could be seen as a grim simulacrum of Weequehela's execution. Another report soon revealed that the trader had survived his hanging. Just days thereafter, word reached the provincial capital that the Shawnees had completely abandoned their towns at the Water

Gap. They had moved with such haste, the report ran, that they left their corn standing. The circumstances of this Shawnee move remain as unclear as those surrounding Weequehela's people's relocation. Six Nations sachems claimed they ordered them west to be under Shikellamy's closer supervision. A few years afterwards, Shawnees themselves said that their neighbors at Minisink had asked them to leave, adding that they had been happy to go since the Minisinks and Iroquois had then been plotting to attack the Pennsylvanians.[26]

Whatever their reasons for going, Shawnees on the Delaware probably had patiently put up with as much Pennsylvanian protection, Iroquois supervision, and colonial neighborliness as they were going to take. There is some evidence suggesting that the Shawnees may have been thinking about moving for some time. On January 4, 1726, Logan directed that a notice be posted at Kingston, New York. The notice stated that word had reached him that people from that place were purchasing some land from Indians "on the west side of the Delaware River above Pechaquealin Hills." Stating that unauthorized purchases were against Pennsylvania law, he warned Kingston residents that his province would only allow purchases from Indians made with proprietary approval.[27]

It appears that Logan was working from good intelligence. A grandson and namesake of the old Hudson Valley land shark Nicholas Depui, who then lived in the hamlet of Keyserike about twenty miles southwest of Kingston, secured a private deed to three thousand acres of Indian land at and around Shawnee Island on September 18, 1727. Signed by two otherwise unknown people identified in the deed as "Waugoanlenneggea and Pemnogque," the younger Nicholas's deed anticipated the Shawnee departure by a year. Nicholas, Jr., parleyed his deed first into a lease and later into a more regular title issued by proprietary owner William Allen for 426 acres that included Depue and Shawnee islands. A couple of years later, on December 26, 1730, another enterprising settler named Johannes Westbrook made a private deal with a man identified as Syacop for some acres of land several miles upriver on the New Jersey side, just across the Binne Kill from Minisink Island.[28]

Whoever sold land at the Water Gap, Canadian documents suggest that French authorities had been trying to draw off Shawnees living there since 1724. It is also clear that a substantial number of Shawnees who left both the Delaware and Susquehanna valleys in 1727 settled far to the west on lands beyond the reach of Shikellamy and the Six Nations. Many moved close to Lake Erie near the sheltering walls of French forts housing traders, trade goods, gunsmiths, and small but mobile garrisons. Others set up new towns in the still-remote heart of the Ohio Valley, where only the most enterprising Iroquois, British, or French intruders might disturb them.[29]

The Shawnees and Weequehela's people were not the only people getting fed up with living near British colonists who insisted they were their protectors in 1728. Schaghticoke people, including several people from Munsee country, grew tired of living under the protection of grasping Albany commissioners. Many had been staying away from the town for increasingly longer periods of time since the end of Queen Anne's War. Their absence was encouraged by hostile New Englanders who did not distinguish them from Abenakis they had been at war with since 1722.

Patience finally turned to anger in the late summer of 1728, when Schaghticoke people returned from their hunting and fishing camps to find their fences broken down, their crops trampled by cattle, and hostile colonists planting their land. Formally greeting Burnet's newly appointed replacement Colonel John Montgomerie at Albany on October 5, 1728, they must have quietly boiled as they listened to the governor blandly assure them of his continuing protection. The attention of his listeners may have perked up when Montgomerie urged them to go to Canada to fetch those of their people who had deserted the province. They politely thanked the governor for his kind words and promised they would leave at the earliest opportunity. The Indians were as good as their word. Leaving Schaghticoke shortly after the meeting, many joined friends and family at the north end of Lake Champlain at Mississiquoi. Others went farther east to Cowas country along the uppermost reaches of the Connecticut River between Vermont and New Hampshire. Although they did not entirely abandon the place, few ever returned to Schaghticoke for more than a brief visit.[30]

Lower River Indians east of the Hudson River started selling off their last remaining tracts of territory in Highland hollows at this time. Robert Livingston made his final three purchases of Indian lands around Taghkanick in the remote hilly back lots of his manor between 1718 and 1724. Nimham I, Wackemane, and several other sachems put their marks on another three deeds between 1723 and 1730 that conveyed much of what remained of their lands in the Berkshire foothills. Most of the sachems signing these and other deeds soon moved with their people east to the still uncolonized uppermost reaches of the Housatonic Valley, where missionaries inspired by the Great Awakening were starting new Indian missions at places like Stockbridge, Massachusetts, and Scaticook, Connecticut.[31]

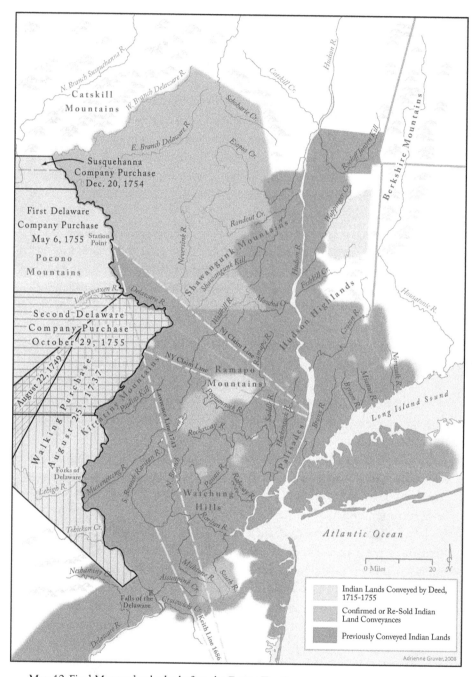

Map 12. Final Munsee land sales before the Easton Treaties

Across the Hudson, Esopus people continued to lodge complaints against Hardenbergh and others failing to pay for or taking too much of their lands at Nicolls Treaty renewal meetings. Renap was raised up as their principal sachem following the death of an elder sachem only identified as Peter at the meeting held in Kingston on January 29, 1723. Farther south in New Jersey, Nowenock, Memerescum, and their compatriots also sold some of their last tracts of land in the upper Passaic River Valley between 1717 and 1729 (see map 12). On November 11, 1721, Nutimus, an increasingly prominent relative of Weequehela, Manawkyhickon, and another young man named Teedyuscung, sold his people's last enclave on the Millstone River in central New Jersey.[32]

Together, these purchases in New Jersey and Esopus country were little more than nips and tucks smoothing out gores and gaps left from earlier sales. Experienced sachems like Manawkyhickon, newcomers like Nutimus and Teedyuscung, and a young man named Daniel who took Nimham as his surname, would soon have to face a new generation of ever more numerous colonists. These would mostly be a mix of ambitious younger sons of old colonial families and impoverished new immigrants from England, Ireland, Scotland, and the German states. Few would have had prior dealings with Indians, and most would share a mutual distaste for them. Unfettered by any sense of obligation or regard for the tiny remnants of Native communities clinging to ancient lands, they would instead concentrate on driving them beyond the pale of settlement.

Manawkyhickon, Nutimus, and the rest would spend the remaining years of their lives defending their people's last pieces of native soil from these newcomers. This critical stage in the struggle between colonists and Indians would furnish the stuff of some of the more iconic moments in American history. Memories of battles, treaties, and land purchases bound up in this climactic conflict still comprise much of the American sense of the colonial past in the present day. Already fading as colonists rushed onto their last lands, memories of earlier Indian efforts to hold onto their territory in the Munsee homeland disappeared as succeeding waves of settlers running roughshod over Indians and British officials flooded across their lost territories in search of new homes of their own farther west.

WALKING PURCHASE

Few land sales in American history weigh more heavily on consciences than the Walking Purchase. The story itself has been told often, and the best accounts leave little out. Although writers consistently identify the Indians involved in the sale as Delawares, very few acknowledge that very nearly all of the Delawares involved in the Walking Purchase were either Munsees or people closely connected to them. This omission has had the same effect on memory as the failure to identify the Indians who sold Manhattan in the most memorable of all American land deals. While use of general terms like Delaware allows scholars to sidestep nitpicking arguments over exactly who owned what, their use has also blotted out memories of significant roles played by Munsee-speaking Delawares in the nation's history.[33]

Munsees were not the only Indians involved in this pivotal purchase. For the first time, the Iroquois Confederacy played a deciding role in a sale of land within the ancestral Munsee homeland. Their involvement began just as the newly arrived proprietary governor Thomas Penn was settling in at Philadelphia. Penn had come to Pennsylvania to drag his family out of debts that had plagued them since the time of his late father. The family had already countenanced sales of large tracts of unpurchased Indian territory in the Lehigh Valley around present-day Allentown to William Allen and several other friends before Thomas sailed to America. Although he was new to the colony, the young Penn knew enough to realize that only the Six Nations were powerful enough to back up these sales and shake loose other lands whose sale monies and quit rents were needed to bail out the financially strapped Penn clan.[34]

Penn, Logan, and representatives of four of the Six Nations met at Philadelphia from August 23 to September 2, 1732, to look into ways they might help each other. Penn proposed that they enter into a new relationship in which the Six Nations would serve as the province's strong arm in all matters involving Indians in Pennsylvania. The new policy would depend upon skilled intermediaries. The Six Nations had men like Shikellamy already in place along the Susquehanna. His provincial counterpart would be a uniquely savvy polyglot son of Palatine German immigrants named Conrad Weiser. Weiser had lived among the Mohawks for sixteen years as a young man and was intimately familiar with their language and customs. Fluent in English as well as German, he also understood Delaware and several other Indian languages. He had begun his career on the frontier in the service of the Six Nations as an intermediary with Pennsylvania.[35]

Having secured Iroquois support, Thomas Penn soon began pressing Nutimus to sell his people's lands in the Lehigh Valley. His first efforts in 1734 failed. One year later, he tried again at a meeting with Nutimus, Lappawinza, and several other sachems at the Penn family country seat at Pennsbury on

May 8, 1735. His secretary, Logan, started by producing a couple of Indian deeds to lands north of Philadelphia to establish a baseline for Penn's purchase request. One was the well-remembered registered deed to land at the Falls of the Delaware signed on July 15, 1682, by sachems Logan identified at the time as "Idaquahon and several other southern Indians." The second was yet another unrecorded and unendorsed surprise deed, this one with blank spaces in critical places. Bearing a date of August 20, 1686, and signed by "Mayhke-erickkishsho, Sayhoppy, and Taughhaughsey, the chiefs or kings of the Northern Indians on Delaware," the document purported to convey land extending "back into the woods as far as a man can go in one day and a half" from a point on Neshaminy Creek in Bucks County. Explaining that the newly arrived governor had just found this latter document in a box of old family papers, Logan had several older settlers come forward to confirm that they had attended the meeting where the deed was signed.[36]

Neither Nutimus nor any other Indian in attendance could remember the fifty-year-old transaction. The use of the travel trope to take bounds was memorably rare, and the Indians knew that their ancestors had signed a deed to land at Neshaminy bounded in part by travel distance sometime around 1700. They could not, however, remember this new document. It was at this time that Logan decided to challenge Nutimus's rights to the land by asking the sachem how a Jersey man like himself could own land in Pennsylvania. This was the incident where Nutimus said he had rights to lands on both sides of the river from both his mother's and father's families. Reflecting on Logan's assertion, Nutimus then asked how the secretary, an Irishman from the old country, could have rights to lands an ocean away in Pennsylvania? The meeting broke up with Nutimus promising he would bring knowledgeable elders to sort things out at their next get-together.[37]

Finally realizing that he could not make Nutimus do what he wanted, Penn authorized Logan to begin working behind the scenes to get the Six Nations to make the Indians at the Forks more tractable. Logan started by directing Weiser to get the Iroquois to sign over lands occupied with their permission by Unami, Shawnee, and other expatriates below the Blue Mountains along the lower Susquehanna River. Although they balked at first, the Six Nations finally deeded over the requested territory on October 11, 1736. Refusing at first to also convey the lands of people they characterized in this instance as their cousins in the Delaware Valley, reluctant Six Nations sachems finally signed over whatever rights they might have to those lands on October 28, 1736. There was only one problem; the Iroquois had no rights to any Delaware Valley lands on the river's main-stem head-waters below present-day Deposit, New York.[38]

This did not matter to Penn and Logan, who took their next steps toward taking the Forks lands at a special session of the provincial council convened on August 24, 1737, in Philadelphia (a meeting not recorded in that body's regular minutes). Speaking for his people, Manawkyhickon presented Penn with a belt of wampum of four rows that affirmed their long-standing "mutual love and friendship." He then proceeded to business. He told the governor that his people did not fully understand what lands were involved in the "deed from Mayhkeerichshoe." A hastily drawn-up map showing a northern border marked by what most commentators affirm was represented to the Indians as Tohickon Creek (but inscribed "west branch of the Delaware," actually the Lehigh River, on the only surviving copy of the map) was shown and accepted. Doubtless informed that the Six Nations would not support them against the Pennsylvanians, Manawkyhickon and the other sachems agreed to sign a confirmation deed acknowledging these boundaries so long as their people "may be permitted to remain on their present settlements and plantations, though within that purchase, without being molested." They were promised that would be the case, and on August 25, 1737, Manawkyhickon, Nutimus, and nearly every other sachem of any consequence with rights to land at the Forks put their marks on the document.[39]

The result was, in hindsight, dismally predictable. Penn had a road cut from the starting place at the present-day Bucks County village of Wrightstown due north and away from the Delaware River, straight into Indian territory. He then had Logan hire the three fastest runners they could find to make the one and a half day walk on September 19, 1737. By noon of the following day, the last remaining runner reached a spot where the borough of Jim Thorpe stands today. The line run during that day and a half extended fifty miles from its starting point. Penn then took advantage of the vague wording describing the conveyance's upper border as a line going from "the utmost extent of the said one day and a half's journey . . . to the aforesaid River Delaware." Rather than run the line due east, he had the line forming the purchase's upper boundary run at a right angle northeast from the walk's endpoint, sixty-five more miles in a straight line to the spot where the Lackawaxen River flows into the Delaware River. In so doing, the Walking Purchase took in more than 1 million acres, five times more land than the Indians had expected to lose. In one day, the Munsees and their kin lost title to nearly all they had left in Pennsylvania.

Outraged, Nutimus and his people returned home, determined to stop any Pennsylvanian trying to move onto land above Tohickon Creek. Initially, earlier purchasers like William Allen took care to privately compensate neighboring Indians before authorizing anyone to occupy any tracts he sold in the Lehigh Valley. Allen had particular success selling suddenly formally registered parcels of lawfully patentable lands to buyers seeking secure titles. Nicholas Depui, the prominent Great Awakening evangelist George Whitefield, and a group of newly arrived followers of the Moravian Brethren patron Nickolaus Ludwig, Count von Zinzendorf, were among his first buyers. The Moravians settled in 1739 at the invitation of Whitefield on a tract he had purchased and christened the Barony of Nazareth. Quickly falling out with Whitefield, the Moravians bought five thousand acres for themselves south of Nazareth on the banks of the Lehigh, where they began building the city they named Bethlehem in 1740. After purchasing Nazareth from Whitefield a year later, Bethlehem remained and continues to be the administrative hub of the Moravian community to the present day.[40]

Penn did not take everything immediately. Partially honoring the promises he had made to Manawkyhickon in 1737, the Pennsylvania governor set aside the sixty-four-thousand-acre Indian Manor reservation on the upper Lehigh River. He later allowed Moses Tunda Tatamy to keep a small three hundred-acre tract at present-day Stockertown, Pennsylvania, that the Christian Indian from central New Jersey had purchased directly from Allen in 1741.[41]

Most of Allen's buyers moving to the Forks wanted to see all Indians leave the area as quickly as possible. Hard words were soon exchanged, and threats of violence made. Doubtless reminding the Six Nations that what Pennsylvanians did to them could be done to others, Indians at the Forks called on their Iroquois uncles to support them in this time of need.[42]

The Six Nations responded by agreeing to come to Philadelphia to discuss the problem. More than four times the expected fifty Iroquois, Munsee, and Unami attendees subsequently gathered in the provincial capital during the last week of June 1742. The Onondaga speaker Canasatego directly addressed his first speech to an expectant Nutimus at the first open session of the meeting on July 12. Nutimus can only have been appalled as Weiser translated the harshest words yet uttered by a sachem from any nation in the presence of colonists in council. Holding up a wampum belt, Canasatego laced into the Forks Indians. He rhetorically shook them by the hair on their heads, called them women with no right to sell land, and upbraided them as selfish children for not sharing goods received for land that had "gone through their guts." Imperiously telling them that "we don't give you the liberty to think about it," Canasatego ordered Nutimus and his people to move immediately to lands the Six Nations had set aside to keep an eye on them at Shamokin or Wyoming.[43]

Pennsylvania authorities almost immediately afterwards moved to violate the pledge they had made in 1737 to not evict the Indians from the Forks. A brother of King Taminy and cousin of Weequehela named Wehheland (known among the colonists as Delaware Captain John) asked to be made exempt from the eviction order. His town of Welagameka, "fine rich soil," lay on the same tract first purchased in 1738 by Whitefield and bought by the Moravians three years later. Receiving word of Wehheland's eviction order on July 3, 1742, the Moravians informed the government that they would allow his people to stay rent-free "because the place has been a settlement of his forefathers." Upon learning that Penn insisted on the eviction, they took care to pay the departing Indians for their land before they left to join their people in new homes on Iroquois land in the upper Susquehanna Valley.[44]

13

SOLD OUT, 1743-1766

Cheated by Penn, abandoned by the Six Nations, and suspected of holding a grudge by nearly everyone, most Indians quickly left the Forks after 1742. More than a few decided to join expatriate Shawnees in the Ohio Valley far from colonists and Iroquois. Some moved to Ochquaga on the North Branch of the Susquehanna River. Nutimus and his family stayed closer, moving to one of the Munsee communities just above the Kittatiny Ridge before relocating to Manawkyhickon's old town at the Great Island between Lock Haven and Williamsport. Manawkyhickon himself remained on the Jersey side of the Delaware, on the shrinking patch of land his people still held at Minisink. Teedyuscung and his people stayed closest of all, remaining in their town of Meniolagomeka, tucked into a small stretch of flat land on Aquashicola Creek at Smith's Gap, just north of the Kittatiny Ridge a few miles west of the Wind Gap.[1]

Other Indians from Munsee country tried to defy the Penn eviction notice and stay in the Lehigh Valley. Some joined the Moravian mission communities at Bethlehem and Nazareth. A few, like Moses Tunda Tatamy, associated themselves with the same David Brainerd that Manawkyhickon laughed at in Minisink on May 10, 1744. Starting his missionary work a year earlier at the mixed Munsee-Mahican town of Kaunaumeek in a small Great Valley cove in the Berkshire foothills, Brainerd moved to the Forks to convert Indians there during the early summer of 1744.[2]

Word of another round of fighting between Great Britain and France reached America at about the same time Brainerd relocated to the Forks. Known in the colonies as King George's War, the new conflict heightened settlers certainty that angry, alienated Munsees would now turn against them. Colonists at the Forks soon joined Penn and Iroquois demanding that all Indians leave the Lehigh Valley. Fearing that their nervous neighbors would attack them now that war had been declared, most of Brainerd's followers decided to leave. Most returned to New Jersey by 1746 to settle in small plots that Weequehela's successor, Andrew Wooley, had held onto between Cranbury and Crosswicks.

Colonists in the Hudson Valley also increasingly regarded their remaining Munsee neighbors with suspicion. To make matters worse, many settlers feared that the Moravians who had set up missions of their own at mixed Munsee-Mahican communities at Shekomeko and Pine Plains near Kaunaumeek in 1740 were secret Catholics in league with the French. Giving in to these fears, Dutchess County officials saw to it that the Moravian missionaries left with any loyal converts willing to follow them in 1746. Most moved to the small Pennsylvania mission town built for them north of Bethlehem, christened Friedenshuetten, "Huts of Peace." Hostile locals near Bethlehem almost immediately forced the Moravians to relocate the community twenty-five miles farther up the Lehigh River to a place the missionaries named Gnadenhuetten, "Huts of Grace." Located at Lehighton, Pennsylvania, just above the Lehigh Gap, astride a key communications route to the Susquehanna Valley, the mission lay just across the river from the Munsee town of Pohopoco.[3]

TURKEYS, WOLVES, AND RUMORS

Indians living among worried settlers in New York's Orange and Ulster counties did not wait to be evicted during the anxious winter of 1745–1746. They fled to their hunting camps at and around Cochecton after Allamaaseeit, a son of Tatapagh, brought news from the west that French and Indians "at Mesasippi" were making large numbers of snowshoes. He told Bernardus Swartwout's son Jacobus on December 15, 1745, that they planned to use the snowshoes to carry them on a midwinter attack "against Albany, Soapus, and Minisink, and likewise the frontiers of Jersey and Pensylvania." A combined French and Indian attack on Saratoga a little more than two weeks earlier on November 28, 1745, gave the report chilling credibility.[4]

The sudden withdrawal of the Esopus and Minisink Indians from the settlements alarmed the already concerned colonists. New York authorities dispatched the elder Swartwout, who was then a major in the Orange County militia, his commander Colonel Thomas De Key, and several other men to find out what was going on. The small party reached the Indian encampment at Cochecton on December 21, 1745. In his subsequent report, De Key stated that he believed the Indians numbered "about 90 or 100 together, with their families." Their speaker told him that they had withdrawn into the interior because they had grown afraid of neighbors who were "always under arms." Assuring the Indians that the settlers were not preparing to attack them, De Key asked that they keep a sharp lookout for any signs of an impending attack. They promised to do so and pledged to help colonists repel any assault launched against the Orange County frontier. Saying that they had recently lost their sachem, they told De Key that they would come to the county seat at Goshen to meet with the governor as soon as they were finished "debating out of which tribe a sachem should be chosen to govern the whole."[5]

The Indians went on to say that they then consisted of two tribes, identified by De Key as wolves and turkeys. This was the first and only time anyone mentioned tribes explicitly named after animals in English in the Munsee homeland. Just what these animal names signified is unclear. Neither were mentioned or drawn as signatures onto the two deeds that finally quieted Indian claims in the Hardenbergh Patent signed shortly thereafter. As mentioned earlier, Esopus sachem Hendrick Hekan was the primary signatory on both instruments. Indians closely associated with the Minisink and Pompton communities, such as Nimham II, Allamaaseeit, and a newcomer named Mottellend, signed the southernmost of the deeds on August 2, 1746, as "Cashichton Indians." Those signing the earlier June 6, 1746, deed to the northernmost part of the purchase, including Renap, "Moonhaw the right Ancrop . . . Tamacapawain and Paskholind, two sons of said Hendrick Hekan," Allamaasseeit, Mottellend, and others, had close associations with the Esopus community.[6]

It could be argued that the wolves were the northernmost group. Many of these people, after all, had close ties to Munsees and Mahicans, whom the French sometimes called Loups. The French, however, almost always employed words like Loup and versions of the Dutch form Mahikander as general cover terms for all Eastern Algonquians. In later years, Americans farther west would often, but not always, use the term "wolf" as synonym for Munsee.

On January 3, 1746, the Indians themselves provided some insight into who the wolves and turkeys in this instance were when their newly selected sachem arrived with twelve of their "chief men" at Goshen as promised. They brought a belt of wampum along to renew their Covenant Chain obligations.

De Key wrote that he spent an hour sitting tied to the sachem by this belt in symbolic assurance that their friendship would last "as long as the sun and moon endures." He did not, however, do more than identify the man and his entourage as "Cashighton Indians."

The identity of these Indians from Cochecton was cleared up twelve years later at another treaty meeting, this one in Easton, Pennsylvania. At the October 21, 1758, treaty-signing session, Teedyuscung held up a wampum belt on behalf of "Nimham the eldest principal chief of the Wappingers or Opings . . . living near Aesopus" who was said to be too sick to attend in person. Three years later, the aged sachem himself, Nimham II, held up the same belt at another meeting. This time, the belt was identified as "a large peace belt of 16 rows with two hearts and the figures 1745 woven into it." The sachem used the belt to announce that his people would be moving with others he called Mohickons to Teedyuscung's town at Wyomink.[7]

Nothing in these references seems to directly indicate that the wolf and turkey tribal names were synonyms for Mahican, Wappinger, Esopus, or Minisink communities. They may instead represent a moiety system of two complementary phratries in a phratry system whose constituent elements contracted or expanded in size and number at different times and places. As in other areas of their lives, such flexibility conferred significant adaptive benefits to Munsees unmoored from ancestral territories and confronting catastrophic population decline.[8]

All this does not mean that turtle tribe people did not live among Munsees at this time. Several could probably be found married to wolf or turkey spouses. Most were probably men who did not have sufficient blood rights, social clout, or numbers needed to break into the cross-cousin marriage system that could maintain wolf and turkey social and political dominance in these communities. A few decades later in Ohio, Moravian missionaries like David Zeisberger would note the almost total political and social dominance of turtle phratry members in mostly Unami-speaking Delaware communities and a corresponding dominance of wolf phratry people where the Munsees were the majority.[9]

LIQUOR, PREACHERS, AND PROPHETS

Little was heard of Munsees in corridors of colonial power in the years immediately following the end of King George's War in 1748. Some Indians in northern and central New Jersey got mixed up with rioting farmers still defying efforts to get them to take out proprietary deeds and pay rents. Andrew Wooley spent years dealing with suits lodged by Lewis Morris's son, Robert Hunter Morris, aimed at evicting Indian people from their land at Cranbury. Indians kept showing up at Rockaway, Merrick, and other places to listen to sermons delivered by another revivalist preacher, Azariah Horton, as he rode his circuit preaching to Native people and enslaved Africans across Long Island.

Most of the time, however, Munsee people quietly traveled virtually unnoticed through their old homeland, continuing to camp in untenanted back lots or lands specially set aside for them. Many made, sold, and traded baskets, brooms, and herbal remedies to settlers. More than a few supplemented this income by hiring out as seasonal laborers, handymen, and house servants. Able-bodied men often joined other Indians on crews of merchantmen and whalers sailing to Arctic oceans, European ports, and more distant destinations.[10]

No matter how much they traded or how hard they worked, they remained a poor people. Sickness and liquor sapped vitality and spread despair. Colonists in the settlements openly defied laws prohibiting sale of liquor to Indians. Few missed any opportunity to take advantage of alcohol-befuddled Munsees as they passed through their neighborhoods. Nakedly manipulative deed deals made at the time were cynically dipped in drink and deceit. Munsees beyond caring sold or pawned furs, guns, and even their clothing for rum and beer. Late winters became starving times as impoverished families ran through their stocks of corn and flour. Malaria and other fevers racked bodies enfeebled by smallpox, hunger, and hard liquor.[11]

Things were little better on the frontiers. Waves of traders sometimes hauling little more than barrels of rum descended on Indian towns along the Susquehanna River as Six Nations sachems schemed to sell the ground out from under them. Reports reaching New York and Philadelphia were filled with accounts of brawls, assaults, thefts, rapes, and killings. Increasing numbers of reports noted Indian withdrawals farther west into the Ohio Valley. Others warned that Indians everywhere along the frontier were listening more closely to French agents urging them to abandon their Covenant Chain allies.[12]

Although many suffered greatly, few gave way to despair. Some Munsees trying to understand why things were going so badly wrong decided to hear what missionaries had to say on the subject. More than a few subsequently moved to the missions established by these preachers. Missions became both homes to converts and way stations along networks traversed by friends and relatives. Diaries chronicling daily life at places like Gnadenhuetten document a constant stream of Indian visitors. Missions became safe zones where harassed people could take refuge, binge drinkers could dry out, and the hungry could be fed. Although missionaries would only permit converts to settle permanently, few turned away visitors willing to work, hunt, carry messages, or provide other services. Indians at the missions built bark-covered longhouses, more substantial log cabins, and frame churches and meeting houses. Many of their buildings had glass windows and hinged doors. They also erected barns, mills, and mill pond dams and races. Many enclosed house lots; fields; apple, peach, and cherry orchards; hog pens; and cattle troughs with stone walls and rail fences.[13]

Only a small percentage of Indians in these mission towns permanently converted to Christianity. Some followed the spiritual path trod by Teedyuscung. He joined the Moravians and accepted the name Gideon given him just after the Six Nations sold his land at Meniolagomeka out from under him. On August 22, 1749, Canasatego and his Iroquois Confederacy colleagues compelled Nutimus and his compatriots to sell Meniolagomeka and all other lands between the Delaware and Susquehanna rivers south of a line formed by the Lackawaxen River and Moosic Mountain (a chain of hills below present-day Scranton, Pennsylvania). Although there is no way of knowing this directly, it seems that Gideon's conversion was inspired by the example set by Tatamy, whose own acceptance of Christianity played a major role in helping him keep his small plot of land at the Forks after other Indians were evicted.[14]

Unable or unwilling to buy his people's land at Meniolagomeka as Tatamy did at Stockertown, Gideon did the next best thing. He invited Moravians to establish a mission at the place in 1750. The mission lasted until 1754, when Pennsylvania authorities finally ordered the Indians to leave. Some of the townspeople moved to Gnadenhuetten. Others followed Teedyuscung, who, after disavowing the new religion that had failed to protect his home and his people, finally moved to land under Six Nations control on the other side of Moosic Mountain at Wyomink in the Susquehanna Valley.[15]

Other Indians forced to leave the Munsee homeland turned elsewhere for spiritual renewal. Many would soon become followers of Neolin, a man colonists knew as the Delaware Prophet. Neolin called on his people to turn away from Europeans and their religion, guns, drink, and wares. He told followers that Kiisheelumukweenk would drive away the colonists and restore things to the way they were before Europeans arrived if they returned to the old ways.[16]

A few followed the young Munsee mystic Papunhank. A son of the Esopus leader Dostou and a grandson of Mamanuchqua, Papunhank was among the earlier Moravian converts at Shekomeko. He was inspired by dreams to seek a middle way incorporating what he thought were the most workable aspects of traditional and European beliefs. Leaving the Moravian brethren, he established a spiritual community of his own at Wyalusing, on the North Branch of the Susquehanna River, in 1752.[17]

Only the most fervent believers permanently moved to religious communities built by prophets or missionaries. Most Munsees caught up in the religious enthusiasms sweeping through their towns chose to remain at home. Moses Tunda Tatamy and his brethren in New Jersey, and most of the Indians scattered across western Long Island, for example, stayed in their own settlements where they could receive or travel to hear circuit-riding clerics and itinerant preachers.

By 1754, neither prophets, missionaries, nor officials charged with enforcing laws meant to kept the peace could stand in the way of the four hundred thousand or so strangers now living on ancestral Munsee lands. Straining to break beyond the Appalachian mountain wall that had hemmed settlers in for more 150 years, they stood ready to sweep down onto the western lands uneasily occupied by displaced Munsees and other Indians under Iroquois suzerainty. Many of these colonists were newcomers alienated in one way or another from the societies they left behind. Most were young. Longing for homes of their own, few wanted to pay rent to Hudson Valley manor lords or buy the high-priced properties then on offer from proprietors in New Jersey and Pennsylvania. Whether they were looking for new lands for themselves or for territory to sell to others, all seemed determined to finally drive Indians from the region.

LAST LAND GRABS

Munsees were not the only people threatened by new immigrants. Imperial officials and longtime residents looked for ways to channel the volatile mix of religion and rapacity that seemed to pulse through this land-hungry multitude. Soon Mohawks found themselves in the path of this demographic wave. Unlike their other Six Nations confederates, who had thus far only been called on to give up tiny albeit strategically placed pieces of land for some forts and missions, the Mohawks faced the specter of utter dispossession. Colonists brandishing deeds, most of them as usual taking in far more than the Indians had agreed to and many of them patently fraudulent, claimed nearly all of their lands. Fed up, the Mohawks came to New York on June 12, 1753, with a long list documenting the worst excesses. They presented their grievances to George Clinton, who was then at the shank end of his ten-year tenure as governor of New York. Clinton supported the colonial claims. On the last day of the meeting on June 16, 1753, an outraged Mohawk sachem, Theyanoguin, known among the colonists as Hendrick, announced that he would be sending a wampum belt to Onondaga demanding that the Covenant Chain be "broken between you and us."[18]

This speech got the attention of the Board of Trade, whose members ordered that every province in British America send representatives to meet with the Six Nations to patch things up. Commissioners from seven colonies met with a comparatively small number of Six Nations and River Indian sachems between June 19 and July 10, 1754, at what became known as the Albany Congress. This was the meeting where Theyanoguin's good friend, the soon-to-be-knighted and already influential Mohawk Valley trader-diplomat William Johnson, came into his own. He used his position as the man charged by congress commissioners to look into Indian claims to help vault himself into the pivotal post of Crown-appointed go-between for all Indians and colonists north of Maryland, a position he held until his death in 1774.[19]

Although the commissioners did not know it at the time, the congress saved the Covenant Chain at a time when they would most need it. Some five hundred miles southwest of Albany, the young Virginian militia officer George Washington surrendered his force of four hundred men to six hundred French troops and one hundred Indian warriors on July 4, 1754, at a hastily constructed stockade he dubbed Fort Necessity. The Virginians were there because the French had just started building a post of their own that they called Fort Duquesne at the Forks of the Ohio, on land claimed by their province.

Washington had built Fort Necessity at a place called the Great Meadow, some miles below the French bastion, after bushwhacking one of their patrols sent to find out what the Virginians were up to on May 28, 1754. Surrendering the place after a one-day siege, he was allowed to march back to Virginia with his men after signing a piece of paper written in French (a language Washington did not understand) admitting that he had assassinated diplomats sent to parley with him on May 28. Like another killing 160 years later at Sarajevo, this incident would spark the outbreak of a world war.

Two deeds signed by Six Nations sachems under shady circumstances in Albany during the conference helped Munsees decide which side they would support when the fighting started. Negotiations for the first of these dragged on for five days. Starting at a local tavern on July 5, 1754, the Pennsylvania contingent led by John Penn, which included a diplomatic neophyte named Benjamin Franklin attending his first big meeting, pressed Six Nations sachems to sell all Indian lands in the western region where Washington had just surrendered to the French. Everyone in the room knew that Indians whom they had already betrayed now lived on those lands under their supposed protection. They also knew to a certainty that these Indians would turn against them and join the French once these last lands were sold out from under them.

None of this stopped either the Pennsylvanians or the Iroquois. By the time Conrad Weiser interpreted the last speech on July 9, 1754, the Iroquois confirmed the earlier October 11, 1736, deed to all lands in the province south of the Kittatinys and signed a new deed accepting £400 for all land they claimed by conquest west of the Susquehanna River, south of a line running from the mouth of Penn's Creek west to the farthest limits of the province's charter bounds. Just two days later, an Albany trader named John Henry Lydius, representing a cartel of nearly eight hundred Connecticut settlers calling themselves the Susquehannah Company, convinced eighteen Six Nations sachems to sign over all lands west of the Susquehanna north of Penn's Creek for £2,000.[20]

Whatever recriminations passed between the signers of these deeds, all stood by the agreements even as word of the Washington's defeat filtered back to the eastern settlements. Pennsylvanian protests lodged immediately after news of Lydius's purchase reached Philadelphia did not deter Connecticut men confident that their sea-to-sea charter gave them the right to buy unpurchased Indian lands at their province's designated latitude west to the Pacific Ocean.

Things soon grew more complicated. Plied with liquor, Nutimus, Allamaaseeit, Mottellend, and several others put their marks on two deeds put before them by representatives of another Connecticut cartel calling itself the Delaware Company between May 6 and October 29, 1755. Nutimus and the rest were identified in the deeds as "sachems and chiefs of the ancient tribe and nations of the Indians called Ninneepauues otherwise and in English known by the name of the Delaware Indians." They accepted a total of 718 Spanish milled dollars and unspecified quantities of trade goods for lands taken from them by the Walking Purchase and subsequent disputed deals. They then returned to the Susquehanna Valley to await developments.[21]

The air must have been electric as everyone waited to see what would happen next. News from the frontier was ominous. During the summer of 1754, Abenakis from Canada burned some houses around Schaghticoke and convinced the sixty or so Indian men, women, and children still living there to leave with them. Thus ended the settlement that Edmund Andros had started nearly eighty years before to protect New York. By winter, Abenakis were traveling through small River Indian encampments below Albany urging their occupants to join them in Canada.[22]

Relieved colonists welcomed thousands of British troops under the overall command of General Edward Braddock landing at Boston, New York, and Potomac River shores during the winter of 1754–1755. Those Indians still living in the settlements looked on with less enthusiasm as militiamen began drilling with regulars on local parade grounds. They, like the British, were still formally at peace with the French. Provincial officials and army officers urged those who would listen to sign up for expeditions that would surely seize Canada and Acadia when the campaigning season reopened in the spring. Politely declining to touch pens to muster rolls, most Munsees chose instead to watch and wait.

They did not have to wait long. On April 15, 1755, Braddock announced his plans to take Fort Duquesne and march north to join another British army, then gathering at Albany to advance on Fort Niagara, at a convocation of governors meeting with him at Alexandria, Virginia. This was also the meeting where Braddock handed William Johnson his long-sought appointment as Superintendent of Indian Affairs for the Northern Department. Sending Johnson back to New York with orders to lead militiamen and Mohawks north to guard the frontier at Lake George, Braddock rejoined his army assembling farther up the Potomac at Fort Cumberland (present-day Cumberland, Maryland). He may have done better if he had ordered Johnson to join him with his mixed force of Mohawks, Stockbridge Indians, and colonial militiamen. As it was, Braddock was only able to get eight Mingo Indians to scout the route ahead for his army.

On May 29, 1755, Braddock began marching his two thousand-man force and its straggling supply train up the wagon road toward Fort Duquesne cut by Washington a year earlier. Washington himself accompa-

nied Braddock as a member of the general's military family. Coming to the
end of Washington's Road on June 16, Braddock decided to send four hundred woodsmen forward to clear the way, following a day later with eight
hundred troopers. The remainder of the force trailed behind with the wag-
ons, supplies, cannon, and women (some of whom brought along children),
known as "camp followers" who saw to the soldiers' personal needs.

Braddock's axemen and regulars collided with 250 French Canadians and
regulars and 640 Western and Canadian Indians near the banks of the Monongahela River on July 9, 1755. It is not known if any Munsees were involved in
the fight. By the time things were sorted out and the firing stopped, nearly
450 of Braddock's men were dead. Another 400 were wounded, many, like
Braddock, mortally. It was one of the most complete defeats suffered at the
hands of Indians that still have no names in American annals. Only 350 out of
1,200 British troops engaged got out of the battle unscathed. The Indians and
the French together suffered fewer than 50 casualties.

It was the beginning of a bad summer for the British. Only the force sent
against Acadia achieved its objective. Like so many commanders before him,
Braddock's successor, Massachusetts governor William Shirley, was unable to
get his part of the plan off the ground. Johnson marched his 1,500 men up to
Lake George, where they erected Fort William Henry at its southern end.
The force did not get any farther. On September 8, 1755, they fought a battle that stopped a French invasion and earned Johnson a knighthood. The
fight was a bloody seesaw affair. Theyanoguin and many Mohawk and Stockbridge Indian warriors were killed, and Johnson was wounded. Although the
French withdrew, Johnson's battered troops could not follow them.

News of these misadventures flashed through the Indian diaspora.
Teedyuscung and other sachems made metaphorical women by the Six
Nations shed their symbolic petticoats and, to paraphrase Jennings, painted
themselves black, summoned their young men to the war dance, grabbed
their hatchets, and turned east. By the time winter closed in, hundreds of
farmsteads along the Delaware and Susquehanna valley frontier lay abandoned, their occupants killed, captured, or driven away by Munsee,
Shawnee, and other war parties.[23]

WAR OF TERROR

The terrible fighting in the forests was already well under way by the time
Great Britain declared war on France on May 17, 1756. France, the British,
and, soon enough, the breakaway provinces that would become the United

States took care to observe the diplomatic niceties that still governed war etiquette in Europe. Frontier combatants with homes and families to lose fought by altogether different sets of rules that made nonsense of notions of just or civilized war. Indians and intruders fought an implacable war that paid only slight regard to formal declarations or solemnly signed treaties. Characterized by wrenching spasms of violence separated sometimes by long months or years of anxious inactivity, their war would only end after 1815, when Great Britain finally cut Indians off from their last sources of support against the Americans. Scattered and exhausted by sixty years of fruitless struggle against overwhelming odds and adversaries, even the most fervent true believers among them finally gave up their last attempts to regain their lost homelands and instead focused on getting through the long years of exile that followed.

Like all wars, fear and hope fueled this struggle. The fuel that kept Indians and colonists fighting one another for sixty years was energized by a singularly toxic and volatile emotional mix. Fear spurred on people increasingly regarding each other as race enemies. Hope, often stoked by charismatic prophets and rapscallion provocateurs, convinced many that eradication of race enemies would end the fear. Murders, massacres, and ranting threats silenced voices of moderation and confirmed the worst stereotypes. Trust in promises of leaders who held up the hope of ultimate victory sustained adversaries unable to prevail decisively on battlefields, in board rooms, or in council rings. The result was the creation of a pervasive atmosphere of terror as dark as the deepest forest morasses christened Shades of Death by colonists.[24]

The shape this war would take was already evident by the summer of 1756. Munsee, Shawnee, and other warriors from Wyoming, Shamokin, and Paxtang (Harrisburg, Pennsylvania) giving themselves to the war sent as many of their families as would go much farther north and west to more remote towns like Kittanning, "The Main Stream," on the Allegheny River. Others went east to join Pompton, Cranbury, Crosswicks, and southern New Jersey Indians who wasted little time assuring New Jersey authorities of their continued friendship. They confirmed their peaceful intentions at a treaty held at Crosswicks on January 8, 1756. Warriors used the closer-in towns at the Great Island on the West Branch of the Susquehanna, at Tioga, Atsinksink, and Sccaughcung in the Chemung Valley, and at Otseningo and Ochquaga farther up the Susquehanna's North Branch as staging areas. There they formed themselves into small raiding parties that initially struck

outlying settlements at Penn's Creek and the Juniata River. By fall, Teedyuscung and others were leading war parties into lost lands in the valleys of the
Minisink and Tulpehocken. On November 24, 1755, a war party raided
Gnadenhuetten, killing eleven of sixteen missionaries and carrying off or
driving away most of the town's nearby Indian neighbors.[25]

Settlers and Indians fleeing the war parties spread fear and terror through
the settlements. The inclination toward vigilantism seen earlier at Maxantawny in 1728 now metastasized into a mindless viciousness that would
soon grow into something much more murderously malignant. On March
2, 1756, a gang of local settlers murdered a family of Indians taking shelter
among colonists at Walden, New York. Six weeks later, another mob murdered an Indian family in their wigwam at Peapack, New Jersey. Unable to
guarantee the safety of River Indians near the settlements, on May 28,
1756, William Johnson urged Indians gathered at Wiccopee on Fishkill
Creek in Dutchess County to move among other River Indians already
settled on Mohawk lands west of the Catskills to towns in the Schoharie
Valley. Those not moving west relocated east to Stockbridge. Few at either
place would ever return to their Hudson Valley homes for more than the
briefest of visits.[26]

The tempo of violence increased as provincial authorities declared war on
the Delawares and Shawnees living out west, authorized bounties for scalps
of Indian enemies, and looked the other way when settlers casually murdered inoffensive Indians in the woods. By the summer of 1756, settlers
were fortifying houses, provincial authorities were building lines of forts on
their frontiers, and raiding parties were attacking Kittanning and the Indian
towns on the West Branch of the Susquehanna. Although the assault on Kittanning managed to do some damage, militia forces undertaking long-range
raids tended to suffer higher casualties than those inflicted on their intended Indian targets.[27]

Trying for Peace

Having exacted a measure of vengeance on the colonists, hard-headed
sachems like Teedyuscung and Nimham II began thinking about how they
might extract their people from the war. The first two years of fighting had
gone badly for the British. Munsees and other Delawares who lived in the
British settlements or had been abroad with British merchantmen and men
of war knew that British sea power and their overwhelming numerical su-

periority on the ground in North America favored the chances for their ultimate victory. They also trusted French promises that they would not take Indian lands about as much as they trusted other promises made by the British.

Trusting the European adversaries to look after their own interests, Teedyuscung and his colleagues started searching for ways to play them against one another in the time-honored way of their ancestors. They knew that Great Britain regarded the French as the more dangerous of their enemies. Letting on that they might consider leaving the French to fend for themselves, Teedyuscung and his colleagues must have been pleased to find British authorities willing to make separate peaces with them. This was the time when Teedyuscung, Tatamy, Weiser, Johnson's deputy George Croghan, and Moravian lay missionary Christian Frederick Post made their reputations as major frontier diplomats. Criss-crossing the frontier, they gradually brought Indians and officials together at a series of meetings.[28]

After several preliminaries at Fort Johnson (built in 1749 by the new superintendent as his seat on the Mohawk River forty or so miles west of Albany), Delawares and Shawnees taking refuge above Tioga made peace with the British at Onondaga during the summer of 1756. The small number of representatives accompanying Nutimus and Wyoming Shawnee leader Paxinosa to the meeting suggests that most Indians refugees were at the very least wary of making any deal with the colonists at that point. Johnson would not be denied, however, and had his supporters among the Six Nations help change their minds. He then ceremoniously removed the petticoats from Nutimus's Tioga Delawares and Paxinosa's Susquehanna Valley Shawnees after both leaders joined Six Nations sachems pledging to join against the French.[29]

Although the British wanted to believe otherwise, most Munsee and many Unami, Shawnee, Conoy, and other Susquehanna Valley expatriates remained hostile and unreconciled. Teedyuscung took the lead in diplomatic efforts on their behalf during 1757 and 1758. His influence over all but his immediate followers, however, was shaky at best. Teedyuscung managed to get a large number of Indians from the Susquehanna country to attend a major peace treaty meeting held at Easton between July 25 and August 7, 1757. Raising the specter of the Walking Purchase, he almost derailed the proceedings. Most scholars agree that Teedyuscung's complaints were spurred on by Quakers trying to recoup lost influence in the province. This was the meeting where an exasperated Lapachpitton told Teedyuscung that land squabbles were "affairs of dirt" and ordered the sachem to get on with the important business of making peace.[30]

It would be awhile before Teedyuscung would be able to use figurative dirt to metaphorically bury axes still being wielded with deadly effect by Munsee warriors nursing grievances over lands lost and relatives killed. Settlers recognized Munsees and Unamis among warriors who continued raiding frontier farmsteads throughout the spring and summer of 1758. These attacks were diminished but not entirely halted as shuttling diplomats persuaded leaders of nearly every Indian community from New York to Ohio to send representatives to Easton for a grand meeting planned for the first weeks of autumn, 1758.

Temporary truces were finally worked out as Munsees and Unamis tied up several loose ends with provincial authorities in New Jersey during the run-up to the meeting. On February 13, 1758, Teedyuscung and other descendants of Weequehela gave their powers of attorney to Tatamy and three other countrymen to settle remaining land claims south of the Raritan River. Belts were then circulated through the Jersey communities and Chemung Valley towns. These invited those with outstanding grievances to settle them at a conference scheduled for late summer at the old West Jersey capital of Burlington.[31]

Delegates representing Minisinks, Delawares, and Senecas from Chemung country met with recently appointed New Jersey royal governor Francis Bernard at Burlington on August 7, 1758. The Minisink speaker greeted the new governor and his council before deferring to messengers from his uncles, the Senecas. After addressing the Minisinks as Munseys and women "who cannot hold treaties by themselves," the Seneca speaker told Bernard that the Six Nations would allow the Munsees to settle remaining land claims in the province with him at the upcoming meeting at Easton. He then displayed a belt and affirmed that the Six Nations, and not Teedyuscung, would represent Indians at Easton.[32]

On September 12, 1758, four men representing their people's interests in New Jersey lands met separately with provincial officials at Crosswicks. They conveyed all but a tract of land owned by Tatamy at the mouth of the Neshanic River and a couple of other small plots south of the Raritan to the New Jersey government. In return, the province promised to purchase lands for a reservation for their people in Burlington county. Using $1,600 allocated for the purpose by the provincial assembly, the officials purchased three thousand acres for the reservation at Edgepillock, soon called Brotherton, in the heart of the pinelands a year later.[33]

Having concluded their business at Crosswicks, Tatamy and his colleagues traveled up the Delaware to join Teedyuscung and the other principals collecting together at Easton. Even as the delegates were gathering, forces under the command of British brigadier general John Forbes were hitting a snag. Forbes had been marshaling an army of seven thousand regulars and militiamen at Carlisle, Pennsylvania, take Fort Duquesne since the beginning of the summer. The snag took the form of a French and Indian repulse of a precipitous night attack made on the fort on September 13–14, 1758, by a flying column under the command of Major James Grant. Forbes felt that he would have to postpone further attacks until the spring if news of a settlement at Easton securing his supply lines did not arrive before winter set in.

On October 7, 1758, more than five hundred Indians representing the Munsees and nearly every other Indian nation on or flanking Forbes's line of march gathered together on the Easton village green. Teedyuscung was noted as the representative of the "Chehohockies, alias Delawares and Unamies." Egohohowen represented the "Munsies or Minisinks," and Nimham II led the "Wapings or Pumptons" at the meeting. Both sides took care to be as clear in their identifications as in their purposes; all had much at stake. Munsee and other Delaware towns stood directly astride the intended British invasion route. They were also still formally at war with Pennsylvania. They wanted to secure their lands and lives. Just as they put their trust in Tatamy and his colleagues to press their claims in New Jersey, the Munsees must have hoped that Teedyuscung would help them get the best possible terms for a peace they very much wanted.[34]

Six Nations sachems also wanted peace. The peace they wanted, however, was one made on their own terms. Still officially neutral even after Seneca and other Iroquois warriors joined the French, they wanted a settlement that would assure their paramount position in the east and consolidate their authority over western lands and nations. The needs of Munsees and other Indians took a back seat to these goals. They pushed Teedyuscung aside and took over the meeting. After a month of private meetings and public declarations, they stood as guarantors for a general peace arranged on behalf of the Munsees and other Indians who had caused such mayhem on the Pennsylvania frontier. The blood shed by these warriors convinced Pennsylvanians to give up claims to lands west of the Appalachians purchased from the Six Nations in 1754 but not yet paid for. Bad feelings left by this latter deal caused many Munsees to join the war on the colonists. Pennsylvania's surrender of this territory to the Six Nations allowed the formally neutral confederacy to bloodlessly claim land reconquered by Munsee and other warriors.

Six Nations diplomats did not prevent colonists from demanding repatriation of captives, whether or not they wanted to return. Requests made by Munsees and other expatriates for secure titles to Susquehanna Valley lands occupied on confederacy or colonial sufferance were put off. Teedyuscung also withdrew his allegations accusing the Penn family of land fraud, blaming the war instead on bad feelings left over from what his people felt was the judicial murder of Weequehela.

The best Munsees were able to do at Easton was to get Six Nations help in negotiating a final deed adjudicating their remaining claims to land in northern New Jersey. On October 23, 1758, Egohohowen, Lappawinza, Hendrick Hekan, and other Minisink and Oping sachems accepted one thousand Spanish pieces of eight for all but their hunting and fishing rights to everything north of a line running from the Raritan River up to the Lamington Falls and west to the Delaware Water Gap. Manawkyhickon and several other sachems confirmed this and the September 12, 1758, deed to all land south of the line two days later (see map 13). This done, the assembled colonial authorities made a point of assuring the sachems that outstanding disputes like the Walking Purchase problem would be submitted to the Crown for resolution.[35]

BETRAYED

The 1758 Treaty at Easton marked the last time Munsees would make decisions that had major consequences in their old homeland. Their decision to sell all but their hunting and fishing rights in the northern half of New Jersey and their assent to the decision accepting a reservation in the southern part of the province ended a relationship that had begun 130 years earlier. And, although they would continue joining other nations resisting westward expansion for the next 50 years, their decision to sign onto the general peace at Easton marked the end of their last serious effort to militarily recover territory in New Jersey and any other part of their ancestral homeland.

Munsee and other Indian acquiescence to Easton Treaty terms had the immediate effect of freeing British armies advancing to the west from the threat of Indian attacks. In Pennsylvania, Forbes pushed his army forward on receiving word of the agreement. Indian allies of the French just as quickly left their camps around the Forks of the Ohio when they got the news. Suddenly abandoned by local Indian allies and grossly outnumbered by the British, the French blew up Fort Duquesne and withdrew north to Fort Niagara as Forbes's army neared the post on November 24, 1758. One year later, another army, led by Sir William Johnson after its original commander was killed by a mortar-shell explosion, took Fort Niagara on July 24, 1759. A few months later on October 4, raiders led by Robert Rogers burned the Abenaki stronghold of St. Francis Odanak, where many Mahicans and their Munsee relatives lived. Other victories that year at Ticonderoga, Crown Point, and Quebec all but ensured final British victory in North America.

Meanwhile, Pennsylvania authorities followed up on their promise to refer the Walking Purchase problem back to the mother country despite Teedyuscung's belated insistence that land had not been the reason they had gone to war in 1755 (he would change his position on this matter several times). Others' interests also were at stake. Imperial authorities were intent on imposing stronger centralized control over the provinces. Proprietors, manor lords, and small freeholders were determined to secure vested rights and interests. Landless tenants and townsfolk looked for ways to get rights that property ownership traditionally conferred on landowners. All had supported Indian claims when they thought it was in their interest to do so. Awareness of their now overwhelming power convinced growing numbers of colonists that the time had come to nullify or ignore Indian rights, especially those claimed by much diminished nations like the Munsees, who had been driven out of their ancestral homelands.

The growing impact of these attitudes was seen in the ways authorities handled the end game in the Walking Purchase dispute. Benjamin Franklin, who represented the Pennsylvania assembly in London at the time, laid the case in front of the Privy Council. The council, in turn, punted the issue to the Board of Trade during the summer of 1759. On August 29, 1759, the board passed the matter onto Sir William Johnson, ordering him to make a final decision on the case. Johnson let three years pass before he got to it. Other problems, like Indian anger over British refusal to honor promises to leave captured French posts once fighting ended and colonial impatience caused by Indian slowness in returning promised captives, made more insistent claims on his time. Johnson was finally able to get "Delawares, Mohiccons, and Opings" represented by Teedyuscung together with Pennsylvania authorities at Easton from June 18 to 28, 1762, to settle the matter.[36]

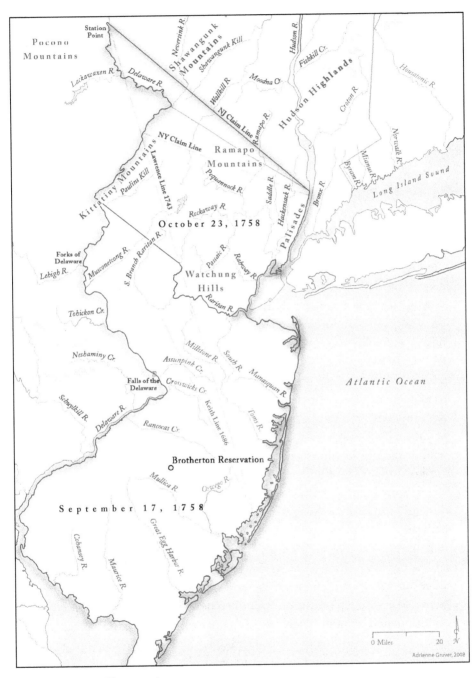

Map 13. Easton Treaty cessions

Johnson had no direct interest in the issue. His decision, however, was a foregone conclusion. He revealed the considerations foremost on his mind when deciding Indian land disputes in a letter penned a few years later. Johnson was then serving as the Crown-appointed arbitrator in another Indian lawsuit, this one brought by Daniel Nimham. A young man who had just succeeded Nimham II as the Oping or Wappinger sachem, Daniel was suing the Philipse family and other manor lords for land taken from them in Dutchess County.

As in the Walking Purchase case, where Indians worked with Quakers against the Penn family, the young Nimham made common cause with rent-rioting tenants intent on breaking up vast manor landholdings in the Hudson Valley. Daniel traveled to Great Britain to place the matter before the Board of Trade after being put off by local authorities. Finding merit in the case, the board acted as they had in the Walking Purchase dispute, ordering Johnson to give the Indians justice in the matter.[37]

More introspective in his writings than most of his contemporaries, Johnson was given to unburdening himself in correspondence with trusted confidants and colleagues. In his 1765 letter, dated August 26, he wrote that he felt that it was his duty to support just claims made by powerful nations or people connected with them capable of resenting what he termed "a neglect." Less than clear-cut claims pressed by weaker "long domesticated" nations, he went on, "had better remain unsupported than that several old titles of his majesty's subjects should therefore be disturbed." Acting on these sentiments, Johnson found for the Pennsylvania proprietors in 1762 and the Hudson Valley manor lords three years later.[38]

Johnson might have made different decisions if militant Munsees still thought capable of resenting neglect had carried on the war despite what he derogatorily called their long domestication. The fact that Johnson was able to make his decisions stick reveals the fundamental shift in attitudes that accompanied imperial victory in the Seven Years' War. Johnson was nearly alone among British commanders, most of whom no longer found it necessary to observe diplomatic niceties when dealing with people belonging to "domesticated" nations. Their refusal to honor British promises to leave the captured posts following the formal end of hostilities in 1763 did not go unnoticed by Indians. In a series of counter-strokes made between 1763 and 1764, Indian warriors captured and destroyed all but two of the British posts west of the Appalachians. Niagara and Detroit, the two forts that drove off initial attacks, were subjected to sieges that were only lifted by British counteroffensives. Chemung Valley Munsees, inspired by their prophet Wangomend, joined in the fighting against the British. Johnson sent a column of 120 Oneida, Tuscarora, and Delaware warriors under the command of a part-Oneida Metis captain named Andrew Montour, married to a Delaware woman, to destroy the Chemung towns during the summer of 1764. As their ancestors had done so many times before, the Munsees and their compatriots abandoned their towns and withdrew in front of the advancing column. And, as other invaders had done in the past, Montour's force plundered and burned the town's houses, destroyed standing crops, and cut down orchards before withdrawing to their base.[39]

This was also the time when vengeful frontier settlers, no longer fearing consequences of either Indian retaliation or provincial retribution, began casually slaughtering Indians wherever they were encountered in the Delaware and Susquehanna valleys. The most prominent victim was Teedyuscung, who burned to death in his cabin as a fire swept through his people's town at Wyoming Valley on April 19, 1763. Although Pennsylvanians suspected that Connecticut arsonists set the fire, no one was ever brought to trial. Elsewhere, individual murderers like Tom Quick and a gang of killers known as the Paxton Boys openly killed inoffensive Indians in the most atrocious ways possible to spread the pall of terror that had hung over the frontier since 1755.[40]

By 1765, most Munsees had moved much farther west to the Allegheny Valley of western Pennsylvania. Not all, however, lived in these towns all the time. Despite the danger of sudden attack, Munsees continued to live near or travel through their old homeland during the final years of British colonial rule. Daniel Nimham and other Wappingers forced to abandon their last homes in Dutchess County moved to Stockbridge. A few Munsees also stayed on with other Delawares on the Brotherton Reservation at Edgepillock. Although Munsees and their fellow expatriates abandoned the Wyoming and the Chemung valleys following the destruction of their towns there, others continued to live farther up the North Branch of the Susquehanna River at places like Otseningo and Ochquaga. Just downriver, Papunhank allowed the Moravians to establish a mission they christened Friedenshuetten next to his town of Wyalusing after his people returned to the locale as the Paxton Boys terror receded in 1765.[41]

Persistent but increasingly smaller groups of families and friends also continued to hunt, fish, camp, and plant in remote places within their ancestral homeland. One of these groups seen near Ringwood, New Jersey, was described by an iron-working German immigrant named Peter Hasen-clever on August 16, 1765. He seemed most impressed by their sense of generosity in the face of what he regarded as extreme poverty. Briefly alluding to their harvests that often seemed to fail, he described them as a people who "dwell in the woods, roaming constantly, and subsisting almost entirely on the chase."[42]

For the first time in their recorded history, Munsees were cut off from all but the most remote and least productive parts of their former homeland. Mostly living far from ancestral graves and sheltering spirits, all they had left was each other. It was enough to see them through the next decades of wanderings and subsequent life on reservations, reserves, and other faraway places. It would not be enough to stop strangers from driving them ever westward. They were adrift on alien terrain far from the ancient hills that had anchored them to the lands of their forebears. Although they would show time and again that they could defend themselves against soldier's bayonets, they would never again have sufficient power to prevent strangers from ultimately intruding into even the most personal parts of their private lives.

14

MANY TRAILS, 1767–TODAY

Very nearly all Munsees had to share their lives with strangers by 1767. The few Munsee families still living on the fringes of their old homeland resided among Unamis at Brotherton in Edgepillock, with Unchechaugs and other eastern Long Island Indians at and around Poosepatuck, with Mahicans and Northern Indians at Stockbridge, and with Western Abenakis at Odanak. Some who had moved thirty years earlier to the small River Indian community in the Schoharie Valley were now wedged between Mohawk Indian towns and Palatine German farmsteads just west of the Catskills. Others still trying to make a go of it in the nearby upper Susquehanna Valley lived at places like the Moravian mission town of Friedenshuetten and Papunhank's nearby revivalist Indian community at Wyalusing. More lived in mixed Indian communities like Tioga, Otseningo, and Ochquaga with Mohawk and Oneida Iroquois émigrés and Tuscarora, Unami, Mahican, Shawnee, Conoy, and Nanticoke expatriates.

The majority of Munsees, probably around one thousand people all told, were now living with different strangers much farther west. Some lived in or near Gekelemukpechink in Ohio. More made their homes in Seneca, Mingo, Wyandot, and Mesquakie settlements at Goschgosching and other upper Allegheny River towns near present-day Tionesta, Pennsylvania. Others lived a bit farther south at and around the large town of Kuskuskies on the Beaver River in present-day Lawrence County, Pennsylvania, with Unami, Mahican, and Mingo neighbors. Many of the people living at Kuskuskies listened attentively to the nativist Delaware prophet and the relocated Chemung Valley revivalist Wangomend. Increasingly, most people living at these other locales began joining kinsmen and women already living farther west at and around places like Gekelemukpechink.

Wherever they lived, Munsees married Indians from foreign nations and other strangers as marriageable partners speaking their own language became harder to find. This necessity created new realities. Old problems of finding places in families of spouses practicing different cultural traditions multiplied in direct proportion to rising numbers of mixed marriages. Clan and family affiliations of one spouse often did not fit easily with those of another. Other difficulties arose when matrilineal Munsees married people belonging to nations organized along patrilineal principles like the Shawnees. Patrilineally inclined families often demanded that wives move into their new husband's households just as determinedly matrilineal Munsee and Unami households expected the opposite arrangement. Couples unwilling to break things off when they could not make such choices increasingly struck out on their own elsewhere.

Wherever they lived and whomever they lived with, Munsees found that their traditional encouragement of fluency in several languages served them well. Munsee children often traditionally grew up in households where multiple dialects, and sometimes entirely different languages, were regularly spoken. Spouses in mixed marriages also often had to learn to speak each other's languages while raising their children in one or the other's family households. Multiple fluency went far in smoothing over rough patches when it came time for people to make difficult choices. In the past, Munsee men often had to decide whether their primary loyalty lay with their mother's family or with the family they married into. This choice could be particularly difficult when the man in question was the sachem of their wife's community. Although primary data documenting choices made by Munsee sachems in their homeland are lacking, the strong allegiances frequently felt by captives adopted into Indian families amply chronicled in colonial records indicate that most sachems probably maintained their closest ties to the communities they guided.

The need to choose one's nationality after marriage made things even more difficult for Munsees living in multicultural communities after 1767. Increasingly, Munsee women as well as men now had to make this decision. Although documentation chronicling such decisions is spotty, their effects can be seen. Decisions to adopt spouse's nationalities played major roles in turning many Munsee family names into surnames later primarily found in other Indian communities. The Munsee Nimham family name, for example, gradually became the prominent Oneida Ninham surname after Munsee Nimham men loosened from the ties of their matrilineages adopted the nationalities of their Oneida wives.

Munsee clans finally lost cohesion and purpose as members married into neighboring communities like the Oneidas and into more distant nations during the nineteenth century. The larger multiclan wolf, turkey, and turtle phratry groups lasted longer. These too, however, fell by the wayside as Munsees and other Delawares found it necessary to look farther afield to find marriageable spouses. Most increasingly chose to adopt the American and Canadian form of bilateral social organization centering on nuclear families as their traditional matrilineal extended family, clan, and phratry organizations lost numbers needed to function effectively.

Traditional phratry affiliations continued to serve as a way to divide up ritual responsibilities among those observing the annual Big House ceremonies in increasingly scattered and shrinking Munsee, Delaware, and Mahican communities in exile. Even the phratries gradually disappeared as Christian conversion and increasing interest in the Native American Church drew adherents away from Big House congregations using them as their organizational base during the last half of the nineteenth century. Associations of particular people and families with particular phratries finally disappeared from all but the memories of a dwindling number of traditionalists speaking their ancestral language after the Eastern Oklahoma Delaware community, the last to observe the ceremony, gathered for its final full-scale Big House observance in 1924.

Paths leading to changes great and small in Munsee life followed many trails after 1766 (see map 14). None, however, traced a direct route. Like the roads and rivers Munsees traveled into exile, their personal lives traversed tortuously twisty terrain. Munsees embarking on these journeys had to develop new habits of mind needed to meet new challenges in strange lands. A bewildering and seemingly ever-changing assortment of parties, coalitions, and interest groups united and divided them along the way. Feelings of love and hate for and against Moravian and Presbyterian missionaries, nativists like the Delaware Prophet, revivalists like Papunhank and Wangomend, and traditional metewak joined and split Munsee families and factions along the Upper Susquehanna during the first decades in exile. Divergent loyalist, neutral, and pro-American sympathies roused during the American Revolution divided Munsees for decades after the war ended. Later on, Munsees living in American reservations and Canadian reserves had to choose between Indian parties advocating continued tribal communal governance and Citizen parties calling on members to take personal ownership of allotted lands and assume rights and obligations of private citizenship. Munsees in a society dominated by racially obsessed whites discriminating against people of color and generally looking down on Indians had to choose a racial identity or have one thrust on them. Munsees have only recently again begun regarding their Indian identity as a good thing.

All this does not mean that Munsee history after 1767 was a confused jumble of random unrelated events. No nation, even one with a track record for flexible adaptability as strong as that held by Munsees, can withstand overwhelming chaos for very long. Difficult as things sometimes were, catastrophically chaotic conditions seldom lasted very long. Munsees confronting change were helped, as Spicer would have said, by their enduring sense of themselves as members of families and communities and, perhaps most important of all, as custodians of cultural traditions worth preserving. Not all Munsees always felt the same way, and many chose paths that took them far from their roots. A sufficient number, however, always thought that preservation of their identities as Munsee people was important enough to maintain.

The few who continued living in the east in mixed communities at Poosepatuck, Stockbridge, Brotherton, Schoharie, and the Upper Susquehanna towns found themselves at the center of the drift toward colonial rebellion in the years immediately following 1767. Many, but not all, of Tackapousha and Suscaneman's descendants moved from Poosepatuck along with other Long Island and Southern New England Indian adherents of the Brothertown Movement to Stockbridge, Scaticook, and other Housatonic River mission towns during the last quarter of the eighteenth century. The Unchechaug language was probably last spoken by Indian people at Poosepatuck sometime after constitutional framer and future president James Madison collected a small vocabulary of their words while visiting the locale in 1801. Several hundred Unchechaug descendants, including some whose ancestors probably spoke Munsee, continue to live on the Poosepatuck Reservation in Mastic.

Other people tracing descent to Indian forebears also continued to live in Brooklyn, Staten Island, and parts of New Jersey and adjacent sections of New York. Although the small reservations in present-day Nassau County completely fell from documentary notice sometime during the 1700s, several families claiming descent from Tackapousha's son Chopeycannows and

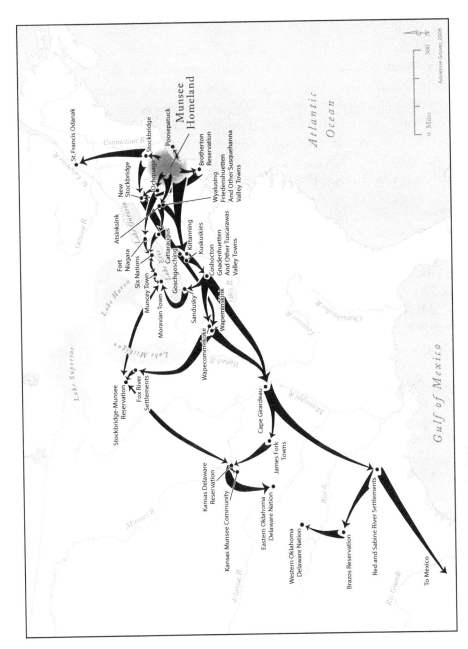

Map 14. Munsee diaspora, 1770s–1860s

Munsee Homeland

St. Francis Odanak

Stockbridge
Poosepatuck

New Stockbridge
Oghquaga
Brotherton
Reservation

Atsinksink
Wyalusing
Friedenshuetten
And Other Susquehanna
Valley Towns

Fort Niagara
Six Nations
Kittanning
Cattaraugus
Kuskuskies

Muncey Town
Goschgoshing
Coshocton
Gnadenhuetten
And Other Tuscarawas
Valley Towns

Moravian Town
Wapeminskink

Sandusky
Wapecommekoke

Stockbridge-Munsee Reservation
Fox River Settlements

Cape Girardeau

Kansas Delaware Reservation
James Fork Towns
Kansas Munsee Community
Eastern Oklahoma Delaware Nation

Western Oklahoma Delaware Nation

Brazos Reservation

Red and Sabine River Settlements

To Mexico

Atlantic Ocean

Gulf of Mexico

Lake Superior
Lake Michigan
Lake Huron
Lake Erie
Lake Ontario

Connecticut R.
St. Lawrence R.
Ottawa R.
Ohio R.
Wabash R.
Mississippi R.
Missouri R.
Arkansas R.
Tennessee R.
Chattahoochee R.
Red R.
Rio Grande

0 Miles   300

Adrienne Grover, 2008

277

other Matinecock ancestors continue to make their homes on western Long Island. Other families tracing ancestry to Munsee ancestors live in small enclaves throughout the Hudson River valley.

At Stockbridge, increasing numbers of Massachusetts settlers flooding into the Berkshires bought or leased much of the town's lands after 1767. Soon outnumbering the Indians, new settlers held a controlling interest at Stockbridge by the time the Revolutionary War broke out in 1775. Daniel Nimham and his son Abraham joined other Stockbridge Indians helping rebel forces drive British troops from Boston, capture Fort Ticonderoga, and defeat Burgoyne's army at Saratoga. Abraham was given command of an all-Indian Stockbridge rifle company formed while Washington's army was encamped at Morristown, New Jersey, during the winter of 1777–1778. Ordered to join troops covering British positions north of New York City, the company participated in several skirmishes. Both Abraham and his father, along with most of the company, subsequently were killed in a fight with British dragoons at Cortlandt Ridge in the north Bronx on August 31, 1778.[1]

Most of the few Munsees living with other River Indians in Mohawk territory at Schoharie sided with the British when the war broke out. Nearly all left in early 1777 after it became clear that Mohawks still mourning the recent death of their patron Sir William Johnson in 1774 would remain loyal to the Crown. A few joined the Delaware main body in Ohio. Some moved in with other Mohawks at Ochquaga and nearby upper Susquehanna towns. Most moved to the Iroquois refugee encampment at Fort Niagara, set up and supplied by the British Indian Office run by the late Sir William's son and successor, Guy Johnson.

Esopus warriors taking refuge at Niagara, like Harman Hekan's descendant Jacob Hagan, joined rangers raiding outlying settlements along the New York, New Jersey, and Pennsylvania frontiers. These men were often led by Mohawk captain Joseph Brant and Loyalist officer Walter Butler. Raiders going to and from Niagara often stopped at Ochquaga for rest and resupply. As much divided in their sympathies as those at Coshocton, Ohio, the inhabitants of Ochquaga suffered the same fate as the people living in the Delaware capital. Like Coshocton, Ochquaga was hastily evacuated during the early fall of 1778, when news of the imminent arrival of a rebel column led by New York militia colonel William Butler (no relation to Walter) reached the town. And, like the soldiers who laid waste to Coshocton and the other Tuscarawas Valley Delaware towns, Butler's militia column systematically destroyed houses, fields, and orchards at Ochquaga and every other Indian town along the upper Susquehanna. The only house they left standing among the forty log cabins (some, Butler noted, with leaded glass windows and hinged doors) at Ochquaga belonged to an Oneida family. It was spared because the Oneidas were the only Iroquois nation openly supporting the American war effort.

Loyalist Indian families burned out of their homes at Ochquaga mostly moved to Niagara for the duration. Pro-American townsfolk subsequently mostly sought shelter in Oneida country. These latter families were probably burned out of their homes a second time when a Loyalist column led by Brant burned the chief Oneida town of Kanonwalohale and the nearby fort built by the Americans in 1780. Many of these people joined other Oneidas swelling Indian refugee ranks at Fort Niagara.[2]

After the war, victorious Americans refused to allow Munsees and other Indian people forced from their homes on the upper Susquehanna to return, no matter what side they had taken. Pro-American Tuscaroras, for example, had to resettle among the Oneidas. Many pro-British Munsee refugees either stayed around Fort Niagara with exiled Mohawks or settled nearby with Senecas at Cattaraugus.

Surviving Stockbridge Indian soldiers returned to a community that was no longer their own. What was worse, they were no longer welcome in their own homes. Some three hundred Indian Stockbridgers, mostly Mahicans but including Nimham family members and a few other people from Wappinger and Esopus countries, took up a long-standing Oneida invitation to settle among them in Madison County, New York, in 1785. Some Stockbridgers also moved north to the Abenaki town at St. Francis Odanak. A few trekked west to join with the Delaware Indian main body in Ohio. Family traditions affirm that a small number of families refusing to leave settled in remote hollows in the mountainous country above Stockbridge.

British authorities set aside land in Ontario for Indians sheltering at Niagara, unable to return to their old homes after the war ended. The overwhelming majority of Munsees at Niagara joined Mohawks and other Loyalist Indians moving to these reserves. Some may have been in the group led by Mohawk leader John Deserontyon relocating to the ninety-four thousand-acre Tyendinaga Reserve established at the Bay of Quinte on the northeast shore of Lake Ontario. Most, however, moved with nearly 450 Mohawks and 1,400 other Iroquois and allied Indians following Joseph Brant to land reserved for them on the Grand River in Ontario during the winter of 1784–1785. Situated some fifty miles west of Niagara, the original bounds of the nearly 1 million–acre Six Nations Reserve extended six miles on either side of the lower fifty miles of the Grand River, from the present-day city of Brantford to its mouth at Lake Erie.

Some 162 Ochquagas and 231 Delawares were living among 1,843 Indians at the Six Nations Reserve by 1785. Although this census does not break these numbers down further, later records noting Esopus and other River Indian residents on the reserve indicates that a goodly number of the enumerated Ochquagas and Delawares were Munsees, Mahicans, and people closely linked to both nations. Some of these people later moved on to other places. More than a few moved to the sites of the upper and lower Muncey towns built on Chippewa land northwest of the Six Nations Reserve near the headwaters of the Thames River. Most staying on at Six Nations moved alongside Cayugas, who established themselves along the lowermost reaches of the Grand River around Dunnville and Port Maitland. Today, many descendants of these Munsee people continue to live in and around the much-reduced reserve farther north near Brantford.[3]

Slightly more than half the Munsee population of one hundred that had held on at Sandusky, Ohio, from the time of the Revolution to the end of the War of 1812 joined the main body when it moved to Missouri, as did the few Munsees left at the Ohio Moravian town of Goshen. The other half of the Sandusky Munsee community moved north to the Muncey towns in Ontario or to the New Fairfield community rebuilt in 1815 by the Moravian Indians across the Thames from the Fairfield mission destroyed by the American army after the Battle of the Thames in 1813.

While these things were going on out west, Munsees and their relatives in New Jersey and New York were finding it impossible to stay in their remaining enclaves. Most of the few Munsees living with Unamis at Edgepillock moved with them to New Stockbridge in Oneida country after they sold their reservation to the State of New Jersey in 1802. Their stay at New Stockbridge was brief. Oneidas who had returned to their lands after the Revolution were under strong pressure to sell them. They were forced to part with all but a few hundred of the original 6 million acres in their homeland in twenty-three treaties concluded in contravention of the 1790 Non-Intercourse Act by the New York government between 1795 and 1846.

In 1818, New Stockbridgers among the Oneidas finally accepted a Miami invitation first made ten years earlier to join the Delaware main body then on the White River in Indiana. A party of seventy-five men, women, and children arrived just after Delawares signed the St. Mary's treaty, selling their Indiana lands and moving west to Missouri. The hapless New Stockbridgers found nothing set aside for them. Unwilling to join the main body on its trek west, they lingered briefly in Indiana until their leaders back east convinced the federal government that they were ideal intermediaries to bring Protestant religion and civilization to the Catholic and pagan Indians in the deep forests of Wisconsin. In 1822, federal authorities brokered a deal in which the Menominee Indians allowed people they called New York Indians (mostly Oneidas, Mahicans, and Munsees) to settle along the Fox River between Green Bay and Lake Winnebago. By 1830, nearly all of the 225 to 350 Indians from New Stockbridge, and a sizable number of Oneidas, were living on Menominee land in Wisconsin.

Stockbridge and Brotherton immigrants were not happy with the swampy ground initially allotted to them. In 1831, they managed to get the federal government to sell them two townships (containing a total of seventy-two square miles) of land in public domain fifty miles farther west. These tracts, sold earlier to the United States by Menominees, were allocated to the mostly Mahican Stockbridge immigrants. An additional adjoining township (thirty-six square miles) was sold to the primarily Delaware Brotherton descendants. One year later, an elder named Bartholomew S. Calvin (his Indian name was Shawuskukhung, "Wilted Grass"), who had been born in New Jersey, petitioned for and received $2,000 from the New Jersey legislature for hunting and fishing rights in northern New Jersey reserved at Easton in 1758. These funds helped impoverished Brothertons tracing ancestry to Weequehela and his kin maintain themselves on lands that became the nucleus of the present-day Stockbridge-Munsee Reservation.[4]

Word of the move to Wisconsin and the relocation of the Delaware main body from Missouri to Kansas in 1832 reached Munsees living at New Fairfield and the Muncey Town settlements in Ontario. Increasingly surrounded by Canadian settlers flooding into Upper Canada, Indians along the Thames finally agreed to see how things stood out west. Some 230 mostly Munsee and Mahican people left the Thames Valley in 1837. Passing through Green Bay, they made their way to the Kansas Delaware Reservation. A party of Stockbridge and Brotherton people from Wisconsin also came to Kansas a year later. Those who liked what they saw elected to stay, purchasing land of their own from the Delawares. The first of these purchases was made in 1851 in what is today Wyandotte County. Three years later, most of these people moved to modern-day Leavenworth County when the Delawares were compelled to sell off a substantial portion of their original reservation. Discouraged by these moves and not particularly fond of life on the prairie, many of these Munsees gradually moved back to Wisconsin and the Thames River Indian towns.[5]

Back in Ontario, Methodists and Baptists were converting most Moravian and pagan Munsees. The last Moravian missionary preached his final sermon in Unami and left New Fairfield on November 6, 1864. Most of the remaining Moravian Indians moved from the already nearly abandoned town shortly thereafter. The majority settled nearby on lands within the present-day reserve of the Moravian of the Thames First Nation. Around the same time, Protestant missionaries finally convinced new converts at Muncey Town to give up their Big House ceremony. Today, a few people still speak Munsee in both reserves, and interest in traditional culture is strong. Some 450 enrolled Moravian Indians live at Moraviantown while another 580 or so live off-reserve, mostly in nearby towns and cities. Farther upriver, 163 of the 524 enrolled members of the Munsee-Delaware First Nation enumerated in the 2000 census live on their band reserve at Muncey Town.

In 1859, a number of Delawares and Munsees, many belonging to the Killbuck family tracing direct descent to Ohio Munsee sachem Gelelemend, decided not to join the main band in its projected move to the new Indian territory in Oklahoma that was delayed by the Civil War in 1866. They joined with Black River and Swan Creek Chippewas to establish a twelve-square-mile reservation of their own at Marais des Cygnes, "Marsh of the Swans," in what is now Franklin County, Kansas. They maintained their reservation there until 1900, when the Chippewas and the seventy Munsees still on the tribal roll (twenty-one of whom were Killbuck family members) accepted a final lump-sum payment of all outstanding federal monies, dissolved the tribe, and became American citizens. Unlike the Stockbridge-Munsees, who in 1934 managed to reverse a similar decision made in 1910, the Kansas Munsees chose to keep their citizenship. The last elders speaking Munsee among them probably passed away shortly after the tribe disbanded, and most descendants married out into other families. At present, Kansas Munsee descendants are developing a growing interest in their Indian ancestry.

Memories of the traditional religion lingered on in several families who continued to speak the Delaware language among themselves. Today, a number of eastern Oklahoma Delaware people maintain their traditional language and culture on and near reservation lands only recently acknowledged as sovereign Delaware territory by both the Cherokee Nation and the United States.

They and other forgotten Munsees possess a considerable history. Today, Americans take pride in remembering nations like the Iroquois Confederacy, celebrated for its determined, if doomed, resistance. Mahicans and Delawares are remembered as tragic figures and wronged friends. Many like to see Indians as valiant opponents whose courageous defense of homeland and tradition does honor both to their memory and the descendants of those who defeated them. More than a few prefer to think of Indians as nature's nobility, exemplars of lost innocence, custodians of ecological wisdom, paragons of spirituality, and role models for right living. Until recently, however, few besides descendants of the Munsees themselves evidently gave much thought to their ancestors' culture or history.

Since much of modern collective memory is preserved on paper, some of this forgetfulness has to be chalked up to bad press. From the beginning, bad experiences helped Europeans and Indians in the Hudson and Delaware valleys regard one another as thievish, murderous, and treacherous. Although it can only be imagined what went on before Hudson sailed into New York Harbor, at least some of it must have been unpleasant. One of the first things Hudson's sailors and Indians living around the harbor tried to do after a Dutch sailor killed an Indian trying to carry off a pillow was slash, shoot at, and club each other. Colonists who followed could not see that they themselves were foreigners, preferring instead to treat Indians as aliens. Thinking they were good, civil Christians, they believed it when they called Indians savages and barbarians.

Unlike other Indians tarred with the same brush, subsequent Munsee responses to European invasion do not seem to have much redeemed them in foreign eyes. Most people like their heroes, both winners and losers, to stride majestically across the pages of history. An American fondness for nobly lost causes goes far in explaining why numbers of books about wars with Indians are only exceeded by those devoted to the Civil War. Munsee warriors who gave themselves totally to battle, like Mayane, who reportedly in 1644 singlehandedly attacked three colonists, killing two before being shot by the third, died early and often. It is difficult to make out what colonists thought of those of his nation whom they surprised in their villages, indiscriminately shot down, and roasted in burning houses and forts. The terse tone of their reports suggests that these brutalizing slaughters gave neither a sense of moral uplift nor feelings of martial glory to their perpetrators.[6]

After colonists broke their power, Munsees did not do the noble thing and suicidally resist, quietly disappear, or join their feeble strength with the Iroquois and other militant nations. Instead, they put up with affronts and abuses and held on to what they could. They endured colonial contumely and Iroquois insult, let pompous governors address them as children, and sat quietly as the Iroquois called them women. When it came to their land, they refused to court certain disaster by defying the colonists. Instead, they put would-be purchasers off and did what they could to hold onto remaining lands. Many sold tracts with overlapping boundaries. They sometimes sold the same ground twice or three times in ways perjoratively called "Indian giving" to the present day.

Colonists buying the land assured themselves that the Indians were submitting to their power and rule. Most would not see that Munsees only accommodated them on their own terms and, as often as possible, at times of their own choosing. This could only baffle and infuriate thwarted colonists, who did not appreciate and could not admit that they were being outmaneuvered by people they often called savages and heathens to their faces. Colonists had greater success plying Munsees with liquor to pry furs, land, and more from them. Settlers comparing their Munsee neighbors to the Iroquois thought that Indians living farther from their settlements were nobler, purer, and somehow better. They increasingly regarded Munsees regularly encountered in their towns and villages as debauched and dissipated drifters.

By the nineteenth century, such attitudes hardened into the venomous species of biological racism equating intimate contact with degeneration. Racial purity was extolled. Intermarriage was condemned. Today, we wince at accounts deploring mixed ancestry of Munsees written at a time when it was thought that one drop of colored blood somehow diminished a person's character and identity. Many Americans today are also ashamed when they compare such intolerance with Munsees who accepted strangers and cried when forced to part with adopted captives, even those whose parents or siblings were killed by members of their adoptive Indian families.

Even this has not been enough to make Americans forget other nations who mingled blood with foreigners and whose people suffered slaughter and insult. Even the murderous Indian hatred that terrorized the frontier could not erase the memories of many of its victims. Why, then, are the Munsees forgotten? Part of the answer lies in the role they played in the early history of the American nation. They frequently appear in accounts as treacherous and dangerous enemies. They are thought to harbor criminals and support rebels and renegades. In many ways, they seem to resemble maroon societies made up of escaped slaves and outcasts in Latin America and the American South, who banded together to form outlaw nations of their own in back country.

Just as accounts of burnings provide the only known descriptions of many Indian towns, chronicles of attacks furnish much of what is known about maroon societies. Like other nations fearing maroon resistance, raids, and possible resurgence, Americans relentlessly sent armies to hunt down and destroy maroon communities. During and after the War of 1812, they defeated and enslaved free blacks who escaped southern bondage. The most extensively documented of these attacks occurred at Fort Mose near St. Augustine in East Florida and at the Negro Fort on the Apalachicola River. The presence of Cherokees among Indians resisting expansion into the Midwest may have helped fuel fears that maroon societies welcoming escaped slaves from the South also might emerge on the Ohio. Munsees with a long history of accepting strangers may have been regarded as a particular dangerous threat. Such fears may account for some of the relentless persistence displayed by Americans, particularly by slave-owning Americans like Virginians and Kentuckians, determined to conquer and control Ohio and the West.[7]

Fears of this sort are not inconsiderable, especially when felt by people who get their histories from books. Anyone looking at the past swiftly realizes that things mostly start from small beginnings. A short millennium ago, English was spoken only by a tiny tribe on a remote island. Armed mainly with swords, spears, and bows and arrows, the few people speaking the Old English tongue barely intelligible to modern-day speakers of the language managed to forge the island's tribes into a formidable nation. Only a few more centuries passed before musket-toting ship-borne English-speaking soldiers, sailors, and settlers carried their language to every part of the world.

What if things had been slightly different before the English or their Dutch cousins showed up in Munsee country? Instead of an Alfred the Great or a Queen Victoria, imagine, say, a particularly enterprising Munsee woman blessed with strong spirit power and an even stronger constitution like Mamanuchqua. She is seized by a dream of imperial proportions. The dream may come fully formed, stirred perhaps by legends and stories. Or she herself may have seen massive cities like Cahokia or Tenochtitlan on her travels. Whatever its source, she would have known how to turn visions into prophetic power mobilizing her people's energies. With the tactical skill and strategic guile shown by Powhatan, Pontiac, Tecumseh, and other great Indian leaders, she could have forged a vast empire by the time European sailors started venturing to Munsee shores. It is not hard to imagine how people belonging to this Munsee-speaking empire, perhaps immune to diseases striking down remnants of European populations already ravaged by the Black Death and other plagues, ultimately may have used their own guns and sailing ships to colonize and dominate "new found Golgothas" in the Old World.[8]

Things, of course, did not turn out that way. But it probably was more of a near thing than might be imagined. And because near things are the very stuff of history, it makes good sense to recover forgotten histories of enduring people like the Munsees, whose past honors their descendants and provides an object lesson for all people.

Appendix

MEASUREMENT CONVERSION CHART

Length

1 link	7.92 inches
25 links	1 rod
100 links	1 chain
4 rods	1 chain
1 chain	66 feet
20 chains	0.25 mile
80 chains	1 mile
1 rod	1 perch
1 perch	16.5 feet
1 ell	3.75 feet
1 fathom	6 feet
1 furlong	660 feet
1 league	3 miles
1 Dutch foot	11 inches, 304/1,000 inch
1 Dutch ell	45 inches
1 Dutch rod	1 foot
1 U.S. or English mile	5,280 feet
1 nautical mile	6,080 feet
1 Dutch mile	3 miles

AREA

1 acre	10 square chains, 160 square perches, or 4,840 square feet
1 morgen	2 acres
1 square mile	640 acres or 6400 square chains

VOLUME

1 gill	5 fluid ounces
1 schepel	0.764 bushel, dry
1 imperial gallon	1.2 U.S. gallons
1 bushel	9.6 U.S. gallons, dry
1 anker	10 U.S. gallons
1 barrel	43 U.S. gallons
1 butt	151 U.S. gallons
1 pipe	151 U.S. gallons
1 last	2 imperial (long) tons or 80 bushels
1 tun	302 U.S. gallons

MASS

1 pennyweight	½ ounce
1 stone	14 pounds
1 hundredweight	100 pounds
1 U.S. (short) ton	2,000 pounds
1 imperial (long) ton	2,240 pounds

MONEY

1 Dutch stiver	2 English pence
1 Dutch guilder	1 English shilling, 8 pence
1 English shilling	12 pence
1 English £ sterling	20 shillings
1 Spanish dollar	4 shillings, 1½ pence

NOTES

TECHNICAL NOTES

1. Inspired by a student malapropism, Lurie (1974) suggests a witty word solution to the contradictory conundrum posed by the allegedly opposite states typified by the terms "savage" and "civilized." Pointing out that the words originally represented terms for forest and city dweller, she proposes that the word "savage" be reclaimed in its original meaning, and a new term, "civilage," be adopted in the place of "civilization" as the more appropriate, and less loaded, contrast word.

1. MUNSEES

1. Delaware is one of several Eastern Algonquian languages spoken by people living along the Atlantic seaboard from Nova Scotia to the Carolinas. Eastern Algonquian, in turn, is part of the widespread Algonquian language family. Shawnees, Illinois, Miamis, and Ottawas in the American Midwest and Crees and Ojibwas living farther north around the Great Lakes and in Canadian forests speak what linguists call Central Algonquian languages. On the Great Plains, Blackfeet, Cheyenne, and Arapaho people speak more distantly related Algonquian languages. See O'Meara (1996) for a key study of the Munsee dialect.

Jennings (1984) used Minisink as a general term identifying all Indian people who lived between the Hudson and Delaware river valleys. He based his choice on three facts. First, the territory surrounding Minisink Island on the upper Delaware was one of the last refuges occupied by the region's first people. Second, colonists frequently used the term to identify Indians from that area during the 1700s. And third, many present-day descendants of these people continue to use the name Munsee, meaning "people from Minisink," to identify themselves. As its adoption by Kraft (2001), Otto (2006), and this volume indicate, Munsee is rapidly becoming the name most widely used by scholars to identify Indians whose ancestral homeland stretched from the lower Hudson to the upper Delaware river valleys.

2. Heckewelder suggested that Pocono comes from the Delaware words *pock-hanne* or *pokohanne,* "a stream issuing from a mountain, or running between two mountains," in LLN:358.

3. Goddard (1971, 1974, and 1978) suggests that Manhattan, Munsee, and Minisink all come from the Delaware word for island, tracing Munsee to the Northern Unami word *men si w,* "person from Minisink," and Minisink from what he suggests is the archaic Delaware expression *menesenk,* "on the island." Several early writers thought Munsee was a Delaware clan name meaning wolf. Minisink was often translated as "mountainous or stony country." Translations of Manhattan have included "hilly island" (Tooker 1901), "place where timber is procured for bows and arrows" (Heckewelder 1841:74), "cluster of islands with channels everywhere" (Beauchamp 1907:129), and "island where we all became intoxicated" (Heckewelder 1876:71–75). This latter example comes from a Delaware story told to Moravian missionary, John Heckewelder, during the late 1700s. The story, a wry, cautionary tale set at the time of Hudson's voyage, summons up memories of their ancestors' first experience with liquor. The reality is less colorful and more prosaic. Manhattan is simply a Delaware word for island. Goddard suggests it has been handed down to the present in its Munsee form, *menatayn.*

Lion Miles (2007, personal communication [hereinafter pc]) makes a strong case for the translation "peninsula people," first noted by Heckewelder in 1801. Miles notes that the Minisink lowlands project like a peninsula into the Pocono-Kittatiny uplands. He also brought my attention to Heckewelder's observation that the "Minsi . . . say [their name] is derived from the word 'Monnisi,' which signifies a peninsula. . . . The Minsi always composed the frontiers, dwelling in a circle-like form from Long Island to and beyond Minnissink." In the appendix to his early study, Barton (1798:2) wrote the following based on correspondence with Heckewelder: "The Minsi or Monsees . . . call themselves Minissi, or the Peninsula-People, because they inhabited the Minnissink. The tradition of these Indians informs us, that they originally dwelled in or under a lake, from whence they have sprung." Pointing out that *bak,* the root of the Dutch name bachom, translated as "extended upper part" by Ruttenber (1906), can also mean "basin or artificial lake," Miles endorsed Eager's (1846) suggestion that Minisink meant "land from where the water had gone." He supported this idea by mixing an ethnographic hypothesis suggesting that Minisinks moved from elsewhere to the upper Delaware River with a geological hypothesis that they arrived after a penned-up lake that formerly filled the upper Delaware River valley burst through the Water Gap at some remote time in the past.

4. People referred to by variant spellings of Mahican include both the original inhabitants of the upper Hudson Valley and Indian refugees from New England who established a separate community in their territory in 1676. Colonists farther west frequently referred to all Eastern Algonquians as Mahicans during the eighteenth century. Today, most Mahican descendants called themselves Mohicans, a variant that came into widespread usage in Wisconsin during the nineteenth century. Scholars, however, continue to use Mahican to distinguish them from the entirely separate Mohegan nation in eastern Connecticut, several of whose members joined Mahi-

cans and other Christian Indian converts at missions like Stockbridge, Massachusetts, from 1734 to 1785 and New Stockbridge, New York, between 1785 and 1822. For histories of the Mahicans, see Brasser (1974 and 1978), S. Dunn (1994 and 2000), and Frazier (1992).

Colonists almost exclusively used variants of the term Mahikander to refer to people from the upper Hudson River valley during colonial times. Until recently, most scholars used the spelling Mahican when talking about these people in and around their homeland. Today, writers like S. Dunn (1994 and 2000) and Frazier (1992) use the spelling Mohican, which first came into widespread use among Stockbridge Indians during the 1800s and that is preferred by many modern-day descendants living in Wisconsin; for Mahican linguistic and social affiliations, see Brasser (1978:198 and 211). For Quiripi-Unquachog, see Goddard (1971) and Salwen (1978:173).

5. The Munsee File is patterned after the Tsimshian File, a compilation of texts and other materials focusing on the importance of names in Tsimshian culture and history on the Northwest Coast of North America. Gathered by Tsimshian community member William Beynon and pioneering Canadian folklorist-anthropologist C. Marius Barbeau during the first half of the twentieth century, the Tsimshian File is currently in the collections of the Canadian Museum of Civilization in Gatineau, Quebec, across the Ottawa River from the Canadian capital of Ottawa, Ontario.

Nelson (1904) was the first writer to compile Indian names in New Jersey. Unpublished compilations of Delaware personal names have been made by William Hunter and Marshall Becker. Most of the personal names of men, women, and children in the Munsee File have been drawn from primary documents in chronicles specifying dates, locations, and additional information. Like other Delaware-speaking people, Munsees assumed a variety of names at different times in their lives. Most were given several formal names and picked up various nicknames, pet names, and titles. Following the dictates of custom, survivors politely refrained from mentioning these names after their owners died, preferring instead to allude to the deceased's qualities or achievements when talking about them (Weslager 1971).

Colonists had no such scruples. Very much concerned with keeping track of people who were sole sources of land and furs, and who might protect or attack them, they made what may be characterized as a fetish of documenting Indian personal, place, and political names. Most of these names, however, were penned by settlers who did not speak the Munsee language. Although some colonists and many Indians in Munsee country were multilingual, settlers and Indians alike usually depended on translators when speaking with one another. Sometimes paths from one language to another took tortuous routes. At some conferences, words from a Munsee speaker might have to be translated by a Dutchman whose interpretation was then translated into English and Iroquois by another person whose first and best language was German. The best translators were people who lived for varying periods among foreign neighbors. The general run of interlocutors often used dumbed-down versions of the Indian or European languages they translated. Less capable interpreters used a pidgin patois like the New Jersey trade jargon (Prince

1912) mostly consisting of Munsee words and simplified Indian expressions with a few English words like "brandywine" mixed in. Skills of later translators, transcribers, indexers, and editors (and the printers and publishers charged with putting their compilations into print) also varied widely (Hagedorn 1988).

Most colonial writers, and Indians literate enough to leave behind writings of their own, tended to spell words as they heard them. All wrote before widespread use of dictionaries significantly standardized spelling. Noting that the first English dictionaries did not appear until the 1600s, Winchester (1998:80–89) observes that dictionaries did not begin to come into wider use until the mid- to late 1700s. Even colonists with dictionaries rarely spelled Indian words the same way twice. Differing sounds, varying accents, and divergent spelling conventions of early Dutch and English colonists and later Swedish and German settlers introduced further variations. Native speakers of one language writing in another, such as writings in English penned by primary German speaker Christian Frederick Post, sometimes produced peculiarly garbled prose more nearly resembling a third language. A representative example of a transcription and transliteration of Post's idiosyncratic orthography may be seen in Grumet (1999:116–120).

Ears of many chroniclers were as ill suited to sound as their pens. Others were more sensitive to subtle speech sounds and shifts. The best scribes rarely spoke or understood Indian languages. More attentive chroniclers could often transcribe the sounds they heard with reasonable fidelity. Most, however, inadvertently spliced together or cut apart Indian words. Sometimes this resulted in separations of Indian equivalents of words like "breathtaking" or "winsome." This often created nonsensical linguistic lumps and fragments.

With one or two exceptions, records written during the twenty years of wars and epidemics that rained down on the people of Munsee country following the end of Kieft's War in 1645 do not provide population statistics. Disappearance after 1663 of nearly one-third ($n = 14$) of the forty-three people identified by name in European records written between 1645 and 1663 in the Munsee File indirectly indicates the magnitude of their losses during these years. Like other leaders mentioned by name in colonial chronicles, most of these people were probably elders by the time they rose to documentary notice. Only one of these, an Esopus leader named Preuwackaman, was clearly identified as a war casualty. The rest fell from prominence, moved away, were disabled, or died.

Particularly large numbers of people included in the Munsee File appear or disappear from colonial records during the middle years of the 1640s, 1660s, 1680s, and 1750s. These years correspond with intervals of time when wars, epidemics, land loss, and forced migration affected their communities. Stresses caused by any one of these disasters could trigger changes. The effect of several striking in quick succession almost certainly sparked significant transformations.

6. For a discussion of Delaware religion at the time of contact, see Kraft (2001:313–351).

7. For Iroquois League name bearers, see Fenton (1998:222). A substantial literature examines women's status in Iroquois societies. See Spittal (1990) for some of

the more influential studies; see Grumet (1980) for a general but still useful survey of women's roles in Eastern Algonquian politics, economy, and spirituality.

8. For an anthropological application of the concept of egalitarianism, see M. H. Fried (1967); for an account describing how one anthropologist learned firsthand how an egalitarian people gently humble excessive pride, see Lee (1969).

Honoring the custom mandating that names of the dead not be mentioned by the living, Mohawk Little Abraham's speech at a treaty meeting held in Lancaster, Pennsylvania, in 1757 did not disturb the memory of the hanging of what everyone called the Indian King of New Jersey by mentioning his name while reminding listeners of past injustices suffered by his people. Colonists belonging to a more rigid kind of society requiring more exact records preserved the name of the man, Weequehela, and the train of incidents that led to his June 30, 1727, execution by hanging in Perth Amboy for killing a neighbor during an argument. The name Perth Amboy is ascribed in LLN:376 to a combination of the Scottish place name Perth and the Delaware word *emboli,* a term for "hollowed out," evidently in reference to the low-lying roundish shape of the locale. For Weequehela, see Grumet (1991b) and Wilk (1993); for Heckewelder's translation of Weequehela as a Delaware expression meaning "to be fatigued," see LLN:834.

9. For marry out or die out, see Tylor (1873).

10. Like Munsee, Unami is the name of a dialect of the Delaware language that only came into use as a social term after its speakers left their homeland. Unami differs from Munsee in vocabulary and a tendency to use the consonant *R* where Munsees use *L.* At the time of contact, Unami and its Northern Unami variant were spoken by Indians living along the tidal estuary of the lower Delaware River below the falls at Trenton, New Jersey (Goddard 1971:14). A single reference made in 1757 used the name Unalimi to identify people living at the Forks of Delaware. See Goddard (1971:14) for Northern Unami and Weslager (1972:47) for Unalimi. Over time, writers have come to use the name Delaware when talking about people who speak variants of the Unami dialect. In this book, the original people of the Lower Delaware Valley and their descendants are referred to as Unamis.

11. A vast literature is devoted to the Iroquois. For their history, see Fenton (1998) and Richter (1992), whose emphasis on locality, factionalism, and distinction between the hereditary Iroquois League of fifty leaders and the political Iroquois Confederacy, which became particularly important in addressing threats to Iroquois survival after the 1690s, is especially useful. Sources on the Susquehannocks include Jennings (1978) and Kent (1984).

12. For enduring people, see Spicer (1971).

13. For culture as an organization of diversity, see A. F. C. Wallace (1952). Although it sounds obvious and simplistic, it is nonetheless true that no people belonging to any culture are ever totally restrained by rules or possessed of unlimited free choice. Those whose cultural values heedlessly embrace self-destructive beliefs and practices or who mire themselves in fanatically intolerant idealism limit ability to pursue potentially useful options. Prolonged insistence on doing things in ways that no longer work almost always leads to collapse. A. F. C. Wallace (1956a) suggests that intolerable stresses caused by strategies that fail often convince people to try new

ways of doing old things, a process he calls revitalization. Successfully revitalized cultures establish routines that maintain more or less stable steady states until catastrophically challenging conditions inspire new revitalization movements.

Catastrophes capable of triggering revitalization movements in Munsee country were in no short supply during the colonial era. Records of seemingly constant warfare show that fighting of varying duration and intensity was endemic in the North Atlantic world. Instances of numerous but considerably briefer outbreaks of disease, by contrast, indicate that sickness was epidemic during this era. One way or another, each war or disease directly or indirectly affected Indian and colonial communities in and around the Munsee homeland. Increasingly lethal wars and newly introduced virulent contagions tended to cause disproportionately high mortality rates among Indians. Land loss posed even greater threats to survival.

The episodic pattern of endemic fighting and epidemic illnesses chronicled in this book is in many ways a chronology of stochastic stutter steps. Periods of comparative stability are shattered at intervals by brief wrenching spasms of convulsive change. Such patterns most closely resemble something evolutionary biologists call punctuated equilibrium. Until recently, scholars saw change as a deliberate, slow, and gradual process requiring ample time for proper adjustment and adaptation. Sudden changes were viewed as occasions for extinction selecting against anything failing to cope with radically changed conditions. Those viewing history, especially that of traditional people, from a gradualist perspective regard steady continuity as a sign of healthful stability. Sudden, substantial, or dramatic changes suggest dislocation, distortion, or worse. Given the seemingly constant turmoil and periodic upheavals that mark Munsee history, not least the fact that they were forced from their homes and driven into exile, it is not surprising that past writers tended to agree that Munsees were not up to the task of contending with colonists.

This gradualist reading of Munsee decline changes when viewed from the vantage point of punctuated equilibrium. Elders preserving accumulated experience and young people representing the future of the Munsee people often were particularly hard hit by wars and epidemics. Massive losses of teachers and pupils at critical intervals cracked, clouded, but did not destroy the cultural lens through which Munsees viewed their world. Continued survival of the Munsees as a people shows that, severe as such losses were, they never completely severed all links to old traditions or past guidance. Enough elders survived to pass on useful knowledge and skills. Young people less restrained by fewer elders increasingly opened themselves to new ideas and beliefs possibly better suited to conditions as they found them. This resulted in periodic emergence of new traditions adapting old knowledge to new realities. These new traditions helped young people pass on much changed but still viable versions of Munsee culture to succeeding generations. The fact of Munsee cultural survival thus allows us to consider the possibility that actions long regarded as chaotic, confused, or feckless actually represent coherent, flexible, and, at times, subtly effective responses to challenging conditions.

For punctuated equilibrium, see Gould (2002). Typical views rationalizing Delaware adjustment difficulties include Newcomb's (1956:78) observation that the

Delawares "were completely unprepared for dealing with the aggressive, techno-logically complex, well-organized, exploitative culture of Europe" and Kraft's (2001:401 and 409) characterization of the Lenapes as hospitable but naive people taken advantage of by self-serving colonists.

Nowhere are the adaptive possibilities revealed by punctuated equilibrium more clearly on view than in studies of Munsee social organization. All investigators agree that Munsee individuals, families, clans, even entire communities changed their names, locations, statuses, structures, functions, and roles at different times. Some scholars believe that inscrutable Indians intentionally took advantage of this to con-fuse colonists. Most recently, Merwick (2006:192) suggests that the mass of names apparently confusing Dutch chroniclers make it difficult, if not impossible, to use Eu-ropean records to reconstruct the contours of Munsee society. Stating that some Dutch merchants had "a minimal knowledge of their strange worlds," Merwick goes on to say "but it mattered to know exactly how the nearby sachems organized them-selves, shifted in and out of the alliances, and controlled the selling of furs—who knew that?"

This is not a majority opinion among specialists. Scholars argue over the mean-ings of the information preserved in the records. Gradualists among them look at the complex, confusing, and occasionally confounding mass of names and see strictly or-dered bands, tribes, and nations thrown into debilitating but still intelligible disar-ray by the rigors of contact. Those favoring a punctuated equilibrium viewpoint, by contrast, see in the same record evidence of a periodically rearranged, flexibly adap-tive social system.

This latter point of view, I believe, provides the most fruitful approach when try-ing to make sense out of the confusing jumble of names marking the different ways Munsees organized their social lives at different times in different places. A Munsee addressed by his dialect's version of lenape, "fellow man," also had other names. These were commonly linked to different locales, kin connections, statuses, and life stages. Depending on who was doing the identifying, this man could also be identified as a Loup, a Mahikander, or a River Indian. Edmund Leach (1954) showed how dif-ferent names used to identify people and groups can document shifting social posi-tions or identities associated with particular sociopolitical integration levels or residence at certain locales.

14. In recent years, several commentators have traced modern-day pejorative use of the word "squaw" to a purported origin as a Mohawk or Sioux vulgar term for vagina; for a discussion of the issue, see Bright (n.d.); for a historical linguistic ety-mology of the word affirming that it was originally a Massachusett word for woman that entered the regional patois during the seventeenth century, see Goddard (1997). For squaw defined as a wife in the mostly Munsee or Northern Unami New Jer-sey trade jargon, see Prince (1912:522).

15. Masthay (1991:155) obtained the words *anapawexkue,* "Indian woman" and *anenapawak,* "Indians," from the late fluent Canadian Munsee speaker Emily John-son in 1981; a reference dated May 6, 1755, records that "the ancient tribe and na-tion of Indians called Ninneepauues otherwise and in English known by the name

of the Delaware Indians" conveyed lands west of the Delaware River between the Delaware Water Gap and the Lackawaxen River to the Connecticut-based Susquehannah Company (SCP 1:260–271). Often translated as "man," anenapawak, Ninneepauue, and Lenape more specifically referred to Indian men. Lenni Lenape came into use among Unami speakers in later years to distinguish Indians from *wapsit lenapewuk,* "white men" and *nesgessit lenapewuk,* "black men" (Whritenour 2007:pc). Munsees and other Delawares used different terms, such as their word for European, *schwannuck,* "salty or bitter people," to identify non-Indians. For Lenapewhihittuck and Kithanne, see LLN:355.

16. An online query for Wappinger Confederacy made on May 17, 2007, yielded more than five hundred hits. Ruttenber named his chieftaincy after what he regarded as its most important tribe and included as Wappingers nations he identified as Weckquaesgeeks, Sint-Sinks, Kitchawongs or Kicktawancs, Tankitekes, Nochpeems, Siwanoys, and a group of Connecticut Valley communities collectively identified as Sequins (Ruttenber 1872:77–85).

Ruttenber largely based this formulation on three pieces of evidence. The first he drew from a claim made by Henry Rowe Schoolcraft that "the prevailing totem of all the Hudson River cantons was the Wolf, borne alike by Minsis, Wappingers and Mahicans, leading the French to call them all Loups or wolves." The second was based on colonial sources identifying lower River Indian leaders like Seyseychkimus as Wappingers. The third originated in an affidavit filed by Wappinger leader Daniel Nimham in 1762. In it, Daniel identified himself as "a River Indian of the tribe of the Wappinoes, which tribe was the ancient inhabitants of the [lower] eastern shore of Hudson's River . . . that another tribe of River Indians called the Mayhiccondas were the ancient inhabitants of the remaining eastern shore . . . [and] these two tribes constituted one nation" (in Ruttenber 1872:51). Although linguists presently agree that most Indians living along the eastern shores of the lower Hudson River valley spoke Munsee, some think members of the Wappinger community in Dutchess County may have been Mahican speakers. Daniel Nimham was descended from Munsee-speaking ancestors from western Long Island and northern New Jersey (Grumet 1992; J. Smith 2000). Originally from Long Island, Seyseychkimus moved to Wiechquaesgeck and later farther upriver to Wappinger country after selling his lands in Brooklyn. Neither fact was available to Ruttenber in 1872. Ruttenber's identification of Nimham I, Seyseychkimus, and the Wappingers as speakers of the Mahican language is understandable in light of the facts as he knew them over a century ago.

Looking farther afield, Ruttenber linked his Wappingers with what he thought were closely related Mahican and Montauk chieftaincies. Like most of his contemporaries, Ruttenber regarded all Algonquian-speaking communities north and east of the Wappingers as Mahicans (often spelled Mohegan). Ruttenber regarded the Hudson River as a major social and linguistic barrier. He located what he called the Minsi tribes in Minisink, Esopus, and Catskill territory. His Unami tribes occupied territory stretching along the western reaches of New York Harbor and the Hudson River from the Navesink Highlands north to present-day Haverstraw, New York. He further lumped both tribes together into a single Lenni Lenape chieftaincy.

See Ruttenber (1872:71–98) for discussions making and supporting each of these tribal and chieftaincy identifications. Ruttenber's Montauk chieftaincy stretched to take in every Indian community on Long Island. Subsequent studies show that Long Island was divided into two or perhaps three speech communities. The Montauks, Shinnecocks, and their neighbors living around Peconic Bay on the east end of Long Island spoke languages similar to those spoken by Pequots, Mohegans, and Narragansetts on the mainland. Mid-island communities may have spoken the Quiripi-Unquachog language also used by Quinnipiacs and other Eastern Algonquians living between the Connecticut and Housatonic river valleys; western Long Islanders mostly spoke Munsee.

Impressed by Ruttenber's scholarship, James E,. Mooney adopted many of his ideas regarding Hudson River valley Indian chieftaincies. He elevated Ruttenber's Wappinger chieftaincy into a confederacy under that name in an entry published in Frederick Webb Hodge's *Handbook of American Indians* (1907–1910, 2:913). Its presence in the authoritative Handbook assured that Mooney's Wappinger Confederacy was universally accepted by nearly every writer on the subject for the next sixty years. The idea was not seriously challenged until 1971, when Robert H. Ives Goddard III disproved the concept in a seminal article. Finding no evidence of a Wappinger Confederacy in colonial records, Goddard showed that Indians living along the lower Hudson River valley spoke Munsee rather than Mahican.

Despite Goddard's linguistic and Grumet's (in NAPN:57–58) analyses showing that the Wappinger Confederacy was created by Ruttenber and Mooney, subsequent writers working as recently as Sivertsen (2007:59–60, 220, 229, and 256–259) continue to use the Wappinger Confederacy concept in their studies of colonial Hudson Valley culture and history.

17. For the April 13, 1670, deed to Staten Island stating that its Indian sellers called the place Aquehonga Manacknong, "high-banked island," see NYCD 13:455–457. For De Rasiere's estimates, see NNN:103; for Wolley's estimates, see the reprint of his pamphlet in NAHC:54.

18. For Danckaerts's thoughts on Indian demography in 1680, see Gehring and Grumet (1987:107). For Denton's observations, referring to the state of things on western Long Island in 1645 and published in London in 1670, see Denton (1670:6–7). For an example of an observation that a populous Indian town in Munsee country could be found empty of inhabitants on occasion, see Robert Hunter Morris's April 22, 1746, letter to James Lyne noting that in 1719 "Cashieghtonk [Cochecton, modern-day Damascus, Pennsylvania] . . . although a town with many Indians at times, it is often abandoned for weeks," in Work Projects Administration (1940, 1:57).

19. For Tomachkapay's September 12, 1681, complaint to English authorities, see NYCD 13:551–552. For Stuyvesant's March 30, 1662, instructions to Oratam and Mattano authorizing both to arrest liquor traders, see NYCD 13:218. For prosecutions at Fort Orange, see Van Laer (1920–1923, 1:286–291 and 2:25–33); Mancall

(1995) provides the most comprehensive survey of the liquor problem among Indians in colonial America.

20. Major studies on the effects of disease on Indian populations include Dobyns (1966 and 1983), Ramenofsky (1987), Thornton (1987), and Henige (1998).

21. For 20,000, see Mooney (1928:2–4). See Kroeber (1939:140) for 22,000 and his 0.75 per square mile population density; for 30,000, see Cook (1976:60–84); for the currently conservative figure of 10,000 to 12,000 Delawares, see Weslager (1972:42); Becker (1993:22) suggests a figure of 5,000 for the total aboriginal Delaware population based on hunter-gatherer demographic density estimates drawn from other cultures in different environments. Becker believes that each of twelve to fourteen of what he called foraging bands of Lenapes (an ethnonym he uses to identify only Delawares living in southeastern Pennsylvania) had from 12 to 40 members and a total population of from 250 to 400. Allowing for the importance of fishing and what he thinks may be the possible practice of horticulture elsewhere in the region, he asserts that his 5,000 precontact population figure suggests that Delawares "suffered no significant long term effects from European disease."

22. See Ceci (1977) and Becker (1988) for Delaware communities as tiny foraging bands; for the 0.66 adjustment of Kroeber's 0.75 per square mile figure for neolithic crude population densities, see Lee and De Vore (1968:11); for crude population density estimates of people in Munsee country, see Grumet (1989b:135).

23. For Eastern Algonquians as bands, see Becker (1986); for tribes, see Thurman (1974:126–127); for chiefdoms, see Potter (1993); and for nations, see Weslager (1972); for discussions of the band, tribe, and chiefdom conundrum, see Leacock (1983:29) and Leacock and Lee (1982). Use of the term "band" to describe groups in and around Munsee country is so widespread that exemplary citations are not necessary. The term is mostly employed as a handy shorthand for identifying constituent parts of more complex social formations like tribes, chiefdoms, or nations. Noting that modern states are not composed of bands, tribes, or chiefdoms, anthropologists taking a less mechanical view of the subject tend to reserve use of the word band to describe a particular type of small-scale hunting, gathering, and foraging society. Band societies are characterized by very low population densities and very high levels of mobility, cooperation, sexual autonomy, social equality, and resource sharing. All band-level societies described by modern-era fieldworkers live in remote places where food cannot be produced without considerable technological assistance. Until a few years ago, such bands were seen as surviving examples of earlier types of human society now confined to the poorest margins of habitable terrain unwanted by more advanced cultures. More recent studies focus on interplay between relatively complex and simpler social formations that have shaped development of both types of society.

24. For impacts of demography on views of social complexity, see Dobyns (1966:395); M. H. Fried (1967) is a good place to start exploring debates about problems with the concept of "tribe."

25. For the April 27, 1677, reference, see NYCD 13:504–505; for the August 27, 1743, reference, see the document filed under that date in the Philhower Collection, Special Collections, Alexander Library, Rutgers University.

Lewis Henry Morgan (in Leacock 1963:176–177) collected the first unambiguously identifiable list of Delaware lineages (groups he called sub-gentes) with the help of a knowledgeable Kansas Delaware man named William Adams while visiting in 1859 and 1860. In 1907, Harrington (1913) found that Delawares in Canada remembered all but two of these terms, though not all were regarded as clan names. Harrington noted that "the names of clans are said to have had their origin in some traditional peculiarity of their ancestors or from some locality once frequented by them."

26. Members striking out on their own helped lineages expand into new territories when things got too crowded. For the classic study looking into the dynamics of expanding segmenting lineage systems, see Sahlins (1961).

27. Like many Northern Unami–speaking people, Nutimus had strong ties with Munsee-speaking communities. His name probably comes from *nutamaes*, "a striker of fish with a spear" (LLN:385).

For the observation that "maternal lineages were the most conspicuous mechanisms of descent and family affiliation among the Delawares," see A. F. C. Wallace (1949:8); for De Rasiere's statement that the Indians of New Netherland reckoned "consanguinity to the eighth degree" and regarded "intercourse with those of their family within the third degree" as incestuous, see NNN:108–109; for Van der Donck's statement "that the children follow their mother," see DONCK:83; observing that succession was "always of the mother's side," William Penn went on to write that "the children of him that is now king, will not succeed, but his brother by the mother, or the children of his sister, whose sons (and after them the children of her daughters) will reign, for no woman inherits; the reason they render for this way of descent is that their issue may not be spurious"; for this and more on Delaware descent principles, see Penn (in WPHOA:35–36).

Several references document matrilineal descent principles at work in Munsee and closely connected Northern Unami communities. A relative of Nutimus's named Teedyuscung used his identification of Andrew Woolley as Weekweyla's sister's son to buttress Andrew's leadership claim in a letter read on August 5, 1757, at a treaty meeting at Easton, Pennsylvania (Minutes of the Third Treaty Council Held at Easton, p. 37, French and Indian War Papers, American Philosophical Society [hereinafter APS]; in a deed signed on April 29, 1666, in NYCD 13:402, and WCH 2:153, Romackqua, a leader's son and successor of the leading Wiechquaesgeck sachem Sauwenaroque, identified himself as the latter's brother on his mother's side; for "Ramaque" as "Janorocket's brother" on February 24, 1671, see ECM 1:70–71; for "Showan Orockett's brother Ramacque" on October 30, 1671, see NYCD 13:460–461 and ECM 1:103–105.

Frequent references to leader's brothers as sachems of neighboring communities are consistent with segmenting lineage systems in which brothers marrying into matrilineages in different communities expand their family's influence and authority over larger areas.

For Nutimus's May 8, 1735, statement, see A. F. C. Wallace (1949:21–22). The existence of patrilineally descended family hunting territories among the Delawares was first suggested by Speck (1915) and explored in depth by his student MacLeod

(1922:452). Reexamining the same land records, A. F. C. Wallace (1947:18) and New-comb (1956:23–24) both thought the evidence more strongly supported the view that hunting territories were inherited along matrilineal lines. More recently, Barnes (1968:15) suggested that both camps were right. She found that the particular de-mands of "the sexual and seasonal division of labor inherent in the Delawares' flex-ible adaptation to their environment created at least two opposing tendencies in social organization. The closely-knit, matrilineal organization favored by agricul-tural activities was countered by the loosely-knit, patrilineal organization that went with hunting and gathering."

The issue of matrilineal descent is not a small one. Sex and descent continue to dominate arguments over relative effects of nature and nurture on human biology and culture. Morgan (in Leacock 1963:393–394) was among many nineteenth-century evolutionary theorists (Marx was another) proposing that the earliest forms of human society were communal matriarchates. Patriarchy, in this view, only emerged with the invention of private property. Speck and MacLeod were part of a reaction to evolutionary thought that set in during the early 1900s. Both men drew on archival and field data documenting the Montagnais and Naskapis (today collectively known as the Innu) of Labrador, the Lenapes of the Lower Delaware Valley, and other peo-ples they regarded as band-level societies thought to be similar to the most basic human social order. They used data suggesting the existence of patriliny in these societies to support the idea that male domination of family-owned hunting terri-tories represented the earliest and perhaps most natural form of society.

This idea remained a dominant paradigm in anthropological kinship studies until the inevitable counter-reaction occurred a generation later. It began after Jenness (1935) suggested that male-managed subarctic family hunting territories emerged only with the coming of the fur trade in historic times. Leacock (1954) carried things further by showing that the earliest records documenting subarctic band fam-ily structure and property values emphasized communal land management and in-cluded female descent. For recent articles by Harvey A. Feit and others calling for a more nuanced view requiring a much harder look at still hazily defined concepts like band, family, ownership, and property, see Bishop and Morantz (1986).

The problem is clearly not an either-or issue. Nutimus's statement of paternal connections suggests an intriguing corroboration of a paternal principle at work in a matrilineal society. This single example, which does not trace property rights be-yond two generations, is not by itself strong enough to support Barnes's suggestion that the Delawares practiced double descent, an exceedingly rare type of bilineal sys-tem in decline everywhere it has been documented. Suggestions of Delaware prop-erty transmission from paternally related fathers to children may more profitably be viewed as examples of complementary filiation, a far more common practice ob-served in most unilineal societies. As set out by Fortes (1953), matrifiliation (the prin-ciple as practiced in matrilineal societies) is a tool for maintaining formal bonds with paternally related fathers and their families (otherwise mere in-laws) that allows the father's family to transmit affinal (i.e., in-law) rights and prerogatives to children with-out resorting to expensive and potentially divisive multigenerational patrilines.

28. For Van der Donck's observation that "100, and frequently many more, dwell together in one house," see DONCK:80; for Danckaerts's observation, see DANCK:56. All other known information on the subject was collected after Delawares were forced from their homeland. These uniformly document existence of nuclear families and neolocal residence patterns. Citing Murdock's (1949:17) classic formulation that "rules of residence reflect general economic, social, and cultural conditions," Newcomb (1956:45–46) felt that neolocality in exiled Delaware communities was caused by "isolation and emphasis placed upon nuclear families, the decrease of polygyny, the scattering of kinsmen, and the individualistic emphasis placed upon economic activity." All but the latter conditions prevailed in the strictly communal eighteenth-century Moravian towns where most of this information was gathered. Prevalence of this suite of conditions in nearby pagan Delaware communities presents the intriguing possibility that mission residence patterns actually encouraged preservation of earlier social forms than those maintained by their non-Moravian brethren.

29. Morgan (in Leacock 1963) was first proposed "phratry" as a term to identify groups of unilineally related family groups like clans in 1877. For a detailed modern-day discussion of the phratry concept, see Fox (1967).

30. For linkages of the three animal-named groups with political and linguistic divisions, see Heckewelder (1876:51–53). Goddard (1978:225) points out that no other writer made the same connections; the problem was compounded when translators Hulburt and Schwarze (1910:27) equally applied the English word "tribe" to Heckewelder's compatriot David Zeisberger's (1780:28) *nationen* (that is, Munsee, Unami, and Unilachtego nations) and his (Zeisberger's) wolf, turtle, and turkey *hauptstamme,* principal tribe or clan. Delawares did not make the same mistake. As early as 1824, Delawares informed Michigan territorial agent Charles C. Trowbridge that members of all three family lines could be found in each Delaware nation. The finding, however, remained buried among Trowbridge's unpublished and unnoticed writings until Weslager (1972:480–481) published them in his own *History.* Morgan's informant in Kansas (in L. White 1959:52) organized what Morgan called Delaware sub-gente lineages into the classic tripartite phratry framework: twelve lineages each in the Wolf and Turkey phratries and ten in the Turtle phratry.

31. See Evans-Pritchard (1940) for his levels of integration concept. Differences in size, composition, and organization at different integration levels of Munsee society can be likened to what some anthropologists call structural poses (Gearing 1962). In this formulation, people organize themselves into temporary task groups to carry out particular economic, military, social, or political goals and objectives. Applying the structural pose concept, we can see groups of men and women putting their marks on deeds to sign away tracts of Munsee territory to colonists as composing land-selling task groups. Those joining together to sign particular treaties may be seen as taking on diplomatic structural poses appropriate to the event; other groups signing trade agreements can be regarded as economic task groups. Largely stable during long periods of equilibrium, destabilizing mortality rates, shifting residence patterns, and other changes can be seen to alter structural pose makeup and configuration.

For one group of closely related Matinecock leaders signing most of the 138 deeds conveying lands within the 160-square-mile town of Oyster Bay in western Long Island to colonists between 1653 and 1703, see Grumet (1996:129). Claims to large tracts made under color of deeds anomalously signed by solitary or otherwise obscure Indian proprietors, such as the unregistered 1686 Walking Purchase Deed discovered nearly fifty years after its alleged creation and the 1709 Hardenburgh Patent, by contrast, often became mired in court and controversy.

Flexibly porous social and political boundaries joining as well as separating interlocking unilineal kinship groups helped Munsees choose task group members from a large pool of potential personnel. Each grouping was shaped, sustained and, on occasion, separated by bonds of blood, affinity, and solidarity. Broader networks linked by common interest and mutual enmity often sustained outnumbered Munsees threatened by settlers who themselves were only restrained by fear of Indian reprisals. Delineation of the size, structure, and extent of Munsee networks can provide clearer understanding of the ways task groups functioned as parts of complex, far-reaching, and ever-changing webs of social, political, economic, and ritual relations rather than as confused incoherent flounderings of a destabilized social order.

For boundaries, see Barth (1969); for networks, see Johnson (1996:855–859); for the Munsee network organization centering around Minisink, see Grumet (1991a).

The structure and makeup of networks and all other aspects of Munsee society changed as forces at the core and periphery of Munsee country joined with war, disease, and depopulation to radically transform Munsee lives at critical points in their history. Changing patterns of archaeological evidence suggest that Iroquois, Powhatan, and other neighboring nations favorably positioning themselves in new markets opened by European merchant-explorers forced Munsees to adjust to changing conditions during the late 1500s and early 1600s. A new set of circumstances confronted Munsee people after 1645, when land sales and war losses forced them to shift the core of their network from coastal salt water shores to inland fresh water rivers. Equally dramatic transformations occurred when changing conditions compelled Munsees to refocus their network organizations from freshwater lowlands to less productive upland foothills during the 1660s, deeper into interior hills and valleys during the 1680s and 1690s, then to the more distant Appalachian Highlands north and west of their ancestral homeland by 1765.

32. The word "sachem" comes from *sachim,* a Narragansett term for leader. Its inclusion in trade jargons used to conduct business in the colonial Northeast resulted in both colonists and Indians using sachem and the closely related term *sagamore* when referring to Indian leaders. The latter term closely resembles the Unami Delaware *sakimawuk.* Munsees used *kihkay* as their word for leader then as now. Colonists used the word "sachem" when referring to Munsee and other Indian leaders everywhere in the Northeast.

33. Initially documented as Mayauwetinnemin, this Massapequa man assumed the name Tackapousha in 1655, at the time when other documents affirmed his rise to prominence. For documents identifying Mayauwetinnemin as another name for Tackapousha, see NYCD 13:58 and 147–149; for other documents naming

Mayauwetinnemin alone, see NYCD 13:18–19 and 14:474; for documents using orthographic fragments Antinome, Witaneywen, and Wittanahom shorn of names' initial sounds, see NYCD 14:79, NYCD 14:60, and Shurtleff and Pulsifer (1855–1861, 2:44–45).

34. Named for the Crow nation on the Great Plains, the "type" society where this system was first identified, Crow kinship terminology "groups together various relatives who are ordinarily distinguished (and assigns) them a common kinship designation" (Murdock 1949:166). Crow systems are characterized by a bifurcate merging kinship terminology in which children use the same word to refer to both their biological father (who is considered an in-law belonging to a different lineage unrelated to them by blood) and their "social" father, a mother's brother who is a member of their matrilineage (Murdock 1949:125).

For the reference dated August 23, 1647, identifying Tackapousha as the son of Mechoswodt, see NYCD 14:79; see NYCD 13:58 for identification on November 27, 1655, of the one-eyed sachem (probably Penhawitz) as Tackapousha's father. Weequehela is another example of a man linked to two men identified as his father. On August 16, 1675 (in EJD Liber 1:197 [142 on verso]), Weequehela (identified as Quicacahuland) was noted as the son of Mattapeck (i.e., Metapis). Several years later, another document identified Irooseeke as Weequehela's father (Stilwell 1903–1932, 3:449). Other sources identify Irooseeke as a son of Metapis's brother Emerus. Following the logic of a bifurcate merging system, Weequehela could use his language's term for father to address both his biological father, Irooseeke (who did not belong to his mother's lineage), and his uncle Metapis, who was a maternal blood relative.

Morgan (in Leacock 1963:176–177 and L. White 1959:52–53) made the only systematic collection of traditional Delaware kin terms during visits to their Kansas reservation in 1859 and 1860. Newcomb (1956:44–48) thought that the kin terms collected by Morgan most closely resembled a matricentered version of what Murdock and succeeding generations of anthropologists call the Hawaiian system. Most anthropologists agree that the Delaware language kin terms collected by Morgan and in recently gathered lexicons reflect a system of terminology significantly different from the aboriginal form and changed, as Newcomb put it, by "altered rules of residence, decreased polygyny, and increased economic and political importance of men."

35. For Chopeycannows' marriage to Suscaneman's sister, see Grumet (1996:125–126). A fuller discussion of these linkages may be found in Grumet (1994:83–87). The heartland of the Matinecock community centered on Oyster Bay. Tooker (in TIN:115) suggests that Matinecock may mean "place of observation," from the Delaware words *latonniken,* "to search or examine," *auke,* "land," and *ut,* "at or near." Initially an obscure group all but unknown to the Dutch as late as 1644, the Matinecocks were identified as refugees living with Nissaquogues farther east on Long Island in 1645. Their sachem Asharoken and his successor Suscaneman became major intermediaries with Oyster Bay, Hempstead, and Huntington townsfolk during the following decades. Suscaneman may have been from Secatogue, where his sister continued to live after her marriage to Tackapousha's younger brother,

Chopeycannows. The well-connected Suscaneman probably took up residence at Matinecock after marrying an equally well-born woman from that place.

36. Keschaechquereren was a major community located near Canarsie in the present-day Flatbush section of southern Brooklyn. Residents at Ryder's Pond (Lopez and Wisniewski 1971–1972) and other places in Flatbush dug up considerable quantities of tools and household debris representing more than six thousand years of occupation in the same general locale, marked by Keskachauwe on the 1639 Manatus map (see below). Writers like Van Wyck (1924) thought the place was the capital of Indian Brooklyn. It is easy to see how they came to this conclusion. Deeds to lands bought by the Dutch West India Company at Maspeth, Governor's Island, and other locales in and around Brooklyn between 1636 and 1638 specifically note that sachems from Keschaechquereren consented to the sales. These include devices dated June and July 16, 1636, conveying three planting lands variously called Castuteeuw or Keskateuw (LP:5–6), June 16, 1637, deeds to Governor's Island and the area around the Brooklyn Navy Yard (LP:6–7), and the August 1, 1638, deed to Maspeth (LP:8–9). Other documents show that Penhawitz, a prominent sachem from the place, wielded considerable influence over Indian affairs on western Long Island. He was evidently well connected. The January 15, 1639, Massapequa deed lists him as a cousin of the influential primary signatory Mechoswodt (LP:9).

Tooker (in TIN:78) supported his argument asserting Keschaechquereren's primacy by suggesting that the name was an analog of the Narragansett word *keesaqunnamune,* "a kind of solemn public meeting." Information on the Manatus map, the last document mentioning the community by this name, has long been though to corroborate this belief. The trail route depicted below the town formed what appears to be the shape of a large heart. Tooker may have taken the pattern as a representation of the heart of Keskachauwe. He certainly thought the locale was important, translating the legend inscribed alongside the town name, *dit fatzoen huysen bewoonen des wilden,* to mean "the principal house of the Indians."

Convincing as these assertions appear, they are not entirely supported by all researchers. Ruttenber (in RIN:90), for example, suggested that the name may have been just as easily derived from the Unami words *k'sch-achquonican,* "great bush net" and *achewen,* "thicket"; Gehring (1985:pc), moreover, regards the heart-shaped trail as a fortuitous pattern and more accurately translates the legend on the Manatus map as "principal way the Indians build their houses." Although these findings challenge assertions suggesting Keschaechquereren was an Indian capital, they do not necessarily diminish the importance of the place to western Long Island Indians at the time. Not mentioned by name after 1639, Keschaechquereren was one of the first Munsee-speaking communities on western Long Island to disappear from Dutch records.

Massapequa survives in the form of the village of the same name in the town of Hempstead, Nassau County. The Massapequa nation initially appeared in Dutch records when Mechoswodt, noted as chief sachem of "Marossepinck," his cousin Penhawitz (identified in the document as Piscawoc), and a number of their people signed rights to their western Long Island lands over to the Dutch West India Company on January 15, 1639. Boundaries set out on the deed ran along the north shore from the East River to Martin Gerritsens Bay (present-day Oyster Bay), then south to Sicketeuw Hacky (Cow Bay) and west to Reckouw Hacky (Rockaway).

See Ruttenber (in RIN:93) and Tooker (in TIN:111) for translations for Massapequa from the Mohegan Massa-pe-auke, "great water land or land at the great cove"; Whritenour (2007:pc) suggests that the orthography Marossepinck indicates that the name is built around the Munsee word *siipuw,* "creek"; see LP:9 for the text of the January 15, 1639, Marossepinck deed.

A nation identified as Mongochkonnome first appeared in Dutch records documenting negotiations at the April 6, 1644, meeting at Fort Amsterdam (NYCD 13:48); the meaning and significance of the word, and of similar-sounding ethnonyms—Mochgonnekonck, mentioned in a document penned that same year, and Mochkeychkonk in another written ten years later—has been the subject of some disagreement among specialists. The name initially appeared in a listing of 1644 meeting participants, including "Mamarranack, Wapgaurin, chief of Kichtawanck, and Mongochkonnome, Pappenoharrow of Wiquaeskeck and Nochpeem, as well as the Wappincx." Placements of commas in the meeting transcript make it appear that Mongochkonnome and Pappenoharrow were names of sachems representing Wiechquaesgeck, Nochpeem, and Wappinger communities. The passage, however, can also be read to suggest that Mamarranack (Munsee for "stream of striped or crooked lines") was a Kichtawanck chief, Wapgaurin of Mongochkonnome was an associate of Gauwaroe of Matinecock, and Pappenoharrow represented the three other nations.

Tooker (in TIN:136–138) thought that the three documented orthographic versions of the word represented a term used by Munsees to identify Shinnecocks from eastern Long Island. The name of the only man explicitly associated with people identified by the word, Wittaneywen, however, is an alias of Tackapousha, the son of Penhawitz and successor to Mechoswodt. No known document identifies Tackapousha as a Shinnecock. The state of present knowledge indicates that Mongochkonnome and its synonyms were either the names of a Wiechquaesgeck sachem, a garbled rendition of Matinecock, another name for Massapequa, or the name of an altogether different western Long Island Indian community.

Goddard (1978:175) makes the most recent connection corroborating Tooker's linkage of Mochgonnekonck with Shinnecock. Tooker also criticized Ruttenber for identifying Wittaneymen as Tackapousha, a linkage that now appears more likely than Tooker's connection of Wittaneymen with the Shinnecock sachem Weenakamin.

37. For "breath of the people," see Penn (in WPHOA:36); for an extensive discussion of the evidence for Indian leadership in Munsee country, see Grumet (1979:98–108); for consensus, see Silberbauer (1982).

For one of the very few references to a leader in Munsee country also mentioned as a medicine person, see Danckaerts's March 4, 1680, reference quoting Hackensack leader Pierwim (identified as Hans by Danckaerts) as saying "I, who am a captain and sakemaker among the Indians, as well as a medicine-man" (in DANCK:268); the near total absence of references of spiritual inclinations of sachems identified by name contrasts with the few accounts describing Munsee religious beliefs and practices. This may well represent a creative misunderstanding that allowed spiritually pure Munsees to deal with ritually impure Christians who were themselves compelled to deal with Indians they regarded as heathens and worse. Interestingly, Danckaerts's status as an outsider uninhibited by provincial attitudes may have made him less reluctant to identify Pierwim as a medicine man.

38. No product manufactured by Indians in the Northeast has fascinated more people than wampum. Also known as sewan, peage, and wampumpeag, wampum are small tube-shaped shell beads. The shiny half-inch or so long, slender tubular beads come in two colors. White beads were produced from whorled centers of whelk shells and midsections of hard clams. Relatively rarer and more highly prized black beads, actually dark purplish blue in color, came from the edges of hard clam. Comparatively large numbers of whites beads of sufficient color quality could be produced from whelks and clams. Only clams possessed the purple color, and only a small number of these exhibited colored edges of sufficient brightness, intensity, and clarity to be considered desirable.

Shells used to produce wampum were found only on beaches and tidal flats. The best places to find them in Munsee country were along ocean beaches, harbor strands, and in ancient heaps marking old clambakes archaeologists call middens. Although people had been producing shell beads long before Europeans landed on Munsee shores, craftsfolk using stone tools could produce them only in small numbers. Vastly larger numbers could be manufactured by cutting shells to shape with iron knives and perforating tiny holes with small awl drills called muxes. Beadmakers used sand and sharkskin to grind beads to the required bright lustrous finish.

Finished beads were strung onto spun fiber or tanned hide strings. Quality was important. Only beads of uniform length, thickness, color, and brightness were acceptable for most uses. Munsees were known to check bead quality by running strings along the bridges of their noses. Those passing muster could be used as single strings or fixed together to form broad belts consisting of several rows. Designs made by threading beads of different colors onto strings and designs woven on belts served as memory aids used to help people remember orally transmitted messages ranging in length from short communications to entire treaty agreements. Like the agreements they signified, the beads themselves were considered powerful things that affected people's lives and destinies.

Colonists as well as Indians came to use wampum. Both Indian and colonial messengers carried wampum strings bearing messages to and from Indian towns. Although people sometimes had to make do with pelts and trade goods, few treaties were negotiated without ceremonial exchanges of strings representing particular points or dramatic presentations of belts symbolizing more portentous propositions of peace, trade, or war. Indians and colonists also repeatedly recycled the rare beads to produce new strings and belts. Colonists constantly short on coin and specie used wampum as a type of currency. Calling wampum the mine of New Netherland, officials established exchange rates and did what they could to regulate quality. Colonial desire for wampum caused bread shortages when bakers stopped producing cheap coarse black bread favored by colonists and switched over to baking more expensive white bread avidly purchased at much higher prices by Indians visiting

New York during the spring trading season. These shortages were so severe that colonial governors periodically had to prohibit sales of white bread to Indians. Despite such restrictions, bakers enriched with wampum and monopolizing production of much-wanted baked goods often grew rich enough to invest in real estate and other business ventures.

Although wampum continued to serve as currency throughout the colonial era, usage fell off dramatically in most places as sufficient amounts of imported coinage became available by the 1700s. Colonial entrepreneurs rather than Indians then controlled most bead production. Continuing Indian demand for the beads during the nineteenth century would be satisfied by factories purpose-built in Paterson, New Jersey, and other cities. More recently, many Indian nations have mounted strenuous efforts to repatriate wampum in museums and other repositories.

See Speck (1919) for the classic text on wampum; for a detailed up-to-date study of wampum in Indian and colonial societies, see Peña (1990); also see Peña (2005:1650–1651) for a handy overview of the subject; for wampum as a post-contact development, see Ceci (1989); for the symbolic significance of wampum, see Hamell (1983) and Snyder (1999); for running wampum across the nose, see Heckewelder (1876); for a lively article sketching out relationships between wampum, baking, and real estate in New Amsterdam, see Middleton (2001).

2. Munsee Country

1. Indian fire ecology has been a subject of particular interest since Day (1953) first brought the practice to widespread attention.

2. Archaeological information presented in this section has largely been abstracted from material in Kraft (2001).

3. Thanks to Whritenour (2007:pc) for his thoughts on the etymology of these and other Munsee place names mentioned in this study.

4. For Heckewelder's suggestion that Pequannock derives from *peckanne*, "dark river," see LLN:375.

5. For Heckewelder's suggestion that Hackensack comes from *hackingsakquik*, "that which unites itself with other water almost imperceptibly," see LLN:375; other translations of the name center on "hook-shaped," from the Unami word *hocquaan*, "hook" (in RIN:104); Oklahoma Unami Delaware speaker Nora Thompson Dean believed the word came from Achkinkas hacky, "sharp ground" (Whritenour 2007:pc). For Heckewelder's suggestion that Musconetcong comes from what he identified as the Monsey word *maskhannecunk*, see LLN:376.

6. For the suggestion that the place name Wallpack comes from *walpeek*, "a turn hole, a deep and still place in a stream," see LLN:375.

7. For Heckewelder's suggestions that Ramapo might come from either *walumopeck*, "round pond or lake," or *lomowopek*, "white on the inside," see LLN:375.

8. For Heckewelder's translation of Wyoming from *m'chueomi* or *m'chewami*, "extensive level flats," see LLN:361; for his translation of Passaic as "valley," from the Delaware words *pasiac* or *pasaiek*, see LLN:375.

9. Esopus country extends across fertile flats and lowlands of the Great Valley from Sussex County in northern New Jersey to Orange and Ulster counties in New York. The lower reaches of the Esopus and Rondout creeks and the Walkill River flow through the most intensively occupied parts of the Esopus heartland. Cornelis Hendrickszen's 1616 map (in IMI 2:c.pl. 24) preserves the earliest known European reference to Esopus. From the very beginning, Europeans regarded Esopus as the site of several Indian communities. Hendrickszen placed Esopus proper on the east bank of the Hudson River, above the Highlands next to the Waoranecks, and across the river from people he called Waranawanka. Both Jan van Wassenaer and Johannes de Laet evidently drew on Hendrickszen for their descriptions of the region. In his February 1624 edition, Van Wassenaer (in NNN:68) wrote "at the Fishers Hook are Pachany, Warenecker, Warrawanankonckx. Near one place, Esopes, are two or three tribes." Writing the first European account noting Esopus at its location on the west bank of the Hudson in 1625, De Laet (in NNN:46) identified the region as the place where "the Waoranecks have their abode." David Pietersz de Vries penned the only other known source mentioning Esopus by name before 1650. In an entry dated May 27, 1640, in NNN:206, he wrote that "we came to Esoopes, where a creek runs in; and there the Indians had much maize land, but all somewhat stony."

The nearly total lack of references to an Esopus region or people in records written by colonists during the following decade suggests that the place remained little more than a name on the map to Europeans during this time. Although their absence from documents chronicling Kieft's War indicates that Indians from the area managed to avoid open involvement in the conflict, later statements made by their sachems during meetings with Petrus Stuyvesant on May 30 and October 15, 1658 (in NYCD 13:84 and 94), noted that many of their people had been killed during the war "waged between them and our nation in Mr. Kieft's time." These statements affirm that at least some of their warriors may have been killed fighting against the colonists.

The people of Esopus finally emerged from documentary obscurity in a French account written in 1650 (in JR 36:101–103). The account listed a people named Notchiuict among five nations from New England and the upper Hudson River promising to support the French in their war against the Iroquois. The others were identified as Mahingan (Mahican), Pagamptagoe (Pocumtucks from the middle reaches of the Connecticut River around Springfield, Massachusetts), Socockoi (Sokokis or Squakheags from the upper Connecticut River in Vermont and New Hampshire), and Penagoc (Pennacooks from New Hampshire). The Notchiuict named in the account were said to live between the Mahingans and Manate (Manhattan) and were described as "very numerous and feared by the Iroquois." Large population and ferocious reputation may account for the absence of European records documenting colonial intrusion into their country before 1650.

The French also called these people Taractons. This name appears in an August 5, 1657, letter cowritten by domines Johannes Megapolensis and Samuel Drisius, in the form of Atharhacton (misspelled as Atkarkarton in NYCD 3:107 and properly transcribed in Corwin 1901–1916, 1:398), as the name Indian people used for Esopus.

Increasing tensions and the outbreak of open warfare at Esopus during the late 1650s soon produced an increased volume of information on the Esopus and their country. Records from the period repeatedly mentioned prominent Esopus sachems like Preuwackaman, Caelcop I, and Sewackenamo by name. Dutch chroniclers, moreover, recorded a succession of battles and skirmishes, describing the sacking of forts and the burning of towns and fields during what became known as the Esopus Wars. They also wrote of paths trod, rivers crossed, and mountains seen as they marched through Esopus country. Writings produced during the Esopus War created a body of documentary material unparalleled in size and detail in surviving Dutch records. Despite this fact, not one observer recorded a single Indian name of any place they saw or heard about before the colony fell to the English in 1664.

10. For Heckewelder's suggestion that Coshocton, Ohio (and, by extension, cognates like Cochecton, Pennsylvania) comes from the Munsee word *gichiechton*, "finished, completed," see LLN:362.

11. Studies in Hart (1998) summarize recent findings in northeastern North American paleobotany.

3. CONTACT, 1524–1640

1. See Wroth (1910:86) for Verrazano.

2. Ibid.

3. Frenchmen like Samuel de Champlain, who got as far as the lake that now bears his name while the *Halve Maen* was cruising up the Hudson River, generally called Indians "sauvage" (from the Latin *sylvan*, "forest"). Hudson and other Englishmen used their equivalent, "savage." Dutch navigators following Hudson often called the Indians *naturallen*, "aboriginals," or, more commonly, wilden. J. Jacobs (2005:22) suggests that this was more in reference to what the Dutch thought was the Indians' wild, that is heathen, religion than anything else. And all used their language's version of Indian, Columbus's case of mistaken identity. Some like Champlain penned the first recorded references to nations like the Iroquois and the Canadian Algonquins. What they did not do, at least initially, was record personal names of Indians or those of their families and kin groups.

4. For the Velasco map, see IMI 2:cpl. 22a. For Juet's journal, see NNN:16–28; for De Laet's extract from Hudson's journal, see NNN:48–49.

5. Workers unearthed the bow of a ship originally thought to be the *Tijger* during excavation of a subway station at Greenwich and Dey streets in 1916. The Museum of the City of New York currently conserves a piece of the vessel sawn off by the workmen. Recent research shows that the fragment actually dates to the 1700s. For Block's map, see IMI 2:c.pl. 23; for the 1612 Smith map, see Barbour (1986, 1:140–141).

6. Like Manhattan, Wiechquaesgeck is an example of a local place name that became a general term for a larger community. Initially thought to be a word signifying bark kettle or birch bark place, most linguists currently think it probably means "at the end of the swamp." The name survives as Wickers Creek, a small brook that

flows into the Hudson River at the village of Dobbs Ferry in Westchester County, New York.

Wiechquaesgeck appears in colonial records as the name of that creek, as the general name for the Dobbs Ferry locale, and most broadly, as a general ethnonym for all Indians living below the Highlands between the Hudson River and westernmost Connecticut. The word may have made its initial appearance as Wikagyl in the Hendrickszen 1616 map (in IMI 2:c.pl. 24). It more identifiably appears in the forms Wiekagjock and Wyeck in Van Wassenaer's 1634 account (in NNN:67). De Laet (in NNN:45) located the Manatthans "on the east side [of the Hudson River], upon the main land" in the same area subsequently identified as Wiechquaesgeck territory.

Three men identified as owners of the Keskeskick tract at the southwest end of the Bronx sold the place to the Dutch West India Company on August 3, 1639 (LP:10). Folk tradition asserts that Swedish ship captain Jonas Bronck, namesake of the borough, first purchased Keskeskick from the Indians. Like many good stories, this one is more fiction than fact. Although Bronck did purchase land in the Bronx, he bought the tract from the company, not the Indians, in 1641.

Wiechquaesgecks in the Bronx and elsewhere soon found themselves pressed in on two sides. Dutch colonists followed Bronck into their territory from the south. English settlers farther east, from New England, began buying lands along Long Island Sound in what they soon called Westchester. Exposed to attack on both flanks, the Wiechquaesgecks suffered devastatingly high losses by the end of Kieft's War in 1645. So heavy were these losses, and so unreconciled were the survivors, that most Wiechquaesgecks moved to the more remote valleys of Raritan country, rather than sign the 1645 treaty. There they joined similarly disaffected Raritan people in attacks on colonists bold enough to venture onto their territories or settle nearby during the years following the end of the war.

Wiechquaesgecks finally returned to their homeland after signing over the eastern half of present-day Westchester and agreeing to sell the remaining western half to Dutch authorities at a later date. This deed, signed on July 14, 1649 (in NYCD 13:24 and LP:62–63), and the treaty made with Stuyvesant five days later, allowed the Wiechquaesgecks to safely return to their homeland. At the treaty, Hackensack speaker Pennekeck gave both an example of the flexible nature of ethnonyms and an indication of the parlous political status of the Wiechquaesgecks when he informed the assembled diplomats that he represented "the tribe called Raritanoos, formerly living at Wiquaeskeck [who] had no chief."

Other sources show that the Wiechquaesgecks did, in fact, still have chiefs at this time. Most of these, however, turned out to be dispossessed Marechkawicks and other Long Islanders who had also moved to Raritan country after the war. One of these, the Nayack sachem Mattano, signed the July 14 deed as Megtegickhama and was noted as "Meijterma, the Chief of Neyick" at the July 19, 1649, treaty; former Marechkawick sachem Seyseychkimus witnessed the latter agreement as a chief sachem. Although neither man signed the July 19, 1649, treaty as a Wiechquaesgeck, Seyseychkimus in particular continued to represent their communities for many years thereafter; identification of "Raritanoos" as former residents of "Wiquaeskeck" can probably be laid at the feet of a scribe who evidently thought all Raritan people used to live at Wiechquaesgeck.

Seyseychkimus's northward-trending career may be traced by following the earliest references to him as a sachem of Keschaechquereren, Marechkawick, and Rockaway (in NYCD 14:5, 14, 62, GTR Book 1:15 and 43–47, and Book 6:9, and OBTR 1:347–349, 351–352), to those mentioning him as a Wiechquaesgeck, Tappan, or Rechgawawanck sachem (in NYCD 13:18–19, 24, 363, and 375–377 and 14:393–394 and EJD Liber 1:115–116 and 254 [85 on verso]). The last references mentioning Seyseychkimus (in NYCD 13:167 and 375–377) called him a Wappinger chief, indicating that he moved even farther north toward the end of his life.

Raritan was also frequently called Sanhican during the colonial era. Block (in IMI 2:c.pl. 23) first located Sangicans on the Bayonne Peninsula across the Hudson from Manhattan Island. The name is a Munsee word for "flint fire striker" (Brinton 1885:43). Heckewelder (1876:99) noted that Munsees and other Delawares also called the Mohawks Sanhicanni, "gunlock people," after the Mohawk name for themselves, Kaniengehaga, "people of the place of the flint." The name also probably served Delawares as a rueful barb recalling the actions of Dutch traders who "sold for furs . . . firearms to the Mohawks for full 400 men, with powder and lead" (in NYCD 1:150) used to dominate Munsees and other Indians denied similar weaponry by colonial authorities.

The two variants of Sanhican on Hendrickszen's 1616 map may be seen in IMI 2:c.pl. 24. Sources penned between 1625 and 1646 used Sanhican both as a name for Indians living at or near the falls and as a place name for the Falls of the Delaware themselves. De Laet (in NNN:57–60) published a brief description and vocabulary of the language of the Sankikans, "who dwell on the upper part of the South River," in the 1633 edition of his book. The vocabulary wholly consists of Northern Unami words.

Proximity probably played a role in the development of hostile relations between Northern Unami–speaking Sanhicans and Munsee-speaking Manhattans noted by early Dutch writers. De Laet (in NNN:45) wrote in the 1625 edition of his book that Sanhicans "are the deadly enemies of the Manathans, and a much better people; they dwell within the sandy hook, and along the bay, as well as in the interior of the country." In 1628 De Rasiere (in NNN:103–104) noted that Indians "in the neighborhood of the Sancicians . . . live in a constant state of enmity with those tribes [west of Newark Bay]."

In 1633 De Vries (in Murphy 1857:25, 29–30) reported that "90 men of the Sankiekans" were killed by a party of six hundred Susquehannock warriors traveling in fifty canoes. European colonists began building outposts of their own on Sanhican lands shortly thereafter. Swedish settlers establishing their New Sweden colony on the banks of the lower Delaware in 1638 regarded Sanhican as one of their most important fur-trade marketplaces. Rumors of precious metals "at the falls at Sanghikans" drew Dutch colonists to the locale. Indians living in the area evidently did not welcome miners. A sachem named Wirackehon, for example, turned away a party of Dutch prospectors from the place on July 12, 1646 (NYCD 12:32).

The location of the Tappans on the west bank of the lower Hudson River was first recognized by Hendrickszen in his 1616 map. Colonists soon used the name to identify Indians living in and around present-day Nyack on the west bank of the Tappan Zee. For other references to the location of the Tappans, see Van Wassenaer (in NNN:67) and De Laet (in NNN:46); orthographic variants include Tappaans in De Laet (in NNN:46), Tapaen in De Vries (in NNN:98), Tappant in Van Wassenaer (in NNN:67), and Top-paun in Wolley 1701 (in NAHC:54). The narrow range of orthographic renderings of the name in these records suggests that it closely matches the sounds heard by Dutch and English chroniclers. Tappan probably comes from the Delaware word *thupane,* "cold stream issuing from springs" (LLN:375); Whritenour (2007:pc) suggests that his translation, "rolling or churning stream," may refer to the flow characteristics of the Sparkill that flows through a gap in the Palisades from its source around present-day Old Tappan, New Jersey.

Like many Indian nations mentioned in the first Dutch records, Tappan remained little more than a name on a map for more than two decades. De Vries (in NNN:205–206) penned the earliest known document recording more than the name. In 1639, he purchased a tract of land, just beyond the northern limits of Dutch settlement on the west bank of the Hudson River, from a group of otherwise unidentified local sachems at Tappan. No copy of a deed, if one was signed, has yet been found. He promptly set up a small patroonship, christened Vriesendael, at the locale. Further efforts to colonize land at Tappan ended abruptly after River Indian warriors burned Vriesendael in 1643 during Kieft's War.

Only a few bold colonists ventured back to the borders of Tappan territory after the Treaty of 1645 returned a measure of uneasy peace to the area. Tappan itself, however, continued to lie on the edge of an exposed and insecure stretch of frontier separating the narrow strip of colonized tidewater riverbank from the vast inland expanses of Indian country beyond. Settlers living on that tideland strip would repeatedly flee their homes as rumors of attack and hostile war parties swept across the lower river during the many times of crisis that disrupted life in New Netherland throughout the final decades of Dutch control. Recurring alarms discouraged further colonization and ensured that the heart of Tappan country remained in Indian hands during these years.

The name of a nearby nation identified as Mechkentiwoom first appears on the west side of the Hudson River a bit above Manhattan on Hendrickszen's 1616 map (IMI 2:24); evidently drawing on this source, Van Wassenaer (in NNN:67) wrote in 1624, "below the Maikans are situated these tribes: Mechkentowoon, Tapants, on the west side." De Laet (in NNN:45nn) also used Hendrickszen as his source in the 1625 and 1633 editions of his book to identify the "Machkentiwomi" as a people living "over against" Manhattan in their final appearance by that name in colonial records.

7. See J. Jacobs (2005:35–38) for the founding of the Dutch West India Company. Also see Rink (1986:51–68) for a survey of the company's history.

8. For the kinds of choices facing the Dutch West India Company during its first decades of existence, see Bachman (1970).

9. For De Laet on Manhattan, see NNN:45.

10. For De Laet, see NNN:45nn.; for the November 5, 1626, report, see NYCD 1:37–38; for Van Wassenaer, see NNN:88.

11. De Rasiere (in NNN:105) is unclear about what he meant by "up the river." It is hard to square his observation of "a high east side" with the physical appearance of the shoreline of the Hudson River, where the Palisades rise far more steeply on its west banks. He may have been simply extending his discussion of Manhattan, whose northern heights still command the east bank.

12. For De Rasiere's statement, see NNN:103; for Van der Donck's observation, see DONCK:92; for corroboration of Van der Donck's view, see the interrogatory of Johannes de la Montaigne (in NYCD 1:198), asking if he fluently spoke "the Manhatans language, which was used by the Indians hereabouts."

The Neversink mentioned by Van der Donck was the Navesink country first described in 1650 by Cornelis van Tienhoven, who wrote that, like the nearby Raritan Valley, what he called Neyswesinck was another abandoned land possessing "right good maize lands which have not been cultivated by the natives for a long time." The word has been subjected to different translations. Some think it is derived from the Unami word *newas*, "point or promontory," in reference to Sandy Hook, the South Bay area's most prominent feature (RIN:102). Tooker (in TIN:115) thought it meant place of observation. It may mean both: places like Nayack in Brooklyn are associated with points; both it and others like Nyack on the banks of the Tappan Zee might be good observation points. Some believe the early spellings of Navesink as Neversink provide evidence that colonial chroniclers using such references thought Navesink was actually the same place as Neversink, the name of the Catskill Mountain stream that flows into the Delaware River at Port Jervis. This belief has fed folklore celebrating the Old Mine Road as America's oldest highway. Its proponents regard early seventeenth-century reports of prospectors searching for minerals in Neversink as evidence that Dutch copper miners at Pahaquarry built the road to transport their ore from the Delaware Water Gap to Kingston, New York. See Kraft (1996) for a critical look at the Old Mine Road and Pahaquarry copper mine traditions.

The location of the Navesink country on the South Bay was first plotted on Visscher's 1651 revision of the Jan Jansson map. The map placed Neve Sincks next to two rectangles symbolizing longhouses on the east bank of what appears to be the South River. Some Old Mine Road enthusiasts believe this South River was the Delaware River, often referred to by that name during the Dutch era. The unnamed tributary of the Raritan on the Jansson-Visscher map is more probably the Middlesex County stream of the same name whose water still flows into the Raritan near the village of South River.

Indian people from Navesink country were frequently linked with others living along the Raritan in accounts written during the last decade of Dutch rule. A source from 1662 singled out Neversinke as "a place where no Christians are residing, but only wild barbarians" (in CHM 1:237). One year later, Marten Kregier noted in his journal that Jacques Corteljou, who had seen the land beyond the Atlantic Highlands firsthand, reportedly claimed that it "was level and good and much of it; there was much old corn land and some Indian corn plantations." Kregier's journal also contained the first reference to a named locality in Navesink country, the "land called Romsingh," later known as Ramenesing at the Forks of the Navesink River near present-day Tinton Falls, New Jersey (NYCD 13:216); for the May 31, 1658, identification of a "Newesink" man living near "Haverstroo" as the killer of a Dutch settler, see NYCD 13:84 and CHM 1:193; for the December 8, 1663, identification of "Sukkurus living at Romsingh by Newsingh Kil" as the man who killed the Dutch settler at Maspeth, see NYCD 13:314–316.

Some of the earliest known sources in the region noted a nation identified as Aquamachukes approximately where Navesink was later located. Aquamachuke is one of the first and most ephemeral names of Indian communities mentioned in early sources. The name may be a Powhatan equivalent of *achquoanatschik,* a Northern Unami word meaning "they who catch things with a net." Block located the Aquamachukes in central New Jersey, in the same general area noted as the Atquanachuks locale on Smith's 1612 map. De Laet identified these people as Indians living "close to the western shore" of New York Harbor in the 1630 edition of his book. Smith later wrote in his 1624 *General History* that Susquehannocks identified them as living north of the Powhatans "on the ocean sea" (Barbour 1986, 2:172). Hendrickszen more specifically situated them in villages just south of Raritan Bay. Details from two globes produced in the Netherlands in the 1620s show them in the same general location (IMI 2:c.pls. 24 and 30). Like many other names chronicled in early sources, Aquamachukes subsequently enjoyed a second life as a cartographic fossil preserved on successive states of the Jansson-Visscher projection and other later maps.

13. For the February 14, 1652, affidavit of the Rev. Wilhelmus Grasmeer, see NYCD 14:160–161.

14. Nayack was in the present-day Fort Hamilton section in Brooklyn. Several documents, including the proceedings of the July 19, 1649, meeting at Fort Amsterdam in NYCD 13:25 and RPS-CM 4:607, the November 11, 1652, deed to land at Nayack in NYCD 14:190, another deed dated May 7, 1654, conveying Gravesend and Coney Island in GTR Book 6:7 and Misc. Records:56–58, and the July 10, 1657, deed to Staten Island in NYCD 14:393–394, identify Mattano as the sachem of Nayack.

Mattano's brothers included a Navesink sachem originally from Long Island named Peropay, a Hackensack sachem who later moved to Raritan country named Neckaock, and Raritan-Navesink sachem Irooseeke, also noted as a father of Weequehela. Andrew Wooley, a Cranbury and Crosswicks sachem who would lead his people to the Brotherton reservation at Edgepillock (now Indian Mills, New Jersey) in 1759, was son of Weequehela's widow, Sarah Store. or a female relative. Many people living on the Stockbridge-Munsee reservation in Wisconsin today directly trace descent to Weequehela Sarah Store, and Andrew Wooley among other ancestors from the Brotherton reservation. For a genealogy, see "The Descendants of

Weequehela," compiled by Caroline Adler in 2003 and online on the Algonkian Church History Blog as of Monday, April 13, 2009.

Mattano and his brothers were sons of Navesink sachem Emerus. At least one of Emerus's possible wives was evidently a sister of a distinguished group of brothers that included Crosswicks sachem Ockanickon (whose deathbed speech was made famous by Quaker chronicler Thomas Budd), Millstone and Minisink sachem Mamarikickon, and Raritan-Navesink sachem Metapis. Married to a sister of the Delaware king Taminy (namesake of New York City's Tammany Hall political club), who sold several tracts of land to William Penn, Metapis was also noted as a father of Weequehela.

One of Ockanickon's brothers, who straddled the boundaries of Munsee and Unami societies, was Sehoppy. Thomas Budd made him famous in colonial Pennsylvania as the feckless successor-designate who preferred to drink rather than comfort Ockanickon on his deathbed. Although Budd stated that he was disowned by the dying sachem, Sehoppy nevertheless continued to pursue a diplomatic career that lasted another twenty-five years. The sachem went by many names during this long career. A deed to land along New Jersey's Millstone River signed on November 28, 1701, identified him as "Comshopey alias Lucke [referenced as Lucky and Luke elsewhere in the deed], known by the English name Captain Charles." A few years earlier, in a deed to land in Pennsylvania at Neshaminy, signed on July 5, 1697, a son of Taminy named Quenameckquid was also identified as Charles. He was frequently identified, often in the same document, as King Charles (a pun on the overbearing late and locally loathed English monarch Charles II) and by variants of Quenameckquid more often spelled like Mechmiquon ("great feather," a pun on a pun on their ceremonial name for William Penn, Miquon, meaning both feather and pen quill). Whoever gave the names to Sehoppy clearly possessed a sense of absurdist humor that may reflect quirks in the sachem's personality. Sehoppy seems to have most frequently gone by the names Mechmiquon and King Charles when dealing with colonists in West Jersey and Pennsylvania. He almost exclusively used the name Sehoppy when conducting affairs farther north and east.

For Ockanickon's choice of a brother's son named Jahkurosoe (probably Irooseeke) as his successor, see Budd (1685:31); for the November 28, 1701, reference linking the names Comshopey, Lucke, and Captain Charles, to the same individual, see EJD Liber H:170; for the July 5, 1697, document linking Quenameckquid with Charles, see PA 1:124–125; for references noting King Charles as Mahomecun on April 11, 1697, Mehemickon on June 18, 1702, and Hymickhond on April 7, 1710, see WJD Liber B:644 and Liber BBB:199 and the June 18, 1702, deed on file under that date in the New Jersey State Library (hereinafter NJSL); for Heckewelder's suggestion that this name comes from *mattemikgun,* "he that has entered a house," see LLN:383.

15. See NAPN:55 for translations of Suanhacky and Metoac as Munsee and Montauk words meaning "place of shells." Whritenour (2007:pc) suggests "scattered wampum shells land" as a more exact translation for Suanhacky; Tooker (in TIN:181) translated Pamanack as "land of tribute" in the belief that the name referred to wampum shell beads used to pay Mohawk, Pequot, and Dutch tribute takers.

Writers in search of a common name for the Indians of western Long Island have referred to them as Canarsees since Silas Wood (1826:50–51) first listed them as the easternmost of his thirteen tribes of Long Island in 1824. The well-known Brooklyn neighborhood name of Canarsie in present-day Flatlands (the Dutch name for the town was Amersfoort) was mentioned as the location of an Indian community in the area only in records written between 1647 and 1667 in NYCD 1:449 and 13:184, RNSH 1:43, FTR Folder 1:71 and 235 and Folder 2:53, FTR Patent Folder 2:45, and FTR Misc. Records:4453; the word Canarsee probably means "long, small, or narrow grasses," perhaps in reference to the broad meadows of salt grass lining Jamaica Bay (RIN:89); on the 1666 Hubbard map, the name of the bay is playfully jumbled into the hybrid Conarie See in the same manner as Tappan Zee and Hobocan Hackingh (NAPN:8).

Waumetompack, one of Tackapousha's sons, was the first man recorded as a sachem of Canarsee. Waumetompack moved to his father's brother's wife's land at Matinecock after signing the last deed to Canarsee land on April 23, 1665. Documents chronicling Waumetompack may be seen in RNSH 1:681–682 and OBTR 1:80–81, 89–90, and 682–687. Other records indicate that small groups of Indians continued to camp in unwanted out-of-the-way, otherwise vacant clearings in the dense hummocky marshlands of Jamaica Bay for a long time afterwards. Taken together, extant evidence indicates that rather than being a general name for all Brooklyn Indians, Canarsee instead was a single locale, one of the last places occupied by the borough's first people. For more information on the Canarsee nation and locality, see NAPN:5–7.

The nearby Rockaway heartland extended from today's Far Rockaway east to present-day Hewlett and East Rockaway. The area includes one of the widest expanses of well-drained land at the western end of Long Island's south shore. The earliest documented forms of the name, Rechouw Hacky in 1639, and Rechqua Akie four years later, almost exactly match the Munsee cognates *leekuwii*, "sand" and *ahkiing*, "land" (TIN:214). *R* words like Rockaway and Merrick may either reflect the presence of Unami *R* dialect speakers in Munsee country or record how Dutch listeners heard the liquid *L* used by Munsee *L* dialect speakers. For an approximation of how the *L* in Munsee may have sounded, see their pronunciation of their word for Pennsylvania, Quaekelilink, "Quaker country," in LLN:374.

Two of Tackapousha's sons, the already mentioned Waumetompack and his successor Monguamy, appear in colonial records as Rockaway sachems. Documents also show that people from Canarsee, Matinecock, and Massapequa lived in and around Rockaway throughout the Dutch regime.

16. De Vries' report of settlers killed by Indians near his farm in 1641 contains the first mention of Hackensacks in Dutch records. Later documents mentioning Oratam and other Hackensack chiefs show that the heartland of their territories stretched across the lower reaches of the Hackensack and Passaic rivers in present-day northeastern New Jersey.

The Hackensack nation, Hackensack country, and the Hackensack sachem Oratam became well known among colonists during the last two decades of Dutch rule. He and they were repeatedly mentioned in land sales, war reports, and treaty proceedings. Places named Ahasimus, Apopcalyck, Aquackenonck Aressick, Communipaw, Hespatingh, Hobokan Hackingh, and Weehawken in and around present-day Jersey City became familiar to settlers moving to the southeastern borders of Hackensack territory at this time. Several sources indicate that Hackensacks also had a fort farther inland. On February 23, 1664, for example, Oratam asked the Dutch to give them a cannon for their castle (in NYCD 13:361). A deposition made on March 5, 1687, recalled the existence of a Hackensack fort in 1666 (Work Projects Administration 1940. 1:10); mention of a since-vanished fortification made in a deed dated April 1, 1694 (WJD Liber B:651) indicates that this or a later fort may have been located somewhere between the Pequannock and Ramapo rivers northwest of Paterson, New Jersey.

A key intermediary between Indians and colonists, Oratam made his first appearance in Dutch records in this capacity as the sachem of "Achkinkes hacky . . . and commissioned by the Indians of Tappaen, Rechgawawanc, Kichtawanc, and Sintsinck," at a meeting at New Amsterdam on April 23, 1643 (NYCD 13:14 and RPS-CM 4:192. For the next twenty years, Oratam and other Hackensack sachems and speakers came to represent nations as far north as Catskill and Esopus and as far west as Minisink.

Europeans interested in Hackensack lands chronicled all-but-forgotten Indian place names like Ahasimus and Aressick long before now-familiar places like Paramus, Passaic, and Totowa were entered onto regional maps. One of the first of these was Hobokan Hackingh. Many writers (including Heckewelder and Du Ponceau, LLN:375) think Hobokan Hackingh is a Delaware pidgin word combining the Unami word for pipe, *hopocan,* with their locative ahkiing, "land." The translation comes from the belief that the place was a riverside council site, where tobacco pipes were ceremoniously smoked. The name is more probably a linguistic hybrid joining the Munsee locative with Hoboken, the name of a formerly important trading port near Antwerp in present-day Belgium.

For the earliest reference identifying Hobokan Hackingh as a linguistic hybrid, see Gatschet (in RIN:108); for Ahasimus, see LP:1 and 3–4; for Heckewelder's suggestion that Aquackenonck comes from *tachquahacanena,* "the place from which we get the wood (gum tree is *tachquacaniminschi* in Delaware), we make our pounding blocks of" see LLN:376; the latter source also notes that the name has also been thought to be a Unami expression meaning "at the stream of lampreys"; for Aressick, see LP:304; for Gweghkongh and Hespatingh, from the Unami, "where we go uphill," see NYCD 14:393–394.

The precise locations and meanings of places named Ahasimus, Aressick, Apopcalyck, and Hespatingh are not presently known. Weehawken was in its present location, and the place repeatedly referred to as Gweghkongh (which might be a garbled form of "Aquackenonck") was probably on a stretch of the Passaic River between Passaic and Paterson. The origin of Communipaw on the Bayonne Peninsula is more problematic. Often considered an Indian name, it does not appear in this form in the earliest Dutch records. The July 11, 1667, document mentioning a sachem of Pau (EJD Liber 1:270 [69 on verso]), the earliest and only appearance of the word, suggests that Pau, like Pavonia, may refer to Pauw's community. Some writers think that the word may come from the Dutch *gemeente paen*, "tillable marshy commons" (Dunlap in RIN:105–106). Most think Pauw's family name derives from *pavo*, the Latin word for peacock and modern Spanish for turkey (in RIN:106).

17. For Dutch involvement in the First Mohawk-Mahican War that led to the killing of the commander at Fort Orange, see Trigger (1971).

18. For the company rule authorizing patroonships, see NYCD 1:96–100.

19. For the July 12, 1630, deed to Hobocan Hackingh, the August 10, 1630, deed to Staten Island, and the November 22, 1630, deed to Ahasimus, see LP:1–4; for Pauw's surrender of patroonship lands to the company in 1635, see J. Jacobs (2005:116).

20. For translated abstracts of the 1636–1637 private party deeds, see LP:5–7; for the August 1, 1638, deed to Bushwick, the January 15, 1639, deed to western Long Island, and the August 3, 1639, deed to Keskeskick in the south Bronx made by Kieft for the company, see LP:8–10.

4. CONFLICT, 1640–1645

1. "Quilipioke" is Quinnipiac, today's New Haven area; see Wojciechowski (1985:89–92) for transcripts of testimonial letters written nearly twenty years after the March 1638 meeting by Englishmen who attended the gathering; the March 20, 1656, reference identifies Sasqua as a locality in Fairfield, Connecticut, sold by "Indians of Poquanuck" (in FCH:279).

2. For Van Tienhoven's instructions, see NYCD 14:28. Ponus and several other sachems from Norwalke and Makentouh just to the west of Norwalk River put their marks on deeds selling lands and islands there on February 26 and April 20, 1640. Sachems of Toquams (later called Rippowams; present-day Stamford), nearby Shippan Point, and the lands between the Asamuck and Patomuck rivers sold land farther west at Stamford and Greenwich on July 1 and July 18, 1640. Ponus signed the April 20, 1640, device as "Pomenate," as Ponus on the July 1, 1640, deed, and as the witness "Pauonohas" on the July 18, 1640, document; Owenoke is identified as Ponus's eldest son in the August 15, 1655, confirmation of the July 1, 1640, deed; see FCH:487 and WCH 1:389–390 for the February 26, 1640, deed; see FCH:482–483 and WCH 1:390 for the April 20, 1640, deed; see FCH:699 and WCH 1:104 for the February 26, 1640, deed; and FCH:366–367 and Mead (1911:5–6) for the July 18, 1640, deed.

3. Trelease (in IACNY:63) followed R. P. Bolton's (1920:232) still undocumented assumption that Van Tienhoven fulfilled his mission to purchase the lands at the Archipelago. See RPS-CM 4:75–77 for the full text of the May 13, 1640, document containing Penhawitz's conversation with Van Tienhoven and the fool's head report.

4. For the September 15, 1639, council resolution, see NYCD 13:6.

5. For Tappan reluctance to pay the levy, see De Vries in NNN:209.

6. A declaration made sometime in the late 1650s by Brant Van Slichtenhorst in an undated court case deposition contains one of the very few explicit statements unequivocally describing the Mohawk custom of taking tribute from other Indians.

In it, Van Slichtenhorst observed that "the cruel, barbaric Indians called the Maquaes . . . receive tribute annually from other nations situated 70 miles [200 English miles] around them and the [Rennselaerswijck] colony" (Gehring 1990:2–3). The original of this document is in Arnhem, the Netherlands. Thanks to Gehring (2007:pc) for providing the quote and citation.

7. Translated transcriptions of this account, written by Harmen Meyndertszen van den Bogaert years later on July 17, 1647, appear in NYCD 13:22–23 and in RPS-CM 2:409; for Van den Bogaert's journal of his journey to the eastern Iroquois towns in 1634, see Gehring and Starna (1988).

The 1640 report was the first mentioning Raritans by name. Linguists currently reject Ruttenber's suggestion (in RIN:103) that Raritan comes from the Narragansett word *nayantukq-ut,* "point on a tidal river." Whritenour (2007:pc) suggests the word most closely resembles *leelachtin,* "mountain in the middle," from the Munsee *leelaa,* "in the middle" and *-ahtun,* "mountain." This translation may be supported by Dutch provincial secretary and Kieft's crony. Van Tienhoven's March 4, 1650, observation that the Raritangs "territory lies between two high mountains, far distant one from the other" (NYCD 1:366). These hills almost certainly belong to the broken range of hills midway between Raritan Bay and the Delaware River that runs from the Sourland Hills on the south above Princeton to Cushetunk Mountain near Clinton to the long ridge of the Musconetcong Mountain, which that runs from the Delaware River north to Lake Hopatcong.

Raritan people figured prominently in Dutch records chronicling warfare in the region. They were repeatedly noted as enemies of the Manhattans. Ten years later, Van Tienhoven wrote that attacks from Southern Indians and floods ruining their stores of corn, beans, and squash forced Raritan people to abandon their country and move farther inland. Interestingly, the people moving inland were probably mostly Wiechquaesgecks, who returned to their inland homes north along the Hudson after making their peace with the Dutch in 1649.

Van Tienhoven's 1650 promotional pamphlet provides the most complete description of Raritan country extant in the Dutch records. The Southern Indians he mentions are almost certainly Susquehannocks. In an effort to draw colonists to the region, he also repeatedly directs readers' attention to Indian cultivation of the land's rich soils and points out that "through this valley pass large numbers of all sorts of tribes, on their way north or east [making the place] very convenient for trade with the Indians" in NYCD 1:366–367.

Although sachems signed deeds to much of the land along the shore of the South Bay between 1650 and 1652, Raritan people did not leave their country at this time. Continued reports of Raritan depredations and hostility discouraged colonists interested in settling on Raritan lands. Other Indians, however, clearly felt comfortable enough to build homes in the area. On December 7, 1663, for example, Marten Kregier, the Dutch military journal keeper who stayed on to become a respected member in the colonial community, saw two houses of Southern Indians at the mouth of the Raritan River. One of Kregier's southern Indian houses may have housed the family of Minqua Sakima, noted in local records as a Hackensack sachem with strong interests in Staten Island. The other may have been the house of a Lower River Indian war captain named Agapou. Identified in the March 4, 1669, deed to land in the Bronx as Achipor Miniquaes, Agapou was reportedly killed a year later by unknown Indians near Albany. Both Agapou and Minqua Sakima either were Susquehannocks or had some sort of close association with them. References to Minqua Sakima may be found in EJD Liber 1:116, NYCD 13:455 and 14:393, WCH 2:504, and ECM 1:43 and 212. References to Agapou appear in NYCD 3:190, 13:455, 14:15, and 393, WCH 2:130 and 504, and ECM 1:43, 81, 212, and 2:478.

Much of the region between Raritan Bay and the Falls of the Delaware was un-known territory to settlers during the Dutch era. Colonists regarded the region's in-habitants as a violent people hostile to intrusion. The place earned its dangerous reputation. Reports reaching New Amsterdam repeatedly carried news of trouble in the area. Susquehannocks and Manhattan Indians warred on its inhabitants at vari-ous times. Settlers moving nearby risked attack when fighting broke out. Although the lowlands running across the center of the region provided the most direct over-land route between the Delaware River and New York Harbor, messengers using it in the greatest numbers during times of direst need were often ambushed along the way.

8. The July 16, 1640, council resolution authorizing force to get satisfaction for Raritan insults that referred to a since-lost treaty made with them in 1634 may be seen in NYCD 13:7. The attack made by men under Van Tienhoven's command on the Raritan town on Staten Island in 1640 started Kieft's War. For accounts of the attack, see De Vries (in NNN:211) and NYCD 1:150. Kieft's War has been the sub-ject of considerable attention. The detailed account in IACNY:60–84 continues to provide the most thorough and succinct overview. More recent studies blaming cul-tural misunderstandings and internal cultural contradictions for both causing the war and making it more ferocious than intended include Otto (2006), Merwick (2006), and Haefeli (1999), who suggests that Kieft mistook what he says was sachem's good-natured corrective joshing as mocking insult. This latter suggestion seems improbable; just as a cigar is sometimes no more than a good smoke, the de-risive intent of sarcastic laughter may also be unmistakable even when crossing cul-tural divides.

9. See De Vries (in NNN:211) for the destruction of his farms on Staten Island on September 1, 1641; see NYCD 13:7 for the head bounty ordinance; see Anony-mous 1647 (in NNN:277) for the reference to Long Island Indian assistance against the Raritan nation.

De Vries' November 2, 1641, document (in NNN:211) reporting that a Tankiteke sachem named Pacham showed up at Fort Amsterdam carrying the hand of a dead Raritan chief on a stick is the first record of a nation called Tankitekes. Their sachem's name almost exactly matches that used to identify "a nation of Indians called Pachami" first recorded on Hendrickszen's 1616 map (in IMI 2:c.p1.24). Hen-drickszen's placement of the Pachamis above the Highlands on the east bank of the Hudson suggests a similar location for the Tankitekes. This location is corroborated by De Vries' 1642 observation (in NNN:216) that the Tankitekes lived two days' journey from his farm at Vriesendael. De Vries' observation represents the last record mentioning Tankitekes. Other early sources mentioning Pachami, including Van Wassenaer (in NNN:68) and De Laet (in NNN:46), evidently draw on the Hendrickszen map.

10. For sources intimating that such a treaty was concluded with the Raritans, see interrogatories addressed to Van Tienhoven, in NYCD 1:199 and 410; see De Vries (in NNN:213–214) and NYCD 1:150 for the Wiechquaesgeck killer; see De Vries (in NNN:215–216) for the involvement of the Hackensacks and Rechgawawancks in the killings at Pavonia; see Anonymous 1647 (in NNN:273–276) for a general account of the troubles.

11. For the conversation with the Hackensack sachem, see De Vries (in NNN:215–216).

12. For the "Witqueschreek" sachem's regret that "20 Christians had not been murdered," see Anonymous 1647 (in NNN:275).

13. For the miscarried missions, see De Vries (in NNN:213–214) and reports in NYCD 1:415 and 13:11–12; for "bit into the mouth of the heathen," see NYCD 13:11–12.

14. The identity of the upriver Indians who attacked the Tappans and Wiechquaesgecks during the winter of 1642–1643 has never been clearly established. The unknown author of the 1647 *Journal of New Netherland* (in NNN:277) wrote that they were "Mahicanders dwelling below Fort Orange." An interrogatory prepared for Johannes de la Montaigne, a leader in the subsequent war against the Indians (in NYCD 1:198), also identified them as Mahicanders. Although De Vries (in NNN:225) identified them as "Mayekander Indians . . . from Fort Orange," he also noted that stunned Indians reeling from the subsequent Dutch attack said that the violence of the assault made them think their attackers were Maquas (Mohawks; in NNN:228). Most other sources, including the formal report made to the Dutch West India Company in 1644 (NYCD 1:151), identify the upriver attackers as Mohawks.

15. For seventeen dead, see Anonymous 1647 (in NNN:277); for the figure of seventy killed, see NYCD 1:151.

16. The community identified as Mareckewich on the 1639 Manatus map was a major Indian town in present-day Brooklyn. The name has variously been translated as "sandy place" (Beauchamp 1907:99) and, more tortuously, as "fortified house" (TIN:102–103). The latter comes from the Unami words *menachka*, "fortified," and *wikink*, "house," and their Massachusett cognates *menehket* and *weekit*. The former translation seems more likely; several Dutch sources (including LP:49 and 57 and De Vries in NNN:255) use Rechkeweck to identify Marechkawick.

Marechkawick encompassed an area of sandy uplands bounded by Williamsburgh on the north and downtown Brooklyn to the south. Colonists used the word as a local place name, calling Wallabout Bay (today's Brooklyn Navy Yard basin) the "bight or bend of Marechkawieck" and referring to the point of land at the bay's mouth as the "cape of Marechkawieck" (Stiles 1867, 2:307). Two sachems from the place,

Seyseychkimus and Numerus, put their marks on a deed selling islands in the East River near the Hellgate on July 16, 1637 (in LP:7) as "Seyseys and Neumers, both chiefs of Mareychkenwikingh"; De Vries (in NNN:255) later identified Numerus as the proprietor of a hostelry across the river at Corlaers Hook, catering to Indians visiting New Amsterdam. After parting with the last of his lands on Long Island, Seyseychkimus would go on to become an influential sachem at Wiechquaesgeck, Tappan, and Rechgawawancks. Unlike Seyseychkimus, the Marechkawick community was last mentioned by name in Dutch records in 1645. For more information on Marechkawick, see NAPN:26–28.

17. The account of the February 25, 1643, massacre published by De Vries, which describes the slaughter of infants, children, and the elderly in heart-rending detail, appears in NNN:226–229. In a footnote, the volume editor points out that the passage was lifted from the *Breeden Raedt* (1649). A translation of an abridged pamphlet version of this anti-Kieft tract appears in DHSNY 4:99–112. Efforts to identify the writer of the *Breeden Raedt* exemplify the kinds of problems encountered when trying to determine authorship of anonymously published work from this period. Earlier writers tended to attribute the account to the pen of Cornelis Melijn. Frijhoff (1998:34) believes that the tract was written by another of Kieft's enemies, Jochem Pietersz Kuijter. Banished from the colony, both men survived the wreck of the ship that claimed the life of Kieft and many of their fellow passengers in 1647. Two years later, Melijn and Kuijter returned to the colony, where Kuijter was killed by Indians in 1654 (J. Jacobs 2005:291). Schmidt (2001:395) thinks that the author of the *Breeden Raedt* might be either Melijn or Kuijter. Whoever its writer, the account's lurid tone and horrific depiction of bestial violence brings to mind similarly graphic descriptions of atrocities committed by rampaging armed bands during the Thirty Years' War that had ended just one year before its publication.

18. For De Vries at Rockaway, see NNN:229–232; for the March 25, 1643, treaty with the Long Island Indians, see NYCD 14:44–45; for the April 22, 1643, treaty signed by Oratam, representing his community of "Achkinckes hacky . . . and commissioned by the Indians of Tappaen, Rechgawawanc, Kichtawanc, and Sintsinck," see NYCD 13:14 and RPS-CM 4:192.

Scholars have argued over the identity of the Rechgawawancks mentioned in the 1643 document since Ruttenber (1872:77–78) first connected them with the Manhattans. I stand with those who think they were Haverstraws, first mentioned in the earliest 1636 state of the Jansson-Visscher map (Grumet 1982). In this map, Haverstroo was located in error at the approximate location of present-day Newark. All other sources place Haverstraw at the northernmost end of the Palisades, which tower above the small valley today that is occupied by the city of the same name. The word is Dutch for "oat straw." Other sources (in De Vries, in NNN:215; RPS-CM 4:192, 279–280, and 608, and NYCD 13:25, 148, 303, and 375–377) specifically identify Remahenonck, Rumachenanck, and Reweghnonck as Indian names for the Haverstraw locale.

De Vries first referred to a group he called "Reckawancks . . . close by me" when he included them among Indians who killed Dutch settlers at Pavonia in 1642. Ruttenber (1872) and a number of other writers prefer to believe that De Vries was talking about people living close by him on the other side of the Hudson. The name Rechgawawanck has been used since 1872 to fill empty spaces on maps of Manhattan and the Bronx. Etymologically related to Marechkawick and Rockaway (see Goddard 1971:18), Rechgawawanck combines the Munsee words *leekuwii* (sand) and *awanck*, "hillside or riverbank." Ruttenber linked the name with Rechgawac, one of the sachems who sold the Keskeskick tract in the Bronx in 1639. Aware of documents showing connections linking Bronx Indians with others nearby, Ruttenber also regarded the Reckeweck and Rechkawyck communities on Long Island as Rechgawawancks. Extension of the name across land identified in early sources as Manhattan territory allowed Ruttenber to suggest that Rechgawawanck was another name for Manhattan Indians. Reginald Bolton (1920:366) used Ruttenber's linkage of the sachem Rechgawac, a signatory to the Keskeskick deed, with Rechgawawanck to situate the Manhattan heartland at the northern end of the island and adjacent sections of the west Bronx.

A closer look at the evidence suggests a different conclusion. Dutch sources clearly linked Reckeweck with Marechkawick, and Rechkawyck with Rockaway. Although both shared similar etymological origins, each place was a distinct community. Neither was ever identified as Rechgawawanck. Variants of the name appear in only four references written between 1642 and 1664. All closely link them with the Hackensack and Tappan communities. The only reference mentioning a Rechgawawanck sachem identifies the man as Sesekemu. The sachem identified as Ses-Segh-Hout, "chief of Rewechnongh or Haverstraw," is mentioned in the May 16, 1664, treaty ending the Esopus Wars. Both Sesekemu and Ses-Segh-Hout were probable spellings of Seyseychkimus, the sachem from Brooklyn who moved upriver to Tappan Zee and Haverstraw Bay after Kieft's War. This evidence links people variously identified as Rechgawawancks, Reckawancks, Remahenoncks, Rumachenancks, and Reweghnoncks with the Haverstraw community. Unlike closer-in locales like Tappan and Hackensack, no parts of Haverstraw territory were sold to settlers during the years of Dutch control. The absence of references to colonists living in Haverstraw at this time indicates that any settlers moving there did so in ways that have since evaded documentation.

All known references to the little known Sintsincks number them among the Lower River estuary nations. The last of these, dated November 15, 1663, notes that they had no chief. Little else is known about this community. References to Sintsinck may be found in NYCD 13:14, 18, and 302; for the terminal reference to "Sinsincqs," see NYCD 13:363.

Although the location of Sintsinck (from *ashunusung*, "place of little stones") was not specified in the record of the 1643 meeting, it was almost certainly present-day Ossining, New York. The name was imprinted into the colonial record after appearing in the form Singsing at the approximate location of Ossining on all versions of the Jansson-Visscher map. The word appears in the January 15, 1639, Massapequa deed as the name of Schouts Bay (today's Hempstead Harbor) and was later applied to a succession of Munsee towns in Pennsylvania, western New York, and Ohio.

19. For the earlier-mentioned August 7, 1643, killing, see RPS-CM 2:153. For Indian dissatisfaction, see De Vries (in NNN:232–233); also see De Vries (in NNN:211) for "best friends." For "Pachem" becoming a determined enemy by May 1643, see *Journal of New Netherland* (in NNN:279).

The August 7, 1643, report describing the settler's killers as "Wappings, who dwell on the North River about half way to Fort Orange" represents the first known identification of Wappingers in their historically chronicled mid-Hudson Valley homeland (in RPS-CM 2:153). Unlike earlier chroniclers using Wappenos as a general term for Eastern Indians, the writer of this report placed the Wappingers in the approximate location of their homeland in and around Dutchess County, New York. Like Oping, Opingona, and Pompton in the Great Valley, linguists trace the etymological origin of Wappinger to the Delaware word for opossum (Goddard 1971:19).

The few colonists bold enough to settle along the Hudson in Wappinger territory left no descriptions of their Indian neighbors. Like the Minisinks, nearly all references to Wappingers during the Dutch period occurred in relation to the wars that ravaged the Hudson Valley between 1655 and 1664. Although later documents show close relations with Esopus people living just across the Hudson, most Wappingers tried to remain neutral during the Esopus War. Their efforts are reflected in the many references to Wappinger messengers and negotiators traveling back and forth from Esopus to the Dutch settlements. Not all Wappingers were fully committed to neutrality, however. Several sources note that Wappingers held prisoners taken by Esopus warriors. Others affirmed that Wappingers were among the Esopus. Despite these evidences of belligerence, the Dutch had their hands full at Esopus. Unable to send forces into Wappinger country, they had to limit themselves to reports of Wappinger activities

For examples of Wappinger involvement in these wars, see the October 18, 1655, report of the Dutch release of a "Wappingh" to encourage a similar release of a European captive in CHM 1:53 during the Peach War; the July 26, 1663, report affirming that two warriors taken prisoner among the Esopus were Wappingers is in NYCD 13:282; and the August 27, 1663, report of Dutch captives mostly held by Esopus and Wappinghs is in NYCD 13:290–29; for examples of Wappinger diplomacy and messenger service during the fighting, see NYCD 13:289, 337, and 354.

20. A considerable body of studies examine Hutchinson's life and thought; for a recent example, see LaPlante (2004).

21. See De Vries' account in NNN:233–234 of the destruction of Vriesendael and his final leave-taking of the colony on October 8, 1643.

22. See Anonymous 1647 (in NNN:280–282) for the abortive Dutch expeditions.

23. See RPS-CM 4:216–217 and NYCD 14:17–18 and 56 for the April 6 and April 15, 1644, meetings. Several investigators, including me (NAPN:11), have suggested that the present-day Brooklyn place name Gowanus preserves the memory of Gauwaroe. Gowanus was actually the family name of local Huguenot settlers.

Secatogue was first mentioned as "Sicketeuw Hacky" in the November 13, 1643, deed (NYCD 14:530). The heart of Secatogue territory centered on the present-day town of Huntington. Documented connections of people linked to the community suggest that Secatogue was a polyglot frontier settlement. At least some of its residents, like its sachem Chopeycannows came from Munsee-speaking families. Cakensickten, also known as Cockenoe-de-Long-Island, was believed to be a Pequot captive adopted by the Montauketts. His activities at Secatogue suggest more easterly connections. For "Conkuskenow" as Cockenoe-de-Long-Island and an example of his involvement in land affairs in western Connecticut, see WCH 1:391; for Cockenoe's biography, see Tooker (1896).

Cakensickten represented the Montaukett sachem as his agent at many meetings with Huntington townsfolk discussing land problems at the locale. Cakensickten further participated in numerous sales of other Indian lands within a radius of fifty miles of Huntington. For "Cackensickten" as the Montaukett sachem's agent, see ECM 2:407, 413–414 and HTR 1:90–91; he and other Secatogues with close connections to Montauketts and other friends and relatives farther east, north, and west were probably people who spoke Munsee, Quiripi-Unquachog, and Montauk, a tongue similar to Pequot and other mainland New England Algonquian languages. Thanks to John Strong (2007:pc) for pointing out that this territory included parts of the towns of Islip and Smithtown that broke away from Huntington during the eighteenth and nineteenth centuries.

Chopeycannows evidently moved to Secatogue after marrying Suscaneman's sister, a woman who, like her brother, belonged to one of the community's most prominent lineages. This connection evidently supported Tackapousha's claim that he spoke for the Secatogues at meetings with colonial authorities. This claim did not go unchallenged, however. Another Secatogue sachem, Keeossechok, refused to recognize Tackapousha's authority. He signed over his rights at Secatogue to Montaukett sachem Wyandanch, with whom he may have had a kinship connection, in June 1657 (in HTR 1:10–11). This was among several actions that gave Wyandanch and his successors a place at the table whenever land affairs were discussed at Huntington, Hempstead, and other places along the frontier separating the Munsee and Montauk countries during the Dutch and succeeding English administrations (Strong 1997:222)

Very little is known about the Nochpeem represented at the April 6, 1644, meeting by the Wiechquaesgeck sachem Pappenoharrow. The only other known reference to the name appears on the Jansson-Visscher map. Nochpeem is placed just north of another little-known community, Keskistkonck. Neither locale is marked by the rectangle signifying an Indian town on any state of the map.

24. The most complete descriptions of the successful expeditions appear in Anonymous 1647 (in NNN:282–284).

25. For the Dutch murders, see NYCD 1:412–413; for the May 24, 1645, meeting, see RPS-CM 4:265–266 and NYCD 14:60.

26. Van Slijck was a prominent Beverwijck trader. He married a Mohawk woman named Otstoch, the daughter of a French father and Mohawk mother. Several of their children grew up to be notable culture brokers along the Mohawk frontier.

The best translation of the August 30, 1645, treaty appears in RPS-CM 4:279–282; compare with NYCD 13:18–19.

27. Minisink appears in early records as the name of an island, a town, a region, and a nation (Grumet 1991a:180). Settlers using it in its broadest application employed the name to refer to the freshwater reaches of the Delaware River above the head of navigation at the falls as Minisink territory. Those using the term to define more limited areas variously regarded Minisink as the portion of the valley above the Forks of Delaware (where the Lehigh River flows into the Delaware at present-day Easton, Pennsylvania) or, more specifically, as the uppermost section of the valley beyond the Delaware Water Gap. In its most specific sense, the name was applied to the two-square-mile Minisink National Historic Landmark containing still well-preserved dense concentrations of archaeological remains in and around Minisink Island at the upper end of the National Park Service's Delaware Water Gap National Recreation Area.

An "Indian from Mechgachkamic" (Munsee for "the red grounds") mentioned at the July 19, 1649, treaty meeting was the first person from a Minisink community documented in colonial records. The alleged malefactor from the place was delicately described as having "involuntarily or unknowingly lately done mischief at Paulus Hook [in Jersey City]." Forgiveness was asked and given (in NYCD 13:25). References to "Maggaghamieck," noted as a half day's journey from "Minnissinck" on February 6, 1694 (in NYCD 4:98), survive today in and around Port Jervis, New York, most memorably to this writer as the name of the fire station next to a diner popular with generations of Delaware River canoe paddlers. The name was soon repeated a couple of years after its first mention in 1651 in the form Meochkonck, a town located in what appears to be the present Basha Kill marshland, in the first version of Visscher's revision of Jansson's New Netherland map. This map also bears the legend "Minnessinck ofte t'landt van Bacham" (Minisink, above the land of Bacham) situated northwest of Meochkonck. This legend represents the first known colonial reference to the Minisink region. Thanks to Gehring (1976:pc) for the Bacham translation; Miles (2007:pc) suggests that the Dutch word ofte translated by Gehring as "above" can mean "or."

The third state of the second version of the Jansson-Visscher map series (the presence of Philadelphia on this state indicates a post-1683 publication date) has the legend "Alter Modus apud Minessincos Ander Manier der Minnessincksche Dorpen" (the other way with the Minisinks [or] other manner of the Minisink Villages) to distinguish a cartouche drawing of a circular fortification around a village from an adjoining drawing of a larger rectangular-shaped enclosure typifying a Mahican fort (Campbell 1965:11). Thanks to Gehring (1989:pc) for providing the alter modus translation from the Dutch; a request for a small piece of ordinance to protect their fort and corn against Seneca attacks made by Minisink sachems during their first known meeting with Stuyvesant at Fort Amsterdam on August 15, 1663 (in NYCD 13:289–290) is the only reference in colonial documents to an Indian fort in the upper Delaware Valley.

No evidence of fortification surrounds the longhouses depicting locations of towns at Meochkonck and the three other nearby named Indian locales drawn on all versions of the Jansson-Visscher map. Local historians long believed that the lowermost of these, t'schichte Wacki, was the location of this fort. The place appears next to two symbols representing longhouses on the east bank of the river at or near Minisink Island. Westfield, New Jersey, school superintendent Charles A. Philhower, an amateur archaeologist who purchased the land around the Minisink site for a country home and who mined the locale for artifacts, believed he found evidence of a fort he dubbed "the fortress of t'schichte Wacki" (Philhower 1953–1954). Subsequent analysis of his field notes (Kraft 1975:21–22) indicates that the twenty-by-twelve-foot oblong-shaped post mold pattern Philhower believed represented a fort was more likely the archaeological footprint of a roundhouse. For Heckewelder's suggestion that "Tschichohacki," the place Delawares of his acquaintance identified as the spot where Burlington, New Jersey, stands today and the first place they say their ancestors settled on the river, see LLN:376; independently, Whritenour and Miles (2007:pcs) suggest that t'schichte Wacki may be another linguistic hybrid, mixing Dutch words *de schichte,* "the arrow," with the Munsee locative *ahkiing.*

Two other rectangles representing Indian houses appear on the map next to Mecharienkonck across the river from Port Jervis, New York, where the village of Matamoras, Pennsylvania stands today. The third name, Schepinaikonck, appears among rectangular-shaped house symbols scattered along the river above Port Jervis. Like so many Indian names on the Jansson-Visscher maps, neither these nor t'schichte Wacki appear in any presently recognizable form anywhere else.

The Minisink nation rose to documentary prominence when Dutch writers repeatedly mentioned their involvement in the Esopus Wars. Other reports made at the same time brought news of Seneca attacks on Minisinks in the Upper Delaware River (NYCD 12:315 and 356). These attacks corroborate sources that include Delaware River Indians among allies of Mahicans and Susquehannocks then at war with Five Nations people. Several other reports document visits to Minisink country during the Dutch era. One states that Stuyvesant visited a place he called Monnesick during an overland journey from New Amsterdam to Fort Orange undertaken in the spring of 1653 (Shurtleff and Pulsifer 1854–1861, 2:44–45). The itinerary follows Stuyvesant's journey from New Amsterdam to "Ackicksack [Hackensack], a great place of Indians from thence to Monessick, thence to opingona, thence to Warranoke [Woaraneck in Esopus country], to Fort Aurania [Fort Orange]." If opingona was the later-mentioned Oping territory, then Stuyvesant probably backtracked slightly from Monessick, possibly to visit people at opingona or approach Warranoke along a more easterly route perhaps more secure than the more direct Neversink River–Rondout Creek valley corridor between Minisink and Esopus (Grumet 1994:84–85).

Another source notes that a colonist named Claes de Ruijter reportedly lived in the area in 1659. In a February 13, 1659, report, he is noted as "having kept house sometime with the Indians living high up the river and about Bachoms country, had understood from them that quicksilver was to be found there" (in NYCD 2:63). Neither this nor any other account written during the Dutch era, however, does more than mention the area.

Only two references document Indian occupation in the interior reaches of the Great Valley in present-day New Jersey between the Hudson Highlands and the Kittatiny Ridge during the same period. Two longhouses identify a town named Pechquakock on the northwestern shore of a large lake (almost certainly Lake Hopatcong) on the Jansson-Visscher map. This may be the earliest reference to Pequest, the current name of the river system, whose headwaters still rise in the uplands above Hopatcong.

As noted above, Stuyvesant's 1653 itinerary states that the director-general passed through a place called Opingona while traveling from Monnesick to Warranoke. The name next appears in later seventeenth- and early eighteenth-century colonial chronicles discussing people identified as Opings, Wappings, and Pomptons living in the upper reaches of the Walkill, Pequannock, and Ramapo river valleys. Taphow, Nimham I, and many other Oping people mentioned in these accounts are closely related to kinsfolk living farther east in the Hudson and Housatonic valleys.

28. For a brief account of the damage done New Amsterdam in Kieft's War, see Jogues (in NNN:263).

29. For the September 10, 1645, deed, see LP:16; a copy of the document containing the endorsement affirming the company's invalidation of the deed may be seen in the GTR Misc. Records:54 and copied in MacLeod (1941).

30. Trelease (in IACNY:86) estimates that the European population in New Amsterdam more than tripled in the ten years following the signing of the August 30, 1645, treaty.

31. Jesuit missionary Jacques Bruyas's 1668 observation that two thirds of all Oneidas were either of Algonquin or Huron origin (in JR 51:123) suggests that many of these Mohawk replacements may themselves have been adopted captives; see the "Relation of 1645" (in JR 27:297) and the "Relation of 1646" (in JR 28:281) for reports documenting Mohawk replacement of Oneida men killed in battle by Algonquin and Huron warriors.

5. DRUMFIRE, 1645–1664

1. From the journal of James Kenny in Jordan (1913:2).

2. The Swedes struck first, forcing the surrender of the nearby Dutch trading post of Fort Casimir during the spring of 1655.

3. For Indians killing three or four messengers sent from the Delaware Valley settlements to Manhattan, see NYCD 2:76 and RPS-CM 4:585–586; for the 1649 treaty, see NYCD 13:25 and RPS-CM 4:607–609.

4. For warfare between the Mohawks and New France, New England, and the Susquehannocks from 1650 to 1653, see Trigger (1976, 2:792).

5. For April 15, 1650, reports of the threatened New England attack, see NYCD 13:27 and 14:124 and JR 36:101–103; for an account of the Fort Hope treaty, see IACNY:105–106.

6. For Stuyvesant's August 16, 1651, letter to the company directors suggesting an alliance with the New Englanders, see AA 4:74–75; for the minutes of a September 21, 1650, meeting at Fort Orange discussing an allegation of a Mohawk plot made by an Indian from Tappan, see Van Laer (1920–1923, 2:127–128); for the 1653 Mohawk peace treaty with New France, see JR 37:109–111.

7. For the reduction of New Sweden, see NYCD 12:85–111; for the September 15, 1655, attack and attackers, see NYCD 12:98–99 and 13:52–57; for Westchester Indian complicity, see NYCD 13:39–40; for Tackapousha's denial of his own people's involvement and his accusation that Onckeway (Fairfield) and Stamford Indians participated in the assault, see NYCD 13:58.

8. For Stuyvesant's letter alleging Swedish encouragement of the attack, see NYCD 12:99; Van Zandt (1998) uses contemporary South River Swedish sources to argue that the September 15, 1655, party actually consisted of Susquehannocks; for English settlers' statements that Indians were out to attack only the Dutch, see NYCD 13:39–43; for Tackapousha's November 27, 1655, request, made through his messenger Adam, for help against the Narragansetts, see NYCD 13:58.

9. See NYCD 13:46–50 for reports of negotiations that succeeded in freeing from sixty to seventy of the more than one hundred prisoners by the end of October 1655; although most remaining captives evidently were released by 1657, Trelease's (in IACNY:147) observation that little documentation exists of their repatriation still holds.

10. For Pennekeck's speeches, see NYCD 13:45–48; evidently impressed by Pennekeck's eloquence, Merwick (2006:225–227) identified him as the Dutch did, as a chief rather than as a speaker; for the March 12, 1656, meeting minutes identifying "Tackpausha being chosen the chief sachem by all the Indian sachems from Marssapege, Maskinekang, Seacutang, Meracock, Rockaway, and Conarisie" as their representative, see RNSH 1:43–45.

Tooker (in TIN:126–127) suggests that Merrick derives from the Massachusett words *mehchi*, "treeless or barren," and *auke*, "land," in reference to the Great Plains of Hempstead or a reference to the suitability of the area as a planting land. More recently, Whritenour (2007:pc) has suggested "snow goose land," from the Unami word *melek*.

Very little is known about the Indian people living at the Merrick locale. Extant references repeatedly link the place with people from Massapequa, Rockaway, Secatogue, and more easterly nations. One of Tackapousha's sons, a man named Pomwaukon closely connected to communities at Maspeth, Massapequa, Matinecock, and Rockaway, signed the November 13, 1643, deed as a sachem of Merrick (NYCD 14:530). Like other nearby localities, Merrick continued to be a place of Indian occupation throughout the Dutch era. For Indian planting land at Merricoke, see NYCD 14:705; for Merrick connections with neighboring communities, see NYCD 14:530, 705, 717, 728, and 735.

11. For the earliest known deed to Indian lands at Esopus, signed on June 5, 1652, see Brink (1905–1914, 1:80–83); for the October 18, 1655, notice of the release of

a "Wappingh" and "an Esopus of Waerinnewaugh" who had been captured on Manhattan during the recent attack in an attempt to encourage reciprocal return of captive settlers, see CHM 1:153; see NYCD 13:73 for the September 15, 1657, letter from the Dutch West India Company directors to Stuyvesant expressing outrage over what they considered extortionate Indian ransom demands for captured children, four or five of which were reportedly held by the Esopus. On September 4, 1659, Esopus sachems told the Dutch that although some of their people were among the Indians who descended on New Amsterdam, none had killed any settlers and all had returned prisoners and reaffirmed friendship with the Dutch and the Mohawks (in NYCD 13:106).

12. For reports of troubles, threats, and fighting at Esopus in May 1658, see NYCD 13:77–80.

13. See NYCD 13:81 for the May 30, 1658, settlers agreement to move their scattered houses into a single fortified settlement and NYCD 13:81–87 for Stuyvesant's account of his activities at Esopus between May 29 and June 25, 1658.

14. See NYCD 13:93–96 for Stuyvesant's account of his second meeting at Esopus.

15. For the summer meetings at Wiltwijck, see NYCD 13:102–103 and 106–107.

References to Southern Indians fill colonial records. Siwanoys are perhaps the best known "southerners" among people interested in the original Indians of greater New York. Although Buckland (2002:65–67) equates Siwanoy with sewan making, most linguists regard the name as a form of the Eastern Algonquian word for southerner. Contemporary documents tend to support this finding. In 1655, for example, Van der Donck (in DONCK:92) listed Savanoo as the language of what he called Southern Nations and featured Siwanoy just inland from Long Island Sound on Visscher's 1655 revision (the name first appeared on the 1651 map) accompanying the second edition of his book printed in 1656. Siwanoy appears in the same general locale in nearly every subsequent version of the map. Despite this, no known colonial chronicle uses the term Siwanoy to identify a particular individual or community.

The widespread acceptance of Siwanoy as the proper name for the original inhabitants of the mainland from Hellgate to Norwalk may like the Wappinger Confederacy, be traced to Ruttenber's writings. Ruttenber (1872:81–82) largely relied on the name's position on the Jansson-Visscher maps to identify Siwanoy as a cover term for all Indians living along the western reaches of the mainland along Long Island Sound. Inspired by Morgan's pioneering social and kinship analyses, Ruttenber used totemic devices to identify and link the variously named individuals and communities in the area. Although Ruttenber's innovative linkages of people and totems remains intriguing, his assertion that Siwanoy was the name they used to identify their nation has not stood the test of time.

A look at colonial records shows that the word Siwanoy first appeared in written form on Block's 1614 map as Sywanois. Block placed Sywanois in northeastern Massachusetts and mentioned Siuanoe maquaas in a note identifying Susquehannocks as southern Mohawks in IMI 2:c.pl. 23. Despite records documenting nearly continual warfare between both nations throughout much of the 1600s, Susquehannocks and Mohawks frequently acknowledged that their two peoples had a common origin. Evidently drawing from Block, De Laet (in NNN:44 and 53) was the first writer to use the name, in prose, placing Siwanois along Long Island Sound and numbering Sauwanoos among nations living near the South (Delaware) River. Sanawanoock, a variant of the latter term, was fixed in the middle of present-day New Jersey on two globes manufactured in the Netherlands during the 1620s (IMI 2:c.pl. 30). Writing in 1628, De Rasiere (in NNN:103) situated Souwenos on Long Island, writing "in some places it is from three to four leagues broad, and it has several creeks and bays, where many Indians dwell, who support themselves by planting maize and making sewan [wampum], and who are called Souwenos and Sinnecox [Shinnecocks]. . . . The tribes are held in subjection by, and are tributary to, the Pyquans [Pequots]."

Siwanoy is not the only community identified by its direction in early records. Most notably, Shawnee also means Southerner. Wampanoag and Abenaki are variously translated as "easterner" and more poetically as "dawnlander." Native New Yorkers often used variants of the Delaware word *wapanow* when referring to Indians from New England as Eastern Indians (Goddard 1971:19). Determining what a writer meant when referring to Eastern Indians is often difficult. It is hard, for example, to determine exactly just who De Rasiere (in NNN:103) was talking about when he referred to Wappenos in 1628. Contemporary references to Wappenos, such as De Laet's reference to people variously identified as Wapenocks and Wapanoos at Narragansett Bay on Block's map (both in NNN:42–43), evidently refer to Indians later known as Wampanoags. De Rasiere's observation that those not driven off by Wappenos "for the most part have died" provides a further clue. Epidemics that ravaged New England Indian communities from 1616 to 1619 (Spiess and Spiess 1987) and again from 1631 to 1634 are not known to have spread to Munsee country. Just as the tidal Hudson today serves as a boundary line separating many northern and southern plant and animal species, it may also have been a barrier to epidemic contagion. If this was the case, and if De Rasiere was talking about Indians living not just on but east of northern Manhattan, these factors may support identification of Wappenos as Wampanoags in particular or as Eastern Indians in general. Van der Donck in DONCK:92 used Wappanoos as a general name for Eastern Indians in the same way he used Minqua to identify all Iroquois-speaking nations. Wappinger sachem Nimham II's 1762 self-identification as "a River Indian of the tribe of the Wappinoes, which tribe was the ancient inhabitants of the [lower] eastern shore of Hudson's River" (see below) shows how similarly spelled names can be used to identify different communities.

The term Northern Indian was often applied by the people of Munsee country and those colonizing their lands to Mahicans and their closely related friends and relatives living along the northern New England–southern Canadian borderlands. People living in the Hudson Valley identified Unamis, Susquehannocks, and Native people sometimes called Virginians as Southern Indians. Indians from the remote interior were called Far Indians. New Amsterdam colonists began using the term North River to identify the Hudson after 1640 (earlier voyagers called it River of the Mountains, Manhattan River, or Mauritius River). The Delaware River was known as the South River throughout the era of Dutch colonization. The name of the estuary christened East River by the Dutch endures to the present day.

These examples show how both Indians and colonists in the Hudson Valley used three of the four cardinal directions to identify people and rivers. Neither people used west for the same purpose, preferring instead to refer to lands in that direction as Far country or as territories of particular peoples like Ottawas, Ojibwas, and Miamis. This may be attributable among Munsees to beliefs that departed souls travel westward (see De Rasiere in NNN:86 for the earliest known reference to Munsee beliefs concerning the western direction). No similar belief among settlers who moved among them explains the absence of references to a western river or nation in their documents.

Virginian is another linguistic fossil that may be put to rest here. Although early European writers sometimes referred to America as Virginia, only one documentary reference refers to Indian sellers of land in Munsee country as Virginians. This reference appears in the earliest known English transcription of the November 22, 1630, deed to land around Newark Bay (in Westbrook and Van Ingen 1841:14) and evidently reproduced in the much-used citation published in NYCD 13:2–3. The absence of the term in the most recent transcription of the original deed document (in LP:3–4) indicates that the term Virginian was added by its original transcriber and repeated by those using his transcription.

16. For reports on the September 20, 1659, attack and the subsequent siege, see NYCD 13:114–121.

17. For reports on the attack at Esopus, see NYCD 13:114–115 and 124; for the Navesink and Long Island killings, see NYCD 2:76 and 78, 12:255, and 13:147–149; for an account of settler panic and Stuyvesant's efforts to put together the scratch force he led to Esopus country, see NYCD 13:124–125.

18. For Mohawk-Mahican diplomacy, see NYCD 13:122–127 and Van Laer (1920–1923, 2:222–223); for Esopus refusal to meet with Stuyvesant in November, see NYCD 13:130–131.

19. For proceedings of the March 6, 1660, meeting, see NYCD 13:147–149; for the March 15, 1660, Wappinger peace proffer, see NYCD 13:150–151; for the letter received on March 9, 1660, containing company permission to make war and the March 25, 1660, proclamation made at Fort Orange announcing Stuyvesant's formal declaration of hostilities, see NYCD 13:149–150 and 152.

20. For accounts of the Dutch raids, see NYCD 13:157–171; for the report noting the deaths of 11 "Minissingh" people among the Esopus, see NYCD 12:306; for the Esopus captives sent to Curacao, see NYCD 13:169 and 178.

21. For the June 3, 1660, truce and associated negotiations, see NYCD 13:171–174; for the May 3, 1660, killing of Preuwamakan (mentioned in the text as Preumaker), see NYCD 13:170–171; for the July 15, 1660, treaty and an account of the treaty talks, see NYCD 13:179–184.

22. For Melijn's arming of Indians on Staten Island and his threats to have Stuyvesant assassinated, see NYCD 14:159–161.

23. For Van Tienhoven's March 4, 1650, observation that the Raritan Valley had been abandoned by the Indians, see NYCD 1:366.

24. For Stuyvesant's letter to the directors dated April 21, 1660, expressing his determination to pay a visit to both nations once he got the chance, see NYCD 13:163. For the April 28, 1660, account of the Susquehannock asylum offer, reportedly made at the urging of Mohawk sachems, see NYCD 12:308; see NYCD 12:430–434 for the 1663 letter mentioning the one hundred River Indians at the Susquehannock fort. See Kent (1984:36–43) for a discussion identifying the fort as the Strickler archaeological site occupied between 1645 and 1665 in Washington Boro, Pennsylvania. Discovery at Strickler of several burials facing westward in the Delaware manner among Susquehannock interments facing east provide possible material corroboration of reports documenting Delaware River Indians at the locale (Kent 1984:43).

25. See NYCD 13:190 for a December 9, 1660, report of the impasse with the Newesinks Indians.

26. For the July 25, 1660, Sinnecke request for prisoner release, see NYCD 13:184; for Stuyvesant's April 16, 1661, order for the release of two prisoners, see NYCD 13:194. The scant nature of extant evidence makes it impossible to identify Indians identified with Dutch names reportedly transported from Curacao to New Netherland during the summer of 1660 as Esopus (Gehring and Schiltkamp 1987:171 and 175).

27. For the establishment of Nieuwdorp, see NYCM-GE Book 10:87; see NYCD 13:243 for the May 10, 1663, letter to Stuyvesant asking that he send gifts to the Esopus.

28. For accounts of the June 7, 1663, attack and the initial Dutch response, see NYCD 13:245–261; for the June 27, 1663, meeting with Oratam and Mattano, see NYCD 13:261–262; for the July 10, 1663, meeting to which Oratam brought Wiechquaesgeck, Kichtawanck, and Staten Island chiefs, see NYCD 13:276–277; for reports of twenty western Long Island warriors and seventeen more from eastern Long Island going to fight alongside the Dutch against the Esopus, see NYCD 13:280 and 285–286.

29. See NYCD 13:328–330 for Kregier's account of the July 27–31, 1663, expedition. Linking documentation with geographical features, Marc B. Fried (1975:66–84) believes the fort was located somewhere near Kerhonkson, New York.

30. For negotiations with Wiechquaegecks on July 26, 1663, see NYCD 13:282; for the August 15, 1663, meeting with three Minisink sachems accompanied by Oratam, see NYCD 13:289–290; for other talks with Minisinks and Wappingers during the summer of 1663, see NYCD 13:288–294 and 337.

31. For the September 5, 1663, attack on the new fort, see NYCD 13:294, 297, and 338–339. Marc B. Fried (1975:87–102) has marshaled evidence indicating that the new fort was located some thirty miles south of Kingston along the Shawangunk Kill, near the hamlet of Bruynswick, New York.

32. For the October 7, 1663, destruction of the abandoned new fort and subsequent truce talks, see NYCD 13:295–296, 304–305, 314, 321–323, and 341–349; for killings of settlers at Communipaw in November 1663 and in Wappinger country the following April, 1664, see NYCD 13:371–372. For trouble between the Mohawks and Mahicans, see NYCD 13:302–304 and 308–310.

33. See NYCD 13:375–377 for minutes of the May 15–16, 1664, treaty meeting.

34. For influenza in New England in 1647, see Winthrop (in Hosmer 1908, 2:326); for malaria on the Delaware in 1658, see NYCD 2:113 and 12:225 and 227; for the January 29, 1661, report of smallpox to Fort Orange, see NYCD 13:192; for its spread among the Susquehannocks nine months later, see NYCD 12:357.

35. For the February 1, 1663, smallpox report, see NYCD 12:423; for smallpox among the Susquehannocks and Senecas in 1663, see NYCD 12:430–433; for the spread of smallpox to the Hudson Valley, see NYCD 12:432–433.

36. Disappearance of Caelcop I from colonial records at this time indicates that he was the old blind sachem represented by Sewackenamo at the May 16, 1664, treaty. The other two who failed to come were either sick themselves or busy tending to others. Repeated appearances of both men in subsequent records show that each lived on for many more years.

37. For compelling discussions of the sociocultural impacts of grief and other passions, see Bailey (1983) and Rosaldo (1989:1–19).

38. For gradual convergence of Indian and European economies, see Cronon (1983:167); for the Protestant ethic, see Weber (1930).

6. Coping, 1630–1664

1. For contrast of customary law in traditional, small-scale, and local societies with statutory law of nation-states, see Moore (1978:20–21).

2. For usufruct among the Delawares, see Cooper (1938).

3. Colonial land concepts are summarized in E. Price (1995); Europeans repeatedly recognized Indian concern for sums and borders. Roger Williams (in Teunissen and Hinz 1973:167) and Penn (in WPHOA:30) both wrote that Indians were punctual and exact observers of boundaries; formative discussions of Northeastern Indian concepts of territoriality and land use rights may be seen in A. F. C. Wallace (1947 and 1957a).

4. Roger Williams provides a brief eyewitness account describing how Narragansett Indians sold land among themselves in Rhode Island in Teunissen and Hinz (1973:167); Penn's description (in WPHOA:36–39) shows how Delaware River Indians conducted themselves at treaties and land sales and describes how they redistributed the proceeds from meetings among themselves.

For a classic statement on Delaware family feelings for one another and their strong devotion "to the head of the universal family, the great and good Manitto" who made the land and all things that come from it, see Heckewelder (1876:101–102).

5. For "deed game," see Jennings (1975:128–145).

6. A succinct legal definition of deed may be seen at The 'Lectric Law Library, www.lectlaw.com/def/d020.htm.

7. Standardized deed components originating in Roman law usually proceed in the following order: *Premises* (names, dates, considerations, property description), *Habendum* (what is granted), *Tenendum* (type of tenure), *Redendum* (reserved rights), *Conditions, Warranty* (protection), *Covenants* (obligations), and *Conclusion* (signatures, dates, seals, and attestations).

8. For a survey of the various and changing structures and practices of colonial land administration apparatuses operating in Middle Atlantic provinces within Munsee country, see E. Price (1995:207–283).

9. For a discussion of colonial land law processes used to acquire Indian territory in New England, see Springer (1986); for a broader survey up to the early twentieth century, see Banner (2005).

10. Belief that Indians did not understand either the meaning or the consequences of land deeds fairly or unfairly foisted on them is nearly universal in the existing literature and needs no further corroboration. For a long time, Paul A. W. Wallace (1981:130) was nearly alone in holding that Indians were "not as naive as . . . sometimes represented." Baker (1989), Banner (2005), Cantwell and Wall (2001), Grumet (1978, 1979, 1989, and 1996), Hoffer (1998), and Shorto (2004) have considered the alternative explanation that both colonists and Indians may have creatively exploited differing interpretations of deeds to establish and maintain reciprocal relationships.

11. See Jorgensen (1984) for the cultural value of land to all Americans; see Collins (1970) for Skagit Indian exchange of spiritually charged substances.

12. For Lapachpitton's identification of land as dirt, see A. F. C. Wallace (1949:158). Douglas (1966) traces cross-cultural understandings of ritual purity and pollution concepts. Studies examining the spiritual significance of European trade goods in Indian societies include Hamell (1983) and Pietak (1995).

13. For the December 3, 1701, deed containing the "to promote the good and general welfare of both nations" passage, see EJD (Liber O:145–148).

Sutton (1975:40) wrote that "early land acquisition for settlers was in the interest of preserving the peace." New Jersey surveyor James Alexander corroborated the practical application of this observation in 1745 when he wrote that "it has ever been the usual practice of the Proprietors of all now settled countries to give the Indians some recompense for their land, and so soon to purchase it of them yet that is not done for want of a sufficient title from the king or prince who has the right of discovery, but out of prudence to make the Indians easy lest otherwise they might destroy the first settlers" in Work Projects Administration (1940, 1:826).

14. See Gehring (1983:97) for Stuyvesant's December 13, 1653, complaint that English townsfolk in Brooklyn endangered the peace of the colony by telling Indians "what a morgen of land is worth to the English and the Dutch, whereby the natives then conclude that they formerly had sold their land too cheaply." For Teedyuscung's speech, see the next note; for "wealth circulateth," see Penn (in WPHOA:30).

15. In a portion of the transcript of a speech made at the third treaty meeting at Easton in November 12, 1756, cited in Grumet (1979:272) in the French and Indian

War Papers on file in the APS and published in slightly different form in CRP 7:313, 324–336, Teedyuscung spoke as follows:

> Though I have sometimes sold land for a few pipes, or clothes, and liquor, and such like trifles, which in a night are broken and gone, yet I look on the bargain as good; but I expect I should not therefore be ill used but when I have sold great tracts of land at unreasonably low rates, to the English, far below what any person would allow to be their value and have borne this with patience, they say the Indians are fools, but we are not so great fools, as not to bear this in mind; farther I would remind you, notwithstanding the Proprietor has purchased the lands so cheap, yet he sells them again too dear to the poor people, that they do not use the Indians well and think they owe us nothing, now he has bought the lands so cheap it would be prudent in him to have let the people know that and to have sold them the game lands cheaper, than he has done ... Besides when you have bought the land so cheap of our forefathers, you will not now allow us to cut a little wood to make a fire and hinder us from getting our livelihood by hunting.

The speech reads like a eulogy to a failed relationship. Teedyuscung starts by giving voice to an unspoken agreement that helped people unable or unwilling to do away with one another to live together in the same country for more than a 150 years. He attributes the bad feelings that drove his people to war on the English after nearly a century of peace to the collapse of this tacitly accepted system of land dealings that established and maintained reciprocal relationships between them.

Just as the way people die does not necessarily reflect the way they lived, collapse of this relationship does not mean that its fatal flaws necessarily brought down people who may have been better served by a more effective system. There were no really reasonable alternatives. People had to make the best of less than ideal choices. Reciprocal relationships built and maintained by deeds helped people live together, albeit uncomfortably. Like everything people do, this strategy had inherent problems and contradictions. It could only last as long as both parties were willing to exchange a limited and differentially valued commodity like land for the dubious and often evanescent benefits of protection. During the early decades of contact, still-powerful Indians overcame the problem of limited acreage by reconquering and reselling tracts of already-sold land like Staten Island. Running out of territory to sell, they could maintain reciprocity by confirming earlier sales and playing off contending claimants. It was an imperfect system that broke down at various points and was at best only partially successful. Reciprocal relationships based on land sales nevertheless helped serve real needs of Indians and colonists in Munsee country for a very long time before the system collapsed under the weight of overwhelming immigration of Europeans into the region during the mid-1700s.

16. See Weiner (1996:1060) for this classic definition of reciprocity. Although the concept has enjoyed a recent vogue in Northeastern Indian studies focusing on the fur trade (Thomas 1985) and broader "interlocking economies—linguistic, religious, as well as material" (Murray 2000), use of the idea to understand Indian land deal-

ings with colonists has not yet gained widespread acceptance. Murray (2000:115) shows how Roger Williams understood that reciprocity rather than economic calculations motivated Indians to give him a gift of land that they would not have sold "for a thousand fathoms" of wampum offered by someone simply wanting to buy it.

Mauss (1967:72) laid out the effects of imbalanced reciprocity, writing that "to give is to show one's superiority, to show that one is something more and higher ... to accept without returning or repaying more is to face subordination, to become a client and subservient."

17. For the January 15, 1639, deed, see LP:9.

18. For reports on the Indian reconquest of Staten Island in 1641, see De Vries (in NNN:211); for Melijn's pious refusal to "pay twice for anything" and his presentation of "a small gift gratis to maintain friendship [of] two coats of duffels containing six ells, four fathoms of wampum, five or six little kettles, and some awls and needles," see Anonymous (1913:124–125); for the reconquest of the island again in 1655, see NYCD 12:98–99; Mattano's brother Neckaock was identified as "Necktan of Hackingsack" on the July 10, 1657, Staten Island deed in NYCD 14:393–394 and Gehring 2003:141–142.

19. Romackqua made this observation while his people were still embroiled in a hotly contested war with the Mohawks. No combatant in this fighting would openly claim anyone's land until the fighting stopped and the adversaries agreed on peace terms. For the statement made by "Ramaque," see NYCD 13:460–461.

Like the feasts and ceremonies used to appease spirits of the dead and more closely bind the living together before occupying land conquered in war in Highland New Guinea (Rappaport 1968), those used by Munsees, Mohawks, and other Indian nations also probably symbolically pacified potentially vengeful ancestral ghosts as they practically reordered relations and boundaries between former combatants.

20. A tip of the hat to Reid (1976) and his characterization of Cherokee law as a better kind of hatchet for inspiring the wording of this subheading.

21. Tackapousha and his associates made the first known deposition in the boundary dispute between Oyster Bay and Hempstead on March 22, 1667, in OBTR 1:677–678; proceedings of the October 6, 1670, trial adjudicating contending claims of Richard Smith and the Town of Huntington provide the earliest known example of acceptance of Indian testimony in New York court proceedings in ECM 2:424–430.

22. First suggested by Bohannan (1966), the concept of creative misunderstanding was developed in the form of working disagreements by Sahlins (1981) and brought to wider attention among historians in R. White (1991). Bailey (1991:128) suggests that evasions show how what people regard as truth and untruth can be deployed in dialogues "between adversaries, who use these words in the contest, each striving to make their own ideas and values prevail."

23. The following discussion substantially draws on findings presented in Grumet (1979 and 1989). Gill's (1990) suggestion that the Mother Earth image in Indian rhetoric originated in an Old World Mother Earth/Father Sky conceptual dichotomy continues to generate strong reactions among many readers.

24. Most recently Merwick (2006:267) suggested that dissonance between corporate mercantile disinterest and the grasping spirit of farmers, free traders, and freebooters caused wars with Indians that made the Dutch feel shame and sorrow.

25. For laws prohibiting trade of liquor to Indians, see CHM 1:85, 98, 109, 117, and 309; for ordinances outlawing unauthorized trade of guns or ammunition to Indians living near New Amsterdam, see CHM 1:93 and NYCD 1:161–162.

26. For examples of settlers punished for robbing Indians in 1648, see CHM 1:115.

27. For Stuyvesant's prosecution of free traders selling guns to Indians at the same time he gave Indians firearms and ammunition, see Anonymous (in NNN:344–345) and Van Tienhoven (in NNN:368–370); for a February 14, 1652, affidavit reporting Indians using arms given by Melijn to threaten settlers in Brooklyn, see NYCD 14:160–161.

28. For the August 23, 1647, meeting at Fort Amsterdam, see NYCD 14:79; for the Hempstead petition to the company written on September 25, 1651, see NYCD 2:156–157; for the Hempstead settlers' December 11, 1653, petition ruing the fact that their requests were being ignored, see NYCD 1:551.

29. For "Rasokon, Sagamore of Matinnicoke" putting his mark on the April 2, 1653, deed to Oyster Bay's Huntington rivals, see HT:9, HTR 1:1–4, and ECM 2:402–403; for Tackapousha's sale to Oyster Bay settlers on March 17, 1658, see OBTR 1:347–349 and 351–352, and for his deed to worried Hempstead settlers concerned about their boundary with Oyster Bay signed on May 11, 1658, see NYCD 14:416–417, OBTR 1:46–48, and Gehring 2003:140–141.

30. For extended discussions of these and other contests between Indian rivals on Long Island at this time, see Grumet (1996:116–139) and Strong (1997:213–266).

31. For allegations that Wyandanch was poisoned, see Lion Gardiner in Orr (1897:146). On November 13, 1643, New England immigrants Robert Fordham and his son-in-law John Carman secured a deed to the Great Plains of Hempstead, the single largest expanse of open ground in western Long Island, from Tackapousha, "sagamore of Masepeage," and Indians from "Merriack or Rockaway." Tackapousha represented various combinations of Merricks, Rockaways, Matinecocks, Secatogues, Unchechaugs, and Mochgonnekoncks in councils with colonists throughout the remaining years of his tenure as Massapequa sachem. Closer to home, he continually used conflicting claims based on the 1639 and 1643 deeds to play Hempstead settlers off first against Dutch authorities and then their English successors after 1664.

Emerus signed the first state of the November 1, 1650, deed in the GTR Patent Book 1:15 as Arremathanus, perhaps the fullest transcription of his name; later states of the same deed (in GTR Patent Book 1:43, 45, and 47) spell the name as Arremackanus; Seyseychkimus's name is the last in the list of sachems, appearing in the form of Sasham, a variant of Sassian, Seiseis, and other forms documented in transactions concluded on Long Island.

32. For Indian killings on May 17, 1652, see NYCD 1:497; for Stuyvesant's June 17, 1652, thoughts on the Nayack claims, see Gehring (1983:28–29).

33. For Mattano's threat, reported on September 18, 1652, see NYCD 1:498.

34. For the July 29, 1652, deed to Thomas Spicer, see GTR Unrecorded Deeds 5:238; for the November 22, 1652, deed to Cornelis van Werckhoven and the December 1, 1652, confirmation, see BTR Patent Book 1:487 and NYCD 14:190.

35. The December 1, 1652, confirmation contained the "condition that they, the Indians, and their descendants remove immediately from the land now occupied by them, called Naieck and never return to live in the limits of the district as described in the foregoing act nor ever make any claim upon it" (BTR Patent Book 1:487 and NYCD 14:190).

36. See EJD (Liber 1:7–9) for Heermann's purchases made March 28, 1651, and December 26, 1652. For Van Dincklagen's August 5, 1650, purchase from Emerus, identified in the deed as Remmatap (a variant of Arremathanus), and his kinsman Natauweer, which if spelled with an *M* in the conjectural form Matauweer may have been Mattano, see EJD (Liber 1:6–7).

37. For the company's August 16, 1652, invalidation of privately purchased deeds to various tracts around the Lower Bay made by Van Dincklagen and other unauthorized buyers, see AA 4:75–76.

38. For the results of Stuyvesant's successful effort to thwart Van der Capellen, see the letter from the company directors dated December 22, 1657, in Gehring 2003:158.

39. The Indians who signed the January 30, 1658, conveyance in EJD (Liber 1:3–6) were local residents; none were prominent sachems; for Van der Capellen's efforts to establish a patroonship in New Netherland, see J. Jacobs (2005:122–123).

Colonial chroniclers tended to record the names and aliases of prominent sachems active in provincial politics with considerable consistency. Thousands of differently spelled names of Indians, however, cannot be linked to particular individuals. Many of these names almost certainly belong to local or less prominent leaders and others who either shunned or were passed over by the spotlight. This was not the case for Waerhinnis Couwee. During a documented career spanning nearly forty years, his name repeatedly appears in fairly recognizable form among Indians involved in affairs concerning Staten Island and the nearby mainland. Several factors seem to account for his greater visibility in these records. He lived on disputed land and participated in many deed sales. He signed, for instance, the Elizabethtown deed as the witness Warinanco. His name appears on the three deeds to Staten Island as Wieromies in 1630, as the Hespatingh sachem Waerhinnis Couwee in 1657, and as the elder Warriner in the final 1670 deed (NYCD 13:2 and 455 and 14:393). Identified as Warimus Cowrue, he was one of the local sachems who resold much of the land around Pavonia to Stuyvesant on January 30, 1658 (EJD Liber 1:3–4); for a 1665 Elizabethtown payment receipt listing him as Wareham, see EJD (Liber 1:1–2). Other deeds bearing his mark as a Native proprietor or witness signed in the general vicinity between 1649 and 1677 may be seen in EJD Liber 1:6–8, 9, 254 (85 on verso) and Liber f-2:370.

Waerhinnis Couwee also attended several meetings and signed a number of treaties. He signed the July 15, 1660, peace agreement as Warrhan of Staten Island and attended the July 20, 1663, meeting where Oratam put off Stuyvesant's demands for the meadowlands as Waerhen van Couwe. Evidence that he spoke either Dutch or the local trade jargon as well as his native tongue appears in several documents identifying him as an interpreter who spoke for Oratam and other Lower River Indian sachems at several important meetings. On May 16, 1664, for example, he served as the interpreter Maerhinnie Tuwe alongside Oratam's friend Sarah Kierstede at the treaty ending the Esopus Wars. Never identified as a major sachem, numerous documents mentioning him by name show that he made sure that he was involved in major developments affecting his land and relations in and around Staten Island. For references to Waerhinnis Couwee's attendance at meetings, see NYCD 13:179, 280, and 375; for references to his role as interpreter, see NYCD 13:147, 167, and 276.

40. For negotiations in Raritan and Navesink country, see Kregier's earlier-mentioned account of his journey there in NYCD 13:314–316; for the December 12, 1663, promissory note phrased in the form of a deed, see NYCD 13:316.

41. For the Navesink four thousand-guilder demand, see CHM 1:257; for Stuyvesant's construction order, see NYCD 13:321–322; for the February 16, 1664, message, see NYCD 13:358; for Echko's message and Stuyvesant's response, see NYCD 13:364–365.

42. For the March 25, 1664, deed, see EJD Liber 1:247 (72 on verso)-246 (73 on verso); and GTR Book 1:72.

43. For the final confirmation deed to Oak Neck and Pine Island, dated 1711, see OBTR 5:650–651; for the original sale, made on November 24, 1658, see OBTR 1:353–354.

7. CONTENTIONS, 1664–1674

1. For the "maelstrom of interests" characterizing colonial politics in New Netherland that only increased in intensity after the English takeover, see Condon (1968:144–172).

2. For the Duke's Laws, see Ritchie (1977).

3. For King Louis XIV dispatching the one thousand men of the Carignan-Salieres regiment to Canada in 1665, see NYCD 9:25–36. A sizable part of this regiment would be lost in an ill-fated expedition against the Mohawks made during the winter of 1665–1666.

4. For accounts of the machinations accompanying Charles's grant to Berkeley and Carteret, see Tanner (1908:2–5) and Pomfret (1962:18–33).

5. For the September 25, 1664, treaty text, see NYCD 3:67–68 and NYBGE:47–49.

6. The most recent transcription of this much-published treaty may be seen in Christoph (1980:3–5). One of the more unusual signatories of the 1665 Nicolls Treaty was one of the "Indian witnesses of the Esopes young men," identified as "Robin Cinnaman, a Pekoit Sachem." No document currently sheds further light on what Robin Cassacinamon's was doing in the area. For a biographical account of the Mashantucket Pequot sachem, see McBride (1996); for a survey of the many subsequent renewals of the Nicolls Treaty, see Scott and Baker (1953).

7. For contemporary documentation of the expedition, see NYCD 3:118–135.

8. See IACNY:242–243 for an assessment of the attacks and the peace negotiations that followed.

9. For the proceedings of the September 10, 1666, treaty, see LIR:33–35.

10. The volatile nature of European politics of the era ensured that belligerents could soon be allies. Within a year, for example, England and Holland would join together in an alliance to stop French efforts to seize the Spanish Netherlands. For an early study of the illicit carrying trade along the smugglers' route between Albany and Montreal, see Buffinton (1922).

11. For proceedings of Nicolls Treaty renewals held between 1668 and 1673, see NYCD 13:401, 417, 435–437, and 452, ECM 1:244, KP 2:489, and NYBGE:172; for the January 25, 1672, order dismissing the fort guard, see KP 2:475.

12. For the August 11, 1669, meeting with Lovelace, see ECM 1:35–36; for Lovelace's August 13, 1669, letter informing Albany officials of the meeting and the peace agreement with the "Maquaes and Synnaks" (i.e., the Mohawks and the four other Iroquois nations to the west), see AA 4:9 and NYCD 13:428.

13. For reports of Josia Chickataubut's defeat and the Mahican and Wiechquaesgeck withdrawals, see NYCD 9:66 and 13:460 and 545.

14. For reports of Mohawk attacks on Wiechquaesgecks during the first years of Nicolls' regime, see NYCD 13:460 and ECM 1:105; for Romackqua's sale offer and the subsequent deed to the same territory Stuyvesant purchased from Sauwenaroque in a July 26, 1655, deed later cancelled before it was registered, see NYCD 13:460–461, ECM 1:70–71 and 103–105, and RPS-CM 3:413–415; the 1670 date of Romackqua's offer to sell land deeded over on October 30, 1671, is probably another example of Old Style–New Style date confusion.

15. Proceedings of the November 8, 1671, treaty have not been found. Notices of the event may be seen in ECM 1:116–117; the difficult path to peace may be followed in reports published in NYCD 13:440 and ECM 1:50, 53, 60, and 379–380.

16. Post-Revolutionary artifacts of Connecticut's ocean-to-ocean claim include Ohio's Western Reserve between Cleveland and the Pennsylvania border, set aside for war veterans from Connecticut, and the Firelands around Sandusky (coincidentally the locale of a major Munsee community during the late eighteenth and early nineteenth centuries), awarded to residents from Danbury, New London, and other Connecticut communities burned by the British during the Revolutionary War. Connecticut did not agree to its current boundary with New York until 1880.

17. Specimens of the particular species of confirmatory deed negotiated by town governments at this time often include information linking signatories with their predecessors. These frequently provide data on rights and connections as useful today as they were to the parties to the original transactions.

For the Amersfoort deed of April 23, 1665, see FTR Book 1:71; for the July 8, 1666, Newtown deed, see Riker (1852:72–73) and ECM 1:235–237; for the April 29, 1666, Harrison deed taking in present-day White Plains, see NYCM-ILP Book 1:10, NYCD 13:402–403, and WCH 2:153; for the September 11, 1666, confirmation of Van der Donck's undocumented previous purchase of Yonkers, see ECM 1:234–235.

18. For Nicolls' February 29, 1665, order, see Howell (1902:154–155); for the October 7, 1665, deposition documenting the Massapequa survey stop, see ECM 2:413–414; For Nicolls' June 16, 1666, proposals to the Hempstead magistrates, see NYCD 14:583–584.

19. For Nicolls' October 1, 1666, order to attend a meeting on October 18, 1666, see NYCD 14:589; for Nicolls' proposals, see ECM 2:569–670; for Tackapousha's March 22, 1667, map, see NYCM-ILP Book 1:30; for the settlers' claim that they had already paid Hempstead for the land, see Matthias Nicolls' letter to John Underhill at Oyster Bay dated April 19, 1667, in NYCD 14:596.

20. In Grumet (1996:128) Suscaneman was identified as the architect of this mass selling strategy in Oyster Bay. Since then it has become evident that Asharoken first began using the tactic. For published transcripts of these deeds, see OBTR 1:80–81, 89–90, and 681–687.

21. For Lovelace's order to Hempstead and his July 8, 1670, permit allowing Oyster Bay to treat for the land, see NYCD 14:621 and 639, ECM 2:570–571, and NYBGE:341 and 360–361; for Tackapousha's defiance on June 26, 1671, see ECM 1:93 and 2:576–577. For Lovelace's remand of the case to the Court of Assizes on September 25, 1671, and the court's finding made on October 4, 1671, see NYCD 14:656 and ECM 2:580–581.

22. For the company's March 26, 1663, approval of Stuyvesant's proposal to acquire the land for English colonists to settle on, see NYCD 13:239; for Oratam's July 20, 1663, demurral, see NYCD 13:280.

23. See NJCD 1:14–15 for the September 26, 1664, Elizabethtown Associates petition and Nicolls' October 1, 1664, permit.

24. For the Elizabethtown deed, see EJD Liber 1:1–2 and NJCD 1:15–16; for the December 1, 1664, patent, see NJCD 6:205–215.

25. For the most recent study examining the course of the Elizabethtown controversy and other conflicts between planters and proprietors in New Jersey, see McConville (1999).

26. Each of these allegations questioning Indian involvement in the Elizabethtown purchase appears in *A Bill in the Chancery of New Jersey* published in 1747. Most were recently revived in Esposito (1976:221–225).

27. Many documents show that Mattano and Waerhinnis Couwee were among the many sachems in Munsee country who demanded payment and received gifts for lands for which they had not been paid, that had been deeded over as sureties for future purchasers, or that their warriors had reconquered in war. These men and others also signed deeds and accepted gratuities for lands that were not settled after their sale or whose patents were voided for other reasons. Although the other two people mentioned in the deed body were not the same persons who signed the deed, all four signed the November 24, 1665, receipt acknowledging payment for the land inscribed in the indorsement on the back of the 1664 deed. All of these people, identified on the indorsement receipt as Wareham, Manamawaone, Kawameck, and Sewah heronos, were experienced diplomats well known to colonial officials and had substantial connections to local communities; for the 1665 indorsement receipt, see the reverse of the Elizabethtown deed on file in the EJD Liber 1:1–2; the mar-

gin of the deed also has a note documenting Augustine Heermann's November 16, 1666, continuing claim to the land based on his 1651 purchase invalidated by the Dutch West India Company directors.

Wareham, who signed the deed as the witness Warinanco, was Waerhinnis Couwee, who as we have already seen, had close connections to the Hackensack community and who often, as we have already seen, served as an interpreter for Oratam and Mattano. He later put his mark next to the name Woraquen on the sale confirmation made at the request of the associates on February 28, 1671. Manamawaone is harder to identify. The presence of a person identified as Machhopwockan in the list of signatories to the 1671 confirmation suggests that Manamawaone may have been Machopoikan, a man who would later become a prominent Raritan sachem.

Kawameck was Querameck, then a young sachem from the Navesink and Raritan countries, who first appeared in colonial records as the man identified as Cowescomen in the Elizabethtown deed. Sewah heronos was Pierwim, the rising Hackensack leader also known to settlers as Hans, who had also taken Sewackenamo's name. As mentioned earlier, Pierwim had participated in the Staten Island sale in 1670 and was identified as Pearawe in the 1671 Elizabethtown confirmation; for the 1671 confirmation, see the reverse and margins of the copy of the Elizabethtown deed on file in the EJD Liber 1:1–2; Pierwim identified himself as Hans in various ways, as "Piewecherenoes alias Hans" in the December 12, 1663, Navesink deed to Stuyvesant in NYCD 13:316; "Hans alias Pieweserenves" in the May 16, 1664, Esopus treaty in NYCD 13:375–377; and "Pewaherenoes alias Hans" in the April 13, 1671, sale at Overpeck Creek in Bergen County in EJD Liber f-2:370 and RCID:39A–39C.

28. For the October 5, 1664, deed to Hackensack Neck, see RCID:34; although Carteret granted Kierstede a patent for 2,260 acres between Overpeck Creek and the Hackensack River on June 24, 1669, no copy of a deed signed by Oratam has yet been found to document her claim. See NJCD 21:8.

29. For Oratam's designation of Hans as his successor as sachem of the Hackensack and Staten Island Indians at the February 23, 1664, meeting, see NYCD 13:361; for the July 8, 1664, meeting, see NYCD 13:386.

30. For "Seweghkamin alias Hans" on May 19, 1671, see EJD Liber 1:115–116 and RCID:40–43. For "Sewackemein alias Hans" as witness to the April 9, 1679, deed, see EJD Liber 1:210 (129 on verso)-209 (130 on verso) and RCID:47B–47D; for "Sewightkamek alias Hans" on April 15, 1685, see RCID:62–65.

Pierwim was not the only Indian man identified as Hans during the colonial era. Tataemshatt, grandson of Esopus sachem Mamanuchqua, signed a deed for land at Claverack, New York as "Hans Vos, or in Indian Tatankenat" on June 5, 1662, in AHC 4:302 and ERA 1:302, and was mentioned as Hans in the Esopus and Wappinger Indian sale of land nearby on September 3, 1683, in KP 1:239–240. Another Indian man named Hans signed a July 18, 1743, deed to land in Monmouth County (Manuscript on file under that date in the New Jersey Historical Society [hereinafter NJHS]).

31. For Carteret's May 26, 1666, letter to Oratam and another letter authorizing Robert Treat to bring the message and view the land, see NJCD 1:55–56; for Treat's deposition made on March 13, 1688, that Perror (i.e., Pierwim) laid claim to the Newark tract and "Oraton being very old but approving of Perror's acting," see EJPBM 2:275: For the July 11, 1667, Newark tract deed, see EJD Liber 1:270 (69 on verso) and RCID:34a–34d.

32. In Grumet (1979:150), I misidentified the person signing this and several other deeds under names variously spelled Waymote, Wawemutting, and Wayweenatan as an individual named Waymutton. Taptawappamund signed the July 11, 1667, deed as Wapamuck; he subsequently put his mark on twenty-one deeds to lands in and around Navesink country. The spelling of his name as Tapatowwowupon in the April 11, 1676, deed to land near Shrewsbury in EJD Liber 1:198 (143 on verso) links him to other documents variously referring to him as Wawapa, who along with Powropa (Peropay) and Emoroas (Emerus) was listed as a chief sachem of Ramesing in the May 26, 1676, deed to lands at the locale in MCD Book B:11–14, as Waymutton in a January 12, 1677, sale in EJD Liber1:235 (104 on verso), as Vowavapon on August 8, 1678, in OTOM:21–22, as Waywanotong on December 16, 1689, in EJD Liber D:418, and as the Ramenesing sachem Waywaramong in June 18, 1675, in EJD Liber 1:250 (49 on verso). For final references identifying him as Waparent in November 18, 1709, and May 9, 1710, deeds to lands in the Ramapo Valley, see EJD Liber I:317–321. For the August 15, 1663, Minisink cannon request, see NYCD 13:289.

33. Memshe signed the Newark deed as Wamesane in EJD Liber 1:270 (69 on verso) and RCID:34a–34d.

34. Other orthographies for Neckaock include Nechtamapepeau in the January 8, 1676, deed to land at New Hackensack in EJD Liber 1:200 (139 on verso); Myanick, a Ramenesing sachem listed in a deed dated September 26, 1676, and Necktoha, noted as a brother of "Powraas and Iraseek, sachems of Wickatunk" on July 16, 1684, both of the latter in OTOM:251. Although Peropay's and Pierwim's names are similar, the fact that both frequently signed the same documents next to names slightly different but distinctively spelled makes separate identifications possible.

35. This was the meeting where Pierwim also presented the Mohawk wampum belt, affirming their separate peace with the Lower River Indians. For the proceedings of this meeting, see ECM 1:35–36.

36. For the July 20, 1668, deed to William Sandford for New Barbados Neck, see EJD Liber 1:42–43 and RCID:35–36; for the February 28, 1672, deed to John Berry for land just above New Barbados Neck, see EJD Liber 1:121–122 and RCID:39.

37. Information for this and the next few paragraphs is mostly drawn from the extensive body of published materials documenting events associated with the last Indian sale of Staten Island, in ECM 1:43–48 and 338–343.

38. Agapou signed as Aquepo for himself, for a young man named Pemantowes, and for an elder who had gambled away his interest in the island identified as Warrenes [Waerhinnis Couwee]; Pierwim signed as Quewequeen; Taptawappamund signed for himself as Wawanecameck and also signed for Minqua Sachemack; the philological route linking Taptawappamund to Wawanecameck proceeds from Way-

waramong (June 18, 1675), Wawemutting (June 4, 1687), Waymutton (January 12, 1677), and Vowavapon (August 8, 1678) to Tapatowwowupon (April 11, 1676).

39. See, for example, the New Jersey Archives entry noting that the license issued on July 30, 1669, by the East Jersey Proprietors to New York Secretary Matthias Nicolls for two thousand acres at Overpeck Creek was voided after Nicolls failed to buy the land from the Indians, settle it, or pay rent before the deadline specified in the license, in NJCD 21:8.

40. For Lovelace's proclamations, which also threw the fur trade open to all New Yorkers, see NYCD 3:188.

41. For the April 13, 1671, deed, see EJD Liber f-2:370–371 and RCID:39A–39C; for the May 19, 1671, deed, see EJD Liber 1:115–116 and RCID:40–43.

42. For Aroorhikan as Ararijkan participating in the sales of three flats at Castuteeuw in Brooklyn on June 16 and July 16, 1636, see NYCD 14:2–4 and LP:5–6; as Ahwaroch participating in the September 28, 1669, sale of land in Fordham in the Bronx, see WCH 2:504 and ECM 1:212; as Auchwarose selling land in the west Bronx on May 10, 1676, see WCH 2:517; as Arrorikan selling Aquegnonke (Aquackenonck, present-day Passaic, New Jersey) on April 9, 1679, see EJD Liber 1:210 (129 on verso); and as Aghwarowes participating in the sale of land at Yonkers, New York, on September 6, 1682, see WCH 1:270; Pierwim signed as "Seweghkamin, also known as Hans" in the May 19, 1671, deed in EJD Liber 1:115–116.

43. Claes's story deserves more attention than it has received. He found many opportunities to exercise an evident talent for languages as a translator in many deed negotiations in the Hudson Valley. He was also the man identified as the Indian called Claus by the Dutch, and Nicholas by the English, who gave Charles Wolley much of the information on Native life included in the journal of his visit to New York between 1678 and 1680 in NAHC:38; he may also have been the Mahigane traveler Klas met by La Salle near the shores of Lake Michigan with a large party of Loups in 1681 in DEF 2:148–149. For the earliest reference to him, a September 21, 1666, deed noting that "Claes the Indian" had an interest in the Yonkers land (i.e., present-day Yonkers, New York), see ECM 1:234.

44. For an account of the Rebellion of 1672, see Pomfret (1962:56–81); see Shomette and Haslach (1988) for an account of the Dutch invasion.

45. For the September 13, 1673, meeting, see NYCD 2:606 and 13:476 and NJCD 1:132; for an account of the Mohawk visit, see NYCD 2:608.

46. Most surviving records documenting Dutch administration of New Orange from 1673 to 1674 are published in NYCD 2:526–740.

47. For an account of this incident, see NYCD 2:682; for Heckewelder's suggestion that Ockanickon's name derives from the Unami word *okanican* or its Munsee equivalent, *woakenican*, "an iron hook, pot hook," see LLN:383.

48. For a brief account of the April 23, 1674, meeting, see NYCD 2:707.

8. Respite, 1674–1679

1. For Andros's commission, issued by the king on July 1, 1674, see NYCD 3:215.

2. For the December 4, 1674, meeting, see AP 1:40; for the January 12, 1675, meeting, see AP 1:316; for the February 14, 1675, Albany meeting, see LIR:37–38; for the drinking problems at Raritan and the two alleged killings on the Millstone River, see NYCD 12:518–519; for the April 20, 1675, meeting in New York, where Porappa was identified as the sachem of Nevesans, Mautaupis and Taptawappaum as sachems of Toponemus, and the latter also as sachem of Kackowackin, see AP 1:131–133 and 291; Kackowackin may be a reference to Waycake near the south shore of Raritan Bay—both orthographies may represent ways the Delaware word for geese sounded to the English (Boyd 2005:172).

3. For the Iroquois request, see NYCD 9:110; for the report of the peace and trade agreement identifying the Seneca town of Gandaschekiagon as the Ottawa trade market, see NYCD 9:117. This was almost certainly Gandachioragon, the westernmost Seneca town and the site of the Jesuit mission of La Conception, established in 1668. Remains dating from 1670 to 1687 at the locale are preserved within the present-day Rochester Junction archaeological site, for which see Wray, Sempowski, and Saunders (1990).

Ottawa country lay at the heart of the lower Great Lakes in the Far country. The Ottawa heartland stretched between lakes Michigan and Erie on land that would later be called Upper Canada. Often called the Ottawawas country at the time, it was home to the eponymous Ottawas as well as many nearby Potawatomis, Anishinabeg (also known as Ojibwas or Chippewas), Mascoutens, Miamis and, by the 1680s, to some River Indians and a few other adventurous Eastern Algonquians. All were often at war with the Iroquois Confederacy, and most were longtime allies of the Susquehannocks and the French.

Ottawa country also centered on the northern end of the upper Ohio River valley route long used by Susquehannocks to bring furs and trade goods from Canada and the Far country to Atlantic Coast entrepôts. The route consisted of navigable rivers with short portages linking the Potomac River; the upper Ohio Valley Youghiogheny, Monongahela, and Allegheny rivers; and Lake Erie tributaries like French Creek and the Cuyahoga River. Competition for this route had been fierce. During difficult times, the area became a vast arena of violence. Various wars consumed entire nations like the Eries, Monongahelas, and Massawomeckes. Conflicts would continue to devastate the region until the United States finally secured control by the close of the eighteenth century.

4. For Frontenac's undated report for the year 1674, which identified the Esopus as "Mohegans of Taracton, a nation bordering on New Netherland" and mentioned the new Ottawa-Iroquois trade accord, see NYCD 9:117; use of Mohegan, the name of the present-day nation in eastern Connecticut, as a spelling for the altogether different Mahican nation and the general use of Mahican as a general name for all Indians living in and around Esopus provide yet another example showing why care must be exercised when associating different spellings for nations with people and places. For the Esopus meeting held between April 21 and 24, 1675, at Kingston to discuss the killings, see KP 2:532.

5. The man identified as "Mawhoscan, Sachem of the Wapping Indyans" in the report of the June 28, 1675, meeting in New York (AP 1:178) was earlier variously

identified as the Kichtawanck sachem Metsewackos on July 10, 1663, in NYCD 13:276–277, Mechtsewach and Messachkewath on November 15, 1663, in NYCD 13:303, and Metsewachset on April 26, 1664, in NYCD 13:371–372; he would later sign a deed to land near New Paltz as Matsiekapie on June 23, 1682, in UCD Book H:629–630, and put his mark to the August 8, 1683, Rumbout Patent at the mouth of Wappinger Creek above the Highlands as Megriskar in Hasbrouck (1909:35–37).

6. Most material used here documenting the Susquehannock move to Maryland and the subsequent Susquehannock diaspora is drawn from Jennings (1984:135–142).

7. For accounts of Bacon's Rebellion, see Washburn (1957) and Webb (1984).

8. For the September 22, 1675, meeting, in which "Mamarakickon" was perhaps pointedly identified as being "from Millstone," the locale of the recent killings, see NYCD 12:541 and AP 1:203–204; for the September 23, 1675, sale of land at the falls, see Holcomb (1926:657–658) and Gehring (1977:99).

9. For the June 2–3, 1676, meeting in Albany, see AP 1:377–378.

10. For the August 4, 1676, NYCM-ECM source noting that the Susquehannocks preferred to move "at the falls or the middle of the river at Delaware," see NYCD 12:553.

11. For the classic account of King Philip's War, see "Flintlock and Tomahawk," D. Leach (1958); for a revisionist perspective, see Jennings (1975); among more recent studies are Bourne (1990), Drake (1999), and Lepore (1998).

12. For the July 23, 1675, meeting where a large delegation of Tappan and Hackensack Indians affirmed friendship with New York and were told that the Long Island Indians had been disarmed because they paid tribute to Northern Indians, see AP 1:195–196; for the September 18, 1675, meeting where the unnamed Rockaway sachem (probably either Waumetompack or Monguamy) affirmed loyalty, see AP 1:202–203; for an October 23, 1675, meeting where Andros again disarmed Tackapousha's Indians after another meeting that failed to resolve the land dispute at Matinecock, see AP 1:238.

13. For the scalp brought by two Indians from Rahway (evidently a slip of the pen for Rakway, i.e., Rockaway) on February 29, 1675 (yet another probable Old Style/New Style calendric mix-up), see AP 1:332.

14. For Warner's account, see AP 1:330–331.

15. For discussions of the Mohawk role in the war, see IACNY:230–236 and Jennings (1975:315); for contemporary reports penned between 1676 and 1678, see AP 1:352, NYCD 3:265, and JR 60:133.

16. The Quintipartite Deed got its name from the five signatories to the deed—John Fenwick and Edward Byllynge for West Jersey, and William Penn, Gawren Lawrie, and Nicholas Lucas for East Jersey. For one of many studies examining the founding of East Jersey and the problems between Andros and Carteret, see Pomfret (1962:82–129).

17. Peropay and Taptawappamund each signed at least fourteen conveyances in and near Navesink between 1674 and 1680; Querameck signed ten, Metapis nine, Emerus eight, Irooseeke seven, and Wassackarous, who eluded punishment for killing a settler in Maspeth in 1660, signed three in 1674 before moving farther south a year

later; for Navesink and lower Raritan country deeds during this period, see EJD Liber 1:197 (142 on verso), 198 (143 on verso), 199 (142 on verso), 232 (107 on verso), 235 (104 on verso), 248 (91 on verso), 251 (88 on verso)-250 (89 on verso), 255 (84 on verso), 257 (82 on verso), 258 (81 on verso)-257 (82 on verso), 264 (75 on verso), 265 (74 on verso), 266 (75 on verso), 271 (68 on verso)-270 (69 on verso), 273 (66 on verso), and 290 (49 on verso)-289 (50 on verso), Liber A:194, and Liber I:105, 401–402, and 402–403, and MCD Book B:11–14, 33–35, 35–36, and 40–43, Book C:178–179, and Book F:203.

18. The route linking Mattum to Taptawappamund progresses from Waymutton (January 12, 1677) and Vowavapon (August 8, 1678) to Tapatowwowupon (April 11, 1676); for the August 16, 1675, deed, see EJD (Liber 1:197 [142]).

19. For the August 5, 1675, opening salvo of this phase of the dispute, see NYCD 14:696 and 2:680.

20. For the inconclusive back and forth between the disputants during Andros's tenure as governor of New York, see NYCD 14:705–707, 720, 728–729, 733–734, and 748, OBTR 1:635–636 and 2:130, 681, and 684, RNSH 1:312–313, and AP 1:235–238, 252–254, and 285 and 2:33–34, 52–53, 77–82, and 154–156.

21. For contemporary Hackensack country deeds, see EJD Liber 1:200 (139 on verso)-199 (140 on verso), 211 (128 on verso)-210 (129 on verso), 210 (129 on verso)-209 (130 on verso), and 254 (85 on verso)-253 (86 on verso) and Liber A:328.

On April 18, 1674, during the brief time the Dutch regained control of Munsee country, a man identified as Harmen Hekam (elsewhere identified as Harman Hekan) purchased two adjoining twenty-acre lots in Marbletown. Then as now, Marbletown lies just beyond the Shawangunk Ridge along the lower Rondout Creek valley just west of what was then called Swaenenburgh (present-day Kingston). The buyer promised to pay five hundred bushels of corn for each plot in two yearly installments. The sellers pledged to plow the fields three days yearly during that time. Transcripts of the two deeds appear in KP 2:741–742. Harman Hekan did not hold onto the land long. For his March 3, 1679, sale deed to a neighbor conveying all but a barn on the property, see UCD Book H:253–254.

These otherwise unremarkable transactions were distinguished by the fact that Harman Hekan was an Indian. The first Esopus Indian, in fact, to buy land from colonists. He was also the first Native person in the Great Valley to agree, as stipulated in the second deed, "to pay all village taxes and obey the laws, and to behave as well as any Christian man." He additionally was the first Indian man chronicled with a surname in local records. Harman the Indian's name was Kawachhijkan. For Kawachhikan as a seller in a June 5, 1652, deed at Esopus, and Kawachhijkan as one of the Indians complaining on September 28, 1669, about nonpayment for lands sold to colonists, see Brink (1905–1914, 1:80–83); For other variations of his Indian name, see Haremamin in UCD Book I:768–774 and 778 and Harmamit in UCD Book H:629–630. Munsees and other Delawares frequently used contractions of names as nicknames. This custom probably helped people in Munsee country accept paired names after the European fashion, putting Dutch or English given names together with truncated Indian surnames. Such shortening also may have helped them accept use of shortened surnames after the full names' original owners died.

Harman Hekan was well known among the colonists. He was noted as "panajrock alias Harmen Hekon" in a September 17, 1683, deed to land in Ulster County in KTR 1:52–53. Colonists most frequently referred to him by his nickname Ankerop during his long life. The first indication that Anckrup was also known as Kawach-hijkan appears in his September 28, 1669, complaint that he was not paid for his lands at Esopus (in NYCD 13:436). The name probably was the Netherlandish equivalent of "bottom's up," the anker being a Dutch liquid measurement unit equivalent to 10 U.S. gallons. This is not the only possible translation. Modern-day Dutch people use the expression when hauling up an anchor. Among Harman Hekan's two documented wives was a daughter of Mamanuchqua named Dostou. Charles Wolley (in NAHC:38) devoted two pages of his journal expressing his amazement at the ease with which Harman's wife gave birth to a child. It is tempting to think that the child may have been Dostou's son Hendrick Hekan. For mention of a woman named Waragkies as Ankerop's wife in the August 18, 1705, sale of land on the Rondout Creek, see UCD Book AA:352; For Doestoe as Ochperawim's mother in the March 5, 1715, deed to land along the Rondout Creek, see UCD Book BB:380–381.

Harman Hekan became the apical ancestor of a family line that extends to the present. His descendants include Hendrick Hekan, also known by the names Aramochtan, Ochperawin, and Cockalalaman, and Jacob Hagan, who fought alongside the British from the Seven Years' War through to the Revolution. Forced into exile after the Revolution, Loyalist Hekan family members moved to the Six Nations Reserve around Brantford, Ontario. For Cockalalaman as a "Munsie" signing over land rights in Northern New Jersey at the Easton treaty meeting in October 23, 1758, see EJD Liber I-2:89–94.

There is another tantalizing possibility that the Hekan family in Esopus country is connected in some way to the contemporary Hegon family from the Saco River valley in western Maine. Esopus people were among Mahicans who periodically took refuge among Northern Indians as far east as Pennacook when warring with the Mohawks. Local chroniclers in both places resorted to the then unusual expedient of identifying members of both families by last names. The prominent sachem Mogg or Mugg Hegon killed while fighting colonists during King Philip's War, for example, was the son of the equally prominent Saco sagamore Walter Higgon. The name of Mary Megonusqua, who may have been Walter or Mogg's wife, mother, or sister, bears a resemblance to what Mamanuchqua's name might look like in another Eastern Algonquian language. Mamanuchqua may have been the otherwise unnamed woman identified as Harman Hekan's mother in a June 23, 1682, deed to land near Marbletown. This would make sense if Mamanuchqua, who was Dostou's mother, was what we call the maternal aunt of Harman Hekan. Such a possibility is reinforced in a deed signed the next day, separately listing Harman Hekan's mother and Mamanuchqua. Such a cross-cousin marriage would keep succession within their two influential families. Whether or not this was the case, succeeding generations in both places respectively adopted variants of Hekan or Hegon as a family surname. It is up to future investigators to see if these similarities are anything more than intriguing coincidences. For Harman Hekan's mother mentioned on June 23 and 24, 1682, deeds and Mamia Rioch (identified as a woman) mentioned in the latter conveyance, see UCD Book H:629–633 and Ulster County Patents on file in the New York State Library (hereinafter NYSL) SC 13274:245–247. For the Hegon family in the Saco Valley, see Baker (2004:87–89).

22. For land affairs in Esopus country at this time, see AP 2:57–59 and UCD Patent Book:15.

23. In AP 1:348–349, Wickerscreeke sachems Wissakano and Ammone (i.e., Wiechquaesgeck leaders Wessecanoe and Amond) first came to New York to answer charges that they were secretly supporting enemy Indians and to ask permission to bring home some of their people taking shelter among friends near Greenwich, Connecticut on March 29, 1676; Andros asked the two sachems to invite Northern Indians and recently displaced Mahicans to settle in New York on April 14, 1676, in AP 1:352–353; for minutes of the May 13, 1676, meeting where Hackensack and Tappan sachems promised to try to bring in "some of the other neighbor Indians" and Andros's May 30, 1676, instructions ordering trusted Mahicans to be sent on the same errand, see AP 1:368 and 375–376.

24. Wayattano was almost certainly the community identified by Brasser (1974:66) as Wyaghtonok, "at the river bend," and by S. Dunn (2000:47–53) as Westenhook, at the headwaters of the upper Housatonic River valley. For the April 27, 1676, meeting, see AP 1:358–359; for the July 20, 1676, Connecticut Council minutes reporting the movement from Powchassuck and their warning letter to Andros, see Trumbull and Hoadly (1850–1890, 2:466–467); for the August 19, 1676, letter reporting that Northern Indian survivors were headed across the Hudson River to a place identified as Paquiage and an examination of a captured Indian during the same month identifying the place as Powquiag, see Trumbull and Hoadly (1850–1890, 2:469–72); Pachquyak was one of five large flats along Catskill Creek sold by sachems representing the Catskill nation on July 8, 1678, in ERA 2:19–21 and 153; for identification of the general locale as Quaiack and the site of the archaeological site at Leeds, New York, see S. Dunn (2000:46).

25. This and the following paragraph synopsize Jennings (1984:149–164).

26. For the absence of aboriginal manufactures in late Susquehannock sites, see Kent (1984); for a cross-cultural examination of technology change in contact situations, see Cobb (2003).

27. For the Susquehannock Indian town on the Schuylkill in 1689, see C. Hunter (1983).

28. For his definition of the Covenant Chain alliance, see Jennings (1971:89–90); also see Jennings (1984) for a comprehensive history of the alliance to 1744.

29. For Mohawk references to the silver Covenant Chain, see Van Laer (1926–1932, 3:363) and LIR:154.

30. For extant Albany meeting minutes taken on April 24, 1677, see LIR:39–40; for the April 27, 1677, Kingston meeting, see NYCD 13:504–505.

31. For the June 4, 1677, Albany meeting minutes, see LIR:40–42; also see Jennings (1984:148–149) for this meeting as the place where the first silver Covenant Chain treaty involving New England was signed.

32. For the New York records of the July-August meetings in Albany, see LIR:42–49; for the Maryland records also mentioning "Mattawass or Delaware Indians" as parties to the agreement, see Browne et al. (1883-present, 5:269) in Jennings (1984:159–160); Mattawass may be a Nanticoke word similar to the Unami *matta awen*, "nobody."

33. For Five Nations depredations in New England, Maryland, and Virginia in the years immediately following the 1677 meetings, see Jennings (1984:162–171); for separate River Indian meetings bypassing Albany during the same period, see the Esopus Nicolls Treaty renewal meetings at Kingston on February 23, 1677, February 23, 1678, and February 5, 1679, in NYCD 13:401–402; for Tackapousha's friendship renewals in New York City on March 28, 1677, see NYCD 14:728 and April 2, 1678, in NYCD 14:735; for the April 25, 1678, meeting with Hackensack sachems in New York, see RCID:14–16; for the May 27, 1679, meeting between Raritan Indians living at Piscataqua (still called Piscataway, New Jersey) and East Jersey authorities at Elizabethtown, see GCOC 1:133.

34. Joris is another of those overlooked figures in Munsee history. He appears second on a list of Mahikander sachems attending a Covenant Chain meeting with Maryland and Virginia officials in Albany on July 19, 1682, in the only generally available published source mentioning his name (LIR:65–68). The only other published reference to the man, the July 10, 1679, statement identifying him as the sachem of the River Indians living below Albany, identifies him as a sachem known to colonists as both Joris and George (RLCC:61). After that, the trail wanders into less clear-cut territory.

Joris is mentioned in a series of unpublished depositions taken between 1726 and 1739 as the Dutch-speaking heir to Maringoman (in unpaginated Kakiac Patent Papers on file in the Goshen Historical Society, Goshen, New York). Maringoman was an influential sachem who signed a series of deeds conveying much of what is now Orange County, New York, to English purchasers between 1685 and 1704. The last manuscript mentioning Joris by name, a March 14, 1745, confirmation of land sales made north of Newark, New Jersey, identifies Yaupis (i.e., Joris) as a descendant of the original sellers, Memshe and Taphow, in EJD Liber E-3:105 .

Mention of an Indian man named Joris during the mid-eighteenth century argues against identifications suggesting that the earlier Joris was also the Catskill sachem Machakniminauw. The connection linking Joris with Machakniminauw is based on the July 8, 1678, sale of land at Leeds, New York, in ERA 2:19–21 and 153, identifying a man named Mamaetcheek as Joris (S. Dunn 2000:355). The former man died sometime before 1709. Joris may, however, have also been Arias Japis, also known as Paponnick, one of the Esopus proprietors who acknowledged receiving payment for the sale of lands near New Paltz on July 23, 1682 (UCD Book H:632). If so, he may also be the Pomponick variously identified as an Esopus, Wappinger, or Catskill Indian who participated in sales of Hudson Valley land north of New Paltz between 1663 and 1683 (UCD Book I:239 and ERA 1:335 and 2:55 and 63).

35. Noting that in matrilineal societies like the Iroquois, "fathers had no power to command children," Jennings (1984:44–46) provides a brief but cogent introduction to the subject.

9. DEVASTATION, 1679–1685

1. For a relation reporting that at least sixty children died of influenza within the space of one month in Seneca country in 1676, see JR 60:175.

2. The earliest report of the epidemic appears in the October 1, 1679, entry in DANCK:129; for the October 31, 1679, report of the disease among the Oneidas, see LIR:55; for the November 6, 1679, report of the epidemic in Quebec, see NYCD 9:129.

3. For Danckaerts's visit to the afflicted settler's house, see his October 1, 1679, entry in DANCK:129; for his great number observation, see the entry dated March 23, 1680, in DANCK:277; Stacy's August 12, 1680, letter to George Hutcheson was published in Anonymous (1681:50).

4. Rosaldo (1984 and 1989:1–19) examines how grief and rage fuel mourning war. Anthropologists have been using the term for at least a century (see Dorsey 1902); most recently, A. F. C. Wallace (1970) and Richter (1992) have used the concept to deepen understanding of motivations for Northeastern Indian warfare.

5. The Spanish Indian territory referred to was almost certainly Georgia or Florida. For the initial March 23, 1680, report, see DANCK:277; for the meeting with Tomachkapay (identified in the document as "the Minnissinke Sachamaker Rathquack") on September 12, 1681, see NYCD 13:551–552. The Minisinks were clearly wary of Brockholls. At a meeting in New York on April 9, 1684, he chided them for not coming earlier to formally welcome him to the province. Apologizing, they politely asked that they wait at Bergen until East Jersey settlers arrived to run a property purchase line (in NJCD 1:458).

6. For the preliminaries preceding the Albany meeting, see LIR:61–65 .

7. For propositions made by the commissioners at the Albany meeting and the Mahikander, Catskill, and Esopus responses, see LIR:65–68 .

8. Indiana University's Glenn A. Black Laboratory of Archaeology preserves English translations of extracts of French text detailing La Salle's dealings with the Loups at Miami first published in DEF 1:524–527 and 2:139–153 and has made them available online at www.gbl.indiana.edu/archives/miamis/.

9. La Salle noted that the Loups he met at the Miami River were Indians "from Boston, of Moraiganoe [Mohegan], Anhangane [Narragansett], of Mahigane [Mahican], of Menissens [Minisink], and from the Manathens, of Destcaraguetaga [Iroquois for Piscataway?], Coiracoitaga [Iroquois for Conoy?], Taractonga [Esopus], and those who live in between Manathes and Virginia" (in DEF 2:148–149).

10. For a brief survey of Grey Lock's life, see Calloway (1990:113–131). Calloway does not make so bold as to suggest the admittedly sketchy linkage between Ouiouilamet and Grey Lock, the man whose resolute resistance sparked Grey Lock's

War in New England between 1722 and 1727. The fact that the Ouiouilamet of 1681 would have been very old by 1722 does not mean the two could not have been one. Grey Lock's name alone suggests advanced age. Other elders like the Powhatan leader Opechcancanough waged vigorous war against the English well into their later years.

Linkages connecting Nanangoucy with Nanacuttin, by contrast, are fairly direct. Orecton served as proxy for an absent interested party identified as Nannacussey in the July 15, 1682, deed to land at the Falls of the Delaware in PA 1:47; Nannechesshon appeared in person to attest to the validity of Orecton's proxy on August 1, 1682, in WPHOA:76; he first appeared in colonial documents as Nenacutton in a deed to land at Little Egg Harbor in August 1674 (in WJD Book B:644); he appeared as Nannacus in the sale of Orecton Island on the Delaware in 1680 (in Bucks County Deeds Book 26:380); and finally as Nanacuttin, the uncle of Sehoppy (identified in the document as Mahomecun or King Charles) in the April 11, 1697, confirmation of the 1674 Little Egg Harbor deed (in WJD Liber B:644); linkage between Klas and Claes is more circumstantial and largely depends on Claes's status as a culture broker and his comparatively brief absence from Hudson Valley records while Klas was on the Miami River.

11. For analysis of European goods documented in mortuary contexts in Munsee country, see Pietak (1995). The fact that few of these graves have been found within the Munsee homeland may be attributed to erosion, destructive development, looting, and, more recently, to newfound respect for Indian interments and religious beliefs reflected in protective laws enacted through legislation like the Native American Graves and Repatriation Act.

12. For the May 4, 1681, sale of land at Raritan east of Bound Brook, see EJD Liber 1:193 (146 on verso); for the May 12, 1681, sale of land west of Bound Brook at Pepametapoke, see EJD Liber 1:192 (148 on verso); for the August 22, 1681, sale of land along the Matawong (i.e., Millstone) River around Manville, see EJD Liber 4:2; for the October 17, 1681, sale of land south of New Piscataway, see New Jersey Historical Society Manuscript Group 7, 1:1; for the November 1, 1681, deed to Ahanderamock at New Brunswick, see EJD Liber 1:187 (152 on verso); for the November 19, 1681, deeds to Matanucka Island at Raritan, and Tuckaramahackinge at the Forks of the Raritan, see EJD Liber 1:186 (153 on verso)-184 (155 on verso) for the April 20, 1682, sale of land at mouth of the South River, see EJD Liber 4:45; for the April 29, 1682, sale of land farther up the South River, see EJD Liber 4:68. For the October 29, 1681, sale of Aschacking in Hackensack country, see EJD Liber 1:188 (151 on verso)-187 (152 on verso); for the sale of Old Tappan on March 13, 1682, see EJD Liber 4:17–18 and RCID:50–52. For the February 16, 1682, letter from the Trustees to Governor Carteret halting purchases and patents, see O'Callaghan (1929:2).

13. Published transcriptions of these deeds may be found in OBTR 1:135–140, 146–156, 173–174, 183–187, 197–198, and 401.

14. For the prominent economic role played by bakers in colonial New York, see Middleton (2001); for Wessecanoe's deeds affirming Frederick Philipse's title to land at Pekantico (present-day Pocantico), Nippizan (present-day Nepperhan Creek),

and Weghqueghe (probably the Wiechquaesgeck locale at Dobb's Ferry, New York) along the east shore of the Hudson signed on December 10, 1681, April 13, 1682, September 6, 1682, and June 5, 1684, see WCH 1:268–271 and 507 and 2:135–136; for the June 3, 1682, deed, see WCD Liber A:181–184 and WCH 1:85; parenthetically, present-day Lake Oscawana is named after Askawanos. The land later came into the possession of the Van Cortlandt family.

15. For Katonah's participation in the December 12, 1680, Hop Ground deed at Bedford, see WCH 1:13–14 and BHR 1:xiv and 1–2; for Mamarranack's deeds to Euketapucuson and Honge near Rye, New York, signed on September 4, 1680, and October 8, 1681, see WCH 2:135–136.

16. For authoritative transcriptions of the much-reproduced early Pennsylvania deeds to lands along the Delaware River signed between July 15, 1682, and December 19, 1683, see R. Dunn et al. (1981–1986, 2:261–269, 353–355, 404–405); also see the map showing the boundaries of these deeds in R. Dunn et al. (1981–1986, 2:491).

17. For deeds signed by Wassackarous (variously spelled Saccatorey on November 17, 1675, Saccotorey on March 14, 1676, Sacotoreys on February 8, 1676, and Seketarius on December 19, 1683) in southern New Jersey and Pennsylvania between 1675 and 1683, see Salem County Deeds (Book 1:18, 19, and 42), New Jersey Historical Society West Jersey Manuscript Group 3:6, WPHOA:60–61 and 93–95, and F. Stewart (1932:62–66); for transcriptions of the July 15, 1682, deed and the August 1, 1682, addendum in which Kekerappamand (Taptawappamund), Pytechay (Peropay), Essepamachatte (Metapis), and Nannechesshon (Nanacuttin) confirmed their approval of the deed and sale price, see PA 1:47 and WPHOA:76–84.

New York governor Thomas Dongan blocked Penn's attempt to get a deed from the Five Nations giving him title to the entire Susquehanna Valley above the present-day New York–Pennsylvania state line. The Five Nations based their right to sell the land on what Jennings (1984:225–230) has shown to be an unproven claim that they conquered the territory from the Susquehannocks. Penn did manage to buy land along the lower Susquehanna from Unami Indians on Pennsylvania's contested southern border with Maryland.

18. Despite the sympathy of the Stuart kings for the many Friends (Quakers) who supported them financially, one enumeration in Pomfret (1962:131) indicates that more than twenty thousand of fifty thousand Quakers living in England were imprisoned at one time or another for refusing to take oaths and for falling afoul of other ordinances running counter to their consciences between 1670 and 1688.

Like many other provincial governors, Rudyard was a deputy of the province's official governor. Many provincial governors elected to remain in Europe, sending deputies or lieutenants to govern in their place. One of these was Scottish Quaker Robert Barclay, official governor of East Jersey and a prime supporter of the policy that brought large numbers of Scots to the province from 1683 to 1688. For developments in East Jersey at this time, see Pomfret (1962:130–198).

19. For the October 8, 1683, order prohibiting private Indian land purchases in West Jersey, see GCOC 1:479; for the similar orders requiring East Jersey settlers "to purchase and take up land in the proprietors' names (and no other) from the Indi-

ans as they see cause, or find it necessary" dated August 1, 1684, and April 9, 1685, see GCOC 1:196 and EJPBM 1:52–53.

20. For the board's July 20, 1683, instructions to Lawrie, see GCOC 1:172–173 and 184–185; for Querameck in the February 26, 1684, sales of two small tracts on the south side of the Raritan, see NJCD 21:57; for Ishavekak, Rumasehekah, and Shapundaqueho in the March 20, 1685, sale of land running six miles on either side of the South River, see NJCD 21:73; for Mindawassa's October 12, 1684, sale, see EJD Liber A:262 and RCID:59A–59C; for Memshe's sale on October 16, 1684, see EJD Liber A:263 and RCID:60–61; for Heckewelder's suggestions that Sehoppy's name either comes from *schwachpi,* "tired of staying in a place," or *scheyachbi,* a word that he translated as "along the water's edge or seashore," see LLN:383.

21. For Irooseeke's lease of Amoskake to Middletown, on July 16, 1684, see MCD Book B:17–21 and OTOM:251; for the May 14, 1685, board decision to buy Wickatunk, see EJPBM 1:59–60; for the February 25, 1686, deed to land at Wickatunk between Cheesquake and the South River, see EJD Liber A:264, NJCD 21:73, and RCID:65A–65B.

22. For Oyster Bay deeds signed between 1683 and 1686, see OBTR 1:172–176, 182–183, 282–289, 292–293 304–305, 313–314, 328–332, 370–371, 494, 502–503, and 545–546, 2:129–130, 248–249, 280–281, 301, and 331, and 5:126 and 130–132. For the October 29, 1683, power of attorney to Suscaneman and Werah for themselves and their sisters and children and the March 6, 1685, document permitting Suscaneman to relinquish all remaining Indian titles on their behalf, see OBTR 1:267 and 283–284; for Suscaneman's January 8, 1684, pledge to give equal shares to Tackapousha and every Indian man and woman with rights to the sold lands, see OBTR 1:182.

23. For examples of Oyster Bay deeds specifying such payments, see OBTR 1:282–283 and 304–305; for the February 19, 1684, deed of gift to Henry Bell, husband of a Narragansett woman living at Matinecock named Jane, see OBTR 1:313–314.

24. For the October 13, 1684, Flushing confirmation, see Thompson (1918, 3:27–28); for the July 20, 1684, Gravesend deed, see GTR Patent Book 1:316 and Book 3:61; for Katonah's November 22, 1683, deed to Quaroppas, see WCH 2:536.

25. Robert Livingston began putting together one of the larger private landholdings in the Hudson Valley during the summer of 1683. He obtained his first deeds from Tataemshatt, Tataemshatt's grandmother Mamanuchqua, and several of their friends and relations, including a number of Mamanuchqua's sons and brothers. They were a closely related mix of people of the kind you might expect to find living in the borderlands between Munsee and Mahican territory. Deed writer Livingston identified them as Mahikanders and Indian owners of Roeloff Jansen's Kill, the stream that continues to bear the same name and that runs through present-day Dutchess and Columbia counties just across the river from the Catskill Mountains. Several of these people, like Mamanuchqua, were clearly associated with Esopus communities. Information contained in the deeds also suggests more far-reaching ties with people elsewhere. Tataemshatt's brother's name, for example, was spelled Michiel after the French manner. The same documents noted that another brother

named Amesett was away "at Canada." Wherever else they lived, in Schaghticoke, Canada, or northern New England, members of this close-knit community continued to claim rights to land that Livingston wanted. He convinced them to give him deeds to six scattered tracts totaling about 10,000 acres around Roeloff Jansen's Kill between July 18, 1683, and August 10, 1685. Including unpurchased lands lying between these tracts, the Albany secretary obtained a manorial patent from Governor Dongan to a vast 160,000-acre holding he named Livingston Manor on July 22, 1686.

Livingston did not have enough money, goods, or credit to purchase all Indian lands in his patent outright. Like most colonists, he was cash poor and deep in debt. Better connected than many of their peers, go-ahead men like Livingston and Philipse often risked defying land laws requiring that they buy lands from Indians before patenting them as property. They felt that the respect, rights, and rents due manor lords justified the risks. They were also, however, painfully aware that angry Indians could expose them at any time. Renters, creditors, and placemen could and would use Indian complaints to pry away land and money for themselves. Bold but not stupid, Livingston would spend the next forty years securing his holdings by discreetly buying up remaining Indian-owned lands within his manor from the original signatories and their descendants. He did not register or record most of these deeds with proper authorities who may have taken offense at the way he disregarded proper procedure. Instead, Livingston quietly filed them for future reference among his personal papers. They were stored among a group of family papers evidently gathered by Philip Livingston to defend the family's estate in 1796. These were later donated by the family's lawyer to what was then the Long Island Historical Society in 1888, where they lay largely unnoticed until they were finally cataloged during the early 1970s.

For Livingston's Indian deeds, see the Brooklyn Historical Society Livingston Family Papers (1974.18), NYCD 13:572, and ERA 2:189–190; see Leder (1961) for the standard biography of Robert Livingston.

26. For the Indian deeds obtained by De Kay and his associates, see WCH 1:88–89 and WCD Liber A:190–194 and 198–199; for Philipse's final deed signed on June 5, 1684, see WCH 1:270–271 and 507; for Morris's February 7, 1685, deed, see WCH 2:463. Although the exceptionally garbled spellings of the scribe who wrote this latter deed make linkages exceedingly tentative, the men who signed as Taquamarke, Wanacapeen, and Awanawis may be Taphow, Wessecanoe, and Askawanos.

Taphance was identified as the son of Ponus in the January 7, 1667, confirmation deed affirming several earlier Indian sales in Stamford, Connecticut, that also reserved twenty acres for continued Indian occupancy in the town (in WCH 2:105 and FCH:700).

27. Extremely variable spellings of the Indian names in these deeds also make linkages more provisional than most. Future research may more clearly determine whether persons variously identified as Saghkaghkemeck, Sackoraghkigh, Sackhewagzien, Wecepwes, Weskkenon, and Wearpeakes as senior Rechgawawanck and Wappinger sachems in these and contemporary deeds in the area were Pierwim and

Wessecanoe; for the July 13, 1683, deed, see National Museum of the American Indian Archives Spec. No. 23/6875, Negative No. 39134, and RCID:53–55; for the August 8, 1683, deed, see Hasbrouck (1909:35–37); for the August 24, 1683, deed, see WCD Liber A:128–131 and WCH 1:86–87.

28. Dongan was much involved in land dealings. His acquisition of vast acreage in Orange and Ulster counties bears further scrutiny. Unlike the other first counties, thinly settled Orange was administered from New York City until 1691. Dongan used his position as acting administrator of the unsurveyed and still ephemeral county to directly acquire these lands. Like many other purchasers unable to fulfill title conditions requiring development within specified periods, Dongan had to let his purchases in Orange and Ulster revert to the Crown. These territories remained Crown lands until 1694, when one of Dongan's successors, Benjamin Fletcher, granted the land to John Evans.

Manuscript copies of Dongan's September 10, 1684, deed to the northern half of what later briefly became the manor of Fletcherdon (see below) may be seen in the Library of the New-York Historical Society (hereinafter NYHS) and in Ulster County Patents:43–44 in NYSL SC 13274. For a published version, see RCID:56–59; for the April 15, 1685, deed, see its manuscript copy in the NYHS under that date and the published transcript in RCID:62–65; beneficiaries of other Dongan patents like Frederick Philipse, Stephanus van Cortlandt, and the governor's secretary, John Knight, were among the witnesses attesting to the validity of the 1684 and 1685 transactions.

Knight bought a tract from the governor called Ketchawong above Croton-on-Hudson on March 20, 1686, that Dongan had purchased from Amond and Askawanos on August, 1685; for the deed and note confirming Dongan's sale of the tract to Knight, see WCH 1:92–93; see Knight's March 9, 1685, sale in NYCM-ILP Book 9:387; for his deed purchasing a tract from Esopus Indians on May 25, 1688, see UCD Book AA:74.

29. For the July 9, 1686, deed, which was later used in disputes over an area claimed by several settlers and two provinces, see RCID:66–69. Nicholas Depui witnessed the May 19, 1671, deed; Hendrick van Bommel interpreted and witnessed the April 13, 1671, and May 19, 1671, transactions. Jacobus de Harte inherited all of the original purchaser Balthazar de Harte's land in his will (Abstract of Wills in the Office of the Surrogate of New York County Book 25:235 on file in the NYHS). In the same will, Balthazar appointed his good friends and later property claimants Hendrick van Bommel and Jacobus Theuniszen de Kay as administrators of his estate.

30. For earlier versions of the analysis supporting these findings, see Grumet (1990a:34–38).

31. For the January 28, 1684, statement made by Witquescheach Indians apologizing to Dongan for not coming sooner "by reason of their sickness," see NYCM-ECM Book 5:43; for La Barre's October 1, 1684, report, see NYCD 9:242; for September 27, 1684, report of fever among the Abenakis, see JR 63:81–99); for Soquans's December 21, 1685, speech, which also informed the magistrates that their

sachem Wamsachko was near death and asking approval for a replacement, see LIR:95–96 .

32. Malaria is Latin for "bad air." Italian physician Francisco Torti made the earliest known use of the word in 1740.

10. SOLDIERING ON, 1686–1701

1. For Dongan's payment of £90, 11s. in goods listed in the September 10, 1684, deed, see RCID:56–57.

2. For Boughton Hill National Historic Landmark, see Grumet (1995:410–411).

3. For the fifty-six men and one hundred women and children coming to Schaghticoke, see LIR:77–79; for the August 4, 1685, River Indian invitation to a second party of Northern Indians returning to the New England frontier to join them at Schaghticoke, see LIR:82; for the Indians from Wawyachtenokse (identified as Detroit in NYCD 4:909), asking to move among the Wappingers on January 24, 1687, see LIR:108–109; for Dongan's August 4, 1687, request to the Five Nations asking that they allow "the Mahikanders that are at Ottowawa and further nations" to return, see Wraxall (in NYCIA:14).

4. For James's June 3, 1686, commission designating Andros as governor-general of the Dominion of New England, see Bartlett (1856–1865, 3:212–218).

5. For the June 24, 1687, Cow Neck reservation deed, see NYCM-ILP Book 4:174; for the June 27, 1687, Hempstead Harbor reservation, see OBTR 1:519.

6. Suscaneman used his other name, noted frequently in Oyster Bay records as Runasuck, to sign the title to the Hempstead Harbor reservation. He used variants of the name in the forms of Wallammassekaman, Olamoeerinck, Rumashekah, and Olomoseecunck in the April 8, 1687, June 4, 1687, March 20, 1689, and December 16, 1689, conveyances to lands in East Jersey on file in the EJD (Liber D:147–148, Liber M:447–449, Liber A:263, and Liber D:418).

7. For background on Coxe and his takeover of the West Jersey proprietary, see Pomfret (1956:150–164).

8. For Coxe's dream of a western fur empire and his other projects in West Jersey, see Pomfret (1956:165–166); for his efforts to open the way west through the Schuylkill River by joining a group of partners that bought land at Phoenixville, Pennsylvania, in 1685 and hired the family of Huguenot refugee Jacques Le Tort to manage the trading post built there, see Jennings (1984:231–232); Suscaneman used the names Lummaseecon and Romasickamon in the March 30, 1688, and April 9, 1688, deeds to Coxe's agent Adlorde Bowde (in WJD Liber B:179–180 and 181).

9. For an example of an inquiry ordering a settler to pay Indians for sold lands, see the minutes of the April 9, 1685, East Jersey proprietary board meeting in EJPBM 1:52–53.

10. For an example of the colonial real estate equivalent of the dog eating homework and the proprietary order issued on June 11, 1685, requiring that settlers bring Indians to testify to their purchases to the proprietary board, and the appearance of those Indians on July 10, 1685, see EJPBM 1:65–66 and 75–77; for an agreement

made with Navesink Patent settlers willing to take out proprietary patents at Manasquan made on July 9, 1685, see EJPBM 1:70; for a similar agreement with John Berry for land above Newark made on September 11, 1685, see EJPBM 1:89–91.

11. Catholicism was not without its divisions. Pope Innocent XI, for example, feared French expansion and floated loans to James's Protestant enemies.

12. For "scratch of a bear's paw," see Whitmore (1868–1874, 3:91–92); for Andros's commission expanding the Dominion of New England to include New York and the Jerseys signed by James on April 7, 1688, see NYCD 3:537–542.

13. For accounts of the 1687 French attack on the Senecas and construction of the first French fort at Niagara, see NYCD 3:453 and 464, 9:358–369, and LIR:99–102. For Dongan's early July 1687 requests that Schaghticokes send warriors to discourage French attacks on Albany and Schenectady and to help protect the Senecas, see LIR:128–132; for his May 1688 order directing Minisink and Long Island Indians to join the Five Nations and Mahicans against the French, see NYCM-GE Book 5:231 and 234.

14. Jesuit fathers who established the first mission towns on the St. Lawrence for mostly Mohawk converts in 1667 moved their key settlement to Caughnawaga near Montreal in 1676; for the measles outbreak at Caughnawaga and the Abenaki missions on the St. Lawrence, see NYCD 9:354; for the French abandonment of Niagara and Five Nations attacks and intrigue, see NYCD 9:384–386, 390–391, 393–396, and 402.

15. For August 14, 1689, depositions of settlers asserting that Andros had paid Wessecanoe to send warriors to attack New York, see NYCD 3:659; for more plausible rumors claiming that Upper River Indians agreed to join Abenaki and Pennacook kinsfolk against the English, see NYCD 3:611.

16. For the force sent by Leisler to Albany, see DHSNY 2:212–216; for "Wessecamer and Wuscawanus of Kightowan" promising to send six men on April 5, 1690, and "Mendoassyn and a captain called Wigworakum of Tappan" on April 19, 1690, reporting that they had sent twelve men to the Maquase and Sinnekes fifteen days earlier, see DHSNY 2:236; for the planned summer assault, see NYCD 3:712–713.

17. For the debacle at Lake Champlain and the spread of the smallpox epidemic, see NYCD 4:193–196 and 9:460–461, 490, and 513–515.

18. For Tackapousha's April 2, 1691, meeting with Sloughter, see NYCM-ECM Book 6:10–11 and Thompson (1918, 3:138); for the Schaghticoke welcome at a Covenant Chain renewal meeting in Albany on June 3, 1691, see NYCD 3:776–780 and RLCC:85; for the Highland Indians' welcome in July, see NYCM-ECM Book 6:33.

19. For Schuyler's journal of the campaign, see NYCD 3:800–805.

20. See NYCD 3:805–809 for the proceedings of the September 2–4, 1691, meeting at Albany.

21. For the ill-fated Dowaganhaes embassy, see NYCD 3:808 and RLCC:85.

22. See O'Callaghan (1861, 1:14) for the October 2, 1691, meeting; for the burn-damaged manuscript of Schuyler's message to Ingoldsby dated August 14, 1692, in CHM 2:227, see NYCM-GE Book 38:165.

23. For Chaouanans on the Miami, see DEF 2:page number illegible.

24. For excavations at the Zimmerman site of the Old Kaskaskia town near Starved Rock, Illinois, see Brown (1961); for a map and general survey of Shawnee movements during this period, see Callender (1978:623 and 630); for the August 18, 1692, meeting in Manhattan and Ingoldsby's commission to Schuyler, see NYCM-ECM Book 6:115–118.

25. For Pieter Schuyler's September 6, 1692, letter to Ingoldsby, see LIR:168–169; for Fletcher's October 25, 1692, meeting with the Five Nations, see Wraxall (in NYCIA:18–20); for Viele's journey west, see Broshar (1920:238–240).

26. For Frontenac's attack and the Anglo-Iroquois response, see IACNY:311–312.

27. The was not the only Indian pun involving an Englishman with a name associated with feathers. As mentioned earlier, William Penn was known by Munsees and Unamis as Miquon and by Iroquois as Onas, both meaning feather in their respective languages, and each referring to feathers used as pen quills. For accounts of Fletcher's ceremonial naming and other developments at Albany, see NYCD 4:19–24.

28. For the April 19, 1693, rumor of "350 Indians of Hagen Sack and Tapan" who could not then field one-tenth that number, see NYCM-ECM Book 6:192.

29. For Fletcher's May 10, 1693, meetings with the otherwise unidentified upper and lower Delaware River Indian delegations in Philadelphia, see CRP 1:372–373.

30. For the July 6, 1693, session with the River Indians, see NYCD 4:46–47. For the proceedings of the meetings held in Albany during June and July, where Fletcher barely managed to stop some of the Five Nations from defecting to the French, see NYCD 4:32 and 38–47 and LIR:170–172.

31. For unrest on Long Island between June 7, 1693, and October 1, 1694, see NYCM-ECM Book 6:205–206 and Book 7:92 and 97–98.

32. For Andrew Hamilton's message, see NYCM-ECM Book 7:52. On December 19, 1693, Fletcher's deputy in Pennsylvania, William Markham, received reports of a planned attack and was told about a packet of suspicious letters sent a year earlier to strange Indians called Shallnarooners in CRP 1:435–436. The latter were almost certainly Shawnees. Viele's outriders reached Albany on February 6, 1694, just one day before Schuyler arrived at Minisink. They brought word that seven nations of Indians numbering one thousand souls were on their way east (in NYCD 4:90). Schuyler's journal of his trip, which contains the earliest known firsthand account of a European visit to Minisink, may be seen in NYCD 4:98–99.

33. On August 17, 1694, Five Nations diplomats confirmed that they made peace with the "Dowangeshaws" and "Deonondas" (another name for Wyandots); no mention was made of Shawnees (Wraxall in NYCIA:26); for Shawnees meeting with Fletcher at Kingston in August 1694, see Calendar of State Papers, Colonial Series, America and the West Indies (1693–1696:1403) cited in IACNY:325; Viele was back east at Onondaga by February 18, 1695, in NYCD 4:123. This suggests that he either left the Shawnees before coming east with them or, more likely, went north to Onondaga to discuss matters with the Five Nations after completing his mission to

bring the Shawnees to Minisink country; for the June 11, 1696, meeting, see NYCM-ECM Book 7:196 and Fernow and Van Laer (1902:150).

Very few eyewitness accounts describing Indian towns in Munsee country survive. Two focus on the Shawnee towns just above Pechoquealin, the name they gave to the Delaware Water Gap. One of these was a very brief notice penned on June 24, 1719, by a member of a party of West Jersey men passing "through low lands of Pahucqualong near to the River side." On the way to meet with New York representatives to establish a mutually acceptable provincial border line, the writer observed "on the farther side of [the Delaware in Pennsylvania] are several small towns of the Shawannoc Indians" (Reading 1915:94).

Lewis Morris included the second, and far longer account in a letter written some twelve years earlier, sent to the secretary of the Society for the Propagation of the Gospel in Foreign Parts in September 1707. Morris, who had just been named president of the West Jersey Society Proprietary Council, shared Coxe and Viele's dream of a western trade empire. A man who easily mixed piety with profit, Morris traveled to the Water Gap to scout out lands targeted for acquisition by the West Jersey Society. Ostensibly inspired by the missionary impulse that had spurred the society's founding just six years earlier, Morris made a point of visiting the Shawnee towns in hopes that he could interest them in accepting a missionary belonging to the society while enlisting their support in westward enterprises.

Morris was surprised by what he saw and heard at the Shawnee town. Although he did not identify them as Shawnees, such an identification may be inferred from his observation that they were a colony of people who "about six or seven years since . . . came from the Bay of Mexico and the country around the great river of Mesasipi." He regarded them as "much more civilized, industrious, and ingenious than our Indians" and contrasted the melodiousness of their singing (possibly Catholic hymns) to what he termed the "barbarous harsh way used by our Indians in their songs." Morris was particularly impressed by the regular layout of their town and the "very large parade kept smooth and clean" at its center. These typical attributes of Indian town plans farther west in the Ohio Valley have not been found in Munsee country, neither in wide area archaeological excavations nor in other written descriptions. For the full transcribed text of Morris's letter, see Sheridan (1991–1993, 1:65–66).

34. For Fletcher's August 22, 1694, request to his brethren of the Five Nations, see NYCM-GE Book 39:185b; for Fletcher's July 15, 1695, order to Schuyler concerning the River Indians, see NYCM-ECM Book 7:146.

35. For the minutes of Fletcher's meetings with the Five Nations, Schaghticokes, and River Indians at Albany from September 29 to October 3, 1696, see NYCD 4:235–241; for his observations written on September 30, 1696, see AA 3:16; for continued River Indian help and Fletcher's knowledge that the Indians were "much inclining to make a peace for themselves," see Fletcher's November 9, 1696, letter in NYCD 4:234; for Fletcher's December 20, 1696, request that they concentrate and stay away from New England, see NYCD 4:248–249; for incidents involving

River Indians in New England during the spring and summer of 1697, see NYCM-GE Book 41:62 and NYCM-ECM Book 9:6.

36. For pre- and postwar population figures of the Five Nations, River Indians, and settlers in Albany County, sent to New York City by Albany officials on April 19, 1698, see NYCD 4:337.

37. For the political context of Fletcher's recall and the subsequent blackening of his reputation by his political enemies, see Leamon (1963); for deeds to lands at and around Fort Neck in Oyster Bay, see OBTR 1:357–359, 472–473, 520–521, 529–530, 2:11–12, 23–26, 29–30, 66–67, 106–108, 140–141, 220–222, and 275–277, and 4:513–514; for deeds in Huntington, see OBTR 1:595 and HTR 2:33–36, 41–43, 48–50, 54–56, 90–92, 95–97, 106–108, 121–122, and 370–371.

38. For Suscaneman's deeds to James Townsend and Moses and Gervis Mudge, see OBTR 1:527–528 and 2:116–117; for Suscaneman's December 6, 1694, complaint using the name Runasark and Fletcher's order, see NYCM-ECM Book 7:109.

39. For the lower Hudson Valley deeds, see WCH 1:22 and 312–313 and 2:140 and 290–292, RCID:72–74, BHR 2:149, Pelletreau (1886:11–12), and WCD Liber B:194–195 and Liber C:308–309; for Taphow's April 1, 1694, deed, see WJD Liber B:651; for Tatapagh's June 6, 1695, deed, see EJD Liber E:306–307; for Nowenock's March 10, 1690, deed, see EJD Liber K-Large:170. Colonists writing at this time used a wide variety of spellings to identify figures like Renap and Nackpunck. The men were identified as Oraghnap and Onagponk in the June 6, 1695, deed first mentioning them by name in EJD Liber E:306–307. Fifty-four years later to the day, Renap, also known as Rinnip, would be identified by his other name Noondauwiharind in UCD Book EE:63–65. Nackpunck would be subject to a similar degree of orthographic variation during his documentary career. For Heckewelder's suggestion that Pompton comes from *pihmtom,* "crooked mouth," see LLN:375.

40. See Leamon (1963:539) for the excessive Mohawk grants to lands largely in Mahican territory north of Albany; see RCID:75–76 for a printed transcript of the Kakiate Patent; a manuscript copy of the deed is preserved in the Kakiac Patent Papers in the Goshen Historical Society, Goshen, New York. Evans was captain of the ship that brought Fletcher to the colony. He became a key placeman in the new governor's administration, hence the reward of manorial status for Dongan's former estate in 1694. Succeeding governors outraged by Fletcher's conveyance of Fletcherdon and other massive estates to cronies managed to get the Crown to annul Evans's patent in 1699. Fletcherdon was broken up and sold piecemeal to other purchasers. Fees paid by subsequent buyers went into the coffers of officials in power at the time of resale.

41. For the Fort Neck deeds, see OBTR 2:260–261, 281–285, 287, and 289–290; for the Huntington deeds, see HTR 2:189–191, 204–210, and 213–216; for the Napanoch deed, see UCD Book CC:145 and Book DD:89–91; for the Fishkill deed, see Frank T. Siebert Collection Sale Catalog (1999:Lot 121), William Reese Company, New Haven, Conn.; for Weequehela's conveyances, see WJD Liber AAA:69, Liber F:534–535 and 573–574, and Liber K-Small:71, and PA 1:124–125.

42. For manor lands in private hands in 1700, see Judd (2005:953).

43. For Suscaneman's September 3, 1698, sale in Oyster Bay, see OBTR 2:54–55; for Charles Pamequa's November 1, 1698, sale in Huntington, see Pelletreau (1898, 1:367–371); for Wackemane's December 29, 1698, deed in Bedford, see BHR 4:225; for an example of a confirmatory Indian deed signed during these years, see Nanacuttin's April 11, 1697, confirmation of the earlier 1674 Little Egg Harbor deed, in WJD Liber B:644; for an example of sachems helping mark borders, see Suscaneman, Samos, and Werah's November 5, 1698, statement in a deed confirming mutually agreed boundaries for a tract sold earlier in Oyster Bay in OBTR 2:204.

44. For deeds to lands at the north end of the province signed between May 10, 1700, and July 29, 1702, see WJD Liber AAA:29–30 and Liber O:145–152, EJD Liber A-2:208–210, Liber C:148–149, and Liber E-3:105–107, and RCID:77–78 and 84–86; the January 12, 1701, deed is on file in the Cooperstown Library in Cooperstown, New York; another copy of the July 29, 1702, deed is on file in New Jersey Historical Society Manuscript Group 3:16.

45. For Weequehela's deed sales made between August 13, 1700, and April 29, 1702, many signed in company within his factotum Quanolam, see EJD Liber C:200 and 231, Liber G:128–129 and 319, and Liber H:170–173 and 220–221; for Caponokonickon's conveyances, see EJD Liber C:273–274; for contemporary Esopus conveyances, see Dostou's April 19, 1700, deed in NYCM-ILP Book 22:276, Cockalalamin's June 3, 1700, deed in UCD Book AA:229–230, and the copy of the August 10, 1700, conveyance on file in the NYHS.

46. For Indian deeds in the town of Huntington signed at this time, see HTR 2:258–262, 263–270, and 272–282; Smith's nickname dated back to 1682, when he served as the last English governor of the city of Tangier in Morocco before their evacuation in 1683; for William Smith's July 2, 1700, reservation grant of fifty acres at Poosepatuck, one hundred acres at Mastic, fifteen acres at Constable's Neck, and ten acres near Indian Point, see Brookhaven Town Records (Book B:358–359).

47. For histories of the Poosepatuck reservation community, see Gonzalez (1984) and Strong (1997:261–293).

48. For Claes the Indian's August 13, 1701, confirmation affirming his mother's rights to lands within the Yonkers purchase, see WCH 2:587–588; for Katonah and company's deeds and deed confirmations to lands in northeasternmost Westchester County, see WCH 1:29–30 and 2:106–108 and BHR 2:160–161.

49. For Heathcote's deeds and confirmations of earlier sales signed by Patthunck and his associates, see NYCM-ILP Book 3:33, WCD Liber C:14, 96–98 and 369–370, and Liber G:108–109, as well as Scheide Library Collection (Indian Deeds:20), Firestone Library, Princeton University, and an original state of Patthunck's February 24, 1702, deed on file in the Richard M. Lederer Local History Room, Scarsdale Public Library; also see De Lancey (1886:33–34). Abstracts of many, but not all, of these deeds are published in WCH 1:29–30, 210, 475–476, and 699–701 and 2:106–108 and 211–212; for a biography of Heathcote, see Fox (1926).

50. For the treaty proceedings, see NYCD 4:896–911; for "dubious privilege," see IACNY:362; for points of view on the treaty taken by different scholars, see Havard (2001:162–163).

51. The long-time standard text on the 1701 Montreal Treaty (A. F. C. Wallace 1957a) has been enlarged by Havard (2001).

11. Great Peace, 1702–1713

1. For the significance of nonevents, see Fogelson (1989).

2. Shoemaker (1999) points out that gender metaphors were widely used in Indian councils during colonial times, noting that Iroquois made symbolic references to Delawares, Catawbas, and Cherokees as women; she suggests that basic similarities in Indian and colonial military divisions of labor in which men went to war and women did not account for what she calls "the gendered language of councils" (Shoemaker 1999:255); for the Shawnee sachem's June 7, 1732, letter stating that the Iroquois put metaphorical petticoats on his people as well as on the Delawares, see PA 1:329–330. Jennings (1984:45–46, 263, 159–162, and 301–302) looks at the primary documents and summarizes the various interpretations of reasons why Iroquois symbolically referred to Delawares as women in councils; also see Miller (1974).

3. For the July 6, 1694, Philadelphia meeting, see CRP 1:447–449; for the Minisink sachem's comment at a meeting in New York on July 19, 1709, see NYCM-ECM Book 10:695.

4. Few views of traditional Munsee society are more widely held than the idea that agriculture was women's work and hunting was a man's preserve. A closer look at this seemingly ironclad dichotomy reveals considerably greater variation. Accounts of actual hunting practices reveal that women participated in game drives, trapping, carcass transport, and, on occasion, in the supposedly exclusively masculine domain of stalking and still hunting. Young men, elders, and children, for their part, often performed farmwork, helping to burn off farm fields, break ground, and stand guard over garden plots. Observations by Rhode Island founder Roger Williams suggest even greater layers of complexity. He wrote that Narragansett children, old men, and loving husbands helped "the woman which (by the custom of the country) they are not bound to." Such examples show how widely accepted concepts like the sexual division of labor often more closely resemble cultural ideals than social realities. For Williams's quote, see Axtell (1981:122–123); for discussion contrasting ideal and real sex roles, see Grumet (1980:54–56).

As mentioned earlier, Mamanuchqua, "striped (blanket?) woman" was the most prominent Esopus woman of her era. She went on to become ancestor to a prominent Wappinger and Mahican lineage. One of her daughter's sons, Tataemshatt, was an influential sachem associated with the Catskill, Wappinger, and Taconic communities. A great-grandchild, Tschoop, was the first Mahican convert baptized by the Moravian brethren in the New World. For more on Mamanuchqua as Esopus sachem, see Grumet (1980:52); for her genealogical position as apical ancestor of the first Mahican Moravian converts, see Merritt (2003:328–329); Tataemshatt's political connections are suggested in a deed to land at the Long Reach in the mid-Hudson Valley dated September 3, 1683, signed by Wappinger and Esopus Indians preserved in KTR Book 1:239–240; only one of the signatories, the Esopus sachem Pemmyrawech, is identified by political affiliation in this document; the name of the man signing as "Kakeroni for his brothers named Hans and Tapowars" appears elsewhere as a resident of Catskill in such forms as Kachketowaa and Kachtowaa (S. Dunn 1994:316). These may be cognates for *Cockalalaman*, the name of a son (Hendrick Hekan) of Dostou and a generational brother of both Tatemshatt and Pemmywrawech. Tataemshatt, Pemmyrawech, and Cockalalaman were all grandsons of Mamanuchqua. Each also had links to the Esopus and Wappinger communities.

5. Pennsylvania authorities were shown how Unami-speaking people metaphorically linked women and children with tribute payment at a meeting at Philadelphia on May 19, 1712. Listening to their speaker recite the messages they were sending to the Five Nations, they noted that the last twenty-four of thirty-two message-bearing wampum belts "were all sent by women, the Indians reckoning the paying of tribute becomes none but women and children" in CRP 2:548.

For references to attacks made on people in Munsee country neglecting to make tribute payments, see the February 1643 attack mentioned earlier in this volume and the February 7, 1694, Minisink concern that Senecas may have attacked one of their hunting parties in retaliation for not making payments in NYCD 4:98–99.

6. Women represented themselves as interest groups at least twice during colonial times. For the first incident where Esopus women and young men referred to as "Barebacks" urged their sachems to make peace with the Dutch in 1663, see NYCD 13:363–364; the second occurred at the abovementioned May 19, 1712, meeting. In both cases men delivered the women's messages.

7. For the concept of the commons, see Hardin (1968).

8. For discussion debunking what he calls the "trek tale tradition" from the mountains to the shore, see Boyd (2005:13–22).

9. For poorhouse production of wampum in Albany, New York, see Peña (1990).

10. Although this is far from the extrapolation of 540 to 900 produced by multiplying the 90 River Indians enumerated in 1697 by factors of 6 to 10, the 294 to 490 figure for Indians in Munsee country includes neither Mahicans nor the several hundred people living at Schaghticoke also part of the 1697 River Indian warrior estimate.

11. For French Indian ambassadors meeting with Loups and other Indians on the Miami River between December 29, 1700, and March 22, 1701, see Havard (2001:100–102).

12. For New York population figures, see Lustig (2005:363).

13. For Mid-Atlantic population figures, see Horn (1993, 2:302).

14. Caleb Heathcote succinctly laid out the problem in a memorial addressed to the Board of Trade on July 16, 1715. Writing of risks run by causing "prodigious numbers" of Indians farther west to defect to the French, he urged that the king should assure them that all grievances would be redressed "till we have our country better settled and secured and the French rooted out, and then we may expect to

have the heathen on better terms," adding, almost as an afterthought, "although justice ought forever to be done them." For Heathcote's memorial, which also called for the construction of a line of frontier forts, see NYCD 5:432–434.

15. The few claims for Indian lands taken for debt could be complicated affairs; a March 25, 1703, claim of Stephanus van Cortlandt's widow Gertruijd and their son Oloft for three necks on the south shore of Long Island (in NYCM-ILP Book 3:117) was followed on June 1 by a deed ceding one of the necks, called Campawis, for £83, signed by Wamehas and fifteen of his people (in the April 12, 2006, sale inventory of the William Reese Company, New Haven, Conn.). The signatories affirmed in a codicil appended to the deed on October 14, 1703, that they had received £53 from Stephanus three years earlier and accepted the additional £30 from his widow to seal the deal. For another example, see Robert Sanders's June 4, 1699, claim that Punguamis pawned his land for "value of seventy beavers and being ten years gone to the Ottowawas and his brother Corpowin now going to the war desires that the said Robert Sanders keep the land of his brother called Oghotackon till his brother pays him the said sum of seventy beavers," in NYCM-ILP Book 3:60. For extensive litigation over this deed, see papers stored in the Frederick Ashton De Peyster Manuscripts, Box 1, Deeds, in the NYHS.

For the two mortgages securing Harman Hekan's land purchases on April 18, 1674, see KP 2:741–742; for Schermerhoorn's January 26, 1675, mortgage of land at Catskill, see AP 1:121 and AHC 3:106–107; for Tapias the Highland Indian's May 16, 1683, mortgage of land in present-day Putnam County, New York, see NYCD 13:572 and ERA 2:182–183.

16. Cornbury arrived in New York at a time when disagreements were most workable in the colonies if the price was right. He had been sent by Queen Anne, his cousin and a sister to Queen Mary (who had died in 1694). Anne, who reportedly detested Cornbury, had just ascended to the English throne following the death of the late Mary's widower, King William III, on March 8, 1702. Infuriated by Louis XIV's recognition of the late James II's son Edward as the rightful king and determined to thwart Louis's plans to place his own grandson on the recently vacated Spanish throne, Anne joined with Holland and Austria to declare war on France on May 14, 1702. Europeans still know the conflict as the War of Spanish Succession. Americans call it Queen Anne's War. Forests of adjectives have grown up around Lord Cornbury and his administration of New York. For a guide through the thicket, see Bonomi (1998).

17. Although they had to give up political authority, East and West Jersey proprietors managed to maintain control over real estate within their charter bounds. Relations in the united royal colony of New Jersey and New York, however, remained testy. Cornbury adopted the Indian Purchase Act passed by the New Jersey Assembly on November 24, 1703, requiring the governor to issue licenses to purchase Indian land in New Jersey only to proprietors or people bearing certificates from them. He refused, however, to accept other legislation known as the Long Bill that invalidated the Elizabethtown and Monmouth patents and granted other advantages favoring proprietors in New Jersey at the expense of investors from New York and England. For this and other developments attending the birth and first years of New Jersey, see Sheridan (1981:35–68).

18. The classic study of the New York fur trade at this time is Norton (1974); also see Parmenter (2005:614–615) for a concise summary.

19. Soquans, speaking for the Schaghticokes at their first meeting with Cornbury on July 20, 1702, in Albany reckoned that they had 110 fighting men at Skachcock. The 87 other fighting men mentioned by Soquans "below the town" were probably Schaghticoke and Mahican Upper River Indians living between Catskill Creek and the Hoosic River. The complete absence of any mention of Lower River Indians in meeting proceedings (they had met with Cornbury earlier in New York City), suggests they were not in attendance. For the Albany conference, see NYCD 4:990–998.

20. Like colonists everywhere, settlers dreamed of finding gold, silver, and diamonds in Munsee country. Although men like Arent Schuyler tried to realize scaled-down dreams of mineral wealth in copper, iron, or lead, practical mining in the region had to wait for the technical advances of the second industrial revolution. Even with modern methods, more recent miners and quarry masters have had to make do with the even more prosaic but still considerable wealth to be found in sand, gravel, shale, trap rock, brownstone, and limestone. Taking a long look at traditions regarding early mining enterprises near the Delaware Water Gap, Kraft (1996) conclusively disproved local legends of old mine roads and ancient copper works at Pahaquarry.

21. For the major Cheesecocks Patent purchases made on December 30, 1702, and June 12, 1704, see OCD Book B:453–455 and RCID:87–88 and 92–93; for the Wawayanda purchase to land east of the Kittatinys made by a syndicate headed by a New York City lawyer on Cornbury's council named John Bridges on March 5, 1703, and patented on the following April 29, see OCD Book B:23–24 and RCID:79–81.

22. For Kierstede's claim, see NYCM-ILP Book 3:26; Kierstede served as one of the interpreters in the June 11, 1703, Minisink deed.

23. For Tietsoort's claim, which he supported with an October 15, 1698, purchase license and a June 30, 1707, Indian deed that have both disappeared in the intervening years, see NYCM-ILP Book 4:104.

24. For the May 28, 1696, orders relating to purchases made at Waghhackemmick by syndicates led by Rutsen and Swartwout, see Fernow and Van Laer (1902:115); for the June 8, 1696, deed to Menissing and Waggackemack, see UCD Book CC:145 and DD:93; for Swartwout's October 18, 1699, petition, see NYCM-ILP Book 2:275.

25. For the September 12, 1702, Aertsen and Swartwout petitions, see NYCM-ILP Book 3:84; for the March 5 and 6, 1703, Wawayanda deeds, see OCD Book B:23–24 and RCID:79–83. Although most of the Wawayanda purchasers signed both deeds, Bridges' syndicate acquired the March 5, 1703, deed; for French's license to buy Minisink, see Fernow and Van Laer (1902:181); for the June 11, 1703, Minisink deed, see RCID:89–91 and Manuscript No. 414 in the Newberry Library's Ayer Collection in Chicago, Illinois. For biographical sketches of the Minisink Patent investors, see La Potin (1974:29–34).

26. Taphow appears as the witness Tapousie, Claes appears as Clauss, Sherikham as Chuckhass, Nowenock as Nannawitt, and Nackpunck as Moghopuck on the March 5, 1703, deed; Renap appears as Rapingonick on the March 5, 1703, deed and Orapequine on the March 6, 1703, conveyance.

Tortured renderings do not necessarily make it impossible to connect differently spelled names with particular individuals; Tindemunge, Samawon, and Pachkiskham in the June 11, 1703, Minisink deed were almost certainly the minor signatories Tindemossigton, Sansman, and Pakiskeham mentioned in the June 8, 1696, Napanoch deed signed by Harman Hekan and Tatapagh on file in the UCD Book DD:90.

27. For the August 1704 Minisink Patent, see NYCM-ILP Book 7:266–270; Wawasowaw and Kisowaw are identified in the March 5, 1703, deed as Wawassowaw and Kisekaw and as Wawastawaw and Quilpaw in the March 6, 1703, conveyance; for Pieter Schuyler's March 30, 1703, letter to Rip van Dam summarizing the interview, see NYCM-ILP Book 3:177; for Wilson's January 1, 1704, petition for a patent for his Minisink land, including Minisink Island, see NYCM-ILP Book 3:163.

28. For Hardenbergh's July 18, 1706, license application, see NYCM-ILP Book 4:88; for Hardenbergh's deed of March 22, 1707, from Nanisinos, see NYCM-ILP Book 4:92; for Rutsen's deed to a large tract extending west to the East Branch of the Delaware River signed by "Nesinos" for £200 on July 31, 1706, and another for an adjacent tract signed by "Shawaghkommin alias Jochem" for £83 on November 2, 1706, see UCD Book AA:400–401. Similarities in the orthographies "Nanisinos," "Nesinos," "Nashingloans," and "Nomalughalan" (see note 9, following chapter) suggest that all are alternative spellings for "Maringoman."

29. For the August 3 and 27, 1743, records of armed Indians barring Hardenbergh's surveyors, see typescripts filed under those dates in the Philhower Collection, Special Collections, Alexander Library, Rutgers University; for the June 6, 1746, conveyance, see UCD Book EE:63–65; for the August 2, 1746, instrument, see UCD Book EE:61–63; Johannis Junior went on to become an officer in the Continental army during the Revolution; one of his sons, named Johannes, is most remembered today as the Ulster County slave owner of Sojourner Truth.

30. For later developments on Hardenbergh and other Hudson Valley patent lands, see Ellis (1946), Kim (1978), and Mark (1940).

31. The vast bulk of the acreage taken up within the Minisink and Hardenbergh patents remained thinly settled for a long time. Only hardier pioneers like Tietsoort and the Swartwout brothers initially chanced it in the upper Delaware Valley. Few others would buy land during wartime on a dangerous frontier astride the bitterly contested New York–New Jersey border, just as few would want to purchase disputed territory still occupied by unwelcoming Munsees and Shawnees once peace returned. Colonists eventually began settling the Upper Delaware Valley above Minisink by the late 1700s. For the time being, however, the region mostly attracted squatters looking for inaccessible out-of-the-way places where they could live unbothered by rental agents or tax collectors.

32. For Taphow, Claes, and Memshe's confirmation on June 1, 1702, and the July 29, 1702, sale, see EJD Liber M:555–556, NJHS MG 3:16, and RCID:84–86; for Heckewelder's suggestion that Whippany comes from *whiphanne,* "arrow creek, where the wood or willow grows of which arrows are made," see LLN:375.

33. For Weequehela's land sales in Monmouth and Middlesex counties, see EJD Liber C:275–276 and Liber H:147, 166–167, and 220–222 and MCD Book E:159–161; for Caponokonickon, Sehoppy, Nimham I, and Weequehela's sales along the Delaware, see WJD Liber AAA:425, 434–435, and 443–445 and EJD Liber C:273–274.

34. For deeds signed by Katonah, Patthunck, Wackemane (who signed some deeds as Sackima Wicker, a pun on Wickers Creek and an assertion in name form of the Wiechquaesgeck sachemship), and others between 1702 and 1705, see WCD Liber E:1–2 and Liber G:531, NYCM-ILP Book 4:58, NYCM-ECM Book 9:556–557, WCH 1:31–33, 211, and 702–703 and 2:142–143, Pelletreau (1886:16–18 and Plate 2), and BHR 2:167 and 172 and 4:404; for Wamehas's deeds in Huntington between 1703 and 1707, see NYCM-ILP Book 3:117, OBTR 2:255–257, and HTR 2:282–294; see the aforementioned Reese and Company Sale Inventory of April 12, 2006, for a copy of the June 1, 1703, deed to Campawis Neck; for deeds at Esopus signed from 1705 to 1707, see UCD Book AA:352–353 and 400–401 and NYCM-ILP Book 4:92.

35. For the April 23, 1702, meeting, see CRP 2:14–18.

36. The July 15, 1703, minute fragment states that "several Indians from the southward called Shawannos Indians made their propositions to his excellency." Cornbury gave them "a present of a gun, 3 bars of lead, 2 pounds of powder, and 4 shillings cash." They left the following day after Cornbury answered their propositions. For what remains of the record of the meeting, see NYCM-ECM Book 9:288–289; for Peter Bezalion's May 18, 1704, message to Pennsylvania authorities in Philadelphia, see CRP 2:145; for the two Shawannais meeting with the governor and council in Philadelphia on May 6, 1705, see CRP 2:183.

37. For the June 20, 1704, Albany meeting with "three Mohoggs and some River Indians and Waganhaer come from Tiogsagrondie," see LIR:196–197. Tiogsagrondie was the Wyandot name for the multinational Indian community that gathered around Detroit after 1701.

38. For the Indians joining Nicholson's force at Schuyler Flatts, see LIR:197.

39. For the April 25, 1709, invitation to the Shawnees and a list of gifts to be presented to them, see NYCM-ECM Book 10:301–302; for New Jersey's May 30, 1709, invitation to Weequehela, the Minisinks, and the Shawnees, see NJCD 13:331; for Weequehela's June 3, 1709, demurral, see NJCD 13:350; for the July 19, 1709, Minisink "squas" response, see NYCM-ECM Book 10:697; for June 21 and July 2, 1709, orders to round up Long Island Indians for service against Canada, see NYCM-ECM Book 10:679 and 687; for sixty River Indian warriors and men from four Iroquois nations receiving presents at Albany on July 16, 1709, see Wraxall (in NYCIA:69).

40. For the visit of the Four Indian Kings to London, see Bond (1952) for what is still the basic history, Garratt (1985) for art and literature produced during the trip, and Hinderaker (1996) for its larger cultural context.

41. For the June 27, 1711, order to raise a force of Long Island Indians and September 12, 1711, report on the problems encountered in recruiting them, see NYCM-ECM Book 10:599 and NYCD 5:253; for a listing of forces gathered for the attack on Canada made on August 20, 1711, including "19 warriors from the Livingston Manor area, 21 from the Hudson Highlands, 38 Schaghticokes, 54 Mahikanders or River Indians, and 26 Shawanoes who are tributary to the Sennekas," as well as 656 Iroquois warriors, see NYCD 5:265–267 and Wraxall (in NYCIA 1915:91).

42. For the June 8, 1711, "Tuscaroroes" visit to "Conestogo," see CRP 2:511–512; for the September 21, 1710, visit to Philadelphia of Ojuncho, "the queen of the Conestogo Indians" announcing the coming of "Connois" refugees among them, see CRP 2:516.

43. For the May 20, 1708, New York invitation carried by a River Indian, see Wraxall (in NYCIA:53); for the June 2 and June 30, 1712, meetings in Kingston discussing rumored conspiracy plots and Shawanno immigrants, see entries under those dates in the Minutes of the Court of Sessions of Common Pleas of Ulster County in the NYSL.

44. For Hunter's July 3, 1712, invitation to the Tuscaroras, see NYCM-ECM Book 11:115–116; for Robert Hunter's life and career, see Lustig (1983); for the September 24, 1714, meeting where it was declared that "Tuscarore Indians are come to shelter themselves among the five nations; they were of us and went from us long ago and are returned," see NYCD 5:387; for the September 15, 1716, statement that "the Sennekas are became a more numerous nation than the rest (by the accession of the Tuscarores and other Indians inhabiting about the Branches of the Susquahanna River)," see Wraxall (in NYCIA:115).

45. Word reached Hunter in New York on May 13, 1714, that the Five Nations had summoned all Indians living between the Jerseys and the Carolinas to a meeting at Onondaga where New Yorkers were barred and all informing them threatened with death. Although Hunter worried that this might be the beginning of an Indian conspiracy, it probably marked the opening moves in a mobilization to send warriors south to avenge the Tuscaroras (NYCM-ECM Book 11:242 and LIR:221–222). Such a purpose was indicated by the thirty recently taken prisoners noted in Hunter's July 25, 1715, letter to the Board of Trade, reporting his intentions to ask the Five Nations and Indians on "Sesquanna" to make war "upon these who have lately attacked Carolina" in NYCD 5:417; for Jayapen (Tatapagh) and Menakahekan listed among the six Susquahanna sachems having captives from the Carolinas mentioned in a letter to Hunter written on October 17, 1715, and received or logged in on November 12, 1715, see NYCD 5:464. For Heckewelder's suggestion that Manawkyhickon's name comes from *monachkhican,* "an instrument for digging the ground—pick axe, grubbing hoe, spade, etc.," see LLN:386.

46. For the Great Southern War, see Aquila (1983); for movements of Saponis, Tuteloes, and others, see Merrell (1989).

12. UNMOORED, 1708–1742

1. For "Catoonah, Sachem of Ramapoo" and Wackemanes's September 30, 1708, sale to the Norwalk men, see WCH 1:392–393 and FCH:631–632; for Nimham I and Sherikham's (signing as Sekomeek) October 8, 1712, sale of land in Dutchess County, see NYCM-ILP Book 5:124; for Livingston's May 13, 1713, deed from "Tataamshat chief sachem of Taghkanik and Roeloff Johnsons kill and Wampopoham, his brother commonly called by the Christians Machiel, another sachem of the said places," and others, see Folder 17 in the Livingston Family Papers on file in the Brooklyn Historical Society.

2. For Mochosconge listed on the July 26, 1708, deed in land at Dock Watch Hollow, see EJD Liber K-Large:131; for Taphaow, Mohusgwungie, and their associates signing the August 13, 1708, Makseta Cohung deed, see EJD Liber I:210–211 and the manuscript copy on file in the NJHS; for Taphow (signing as Pecca Chica, a variant of his other name, usually spelled Papejeco) and company's September 16, 1709, sale of the Wagaraw tract in the Pequannock Valley, see RCID:94–96; for Sherikham, Memereskum, and Tapheem signing the November 18, 1709, sale of land at Ramapo, which also contained the last documentary appearance of Claes, signing as Touwitwitch, see EJD Liber I:319–321 and RCID:97–104; for "Memerescum sole Sachem of all the Nations of Indians on Remopuck River, and on the West and East Branches thereof, on Sadle River, Pasqueek River, Narashunk River, Hackinsack River, and Tapaan," Taphome, and others selling land next to the Ramapo tract on May 9, 1710, see EJD Liber I:317–319, the manuscript copy on file in the NJHS, Anonymous (1924:300–304), and RCID:105–108; for Arent Schuyler's April 12, 1712, purchase of land near Wawayanda in New Jersey from Tapgow and several others, see National Museum of the American Indian Archives, Specimen Number 24/6665, Negative Number 40047; for "Papesecop commander or sachem of the Indians inhabitants of a part of what the English call the north part of Jersey," and others' September 3, 1714, deed to land from Singac to Pompton Falls, see BCD Book A:5 and RCID:109–111; a transcript of the November 10, 1714, deed from Nowenike and Tokuny for land at the Dead River was produced by Richard S. Walling from an original copy in the Middlesex County Early Records (Land Deeds 1714–1722:234–236) in the Special Collections of the Alexander Library, Rutgers University.

For Hippaquonon, Shushkamin (Nimham I), Ochquaolon (Weequehela?), and Succolum (Quanolam) signing the May 31, 1709, sale of land at Rocky Hill, see Works Projects Administration 1940, 1:12; for Hippoquanow in the June 1, 1709, deed to land at Crosswicks, see EJD Liber I:234–235; for Weequehela signing as Wickwala in the July 15, 1709, deed to land in the upper Millstone Valley, see MCD Book E:161–163; for Nimham I putting his mark on the October 7, 1709, sale of three hundred acres west of Flemington as Squahikkon, see WJD Liber BB:323–324; for Memerescum signing as Matamisco on the October 13, 1709, deed to land at Lamington, see WJD Liber B-2:274–275.

3. For Lewis Morris's deed to land west of the Lamington Falls signed by Memerescum as Matamisco on November 13, 1709, see WJD Liber BBB:207–208; for Manawkyhickon signing as "Minckhockamack commonly called and known by

the name of Indian Tom" on the August 16, 1711, "Great Patent" in Hunterdon County made out to Lewis Morris's agent, see WJD Liber BBB:206–207; for Morris's January 17, 1712, purchase of land between the Lamington and Musconetcong rivers from Quinomeck, see WJD Liber GG:458–460.

For Daniel Coxe and company's first August 18, 1713, deed to land from the Musconetcong River north to a point well above the Delaware Water Gap, from Monaukahukon (Manawkyhickon) and Massamiska (Memerescum); their second deed from Laparomza (Lappawinza), Nawoonaka, (Nowenock), Sasakaman (Nimham I), and a person identified as Wowopkoshot; their third from Wenacanikoman (Manawkyhickon); and their fourth from Quonamaka (Quinomeck) and Tolakamis, see WJD Liber BBB:140–147. For Namaliskont (Maringoman) along with Nawishawan (Nowennock), Paquasha (Taphow), Shopawa (Sehoppy), and Walough Pekomon (Manawkyhickon) selling land north west of the rivers Pesaick (Passaic) and Pequanake (Pequannock) on November 1, 1714, see WJD Liber N:179–183. For Heckewelder's suggestion that Lappawinza's name comes from *lapawinzoe*, "he is gone again, gathering nuts, corn, or anything eatable," see LLN:386.

4. For Heckewelder's suggestion that Shamokin comes from *shahamoki* or *shahamokink*, "place of eels," see LLN:363; for the belated December 16, 1714, proclamation issued by Governor Hunter, a political enemy of Coxe's, asserting his sole authority to issue licenses for purchasing land from Indians in New York and New Jersey, an act that put a virtual halt to all further Indian sales during the remaining four and one-half years of his administration, see NYCM-ECM Book 11:284.

5. For Manawkyhickon's signing of the already cited deeds to lands in New Jersey along the middle Delaware River valley in present-day Hunterdon, Warren, and Sussex counties finalized between 1711 and 1713 under the orthographies Minckhockamack alias Indian Tom, Menakahikkon, and Wenacanikoman, see WJD Liber BBB:140–145 and 206–207; for his presence on the Susquehanna in 1715, see NYCD 5:464; Logan mentioned his actions in April 18, 1728, at Chenastry as Chenasshy, a probable reference to Genesee, whose headwaters lay near those of West Branch tributaries, in PA 1:210–211; and for the report of his war belt circulation in 1728, see James Logan Papers on file in the Historical Society of Pennsylvania (Book 4:206), PA 1:214, and CRP 3:349 and 4:330.

6. For Manawkyhickon's part in Walking Purchase discussions, see PA 1:539 and 541–543; for mention of him as the uncooperative Indian King at Minisinck in 1740, see CRP 4:447; for the May 10, 1744, reference to the laughing sachem at "a place called Miunissinks," see Brainerd in Edwards and Dwight (1822:174); for Wona Waleckon as a Munsee or Minisink sachem consenting on October 25, 1758, to the final settlement sale of northern New Jersey, see EJD Liber I-2:94 and WJD Liber O:469.

7. For "Metapas's Wigwam," see the May 4, 1681, deed to land on the Raritan River in EJD (Liber 1:193 [246]; for "Amirent's [Emerus's] Plantation," see the April 9, 1688, deed to land by the Millstone River in WJD (Liber B:181). Becker (1987:89–93) argues that colonial mention of Indians at Lehigh only after 1692 is evidence that the area was an unoccupied buffer zone before that time.

8. Reading was the eldest son of Colonel John Reading, one of the senior investors in the cartel led by Daniel Coxe that purchased dominant interest in West Jersey in 1687. The younger Reading was one of the West Jersey's first surveyors. Rising gradually in the proprietary hierarchy, he ultimately became the first native-born New Jersey man to become governor of the province in 1747.

9. The man identified as Nomalughalan at the Tohokkonetkong in Reading (1915:43) was probably Maringoman.

10. Although Pennsylvania was not formally involved in the 1719 boundary line survey, provincial authorities thought it prudent to send two of their own surveyors to join the party. Their December 22, 1719, report may be seen in PA 19:660–662; see Reading (1915) for his account of the 1719 boundary survey; for preservation of hunting and fishing rights in the October 23, 1758, deed signing over northern New Jersey, see EJD Liber I-2:89–94 and WJD Liber O:464–469.

11. For Schuyler's January 19, 1702, deed claim, see AA 4:170; for the February 28, 1707, deed, see AA 5:147–148.

12. For speeches recorded at the September 27, 1714, meeting, see NYCD 5:387–389.

13. Wyalusing was located in the present-day village of the same name in Bradford County, Pennsylvania; Heckewelder suggested the name came from the Delaware *m'chwhillusink,* "place of the hoary veteran," in reference to an elderly warrior who lived there earlier; Tioga, an Iroquois word meaning "gate, entrance, place to enter in at," was located at the southern approach of the Susquehanna route into confederacy country, farther upriver in Bradford County where the Chemung River flows into the North Branch at the present site of Athens, Pennsylvania; for translations of Wyalusing and Tioga, see LLN:362; Ochquaga was located fifty miles farther on in and around Windsor in Broome County, New York

14. Although the ten Indian Nations refused to end their war with the Southern Indians, they promised to travel farther westward to reduce the chances of trouble with colonists and Indians under their protection along the Warrior's Path. The colonial nations politely referred to by the Iroquois speaker were the ten provinces represented at the meeting. For minutes of the meeting held between August 27 and September 10, 1722, see NYCD 5:657–681; for a biography of Shikellamy, see Merrell (1996).

15. For Dongan's August 4, 1687, request, see Wraxall (in NYCIA:14); for Dubuisson's account identifying the nations involved on both sides in the 1712 siege that touched off the Fox Wars, see Thwaites (1902:267–288).

16. For the minutes of the two days allotted to River Indians, who accepted gifts that were divided equally between those living above and below Albany at the Covenant Chain meeting held in Albany between August 27 and September 10, 1722, see NYCD 5:661–664.

17. For a murder complaint made by Nappaner (Napanoch) and other River Indians living in Ulster County at a Nicolls Treaty renewal meeting held with the governor in New York, who condoled them for their loss on June 9, 1719, see

NYCM-ECM Book 11:607–613. No evidence of further proceedings has been found.

18. For Mohawk speaker Little Abraham's May 19, 1757, account averring that the "Delaware chief's" gun accidentally went off while he was reaching out to shake his neighbor's hand, see SWJ 9:754–766; for Weequehela's descendant Marian Peter's June 20, 1864, letter sent to the Reverend Marsh in Keshena, Wisconsin, expressing the same point of view, see Honeyman (1928:410–414).

19. For records of Weequehela's purchases and debts, see NJCD 23:53 and David Lyle's account book in the Stevens Family Papers, on file in the New Jersey Historical Society; for Samuel Smith's account of Weequehela's home furnishings and lifestyle, see S. Smith (1765:440–441).

20. Proceedings of Weequehela's trial are not in provincial or county court records on file in Trenton or New Brunswick. Contemporary newspaper accounts containing most known information may be seen in NJCD 11:129–135.

21. It is tempting to speculate that the Snake Town mentioned in 1727 was the same place called Snake Hole by colonists and Aschkokwawalochtet (a Munsee place name referring to snakes) by Indians, just up the Chemung River from Tioga, visited by Christian Frederick Post and his party on May 22, 1760. For Aschkokwawalochtet, see Grumet (1999:54–55); for the September 27, 1727, message, see CRP 3:285–287; for the December 6, 1727, dispatch reporting Indians driving surveyors off at gunpoint at Durham, see James Logan Papers (Book 4 under that date on file in the American Philosophical Society [APS], Philadelphia, Penn.); for a copy of the September 17, 1718, deed in provincial files, see Pennsylvania Land Office Records (Book 1:29) on file in the Pennsylvania Archives in Harrisburg; for Logan's reading of the September 17, 1718, deed to Sassoonan and other sachems meeting with the governor at Philadelphia on June 5, 1728, see CRP 3:320–322; for later mention of the September 17, 1718, deed and the June 4–5, 1728, treaty entered into evidence at the Philadelphia Treaty meeting in July 1742, see George Croghan's memorandum filed under the date July 25, 1757, in the French and Indian War Papers on file in the APS; for Heckewelder's suggestion that Sassoonan's name means "our uncle," see LLN:385.

22. For Heckewelder's translation of Maxantawny as "bear's path creek, or the stream on which the bears have a path," see LLN:360; for a summary of the incidents presented to the assembled chiefs by the governor of Pennsylvania at the Philadelphia Treaty meeting session on June 4, 1728, see CRP 3:318; for initial reports of the murders and the arrest, examination, and conviction of the suspects, see PA 1:215–225 and PAPG 1:444–450; for Manawkyhickon's desire to stir up Miami and Iroquois support to avenge his relative Weequehela reported on September 1, 1728, see CRP 3:330; for Manawkyhickon's war belts, see Logan's April 18, 1728, letter to Governor Burnet in the James Logan Papers (Book 4:206) on file in the APS and printed in CRP 3:296; for Manawkyhickon's May 10, 1728, statement to Sassoonan that if he wanted "war he could make a handle to his hatchet 70 fathoms long, and I should see what he would do," see PA 1:214–215.

23. Keith had become lieutenant governor of Pennsylvania just before William Penn's death in 1718; for the May 12, 1728, proclamation text, see CRP 3:307–308. The Susquehanna Indians at the May 26–27, 1727, meeting told the governor that the killers of the settler the previous year were "Menysincks, who are of another nation, and therefore they can say nothing to it." For the May 26–27, 1728, Conestoga meeting minutes, see CRP 3:310–315 and PAPG 1:444–447. The sachems at the June 4–5, 1728, meeting also identified the killers as "Menysineks [who] live at the Forks of Sasquehannah above Meehayomy [Wyoming], and that their king is Kindassowa." For the June 4–5, 1728, Philadelphia meeting minutes, see CRP 3:316–326 and PAPG 1:447–450; Kindassowa was later identified as Kendaskond at the largely Minisink village of Atsinksink on the Chemung River on July 11, 1760 (in CRP 8:484) and as the Munsie chief Kendasseong in the June 24, 1768, report of a conference at Fort Pitt in CRP 9:56.

24. For an account of the hangings of John and Walter Winters for the murders of Toka Collie, his wife, and another Delaware woman, see PA 1:225–226 and PAPG 1:451–452; for friendly relations between Pennsylvania and the "Delawares, Shawanese, and Mingoes amongst us" formally reestablished at the promised fall general meeting held at Philadelphia between October 10 and 11, 1728, see CRP 3:333–337.

25. For James Logan's April 18, 1728, message to Manawkyhickon and other sachems at Chenasshy, see PA 1:210–211; for Gordon's May 21, 1728, message to Kakowatchy, see PA 1:223–224.

26. For the August 27, 1728, report that "Suanos" had hanged a trader named Timothy Higgins in a cabin at "Siamocon" [Shamokin], see PA 1:227; for messages dated September 3, 1728, and October 9, 1728, affirming that Higgins had escaped with his life, see PA 1:232 and CRP 3:333; for the September 1, 1728, report that the Shawnees left with their corn still standing, see CRP 3:330; for the Philadelphia message of the same date, sent to make inquiries into the reasons why Kakowatchy and his people left Pechoquealin, see PA 1:229–230; for the June 7, 1732, message from Shawnee chiefs stating that they had been asked to leave by the Munsees, see PA 1:329–330.

27. For the January 4, 1726, text, see Logan's January 11, 1726, advertisement in the James Logan Papers on file in the Historical Society of Pennsylvania in Philadelphia.

28. If the deed was actually signed by Shawnees, it represents their only known conveyance of land on the Delaware. The existence of several Nicholas Depuis, Depews, and Depues in contemporary colonial documents makes it difficult to pin down exactly which one got the land conveyed in the September 18, 1727, deed. Identification of Kizerrick, Ulster County (present-day Keyserike, just south of High Falls, New York) as the residence of the Niklas Depue in the 1727 deed suggests he was the son born on March 12, 1682 to the elder Nicholas's son Moses Depui in Kingston; for an abstract of the September 18, 1727, deed that Nicholas Depui later parlayed into a proprietary title in 1733, see Anonymous (1898:504); Syacop may have been Ankerop, i.e, Harman Hekan or Nimham I, one of whose

Indian names, Squahickkon, was sometimes spelled Sasakaman or Shushkamin by settlers; for Syacop signing the December 26, 1730, deed to Westbrook in the private family papers of local landowner Burson Bell, see Kraft (1977:39–40).

29. For the August 1, 1728, French report observing that Canadian authorities had been trying to induce "Chaouanons" to defect from the British interest since 1724 and affirming that 150 Shawnee men and their families "had begun a village on the River Ohio," see NYCD 9:1013; also see Wraxall's May 7, 1729, report in NYCIA:176 that three hundred "Makindus and Showanoes" were momentarily expected to settle among the Six Nations.

30. For the minutes of the October 5, 1728, Covenant Chain renewal session with the "Schaahook and River Indians," see NYCD 5:868–870.

31. For the final three Livingston Manor Indian deeds, see Folders 18, 20, and 21 in the Livingston Family Papers on file in the Brooklyn Historical Society; for the last deeds signed by Nimham I, Wackemane, and their people in the Berkshires, see WCH 1:35 and 393–394, FCH:637–638, and McDermott and Buck (1979:109–113); for a discussion of the new missions started at Scaticook (Kent, Connecticut) and Stockbridge in 1734 and elsewhere in and around the Housatonic Valley a few years later, see Frazier (1992).

32. For "Roondaghneere" being "put in the room" of the recently deceased Peter at the January 29, 1723, meeting, see the typescript filed under that date in the Philhower Collection (Special Collections of the Alexander Library, Rutgers University). Although no document currently links a man named Peter with any other Esopus person before 1723, the prominent position held by the man suggests that he may have been Tatapagh, the Esopus sachem who was last mentioned by that name in 1715 and the only important Esopus sachem besides Harman Hekan to disappear from European records around this time; for other Esopus deeds signed during this period, see the sale made by Doesto, her sons Awarawat and Ochperawim (Hendrick Hekan), and her daughter Asuctwichtogh on March 5, 1715, in UCD Book BB:380–381, and the June 15, 1728, sale of four hundred acres containing a lead mine in Nepenagh [Napanoch] made by Sateuw, Ochangues (Hendrick Hekan), and Neckarind [Renap] in UCD Book DD:6–7; for Nowenock's June 24, 1717, deed to land on the Dead River, see EJD Liber A-2:133–135; for Nutimus's November 11, 1721, sale of land on the Millstone, see the deed filed under the same date in the NJHS; for Memerescum's deeds to lands on the Ramapo River signed on May 17, 1723, April 23, 1724, and April 21, 1727, see NJHS MG 7:72, RCID:111, and EJD Liber E-2:152; for Nowenock's September 8, 1729, deed to land at Wanaque, see Roome (1883:20–21 and 1897:24).

33. For studies substantiating the current majority view of the Walking Purchase as a swindle of heroic proportions, see A. F. C. Wallace (1949:18–30) and Jennings (1970 and 1984:325–346); Becker (1987:114–177 and 133–134) mostly stands alone as the current proponent of the view that the deed and the deal were just and valid (see W. Hunter 1960:6 and 181 for an earlier expression of this viewpoint).

34. For Allen's and other purchases of land in the Lehigh Valley from Penn family agents made between August 28, 1728, and April 16, 1729, see Pennsylvania Patents (Book F-5:92 and 562 and Book F-6:1), on file in the Pennsylvania Archives, Har-

risburg; for the January 22, 1735, patent of these lands, see Northampton County Deeds (Book A-1:149–152), on file in Easton, Penn.

35. For a biography of Weiser, see P. A. W. Wallace (1945); for Weiser's original role as a Six Nations representative, see Jennings (1984:313).

36. The most complete of the numerous official copies of the July 15, 1682, deed appears in R. Dunn et al. (1981–1986, 2:261–269). The original August 20, 1686, deed has disappeared. Sir William Johnson sent a copy of this deed to the Board of Trade in 1762. An abstract of the document appears in the "Documents Relating to the Wyoming Controversy 1751–1814," p. 123, on file in the APS. Mayhkeerickk-ishsho, Sayhoppy and Taughhaughsey are listed as "the chiefs or kings of the North-ern Indians on Delaware" in the subsequent August 24, 1737, Walking Purchase deed in PA 1:541–543. The area taken up by the July 5, 1697, deed to land between the Pennypack and Neshaminy creeks extended "in length from the said River Delaware, so far as a horse can travel in two summer days" (in PA 1:124–125).

37. The 1686 and 1697 documents are two of only three deeds attributed to Munsee signatories known to use distance traveled to mark a boundary. For the third, see the February 26, 1640, deed to a tract at Norwalk extending "from the sea a day's walk into the country" in WCH 1:389–390 and FCH:487.

38. In his letter to Weiser on October 18, 1736, Logan characterized Nutimus as a "turbulent fellow . . . from Jersey much like such another as Manawkyhickon who was also of Jersey, . . . This man while he lived in Jersey pretended that a relation of his on this side of Delaware left him land by will and accordingly came over and claimed a great quantity to which he had no right" (in the Logan Papers 4:62–64, on file in the APS). In his October 28, 1736, response describing the Iroquois posi-tion, Weiser informed Logan that "it went very hard about signing over their right upon Delaware because they said they had nothing to do there about the land and they were afraid they should do anything amiss to their cousins the Delawares" (in the James Logan Papers 4:64, APS). The October 11 and 25, 1736, Six Nations deeds are mentioned in CRP 4:481. For discussions of these and other Walking Purchase documents, see Jennings (1970 and 1984:388–397).

39. Heckewelder suggested Tohickon comes from the Delaware *tohickhan* or *to-hickhanne*, "the stream over which we pass by means of a bridge of driftwood," in LLN:356; for the minutes of the August 24, 1737, Philadelphia council, see PA 1:539–541; for the August 25, 1737, deed signed as "a further confirmation thereof . . . for ourselves and all other the Delaware Indians," see PA 1:541–543.

40. Financial constraints compelled Whitefield to sell Nazareth to the Moravians in 1741. For the founding of Bethlehem, see Smaby (1989).

41. For a map showing locations of the Indian Manor and Tatamy tracts at the Forks, see Chidsey (1937:map). Evidently seeing handwriting on the wall, Tatamy privately purchased his tract on March 24, 1733, from William Allen for £48, 16s., and 5p. He had the land surveyed on December 30, 1736, and registered his patent on April 28, 1738 (W. Hunter 1974:72). Tatamy later petitioned the Pennsylvania government on November 20, 1742, for permission to remain on the land. For their response giving him provisional permission, pending approval of the Six Nations, see CRP 4:624–625.

42. For more on the troubles at the Forks in the years immediately following the Walking Purchase, see Jennings (1984:347–350).

43. For proceedings at the 1742 Philadelphia Treaty meeting, see CRP 4:559–586; for Canasatego's speech, see CRP 4:578–583; for a biography of Canasatego, see Starna (in Pencak and Richter 2004:144–167).

44. For Heckewelder's translation of Welagameka, see LLN:359; for developments at Nazareth, see Hamilton (1971:31–32 and 42) and Levering (1903:50–51 and 154–155); for the Pennsylvania government's refusal to honor Wehheland's request that his people be allowed to stay at Welagameka made at the same meeting with Tatamy, see CRP 4:624–625.

13. SOLD OUT, 1743–1766

1. For Heckewelder's translations of Aquashicola as "the brush-net fishing creek" and Meniolagomeka as "rich or good spot of land within that which is bad or barren," see LLN:358–359; for Nutimus signing the August 22, 1749, deed to lands above the Kittatinys, see PA 2:33–37. He was identified both as Nutimus and as Lawichcomet and Lawpays, variants of his other name (he was listed in the 1742 Philadelphia Treaty as "Nudimus alias Lawye-Quowhon") in CRP 4:582, and in documents recording affairs in and around the Great Island on the West Branch of the Susquehanna River between 1761 and 1763 in CRP 8:565 and PA 7:435 and 438; for Heckewelder's suggestion that Nutimus's earlier name comes from *lawiequaham*, "in the middle of the house," the favored place reserved for sachems, see LLN:385; for Teedyuscung at Meniolagomeka, see Anonymous (1905) and Heckewelder (1820:145).

2. For an account of the move made by most of the Kaunaumeek congregation to Stockbridge in 1744, see Frazier (1992:58–59).

3. For a classic account of the Moravian missions to the Mahicans and Munsees in New York between 1740 and 1746, see D. Smith (1948:52–115).

4. For Allamaaseeit's initial December 2, 1745, report sent by Swartwout to New York, New Jersey, and Pennsylvania, see NYCM-ECM Book 21:67, Sheridan (1991–1993, 3:427–428), and CRP 5:1 and 26. Thanks to John Michael Smith (pc May 25, 2009) for identification of Allamaaseeit as Tatapagh's son.

5. Thomas De Key was the grandson of New York baker and Munsee land purchaser Jacobus Theuniszen de Kay; for De Key's January 17, 1746, report, see NYCM-ECM Book 21:71–72; the report is discussed in Ruttenber (1906:182).

6. Mottellend's documented career illustrates something of the variety of political identities assumed by some Munsees at different times. This was particularly the case for more cosmopolitan types like Mottellend, who was noted on April 29, 1761, as a speaker of good English (SCP 2:81). He was identified as a Sopus Indian named "Mathalane alias Jan" in the June 6, 1746, deed (UCD Book EE:63–65); as the Cashichton Indian Makohin in the August 2, 1746, deed (UCD Book EE:61–63); as the Ninneepauues [Lenape] sachem Mottellend in the May 6, 1755, deed to the upper Delaware River in SCP 1:260–271; as the fifteen-year resident living among

the Mohawks at Tioga noted on May 10, 1756; as the Menisink Indian Modelee-
and who returned to his birthplace as often as possible (in the unpublished papers
of the Pennsylvania Provincial Council, Pennsylvania Archives, under that date); as
Maulcey, a Mohickon captain at the April 6–12, 1760, Fort Pitt Conference (in SWJ
3:208–217); and as Maudlin, for whose murder Pennsylvania authorities condoled
Eichokohoon and other Munsey chiefs on October 29, 1762 (in Box 9, Miscellaneous Documents, NJSL).

For Cacawalomin alias Hendrick Hekan, Noondawcharind alias Rinnip, and
Lamaseeth alias William Crom also signing the June 6, 1746, conveyance, see UCD
Book EE:63–65; for the August 2, 1746, instrument signed by Hendrick Hekan as
Kakalarimme, Nimham II as Elman, and Allamaaseeit as Aloamsek, see UCD Book
EE:61–63.

7. Teedyuscung reported "that the belt was given them by the government of
New York and represented their union, which was to last as long as the sun should
continue in the firmament." For the most complete sets of minutes of the October
1758 Easton meeting, see EJD Liber I-2:89–94 and WJD Liber O:438–469.
Abridged minutes are published in CRP 8:175–223 and S. Smith (1765:455–483);
for the minutes of the October 1–11, 1761, meeting at Bush Hill, a country estate
one mile from Philadelphia's city center, where Teedyuscung introduced "Nime-
ham, chief of the Opies," and presented two since-lost certificates attesting to his
people's loyalty to Great Britain that he had also shown at Easton, see CRP 8:667–
670. One of the certificates, dated 1745, was signed by New York governor George
Clinton; the other from 1756 was above the signature of his successor, Charles Hardy.

Heckewelder identified the man whose name was spelled Nihmha in LLN:387
as "a Monsey chief, born at Minisink, on Delaware; afterwards a chief on Susquehanna and on Ohio."

8. Thanks to Daniel K. Richter (2007:pc) for the moiety insight. Also thanks to
Miles (2007:pc) for pointing out the passage in the appendix in Barton (1798:2)
based on information supplied by Heckewelder that the Delawares formerly had a
fourth crow tribe that "was the last in rank and respectability." Barton wrote that the
turtle tribe was held in highest esteem, an assertion reinforced by Morgan's translation (in Leacock 1963:176) of the turtle phratry lineage, O-ka-ho-ki, as "ruler." Barton went on to state that although crow tribe leaders could call councils together,
their last formal ceremonial responsibilities before their dissolution centered on
lighting pipes for leaders of the turtle, wolf, and turkey tribes. Years later in Kansas,
Charles Journeycake's mother, a member of the wolf tribe, told Morgan (in L. White
1959:52) that the crows were a subdivision of the turkeys. She went on to say that
Delawares only married within their tribes, and as one example offered that crows
married only turkeys. These data can be interpreted to indicate that at some point
in time, the crow phratry was absorbed into the turkeys as a lineage, and that later
in Kansas, the three phratries became localized endogamous ceremonial organizations that no longer functioned as kinship units.

9. For turtle and wolf *freundschaft* people as Unami community leaders in Ohio,
see Wellenreuther and Wessel (2005); for moieties, see Fox (1967).

10. For the August 22, 1749, deed to land between the Delaware and Susquehanna rivers, signed by Canasatego, several other prominent Six Nations leaders, Nutimus, two of his people, and representatives of the Delawares at Shamokin and the Shawnees, see PA 2:33–37; for evidence that the August sale did not go down well with some Aesopus or Mohiccon Indians identified as Captain Allamouse (Allamaaseeit), Captain Clitches (Kattias), and King Tattenhick (Teedyuscung), who blocked surveyors trying to lay out land at the Lackawaxen River on October 28, 1749, see CRP 5:489–490; thanks to John Michael Smith (pc, May 25, 2009) for identifying Kattias; for brief accounts of Indian involvement in troubles in northern and central New Jersey between 1744 and 1755, see McConville (1999:146, 155, 166–169, and 191–193); for Azariah Horton's mission to the Long Island Indians beginning in 1741, see Strong (in Stone 1993:191–220). Although much is known about Indian involvement in colonial maritime affairs, documentation of particular Munsee activity at sea awaits future studies.

11. For alcohol abuse among Indians, see Mancall (1995).

12. For a June 12, 1753, report that six colonists and fourteen Indians, Showammers and Mehihammers, had been killed in brawls that spring in Ohio, see NYCD 6:782; for conditions in the Ohio and Susquehanna valley Indian towns, see Mancall (1991), McConnell (1992), and R. White (1991).

13. For numerous references chronicling the stream of visitors passing through Moravian missions, see Fliegel (1978:passim).

14. For the August 22, 1749, deed, see PA 2:33–37.

15. For the Moravian interlude at Meniolagomeka, see Anonymous (1905) and Heckewelder (1820:145).

16. For studies of Delaware prophetic movements, see A. F. C. Wallace (1956b), Cave (2006), C. Hunter (1971), and Miller (1997).

17. For Papunhank, see Papunhank (2005) and Merritt (1997).

18. For the June 12–16, 1753, New York meeting proceedings and Theyanoguin's speech, see NYCD 6:783–788; for a biography of Theyanoguin, see Snow (1996).

19. For the Schaghticoke and River Indian sachems' welcomes on July 6, their presentation of compliments, brief history of relations with colonists, and complaints over liquor trade and land abuses on July 8, and their receipt of the meeting commissioners' answers and presents the next day, see NYCD 6:877–885 and CRP 6:92–100. Commissioners from every colony except New Jersey (which had again become a separate royal colony in 1738), Virginia, and the Carolinas attended the meeting; for proceedings of the Albany Congress, see NYCD 6:853–899; for the meeting and its significance, see Shannon (2000); for Johnson's life and career, see Flexner (1959).

20. For the July 5–9 land talks and deeds, reserving small plots for Indians living at Shamokin and Wyoming and promising that further payments when settlers began moving onto the westernmost parts of this land, see CRP 6:114–129; for the July 11, 1754, Susquehannah Company deed see SCP 1:4–5.

21. For the December 10, 1754, sale of the disputed western part of Minisink Patent land between the Hardenbergh Patent line and the west side of the Shawangunk Ridge for 108 Spanish milled dollars by Noleatock (Nutimus), Mactkka (Mot-

tellend), and two others, see SCP 1:196–200; for the May 6, 1755, deed in which Allamaaseeit, Nutimus [identified as Mumgerchass], Mottellend, and several others accepted "500 and upwards Spanish milled dollars" for land north of the Lackawaxen River to Mohawk country between the Delaware River and Moosic Mountain, see SCP 1:260–271; for the October 29, 1755, sale of land between the Lackawaxen River and the Delaware Water Gap for "110 Spanish milled dollars and certain English goods [paid to] Mackeus [Mottellend?], Kalestias [Kattias], Wescollong [Teedyusung?], and Mechokenous [Nutimus], sachems and chiefs of the tribe and nation of the Indians called Ninnepauues otherwise and in English known by the name of the Delaware Indians planted and inhabiting in the western continent of North America," see SCP 1:308–314.

22. For the October 8, 1754, report from acting New York governor James De Lancey, informing the Board of Trade that Abenakis had carried off the Schaghti-cokes on August 28, see NYCD 6:909; for the December 26, 1754, letter from the Marquis du Quesne telling De Lancey that he had given permission allowing a party from St. Francis and Becancourt to visit "their brethren, the Loups settled near Orange," see NYCD 6:936.

23. For painting themselves black, see Jennings (1965:453); for a partial list of settlers killed and captured between 1755 and 1756, see Anonymous (1908).

24. For the rise of race prejudice as a prime force driving intercultural relations in the region at this time, see Merritt (2003:282–295).

25. For Heckewelder's translation of Tulpehocken from *tulpewhihacki,* "the land abounding with turtles," see LLN:360; for his translation of Kittanning from the Unami word *kithanne* and the Munsee form *gichthanne,* see LLN:366; for the January 8, 1756, Crosswicks Treaty, whose participants did not include influential sachems like Nimham II of the Pomptons, see the copy of the treaty filed under that date in the NJSL. Much of the material on the Seven Years' War in America used here is drawn from Anderson (2000) and Jennings (1988).

26. For the March 2, 1756, attack at Walden, see CHM 2:650–651 and Fernow and Van Laer (1902:425–426); for the April 12, 1756, murders at Peapack, see NJCD 20:27–28 and 39–44; for Johnson's May 28, 1756, letter to the magistrates at "Fish Kilns," see SWJ 2:477–478.

27. For a map of Kittanning at the time of the Pennsylvania militia attack, see Weslager (1978:7).

28. For these and other frontier diplomats and diplomatic efforts at this time, see W. Jacobs (1950), Merrell (1999), and P. A. W. Wallace (1945). For Teedyuscung, see A. F. C. Wallace (1949); for Tatamy, see W. Hunter (1974); for Croghan, see Wainwright (1959); for Post, see Chase (1980).

29. No set of minutes for the summer 1756 meeting at Onondaga has survived. A. F. C. Wallace (1949:96–100) pieced together the most complete account from information in Thomson (1759) and several other sources discussing the meeting.

30. Teedyuscung first blamed the war on the Walking Purchase in his "we are not so great fools" speech on November 12, at the third meeting at Easton held between November 8 and 17, 1756. (Manuscript on file in the French and Indian War Papers, APS, and published in slightly different form in CRP 7:313 and 324–

336.) At the July 25–August 7, 1757, Easton meeting, Teedyuscung styled himself "King of the Delawares, living on Susquehannah, who is empowered by the ten following nations, vizt Lenopi, Wename, Munsey, Mawhickon, Tiawco, or Nanticokes and the Senecas, Onondagoes, Cayougas, Oneidoes, and Mohawks" in the copy of the minutes prepared for him at his insistence by Charles Thomson, future secretary to the First Continental Congress in CRP 7:665–714. A transcript of another version written by a different scribe appears in NYCD 7:287–321. The young Thomson's subsequent account of the conference published in England (Thomson 1759) would bring the grievances of the Delawares and Shawnees to international attention. In another unpublished manuscript written a year later, Thomson (1760) focused on Papunhank's theological experiment and the reasons why Munsees went to war against the colonists.

31. For the August 4–5, 1758, meeting between Pennsylvania authorities and belt-carrying Minisink, Delaware, and Seneca messengers, first coming to Philadelphia to announce that the Six Nations represented all Indians on their way to Easton before going on to Burlington, see CRP 8:149–155. For the February 23, 1758, power of attorney, see EJD Liber I-2:45–47.

32. For the August 7–8, 1758, meeting in Burlington, see CRP 8:157–161. One of the two Seneca messengers (the one who did not speak) was a Delaware Indian identified as Samuel, who may have been the Samuel Evans who participated in earlier meetings at Philadelphia on July 20, 1756 (also identified as Petaghchdaqua in the manuscript filed under that date in the Collection of Treaties on file in the APS), at present-day Harrisburg, Pennsylvania on April 1, 1757 (in SWJ 9:728), and at the July-August 1757 Easton council (in NYCD 7:287–321).

33. For the September 12, 1758, deed to southern New Jersey, see EJD Liber O:458–464.

34. For proceedings of the October 7–26, 1758, Easton Treaty conference, see CRP 8:174–223.

35. Oneida speaker Thomas King and Seneca speaker Tagashata managed to get the New Jersey authorities to raise their original offer of 800 pieces of eight; Manawkyhickon signed both October 25, 1758, postscripts as Wona Weleckon. Consideration of Weequehela's execution in the proceedings must have opened and soothed his now elderly kinsman's old wounds: Nimham II was reportedly too ill to participate in the October 23, 1758, deed signing; he later signaled his approval of the deal as the "eldest principal chief of the Wappingers or Opings" in a postscript on the October 23, 1758, deed; for manuscript copies of the October 23, 1758, deed, see EJD Liber I-2:89–94 and WJD Liber O:464–469; an original on parchment is in the collection of Forbes, Inc., in New York.

36. For the August 29, 1759, order, see SWJ 3:837; for the June 18–28, 1762, meeting at Easton, see SWJ 3:760–791.

37. For Johnson's August 26, 1765, letter to Roger Morris (no relation to Lewis), see Pocket XIII, No. 55, in the Philipse-Gouverneur Papers on file in the Library of Columbia University, New York.

38. For Johnson's subsequent correspondence and reports on the June 18–28, 1762, Easton Meeting, Pennsylvania's refusal to pay anything, Teedyuscung's demand

reductions from £600 to £400, and his ultimate acceptance of £200 and the promise of a later gift, see SWJ 3:794–818, 827–828, 837–852, and 865–869; for the Wappinger suit and Johnson's decision on the Dutchess County land claim, see Handlin and Mark (1964) and Nammack (1969:70–85).

39. For descriptions of the Chemung towns in 1760, see Post's and Hays's accounts in Grumet (1999); for biographies of Andrew Montour and accounts of the burning of the Chemung towns, see Hagedorn (1994) and Lewin (1966); for Wangomend, see A. F. C. Wallace (1956b:9–10); for Heckewelder's suggestion that Wangomend's name means "he who is saluted, is met with friendship," see LLN:395.

40. For events leading up to Teedyuscung's suspicious death and its aftermath, see A. F. C. Wallace (1949:252–266); for Heckewelder's suggestion that the place name Paxton comes from the Delaware word *peekstunk*, "the standing or dead water, a deep or stagnant spot of water in a stream, a pool, etc.," see LLN:373.

Tom Quick was a most notorious murderer of Munsees in local legends. The luster of this legend has tarnished in recent years. Unreconstructed storytellers, however, almost surely continue to tell tales of his exploits around Delaware Valley campfires. They center on Quick's efforts to fulfill his vow to kill one hundred Indians to avenge the killing of his father by Indian neighbors at his cabin in Milford, Pennsylvania, in 1755. The real Tom Quick was the son and namesake of a second-generation settler originally from the Keyserike locale in Ulster County. Tom's father's accomplishments included service as an interpreter for the Delaware Company purchase in 1754. Like the runners of the 1737 Walking Purchase, the elder Quick was evidently targeted by Indians resenting Delaware Company colonization. His son, who stood frontier defense during the war that broke out in 1755, refused to recognize the peace concluded at Easton with the Munsees and other Delawares in 1758. Although he was never indicted for any of the murders he claimed to have committed, he identified himself as the man who murdered his old friend Mottellend near Minisink sometime in the fall of 1761. Quick's assertion that Mottellend killed his father gives an indication of how bitter feelings had become. For New Jersey's presentation of presents condoling the killing of Mottellend (identified in the document as Maudlin) to "Munsey chief Eichokohoon" (Egohohowen) at Cole's Fort in the upper Delaware Valley on October 29, 1762, see the document filed under that date in Box 9, Miscellaneous Documents, NJHS.

Like Bacon's murderous followers before them, men like Quick were lionized as defenders of the helpless, sons of liberty, and proto-patriots by later writers. Contemporaries had a more clear-eyed view. Most, especially those living in cities and settlements, regarded Quick and those like him as unsavory renegades who figuratively as well as literally lived on the fringes of colonial society. The worst of them, the Paxton Boys, started out as a band of fifty vigilantes who murdered twenty inoffensive Conestoga Indians taking refuge in the Lancaster county workhouse in December 1763. Tapping into a deepening well of growing race hatred, they quickly attracted large numbers of angry frontiersmen. Some five hundred Paxton rioters marched on Philadelphia in January 1764, demanding that authorities turn over Papunhank and 140 Munsees, Unamis, and other Indians taking refuge in the city.

Derided in the press and provincial council houses as frontier banditti (see Vaughan 1984), they were stopped by authorities and ordered back to their homes.

Quick himself evidently stayed under the radar as much as possible. Official records note little more than the fact that he, like many other men at the time, enlisted in and later deserted from the local militia during the Revolutionary War. Virtually everything else we know about him comes from stories he told or that were told about him. For the earliest published compilation of these legends, see Quinlan (1851).

41. For Papunhank and the Wyalusing community, see Schutt (1999).

42. For Hasenclever's August 16, 1765, letter, see Heusser (1923).

14. MANY TRAILS, 1767–TODAY

1. See Walling (1996) for an account of the Stockbridge Indian rifle company.

2. For Ochquaga and the other upper Susquehanna Indian towns during the Revolution, see Calloway (1995:108–128) and Hinman (1975); for Indian refugee towns around Fort Niagara, see Calloway (1995:129–157).

3. For documents and an overview of the first fifty years of life on the Six Nations Reserve at Grand River, see Johnston (1964); for the 1785 Grand River census, see Calloway (1995:155).

4. Thanks to Stockbridge-Munsee historian Sheila Miller (2007:pc) for providing the surnames of several families in Wisconsin tracing descent to Weequehela; For a genealogy of descendants of Weequehela and other Brotherton ancestors from the Stockbridge-Munsee community, see web pages entitled "The Genealogy of the Indians of Brothertown, New York" maintained by Caroline K. Alder on www.genealogy.com.

5. For the Canadian Munsee and Mahican journey to Kansas, see Gray and Gray (1956:276–278).

6. For the Mayane incident, see *Journal of New Netherland* (in NNN:281).

7. For maroon societies, see R. Price (1996).

8. For Thomas Morton's observation, published in 1632, noting that bones of Indian people killed by epidemics strewn unburied on the ground made New England look like a newfound Golgotha, see Adams (1883).

REFERENCES

Sources Cited by Abbreviation

AA   Munsell, Joel, ed.
1850–1859 *The Annals of Albany*. 10 vols. Albany.

AHC   Munsell, Joel, ed.
1865–1871 *Collections of the History of Albany*, New York. 4 vols. Albany.

AP   Christoph, Peter R., Florence A. Christoph, and Charles T. Gehring, eds.
1989–1991 *The Andros Papers: Files of the Provincial Secretary of New York during the Administration of Governor Sir Edmund Andros, 1674–1680.* 3 vols. New York Historical Manuscript Series. Syracuse: Syracuse University Press.

BCD   Bergen County Deeds. On file in the Bergen County Hall of Records, Hackensack, N.J.

BHR   Marshall, Donald W., et al., eds.
1962–1978 *Bedford Historical Records.* 4 vols. Bedford Hills, N.Y.: The Town of Bedford.

BTR   Brooklyn Town Records. On file in the Municipal Archives, New York, N.Y.

CHM   O'Callaghan, Edmund Burke, ed.
1865–1866 *Calendar of Historical Manuscripts in the Office of the Secretary of State, Albany, New York.* 2 vols. Albany: Weed, Parsons, and Co.

CRP   Pennsylvania, The State of, ed.
1851–1853 *Minutes of the Provincial Council of Pennsylvania From the Organization to the Termination of the Proprietary Government* (Vols. 6–16 titled *Minutes of the Supreme Executive Council of Pennsylvania From Its Organization to the Termination of the Revolution*). Printed by the

State. 16 vols. Harrisburg: Jo. Severns and Co. (Vols. 1–3, 1852) and Theo. Fenn and Co. (Vols. 4–16, 1851–1853) The first three volumes were originally published separately with different pagination between 1838 and 1840.

DANCK Murphy, Henry C., ed.
1867 *Jasper Danckaerts and William Sluyter, Journal of a Voyage to New York in 1679–1680.* Memoirs of the Long Island Historical Society, Vol. 1. Brooklyn. Facsimile reprint in 1966 as No. 27 in the March of America Facsimile Series, University Microfilms, Ann Arbor. Also released in 1913 and reprinted in 1941 with a new introduction by Bartlett Burleigh James and J. Franklin Jameson by Charles Scribner's Sons, New York and reprinted again in 1967 by Barnes and Noble, New York.

DONCK O'Donnell, Thomas F., ed.
1968 *Adriaen Van der Donck, A Description of the New Netherlands.* Syracuse: Syracuse University Press. First published in 1655. A second edition was published in 1656.

DEF Margry, Pierre
1876–1886 *Decouvertes et Etablissements des Francais dans l'Ouest et dans le Sud de l'Amerique Septentrionale (1614–1754).* 6 vols. Paris.

DHSNY O'Callaghan, Edmund Burke, ed.
1849–1851 *The Documentary History of the State of New York.* 4 vols. Quarto edition. Albany: Weed, Parsons, and Co.

ECM Paltstits, Victor Hugo, ed.
1910 *Minutes of the Executive Council of the Province of New York: Administration of Francis Lovelace, 1668–1673.* 2 vols. Albany: J. B. Lyon Company, State Printers.

EJD East Jersey Deeds on file in the New Jersey Archives, Trenton.

EJPBM Miller, George J., Maxine N. Lurie, and Joanne R. Walroth, eds.
1949–1985 *The Minutes of the Board of Proprietors of the Eastern Division of New Jersey, 1685–1794.* 4 vols. Perth Amboy and Newark: General Board of Proprietors of the Eastern Division of New Jersey and the New Jersey Historical Society.

ERA Pearson, Jonathan, and Arnold J. F. van Laer, eds.
1869–1919 *Early Records of the City and County of Albany.* 3 vols. Albany: J. Munsell and the University of the State of New York.

FCH Hurd, D. Hamilton
1881 *The History of Fairfield County, Connecticut: With Illustrations and Biographical Sketches of Its Prominent Men and Pioneers.* New York: J. W. Lewis. Reprinted in 1988 by the Higginson Book Company.

FTR Flatlands Town Records. On file in the Municipal Archives, New York, N.Y.

GCOC Leaming, Aaron, and Jacob Spicer
1881 *The Grants, Concessions, and Original Constitutions of the Province of New Jersey.* 2 vols. Philadelphia.

GTR Gravesend Town Records. On file in the Municipal Archives, New York, N.Y.

HT Street, Charles R.
1882 "The Town of Huntington," in *The History of Suffolk County.* W. W. Munsell, ed., pp. 1–90. New York: W. W. Munsell. Individual town histories separately paginated.

HTR Street, Charles R., ed.
1887–1889 *Huntington Town Records.* 3 vols. Huntington, N.Y.

IACNY Trelease, Allen W.
1960 *Indian Affairs in Colonial New York: The Seventeenth Century.* Ithaca: Cornell University Press. Reprinted in 1997 by University of Nebraska Press, Lincoln.

IMI Stokes, Isaac Newton Phelps
1915–1928 *The Iconography of Manhattan Island, 1498–1909.* 6 vols. New York: Robert H. Dodd. Reprinted in 1967 by Arno Press, New York, and in 1998 by Oak Knoll, New York.

JR Thwaites, Rueben Gold, ed.
1896–1901 *The Jesuit Relations and Allied Documents: Travels and Explorations of the Jesuit Missionaries of New France, 1610–1791.* 73 vols. Cleveland: Burrows Brothers.

KP Christoph, Peter R., Kenneth Scott, and Kenn Stryker-Rodda, eds.
1976 *Kingston Papers.* 2 vols. Baltimore: Genealogical Publishing Company.

KTR Kingston Town Records on file in the Ulster County Hall of Records, Kingston, N.Y.

LIR Leder, Lawrence H., ed.
1956 *The Livingston Indian Records, 1666–1723.* Gettysburg: Pennsylvania Historical Association.

LLN Heckewelder, John Gottlieb Ernestus, and Peter S. Du Ponceau
1834 "Names Which the Lenni Lenape or Delaware Indians, Who Once Inhabited This Country, Had Given to Rivers, Streams, Places, &c. &c. Within the Now States of Pennsylvania, New Jersey, Maryland and Virginia: And Also Names of Chieftains and Distinguished Men of That Nation; With the Signification of Those Names, and Biographical Sketches of Some of Those Men. By the Late Rev. John Heckewelder, of Bethlehem, Pennsylvania. Communicated to the American Philosophical Society April 5, 1822, and Now Published by Their Order. Revised and Prepared for the Press by Peter S. Du Ponceau." *Transactions of the American Philosophical Society*, New Ser., Vol. 4, pp. 351–396.

LP   Gehring, Charles T., trans. and ed.
            1980 *Land Papers: Volumes GG, HH, and II.* New York Historical
            Manuscripts: Dutch. Baltimore: Genealogical Publishing Company.
MCD   Monmouth County Deeds. On File in the Monmouth County Hall
            of Records, Freehold, N.J.
NAHC   Jaray, Cornell, ed.
            1968 *Historical Chronicles of New Amsterdam, Colonial New York, and
            Early Long Island.* Port Washington, N.Y.: Ira J. Friedman.
NAPN   Grumet, Robert S.
            1981 *Native American Place Names in New York City.* New York: Mu-
            seum of the City of New York.
NJCD   Whitehead, William A., William N. Nelson, Frederick W. Ricord, and
            A. Van Doren Honeyman, eds.
            1880–1931 *Documents Relating to the Colonial History of the State of
            New Jersey.* 2 series, 35 vols. Newark, Trenton, and Paterson: Daily
            Advertiser Printing House, John L. Murphy Publishing Company,
            Printers, and the Press Printing and Publishing Company.
NNN   Jameson, J. Franklin, ed.
            1909 *Narratives of New Netherland, 1609–1664.* New York: Charles
            Scribner's Sons. Reprinted in 1967 by Barnes and Noble, New
            York.
NYBGE   Christoph, Peter R., and Florence A. Christoph, eds.
            1982 *Books of General Entries of the Colony of New York, 1664–1673:
            Orders, Warrants, Letters, Commissions, Passes, and Licenses Issued by Gov-
            ernors Richard Nicolls and Francis Lovelace.* New York Historical Man-
            uscripts: English. Baltimore: Genealogical Publishing Company.
NYCD   O'Callaghan, Edmund Burke, and Berthold Fernow, eds.
            1853–1887 *Documents Relative to the Colonial History of the State of
            New-York: Procured in Holland, England, and France, by John Romeyn
            Brodhead, Esq.* 15 vols. Albany: Weed, Parsons and Co.
NYCIA   McIlwain, Charles Howard, ed.
            1915 *An Abridgement of the Indian Affairs Contained in Four Folio Vol-
            umes, Transacted in the Colony of New York, From the Year 1678 to the
            Year 1751, by Peter Wraxall.* Harvard Historical Studies, Vol. 21, Cam-
            bridge. Reprinted in 1968 by Benjamin Blom, N.Y.
NYCM-ECM Executive Council Minutes. In New York Colonial Manuscripts on
            file in the New York State Archives, Albany.
NYCM-GE   General Entries. In New York Colonial Manuscripts on file in the
            New York State Archives, Albany.
NYCM-ILP   Indorsed Land Papers. In New York Colonial Manuscripts on file in
            the New York State Archives, Albany.
OBTR   Cox, John, Jr., ed.
            1916–1940 *Oyster Bay Town Records.* 8 vols. New York: Tobias A.
            Wright.

OCD   Orange County Deeds. On file in the Orange County Office Building, Goshen, N.Y.

OTOM   Salter, Edwin, and George C. Beekman
1887 *Old Times in Old Monmouth: Historical Reminiscences of Old Monmouth County, Being a Series of Historical Sketches of Old Monmouth County (Now Monmouth and Ocean).* Freehold, N.J. Reprinted by Genealogical Publishing Company, Baltimore, Md., and Clearfield Company in 1994 and Heritage Books, Bowie, Md., in 1999.

PA   Hazard, Samuel, ed.
1852–1860 *Pennsylvania Archives Selected and Arranged From the Original Documents in the Office of the Secretary of the Commonwealth.* First Series. 12 vols. Harrisburg: John Severns.

PAPG   Reed, George E., ed.
1900–1902 *Pennsylvania Archives: Papers of the Governors.* Fourth Series. 12 vols. Harrisburg.

RCID   Budke, George H., ed.
1975 *Indian Deeds: 1630 to 1748.* New City, N.Y.: Library Association of Rockland County.

RIN   Ruttenber, Edward Manning
1906 "Indian Geographical Names of the Valley of the Hudson's River." *Proceedings of the New York Historical Association,* Vol. 6, pp. 1–241. Newburgh.

RLCC   Richter, Daniel K.
1982 "Rediscovered Links in the Covenant Chain: Previously Unpublished Transcripts of New York Indian Treaty Minutes, 1677–1691." *Proceedings of the American Antiquarian Society,* Vol. 92, Pt. 1, pp. 45–85. Worcester, Mass.

RNSH   Hicks, Benjamin D., ed.
1896–1904 *Records of the Towns of North and South Hempstead, Long Island, New York.* 8 vols. Jamaica, N.Y.: Long Island Farmer Printer.

RPS-CM   Scott, Kenneth, and Kenn Stryker-Rodda, eds.
1974 *Register of the Provincial Secretary, 1638–1660, and Council Minutes, 1638–1649.* New York Historical Manuscripts: Dutch Period. 4 vols. Baltimore: Genealogical Publishing Company.

SCP   Boyd, Julian P., and Robert J. Taylor, eds.
1930–1971 *The Susquehannah Company Papers, 1753–1803.* 11 vols. Wilkes Barre: Wyoming Historical and Geological Society.

SWJ   Sullivan, James, Alexander C. Flick, Almon W. Lauber, Milton W. Hamilton, and Albert B. Corey, eds.
1921–1965 *The Papers of Sir William Johnson.* 15 Vols. Albany: University of the State of New York.

TIN   Tooker, William Wallace
            1911 *The Indian Place-Names of Long Island and Islands Adjacent with Their Probable Significations.* New York: G. P. Putnam's Sons for the John Jermain Memorial Library. Reprinted in 1962 by Ira J. Friedman, Port Washington, N.Y.
UCD   Ulster County Deeds. On file in the Ulster County Hall of Records, Kingston, N.Y.
WCD   Westchester County Deeds. On file in the Westchester County Archives, Elmsford, N.Y.
WCH   Bolton, Robert
            1881 *The History of the Several Towns, Manors, and Patents of the County of Westchester, New York.* 2 vols. Second edition. New York. First published in 1848.
WJD   West Jersey Deeds. On file in the New Jersey Archives, Trenton.
WPHOA   Myers, Albert Cook, ed.
            1937 *William Penn: His Own Account of the Lenni Lenape or Delaware Indians, 1683.* Moylan, Pa. Reprinted in 1970 by the Middle Atlantic Press, Wallingford, Pa.

Sources Cited by Author and Date

Adams, Charles Francis, ed.
    1883 *New English Canaan.* Boston. First published in 1632. Multiple reprints.
Alexander, James, and Joseph Murray
    1747 *A Bill in the Chancery of New Jersey, At the Suit of John Earl of Stair, and Others, Proprietors of the Eastern Division of New Jersey; against Benjamin Bond, and Some Persons of Elizabeth Town, Distinguished by the Name Clinker Lot Right Men.* New York: James Parker, printer.
Anderson, Fred
    2000 *Crucible of War: The Seven Years' War and the Fate of Empire in British North America, 1754–1766.* New York: Alfred A. Knopf.
Anonymous
    1681 *An Abstract or Abbreviation of Some Few of the Many Testimonies from the Inhabitants of New Jersey and other Eminent Persons.* London.
    1898 "Abstract of an Indenture of 1727." *Pennsylvania Magazine of History and Biography,* Vol. 22, No. 4, p. 504.
    1905 "Dedication of the Monument at Meniolagomeka, October 22, 1901." *Transactions of the Moravian Historical Society,* Vol. 7, No. 1, pp. 4–12.
    1908 "List of Pennsylvania Settlers Murdered, Scalped, and Taken Prisoner by the Indians, 1755–1756." *Pennsylvania Magazine of History and Biography,* Vol. 32, No. 3, pp. 309–319.
    1913 "Melyn Papers: 1640–1699." *Collections of the New-York Historical Society for the Year 1913,* pp. 95–138. New York.

1924   "Ramapo Indian Deed." *Proceedings of the New Jersey Historical Society*, Vol. 9, No. 2, pp. 300–304.

Aquila, Richard
1983   *The Iroquois Restoration: Iroquois Diplomacy on the Frontier, 1701–1754.* Detroit: Wayne State University Press. Reprinted in 1997 by University of Nebraska Press, Lincoln.

Axtell, James, ed.
1981   *The Indian Peoples of Eastern America: A Documentary History of the Sexes.* New York: Oxford University Press.

Bachman, Van Cleaf
1970   *Peltries or Plantations: The Economic Policies of the Dutch West Indian Company in New Netherlands, 1621–1638.* Baltimore: Johns Hopkins University Press.

Bailey, Frederick G.
1983   *The Tactical Uses of Passion: An Essay on Power, Reason, and Reality.* Ithaca: Cornell University Press.
1991   *The Prevalence of Deceit.* Ithaca: Cornell University Press.

Baker, Emerson W.
1989   "'A Scratch with a Bear's Paw': Anglo-Indian Land Deeds in Early Maine." *Ethnohistory,* Vol. 36, No. 3, pp. 235–256.
2004   "Finding the Almouchiquois: Native American Families, Territories, and Land Sales in Southern Maine." *Ethnohistory,* Vol. 51, No. 1, pp. 73–100.

Banner, Stuart
2005   *How the Indians Lost Their Land: Law and Power on the Frontier.* Cambridge: Harvard University Press.

Barbour, Phillip L., ed.
1986   *The Complete Works of Captain John Smith (1580–1631).* 3 vols. Chapel Hill: University of North Carolina Press.

Barnes, Carol
1968   "Subsistence and Social Organization of the Delaware Indians: 1600 A. D." *Bulletin of the Philadelphia Anthropological Society,* Vol. 20, No. 1, pp. 15–29.

Barth, Fredrik
1969   "Introduction." In *Ethnic Groups and Boundaries: The Social Organization of Cultural Difference,* Fredrik Barth, ed., 9–38. Boston: Little, Brown.

Bartlett, John R., ed.
1856–1865   *Records of the Colony of Rhode Island and Providence Plantations in New England (1636–1792).* 10 vols. Providence: A. C. Green and Brothers.

Barton, Benjamin Smith
1798   *New Views of the Origin of the Tribes and Nations of America.* Revised second edition. First edition published in 1797.

Beauchamp, William Morris
1907   *Aboriginal Place Names of New York.* New York State Museum Bulletin, No. 108. Albany.

Becker, Marshall Joseph

1986   "The Okehocking Band of Lenape: Cultural Continuities and Accommodations in Southeastern Pennsylvania." In *Strategies for Survival: American Indians in the Eastern United States*, Frank W. Porter, III, ed., pp. 43–83. Westport, Ct.: Greenwood Press.

1987   "The Moravian Mission in the Forks of Delaware: Reconstructing the Migration and Settlement Patterns of the Jersey Lenape during the Eighteenth Century through Documents in the Moravian Archives." *Unitas Fratrum*, Nos. 21–22, pp. 83–168. Friedrich Wittig Verlag, Hamburg, Ger.

1988   "A Summary of Lenape Socio-Political Organization and Settlement Pattern at the Time of European Contact: The Evidence for Collecting Bands." *Journal of Middle Atlantic Archaeology*, Vol. 4, pp. 79–83.

1993   "The Lenape and Other 'Delawarean' Peoples at the Time of European Contact: Population Estimates Derived from Archaeological and Historical Sources." *The Bulletin: Journal of the New York State Archaeological Association*, No. 105, pp. 16–25.

Bishop, Charles A., and Toby Morantz, eds.

1986   "Who Owns the Beaver? Northern Algonquian Land Tenure Reconsidered." *Anthropologica*, Vol. 28, Nos. 1–2, pp. 1–219.

Bohannan, Laura

1966   "Shakespeare in the Bush." *Natural History*, Vol. 75, pp. 28–33. Multiple reprints.

Bolton, Reginald Pelham

1920   *New York in Indian Possession*. Indian Notes and Monographs, Vol. 2, No. 7. Museum of the American Indian, Heye Foundation. Second edition published in 1975 by the Museum of the American Indian, Heye Foundation. New York.

Bond, Richmond P.

1952   *Queen Anne's American Kings*. Oxford: Oxford University Press. Reprinted in 1974 by Octagon Books, N.Y.

Bonomi, Patricia U.

1998   *The Lord Cornbury Scandal: The Politics of Reputation in British America*. Chapel Hill: University of North Carolina Press.

Bourne, Russell

1990   *The Red King's Rebellion: Racial Politics in New England, 1675–1678*. New York: Atheneum.

Boyd, Paul D.

2005   "Settlers along the Shores: Lenape Spatial Patterns in Coastal Monmouth County, 1600–1750." Unpublished Doctoral Dissertation, Department of Geography, Rutgers University, New Brunswick, N.J.

Brasser, Theodore J. C.

1974   *Riding on the Frontier's Crest: Mahican Indian Culture and Culture Change*. National Museum of Man, Mercury Series, Ethnology Division Paper, No. 13, Ottawa.

1978   "Mahican." In *Northeast*, Vol. 15, Bruce T. Trigger, ed., pp. 198–212. William C. Sturtevant, gen. ed., *Handbook of North American Indians.* Washington, D.C.: Smithsonian Institution Press.

Bright, William
n.d.   "The Sociolinguistics of the 'S-Word': 'Squaw' in American Place Names." Online article at www.ncidc.org/bright/Squaw_revised.doc.

Brink, Benjamin Myer, ed.
1905–1914   *Olde Ulster: An Historical and Genealogical Magazine.* 10 vols. Kingston, N.Y.

Brinton, Daniel Garrison
1885   *The Lenape and Their Legends: With the Complete Text and Symbols of the Walam Olum, a New Translation, and an Inquiry into Its Authenticity.* Brinton's Library of Aboriginal Americana, No. 5. Philadelphia. Reprinted in 1969 by AMS Press, New York.

Broshar, Helen
1920   "The First Push Westward of the Albany Traders." *The Mississippi Valley Historical Review,* Vol. 7, No. 3, pp. 228–241.

Brown, James A., ed.
1961   *The Zimmerman Site: A Report of Excavations at the Grand Village of Old Kaskaskia, La Salle County, Illinois.* Report of Investigations, No. 9, Illinois State Museum. Springfield.

Browne, William Hand, et al., eds.
1883-present   *Archives of Maryland.* 72 vols. Baltimore: Maryland Historical Society.

Buckland, John Alexander
2002   *The First Traders on Wall Street: The Wiechquaeskeck Indians of Southwestern Connecticut in the Seventeenth Century.* Bowie, Md.: Heritage Books.

Budd, Thomas
1685   *Good Order Established in Pennsilvania and New Jersey.* Philadelphia: William Bradford. Reprinted in 1902 by Frederick J. Shepard in Cleveland and in 1966 by Readex Microprint, Ann Arbor, Mi.

Buffinton, Arthur H.
1922   "The Policy of Albany and English Westward Expansion." *Mississippi Valley Historical Review,* Vol. 8, No. 4, pp. 327–366.

Callender, Charles
1978   "Shawnee." In *Northeast,* Vol. 15, Bruce T. Trigger, ed., pp. 622–635. William C. Sturtevant, gen. ed., *Handbook of North American Indians.* Washington, D.C.: Smithsonian Institution Press.

Calloway, Colin G.
1990   *The Western Abenakis of Vermont, 1600–1800: War, Migration, and the Survival of an Indian People.* Norman: University of Oklahoma Press.
1995   *The American Revolution in Indian Country: Crisis and Diversity in Native American Communities.* New York: Cambridge University Press.

Campbell, Tony

   1965   "New Light on the Jansson-Visscher Maps of New England." *The Map Collectors Circle*, No. 24. London.

Cantwell, Anne-Marie, and Diane DiZerega Wall

   2001   *Unearthing Gotham: The Archaeology of New York City.* New Haven: Yale University Press.

Cave, Alfred A.

   2006   *Prophets of the Great Spirit: Native American Revitalization Movements in Eastern North America.* Lincoln: University of Nebraska Press.

Ceci, Lynn

   1977   "The Effect of European Contact and Trade on the Settlement Pattern of Indians in Coastal New York, 1524–1665: The Archaeological and Documentary Evidence." Unpublished Doctoral Dissertation, Department of Anthropology, Graduate Center of the City University of New York. Published in 1990 by Garland Publishing Company, New York.

   1989   "Tracing Wampum's Origins: Shell Bead Evidence From Archaeological Sites in Western and Coastal New York." In *Proceedings of the 1986 Shell Bead Conference*, Charles F. Hayes, III, ed., pp. 63–80. Rochester Museum and Science Center.

Chase, Thomas C.

   1980   "Christian Frederick Post, 1715–1785: Missionary and Diplomat to the Indians of America." Unpublished Doctoral Dissertation, Department of Education, Pennsylvania State University, State College.

Chidsey, Andrew Dwight

   1937   *The Penn Patents in the Forks of the Delaware.* Easton, Pa.: Northampton Historical and Genealogical Society Publications.

Christoph, Peter R., ed.

   1980   *Administrative Papers of Governors Richard Nicolls and Francis Lovelace, 1664–1673, Volume XXII.* New York Historical Manuscripts: English. Baltimore: Genealogical Publishing Company.

Cobb, Charles R., ed.

   2003   *Stone Tool Traditions in the Contact Era.* Tuscaloosa: University of Alabama Press.

Collins, June

   1970   *Valley of the Spirits: The Skagit Indians of Western Washington State.* Seattle: University of Washington Press.

Condon, Thomas J.

   1968   *New York Beginnings: The Commercial Origins of New Netherland.* New York: New York University Press.

Cook, Sherburne F.

   1976   *The Indian Population of New England in the Seventeenth Century.* University of California Publications in Anthropology, Vol. 12. Berkeley.

Cooper, John M.

   1938   "Land Tenure among the Indians of Eastern and Northern North America." *Pennsylvania Archaeologist*, Vol. 8, No. 3, pp. 55–59.

Corwin, Edward T., ed.
    1901–1916   *Ecclesiastical Records State of New York.* 7 vols. Albany: University of the State of New York.

Cronon, William
    1983   *Changes in the Land: Indians, Colonists, and the Ecology of New England.* New York: Hill and Wang.

Day, Gordon F.
    1953   "The Indian as an Ecological Factor in the Northeastern Forest." *Ecology,* Vol. 34, No. 2, pp. 329–346.

De Lancey, Edward F.
    1886   "The Origin and History of Manors in New York, and in the County of Westchester." In *History of Westchester County, New York.* 2 vols. J. Thomas Scharf, ed., Vol. 1, pp. 31–160. Philadelphia: L. E. Preston. Reprinted in 1992 by Picton Press, Camden, Me.

Denton, Daniel
    1670   *A Brief Description of New-York: Formerly Called New Netherlands.* London. Reprinted in 1966, March of America Facsimile Series, No. 26, University Microfilms, Ann Arbor, Mi.

Dobyns, Henry F.
    1966   "Estimating Aboriginal American Populations: An Appraisal of Techniques with a New Hemispheric Estimate." *Current Anthropology,* Vol. 7, No. 3, pp. 395–416.
    1983   *Their Number Become Thinned: Native American Population Dynamics in Eastern North America.* Knoxville: University of Tennessee Press.

Dorsey, George A.
    1902   "The Osage Mourning-War Ceremony." *American Anthropologist,* Vol. 4, No. 3, pp. 404–411.

Douglas, Mary
    1966   *Purity and Danger: An Analysis of Concepts of Pollution and Taboo.* London: Routledge and Kegan Paul.

Drake, James D.
    1999   *King Philip's War: Civil War in New England, 1675–1676.* Amherst: University of Massachusetts Press.

Dunn, Richard S., Mary Maples Dunn, Edwin B. Bronner, and David Fraser, eds.
    1981–1986   *The Papers of William Penn.* 5 vols. Philadelphia: University of Pennsylvania Press.

Dunn, Shirley W.
    1994   *The Mohicans and Their Land: 1609–1730.* Fleischmanns, N.Y.: Purple Mountain Press.
    2000   *The Mohican World, 1680–1750.* Fleischmanns, N.Y.: Purple Mountain Press.

Eager, Samuel
    1846   *An Outline History of Orange County.* Newburgh, N.Y.: S. T. Callahan. Reprinted in 1969 by Trumbull Printing, Middletown, N.Y., and in 2007 by Apple Manor Press, Markham, Va.

Edwards, Jonathan, and Sereno Edwards Dwight, eds.

1822   *Memoirs of the Reverend David Brainerd: Missionary to the Indians on the Border of New York, New Jersey, and Pennsylvania.* New Haven: S. Converse. Multiple reprints.

Ellis, David Maldwyn

1946   *Landlords and Farmers in the Hudson-Mohawk Region, 1790–1850.* Ithaca: Cornell University Press. Reprinted in 1967 by Octagon Books, N.Y.

Esposito, Frank J.

1976   "Indian-White Relations in New Jersey." Unpublished Doctoral Dissertation, Department of History, Rutgers University, New Brunswick, N.J.

Evans-Pritchard, Edward E.

1940   *The Nuer.* London: Cambridge University Press.

Fenton, William N.

1998   *The Great Law and the Longhouse: A Political History of the Iroquois Confederacy.* Norman: University of Oklahoma Press.

Fernow, Berthold, and Arnold J. F. Van Laer, eds.

1902   *Calendar of Council Minutes, 1668–1783.* Bulletin 58, History Bulletin 6. Albany: University of the State of New York. Reprinted in 1987 by Harbor Hill Books, Harrison, N.Y.

Fiedel, Stuart J.

1987   "Algonquian Origins: A Problem in Archaeological-Linguistic Correlation." *Archaeology of Eastern North America,* Vol. 15, pp. 1–11.

Flexner, James Thomas

1959   *Mohawk Baronet: A Biography of Sir William Johnson.* New York: Harper and Brothers. Little, Brown published a revised version entitled *Lord of the Mohawks* in 1979. Syracuse University Press published the revised edition under its original title in 1989.

Fliegel, Carl John, ed.

1978   *Guide to the Records of the Moravian Mission among the Indians of North America.* New Haven: Gale/Primary Source Microfilm.

Fogelson, Raymond D.

1989   "The Ethnohistory of Events and Nonevents." *Ethnohistory,* Vol. 36, No. 2, pp. 133–147.

Fortes, Meyer

1953   "The Structure of Unilineal Groups." *American Anthropologist,* Vol. 55, No. 1, pp. 25–39.

Fox, Dixon Ryan

1926   *Caleb Heathcote, Gentleman Colonist, Lord of the Manor of Scarsdale: The Story of a Career in the Province of New York, 1692–1721.* New York: Charles Scribner's Sons. Reprinted in 1971 by Cooper Square Publishers, N.Y., and in 1989 by Harbor Hill Books.

Fox, Robin

1967   *Kinship and Marriage: An Anthropological Perspective.* Baltimore: Penguin. Cambridge University Press published a new impression edition in 1984.

Frazier, Patrick
    1992   *The Mohicans of Stockbridge*. Lincoln: University of Nebraska Press.

Fried, Marc B.
    1975   *The Early History of Kingston and Ulster County, New York*. Marbletown, N.Y.: Ulster County Historical Society.

Fried, Morton H.
    1967   *The Evolution of Political Society: An Essay in Political Anthropology*. New York: Random House.

Frijhoff, Willem
    1998   "New Views on the Dutch Period of New York." *De Halve Maen*, No. 71, pp. 23–34.

Garratt, John G.
    1985   *The Four Indian Kings*. Ottawa: Public Archives Canada.

Gearing, Fred O.
    1962   *Priests and Warriors: Social Structure for Cherokee Politics in the Eighteenth Century*. Memoirs of the American Anthropological Association, Vol. 64, No. 5, Pt. 2. Memoir 93. Menasha, Wisc.

Gehring, Charles T., trans. and ed.
    1977   *Delaware Papers (English Period): Volumes 20–21*. New York Historical Manuscripts. Baltimore: Geneaological Publishing Company.
    1983   *Council Minutes, 1652–1654: Volume 5*. New York Historical Manuscripts, Dutch. Baltimore: Genealogical Publishing Company.
    1990   "Brant Van Slichtenhorst Deposition." *Marcurious: Newsletter of the New Netherland Project*, Vol. 6, No. 3, pp. 2–3.
    2003   *Correspondence of Petrus Stuyvesant, 1654–1658: Volume 12*. New Netherland Documents Series. Syracuse, N.Y.: Syracuse University Press.

Gehring, Charles T., trans., and Robert S. Grumet, ed.
    1987   "Observations of the Indians From Jasper Danckaerts's Journal, 1679–1680." *William and Mary Quarterly*, Vol. 44, No. 1, pp. 104–120.

Gehring, Charles T., and Jacob Adriaan Schiltkamp, trans. and eds.
    1987   *Curacao Papers, 1640–1665*. New Netherland Documents, Vol. 17. Interlaken, N.Y.: Heart of the Lakes Publishing.

Gehring, Charles T., trans., and William A. Starna, ed.
    1988   *A Journey into Mohawk and Oneida Country, 1634–1635: The Journal of Harmen Meyndertszen van den Bogaert*. Syracuse, N.Y.: Syracuse University Press.

Gill, Sam M.
    1990   *Mother Earth*. Chicago: University of Chicago Press.

Goddard, Robert H. Ives, III
    1971   "The Ethnohistorical Implications of Early Delaware Linguistic Materials." *Man in the Northeast*, No. 1, pp. 14–26. Reprinted in 1978 in *Neighbors and Intruders: An Ethnohistorical Exploration of the Indians of Hudson's River*, Laurence M. Hauptman and Jack Campisi, eds., pp. 88–102. National Museum of Canada Mercury Series, Canadian Centre for Folk Culture Studies Paper No. 39. Ottawa.

1974   "The Delaware Language, Past and Present." In *A Delaware Indian Symposium*, Herbert C. Kraft, ed., pp. 103–110. Anthropological Series No. 4, Pennsylvania Historical and Museum Commission. Harrisburg.

1978   "Delaware." In *Northeast*, Vol. 15, Bruce T. Trigger, ed., pp. 212–239. William C. Sturtevant, gen. ed., *Handbook of North American Indians*. Washington, D.C.: Smithsonian Institution Press.

1997   "Since the Word Squaw Continues to Be of Interest." *News From Indian Country*, Mid-April, p. 19. An expanded version entitled "The True History of the Word Squaw" is posted online at www.nmhm.si.edu/anthro/Goddard/Squaw_1.pdf.

Gonzalez, Ellice

1984   "From Unkechaug to Poospatuck." Manuscript on file, Fire Island National Seashore, National Park Service, Patchogue, N.Y.

Gould, Stephen Jay

2002   *The Structure of Evolutionary Theory.* Cambridge: Harvard University Press.

Gray, Elma E., and Leslie Robb Gray

1956   *Wilderness Christians: The Moravian Mission to the Delaware Indians.* Ithaca, N.Y.: Cornell University Press.

Grumet, Robert S.

1978   "An Analysis of Upper Delawaran Land Sales in Northern New Jersey, 1630–1758." In *Papers of the Ninth Algonquian Conference*, William Cowan, ed., pp. 25–35. Ottawa: Carleton University Press.

1979   "'We Are Not So Great Fools': Changes in Upper Delawaran Socio-Political Life, 1630–1758." Unpublished Doctoral Dissertation, Department of Anthropology, Rutgers University, New Brunswick, N.J.

1980   "Sunksquaws, Shamans, and Tradeswomen: Mid-Atlantic Coastal Algonkian Women during the Seventeenth and Eighteenth Centuries." In *Women and Colonization: Anthropological Perspectives*, Mona Etienne and Eleanor Burke Leacock, eds., pp. 43–62. New York: Bergin and Praeger Scientific.

1982   "On the Identity of the Rechgawawanck." *The Bulletin and Journal of Archaeology for New York State*, No. 83, pp. 1–7.

1989a   "The Selling of Lenapehoking." *Bulletin of the Archaeological Society of New Jersey*, No. 44, pp. 1–6. Reprinted in 1994 in *Proceedings of the 1992 People to People Conference: Selected Papers*, Charles F. Hayes III, Connie Cox Bodner, and Lorraine P. Saunders, eds., pp. 19–24. Research Records No. 23, Rochester Museum and Science Center. Rochester, N.Y.

1989b   "'Strangely Decrease by the Hand of God': A Documentary Appearance-Disappearance Model for Munsee Demography, 1630–1801." *Journal of Middle Atlantic Archaeology*, Vol. 5, pp. 129–145.

1990a   "A New Ethnohistorical Model for North American Indian Demography." *North American Archaeologist*, Vol. 11, No. 1, pp. 29–41.

1990b   "'That Their Issue Be Not Spurious': An Inquiry into Munsee Matriliny." *Bulletin of the Archaeological Society of New Jersey*, No. 45, pp. 19–24.

1991a   "The Minisink Settlements: Native American Identity and Society in
the Munsee Heartland, 1650–1778." In *People of Minisink: Papers from the
1989 Delaware Water Gap Symposium*, David G. Orr and Douglas V. Campana,
eds., pp. 175–250. Philadelphia: Mid-Atlantic Region, National Park Service.

1991b   "The King of New Jersey." In *The Archaeology and Ethnohistory of the
Lower Hudson Valley and Neighboring Regions: Essays in Honor of Louis A. Bren-
nan*, Herbert C. Kraft, ed., pp. 223–231. Occasional Publications in Northeastern Anthropology, No. 11. Bethlehem, Ct. Reprinted in 1993 in the
Bulletin of the Archaeological Society of New Jersey, No. 48, pp. 45–52.

1992   "The Nimhams of the Colonial Hudson Valley, 1667–1783." *The Hudson Valley Regional Review*, Vol. 9, No. 2, pp. 80–99.

1994   "New Information From an Old Source: Notes on Adam the Indian's
May 11, 1653, Testimony in the New Plymouth Colony Records." *Bulletin of
the Archaeological Society of New Jersey*, No. 49, pp. 83–87.

1995   *Historic Contact: Indian People and Colonists in Today's Northeastern United
States in the Sixteenth through Eighteenth Centuries.* Norman: University of
Oklahoma Press.

1996   "Suscaneman and the Matinecock Lands, 1653–1703." In *Northeastern
Indian Lives, 1631–1816*. Robert S. Grumet, ed., pp. 116–139. Amherst: University of Massachusetts Press.

Grumet, Robert S., ed.
1999   *Journey on the Forbidden Path: Chronicles of a Diplomatic Mission to the Allegheny Country, March-September, 1760.* Transactions of the American Philosophical Society, Vol. 89, Pt. 2. Philadelphia.

Haefeli, Evan
1999   "Kieft's War and the Cultures of Violence in Colonial America." In
Lethal Imagination: Violence and Brutality in American History. Michael A. Belle-
siles, ed., pp. 17–40. New York: New York University Press.

Hagedorn, Nancy L.
1988   "'A Friend to Go between Them': The Interpreter as Culture Broker
during Anglo-Iroquois Councils, 1740–1770." *Ethnohistory*, Vol. 35, No. 1, pp.
60–80.

1994   "Faithful, Knowing, and Prudent: Andrew Montour as Interpreter and
Culture Broker, 1740–1772." In *Between Indian and White Worlds: The Culture
Broker*, Margaret Connell Szasz, ed., 44–60. Norman: University of Oklahoma
Press.

Hamell, George R.
1983   "Trading in Metaphors: Another Perspective Upon Indian-European
Contact in Northeastern North America." In *Proceedings of the 1982 Glass
Trade Bead Conference*. Charles F. Hayes, III, ed., pp. 5–28. Research Records
No. 16, Rochester Museum and Science Center. Rochester, N.Y.

Hamilton, Kenneth G., trans. and ed.
  1971   *The Bethlehem Diary, Volume 1, 1742–1744.* Bethlehem: Archives of the Moravian Church.

Handlin, Oscar, and Irving Mark, eds.
  1964   "Chief Nimham v. Roger Morris, Beverly Robinson, and Philip Philipse—An Indian Land Case in Colonial New York, 1765–1767." *Ethnohistory,* Vol. 11, No. 3, pp. 193–246.

Hardin, Garrett
  1968   "The Tragedy of the Commons." *Science,* Vol. 162, No. 3859, pp. 1243–1248.

Harrington, Mark Raymond
  1913   "A Preliminary Sketch of Lenape Culture." *American Anthropologist,* Vol. 15, No. 2, pp. 208–235.

Hart, John P., ed.
  1998   *Current Northeast Paleobotany.* New York State Museum Bulletin, No. 494. Albany.

Hart, John P., and Hetty Jo Brumbach
  2003   "The Death of Owasco." *American Antiquity,* Vol. 68, No. 4, pp. 737–752.

Hasbrouck, Frank, ed.
  1909   *The History of Dutchess County, New York.* Poughkeepsie, N.Y.: Samuel A. Matthieu.

Havard, Gilles
  2001   *The Great Peace of Montreal of 1701: French-Native Diplomacy in the Seventeenth Century.* Translated by Phyllis Aronoff and Howard Scott. Montreal: McGill-Queens University Press.

Heckewelder, John Gottlieb Ernestus
  1820   *A Narrative of the Mission of the United Brethren among the Delaware and Mohegan Indians, From Its Commencement, in the Year 1740 to the Year 1808.* Philadelphia: McCarty and Davis. Second edition edited by William E. Connelley, published in 1907 in Cleveland, Oh.
  1841   "Indian Tradition of the First Arrival of the Dutch at Manhattan Island, New New York." *Collections of the New-York Historical Society,* Second Series, Vol. 1, pp. 68–74.
  1876   *History, Manners, and Customs of the Indians Who Once Inhabited Pennsylvania and the Neighbouring States.* Second edition. Memoirs of the Historical Society of Pennsylvania, Vol. 12, William C. Reichel, ed. Philadelphia. First published in 1819 in *Transactions of the Historical and Literary Committee of the American Philosophical Society,* Vol. 1, Philadelphia and reprinted by Arno Press and the New York Times in 1971.

Henige, David P.
  1998   *Numbers from Nowhere: The American Indian Contact Population Debate.* Norman: University of Oklahoma Press.

Heusser, Albert H.
  1923   *Homes and Haunts of the Indians*. Paterson, N.J.: Benjamin Franklin
  Press.

Hinderaker, Eric
  1996   "The 'Four Indian Kings' and the Imaginative Construction of the
  First British Empire." *William and Mary Quarterly*, Vol. 53, No. 3, pp. 487–526.

Hinman, Marjory Barnum
  1975   *Onaquaga: Hub of the Border Wars of the American Revolution in New York
  State*. Windsor, N.Y.: Privately printed.

Hodge, Frederick Webb, ed.
  1907–1910   *Handbook of American Indians North of Mexico*. 2 vols. Bureau of
  American Ethnology, Bulletin 30. Washington, D.C.: Government Printing
  Office.

Hoffer, Peter Charles
  1998   *Law and People in Colonial America*. Revised edition. Baltimore: Johns
  Hopkins University Press. First published in 1992.

Holcomb, Richmond C.
  1926   "The Old York Road." In *Bucks County Historical Society*, Vol. 5, pp.
  657–658. Doylestown, Pa.

Honeyman, A. Van Doren, ed.
  1928   "Letter of Marian Peters to the Reverend Mr. Marsh, Keshena, Wisconsin, June 20, 1864." *Proceedings of the New Jersey Historical Society*, Vol. 8, No.
  4, pp. 410–414.

Horn, James
  1993   "Repeopling the Land: The British and Dutch Colonies." In *Encyclopedia of the North American Colonies*. Vol. 2, James Ernest Cooke, ed., pp. 301–
  317. New York: Charles Scribner's Sons.

Hosmer, James K., ed.
  1908   *Winthrop's Journal, History of New England, 1630–1649*. 2 vols. New
  York: Charles Scribner's Sons.

Howell, George Rogers, ed.
  1902   *Colonial Records: General Entries, Volume 1, 1664–1665*. New York State
  Library History Bulletin 1, No. 2. Albany.

Hulburt, Archer Butler, and William Nathaniel Schwarze, eds.
  1910   "David Zeisberger's History of the Northern American Indians,
  1779–1780." *Ohio State Archaeological and Historical Quarterly*, Vol. 19, pp. 1–189.
  Reprinted in 1999 by Wennawoods Publishing, Lewisburg, Pa..

Hunter, Charles E.
  1971   "The Delaware Nativist Revival of the Mid-Eighteenth Century."
  Ethnohistory, Vol. 18, No. 1, pp. 39–49.
  1983   "A Susquehanna Indian Town on the Schuylkill." *Pennsylvania Archaeologist*, Vol. 53, No. 3, pp. 17–19.

Hunter, William A.

1960   *Forts on the Pennsylvania Frontier, 1753–1758.* Harrisburg: Pennsylvania Historical and Museum Commission.

1974   "Moses (Tunda) Tatamy, Delaware Indian Diplomat." In *A Delaware Indian Symposium,* Herbert C. Kraft, ed., pp. 71–88. Anthropological Series No. 4, Pennsylvania Historical and Museum Commission. Harrisburg. Reprinted in 1996 in *Northeastern Indian Lives, 1632–1816,* Robert S. Grumet, ed., pp. 258–272. Amherst: University of Massachusetts Press.

Jacobs, Jaap

2005   *New Netherland: A Dutch Colony in Seventeenth-Century America.* Leiden: Brill.

Jacobs, Wilbur

1950   *Diplomacy and Indian Gifts: Anglo-French Rivalry along the Ohio and Northwest Frontiers, 1748–1763.* Stanford, Calif.: Stanford University Press. Reprinted in 1966 by the University of Nebraska Press, Lincoln, Neb., and in 2001 by Wennawoods Publishing, Lewisburg, Pa..

Jenness, Diamond

1935   *The Ojibwa Indians of Parry Island, Their Social and Religious Life.* National Museum of Canada Bulletin No. 78, Anthropological Series, No. 17. Ottawa, Ont.

Jennings, Francis

1965   "Miquon's Passing: Indian-European Relations in Colonial Pennsylvania, 1674–1755." Unpublished Doctoral Dissertation, Department of History, University of Pennsylvania, Philadelphia.

1970   "The Scandalous Policy of William Penn's Sons: Deeds and Documents of the Walking Purchase." *Pennsylvania History,* Vol. 37, No. 1, pp. 19–39.

1971   "The Constitutional Evolution of the Covenant Chain." *Proceedings of the American Philosophical Society,* Vol. 115, No. 2, pp. 88–96. Philadelphia.

1975   *The Invasion of America: Indians, Colonialism, and the Cant of Conquest.* Chapel Hill: University of North Carolina Press. Reprinted in 1976 by W. W. Norton, N.Y.

1978   "Susquehannock." In *Northeast,* Vol. 15, Bruce T. Trigger, ed., pp. 362–367. William C. Sturtevant, gen. ed., *Handbook of North American Indians.* Washington, D.C.: Smithsonian Institution Press.

1984   *The Ambiguous Iroquois Empire: The Covenant Chain Confederation of Indian Tribes with English Colonies from Its Beginnings to the Lancaster Treaty of 1744.* New York: W. W. Norton.

1988   *Empire of Fortune: Crowns, Colonies, and Tribes in the Seven Years' War in America.* New York: W. W. Norton.

Johnson, Jeffrey C.

1996   "Network Analysis." In *Encyclopedia of Cultural Anthropology,* Vol. 3, David Levinson and Melvin Ember, eds., pp. 855–859. New York: Henry Holt.

Johnston, Charles M., ed.

    1964   *The Valley of the Six Nations: A Collection of Documents on the Indian Lands of the Grand River.* Toronto: Champlain Society for the Government of Ontario and the University of Toronto Press. Reprinted in 1971.

Jordan, John W., ed.

    1913   "James Kenny's Journal, 1761–63." *Pennsylvania Magazine of History and Biography,* Vol. 37, No. 1, pp. 1–47; No. 2, pp. 152–201.

Jorgensen, Joseph G.

    1984   "Land is Cultural, So Is a Commodity: The Locus of Differences Among Indians, Cowboys, Sod-Busters, and Environmentalists." *Journal of Ethnic Studies,* Vol. 12, No. 3, pp. 1–21.

Judd, Jacob

    2005   "Manor System." In *Encyclopedia of New York State,* Peter Eisenstadt and Laura-Eve Moss, eds., pp. 952–954. Syracuse, N.Y.: Syracuse University Press.

Kent, Barry C.

    1984   *Susquehanna's Indians.* Anthropological Series, No. 6, Pennsylvania Museum and Historical Commission. Harrisburg.

Kim, Sung Bock

    1978   *Landlord and Tenant in Colonial New York: Manorial Society, 1664–1775.* Chapel Hill: University of North Carolina Press.

Kraft, Herbert C.

    1975   *The Archaeology of the Tocks Island Area.* South Orange, N.J.: Seton Hall University Archaeological Research Center.

    1977   *The Minisink Settlements: An Investigation into a Prehistoric and Early Historic Site in Sussex County, New Jersey.* South Orange, N.J.: Seton Hall University Archaeological Research Center.

    1996   *The Dutch, the Indians, and the Quest for Copper: Pahaquarry and the Old Mine Road.* South Orange, N.J.: Seton Hall University Museum.

    2001   *The Lenape-Delaware Indian Heritage: 10,000 B. C. to A. D. 2000.* Elizabeth, N.J.: Lenape Books.

Kroeber, Alfred Louis

    1939   *Cultural and Natural Areas of Native North America.* University of California Publications in American Archaeology and Ethnology, Vol. 38. Berkeley. Reprinted in 1947 by University of California Press.

La Potin, Armand Shelby

    1974   "The Minisink Patent: A Study in Colonial Landholding and the Problems of Settlement in Eighteenth Century New York." Unpublished Doctoral Dissertation, Department of History, University of Wisconsin, Madison. Published in 1979 by the Arno Press, New York. A greatly abridged version was published in 1978 in *Neighbors and Intruders: An Ethnohistorical Exploration of the Indians of Hudson's River,* Laurence M. Hauptman and Jack Campisi, eds., pp. 210–223. National Museum of Canada Mercury Series, Canadian Centre for Folk Culture Studies Paper No. 39. Ottawa.

LaPlante, Eve

    2004   *American Jezebel: The Uncommon Life of Anne Hutchinson, the Woman Who Defied the Puritans.* New York: HarperOne.

Leach, Douglas Edward

1958   *Flintlock and Tomahawk: New England in King Philip's War.* New York: McMillan. Reprinted in 1966 by W. W. Norton, New York, and in 1992 by Parnassus Press, Berkeley.

Leach, Edmund R.

1954   *Political Systems of Highland Burma: A Study of Kachin Social Structure.* London: G. Bell and Son. Reprinted in 1970 by the Athlone Press, London.

Leacock, Eleanor Burke

1954   *The Montagnais "Hunting Territory" and the Fur Trade.* Memoirs of the American Anthropological Association, No. 78. Menasha, Wisc.

1983   "Ethnohistorical Investigation of Egalitarian Politics in Eastern North America." In *The Development of Political Organization in Native North America: 1979 Proceedings of the American Ethnological Society,* Elisabeth Tooker, ed., pp. 7–31. Washington, D.C.: American Ethnological Society.

Leacock, Eleanor Burke, ed.

1963   *Lewis Henry Morgan: Ancient Society, or Researches in the Line of Human Progress From Savagery through Barbarism to Civilization.* Cleveland: Meridian Books. First published in 1877 and reprinted with a new introduction by Robin Fox in 2000 by Transaction Publishers, New Brunswick, N.J.

Leacock, Eleanor Burke, and Richard Borshay Lee, eds.

1982   *Politics and History in Band Societies.* New York: Cambridge University Press.

Leamon, James S.

1963   "Governor Fletcher's Recall." *William and Mary Quarterly,* Vol. 20, No. 4, pp. 527–542.

Leder, Lawrence H.

1961   *Robert Livingston, 1654–1728, and the Politics of Colonial New York.* Chapel Hill: University of North Carolina Press.

Lee, Richard Borshay

1969   "Eating Christmas in the Kalahari." *Natural History,* Vol. 78, pp. 14, 16, 18, 21–22, 60–63. Multiple reprints.

Lee, Richard Borshay, and Irven De Vore, eds.

1968   *Man the Hunter.* Chicago: Aldine.

Levering, Joseph M.

1903   *A History of Bethlehem, Pennsylvania, 1741–1892.* Bethlehem.

Lewin, Howard

1966   "A Frontier Diplomat: Andrew Montour." *Pennsylvania History,* Vol. 33, No. 2, pp. 153–186.

Lopez, Julius, and Stanley Wisniewski

1971–1972   "The Ryder's Pond Site: Kings County, New York." *New York State Archaeological Association Bulletin,* No. 53, pp. 1–21, and No. 55, pp. 6–20.

Lepore, Jill

1998   *The Name of War: King Philip's War and the Origins of American Identity.* New York: Alfred A. Knopf.

Lurie, Nancy O.
1974   "Forked Tongue in Cheek or Life Among the Noble Civilages." *Indian Historian,* Vol. 7, No. 2, pp. 28–40 and 52.

Lustig, Mary Lou
1983   *Robert Hunter (1666–1734): New York's Augustan Statesman.* Syracuse, N.Y.: Syracuse University Press.
2005   "Colonial New York." In *Encyclopedia of New York State,* Peter Eisenstadt and Laura-Eve Moss, eds., pp. 326–368. Syracuse, N.Y.: Syracuse University Press.

MacLeod, William Christie
1922   "The Family Hunting Territory and Lenape Political Organization." *American Anthropologist,* Vol. 24, No. 3, pp. 448–463.
1941   "The Indians of Brooklyn in the Days of the Dutch." Historical Records Survey, U.S. Work Projects Administration. Manuscript on file, Brooklyn Historical Society. Brooklyn.

Mancall, Peter C.
1991   *Valley of Opportunity: Economic Culture along the Upper Susquehanna, 1700–1800.* Ithaca, N.Y.: Cornell University Press.
1995   *Deadly Medicine: Indians and Alcohol in Early America.* Ithaca, N.Y.: Cornell University Press.

Mark, Irving
1940   *Agrarian Conflicts in Colonial New York, 1711–1775.* New York: Columbia University Press. Second edition published in 1965 by Ira J. Friedman, Port Washington, N.Y.

Masthay, Carl, ed.
1991   *Schmick's Mahican Dictionary.* Memoirs of the American Philosophical Society, Vol. 197. Philadelphia.

Mauss, Marcel
1967   *The Gift: Forms and Functions of Exchange in Archaic Societies.* Ian Cunnison, trans. New York: W. W. Norton. First published in 1925 as *Essai sur le don: forme archaique de l'echange.* Paris.

McBride, Kevin A.
1996   "The Legacy of Robin Cassacinamon: Mashantucket Pequot Leadership in the Historic Period." In *Northeastern Indian Lives, 1632–1816,* Robert S. Grumet, ed., pp. 74–92. Amherst: University of Massachusetts Press.

McConnell, Michael N.
1992   *A Country Between: The Upper Ohio Valley and Its People, 1724–1774.* Lincoln: University of Nebraska Press.

McConville, Brendan

1999   *These Daring Disturbers of the Public Peace: The Struggle for Property and Power in Early New Jersey.* Ithaca, N.Y.: Cornell University Press. Reprinted in 2003 by the University of Pennsylvania Press.

McDermott, William J., and Clifford Buck, comps.

1979   *Eighteenth-Century Documents of the Nine Partners Patent, Dutchess County, New York.* Poughkeepsie, N.Y.: Dutchess County Historical Society.

Merrell, James H.

1989   *The Indian's New World: Catawbas and Their Neighbors from European Contact through the Era of Removal.* Chapel Hill: University of North Carolina Press.

1996   "Shikellamy: 'A Person of Consequence.'" In *Northeastern Indian Lives, 1632–1816*, Robert S. Grumet, ed., pp. 227–257. Amherst: University of Massachusetts Press.

1999   *Into the American Woods: Negotiators on the Colonial Pennsylvania Frontier.* New York: W. W. Norton.

Merritt, Jane T.

1997   "Dreaming of the Saviour's Blood: Moravians and the Indian Great Awakening in Pennsylvania." *William and Mary Quarterly,* Vol. 54, No. 4, pp. 723–746.

2003   *At the Crossroads: Indians and Empires on a Mid-Atlantic Frontier, 1700–1763.* Chapel Hill: University of North Carolina Press.

Merwick, Donna

2006   *The Shame and the Sorrow: Dutch-Amerindian Encounters in New Netherland.* Philadelphia: University of Pennsylvania Press.

Middleton, Simon

2001   "'How It Came That the Bakers Bake No Bread': A Struggle for Trade Privileges in Seventeenth-Century New Amsterdam." *William and Mary Quarterly,* Vol. 58, No. 2, pp. 347–372.

Miller, Jay

1974   "The Delaware as Women: A Symbolic Solution." *American Ethnologist,* Vol. 1, No. 4, pp. 507–514.

1997   "Old Religion among the Delawares: The Gamwing (Big House Rite)." *Ethnohistory,* Vol. 44, No. 1, pp. 113–134.

Mooney, James E.

1928   *The Aboriginal Population of America North of Mexico.* Smithsonian Miscellaneous Collections, Vol. 80, No. 7. Washington, D.C.

Moore, Sally Falk

1978   *Law as Process: An Anthropological Approach.* London: Routledge and Kegan Paul.

Murdock, George Peter

1949   *Social Structure.* New York: MacMillan.

Murphy, Henry C., ed.

1857   "David Peterszen de Vries: Voyages from Holland to America, A.D. 1632 to 1644." *Collections of the New-York Historical Society,* Vol. 3, No. 1, pp. 1–136.

Murray, David
  2000   *Indian Giving: Economies of Power in Indian-White Relations.* Amherst: University of Massachusetts Press.

Nammack, Georgiana C.
  1969   *Fraud, Politics, and the Dispossession of the Indians: The Iroquois Land Frontier in the Colonial Period.* Norman: University of Oklahoma Press.

Nelson, William N.
  1904   *Personal Names of Indians of New Jersey.* Paterson, N.J.: Paterson History Club.

Newcomb, William W., Jr.
  1956   *The Culture and Acculturation of the Delaware Indians.* Anthropological Papers of the University of Michigan, Vol. 10. Ann Arbor. Reprinted in 1970 by the University of Michigan.

Norton, Thomas E.
  1974   *The Fur Trade in Colonial New York, 1686–1776.* Madison: University of Wisconsin Press.

O'Callaghan, Edmund Burke, ed.
  1861   *Journal of the Legislative Council of the Province of New York.* 2 vols. Albany.
  1929   *Calendar of New York Colonial Commissions, 1680–1770.* New York: New-York Historical Society.

O'Meara, John
  1996   *Delaware-English/English-Delaware Dictionary.* Toronto: University of Toronto Press.

Orr, Charles, ed.
  1897   *History of the Pequot War.* Cleveland, Ohio: Helman-Taylor.

Otto, Paul
  2006   *The Dutch-Munsee Encounter in America: The Struggle for Sovereignty in the Hudson Valley.* New York: Berghahn.

Papunhank, John
  2005   *John Papunhank, a Christian Indian in North America: A Narrative of Facts in 1820.* London: Kessinger Publishing

Parmenter, Jon
  2005   "Fur Trade." In *The Encyclopedia of New York State.* Peter Eisenstadt and Laura-Eve Moss, eds., pp. 614–615. Syracuse, N.Y.: Syracuse University Press.

Pelletreau, William Smith
  1886   *History of Putnam County, New York: With Biographical Sketches of Its Prominent Men.* Philadelphia: W. W. Preston. Reprinted in 1975 by the Landmarks Preservation Committee of Southeast Museum, Brewster, N.Y.

Pelletreau, William Smith, ed.
  1898   *Records of the Town of Smithtown, Long Island, New York.* Huntington, N.Y.

Peña, Elizabeth Shapiro
  1990   "Wampum Production in New Netherland and New York: The Historical and Archaeological Context." Unpublished Doctoral Dissertation, Department of Anthropology, Boston University.

2005   "Wampum." In *The Encyclopedia of New York State*, Peter Eisenstadt and Laura-Eve Moss, eds., pp. 1650–1651. Syracuse, N.Y.: Syracuse University Press.

Pencak, William A., and Daniel K. Richter, eds.

2004   *Friends and Enemies in Penn's Woods: Indians, Colonists, and the Racial Construction of Pennsylvania*. College Park: Pennsylvania State University Press.

Philhower, Charles A.

n.d.   Charles A. Philhower Collection. Manuscript group on file in the Special Collections of the Alexander Library, Rutgers University, New Brunswick, N.J.

1953–1954   "The Historic Minisink Site." *Bulletin of the Archaeological Society of New Jersey*, Nos. 7 and 8.

Pietak, Lynn Marie

1995   "Trading with Strangers: Delaware and Munsee Strategies for Integrating European Trade Goods, 1600–1800." Unpublished Doctoral Dissertation, Department of Anthropology, University of Virginia, Charlottesville.

Pomfret, John E.

1956   *The Province of West Jersey, 1609–1702: A History of the Origins of an American Colony*. Princeton, N.J.: Princeton University Press.

1962   *The Province of East Jersey, 1609–1702: The Rebellious Proprietary*. Princeton, N.J.: Princeton University Press.

Potter, Stephen R.

1993   *Commoners, Tribute, and Chiefs: The Development of Algonquian Culture in the Potomac Valley*. Charlottesville: University of Virginia Press.

Price, Edward T.

1995   *Dividing the Land: Early American Beginnings of Our Private Property Mosaic*. The University of Chicago Geography Research Paper No. 238. Chicago: University of Chicago Press.

Price, Richard, ed.

1996   *Maroon Societies: Rebel Slave Communities in the Americas*. Third edition. Baltimore: Johns Hopkins University Press. First published by Doubleday in 1973. Johns Hopkins University Press published the second edition in 1979.

Prince, J. Dyneley

1912   "An Ancient New Jersey Indian Jargon." *American Anthropologist*, Vol. 14, No. 4, pp. 508–524.

Quinlan, James E.

1851   *Tom Quick, the Indian Slayer and the Pioneers of Minisink and Wawarsink*. Monticello, N.Y. Abridged Second edition published in 1894 by the Deposit Journal, Deposit, N.Y.

Ramenofsky, Ann F.

1987   *Vectors of Death: The Archaeology of European Contact*. Albuquerque: University of New Mexico Press.

Rappaport, Roy A.

1968   *Pigs for the Ancestors: Ritual in the Ecology of a New Guinea People.* New Haven, Conn.: Yale University Press.

Reading, John, Jr.

1915   "Journal of John Reading." *Proceedings of the New Jersey Historical Society,* Vol. 10, No. 1, pp. 34–46, No. 2, pp. 90–110, No. 3, pp. 128–133.

Reid, John Phillip

1976   *A Better Kind of Hatchet: Law, Trade, and Diplomacy in the Cherokee Nation during the Early Years of European Contact.* University Park: Pennsylvania State University Press.

Richter, Conrad

1953   *Light in the Forest.* New York: Alfred A. Knopf. Multiple reprints.

Richter, Daniel K.

1992   *The Ordeal of the Longhouse: The Peoples of the Iroquois League in the Era of European Colonization.* Chapel Hill: University of North Carolina Press.

Riker, James

1852   *Annals of Newtown in Queens County, New York.* New York: D. Fanshaw.

Rink, Oliver A.

1986   *Holland on the Hudson: An Economic and Social History of Dutch New York.* Ithaca, N.Y.: Cornell University Press.

Ritchie, Robert C.

1977   *The Duke's Province: A Study of New York Politics and Society, 1664–1691.* Chapel Hill: University of North Carolina Press.

Roome, William

1883   *Early Days and Early Surveys of East Jersey.* Morristown, N.J. Second edition published in 1897.

Rosaldo, Renato

1984   "Grief and a Headhunter's Rage." In *Text, Play, and Story: 1983 Proceedings of the American Ethnological Society,* Edward Bruner, ed., pp. 178–195. Washington, D.C.

1989   *Culture and Truth: The Remaking of Social Analysis.* Boston: Beacon Press.

Ruttenber, Edward Manning

1872   *History of the Indian Tribes of Hudson's River.* Albany. Reprinted in 1971 by Kennikat Press, Port Washington, N.Y., by Hope Farm Press in 1992, and by Kessinger Publishing, LLC in 2007.

1906   "Cochecton." *Historical Papers of the Historical Society of Newburgh Bay and the Highlands,* Vol. 13, pp. 178–184. Newburgh.

Sahlins, Marshall D.

1961   "The Segmentary Lineage: An Organization of Predatory Expansion." *American Anthropologist,* Vol. 63, No. 2, pp. 332–345. Multiple reprints.

1981   *Historical Metaphors and Mythical Realities: Structure in the Early History of the Sandwich Islands Kingdom.* Association for Social Anthropology in Oceania, Vol. 1. Ann Arbor: University of Michigan Press.

Salwen, Bert

1978   "Indians of Southern New England and Long Island: Early Period." In *Northeast,* Vol. 15, Bruce T. Trigger, ed., pp. 160–176. William C. Sturtevant, gen. ed., *Handbook of North American Indians.* Washington, D.C.: Smithsonian Institution Press.

Schmidt, Benjamin

2001   *Innocence Abroad: The Dutch Imagination and the New World, 1570–1670.* New York: Cambridge University Press.

Schutt, Amy C.

1999   "Tribal Identity in the Moravian Towns on the Susquehanna." *Pennsylvania History,* Vol. 6, No. 4, pp. 378–398.

Scott, Kenneth, and Charles E. Baker

1953   "Renewals of Governor Nicolls's Treaty of 1665 with the Esopus Indians at Kingston, New York." *New-York Historical Society Quarterly,* Vol. 37, No. 3, pp. 251–272.

Shannon, Timothy J.

2000   *Indians and Colonists at the Crossroads of Empire: The Albany Congress of 1754.* Ithaca, N.Y.: Cornell University Press.

Sheridan, Eugene R.

1981   *Lewis Morris, 1671–1746: A Study in Early American Politics.* Syracuse, N.Y.: Syracuse University Press.

Sheridan, Eugene R., ed.

1991–1993   *The Papers of Lewis Morris.* 3 vols. Newark: New Jersey Historical Society.

Shoemaker, Nancy

1999   "An Alliance between Men: Gender Metaphors in Eighteenth-Century American Indian Diplomacy East of the Mississippi." *Ethnohistory,* Vol. 46, No. 2, pp. 239–263.

Shomette, Donald G., and Roger D. Haslach

1988   *Raid on America: The Dutch Naval Campaign of 1672–1674.* Columbia: University of South Carolina Press.

Shorto, Russell

2004   *The Island at the Center of the World: The Epic Story of Dutch Manhattan and the Forgotten Colony that Shaped America.* New York: Doubleday.

Shurtleff, Nathaniel B., and David Pulsifer, eds.

1854–1861   *Records of the Colony of New Plymouth, in New England.* 12 vols. Boston: William White.

Silberbauer, George

1982   "Political Process in G/wi Bands." In *Politics and History in Band Societies*, Eleanor Burke Leacock and Richard Borshay Lee, eds., pp. 23–35. New York: Cambridge University Press.

Sivertsen, Karen
2007   "Babel on the Hudson: Community Formation in Dutch Manhattan." Unpublished Doctoral Dissertation, Department of History, Duke University, Winston-Salem.

Smaby, Beverly Prior
1989   *The Transformation of Moravian Bethlehem: From Communal Mission to Family Economy*. Philadelphia: University of Pennsylvania Press.

Smith, DeCost
1948   *Martyrs of the Oblong and the Little Nine*. Caldwell, Idaho: Caxton Printers.

Smith, J. Michael
2000   "The Highland King Nimhammaw and the Native Proprietors of Land in Dutchess County, N.Y.: 1712–1765." *Hudson Valley Regional Review*, Vol. 17, No. 2, pp. 69–108. Reprinted in 2004 in *The Continuance: An Algonquian Peoples Seminar: Selected Research Papers, 2000*, Shirley W. Dunn, ed., pp. 39–76. New York State Museum Bulletin 501, Albany.

Smith, Samuel
1765   *The History of the Colony of Nova-Caesaria or New-Jersey: Containing an Account of Its First Settlement, Progressive Improvements, the Original and Present Constitution, and Other Events, to the Year 1721. With Some Particulars Since: And a Short View of Its Present State*. Trenton. Multiple editions and reprints.

Snow, Dean R.
1996   "Theyanoguin." In *Northeastern Indian Lives, 1632–1816*, Robert S. Grumet, ed., pp. 208–226. Amherst: University of Massachusetts Press

Snyder, Gary S.
1999   "Wampum: A Material Symbol of Cultural Value to the Iroquois Peoples of Northeastern North America." In *Material Symbols: Culture and Economy in Prehistory*, John E. Robb, ed., pp. 362–381. Southern Illionis University, Occasional Paper No. 26. Carbondale, Center for Archaeological Investigations.

Speck, Frank Gouldsmith
1915   "The Family Hunting Territory as the Basis of Algonkian Social Organization." *American Anthropologist*, Vol. 17, No. 3, pp. 293–305.
1919   *The Functions of Wampum among the Eastern Algonkian*. Memoir 6, American Anthropological Association. Washington, D.C.

Spicer, Edward H.
1971   "Persistent Cultural Systems." *Science*, Vol. 174, pp. 795–800.

Spiess, Arthur E., and Bruce D. Spiess
1987   "New England Pandemic of 1616–19: Cause and Archaeological Implications." *Man in the Northeast*, No. 34, pp. 71–83.

Spittal, W. G., ed.

1990   *Iroquois Women: An Anthology.* Oshwekon, Ont.: Irocrafts.

Springer, James Warren

1986   "American Indians and the Law of Real Property in Colonial New England." *American Journal of Legal History,* Vol. 30, No. 1, pp. 25–58.

Stearns, Peter N., comp. and ed.

2002   *An Encyclopedia of World History.* Second edition. London: James Clarke. German edition by Karl Ploetz; published in English in 1883 by Houghton Mifflin as *An Epitome of Ancient, Medieval, and Modern History,* revised in 1923 by Harry Elmer Barnes, and updated in 1948 by William L. Langer.

Stewart, Frank H.

1932   *Indians of Southern New Jersey.* Woodbury, N.J.: Gloucester County Historical Society.

Stiles, Henry Reed

1867   *A History of the City of Brooklyn: Including the Old Town and Village of Brooklyn, the Town of Bushwick, and the Village and City of Williamsburgh.* 3 vols. Brooklyn. Facsimile reprint published in 1993 by Heritage Books, Bowie, Md.

Stilwell, John F., ed.

1903–1932   *Historical and Genealogical Miscellany: Data Relating to the Settlement and Settlers of New York and New Jersey.* 5 vols. New York: Privately printed.

Stone, Gaynell, ed.

1993   *The History and Archaeology of the Montauk.* Readings in Long Island Archaeology and Ethnohistory, Vol. 3, second edition. Stony Brook, N.Y.: Suffolk County Archaeological Association and Nassau County Archaeological Committee.

Strong, John A.

1996   *"We Are Still Here": The Algonquian Peoples of Long Island Today.* Interlaken, N.Y.: Heart of the Lakes Publishing. Revised second edition published in 1998 by Empire State Books, Interlaken, N.Y.

1997   *The Algonquian Peoples of Long Island from Earliest Times to 1700.* Interlaken, N.Y.: Empire State Books–Heart of the Lakes Publishing.

Sutton, Imre

1975   *Indian Land Tenure: Bibliographical Essays and a Guide to the Literature.* Broomfield, Colo.: Clearwater Publishing Company.

Tanner, Edwin P.

1908   *The Province of New Jersey, 1664–1738.* Published Doctoral Dissertation, Department of Political Science, Columbia University. New York.

Teunissen, John J., and Evelyn J. Hinz, eds.

1973   *Roger Williams, A Key into the Language of America.* Detroit: Wayne State University Press. First published by Williams in 1643.

Thomas, Peter A.

1985   "Cultural Change on the Southern New England Frontier, 1630–35." In *Cultures in Contact: The Impact of European Contacts on Native American Cul-*

tural Institutions, A.D. 1000–1800. William W. Fitzhugh, ed., pp. 131–161. Washington, D.C.: Smithsonian Institution Press.

Thompson, Benjamin F.
1918   *The History of Long Island.* 3 Vols. Charles J. Werner, ed. Rahway, N.J.: Quinn and Boden Press. First published by Thompson in 1843.

Thomson, Charles
1759   *An Inquiry into the Causes of the Alienation of the Delawares and Shawanese Indians from the British Interest, and into the Measures Taken for Recovering Their Friendship. . . .* London: J. Wilkie. Reprinted in 1867 by John Campbell, Philadelphia.
1760   "Some Account of the Behavior and Sentiments of a Number of Well-Disposed Indians Mostly of the Minusing-Tribe." Manuscript on file in the Miscellaneous Manuscripts Group, Friends Historical Society, Haverford, Pa.

Thornton, Russell
1987   *American Indian Holocaust and Survival: A Population History since 1492.* Norman: University of Oklahoma Press.

Thurman, Melburn Delano
1974   "Delaware Social Organization." In *A Delaware Indian Symposium,* Herbert C. Kraft, ed., pp. 111–134. Anthropological Series No. 4, Pennsylvania Historical and Museum Commission. Harrisburg.

Thwaites, Rueben Gold, ed.
1902   *The French Regime in Wisconsin, 1634–1727.* Collections of the State Historical Society of Wisconsin, Vol. 16. Madison.

Tooker, William Wallace
1896   *John Eliot's First Indian Teacher and Interpreter, Cockenoe-de-Long-Island, and the Story of His Career from the Early Records.* New York: Francis P. Harper. Reprinted in 1980 in *Languages and Lore of the Long Island Indians,* Gaynell Stone Levine and Nancy Bonvillain, eds., pp. 176–189. Stony Brook, N.Y.: Suffolk County Archaeological Association.
1901   *Indian Names of Manhattan.* New York.

Trigger, Bruce G.
1971   "The Mohawk-Mahican War (1624–1628): The Establishment of a Pattern." *Canadian Historical Review,* Vol. 52, No. 3, pp. 276–286.
1976   *Children of Aataentsic: A History of the Huron People to 1660.* 2 vols. Montreal: McGill-Queens University Press.

Trigger, Bruce G., ed.
1978   *Northeast.* Vol. 15 of *Handbook of North American Indians,*, William C. Sturtevant, gen. ed. Washington, D.C.: Smithsonian Institution Press.

Trumbull, J. Hammond, and Charles J. Hoadly, eds.
1850–1890   *The Public Records of the Colony of Connecticut.* 15 vols. Hartford.

Tylor, Edward B.

1873   "Primitive Society." *Contemporary Review*, Vol. 21, pp. 701–718, and Vol. 22, pp. 53–72. London.

Van Laer, Arnold J. F., ed.

1920–1923   *Minutes of the Court of Fort Orange and Beverwyck, 1652–1660*. 2 vols. Albany: University of the State of New York.

1926–1932   *Minutes of the Court of Albany, Rensselaerswyck, and Schenectady, 1668–1673*. 3 vols. Albany: University of the State of New York.

Van Wyck, Frederick

1924   *Keskachauge, or the First Settlement on Long Island*. New York: G. P. Putnam's Sons. Two vol. facsimile reprint (n.d.) published by Higginson Book Company, Salem, Mass.

Van Zandt, Cynthia J.

1998   "Negotiating Settlement: Colonialism, Cultural Exchange, and Conflict in Early Colonial Atlantic North America, 1580–1660." Unpublished Doctoral Dissertation, Department of History, University of Connecticut, Storrs.

Vaughan, Alden T.

1984   "Frontier Banditti and the Indians: The Paxton Boy's Legacy, 1763–1775." *Pennsylvania History*, Vol. 51, No. 1, pp. 1–29.

Wainwright, Nicholas B.

1959   *George Croghan: Frontier Diplomat*. Chapel Hill: University of North Carolina Press.

Wallace, Anthony F. C.

1947   "Women, Land, and Society: Three Aspects of Aboriginal Delaware Life." *Pennsylvania Archaeologist*, Vol. 17, Nos. 1–4, pp. 1–35.

1949   *King of the Delawares: Teedyuscung, 1700–1763*. Philadelphia: University of Pennsylvania Press. Reprinted in 1991 by University of Nebraska Press, Lincoln.

1952   *The Modal Personality Structure of the Tuscarora Indians, as Revealed by the Rorschach Test*. Bureau of American Ethnology, Bulletin 150. Washington, D.C.

1956a   "Revitalization Movements: Some Theoretical Considerations for Their Comparative Study." *American Anthropologist*, Vol. 58, No. 2, pp. 264–281. Multiple reprints.

1956b   "New Religions among the Delaware Indians, 1600–1900." *Southwestern Journal of Anthropology*, Vol. 12, No. 1, pp. 1–21.

1957a   "Political Organization and Land Tenure among the Northeastern Indians." *Southwestern Journal of Anthropology*, Vol. 13, No. 3, pp. 300–321.

1957b   "Origins of Iroquois Neutrality: The Grand Settlement of 1701." *Pennsylvania History*, Vol. 24, No. 2, pp. 223–235

1970   *The Death and Rebirth of the Seneca*. New York: Alfred A. Knopf.

Wallace, Paul A. W.

1945   *Conrad Weiser, 1696–1760: Friend of Colonist and Mohawk*. Philadelphia: University of Pennsylvania Press. Reprinted in 2001 by Wennawoods Publishing, Lewisburg, Pa.

1958   *Thirty Thousand Miles with John Heckewelder, or Travels among the Indians of Pennsylvania, New York, and Ohio in the Eighteenth Century.* Philadelphia: University of Pennsylvania Press. Reprinted in 1985 as *The Travels of John Heckewelder in Frontier America* by the University of Pittsburgh Press and in 1998 under its original title by Wennawoods Publishing, Lewisburg, Pa.

1981   *Indians in Pennsylvania.* Second Edition, Revised by William A. Hunter. Harrisburg: Pennsylvania Museum and Historical Commission. First published in 1961.

Walling, Richard S.

1996   "Death in the Bronx: The Stockbridge Indian Massacre, August 1778." Online article at www.americanrevolution.org/ind3.html.

Washburn, Wilcomb E.

1957   *The Governor and the Rebel: A History of Bacon's Rebellion in Virginia.* Chapel Hill: University of North Carolina Press.

Webb, Stephen Saunders

1984   *1676: The End of American Independence.* New York: Alfred A. Knopf.

Weber, Max

1930   *The Protestant Ethic and the Spirit of Capitalism.* Talcott Parsons, trans. New York: Scribner. First published in 1904.

Weiner, Annette B.

1996   "Reciprocity." In *Encyclopedia of Cultural Anthropology*, Vol. 3, David Levinson and Melvin Ember, eds., pp. 1060–1068. New York: Henry Holt.

Wellenreuther, Hermann, and Carola Wessel, eds.

2005   *The Moravian Mission Diaries of David Zeisberger, 1772–1781.* Max Kade German-American Research Institute. University Park: Pennsylvania State University Press.

Weslager, Clinton Alfred

1971   "Name-Giving Among the Delaware Indians." *Names*, Vol. 19, No. 4, pp. 268–283.

1972   *The Delaware Indians: A History.* New Brunswick: Rutgers University Press.

1978   *The Delaware Indian Westward Migration.* Wallingford, Pa.: Middle Atlantic Press.

Westbrook, Cornelius, and John Van Ingen, eds.

1841   "Copies of Indian Deeds, Grants, Transports, and Conveyances in the Secretary's Office at Albany Translated from the Original Dutch: Book GG." Manuscript on file at the Library of the New-York Historical Society. New York.

White, Leslie A., ed.

1959   *Lewis Henry Morgan: The Indian Journals, 1859–1862.* Ann Arbor: University of Michigan Press.

White, Richard

    1991   *The Middle Ground: Indians, Empires, and Republics in the Great Lakes Region, 1650–1815.* Cambridge: Cambridge University Press.

Whitmore, W. H., ed.

    1868–1874   *The Andros Tracts, with Notes and a Memoir of Sir Edmund Andros.* 3 vols. Boston: Prince Society. Reprinted in 1968 by Burt Franklin, N.Y.

Wilk, Stephen R.

    1993   "Weequehela." *New Jersey History*, Vol. 111, Nos. 3–4, pp. 1–16.

Winchester, Simon

    1998   *The Professor and the Madman: A Tale of Murder, Insanity, and the Making of the Oxford English Dictionary.* New York: Harper Collins.

Wojciechowski, Franz L.

    1985   *The Paugusett Tribes: An Ethnohistorical Study of the Tribal Interrelationships of the Indians of the Lower Housatonic River Area.* Social Anthropology Studies, No. 19, Department of Cultural and Social Anthropology, Catholic University of Nijmegen, The Netherlands.

Wood, Silas

    1826   *A Sketch of the First Settlement of the Several Towns on Long Island: With Their Political Conditions, to the End of the American Revolution.* Second edition. Brooklyn. First published in 1824 and revised and reprinted by Alden Spooner, Brooklyn in 1828, and again by the Furman Club, Brooklyn in 1865 and Ira J. Friedman, Port Washington, N.Y. in 1967.

Work Projects Administration

    1940   *Calendar of the Stevens Family Papers: Stevens Institute of Technology Library, Lieb Memorial Room, Hoboken, New Jersey.* 2 vols. Newark, N.J.: Historical Records Survey.

Wray, Charles F., Martha L. Sempowski, and Lorraine P. Saunders

    1990   *Two Early Contact Era Seneca Sites: Tram and Cameron.* C. F. Wray Series in Seneca Archaeology, Vol. 2, Research Record 21, Rochester Museum and Science Center, N.Y.

Wroth, Lawrence C., ed.

    1910   *The Voyages of Giovanni da Verrazzano, 1524–1528.* New York. Reprinted in 1970 by Yale University Press.

Zeisberger, David

    1780   "Von der Indianer Gestalt u. Lebensart." Indian Mission Records, Box 2291. Manuscript on file in the Archives of the Moravian Church, Moravian College Library, Bethlehem, Pa.

INDEX

Abenaki Indians, 168, 193, 235, 241, 259,
  268, 279, 331n15, 357n31, 359nn14–15,
  381n22
Acadia, 208, 211, 223–24, 259–60
Accokeek Creek National Historic
  Landmark, 137
Ackinckes hacky. *See* Hackensack
Act of Union (1707), 225
Adam, the Indian, 329n8
Adams, William (1833–1902), 299n25
Adena archaeological phase, 29
Adoption, 10, 64, 156
Aepjen (fl. 1645–65), 61
Aertsen, Gerrit (1651–1723), 217, 367n25
Africans and descendants of, 211, 227, 238,
  254, 284–285
Agapou. *Also* Achipor Miniquaes, Aquepo
  (d. 1670), 124, 320n7, 344n38
Ague. *See* Malaria in epidemics
Ahanderamock, 353n12
Ahasimus, 317n16, 318n19
Albania (original name of New Jersey), 111,
  116, 119–20, 123
Albany, Albanians. *Also* Beverwijck,
  Orange, 45, 48, 50, 114, 134–36, 139,
  141–42, 146, 148–49, 153, 164, 175,
  184–87, 189–93, 196, 202, 208–10,
  213–14, 219, 223–24, 227, 232, 236,
  242, 251, 258–59, 263, 320n7, 325n26,
  341n10, 341n12, 345–46n2, 347n9,

350–51nn30–31, 351nn33–34, 352nn6–
  7, 356n25, 359n13, 359n16, 359n18,
  359n20, 360n27, 360n30, 360n32,
  361–62nn35–36, 362n40, 365n9,
  367n19, 369n37, 369n39, 373n16,
  381n22
Albany Board of Indian Commissioners,
  149, 175, 235, 241, 352n7
Albany Congress (1754), 257, 380n19
Alcohol consumption and smuggling.
  Also Beer, Brandy, Liquor, Rum, Strong
  Drink, Wine, 15, 38, 40–41, 58, 72–73,
  94, 97–98, 129, 135, 147, 173, 175, 191,
  212, 223, 238, 254–56, 259, 284, 297–
  98n19, 338n25, 346n2, 380n11
Algonquian language family, 9, 289n1,
  296n16; Central Algonquian languages, 9,
  289n1; Eastern Algonquian languages, 3,
  9–10, 29–30, 289n1, 297n16, 330n15;
  New England Algonquian languages,
  325n23; proto-Algonquian language
  reconstruction, 29
Algonquin Indians, 64, 309n3, 328n31
Allamaaseeit. *Also* Aloamsek, Captain
  Allamouse, Lamaseeth, William Crom (fl.
  1745–61), 251–52, 258, 378n4, 379n6,
  380n10, 381n21
Allamuch-Ahokkin Indian Town, 234
Allegheny River and Valley, 192, 207, 261,
  270, 273, 346n3

Eastern Algonquian Indians, 153–55, 188,
205, 207, 252, 290n4, 298n23, 346n3,
349n21
Eastern Algonquian languages. *See*
Algonquian language family
Eastern Indians, 324n19, 331n15
Eastern Oklahoma Delaware community,
275, 282
Easton, Penn., 35–36, 90, 253, 264–66, 268,
326n27, 335–36nn14–15, 379n7, 381–
82nn30–32, 382n38
Edgepillock, N.J., 266, 271, 273, 280,
314n14
Egalitarianism, 8–9, 17, 20, 293n8
Egohohowen. *Also* Eichokohoon (fl. 1758–
62), 265, 379n6, 383n40
Elizabethtown, N.J., 116, 120, 123, 130,
149, 180, 351n33
Elizabethtown Purchase and associates, 119,
122–23, 230, 339n39, 342–43nn23–27,
366n17
Elizabethport, N.J., 123
Emerus. *Also* Amirent, Arremackanus,
Arremathanus, Emeroas, Remmatap (fl.
1650–88), 99–100, 123, 143, 157, 233,
303n34, 315n14, 338n31, 339n36,
344n32, 347n17
English, England, 7, 10, 12, 15, 43, 53–54,
59, 69–70, 95–97, 101–103, 109–11,
116–19, 128, 133–34, 136–37, 143, 152,
159, 161, 181, 183–84, 186–87, 190, 192,
194, 198–99, 201–203, 205, 210–11, 213,
225, 244, 291–92n5, 297n19, 310n6,
312n6, 315n14, 318n1, 325n23, 329n8,
332n15, 335–36nn14–15, 338n31,
340n1, 341n10, 342n22, 345n43, 346n2,
348n21, 351n34, 352n8, 353n10, 354n18,
359n15, 360n25, 360n27, 363n46,
366nn16–17; English Channel,133
Epidemics, 10, 15, 63–64, 81, 130–31, 135,
150, 159, 254, 292n5, 298n20, 331n15,
384n8; influenza, 16, 151, 334n34, 352n1;
malaria, 152, 167–68, 254, 334n34, 357–
58nn31–32; measles, 182, 359n14;
smallpox, 16, 64–66, 78, 122, 151–53,
156–57, 168–69, 185–86, 188, 194, 213–
14, 254, 334nn34–35, 352nn2–3, 359n17
Esopus archaeological sites, 35–36

Esopus Creek, 32–33, 36, 76, 308n9
Esopus Fort, 76
Esopus Indians and country. *Also* Aesopus,
Atharhacton, Esopes, Esoopes, Mohegans
of Taracton, Notchiuict, Soapus, Sopus,
Taractonga, Taractons, 32, 45, 61–62, 69–
77, 90, 102, 112–14, 122, 135–36, 140,
144–45, 148–49, 153, 165, 168, 188, 199,
209, 222, 227, 242–44, 251–53, 278–80,
292n5, 296n16, 308–309n9, 317n16,
324n19, 329–30nn11–14, 332nn17–18,
332n20, 333nn26–27, 343n27, 343n30,
346n4, 348–50nn21–22, 351nn33–34,
352n7, 352n9, 355n25, 357n28, 363n45,
364–65n4, 365n6, 369n34, 376n32, 378–
79n6, 380n10
Esopus Wars, 67, 71–77, 90, 102–103, 135,
309n9, 323–24nn18–19, 327n27,
340n39, 343n27
Essakauqueamenshehikkon Indian town,
234
Euketapucuson, 354n15
Evans, John, 196, 198, 357n28, 362n40
Evans, Samuel. *Also* Petaghclidaqua, 382n32
Evertsen, Cornelis, the Younger (1628–
1706), 128–29, 183
Exogamy, 9, 18, 274–75, 284, 293n9,
299n27

Fairfield community and County (Conn.),
61, 318n1, 329n7
Fairfield Indian mission, Ont., 280
Falls of the Delaware, 32, 37, 45, 48, 61, 74,
138–39, 152, 160, 179, 222, 245, 311n6,
320n7, 347n10, 353n10
Falls of the Passaic, 37
Family, families, 17–20, 64, 233, 238, 246,
270, 273–76, 278–79, 299n27, 300n29,
309n3, 334n4
Far Indians and country, 131, 174, 188–89,
208, 331–32n15, 346n3
Fauconnier, Peter (1686–1746), 230
Finns, Finland, 70, 85
Fire Island National Seashore, 201
Fishkill Creek and locality. *Also* Fish Kilns,
32, 197, 206–207, 262, 362n41, 381n26
Flatbush, Brooklyn, 50, 99–100, 304n36
Flemington, N.J., 371n2

INDEX

428   INDEX

Kendaskond. *Also* Kendasseong,
    Kindassowa, 375n23
Kent, Conn., 376n31
Keschaechquereren Indians and locality.
    Also Keskachauwe, 20, 22, 49, 58, 62, 206,
    304n36, 311n6
Keshena, Wisc., 374n18
Keskeskick, 310n6, 318n20, 323n18
Keskistkonck, 325n23
Kettyspowy family, 17
Keyserike, N.Y.. *Also* Kizzerick, 242,
    375n28, 383n40
Kichtawanck Indians and country. *Also*
    Ketchawong, Kightowan, Kichtawanc,
    Kicktawancs, Kitchawongs, 58–60,
    296n16, 305n36, 317n16, 322n18,
    333n28, 346n5, 359n16
Kidd, William (d. 1701), 186, 211
Kierstede: Lucas (1679–1758), 216–17, 230,
    367n367n22; Sarah Roeloffse (1627–93),
    122, 217, 340n39, 343n28
Kieft, Willem (1597–1647), 47, 51, 53, 55–
    60, 63, 66, 68, 70, 74, 97, 100, 133,
    308n9, 318n20, 319n7, 322n17
Kieft's War, 56–68, 96, 99–100, 144, 308n9,
    310n6, 312n6, 320n8, 328n28
Kighshepaw. *See* Kettyspowy family
Kiisheelumukweenk, 84, 255
Kil Muscota. *See* Harlem River
Killbuck Family, 282
Killings, homicides, 15, 46, 49, 52, 57–61,
    63–65, 68–69, 71, 73–75, 77–80, 100–
    101, 136–38, 141–42, 145, 149, 152–53,
    184, 186, 189, 192–93, 227, 239–40,
    258, 261, 263, 271, 283, 293n8, 311n6,
    314n12, 316n16, 318n17, 320n7,
    321n10, 321n15, 322nn17–18, 324n19,
    328n3, 322n17, 322n21, 334n32,
    338n32, 346,2, 346n4, 347n8, 348n17,
    374–75nn22–24, 379n6, 380n12,
    381n23, 381n26, 383n40
Kinaquariones, battle at (1669), 115
King, Thomas, 382n35
King Charles. *See* Sehoppy
King George's War, 250–51, 253
King Philip. *Also* Metacom, 139, 142
King Philip's War, 139, 347nn11–15,
    349n21

Kings County. *See* Brooklyn
Kingston, N.Y., 17, 35, 71, 111, 113–114,
    128, 134, 136, 144, 148–49, 210, 227,
    232, 241–42, 313n12, 333n31, 346n4,
    348n21, 350n30, 351n33, 360n33,
    370n43, 375n28
King Taminy (fl. 1683–97), 248, 315n14
King Tattenhick. *See* Teedyuscung
King William's War, 184, 198, 209, 236
Kisowaw. *Also* Kisekaw, Quilpaw, 218,
    368n27
Kipp Island archaeological phase, 29
Kittanning Indian town, 261–62, 381n25,
    381n27
Kittatiny Ridge and Mountains. *Also* Blew
    Hills, 31, 206, 216, 227, 231, 246, 250,
    258, 328n27, 378n1
Klas. *See* Claes de Wilt
Knight, John, 357n28
Kregier, Marten (1617–1713), 76–77, 102,
    122, 314n12, 319n7, 333n29, 340n40
Kuijter, Jochem Pietersz (d. 1654), 69,
    322n17
Kuskuskies Indian town, 273

La Barre, Antoine-Lefebvre, Sieur de
    (1622–90), 167–68, 357n31
La Salle, Rene-Robert Cavalier, Sieur de,
    153–56, 188, 209, 345n43, 352nn8–9
Labadists, 15, 152
Lachine, Montreal, Quebec, 184, 193
Lackawack River, 33
Lackawanna River, 33
Lackawaxen River, 33, 247, 255, 296n15,
    380n10, 381n21
Laet, Johannes de (1582–1649), 47
Lake Champlain, 185–186, 224, 242, 309n3,
    359n17
Lake Erie, 155, 241, 280, 346n3
Lake George, 259–60
Lake Hopatcong, 319n7, 328n27
Lake Michigan, 155, 345n43, 346n3
Lake Ontario, 231, 279
Lake Oskawana, 354n14
Lake Winnebago, 281
Lamington Falls, 266, 371n3
Lancaster city and County, Penn., 147,
    383n40

Quinnipiac Indians. *Also* Quilipioke,
Quiripeys, 45, 53, 297n16, 318n1
Quinomack. *Also* Quonamaka (fl. 1712–
15), 372n3
Quintipartite deed, 143, 347n16
Quiripi-Unquachog dialect, 9, 33, 40,
291n4, 297n16, 325n23
Quit-rents, 87, 117, 120, 161, 245, 254, 256

Race, 49, 262, 276, 284, 381n24, 383n40
Rahway River, 161
Ramapo River and Valley. *Also* Remopuck,
34, 36, 230, 234, 307n7, 317n16, 328n27,
344n32, 371n2, 376n32
Ramapoo (Conn.), 371n1
Ramenesing Indian town. *Also* Ramesing,
Romsingh, 102, 123, 143, 206, 314n12,
344n32, 344n34
Ranachquahung (hypothetical community
reconstruction), 37–40
Raresquash (fl. 1700–1705), 222
Raritan Bay, 48, 61, 74, 100, 122, 135, 143,
179, 314n12, 319–20n7, 339n37, 346n2
Raritan Corridor, 48, 61, 74, 78, 179
Raritan Indians and country. *Also* Bay
Indians, Raretany, Raritangs, Raritanoos,
49, 56, 58, 60, 68, 74–75, 92, 97, 100–
103, 119, 135, 157, 168, 206, 210,
310–11n6, 314–15n14, 319–21nn7–10,
340n40, 343n27, 348n17, 351n33
Raritan River and Valley, 102, 119, 143,
157, 160, 230, 233, 264, 266, 313n12,
319n7, 333n23, 346n2, 353n12, 355n20,
372n7
Rasiere, Isaack de (1595–1669), 14, 48
Reading, John, Jr. (1686–1767), 233–34,
373n8
Reading Prong, 33
Rebellion of 1672, 127, 345n44
Rechgawac, 323n18
Rechgawawanck Indians and country. *Also*
Haverstraws, Rechgawawanc,
Reckawancks, Remahenonck,
Reweghnonck, Rumachenanck, 58, 60,
68, 126, 311n6, 317n16, 321n10, 322n16,
322–23n18, 356n27
Rechkawyck. *See* Rockaway
Reciprocity, 90, 150, 336–37nn15–16

Reckeweck. *See* Marechkawick
Renap. *Also* Nerkarind, Noondauwiharind,
Noondawcharind, Orapequine,
Rapingonick, Rinnip, Roondaghneere
(fl. 1695–1753), 196–97, 218, 222, 242,
362n39, 368n26, 376n32, 379n6
Rensselaer, van: Alida (1656–1727), 164;
Jeremias (1632–74), 164; Maria (1645–
89), 164; Rensselaerswijck, 164, 319n6;
van Rensselaer family, 164, 198
Revolutionary War. *See* American
Revolution
Ringwood, N.J., 271
Rippowams. *See* Toquams
River Indians. *Also* Lower River Indians,
12, 32, 59, 61–63, 69–70, 73, 76, 79, 81–
82, 90, 92, 102, 112, 115–17, 128,
130–31, 134–36, 140, 146–52, 159, 165,
174–75, 182, 184–88, 191, 193–94, 198,
201, 204–206, 208–209, 214, 224–28,
242, 257, 259, 262, 273, 278, 280,
295n13, 296n16, 312n6, 319n7, 323n18,
331n15, 333n24, 344n35, 346n3,
351nn33–34, 358n3, 360n30, 361–
62nn35–36, 365n10, 367n19, 369n37,
370n41, 370n43, 373–74nn16–17,
376n30, 380n19
Roanoke Colony, 43
Roanoke River and Valley, 137, 228
Rochester Junction archaeological site,
346n3
Rockaway Indians and country. *Also*
Rakway, Rechkawyck, Rechqua Akie,
Reckonhacky, Reckouw Hacky, 31, 49,
58–61, 71, 177, 232, 254, 305n36, 311n6,
316n15, 322–23n18, 329n10, 338n31,
347nn12–13
Rockaway River, N.J., 199, 221
Rockland County (N.Y.), 34
Rocky Hill, N.J., 371n2
Roeloff Jansen's Kill, 355–56n25, 371n1
Rogers, Robert (1731–95), 268
Romackqua. *Also* Ramaque, Ramacque (fl.
1660–83), 92, 115, 168, 299n27, 337n19,
341n14
Rombouts, Francis (1631–91), 165
Rondout Creek and Valley, 32, 71, 308n9,
327n27, 348n21

Spanish pieces of eight, 266
Sparkill Gap, 125, 312n6
Spotswood, Alexander (1676–1740), 236
Spuyten Duyvil, 165
Squaw, jargon word, 13, 295n14
Sachems, 20
Stacy, Mahlon (1638–1704), 152, 352n3
Stamford, Conn., 59, 61, 70, 318n2, 356n26
Stamford Indians, 329n7
Starved Rock, Ill., 188, 360n24
Staten Island. *Also* Aquehonga
    Manacknong, 26, 35, 43, 48–49, 51, 56,
    59, 70, 74, 92, 110, 119, 124–26, 276,
    297n17, 314n14, 318n19, 320nn7–9,
    333n22, 336n15, 337n18, 339–40n39,
    343n27, 344nn37–38
Staten Island Indians, 14, 92, 100–101, 119–
    20, 124, 333n28, 343n29
Stockbridge Indian Rifle Company, 278,
    384n1
Stockbridge Indians, mission, and town,
    242, 259–60, 262, 270, 273, 276, 278–79,
    291n4, 376n31, 378n2
Stockbridge-Munsee Indians and
    reservation, Wisc., 281–82, 384n4
Stockertown, Penn., 248, 255
Store, Sarah (b. 1724), 314n14
Strickler archaeological site, 333n24
Strickler Ceramics, 147
Stuyvesant, Petrus (1612–72), 66, 68–76,
    93–94, 97, 99–103, 109, 116, 119, 122–
    24, 133, 297n19, 308n9, 310n6,
    326–27n27, 329n6, 329n8, 330n11,
    330nn13–4, 332nn17–19, 333n22,
    333n24, 333nn26–27, 335n14, 338n27,
    338n32, 339nn38–39, 340n41, 341n14,
    342n22
Suanhacky. *See* Long Island
Suffolk County (N.Y.), 199, 224
Sukkurus. *See* Wassackarous
Sullivan County (N.Y.), 219
Superintendent of Indian Affairs for the
    Northern Department, 259
Surinam, 114
Surrukunga (fl. 1683–1711), 163, 194
Suscaneman. Also Lummaseecon,
    Olamoeerinck, Olomoseecunck,
    Romasickamon, Rumashekah, Runasark,

Runasuck, Wallammassekaman (fl. 1653–
    1703), 22, 98, 103, 117–118, 158, 163,
    173, 179, 194, 196, 198, 207, 210, 276,
    303n35, 342n20, 355nn20–22, 358n6,
    358n8, 362n38, 363n43; sister of, 303–
    304n35, 325n23
Susquehannah Company, 258, 296n15,
    380n20
Susquehanna River and Valley. *Also*
    Sesquanna, Susquahanna, 4, 10, 33–34,
    75, 139, 159, 192, 207, 226–28, 236–41,
    246 249–51, 255, 258–63, 266, 270, 273,
    275, 279, 354n17, 370nn44–45, 372n5,
    373n13, 379n7, 380n10; North Branch
    of, 235, 250, 256, 261, 270, 373n13
Susquehanna Valley Indian towns, Indians,
    and missions, 192, 207, 226–28, 231–33,
    236, 239, 249, 254, 263, 270, 273, 276,
    278, 375n23, 380n12, 382n30, 384n2
Susquehannock Indians. *Also* Minquas,
    Minquaes, Minquays, Sasquehannah,
    Siuano maquaas, 9–10, 33, 40, 45, 68, 70,
    72, 74–75, 78–79, 96, 112, 114, 131, 135–
    39, 146–49, 151, 222, 245–46, 293n11,
    311n6, 314n12, 319–20n7, 327n27,
    328n4, 329n8, 330–31n15, 333n24,
    334nn34–35, 346n3, 347n6, 347n10,
    350nn26–27, 354n17
Sussex County (N.J.), 308n9, 372n5
Swaenenburgh (Kingston, N.Y.), 128,
    348n21
Swartwout: Bernardus (1673–1760), 217,
    251–52, 367nn24–25, 368n31; Jacobus
    (1726–75), 251, 378n4; Thomas (1658–
    1723), 216–17, 368n31
Swedes, Sweden, 67, 292n5, 310–11n6,
    328n2, 329n8
Syacop, Sateuw, 375–76n27, 376n32
Syhar (fl. 1655–98), 158, 163, 194

Tacitus, Publius Gaius Cornelius (ca. 56–
    117), 62
Tackapousha. *Also* Antinome,
    Mayauwetinnemin, Wittanahom,
    Wittaneywen (fl. 1643–99), 20–22, 60–
    61, 70–71, 73, 76, 94, 98–99, 103,
    117–18, 134, 140–41, 144, 158, 163, 168,
    173, 177, 186, 191, 194, 197, 199, 207,

CPSIA information can be obtained
at www.ICGtesting.com
Printed in the USA
LVHW091728040122
707834LV00012B/1601